MULTISTATE EXAMINATION WORKBOOK

Volume II

By

Jeff A. Fleming
Attorney at Law

Edited by

Susan P. Sneidmiller
Attorney at Law

Published by: FLEMING'S FUNDAMENTALS OF LAW
26170 Enterprise Way, Suite 500, Lake Forest, CA 92630
(949) 770-7030 • (800) LAW EXAM
FAX (949) 454-8556
WEB www.lawprepare.com • EMAIL info@ffol.com

Distributed by: LEGAL BOOKS DISTRIBUTING
4247 Whiteside Street
Los Angeles, CA 90063
(800) 200-7112

SUPERVISING WRITER AND EDITOR

Jeff A. Fleming
Attorney at Law

MANAGING WRITER AND EDITORS

Susan P. Sneidmiller
Attorney at Law

LAYOUT:

Donald F. Bayley II
IMAGEN Company   Irvine, CA.

CONTRIBUTING WRITERS:

Professor Todd Brower
Standford University School Of Law, J.D.

Josh Effron
Loyola Law School of Los Angeles, J.D.

Jarod Gross
University Of Santa Clara School Of Law, J.D.

Professor Glenn Koppel
Harvard Law School, J.D.

Professor Jeremy Miller
Tulane School Of Law, J.D.

Professor Anita Stuppler
University of Baltimore School of Law, J.D.

CONTENTS - Volume II

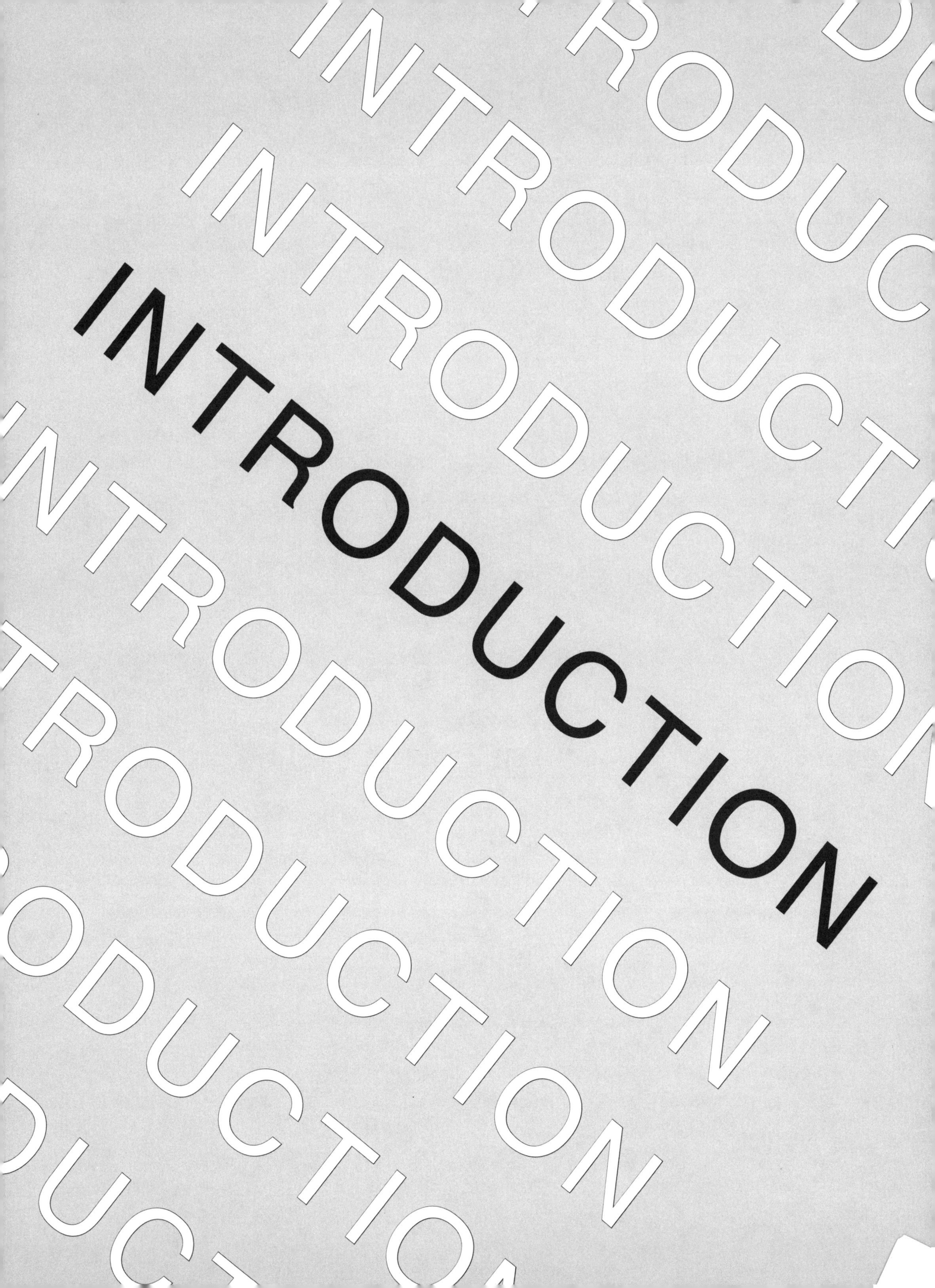

INTRODUCTION

THE RULES OF THE ROAD - AN INTRODUCTION TO THE MULTISTATE METHOD

As we traveled down the road of higher education, each milestone had a cryptic name – the PSAT, the SAT, and the LSAT, among others. Although each successive exam seemed to intimidate more than the last, with some determination, we arrive at the ultimate milestone – the Multistate Bar Examination, or MBE.

Created in 1972 by the National Conference of Bar Examiners (or NCBE), in cooperation with the Educational Testing Service, the MBE is a full-day, 200-question, mind numbing, multiple choice exam. One hundred questions are administered, randomly as to subject area, in two three-hour testing sessions. The exam seeks to cover a breadth of subjects that would be impossible to cover in a few selected essays.

The MBE has become the standard for most multiple choice exams that seek to test on legal reasoning skills, as well as familiarity with generally accepted legal principles. Presently, it covers the seven core areas of Torts, Criminal Law and Procedure, Contracts, Real Property, Constitutional Law, and Evidence. As constituted, the MBE is a major portion of the bar exam in virtually every jurisdiction, with Indiana, Louisiana and Washington being the exceptions.

The MBE has also been the model for countless objective law school exams, as well as the California First Year Law Student Exam administered by the State Bar (also referred to as the Baby Bar). However, the MBE is perhaps the most subjective objective test ever created. It attempts to test those analytical skills that we have honed and perfected, or have attempted to perfect, in the law school classroom through case study.

This introduction will review preparation methods and offer test-taking techniques that will also be of value to the law student facing objective testing in virtually any area of the law and California students preparing for the Bar and/or Baby Bar Exam. The methodology discussed herein can be applied to any multiple choice testing format that uses the MBE as a model.

RULE #1 – FAMILIARIZE YOURSELF WITH THE MBE TERRAIN

Material released by the NCBE indicates, in an almost lawyer-like disclaimer fashion, that the MBE is:

1. Not a multiple-guess test, or a test of test-taking skills, but of legal skills and knowledge, with a high correlation to performance on the essays;
2. Not a needlessly difficult, arcane or tricky test, but is designed to be a fair and unbiased index of whether the applicant has the ability to practice law, regardless or race or ethnicity;
3. Not a test in which time is a statistically significant factor, as the time allotted is sufficient for 99 percent of the test takers;
4. Not inferior to essay and performance exams as a measure of minimum competency to practice law, because the MBE can cover a greater breadth of subjects, can be scored objectively and scaled to account for variations in difficulty from test to test; and
5. Not getting easier from year to year.

Perhaps this last representation can go without dispute, but even the less gifted advocates among us may, after a trip down the MBE road, be able to raise an issue or two.

The landscape on the MBE road looks something like this:

A. **<u>TORTS</u>** (34 questions)

50% - Negligence, Proximate Cause, Damages (Apportionment), Defenses, Vicarious Liablility
50% - Divided among remaining Tort areas

Questions here are based on the common law, the majority rule, and, increasingly, on the Restatement 2d, Torts. The importance of Torts, and specifically of negligence, cannot be overstated. The remaining emphasis is primarily on the intentional torts and strict liability, with nuisance, defamation, privacy and misrepresentation also being represented. You can count on at least one question from each of these seven topics.

The specifications (i.e., subject matter outline) for the Torts MBE questions feature five main headings. Nuisance, defamation, privacy and misrepresentation fall under a single heading of Other Torts. Products liability is segregated from strict liability, and the Other Torts heading also includes intentional interference with business relations. The significance of the headings is that the examiners will always post at least one entry from each category. Of the 34 Torts questions, 50% will test on negligence.

B. **CRIMINAL LAW AND PROCEDURE** (33 questions)

15% - Pre-Commission Crimes
15% - Homicide
15% - Real/Personal Property/Theft Crimes
15% - Mena Rea, Defenses - Justification/Excuse
40% - Criminal Procedure - Fourth, Fifth and Sixth Amendment

The common law, the modern law, the majority rule, the Model Penal Code, and, sometimes, a statute contained within the problem form the basis for the Criminal Law questions. The decisions of the U.S. Supreme Court are the basis for the Criminal Procedure questions. In the other crimes area, theft crimes predominate. In Criminal Procedure, search and seizure issues are emphasized.

The MBE includes 33 questions in Criminal Law and Procedure, 40% testing on Criminal Procedure, the remaining questions divided equally among the four remaining areas of Criminal Law.

C. **CONTRACTS** (34 questions)

60% - Mutual Assent, Defenses, Warranties, Conditions, Breach, Remedies (U.C.C.)
20% - Consideration, Statute of Frauds, Third Party Rights
20% - Parol Evidence, Impossibility of Performance, Frustration of Purpose, Discharge of Contractual Duties

The source of law in this area is the common law, the majority rule, the Restatement 2d, Contracts, and the Uniform Commercial Code (U.C.C.) Articles 1 and 2. The bad news is that the questions in this area feature some of the longest, most complex fact patterns on the MBE; the good news is that the concepts tested generally tend toward the basic.

The MBE includes 34 questions in Contracts, roughly 60% covering formation, conditions and remedies, and with about eight or nine questions based on U.C.C. Articles 1 and 2.

D. **REAL PROPERTY** (33 questions)

- 75% - Interests in Land, Co-Tenancies, Landlord & Tenant, Ownership in Trusts, Easements, Profits, Licenses, Covenants, Servitudes, Water and Land Rights, Zoning, Fixtures (Article 9, U.C.C.), Adverse Possession, Deed, Conveyancing by Will, Recording Act
- 25% - Land Sales Contract/Risk of Loss/Marketable Title/Mortgages

The common law, the modern law, the majority rule, and the U.C.C. (Article 9 – Fixtures) are tested in Real Property. The problems are, along with Contracts, the longest and most complex on the MBE; unfortunately, most students would agree that the concepts tested are anything but basic. Traditionally, the lowest percentages come out of Real Property. On recent MBE's, there has been a significant rise in testing on mortgages.

The 33 Real Property questions will draw on the areas of ownership, rights in land and title for 75% of the questions, land sale contracts and mortgages for the remainder. Newly tested subjects include zoning, conveyance by will and ownership interests in trusts.

E. **CONSTITUTIONAL LAW** (33 questions)

- 50% - State Action, Due Process, Equal Protection, Privileges and Immunities, Bill of Attainder, Ex-Post Facto, Contract Clause, First Amendment (Speech, Association, Press, and Religion)
- 17% - Federal/State Conflict
- 16% - Separation of Powers
- 16% - Procedure

The principles tested in Constitutional Law are derived from the U.S. Constitution, the decisions of the U.S. Supreme Court, and, apparently, from obscure footnotes in Nowak's hornbook on Constitutional Law. The good news is that the questions in this area tend to be the most straight forward on the MBE, accounting for the highest percentage scores.

The MBE includes 33 questions in Constitutional Law, approximately 50% of which will test on "individual rights": due process, equal protection and first amendment freedoms.

F. **EVIDENCE** (33 questions)

- 33% - Hearsay
- 33% - Relevancy, Real and Demonstrative & Scientific Evidence, Authentication, Expert Testimony, Privileges, Best Evidence Rule
- 33% - Impeachment, Rehabilitation, Opinion, Burdens and Presumptions, Judicial Notice, Direct Examination, Cross-Examination

The questions are based on the Federal Rules of Evidence. Throw out those old outlines based on the common law, with one possible exception – From time to time, you may see a federal court sitting in diversity jurisdiction. In those situations, apply state rules of procedure that may be outcome determinative, including state rules of Evidence, as spelled out in the problem.

Note that if the questions testing on character evidence (from relevance and impeachment) are combined with the hearsay questions, the total is generally 60% or more of the testing in Evidence. The questions tend to be the shortest, yet most devious, on the MBE.

The MBE includes 33 questions in Evidence, one-third based on presentation of evidence, one-third based on hearsay, and one-third based on relevancy, privileges and writings.

The subjects of Crimes, Evidence and Torts tend to emphasize, and will likely continue to emphasize, the elements of the rule invoked by the facts; in Constitutional Law, Contracts, and Real Property factual analysis and reading comprehension is emphasized.

Unlike the essays, cross-over testing is the exception rather that the rule. This is due, at least in part, to the fact that the questions are drafted by individual committees, each responsible for one of the MBE areas.

Currently, Civil Procedure is not considered a testable subject. A recent trend has been to get to Torts by means of a motion for a directed verdict (known as a motion for judgment as a matter of law), a motion to dismiss, or a motion for summary judgment. For example, a question may require you to know that the doctrine of res ipsa loquitur will raise an inference of negligence sufficient to turn the matter over to the jury, and overcome a directed verdict motion.

Prior MBE questions have tested the Erie doctrine in Constitutional Law, have used a will or trust to get to an issue in Real Property, have used a federal court sitting in diversity jurisdiction to get to an Evidence issue, or have used a contract to get into a Real Property issue. Expect to see as many as three or four questions that could cross-over between Evidence and Criminal Procedure. Remedies, including damages and equitable relief, will arise in the context of in Contracts, Real Property (e.g., specific performance), Torts, and, possibly, Constitutional Law (e.g., injunctive relief).

It is highly unlikely that anything resembling a cross-over pattern will be seen on the Baby Bar, as the examiner is unable to assume that you have any knowledge beyond the Contracts, Crimes or Torts material covered in your first year of law school.

Note:

Effective with the February 2015 administration of the Multistate Bar examination (MBE), a seventh content area – Civil Procedure – will be covered for the first time.

The MBE consists of 200 multiple-choice questions, of which 190 are scored items and 10 are unscored pretest items. The current list of topics include Constitutional Law, Contracts, Criminal Law and Procedure, Evidence, Real Property, and Torts. The addition of Civil Procedure will mean that the number of questions per topic will decrease. Starting in 2015, there will be 28 questions covering Contracts, and 27 questions covering each of the six remaining topics, for a total of 190.

RULE #2 – PREPARE FOR THE LONG HAUL (or, You Have to Get out of the Driveway before You Can Ride the MBE Fast Lane)

The foregoing subject breakdowns are to be used as study guides, along with comprehensive outlines, such as the Gilbert series recommended by Fleming's Fundamentals of Law in the MBE areas. It is recommended that one outline be reviewed every one and one-half weeks for long term and review two outlines per week for short term. Greater emphasis should be placed on any weak or highly testable areas, combined with practice problems as discussed below.

The essentials of preparation for the MBE can be addressed in three words – **practice, practice, practice.**

In gearing up for the practice runs, the student must sort through a potentially overwhelming assortment of materials. At the outset, a schedule should be prepared that considers the outlines to be covered, as well as the practice problems to be done. A series of goals, both long term (overall) and short term (daily), will be helpful, but only if these goals are realistic and within reach.

A successful performance on the MBE requires more than the ability to regurgitate rules of law and a rote memorization of the outlines. An examinee must be able to master the rules, the exceptions, the exceptions to the exceptions, the footnotes in the hornbooks, the Restatement comments and illustrations, the ability to function in a stress-filled environment, the ability to think on one's feet, and the ability to apply all of this in 1.8 minutes per question.

Unquestionably, success on the MBE is grounded on a solid foundation of the black letter law. By itself, however, this is not enough. Each rule, as it is studied, must be put into a factual context so that the application of the rule is understood and the associative process is enhanced.

Generally, the commercial outlines, such as the Gilbert series, or the bar review outlines, will be a sufficient source of the law needed. Despite all of our experience with last-minute cramming, merely reading the outlines will not be enough to vanquish the MBE. The study of the law must be incorporated into an approach that contemplates problem-solving as the goal, rather than rote memorization.

The recommended **first step** is to break down each subject area into its component parts and to master each of these areas before moving on to the next. For example, one cannot learn Crimes without first mastering the general requirements of **actus reus** (the criminal act) and **mens rea** (the mental state) **before** moving on to homicide and theft crimes.

While studying the outline materials, take the time to discern the necessary elements of each rule reviewed. List these elements in your mind, on a piece of paper or on a flash card and then **contextualize**. This means putting the outline aside for a moment to consider or imagine a set of facts that will call up the rule, element or exception to be applied. For example, while reviewing contract offers, consider a number of situations in which an offer may or may not exist, such as Do you want to go to the movies? (merely an inquiry); If you pay for the movies, I'll pay for the food (possibly an offer, despite its indefiniteness, if another would be justified in believing that a power of acceptance has been created); or I'll pay you $5.00 an hour to come over at 7:00 P.M. this Saturday and watch my kids while I go to the movies (clearly an offer). If at first this seems difficult, there are a number of flash card sets, such as those published by Law-in-a-Flash or PMBR that list examples or hypotheticals that may prove helpful in helping initiate the process.

The **next step** is to turn to a source of practice questions, such as the Finz Multistate Method book utilized by Fleming's Fundamentals of Law, starting with the table of contents. You will see, for example, in the Criminal Law section, that following the heading **General Principles** is a listing of 13 questions that test in that specific area. Working questions in the subtopic immediately following its review will not only help you place the rules in context, i.e., to apply the rules, it will also help you to determine whether or not there is sufficient comprehension of the rules so as to allow you to move on to the next area of testing. Again, it is vital to achieve some sense of mastery in each area before moving to the next.

When taking the practice test questions, always time yourself, allowing no more than 1.8 minutes per question. If you are aware of the time pressure from the very beginning, then you will start to develop a rhythm or an almost instinctive awareness of the passage of time as you work the problems.

RULE #3 – KEEP YOUR EYES ON THE ROAD (or, the Zen of testing)

One of the attributes of the successful examinee is the ability to **focus**, to the exclusion of all else, while in testing mode. This can be thought of as finding a quiet place, both externally and internally, in which to perform. The distractions may be external, such as the continued groans of a neighboring test taker; or the distractions may be internal, such as wondering what impulse possessed you to sit for the exam.

The key is to block out everything but the test question, and to be able to do that for an extended period of time. By doing test questions in blocks of no less than 17 at a time, one half hour per set, you can consciously put yourself in the exam for that period of time to the exclusion of all else. Consider continuing to practice the half hour sets until you have mastered the ability to go for thirty minutes without thinking about anything but the test questions. Once you have mastered this ability, then expand to one hour of testing, or 33 questions, and so on, until you can sit for three hours without a significant break in concentration.

This does mean, however, that no matter how great the temptation, you cannot look at the answer key until you have completed the set. When you do review the answers, look at the explanations for both the correct and incorrect responses to ensure a well-reasoned basis for your selections and to reinforce your grasp of the rule being tested.

Some students will find it helpful to write out the rule on a flash card for those problems they got wrong. This, again, helps to reinforce your grasp of the rule, will help you keep track of areas of difficulty, and will create a valuable study tool.

It is also important to sit for at least one simulated exam so as to test your ability to focus over the long haul. Use the simulation as an opportunity to diagnose areas of weakness, not only substantively, but technically or procedurally as well, i.e., Does the brain completely fade somewhere around question 75? Does it take 10 to 15 questions to establish a rhythm? Does the brain think of nothing but lunch as the clock nears the noon hour?

As the exam draws nearer, the emphasis should shift from outline review to problem solving, with the outlines being used primarily as a refresher or supplement to the problems. Again, the exam is testing on problem solving skills, not the ability to regurgitate the black letter law. The final month should be devoted to doing practice MBE's.

RULE #4 – MAXIMIZE YOUR FUEL EFFICIENCY

As mentioned above, study time should be allotted to reflect the relative importance of each subject area. Of the 200 questions on the current MBE, there are 34 each in the areas of Contracts and Torts, and 33 each in the areas of Constitutional Law, Criminal Law and Procedure, Evidence and Real Property.

Factor in the testing on the essays, where typically three out of the six one-hour questions test on the same rules as the MBE, and that you cannot study law for the performance essays, and the result is that at least 75% of the black letter law needed to pass the California Bar Exam comes out of the MBE areas. This same basic principle, that studying for the MBE will help on the essays, also applies to the Baby Bar essay questions, but is limited to the topics of Contracts, Crimes and Torts.

Emphasis in study time for the California Bar Exam should be placed on the MBE areas. Generally, each MBE area should be studied three times as much as any individual essay-only subject, such as Wills or Community Property.

As we saw in the subject breakdowns, above, within each MBE subject can be found certain key areas, for example:

CONSTITUTIONAL LAW:.... Individual Rights And The First Amendment................................ 16 Questions

CONTRACTS: .... Formation (Including U.C.C.), Defenses ... 15 Questions

EVIDENCE: .... Hearsay And Character Evidence .... 15 Questions

TORTS: .... Negligence .... 17 Questions

PROPERTY:............................ Establishing And Conveying Title .... 20 Questions

(Note: While Criminal Law has a somewhat emphasized area, the general requirements and defenses will likely be tested directly or indirectly on the bulk of questions, and should therefore be considered key, both in study and in the review of the elements of each criminal offense.)

Obviously, the key areas require a greater expenditure of time. Again, the subject breakdowns will be an important tool in emphasizing specific areas, and getting the most efficient use of your study time.

RULE #5 – KNOW WHERE YOU ARE HEADED (Before You Leave the House)

In order to maximize your reading comprehension and initiate your analysis of an MBE test question, it will help to know the area of testing, and, if possible, to determine the rule of application, before you start to read the facts. The area being tested will not be specifically identified for you.

The typical MBE question is composed of three parts – the **root/stimulus** (fact pattern); the **stem** (call of the question); and the **options** (answer choices), as in the following example:

Question 1 is based on the following facts:

Archie, a candidate for Student Body President at the exclusive Riverdale Academy, was scheduled to debate the other presidential candidates before the assembled student body in the school's auditorium. After the students had taken their seats, Ms. Grundy, the faculty advisor, called Archie to the podium. Just as Archie was crossing the stage to get to the podium, his opponent Reggie stuck out his foot, causing Archie to fall off of the stage. As a result, Archie was deeply humiliated, but suffered no physical harm.

1. If Archie asserts a claim against Reggie due to the humiliation that he suffered, will Archie prevail?

   A. Yes, if Reggie knew that Archie had to walk across the stage in front of Reggie at the precise moment Reggie stuck out his foot.

   B. Yes, if Reggie carelessly failed to notice that Archie had to walk across the stage in front of Reggie.

   C. No, because Archie suffered no physical harm.

   D. No, only if in sticking out his leg Reggie did not intend to cause physical harm to Archie.

The answer to this example can be found in the Rule #7 Section that follows.

Prior to reading the facts, read the stem. In the above example, the asserts a claim language identified the area of testing – Torts. Now the root can be read with a eye toward the appropriate cause of action. This is essentially the same as issue spotting an essay. The facts are designed to trigger the application of a rule. The examinee's job is to recognize those trigger facts and apply the appropriate rule.

Getting a sense of the ultimate destination helps to initiate the reasoning process that goes into analyzing the facts. Again, this is the same process that goes into issue spotting an essay, i.e., Do the facts support a particular outcome or result? Have all elements been satisfied? Are there additional facts that must be evaluated? Are there missing facts that must be considered before the outcome can be determined? Is there an exception that will apply?

In the above Archie-Reggie example, once the area of law was established, we can now consider the various rules which might apply, e.g., negligence, intentional tort or strict liability. Which facts become significant? The facts state that as Archie was crossing the stage, his opponent Reggie stuck out his foot. There is no mention of whether or not it was intentional or accidental. It does not appear that any of the categories of strict liability (products liability, wild animals, abnormally dangerous activities) can be supported by the facts, so this area can be eliminated. Negligence is possible, but given the lack of physical harm, we will need to continue the search for a more appropriate rule. The claim asserted will likely arise out of the intentional torts, perhaps battery or intentional infliction of emotional distress. The facts must be scrutinized to see if they will support the claim, or if something more will be needed.

On occasion, the stem may go further in establishing the rule of application, e.g., if Defendant is charged with murder..., or if Plaintiff asserts a claim in strict liability due to the injuries caused by the defective product.... This may allow you to get further along in the distillation process, but it does not mean that your analytical skills will not be called into play.

In those problems where the root is followed by more than one stem, i.e., multiple questions follow a single fact pattern, try to read each stem so as to get a general sense of the issues or areas being tested. Later, when working through the responses, you can deal with each stem independently.

If the stem does not provide you with sufficient information to determine the area of testing, glance at the options. This means allowing your eyes to drop down an imaginary centerline through the potential responses, so that you recognize key words. This should be enough to enable you to determine, at a minimum, the area of testing. In the above example, you may have noted the words know and carelessly in the first two options, suggesting that the key, or correct answer, will be coming out of intentional torts or negligence, and may possibly require a distinction to be made as to those two areas.

Consider the following example:

2. In a common-law jurisdiction, Defendant should be found guilty of:

   A. Burglary only

   B. Arson only

   C. Burglary and arson

   D. Neither burglary nor arson

As you have likely observed, the stem did identify the rule of application, the common-law rules. It did not identify the rule of law; however, a quick glance at the options clarified the area (Criminal Law) and the crimes of burglary and arson. Once you have identified the rule or rules of application, your job may merely be the accounting of all essential elements.

In some examples, the stem essentially replaces or supplements the existing facts by asking you to assume additional facts. In this situation, reading the entire stem first may not be as desirable. It may be helpful to first read the last sentence or phrase of the longer stem, so as to learn the objective of the problem, and then read the additional facts contained in the stem. Consider the following example:

Assume for the purposes of this question only that instead of doing the job herself, Builder delegated the remodeling work to Framington, who was an experienced cabinetmaker. Although Framington had never worked on a job of this exact type, size and complexity, she eagerly accepted the delegation because she owed a sizable gambling debt to Builder. Builder did not inform Owner of the delegation. Builder then assigned the contract proceeds to Karman to pay off her car loan.

3. Will Owner be required to accept Builder's delegation of duties to Framington?

In this example, glancing at the last sentence identifies this stem as testing on a delegation of contract duties. By having this knowledge, the important facts are easily distinguished from those immaterial to the inquiry (e.g., that Framington was inexperienced with the type of job versus Framington's experience as a cabinetmaker or the assignment to Karman). Note also that where the stem instructs you to Assume for the purposes of this question only **do not** carry those additional facts on to other questions and **do not** allow the new facts to influence your reading of the basic fact pattern.

RULE #6 – USE ROAD MAPS

Reading the stem, or glancing at the answers, to establish the objective or direction the problem is taking will help boost your reading comprehension. This can be compared to using a road map to establish which direction to take in order to reach your ultimate destination, i.e., the objective of the problem.

Reading comprehension is enhanced if you have a sense of direction, that is, an idea of which facts are likely to be important and which facts are set forth as mere distracters. Whole paragraphs may be skimmed if you know in advance that such paragraphs will not have a bearing on the result. Parties are more easily identified, issues are more easily narrowed.

Once the objective has been established, it becomes easier to recognize the details that may be important in resolving the issues presented. For example, the fact that the plaintiff was an anticipated or known trespasser, and thus a duty was owed, may be determinative in Torts; or that the seller was an unemployed ballerina, and thus not a merchant, may help resolve the issue as to whether or not a written option contract not supported by consideration is enforceable; or that the seller was planning to sell, rather than presently intending to sell, may indicate that there is no offer on which to base a contract.

As indicated above, a fact critical to the outcome may be buried within the details of the fact pattern which, in essence, is identical to the essays. These details may be seen in adjectives, verbs, adverbs, times, dates, places, quotations, personal characteristics, names, or intentions. The question to ask is: What is the **legal significance** of each fact or detail as it relates to our inquiry or call of the question?

In some problems, but not all, a simple, quickly executed diagram may be helpful to set out, for example, the chronology or the relationships that are central to the question. This can be done right in the test booklet, or on the scratch paper provided by the proctors. Consider the following example:

Question 4 is based on the following facts:

Buss is the owner in fee simple absolute of Lakeracre, a 13,000 acre ranch in Kern County, in the state of Golden. On May 2, despondent over the playoff loss of her beloved Magicians basketball team to their archrivals, the Missiles, Buss conveyed Lakeracre to Johnson for the price of $150,000.00 by means of a quitclaim deed. Johnson did not immediately record this conveyance. On June 16, Buss conveyed Lakeracre by warranty deed to Nelson in consideration of a $250,000.00 debt owed by Buss to Nelson, which Nelson forgave. Nelson recorded this conveyance immediately. On July 1, Johnson recorded his quitclaim deed.

On July 10, Johnson conveyed Lakeracre to his friend Threatt as a gift.

Threatt recorded the conveyance immediately. On July 15, Nelson conveyed Lakeracre to Peeler by quitclaim deed for the price of $300,000.00. Peeler recorded immediately.

4. Assume for the purposes of this question only that Golden has a recording statute that reads as follows:

   > *No conveyance is good as against a subsequent purchaser for valuable consideration and without notice, unless such conveyance be recorded prior to subsequent purchase.*

   If all necessary parties are joined in a quiet title action, title will be found in which of the following of the following parties?

This problem can be diagrammed to strip the facts down to the essentials. The key is to identify the bona fide purchasers, and when each recorded relative to the other, so as to establish the absence or presence of notice in this race notice jurisdiction. A diagram may look something like the following:

B to J/BFP B to N, N rec J rec J to T/gift, T rec. N to P/BFP, P rec
–|––––––––––|––––––––––|––––––––––|––––––––––|–

Of course, the diagram can be distilled further by using arrows instead of to, or abbreviating recorded to the letter R, so long as there is no confusion as to meaning or a party.

The areas that are most likely to call on diagramming skills would be Contracts and Real Property. It is recommended that you practice diagramming, if that technique is to be employed, wherever appropriate in the practice questions. The objective to distill the information into a useful format as quickly as possible, keeping in mind that if you spend more than 1.8 minutes with each stem following the root, that time must be made up elsewhere.

Some students may wish to highlight or underline the facts. This can either be helpful, or a waste of time. In order to highlight effectively, there must still be some awareness of the relative importance of the material highlighted. You may recall how much material you highlighted in your casebooks during the first weeks of law school. Soon, as you grew more sensitive to the relevant facts and law, less and less was being highlighted. This was a product of learning how to read a case. In much the same way, you will learn how to recognize the vital facts, and disregard the immaterial.

In reading the root of the Archie-Reggie example, above, it may not be as important to note that Archie was running for office as it was to note that the accident occurred in front of the assembled student body, thus increasing the probability that Archie would be humiliated. This is not to completely discount the Archie's purpose for being in the auditorium, or that Reggie was his opponent. The fact that Archie was there to participate in a debate makes it clear that the audience would likely watch Archie's every move. The facts are not clear on Reggie's intent in sticking out his leg; while it might appear that he intended to trip Archie, we have to be careful in making an unwarranted assumption. In this example, we appear to be missing a critical fact, and cannot make up for it with imagination. The resolution of this issue is likely the key to the problem, and will be dealt with in the answer choices.

It is important that you follow the facts and do not fight or respond emotionally to the facts that are given. This means taking the facts at face value, without reading too much into the facts. In this regard, you may need to stifle some of the natural inclinations of an advocate, as arguing or assuming facts may do little except waste time or lead to an incorrect response. Where the facts state that the arresting officer had a valid warrant, do not attempt to challenge the warrant. Where the facts state that the police made a random stop, do not go on to consider the possible exceptions to the warrant requirement. Where the facts state that a deed is valid and has been properly executed, there is no need to ask if the description is sufficient.

Some rules may seem unfair, perhaps even illogical, in applying the facts. For example, Why shouldn't a physician be required to act to render assistance to another who may be seriously injured as a result of the physician's inaction, where there is no risk to the physician, and despite the fact that the victim was placed in peril by another? Why shouldn't a party be allowed to prove up a subsequent remedial measure to prove negligence or culpability, when such remedy is logically connected to the dangerous condition causing injury? The MBE is not the place to argue policy, and attempting to do so will exact a very high toll. Again, do not respond with emotion, but rather a reasoned approach to applying the law to the facts.

If a straight forward interpretation is available, do not over-analyze or seek out an unnecessarily convoluted interpretation. A reasonable, logical inference may, however, be required. Ensure that the inferred fact logically and necessarily follows from the information given. Making assumptions, creating new facts, or working with conclusions that are not warranted by the existing facts will, in most instances, generate an incorrect response.

Constitutional Law, Contracts and Real Property are where the subjects that are more demanding on reading comprehension, given the nature of the subject matter and the tendency that the examiners have to use longer, more complex fact patterns with multiple parties to test in these areas. Fact patterns in these areas will often require greater scrutiny, and therefore require more time.

Testing in Crimes, Evidence and Torts tends to emphasize elements and command of the black letter law. As a result, the fact patterns tend to be shorter, and may require less in the way of reading comprehension, and more in the way of substantive knowledge of the rules of law.

When reading the facts, regardless of the subject, keep in mind that the examiner is testing on lawyering skills. Cases very often turn on details, so an effective reading of the facts will often depend on the examinee's ability to discern the operative from the inoperative, the relevant from the immaterial, and the substantial from the inconsequential. Also, you must be as flexible and as adaptable as conditions may demand. This is known as thinking on one's feet. These are qualities that lead to a successful performance.

As with all the methods and techniques discussed in this introduction, including the following materials on selecting a response, success is dependent on practicing until the approach is virtually unconscious. Techniques must be adjusted to fit each individual's approach, and that only comes through practice. You must sort through each suggestion, and incorporate only that which has produced the greatest result with the practice questions.

Arguably, if the work done in reading the facts and the call of the question has been successful, then there should be little effort expended in reaching your destination, i.e., selecting a correct answer. In the most basic terms, we are usually seeking the best legal basis on which to support a particular or given outcome.

RULE #7 – DON'T GET SIDETRACKED

On occasion, the correct answer may appear obvious. Certainly, if the answer is obvious, do not fight it. In other instances, however, it will seem as though the examiner has taken great pains to hide the ball. The incorrect answers, referred to as distracters by the examiners, are aptly named.

Consider the Archie-Reggie example (Question 1) above. It would appear that Reggie acted intentionally to trip Archie; however, the facts say nothing about Reggie's state of mind, and we cannot afford to guess at what Reggie was thinking. The facts state that Archie was not injured, so the (B) response, based on negligence, is improbable. The (C) response can be ruled out, because an action for battery or intentional infliction of emotional distress can be maintained even in the absence of actual physical harm. The (D) response can also be eliminated, as it limits liability to intent to cause physical harm; however, a cause of action can be based on the offense to Archie's dignity or the intent to cause emotional distress. The (A) response, therefore, is the **key**, or correct response. By using the word know it addresses the missing element of intent.

Typically, the person drafting the question is or has been a law professor. As a result, he or she has ample experience with the phrasings that are likely to lure an examinee into an incorrect response. There must be something attractive in a distracter. It may be an inaccurate or incomplete statement of the law. It may trigger some faint memory of an arcane rule. It may be a concept that has been drilled into you. Or, more likely, the distracter may reflect an incomplete understanding of a rule that has traditionally led to confusion.

In the Archie-Reggie example, the examiner may have been counting on the difficulty some students may have in distinguishing negligence and the intentional torts, or the requirement of physical harm that accompanies a negligence action.

One concept that routinely turns up in distracters is promissory estoppel. Those same people who taught you to love and cherish the concept, law professors, now turn it against you. In the absence of a promise and a reasonable expectation on the part of the promisor that the promise will induce some action or inaction, the doctrine does not apply. Yet students have routinely attempted to use promissory estoppel as an all-purpose substitute for consideration, despite the absence of a promise, or the presence of a more appropriate response that has very real consideration.

In other situations, the distracter may prey on an examinee's confusion as to the identity of the holder of a right, or when the right arises. In a problem where the government is maintaining an action in inverse condemnation, an examinee must realize the action is one properly maintained against the government. In a problem where a defendant seeks to assert the last clear chance doctrine, an examinee must realize that only a plaintiff can assert the doctrine. Where there is a claim of privilege against self-incrimination, be sure that there is a statement in issue, and that the statement is testimonial in nature.

Other distracters may seek to create whole new, incorrect concepts. Only a student with sufficient familiarity with the hearsay exceptions under the Federal Rules will know that there is no exception for a recent sense impression. Bargained-for reliance, a concept that withers in daylight, might get a second glance from the examinee who is unsure of his or her knowledge of Contracts. Keep in mind that after reading outlines in each of the subject areas, and doing thousands of practice questions, if there was such a thing as bargained-for reliance you would recognize the concept.

This is not intended to mean that you will necessarily be familiar with all potential phrasings. In an area such as negligence we cannot expect to see 17 problems that may be answered Liable, if negligent. Some synonyms are in order, such as recklessly, carelessly, unreasonably, without due care, and so on. This does not mean, on the other hand, that new, special duties can be created, e.g., in a negligence action, the defendant owes the highest or an utmost duty of care.

Ultimately, the best cure is a thorough substantive review, followed by judicious amounts of practice questions. Adequate preparation will thwart the intentions of the examiner seeking to trap the unwary examinee.

RULE #8 – REMEMBER TO READ THE TRAFFIC SIGNS

A clear understanding of the language in the stem and the options will be critical to achieving a sense of direction, or, in other words, the objective of the problem and arriving at the correct response.

The language in the stem may cast the examinee in a specific role, which in turn will have a bearing on which response is the most appropriate. For example, a stem that asks for the best basis on which to support a judge's decision is asking you, in essence, to act as that judge's law clerk. A question asking for the strongest or weakest argument is calling for an advocate. On the other hand, a stem seeking the most probable outcome may require a neutral approach in analyzing the most appropriate response.

Consider the following example to determine how much information is contained in the stem:

Question 5 is based on the following facts:

Dennis and Joey operate a private courier service in the city of Metropolis. They entered into a contract with the law firm of Ketcham and Wilson for the delivery of the firm's promotional calendars to clients throughout the city. Prior to commencing the deliveries, Dennis suggested to Joey that the two of them throw away the calendars, pocket the money paid for the deliveries, and spend the rest of day at the local race track. Joey said nothing. Dennis then proceeded to dispose of the calendars.

5. If Dennis and Joey are charged with conspiracy to commit larceny in a common law jurisdiction, which of the following constitutes Joey's **weakest** defense?

   A. Joey did not have the required intent.

   B. Joey did not form an agreement with Dennis, either explicitly or implicitly, as to a criminal objective.

C. Joey did not act to take the calendars out of Ketcham and Wilson's possession.

D. Joey was feigning agreement.

In the above example, the question stem is identifying the following: (1) the area of law, (2) the specific rule being tested, (3) the law of the jurisdiction, (4) the defendant to focus on in applying the rule, and (5) the role to assume in responding to the question. Actually, very little is needed from the root in this example. The criminal charge has been set out, so in order to respond, apply the rule of conspiracy.

The fact that the question seeks the weakest defense should not dramatically affect your analysis. This question may be more easily solved by working it in reverse; in other words, re-phrase the call to read Which of the following constitutes Joey's **strongest** defenses? In this example, the (A), (B) and (D) responses are all negating an element of conspiracy, i.e., the specific intent to commit larceny or the agreement between two or more actors, and as such, are very strong defenses. Option (C) appears to be dealing with the crime of larceny, and not the inchoate crime of conspiracy, and would not be an adequate defense, is therefore the key in this example. Note that in the areas of Crimes and Torts the strongest, best defenses are those which negate an element of the charge or claim.

The same care must be used in analyzing the options. Consider the following example:

Question 6 is based on the following facts:

Peters was skiing in the exclusive resort of Deer Park, an area which he was not familiar with, and inadvertently skied out of bounds. As he attempted to get back on the ski trail, a blizzard started, making it impossible for him to find his way back. As darkness descended, Peters started to fear that he would suffer from hypothermia unless he found shelter. As he was making his way through the waist-high snow, Peters spotted a ski cabin owned by Denver. Despite seeing a sign which read Private Property – Keep Out!, Peters immediately made his way to the cabin and was able to gain entry by forcing the door open. The cabin was unoccupied.

Once inside the cabin, Peters started a fire in the fire place. Without realizing there was a defect in the fire place screen which allowed sparks to escape, Peters went to sleep. A fire broke out, which destroyed the cabin and caused serious injury to Peters.

6. If Peters asserts a claim against Denver for his injuries, will he be successful?

    A. Yes, **if** Denver was aware of the defective fire place screen.

    B. Yes, **only if** Denver could have discovered the defective fire screen by a reasonable inspection.

    C. No, **unless** Denver had reason to anticipate a skier might break into the cabin.

    D. No, **because** Peters assumed the risk that a fire might break out when he went to sleep.

In this example, notice that each option has a result, followed by a suggested basis on which to support that result. This is the most common formulation of answers on the MBE. Look closer, and you will notice that each outcome is joined to the basis by a conjunction, which can be referred to as the modifier, or operative term. Each different modifier has its own connotation or usage.

The modifier in option (A), **if,** suggests that the outcome **must** follow as a result of the statement of law of fact given, and no other outcome is possible. The determination that must be made is whether the logical connection is sufficient to justify the result. In a problem where there is one missing element in order for the plaintiff to prevail, and that missing element is preceded by an if modifier, then no other result is possible. This would be a very strong choice. The if modifier may be followed by a new fact, in which case the inquiry is whether no other result logically follows the new information. In the above example, we do not need to question whether or not Denver actually knew of the defect. The inquiry is whether or not Denver would necessarily be liable, given this awareness. Your knowledge of Torts will tell you that absent some duty owed, this result does not necessarily follow, and this answer may be rejected.

The **only if** modifier in option (B) suggests that the basis which follows the outcome is the exclusive means of arriving at the outcome, and that there is no other way to logically arrive at the outcome. The word only is a word of restriction or limitation. If there is another way to arrive at the outcome, then this modifier would indicate an incorrect response. In this example, the duty to inspect (owed to invitees) would not be the exclusive basis on which to predicate Denver's liability to Peters, and therefore must be rejected.

Option (C) features the **unless** modifier, which requires a reversal of the analysis of the only if modifier in options (A). In other words, the outcome stated can only be avoided by the statement which follows. The unless modifier should be treated as the logical opposite of only if. Your knowledge of Torts will tell you that Denver will prevail if Peters is unable to satisfy all of the elements of negligence. All of the elements needed to find for Peters have been supplied except one – duty. Another way to view this option is to rephrase it to Peters will recover **only if** Denver had reason to anticipate Peters presence in the cabin. This logically follows, because, based on the facts, duty to the trespassing Peters will only arise where Denver has reason to know or anticipate his presence in the cabin; therefore, this is the key response.

The modifier in option (D), **because**, can be used interchangeably with the conjunctions since and as. Here the inquiry is two-fold. First examine the basis as a correct statement of law or fact. If it is correct, then ask if the outcome stated logically and necessarily follows from the basis. In this example, there is nothing in the facts that indicates Peters voluntarily and unreasonably encountered the known risk of a defective fire place screen. As a result of this, this option must be rejected.

The analysis of the language above may seem awkward, even somewhat convoluted at first. After working through a substantial number of practice questions, you will find that familiarity and comfort with the language increases at a rapid pace.

RULE #9 – BE ALERT FOR CHANGING ROAD CONDITIONS

The three complete examples above followed a fairly standard format. The root was followed by the stem, which in turn was followed by options which each listed an outcome followed by a proposed basis on which to support the outcome. The method used to arrive at the correct response in the explanations above was the process of elimination. Once we eliminated the false statements, whatever remained became our selection.

Another way to view the exam is as a multiple true-false test, rather than multiple choice. That means looking at each option, independently, as a true-false question. It will be helpful to mark a T or an F next to each option as you read through them. Alternately, you might use a system of pluses or minuses, or crossing out the false statements. Selecting the correct option then becomes a function of looking for a T, a plus, or an option which has not been crossed out.

But what about the options with a question mark next to them? What if you can only narrow it down to two choices?

If you are able to narrow it down to two choices, one of which is correct, you are definitely on the right track. You will have increased the odds of getting the problem correct by 100%. This is one reason why you may wish to indicate your second choice as you work through the practice questions. As you read through the explanatory answers, you will seek to develop a sense of why the examiner prefers one choice over another.

Remember that the examiner, at least in the problem types we have reviewed so far, is putting you on the hunt for the **best legal basis** on which to support a given outcome. Consequently, the answer which is narrower or more specific to the result is usually preferred; the same is true when comparing a legal basis with a factual basis. The legal basis is generally preferred. For example, Not guilty, because the facts do not state that Defendant had an improper motive does not present as good a legal basis as Not guilty, because Defendant lacked the intent to steal in exculpating the defendant in an example testing on larceny.

Be on the alert for those answer choices that are underinclusive or overinclusive in stating the basis for the outcome. For example, the option stating Constitutional, because the 1st Amendment only protects words is likely to be wrong in a Constitutional Law problem, because certain acts of expressive conduct may be within the scope of 1st Amendment protection. If you find that the rationale in an option eliminates a right which ought to be included, or encompasses a right or result which does not follow from your understanding of the law, then such option is to be avoided.

The examiners use a number of variations on the problem-types illustrated above, such as where the result is the only thing contained in the option. Consider the following example:

Question 7 is based on the following facts:

During the night, Dexter, a drug addict, broke into Gordon's apartment, a reputed drug dealer, with the intention of stealing Gordon's supply of rock cocaine. Although Dexter did not find any cocaine, he did find some methedrine, an illegal stimulant. Dexter took the methedrine with him when he left the apartment.

7. In a common law jurisdiction, Dexter is guilty of:

   A. Burglary only

   B. Larceny only

   C. Burglary and larceny

   D. No crime

Although the options are not the compound type that we have looked at, the approach is similar, in that we must still go through each possible response and deem it either true or false. We do this by reviewing the elements of each charge, and determining whether or not the facts will support the charge. Where there are multiple charges (or outcomes), deal with the elements of each individual charge.

In this example, we are in a common-law jurisdiction, and the facts state that Dexter broke in to Gordon's apartment at nighttime with the intent to steal drugs. We do not have to struggle with the elements of breaking and entering because they are there in the facts. The examiner is hoping for an emotional response, that somehow stealing illegal drugs is not morally wrong. But the facts make it clear that Dexter had the intent to commit a larceny at the time of breaking and entering, therefore Dexter has committed burglary. He has also taken the drugs, which are the personal property of another, with the intent to steal; therefore Dexter has also committed larceny, and choice (C) is correct. Keep in mind that each crime requires satisfaction of an element the other does not, so there is no double jeopardy prohibition.

Another problem type incorporates the facts into the options themselves, which may be referred to as a **squib-option** format, as in the following example:

8. In which of the following fact situations will the contract most likely be enforceable despite the absence of a written agreement?

   A. Homeowner and Cable Company have a dispute over the placement of Cable's use of the utility poles on Homeowner's land. In an effort to settle the matter, Cable offers to purchase an easement from Homeowner, and Homeowner accepts.

   B. Vendor operates vending machines throughout the city of Sierra Vista. Supplier offers to sell $5,000.00 worth of snack foods to Vendor for only $3,000.00. Vendor accepts.

   C. Agent hears Singer perform in a nightclub and on the spot offers her a two-year recording contract. In reliance on the offer, Singer quits her job at the nightclub, and accepts the offer.

   D. Owner asks Builder to submit a bid for the construction of addition to Owner's house. Builder offers to build the addition for $10,000.00. Owner accepts.

Problems of this type can generally be attacked with a two-step approach. Ask yourself the following: What is the rule being tested (as identified by the stem)? And, How is it to be applied, i.e., what is the task to perform? In this example, the stem indicates that the rule being tested is the Statute of Frauds (requiring a writing in order to enforce certain types of agreements), and the task is to classify each contract to see whether it falls within the Statute. Options (A), (B), and (C) each reflect an agreement that requires a writing under the Statute of Frauds – a contract for the sale of an interest in land, a contract for the sale of goods for the price of $500 or more, and a contract that is not to be performed within one year from the making thereof, respectively. Only (D), involving a construction contract, clearly falls outside of the Statute, and is the key response.

Answer choice (C) may present a problem for some students, as they might want to argue the element of reliance. The examiners are counting on this, expecting some students will waste time wanting to argue. If you have an arguable response, versus a clear cut response, do not waste time. Answer the question, and then completely erase it from your mind. One of the pitfalls of the exam is that certain problems are so challenging that a student will continue to work it in the back of the head long after a response has been marked. Resist this temptation, as it will only slow you down, frustrate you and destroy your effectiveness.

Another problem type the examiners have used is the **tiered** question, as in the following example:

Question 9 is based on the following facts:

Thanatos operates a factory in the city of Olympia which manufactures air conditioners. One of the ingredients used in the manufacturing process is freon gas, which when exposed to the welding torches necessary to the manufacturing process creates the highly toxic phosgene gas. The phosgene gas is pulled out of the inside of the factory by means of large exhaust fans, which are vented directly to the atmosphere. No other means are available to Thanatos for the removal of the phosgene gas. Morpheus, who lives next to the factory, inhaled the fumes and was severely injured.

9. If Morpheus asserts a claim against Thanatos for her injuries, which of the following **must** be established if she is to be successful?

   I. Thanatos operated the factory in a negligent manner.

   II. The factory constituted a public nuisance.

   III. The toxic gas released by Thanatos caused her injuries.

   A. III only

   B. I and III only

   C. II, and III only

   D. I, II, and III

The most efficient, effective way to work this problem is to treat it in the same way that we have already seen, that is, to treat it as a compound true-false question. The stem is asking which of the following is an absolute requirement, regardless of the cause of action. We can cross out or write an F next to statement I and statement II, because Thanatos is involved in an abnormally dangerous activity giving rise to strict liability, i.e., disbursing highly toxic gases into the atmosphere in a populated area. Morpheus can therefore prevail even in the absence of proof of negligence or nuisance. Option (A) is therefore correct.

Yet another problem type is the **complex case precedent**. In this problem type, a series of case precedents are set out, with the stems being fact patterns, and the options designating which of the precedents will be controlling, as in the following example:

Questions 10 - 12 are based on the following facts:

Read the summaries in the four cases (A – D) below. Then decide which is the most applicable as a precedent to each of the cases in the questions that follow, and indicate each choice by marking the corresponding space on your answer sheet.

(A) Defendant, while in the process of robbing a liquor store, dropped his revolver. The gun discharged, and the bullet struck and killed a customer in the store. Defendant fled, but is later apprehended and charged with murder. At trial, Defendant testifies that the killing was accidental, and requests that an instruction for manslaughter be given. **Held**: Guilty of murder.

(B) Defendant, angered over not being invited to her next-door neighbor's housewarming party, discharged her gun into their common wall while the party was ongoing. The bullet struck a lighting fixture, and the shards of glass in turn struck and killed a partygoer. Defendant was apprehended and charged with murder. At trial, Defendant testifies that she never intended to harm anyone and requests that an instruction for manslaughter be given. **Held**: Guilty of murder.

(C) Defendant, while in the Mojave Desert region of Southern California, decided to practice target shooting with her new rifle. Taking aim at a cactus, she discharged a round. The bullet struck a rock, ricocheted off of another rock, and struck and killed a person standing 10 yards behind Defendant. Defendant is apprehended and charged with murder. At trial, Defendant testifies that she did not know that the victim was present, and requests that an instruction for manslaughter be given. **Held**: Guilty of manslaughter.

(D) Defendant was away on a two-week lecture tour. On her return home, she discovered her husband having sex with her sister. Defendant then removed a revolver from her briefcase and fired it in the general direction of her husband and sister. The sister is struck by the bullet and dies. Defendant is apprehended and charged with murder. At trial, Defendant testifies that she only intended to shoot her husband, that the shooting of her sister was accidental, and she only discharged the gun because she had lost control and was unable to regain her composure. Defendant also requested an instruction for manslaughter. **Held**: Guilty of manslaughter

10. Defendant, intending to collect on an insurance claim, sets fire to his warehouse. The fire spreads to an adjoining building, which apparently had been abandoned several years earlier. A vagrant who was living in this adjoining building was sleeping at the time and was overcome by the smoke. As a result, the vagrant was unable to escape in time, and was killed in the ensuing blaze. A statute in the jurisdiction defines arson as the malicious burning of any structure.

11. Defendant, while driving his car at the posted speed limit on the Golden State Freeway, began to be perturbed at the close proximity of the car, driven by Victim, immediately behind him. In an effort to send a message to the tailgating driver, Defendant abruptly slammed on his brakes. Victim attempted to avoid the impact by swerving his car, but instead struck the concrete center median barrier and Victim was killed.

12. Defendant and Victim were fellow employees of IDF, a communications software developer. One night the two of them began to argue over which long distance telephone service the company should choose. Victim then reached into her desk drawer, and started to pull out something that appeared metallic. Defendant believed that Victim was pulling out a gun and was about to shoot her, so Defendant reached into her purse and pulled out a gun and shot Victim. Victim, who was merely taking out a letter opener, died.

The temptation will be to match the facts in the stems with the facts in the precedents, which will usually result in confusion and one or more incorrect answers. In the above example, the facts in the question cases did not closely resemble the precedents. The key is to distinguish each precedent as to the legal basis as it relates to the result, use your knowledge of the law to determine the result in each stem, and then match result for result. In the above example, this means identifying the following:

A. Murder/Felony murder rule – robbery

B. Murder/Depraved heart murder

C. Manslaughter/involuntary – act of criminal recklessness

D. Manslaughter/voluntary – adequate provocation

Now, it becomes a task of matching result and basis with each of the ensuing fact patterns. This means that the correct answer to Question 10 is (A), because the accidental killing arose as a foreseeable consequence of the commission of an inherently dangerous felony, arson. Question 11 was an example of involuntary manslaughter involving criminal recklessness, and not depraved heart murder, because the necessary showing of the Defendant's awareness of the high probability of death was not present; thus, option (C) is correct. Finally, Question 12, is an example of voluntary manslaughter because of mistaken justification – Defendant had a mistaken belief in an imminent threat of death or serious bodily injury. The result must be matched with the result in one of the precedents; consequently, option (D) is correct. Thankfully for many students, this question type does not appear with frequency; when it does, usually in Criminal Law/Procedure, you may recognize that with a workable approach, these questions will not seem overly difficult.

In the **supposition stem** problem type, the stem will ask which of the facts contained in the options, if true, will best support a particular result. The goal here is to treat each of the options as true, combine it with the existing facts, and determine if it logically and necessarily leads to the desired outcome, as in the following example:

Question 13 is based on the following fact situation:

On May 28, Pilcher and Dante, a dealer of vintage cars, entered into a written, signed agreement whereby Dante offered to give Pilcher 30 days in which to decide whether or not to purchase Dante's rare BMW 507 automobile for $100,000.00. Only 50 BMW 507s were imported to the United States, and only five are currently known to exist. On June 1, Pilcher tendered a cashier's check for $100,000.00. Dante refused to convey title to the automobile. Pilcher brings an action for specific performance.

13. Which of the following facts, if true, would provide Dante with his **strongest** defense?

    A. Pilcher did not give any form of consideration for the option to purchase the BMW 507.

    B. Pilcher had entered into an agreement with another dealer for the purchase of a different BMW 507 after May 28, and had communicated that fact to Dante.

    C. At the time of commencing the action, Pilcher knew that another BMW 507 was available for $150,000.00.

    D. Both parties thought the agreement was for the purchase of Dante's Maserati Ghibli.

Again, as each option is examined, it is assumed that it is true. Option (A) does not have legal significance, as the facts state that Dante was a dealer in this type of automobile. Under the U.C.C., a merchant who gives assurance in a signed writing that an offer will not be revoked cannot later claim lack of consideration as a defense to an option contract. Option (B) appears to state that Pilcher revoked his offer; however, this does not follow from the facts, as Pilcher is an offeree who has not yet rejected Dante's offer. Option (C) cuts against the remedy of specific performance, yet it is incomplete in that it does not state that the two automobiles were alike in all practical respects. Option (D), although it flies in the face of the facts, is the key response, because if mutual mistake is present, the contract is necessarily voidable at the election of either party. Remember, in this problem type each additional fact must be treated as true.

In the **three-one split** problem type, there will be one option that stands alone as to result. Do not attach any special significance to this, as it probably has a one in four chance of being correct. Work it through as you would any other example, but pay special attention to the modifiers, particularly one that would affect the result such as unless. If one option does not include a basis or rationale, select it only if the facts provide sufficient support for the outcome. Consider the following example:

Question 14 is based on the following fact situation.

Divac, a skater with the Ice Follies, a traveling troupe of ice skaters, stopped into the Fern Bar for a drink after performing one evening. After having several drinks, Divac began to speak with Vlade, who was seated next to him at the bar. The topic turned to the greatest hockey goalkeeper of all time, and the disagreement was so fierce that Divac took a swing at Vlade. The contact was slight, but it was enough to knock Vlade off of his bar stool. Unbeknownst to Divac, Vlade was an undercover officer for the federal Drug Enforcement Agency, and was at the Fern Bar in order to make a drug buy.

Subsequently, Divac was arrested and charged with assaulting a federal officer. At trial, Divac testified that he was unaware that Vlade was a federal officer, and that if he had known, he would have never struck him.

14. If the jury believes Divac, it should find him:

   A. Guilty.

   B. Not guilty, because he lacked the specific intent to assault a federal officer.

   C. Not guilty, unless assault of this type is considered a general intent crime.

   D. Not guilty, because Divac was mistaken as to Vlade's identity.

In the above example, the only requirement as to mens rea is that Divac intended the assault. Divac's awareness of Vlade as a federal officer is immaterial. No mental awareness of the jurisdictional element of this type of offense is necessary to convict. Note that option (B) can be eliminated on this basis. Option (C), which has the modifier unless, can be eliminated on the basis that the facts indicate that Divac intended the assault, and so the classification does not have a bearing on guilt. Option (D) is incorrect, because mistake is no defense on these facts. Again, only after eliminating all other choices can we properly arrive at the correct answer, option (A).

Other problem types may appear from time to time. It is the ability to think on your feet and apply the law to the facts in a lawyer-like fashion that will allow you to vanquish each problem, and, ultimately, the MBE.

RULE #10 – ENSURE THAT SPEED IS ADEQUATE TO PASS

Be aware that a number of problems do not appear to test your minimum competency to practice, but rather are designed to screw with your mind. As the exam is a test against time, you cannot afford to get bogged down on any one problem. If the answer proves elusive, mark down a response, and move on. If the facts are lengthy, and there is only one problem, consider skipping it to conserve time, especially if it is testing on arcane or obscure material. For example, if the problem has two full columns of facts, and a single question testing on planned unit developments and the mutuality of equitable servitudes in Real Property, Burby himself might skip it. Before moving on, though, glance at the options to see if any can be eliminated as clear false statements of law, so as to improve the odds of a guess.

Always be sure to mark down an answer so as to avoid skewing the Scantron. If you have skewed the answer grid, say around problem 15, you cannot afford to discover this as the proctor is calling time. You must always be aware of time and speed, so that you do not run into the situation where no time remains, and yet you are still trying to fill in the bubbles.

Avoid changing answers unless you specifically see where you have misread a problem, or later remember the formulation of a rule that applies in a earlier problem; however, if you are still thinking about an earlier problem, the concentration is not there, and speed is likely lagging. If you spend enough time practicing, your first guess will probably be correct anyway.

Remember, no one gets them all, not even the law professors who take the exam. In fact, the examiners will typically throw out two to three questions on each exam due to ambiguity or inconsistency. Of the 200 questions on the bar exam MBE, most examinees will get at least 100 correct. The key to success is getting the next 40 to 60 problems correct.

Always, always remain positive. Indicate to yourself that you are ready to pass by doing the things that you, and only you, know you need to do.

Treat the exam like a game, and do it for the sake of the game. Don't think about the result or the stakes, just enjoy the ride.

THE RULES OF THE MBE ROAD, IN REVIEW:

1. Familiarize Yourself With The MBE Terrain
2. Prepare For The Long Haul
3. Keep Your Eyes On The Road
4. Maximize Your Fuel Efficiency
5. Know Where You Are Headed
6. Use Road Maps
7. Don't Get Sidetracked
8. Remember To Read The Traffic Signs
9. Be Alert For Changing Road Conditions
10. Ensure That Speed Is Adequate To Pass

Good luck on the MBE!

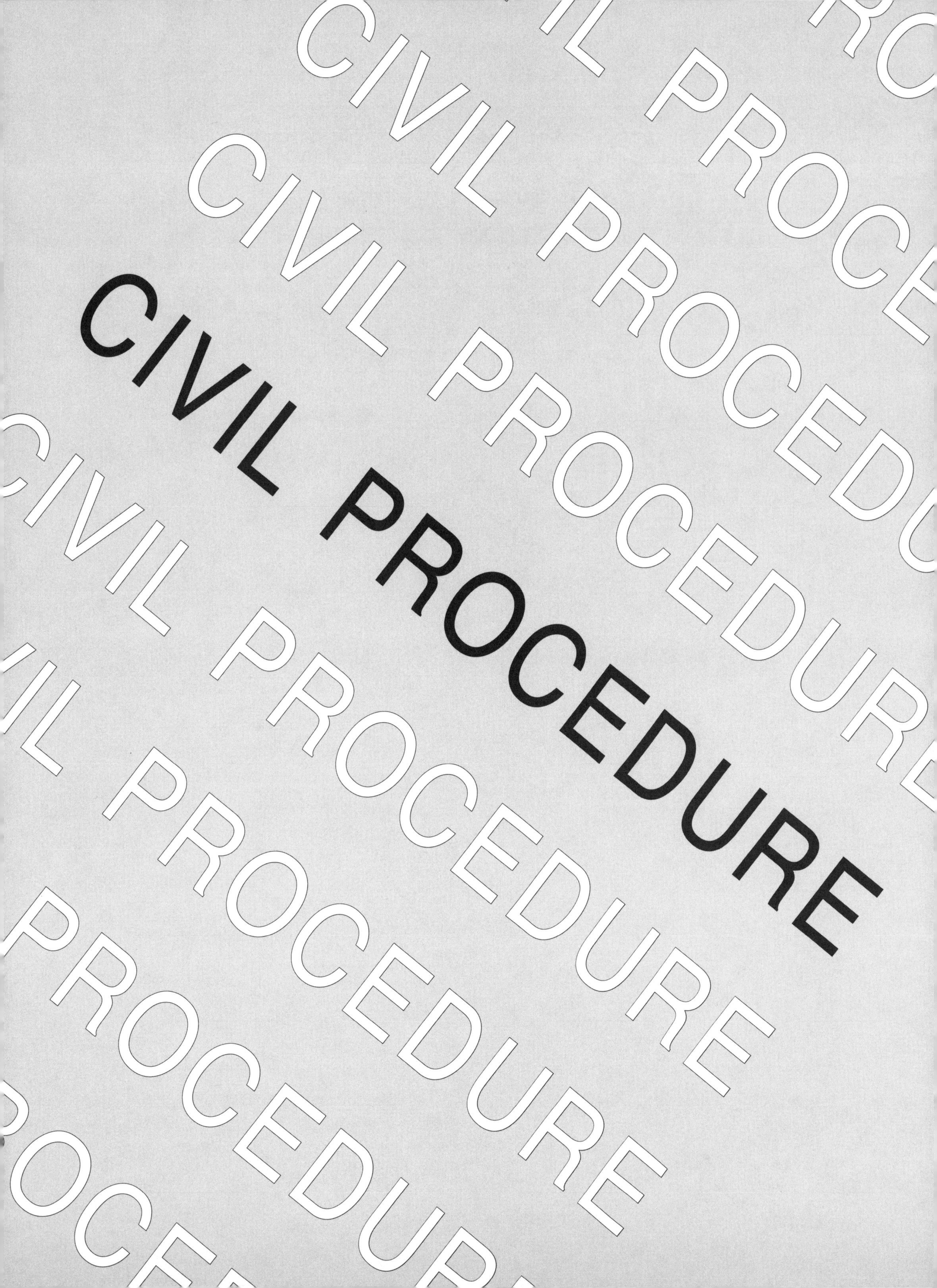
CIVIL PROCEDURE

CIVIL PROCEDURE – QUESTION BREAKDOWN

1. Personal Jurisdiction – Consent
2. Personal Jurisdiction – Domicile
3. Supplemental Jurisdiction – Impleader
4. Supplemental Jurisdiction – Federal Question
5. Subject Matter Jurisdiction – Diversity of Citizenship
6. Personal Jurisdiction – Minimum Contacts
7. Personal Jurisdiction – Long Arm Statute
8. Personal Jurisdiction – Quasi-In-Rem Jurisdiction
9. Removal
10. Personal Jurisdiction – Minimum Contacts
11. Personal Jurisdiction – Minimum Contacts
12. Venue – Waiver
13. Joinder
14. Subject Matter Jurisdiction – Diversity of Citizenship
15. Venue
16. Removal – Convenience of the Parties and Witnesses
17. Personal Jurisdiction – Quasi-In-Rem
18. Supplemental Jurisdiction
19. Subject Matter Jurisdiction
20. Impleader – Personal Jurisdiction
21. Joinder of Claims
22. Subject Matter Jurisdiction – Diversity of Citizenship
23. Supplemental Jurisdiction
24. Joinder – Impleader
25. Joinder – Necessary and Indispensable Parties
26. Class Action – Adequate Representation
27. Class Action – Damages
28. Discovery – Interrogatories
29. Discovery – Disclosure
30. Discovery – Depositions

31. Discovery – Expert Witness Reports

32. Discovery – Questioning Employees about Work Performed in the Ordinary Scope of the Employee's Duties

33. Discovery – Production of Documents

34. Class Action – Collateral Estoppel

35. Right to a Jury Trial

36. General Appearance

37. Pretrial Disposition – Voluntary Dismissal

38. Pretrial Disposition – Summary Judgment

39. Pleadings – Leave to Amend

40. Motion for Judgment as a Matter of Law

41. Jury

42. Appellate Review

43. Appellate Review

44. Joinder

45. Pretrial Disposition – Summary Judgment

46. Split Cause of Action

47. Alienage Jurisdiction

48. Res Judicata – On the Merits

49. Res Judicata – Same Transaction or Occurrence

50. Res Judicata

51. Pleadings

52. Discovery – Disclosures

53. Discovery – Deposition of Experts

54. Discovery - Documents

55. Discovery – Disclosure of Witnesses

56. Summary Judgment

57. Res Judicata – Split Cause of Action

58. Res Judicata – Same Parties or Privies

59. Summary Judgment

60. Discovery – Witness Statement

61. Discovery – Work Product

62. Discovery of Subsequent Remedial Measures

63. Discovery – Work Product

64. Discovery – Attorney-Client Privilege

65. Subject Matter Jurisdiction – Diversity of Citizenship and Amount in Controversy

66. Subject Matter Jurisdiction – Diversity of Citizenship

67. Supplemental Jurisdiction

68. Impleader

69. Supplemental Jurisdiction

70. Counterclaims and Supplemental Jurisdiction

71. Counterclaims

72. Subject Matter Jurisdiction – Federal Question

73. Class Action - Subject Matter Jurisdiction

74. Class Action – Notice

75. Class Action – Representative

76. Class Action – Notice

77. Discovery – Relevance

78. Discovery – Automatic Disclosure

79. Judgment as a Matter of Law

80. Discovery – Physical Examination

81. Discovery – Physical Examination

82. Summary Judgment – Burden of Persuasion

83. Renewed Judgment as a Matter of Law

84. Juror Misconduct

85. Subject Matter Jurisdiction – Diversity of Citizenship

86. Jurisdiction – Personal/Subject Matter

87. Res Judicata – Judgment on the Merits

88. Personal Jurisdiction – Due Process

89. Subject Matter Jurisdiction

90. Res Judicata – Multiple Defendants

91. Collateral Estoppel

92. Subject Matter Jurisdiction

93. Class Action Lawsuits - Settlements

94. Erie

95. Res Judicata

96. Collateral Estoppel

97. Summary Judgment - Burdens of Proof in Criminal and Civil Cases

98. Mutuality of Estoppel

99. Jurisdiction

100. New Trial Motion

CIVIL PROCEDURE QUESTIONS

1. A woman from State X sued a man from State Y for personal injuries that she sustained in an automobile accident when his automobile collided with her truck. This was the man's only trip to State X. She sued him in State X court. The man personally appeared (marking his second time in State X) and answered the complaint, stating that he was not liable, for a whole host of reasons. Four months later, at one of the hearings connected to this lawsuit, the man made a motion to dismiss based on lack of personal jurisdiction. How should the court rule on the man's motion?

   A. The court should grant the man's motion because the man did not consent to State X jurisdiction over him.

   B. The court should grant the man's motion because challenges to personal jurisdiction can be raised at any time.

   C. The court should grant the man's motion because there were no minimum contacts.

   D. The court should deny the man's motion because he consented to State X jurisdiction over him.

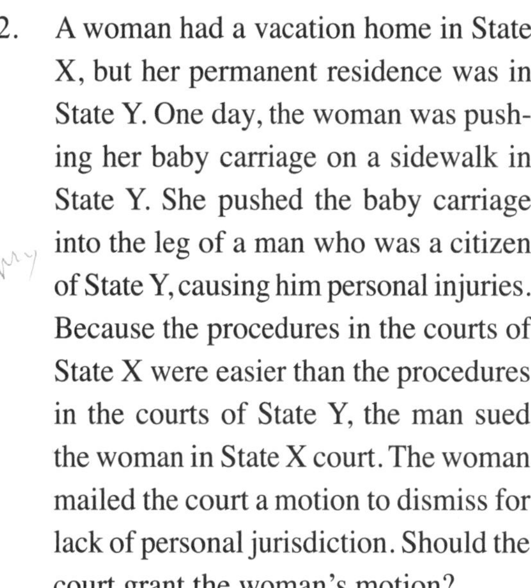

2. A woman had a vacation home in State X, but her permanent residence was in State Y. One day, the woman was pushing her baby carriage on a sidewalk in State Y. She pushed the baby carriage into the leg of a man who was a citizen of State Y, causing him personal injuries. Because the procedures in the courts of State X were easier than the procedures in the courts of State Y, the man sued the woman in State X court. The woman mailed the court a motion to dismiss for lack of personal jurisdiction. Should the court grant the woman's motion?

   A. No because the woman had a vacation home in State X.

   B. No because the woman consented to the personal jurisdiction of the State X court by mailing a motion to the State X court.

   C. Yes because the court lacked personal jurisdiction over the woman.

   D. Yes because the court lacked subject matter jurisdiction over the woman.

3. A woman, a California citizen, purchased a hamburger from a fast food chain in California. She became violently ill after eating the hamburger and filed a lawsuit against the fast food chain in federal district court. The fast food chain was a corporation and a citizen of Florida. The fast food chain believed that meat that was supplied by

its meat supplier was the cause of the woman's injury. The meat supplier was a corporation and a citizen of California. The fast food chain impleaded the meat supplier by serving a third-party complaint and summons on the meat supplier. The woman moved to dismiss the fast food chain's third-party complaint and summons on the meat supplier. How should the court rule?

A. The woman's motion to dismiss should be denied because impleading the meat supplier did not destroy diversity.

B. The woman's motion to dismiss should be denied because a plaintiff can never object to a defendant's impleading another party.

C. The woman's motion to dismiss should be granted because impleading the meat supplier destroyed diversity.

D. The woman's motion to dismiss should be granted because the meat supplier caused her injury.

4. A woman sued her employer in federal district court for discriminating against her on the basis of her gender in violation of a federal civil rights statute. The woman based her lawsuit on the actions of her supervisor. The woman was a citizen of Wyoming, and the employer, a corporation, was a citizen of Nevada. After the lawsuit commenced, the woman added the supervisor as an additional defendant. The supervisor was a citizen of Wyoming. The employer then moved to dismiss the lawsuit for lack of jurisdiction. How should the court rule on the employer's motion?

A. The motion should be dismissed because it was the defendant who was bringing the motion, rather than the plaintiff.

B. The motion should be dismissed because the court had subject matter jurisdiction.

C. The motion should be granted because the addition of the supervisor destroyed diversity.

D. The motion should be granted because the employer should have impleaded the supervisor, rather than the woman adding the supervisor as an additional defendant.

5. A woman went to a Federal Express (FedEx) office to mail a package. While she was waiting in line, she encountered her next-door neighbor who punched her in the face, accusing her of cutting in line. She suffered injury to her face and had $76,000 of medical bills. She brought a lawsuit against the neighbor in federal district court. The neighbor moved to dismiss for lack of subject matter jurisdiction. Will the neighbor prevail?

A. Yes because there was no subject matter jurisdiction here.

B. Yes because there was no personal jurisdiction here.

C. No because there was subject matter jurisdiction here.

D. No because there was personal jurisdiction here.

6. A man commuted to work on a daily basis. The man was a citizen of State X, but he worked in State Z. In order to get to work, he drove on the roads of State Y every day. One day, the man was driving his vehicle in State Y, far in excess of the posted speed limit, in an effort to get to an early meeting at work. His vehicle struck the rear end of a woman's vehicle while the woman was inside that vehicle. The woman suffered severe injuries. She brought a lawsuit against the man in State Y. The man made a motion to dismiss, based on lack of personal jurisdiction. Will his motion be granted?

A. No because the court did not have subject matter jurisdiction here.

B. No because there was personal jurisdiction here.

C. Yes because there was no personal jurisdiction here.

D. Yes because it was inconvenient for the man to defend in State Y.

7. A man sued a woman for defamation after the woman published an article in a Connecticut newspaper stating that the man had attacked her in Connecticut and had stolen her diamond ring. The man was a citizen of Massachusetts, and the woman was a citizen of Connecticut. In fact, the woman had never been to Massachusetts. The man, nonetheless, brought his lawsuit in Massachusetts.

In her answer to the man's complaint, the woman alleged lack of authorization by the Massachusetts Long Arm Statute. The relevant section of the Long Arm Statute provided:

"As to a cause of action arising from any of the acts enumerated in this section, a court may exercise personal jurisdiction over any non-domiciliary who commits a tortious act outside the state causing injury to person or property within the state if he regularly does or solicits business, or engages in any other persistent course of conduct, or derives substantial revenue from goods used or consumed or services rendered in the state."

Which of the following are plausible arguments for the woman to make under the Massachusetts Long Arm statute?

A. The woman did not cause injury to person or property within Massachusetts. In addition, she did not derive substantial revenue from goods used or consumed or services rendered in Massachusetts. Lastly, she did not regularly do or solicit business in Massachusetts.

B. The woman did not transact business within Massachusetts.

C. The woman did not purposefully avail herself of the benefits and protections of Massachusetts law.

D. The woman was not a citizen of Massachusetts.

8. A woman sued a man in California state court for personal injury arising from an auto accident in Ilinois. For the purpose of securing quasi-in-rem jurisdiction, she had the sheriff seize stock certificates that the man had in a California corporation. The man had never been to California and had no contact with California other than his purchase of the stock certificates. The man made a motion to dismiss for lack of quasi-in-rem jurisdiction under the Due Process Clause of the Fourteenth Amendment to the United States Constitution. How should the court rule on the man's motion?

A. The court should dismiss the man's motion because the corporation is a citizen of California.

B. The court should dismiss the man's motion because the man had sufficient minimum contacts with California for the California court to be able to exercise quasi-in-rem jurisdiction here.

C. The court should grant the man's motion because, while the man had sufficient minimum contacts with California, quasi-in-rem jurisdiction is not based on minimum contacts with the forum state.

D. The court should grant the man's motion because the man did not have sufficient minimum contacts with California for the California court to be able to exercise quasi-in-rem jurisdiction here.

9. A woman who was a citizen of Montana filed a lawsuit against a man who was a citizen of Hawaii, alleging $76,800 in damages after the man knocked her down on the sidewalk as he was attempting to steal her purse. The woman brought the lawsuit in Hawaii state court.

The man filed a petition to remove the action to the federal district court in Hawaii. How should the court rule on the man's motion?

A. The man's motion should be granted because there was supplemental jurisdiction.

B. The man's motion should be granted because there was subject matter jurisdiction.

C. The man's motion should be denied because the woman was a citizen of Montana.

D. The man's motion should be denied because the man was a citizen of Hawaii.

10. An American woman visited a foreign country located thousands of miles from the nearest U.S. border. She purchased ten small toys in a local toy store in that country. This toy store had never sold any toys in the United States, nor did it ever plan to do so. When she returned to the USA, she gave the toys to her friends' children as presents. When one of the children was playing with the toy, a piece of glass in the toy injured the child's eye. The child's parents, on behalf of the child, filed a lawsuit in United States district court against the toy store. The lawsuit claimed $76,400 in damages. The toy store made a pre-answer motion under Rule 12(b)(2) of the Federal Rules of Civil Procedure to dismiss the claim against it for lack of personal jurisdiction. Which of the following is (are) a plausible argument(s) in support of the motion?

    A. Whether or not the toy store purposefully availed itself of the U.S. market, it would be fundamentally unreasonable and unfair for a court in the United States to exercise personal jurisdiction because the interests of the plaintiff and the forum in the assertion of jurisdiction by the federal court in the U.S. is slight, and the burden on the toy store in defending thousands of miles from the toy store's home country and in a foreign legal system (i.e., the U.S. legal system) is great.

    B. The toy store did not purposefully avail itself of the U.S. market because it performed no action that was purposefully directed at the U.S. Therefore, the court cannot exercise personal jurisdiction over the toy store.

    C. Even though the toy store did not purposefully avail itself of the U.S. market, the court can exercise personal jurisdiction over the toy store because it is fair and reasonable in light of the great interest to both the plaintiff and the forum state (the U.S.) in having the child's claim adjudicated in a U.S. court.

    D. The toy store did purposefully avail itself of the U.S. market by deliberately placing the ten toys into the stream of commerce when it reasonably knew that such toys would flow to the U.S. where they would be used by children in the U.S.

11. A meat packer in Nebraska sold meat to a restaurant in Oklahoma on a regular basis. A man went to the restaurant for dinner. He ordered and ate a steak containing meat from the Nebraska meat packer. When he returned home that night, he became violently ill as a result of consuming the meat. He was

hospitalized for food poisoning. He brought a lawsuit in Oklahoma, naming the meat packer as the defendant. The meat packer filed a motion to dismiss for lack of personal jurisdiction. How should the court rule on the motion?

A. The court should deny the motion because it had personal jurisdiction over the meat packer.

B. The court should deny the motion because it had personal jurisdiction over the man.

C. The court should grant the motion because it did not have personal jurisdiction over the meat packer.

D. The court should grant the motion because it did not have personal jurisdiction over the man.

12. A woman sued a man in federal district court, alleging that the man had dropped a safe on her automobile, destroying the vehicle. The court was located across the street from where the incident had occurred in the same state of which the woman was resident, but not in the same state of which the man was a resident.

The man made a motion to dismiss based on lack of personal jurisdiction and lack of subject matter jurisdiction. The court denied the man's motions. The man then moved to dismiss based on improper venue. How should the court rule on the man's motion to dismiss for improper venue?

A. Venue was proper because the woman resided in the forum state. In addition, the incident occurred in the forum state.

B. Venue was improper because the woman and the man resided in different states.

C. Venue was improper because the man did not reside in the forum state.

D. The man waived his venue objection.

13. One afternoon, a cannibal who was a citizen of Maine went up to a woman who was a citizen of Wyoming, knocked her out with drugs, and cut off both of her ears, which he fried and cooked in a barbeque sauce that he had created to sell to stores throughout the state.

When the woman woke up, she was horrified to find herself without any ears. She brought a personal injury lawsuit in federal district court against the man, alleging $500,000 in damages.

After bringing her lawsuit, the woman added an additional claim against the man – namely, that he had violated her intellectual property rights under federal law to the barbeque sauce recipe and that she had created this recipe before the man had done so.

The man moved to dismiss the first claim for lack of jurisdiction, and he moved to dismiss the second claim because it did not arise out the same transaction as the main claim. How should the court rule on the man's motions?

A. Both the first and second claims should be dismissed.

B. The second claim should be dismissed because it is an improper cross-claim. It does not arise out of the same transaction as the woman's main claim.

C. Neither the first claim nor the second claim should be dismissed.

D. The first claim should be dismissed for lack of subject matter jurisdiction.

14. A man from North Carolina sued a company whose headquarters were in South Carolina for injuries that occurred in Nevada as a result of the company's actions. The total damages were $80,000, and the man brought his lawsuit in federal district court. About eight months later, while the man's lawsuit was still pending, it came out that the owner of the company, who lived in North Carolina, may be personally liable for the man's damages if the man were to prevail in his lawsuit against the company. As a result, the owner made a motion to intervene in the man's lawsuit. Will the owner's motion be granted?

A. Yes because the intervention motion was proper under these facts.

B. Yes because people can always intervene in lawsuits, regardless of the effects on subject matter jurisdiction.

C. No because this would destroy subject matter jurisdiction.

D. No because it would destroy personal jurisdiction.

15. A woman brought a lawsuit in federal district court against four defendants, who were all from the same state as the forum court. The state had four federal judicial districts. The woman's lawsuit was brought in the southern judicial district where both she and one of the defendants lived and where the incident that was the subject of the woman's lawsuit had occurred.

One of the other defendants resided in the northern district, another resided in the central district, and the last defendant resided in the eastern district. Before answering the woman's complaint, these three defendants immediately made a motion to dismiss for improper venue. Which of the following rulings is correct?

A. All three of these defendants waived their venue objection because they failed to raise it in a pre-answer motion.

B. Venue was improper because only one of the defendants resided in the southern district.

C. Venue was proper because all defendants were subject to personal jurisdiction in the southern district at the time that the action was commenced.

D. Venue was proper because one defendant could be found in the southern district, and there was no district in which the action could have otherwise been brought.

16. A woman who was a citizen of the United States and a resident of Minnesota brought a lawsuit against a man who was a U.S. citizen, but a resident of Istanbul, Turkey. The woman's lawsuit alleged that the man, while visiting Minnesota, met with other individuals for the purpose of violating the Sherman Antitrust Act. The woman filed the case in United States district court in Minnesota.

The man then moved to dismiss the case invoking the doctrine of *forum non conveniens*.

Turkey has a body of law that is roughly the equivalent of U.S. antitrust law. How should the court rule on the man's motion?

A. The man's motion should be denied because, even though the relevant law in Turkey is roughly the same as the law in the United States, it would be somewhat more difficult for the woman to win a judgment against the man under substantive Turkish law.

B. The man's motion should be denied because the woman, as the plaintiff, controls where the case is brought.

C. Because the man was a resident of Turkey and was only visiting the United States at the time of the alleged incident, U.S. courts have no jurisdiction over the man. Thus, the man's motion should be granted because Turkish courts are the only courts that can hear this case.

D. The man's motion should be granted, even if it would be more difficult for the woman to win a judgment against the man under substantive Turkish law.

17. A woman sued a man for personal injuries arising out of the man's misuse of handcuffs while on vacation in Nevada. The woman was from Rhode Island, and the man was from Vermont. The woman brought the lawsuit in Rhode Island, after discovering that the man had a bank account in Rhode Island. The man had opened the bank account after receiving an inheritance from his father ten years prior. Since opening the bank account, the man had not made any deposits to or withdrawals from the bank account. Furthermore, since opening the bank account, the man had never returned to Rhode Island and had no other contacts with the state.

The woman attached the man's bank account for the purpose of securing quasi-in-rem jurisdiction. Rhode Island granted the man the right to enter a limited appearance for the purpose of contesting jurisdiction. He timely moved to dismiss for lack of quasi-in-rem jurisdiction. How should the court rule on the man's motion?

A. The court should grant the man's motion because the man had no contacts with Rhode Island, other than going there ten years earlier to open up the bank account.

B. The court should grant the man's motion because quasi-in-rem is always a basis for subject matter jurisdiction.

C. The court should deny the man's motion because quasi-in-rem is still sometimes a basis for jurisdiction.

D. The court should deny the man's motion because quasi-in-rem is no longer a basis for personal jurisdiction.

18. A man who was a citizen of Maine sued a woman who was a citizen of New Hampshire in federal district court for defamation. After the lawsuit commenced, the man discovered that the woman's daughter, who was a citizen of Maine, may have assisted the woman in defaming the man. The man brought a motion to add the daughter as an additional defendant. The woman moved to dismiss the lawsuit. How should the court rule on the woman's motion?

A. The court should deny the woman's motion because subject matter jurisdiction was not destroyed.

B. The court should deny the woman's motion because only the woman could have added the daughter.

C. The court should grant the woman's motion because subject matter jurisdiction was destroyed.

D. The court should grant the woman's motion because subject matter jurisdiction was based on federal question.

19. A woman from San Francisco, California, sued a man from San Diego, California, in federal court. She asked for $74,000 in damages. The basis of the lawsuit was that the man had violated the woman's copyrights;. The man moved to dismiss for lack of subject matter jurisdiction. Will he prevail?

A. Yes because both the woman and the man are from California.

B. Yes because the amount in controversy is less than $75,000.

C. No because there was personal jurisdiction here.

D. No because there was subject matter jurisdiction here.

20. A woman who was a citizen of Nevada sued a man who was a citizen of California for injuries that she suffered in an automobile collision that was allegedly caused by the man's vehicle while it was being driven in Nevada. The woman brought her lawsuit in federal district court in California.

The man subsequently served a timely third-party complaint and summons on his cousin, who was a citizen of Nevada, while the cousin was visiting his college roommate in California. The man's third-party complaint stated a claim for contribution among joint tortfeasors, a state law tort, alleging that the cousin who had been driving the man's vehicle at the time of the collision was 50% at fault for the woman's injuries.

In response, the cousin served on the man a third-party answer in which the cousin denied any responsibility for the collision, stating that the accident had occurred because the brakes in the man's vehicle had failed, which was a result of the man failing to maintain his vehicle in proper working order. The cousin's third-party answer also included a defense of lack of personal jurisdiction.

The cousin then moved to dismiss the third-party complaint. How should the court rule on the cousin's motion?

A. Because the sole basis for subject matter jurisdiction over the man's third-party claim was diversity jurisdiction, *Erie* requires that the court apply California's state court "special appearance" rule. Applying such rule, the cousin waived his defense of lack of personal jurisdiction.

B. The court cannot exercise personal jurisdiction over the cousin, a non-resident of California because the man's contribution claim against the cousin arose out of the cousin driving a car in Nevada, not in California.

C. The man improperly impleaded his cousin because it is solely the prerogative of the plaintiff which of the several joint tortfeasors to sue.

D. The cousin was properly impleaded and was subject to personal jurisdiction because he was served with process in California.

21. A woman was scared to death by a man when the man put on a scary mask and scared her so much that she had a heart attack and died. The woman's estate brought a wrongful death lawsuit against the man, in federal district court, alleging $35,000 in damages.

As it happens, the man had also been the woman's boss in a large interstate corporation, and he had terminated her employment the week before her death. The woman's estate thus brought an additional claim against the man for wrongful termination, alleging $70,000 in damages.

The woman was a citizen of Hawaii, and the man was a citizen of Alaska.

The man moved to dismiss the entire lawsuit for lack of subject matter jurisdiction. He also moved to dismiss the second claim because it was wholly unrelated to the first claim.

How should the court rule on the man's motions?

A. The court should deny the man's first motion, but grant the man's second motion.

B. The court should grant the man's first motion but deny the man's second motion.

C. The court should deny both of the man's motions.

D. The court should grant both of the man's motions.

22. A woman worked for the post office in California. She had to quit her job because her boss, a man, was constantly asking her for sexual favors. Both the woman and the man were citizens of California. The woman sued the man in federal district court in California for sexual harassment, alleging $100,000 in damages. The man brought a motion to dismiss based on lack of subject matter jurisdiction. How should the court rule on the man's motion?

A. The court should dismiss the man's motion because there was subject matter jurisdiction.

B. The court should dismiss the man's motion because there was personal jurisdiction here.

C. The court should grant the man's motion because there was subject matter jurisdiction here.

D. The court should grant the man's motion because there was no subject matter jurisdiction here.

23. A woman sued a man in federal district court for negligence, alleging $500,000 in damages. The woman was a citizen of Nevada, and the man was a citizen of New Mexico. Subsequently, the man served a third-party complaint and summons on the woman's neighbor, also a citizen of Nevada, asserting a claim for contribution alleging that the woman's neighbor is 50% at fault and that, if the man is liable to the plaintiff, then the woman's neighbor is liable to the man for half the damages. Then, the plaintiff amended her complaint to add the neighbor as an additional defendant. How should the court rule?

A. The neighbor's motion will be denied because the woman's

claim against her neighbor was supported by supplemental jurisdiction, since this "Rule 14" jclaim was sufficiently related to her claim against the man.

B. The neighbor's motion will be denied because there was ancillary jurisdiction over the woman's claim against her neighbor.

C. The neighbor's motion will be granted because there was no pendent jurisdiction over the woman's claim against her neighbor.

D. The neighbor's motion will be granted because the court had no supplemental jurisdiction over the woman's claim against the neighbor.

24. A company owned seven commercial fishing vessels. Each of these boats was operated by a captain and two crewmen. The Internal Revenue Service assessed and collected employment taxes for the crewmen from the company, taking the position that the company was the "employer" of the crewmen. The company then sued the U.S. Government for the refund of the employment taxes. The U.S. Government served a third-party complaint and summons on each of the captains, alleging that if the company were able to prove that it was not the "employer" of the crewmen and, thus, not liable for their employment taxes, it would automatically follow that the captains were the "employers" of the crewmen and would be liable to pay the U.S. the very employment taxes the U.S. would have to refund to the company. The captains moved to dismiss the third-party complaint against themselves. Which of the following rulings is most nearly correct?

A. Impleader of the captains was proper because the liability of the captains arose out of the same operative facts as the company's refund claim against the U.S. Government.

B. Impleader of the captains was proper because either the company or the captains were liable as "employers" for the crewmen's employment taxes.

C. Impleader of the captains was improper because the U.S. Government's claim against the captains was not a contingent or derivative claim but, rather, an independent claim based upon the captains' liability to the U.S. (under the tax code).

D. Impleader of the captains was proper, because, otherwise, the U.S. would be exposed to the risk of inconsistent judgments if it had to assert its claim against the captains in a separate lawsuit with a separate trial.

25. A man underwent surgery in which a "plate and screw" device was implanted

in his lower spine. The surgical procedure caused him greater discomfort than did his previous condition. The device was manufactured by a device company. The surgery was performed by a doctor in a hospital.

The man brought a state court lawsuit against the doctor and the hospital, alleging malpractice and negligence. He also filed suit in federal district court against the device company, alleging defective design and manufacture of the device. The company filed a motion: (1) to require the man to join the doctor and the hospital as defendants arguing that they are "necessary parties" under Rule 19(a) of the Federal Rules of Civil Procedure; and (2) if the man were unable to join the doctor and hospital, the court must dismiss the man's lawsuit because the doctor and hospital were "indispensable" parties under Rule 19(b) of the Federal Rules of Civil Procedure. Which of the following rulings is most nearly correct?

A. The motion should be denied because joint tortfeasors are not "necessary" or "indispensable" parties.

B. The motion should be granted because the public's interest in judicial economy will be harmed by multiple lawsuits where one federal suit can resolve the controversy.

C. The motion should be granted because it is prejudicial to the defendants to have the two separate lawsuits being carried on simultaneously. The company's defense will be that the plate was not defective, but that the doctor and hospital were negligent. On the other hand, the doctor's and the hospital's defense will be that they were not negligent, but that the plate was defective.

D. The motion should be granted because joint tortfeasors are "necessary" or "indispensable" parties.

26. A group of mine workers developed lung cancer after years of working in the mines. One of the mine workers was a law student who worked in the mine during summers when he was in law school. Once he became an attorney, he specialized in class action lawsuits involving former mine workers who developed lung cancer. Ironically, he himself later developed lung cancer around the same time as his other former colleagues from the mines. The former mine workers brought a class action lawsuit against the mine company for causing their lung cancer, asking for $75,000 in damages. Because he was now an attorney, he acted both as counsel for the class and as the named class representative.

At the class certification hearing on the issue of the adequacy of class representation by this former mine worker-turned attorney, which of the following arguments is correct?

A. Class representation by this individual would be adequate because he has extensive experience as an attorney in these types of class action lawsuits.

B. Class representation by this individual would be adequate because his law firm gives the class access to substantial financial and clerical resources.

C. Class representation by this individual would be inadequate because the class claims only $75,000 in damages.

D. Class representation by this individual would be inadequate because having him serving as class counsel and as class representative would present a conflict of interest.

27. Five thousand individuals were allegedly injured at a concert when several microphones and speakers malfunctioned and tipped over. Some individuals who had been standing close to the speakers at the time in question alleged that they had suffered hearing loss, while the individuals who had been standing close to the microphones alleged damages from electrocution. Other individuals alleged that they had been injured when they were crushed by the falling speakers.

A number of individuals who had allegedly been crushed by the falling speakers at the concert sought to sue the company that managed the venue in federal district court as representatives of the entire class of 5,000 individuals who had allegedly been injured at the concert. How should the court rule?

A. The court should find that these individuals may represent the entire class of 5,000 people because the class is so numerous that joinder of all members is impracticable.

B. The court should find that these individuals may represent the entire class of 5,000 people because the representative parties will fairly and adequately protect the interests of the class.

C. The court should find that these individuals may not represent the entire class of 5,000 people because these individuals do not have identical – or virtually identical – claims.

D. The court should find that these individuals may not represent the entire class of 5,000 people because the multitude of plaintiffs rule prevents such a large number of individuals from comprising a class.

28. A woman brought a lawsuit against a man, in federal district court based on the fact that the man's dog had bitten her leg. The woman served interrogatories

on the man, one of which stated:

"Please provide us with a list of all of the dates on which your dog has received rabies vaccinations in the past ten years."

The man responded to the above interrogatory. In his response, he wrote:

"This interrogatory is objectionable. As a result, I refuse to answer."

LACKS SPECIFICITY

The woman made a motion to compel the man to answer this interrogatory. How should the court rule on this motion?

A. The motion should be denied because the man's objection to the interrogatory was proper.

B. The motion should be denied because the woman exceeded the maximum number of interrogatories.

C. The motion should be granted because the woman did not exceed the maximum number of interrogatories.

D. The motion should be granted because the man should have answered the interrogatory.

29. During the discovery phase of a lawsuit, which of the following information is a plaintiff entitled to receive under the mandatory ("required") disclosure rules?

A. The name and, if known, the address and telephone number of each individual likely to have discoverable information—along with the subjects of that information—that the disclosing party may use to support its claims or defenses, unless the use would be solely for impeachment.

B. An action by the United States to collect on a student loan guaranteed by the United States.

C. A forfeiture action in rem arising from a federal statute.

D. A petition for habeas corpus or any other proceeding to challenge a criminal conviction or sentence.

30. During the discovery phase of a lawsuit that was pending in federal district court, the plaintiff and his attorney started to depose the defendant. The deposition was taken before a notary public whose commission came from the state in which they were located. The notary public did not have any special commission from the federal government. The defendant objected to having his deposition taken before a notary public and demanded that his deposition be taken before someone with authorization from the federal court. The deposition was then terminated until the judge could rule on the defendant's objection. How should the judge rule?

A. The judge should overrule the objection and officiate at the deposition himself.

B. The judge should overrule the objection and rule that the deposition can resume because the notary public is allowed to hear depositions.

C. The judge should deputize the notary public and then overrule the objection to allow the notary public to hear the deposition.

D. The judge should sustain the objection.

31. A woman was injured in an explosion. She brought a lawsuit in federal court against the company that owned the building where the explosion had taken place, asking for $5,000,000 in damages. The woman alleged that the explosion had been caused by chemicals that had been negligently stored inside the building.

The company owners sent a chemist to the former site of the building for the purpose of determining whether he would make a good trial expert witness. The chemist spent two hours investigating the wreckage and wrote a five-page report concluding that chemicals were the sole cause of the explosion. The chemist was paid an agreed honorarium of $200 and was never contacted by the building owners again. The woman demanded a copy of the chemist's report to the company owners through the appropriate method. The company owners objected, and the woman moved to compel production of the report. Which of the following rulings on the woman's motion is correct?

A. The report should be produced, only if the woman could show a substantial need for it and an inability to get the substantial equivalent of the report's contents without undue hardship.

B. The report should be produced because its contents were relevant to the subject matter and it had not been prepared in anticipation of litigation.

C. The report should be produced, only if the woman could show exceptional circumstances.

D. The report should not be produced under any circumstances because the chemist was an informally consulted expert.

32. A train crashed into a man's living room. The man, while not injured, was severely traumatized, and his living room was completely wrecked. The man sued the train company in federal district court. He served a notice of deposition on an employee of the train company who worked in the company's accident prevention department. The employee had a degree in mechanical engineering and was the person who

first examined the wreckage of the train immediately after the crash to determine the cause of the crash, as part of his accident prevention duties.

Two months later, the employee was assigned to the train company's legal team as an expert whose duties were to re-examine the wreckage to assist the train company's attorneys in the preparation of the train company's defense to the man's lawsuit. The employee will not testify for the train company at trial. The train company moved for a protective order that the train company's deposition not take place. The train company argued that the employee was a non-testifying expert who the train company specially employed in preparation for trial and, therefore, the man needed to make a showing of "exceptional circumstances" under which it was impracticable for the man to obtain the employee's facts and opinions by other means. The man responded that he wanted to question the employee solely about the facts acquired by the employee during the employee's initial examination of the wreckage immediately after the crash. Which of the following rulings is most nearly correct?

A. The train company's motion should be denied, but only if the man could show substantial need for the employee's deposition and that the man was unable without undue hardship to obtain the substantial equivalent of the information known to the employee by other means.

B. The train company's motion should be denied because the employee was an ordinary percipient witness with respect to the facts sought to be discovered by the man on deposition.

C. The train company's motion should be denied, but only if the man could show exceptional circumstances for deposing the employee.

D. The train company's motion should be granted because the facts the man sought to discover from the employee's deposition were irrelevant to the subject matter of the lawsuit.

33. A mechanic employed by an airport witnessed an airplane crash at that airport. Believing that the airline would likely be facing a lawsuit by the injured passengers, the mechanic sent the airline's lawyers a signed note recounting what he had observed. The mechanic was correct, and a lawsuit ensued in federal district court. One of the plaintiffs, an injured passenger, sought to discover this note, and the airline objected. On a motion by that plaintiff to compel production of the note, which of the following rulings is correct?

A. The note was discoverable because it was relevant to the subject matter.

B. The note is not discoverable because the mechanic's status

as an expert mechanic protected the note under Rule 26(b)(4) of the Federal Rules of Civil Procedure.

C. The note was not discoverable because it was a written witness statement that was protected as ordinary work product.

D. The note was not discoverable because it was protected under the attorney-client privilege.

34. A class of individuals sued a bus company, in federal district court in Iowa, for injuries suffered in a highway accident in that state, alleging that the bus driver had been negligent. One of the passengers, a woman, opted out of the class action while the lawsuit was still in its preliminary stages. However, in response to the class action notice that she had received from the class representatives, the woman brought a personal injury suit against the bus company in Iowa state court for damages arising out of the highway accident, also alleging that the bus driver had been negligent.

The class action went to trial, and the plaintiff class won. Judgment was entered for the class. After judgment had been entered for the class in the federal class action suit, the woman moved for partial summary judgment in her lawsuit against the bus company, requesting the court to order that, based upon the federal class action judgment, it had been conclusively established in the woman's lawsuit that the bus company was liable in negligence to the woman (leaving only damages to be determined). Which of the following statements is not correct?

A. If the case law of the Federal Court of Appeals for the Eighth Circuit clearly forbids plaintiffs who opt out of a class action from using collateral estoppel offensively, but Iowa state case law does allow such plaintiffs to use collateral estoppel offensively, the Iowa court could not grant the woman's motion.

B. The Due Process Clause of the United States Constitution prevented the woman from invoking collateral estoppel against the bus company in reliance upon the class action judgment.

C. If the Iowa state court determined that the woman had been motivated to opt-out in order to "wait and see" whether the class action turned out to be successful, the court would likely deny the woman's motion.

D. If the federal courts would have preventedjk the woman from relying on the previous judgment in favor of the class, then the Iowa court could not grant the woman's motion.

35. A bill is pending before Congress to deter sexual harassment in the workplace. During the debates surrounding this bill, an issue arose as to whether juries or judges should determine factual issues in trials involving lawsuits brought under the new Act. Which of the following versions of the statute would violate the Seventh Amendment to the U.S. Constitution?

    A. The statute creates a new private right of action for sexual harassment, allows both injunctive relief and damages, and provides that all issues of fact will be tried by a judge without regard to the remedy sought.

    B. The statute creates a new private right of action for sexual harassment, allows both injunctive relief and damages, and provides that all questions of fact shall be tried by a jury (or, if the right to a jury trial is waived, by a judge) without regard to the remedy demanded.

    C. The statute creates a new private right of action for sexual harassment, allows both injunctive relief and damages, and is silent on the issue of who shall be the trier of fact, judge or jury.

    D. The statute creates a comprehensive federal regulatory program intended to stop sexual harassment in the workplace and permits the federal government to bring suit against violators before the federal Sexual Harassment Agency seeking the imposition of fines. All actions brought under the statute shall be tried before the federal Sexual Harassment Agency.

36. A creditor sued a debtor for money owed. The creditor served the complaint upon the debtor. Rather than file an answer, the debtor engaged in settlement negotiations with the creditor. The settlement negotiations lasted for six weeks, which exceeded the period for the debtor to file an answer to the creditor's complaint.

    The creditor, without indicating any previous intent to do so, then filed a motion for default judgment against the debtor in federal district court. The court granted the creditor's motion. The debtor then moved to set aside the default judgment under Rule 60(b) of the Federal Rules of Civil Procedure. Which of the following rulings is correct?

    A. The default judgment should be set aside because the debtor's act of entering into settlement negotiations shows that he was not in default.

    B. The default judgment should be set aside because the debtor's act of entering into settlement negotiations constitutes an appearance by the debtor.

C. The default judgment should not be set aside because the settlement negotiations did not prevent a default judgment from being entered.

D. The default judgment should not be set aside because there is no way to avoid a default judgment if one fails to answer in a timely manner.

37. A woman sued a man in federal district court for intentional infliction of emotional distress. The man served an answer to the complaint, denying the operative allegations of the complaint. Shortly thereafter, the woman filed a notice of dismissal, and the man moved to quash and vacate the notice of dismissal. Which of the following statements is most nearly correct?

A. The motion should be denied because the man had not yet moved for summary judgment.

B. The motion should be denied because the action had not proceeded to the point in which the man would be prejudiced.

C. The motion should be granted because the man had previously answered the complaint.

D. The motion should be granted because plaintiffs never have an absolute right to voluntarily dismiss their own actions.

38. A woman sued a doctor in federal district court, alleging malpractice. In her complaint, she alleged that, during surgery performed by that doctor, a sponge had been left in her abdomen.

The doctor answered the complaint with a general denial. He then made a motion for summary judgment, alleging that the woman had failed to show that the sponge had been left in her abdomen during the surgery in question, as she had had other surgeries in the recent past. The woman responded by submitting her complaint.

How should the court rule on the doctor's motion for summary judgment?

A. The motion should be denied because of the doctrine of *res ipsa loquitur*.

B. The motion should be denied because the doctor did not meet his movant's burden.

C. The motion should be granted because the woman did not meet her respondent's burden.

D. The motion should be granted because the absence of affidavits or deposition testimony means that there were no credibility issues to resolve.

39. A woman sued a man in federal district court. The court held a pre-trial conference. The pre-trial order that

resulted from the conference specified that copyright infringement under the Federal Copyright Act was the woman's only cause of action.

On the third day of trial, the woman sought to amend the pre-trial order to add certain state common law claims. Which of the following statements is correct?

A. The woman had a right to amend the pre-trial order to add another related cause of action.

B. The woman could amend the pre-trial order provided she could show exceptional circumstances for doing so.

C. Leave of court to allow plaintiffs to amend the pre-trial order shall be freely granted, as a matter of policy.

D. Leave of court to amend the pre-trial order is granted only to prevent manifest injustice.

40. A client sued his lawyer in federal district court for malpractice for failing to file a lawsuit before the statute of limitations had run. The case went to trial. The client's sole evidence was his own testimony that the lawyer had not filed the lawsuit prior to the running of the statute of limitations, that the client had had a strong case and, had the lawsuit been filed been filed prior to the running of the statute of limitations, the client would likely have prevailed.

In rebuttal, the lawyer testified not only that the client had such a weak case that the client would not have won his case even if the case had been filed prior to the running of the statute of limitations, but also, that the lawyer had filed the client's lawsuit prior to the running of the statute of limitations. In addition, four other attorneys who were disinterested each testified for the lawyer that they had been present at the courthouse and witnessed the lawyer file the case on a date that was prior to the running of the statute of limitations.

At the close of all the evidence, the lawyer moved for a judgment as a matter of law. Which of the following rulings is correct?

A. The court should grant the motion because the lawyer presented corroborated and disinterested testimony, which overwhelmed the client's sole testimony on the issue.

B. The court should grant the motion because the client's testimony was not credible as a matter of law.

C. The court should deny the motion because the lawyer did not make the motion before the close of the client's case.

D. The court should deny the motion because the jury should have had the opportunity to determine the credibility of the client's testimony.

41. A man sued a woman in federal district court. The jury ultimately rendered a verdict in favor of the woman. The man moved for a new trial. He submitted the affidavits of three jurors each stating: (1) that each had observed that the man had shifted uncomfortably in his seat at plaintiff's counsel table throughout the trial; and (2) that the man had looked scared— which caused each of the three jurors to believe that he was lying on the stand. Which of the following rulings is correct?

   A. The motion should be granted because jurors are not allowed to base their decisions on their observations of the parties' demeanors.

   B. The motion should be granted because what the jurors observed in the courtroom amounted to extraneous prejudicial information improperly brought to the jury's attention.

   C. The motion should be denied because the jurors' three affidavits contained no evidence of jury misconduct.

   D. The motion should be denied because, even though the jurors had engaged in jury misconduct, that misconduct was not prejudicial.

42. A woman sued a man in federal district court. The jury ultimately returned a verdict in favor of the man. The woman appealed, raising for the first time the objection to the admission into evidence of testimony that she considered to be hearsay. Which of the following rulings by the Court of Appeals is correct?

   A. The objection was not reviewable because the woman did not raise it in the trial court.

   B. The objection was not reviewable because the trial judge committed the error during the middle of the trial; therefore, it was interlocutory.

   C. The objection was reviewable because, if the testimony was hearsay, it could have prejudiced the verdict.

   D. The objection is reviewable because this was an "exceptional circumstance" where justice might otherwise not result.

43. A woman sued a man in federal district court. Before the verdict was rendered, the man also moved for attorney's fees to be included in his verdict should he be the prevailing party. In the end, a verdict was rendered in favor of the man. However, the court denied the man's motion for attorney's fees.

The woman then appealed the judgment. The man subsequently appealed the denial of his motion for attorney's fees. How should the Court of Appeals rule?

A. The error was reviewable because the man was not attacking the trial judge on the underlying merits of the court's judgment in favor of the man.

B. The error was reviewable because the man had previously raised the error in the district court.

C. The error was not reviewable because this is not the kind of attack that the man could make on the trial court's findings.

D. The error was not reviewable because it was harmless error.

44. A woman who was a citizen of Arizona was walking on a sidewalk with her purse open. A man who was a citizen of New Mexico ran alongside the woman, reached into her purse and pulled out an expensive fountain pen. The woman spat in the man's face, so he opened the pen and used it to draw all over the woman's face.

The woman sued the man in federal district court for battery. She alleged $80,000 in damages. The woman was ultimately successful in her battery claim against the man.

The man then brought a lawsuit against the woman for battery because she had spat in his face. He alleged $76,000 in damages.

The woman moved to dismiss the man's battery lawsuit, alleging that the man's battery claim against the woman should have been raised as a counterclaim in the woman's original lawsuit. How should the court rule?

A. The court should deny the woman's motion, vacate the original judgment in the woman's favor, and require the woman to relitigate her battery claim against the man.

B. The court should deny the woman's motion, but leave undisturbed the original judgment in the woman's favor.

C. The court should deny the woman's motion and vacate the original judgment in the woman's favor.

D. The court should grant the woman's motion because the man's battery claim constituted a compulsory counterclaim.

45. A man sued a woman in federal district court, alleging breach of contract and interference with perspective commercial advantage. The woman moved for partial summary judgment on the issue of interference with perspective commercial advantage, alleging that she had not known that her alleged breach

of contract would negatively affect the man's other business. The man failed to respond to the woman's motion for partial summary judgment. How should the court rule on the woman's motion?

A. The court should grant the woman's motion because the court can consider the issues raised in the woman's motion to be undisputed.

B. The court should grant the woman's motion because a partial summary judgment still allows the man to proceed to trial.

C. The court should deny the woman's motion because partial summary judgments are no longer permitted in federal courts.

D. The court should deny the woman's motion because of the rule in *Hadley v. Baxendale*.

46. A woman and a man were involved in an automobile collision. The woman's automobile was damaged, and she suffered personal injury. The woman sued the man in federal district court for property damage, demanding $78,000 in damages. Judgment was entered in favor of the woman. The woman then sued the same man, again in federal district court, for her personal injuries arising out of the same accident. The man made a motion for summary judgment to dismiss the woman's claim for personal injury in reliance on the prior judgment in the property damage lawsuit. Which of the following rulings is most nearly correct?

A. The man's motion should be granted because allowing the woman's personal injury claim to move forward would violate the Double Jeopardy clause of the United States Constitution.

B. The man's motion should be granted because the woman's claim for personal injury was part of the same cause of action as her claim for property damage.

C. The man's motion should be denied because the woman's claim for personal injury was not part of the same cause of action as her claim for property damage.

D. The man's motion should be denied because a plaintiff can bring any cause of action at any time, since the plaintiff always controls the lawsuit.

47. A man was a German citizen and a lawful permanent resident of the United States, and his domicile was in California. One afternoon, the man was out for a stroll on a street in Los Angeles, California, swinging his car keys as he walked. A woman who was a citizen of California was walking behind the man found herself in the path of the man's swinging keys; one of the keys stabbed

the woman in her left eye, causing her to completely lose her vision in that eye.

The woman brought a lawsuit for negligence against the man in the federal district court for the Central District of California, located in Los Angeles, asking for $500,000 in damages. The man moved to dismiss for lack of jurisdiction. How should the court rule on the man's motion?

A. The man's motion should be denied because the incident in question took place in Los Angeles, California, which was also where the court was located.

B. The man's motion should be denied because the court had alienage jurisdiction.

C. The man's motion should be granted because federal district courts do not have jurisdiction over negligence actions.

D. The man's motion should be granted because the court lacked jurisdiction under these facts.

48. A woman from Nevada brought a trespass action against a man from Wyoming in federal district court in Nevada. The man moved to dismiss the woman's case on the grounds that the court lacked personal jurisdiction over him, which motion the court granted.

The woman then brought another trespass action against the same man in the federal district court in Wyoming and served the man with a summons while he was visiting the Hoover Dam in Nevada. The man's answer asserted the following by way of defense against the woman's claim: (1) that she did not own the property on which he was alleged to have trespassed; (2) that the man had never trespassed on the property in question, and (3) that the woman's claim was barred by res judicata.

The man then moved to dismiss the woman's suit on grounds of res judicata. Which of the following is the most likely ruling of the court?

A. The court should grant the man's motion because the woman previously sued him on the same cause of action in the Nevada court, and the Nevada federal court rendered a final judgment on the merits.

B. The court should grant the man's motion because the man was not personally served with process in Wyoming.

C. The court should deny the man's motion because trespass actions can be brought in any state.

D. The court should deny the man's motion because the Nevada federal court's judgment was not a judgment on the merits.

49. A man sued a woman in federal district court for defamation based on alleg-

edly false statements that she had made about him to a third party. The case went to trial, and the court ruled in favor of the woman.

The man then sued the same woman, again in federal district court, for invasion of privacy based on false light based on the same allegedly false statements. The woman moved to dismiss. How should the court rule?

A. The court should grant the woman's motion because the defamation and false light invasion of privacy are part of the same transaction or occurrence.

B. The court should deny the woman's motion because defamation and false light invasion of privacy are different transactions.

C. The court should deny the woman's motion because defamation and false light invasion of privacy are based upon different wrongful acts by the woman.

D. The court should deny the woman's motion based on collateral estoppel.

50. A woman claimed ownership through adverse possession of a piece of property. At the same time, a man had a deed to the same piece of property, bearing his name on file in the County Recorder's office. A lumberjack came onto the property without the permission of either the woman or the man and cut down timber, which the lumberjack hauled away and sold.

The woman brought a trespass lawsuit against the lumberjack. The jury ultimately determined that the lumberjack had not trespassed.

The man then brought a trespass lawsuit against the lumberjack in federal court. The lumberjack moved for summary judgment based on res judicata, asking the court to find that it had been conclusively established by the judgment in the lawsuit by the woman against the lumberjack, that the lumberjack had not trespassed. How should the court rule on the lumberjack's motion for summary judgment based on res judicata?

A. The court should grant the lumberjack's motion because the jury, in the lawsuit by the woman against the lumberjack, had already determined that the lumberjack had not trespassed on that piece of property.

B. The court should grant the lumberjack's motion because allowing the issue of trespass to be relitigated would violate the lumberjack's right against double jeopardy.

C. The court should deny the lumberjack's motion because, whether or not the jury actually determined that the lumberjack had not trespassed, the man had not been a party in the lawsuit by the woman against the lumberjack.

D. The court should deny the lumberjack's motion because the lumberjack could not show that the jury, in the lawsuit by the woman against the lumberjack, had actually determined that the lumberjack had not trespassed on that piece of property.

51. A man was driving his automobile on a turnpike when the engine suddenly quit and the automobile slowed down to a stop before the man could steer the automobile to the shoulder of the road. Consequently, the automobile was rear-ended, causing injury to the automobile and to the man.

The man brought a products liability suit in federal district court against the manufacturer of his automobile. The complaint alleged, in pertinent part, that the automobile had been defectively designed and manufactured, without specifying the nature of the defects, and that said defects were the proximate cause of injury to the man and his automobile.

The manufacturer did not make a pre-answer motion but instead filed and served a timely answer to the man's complaint. In addition to denying the allegations of the man's complaint, the answer stated, as a defense, that the allegations regarding the automobile's defects were vague and conclusory and, that because they were central to the man's products liability claim, the complaint should be dismissed.

How should the court rule on a motion by the manufacturer to dismiss the complaint?

A. The motion should be granted, if the court views the allegations regarding the car's defects to be conclusory, which the court need not accept as true and further finds that there are no factual allegations that plausibly suggest that the man is entitled to relief.

B. The motion should be denied because the "defect" allegations were adequately pleaded.

C. The motion should be denied because the manufacturer should have attacked the sufficiency of the allegations in the man's complaint through a pre-answer motion under Rule 12(b)(6) of the Federal Rules of Civil Procedure.

D. The motion should be denied because the manufacturer waived any objection to the sufficiency of the complaint when it responded to the complaint's allegations by denying them.

52. A man was injured when the brakes failed on the bicycle he was riding. Because

the bicycle would not stop, the bicycle crashed into a curb, and the man was thrown off of the bicycle, breaking both of his arms. He then sued the bicycle manufacturer in federal district court. As required by Rule 26(f) of the Federal Rules of Civil Procedure, the parties met, in part, to arrange for the "disclosures" required under Rule 26(a)(1).

At this conference, the man insisted that the bicycle manufacturer had an obligation under Rule 26(a)(1), to "disclose" to the man all persons possibly involved in, and all documents affecting the design, manufacture, and assembly of the same model and year of the bicycle that the man had been riding. The bicycle manufacturer adamantly refused, contending (1) that it did not have a duty to disclose until the man's complaint alleged with particularity the defects in the bicycle, and (2) that the bicycle manufacturer did not have to identify persons with discoverable information who would support the man's claim. Which of the following statements is correct?

A. The bicycle manufacturer was obligated to disclose the identity of each individual with discoverable information, but only as to disputed facts alleged with particularity in the man's complaint.

B. The bicycle manufacturer was obligated to disclose the identity of each individual with discoverable information relevant to the case.

C. The bicycle manufacturer was obligated to disclose the identity of each individual likely to have discoverable information that the bicycle manufacturer could use to support its defenses.

D. The bicycle manufacturer was obligated to disclose the identity of each individual likely to have discoverable information that the bicycle manufacturer could use to support its defenses, but only as to facts alleged with particularity in the man's complaint.

53. A woman purchased a hair dye. Upon applying it to her hair, the majority of her hair fell out. She sued the hair dye manufacturer in federal district court. The manufacturer retained an expert to provide expert testimony on behalf of the hair dye manufacturer at trial. After being retained by the hair dye manufacturer, the expert inspected tested samples of the hair dye. The hair dye manufacturer disclosed to the woman the identity of the expert and provided a report prepared and signed by the expert containing all the information required by Rule 26(a)(2)(B) of the Federal Rules of Civil Procedure.

The woman now sought to depose the expert. The hair dye manufacturer moved for a protective order to bar the deposition of the expert. Which of the following statements is correct?

A. The hair dye manufacturer's motion should be granted because the woman should have hired her own expert to examine samples of the hair dye.

B. The hair dye manufacturer's motion should be granted because the woman failed first to serve interrogatories on the hair dye manufacturer inquiring into the facts and opinions to which the expert would testify at trial.

C. The hair dye manufacturer's motion should be granted because the facts and opinions of the hair dye manufacturer's expert were protected by the work product immunity.

D. The hair dye manufacturer's motion should be denied.

54. A woman burned her hair while using a blowtorch. She sued the manufacturer of the blowtorch in federal district court, alleging that a defect in the design of the blowtorch caused the burns. Immediately thereafter, the blowtorch manufacturer sent the woman a list identifying all of the manufacturer's employees with knowledge of the design of the blowtorch in question that the blowtorch manufacturer could may use in support of its defense and describing by category and location all documents in the possession, custody and control of the blowtorch manufacturer relating to the design of that blowtorch that the blowtorch manufacturer could use in support of its defense. On motion by the woman to impose sanctions against the blowtorch manufacturer, the woman asserted that the blowtorch manufacturer was obligated by the "disclosure" requirements of Rule 26 of the Federal Rules of Civil Procedure to provide her with actual copies of these documents, not merely a description. Which of the following statements is correct?

A. The blowtorch manufacturer was not obligated under the "disclosure" rules to provide copies of the documents in question, as long as it provides a description of the documents by category and location.

B. The "disclosure" rules only allowed the blowtorch manufacturer to provide the woman with a description of the documents in question, but not copies; to obtain copies, the woman had to serve on the blowtorch manufacturer a formal request under Rule 34 of the Federal Rules of Civil Procedure.

C. By providing the woman with a description of the documents in question, pursuant to the "disclosure" rules, the blowtorch manufacturer waived its right to object to production of those documents on the basis of privilege and work product protection.

D. The blowtorch manufacturer was obligated under the "disclosure" rules to provide copies of the documents in question.

55. A woman sued a man in federal district court for false imprisonment. Twenty days before the commencement of trial, the man had not received a list of the woman's trial witnesses. The man told the woman by telephone and letter that she was obligated by Rule 26(a) of the Federal Rules of Civil Procedure to "disclose" this information, but she adamantly refused.

The man moved for sanctions against the woman under Rule 37(a)(3)(A) and included a certification that he had attempted to confer with the woman in an effort to secure disclosure without court action. Which of the following statements is correct?

A. The man's motion should be denied because the woman's trial strategy constituted mental impressions and, as such, were protected from discovery.

B. The man's motion should be denied because he should have sought this information by serving a formal interrogatory.

C. The man's motion should be granted because the identity of the woman's trial witnesses was relevant information and was not protected from discovery as the woman's trial strategy.

D. The man's motion should be granted because the woman was obligated to provide this information to him under the "disclosure" rules.

56. A woman sued a man in federal district court for false imprisonment. Both the woman and the man acknowledged that at the time of the alleged incident, the woman had been free to leave at any time and had been aware of this fact. However, the woman's complaint alleged that the room where the alleged incident had taken place was scary and later gave the woman nightmares.

The man moved for summary judgment. How should the court rule on the man's motion?

A. The motion should be granted because there were no disputes as to the facts.

B. The motion should be granted because false imprisonment claims can only be made against police agencies.

C. The motion should be denied because the woman, as the plaintiff, had a right to have her claim fully litigated in court.

D. The motion should be denied because this case was being litigated in federal court, and summary judgment no longer exists in the federal court system.

57. A tenant was in arrears for his rent for January, February, and March. His landlord, who lived in a different state, brought a lawsuit against the tenant in federal district court, seeking rent payments for January and February. A judgment was entered in favor of the landlord.

The following month, the landlord brought another lawsuit in federal district court against the same tenant for the March rent. The tenant brought a motion to dismiss. How should the court rule on the tenant's motion?

A. The tenant's motion should be denied because rent arrearage can always be collected.

B. The tenant's motion should be denied because each monthly obligation to pay rent constitutes a separate "cause of action."

C. The tenant's motion should be granted because the landlord split his cause of action.

D. The tenant's motion should be granted because rent arrearage can never be collected.

58. A landlord sued a tenant for rent that was in arrears. A final judgment was entered in favor of the tenant. Subsequently, the landlord learned that the tenant was sharing the same apartment with his girlfriend. The landlord then brought a lawsuit against the girlfriend for the same rent that the landlord still alleged was in arrears. The girlfriend made a motion for summary judgment based on the previous decision against the landlord.

How should the court rule on the girlfriend's motion?

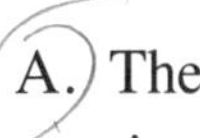

A. The court should grant the motion.

B. The court should grant the motion because there was no final judgment in the landlord's previous lawsuit against the tenant.

C. The court should grant the motion because the landlord already had his day in court.

D. The court should deny the motion.

59. A woman sued a man for intentional infliction of emotional distress. The court found in favor of the man. The woman then sued the man for defamation and for intentional infliction of emotional distress based on the same incident as her original lawsuit against the man. The man then made a motion for summary judgment based on the fact that he had prevailed in the woman's prior lawsuit against him. How should the court rule on the man's motion?

A. The court should grant the motion for summary judgment on the issues of defamation and in-

tentional infliction of emotional distress.

B. The court should grant the motion for partial summary judgment on the issue of intentional infliction of emotional distress only.

C. The court should deny the motion for summary judgment on the issues of defamation and intentional infliction of emotional distress.

D. The court should deny the motion for partial summary judgment on the issue of intentional infliction of emotional distress.

60. A woman sued a man in federal district court for assault. The woman's friend who had been with the woman at the time of the incident claimed to have seen what happened. The friend gave a written statement to the man immediately after the incident. Neither the woman nor the friend had a copy of the friend's statement. The woman, who was *in pro per*, properly served on the man a discovery demand for the friend's statement. After the man objected to producing the friend's statement on work product grounds, the woman moved to compel production. Which of the following statements is correct?

A. The woman's motion should be granted because the woman, but not the friend, had an unqualified right to discover the friend's statement.

B. The woman's motion should be denied because the friend, but not the woman, had an unqualified right to get a copy of the friend's statement from the man.

C. The woman's motion should be denied because the woman was not a lawyer.

D. The woman's motion should be denied because neither the woman nor the friend had an unqualified right to get a copy of the friend's statement from the man.

61. A man sued a woman in federal district court for battery. The woman's lawyer tracked down a witness to the incident and obtained a written statement from the witness. The man properly served on the woman a discovery demand for the witness' statement. The woman objected, and the man moved to compel production. Which of the following statements is correct?

A. The witness' statement is not discoverable because it is protected by the attorney-client privilege.

B. The witness' statement is not discoverable because it is protected by the work product doctrine.

C. The witness' statement is not discoverable because it is irrelevant.

D. The witness' statement is discoverable because it is relevant.

62. A woman was severely injured when the blender she was using exploded and cut off her left arm. She sued the manufacturer of the blender in federal district court for her injuries. The manufacturer made numerous adjustments to subsequent blenders, so that these types of accidents could not occur in the future. Although the woman's case had not yet reached the trial phase because the parties were still in discovery, the woman made a formal request for copies of any materials regarding the adjustments to subsequent blenders. The manufacturer objected to the request, and the woman moved to compel production. Which of the following statements is correct?

A. The materials were not discoverable because they contained the mental impressions of an expert.

B. The materials were not discoverable because their purpose was to avoid future litigation.

C. The materials were discoverable.

D. The materials were not discoverable because they were irrelevant.

63. A woman slipped on some fruit on the floor of a supermarket that was part of a national chain of supermarkets. She brought a personal injury lawsuit in federal district court against the supermarket.

The woman sought to discover a report by a city Health Department officer regarding fruits and vegetables that the officer had found on the floors of all of the chain's supermarkets, including the location where the woman had slipped. The supermarket objected to the woman's discovery request, and the woman moved to compel production of the report. Which of the following statements is correct?

A. The report was not discoverable because it was irrelevant.

B. The report was not discoverable because it was confidential.

C. The report was not discoverable because it was protected by the work product immunity.

D. The report was discoverable.

64. A woman sued her neighbor in federal district court for encroachment on her property. In preparation for the lawsuit, the neighbor contacted his attorney and admitted that he was, in fact, encroaching on the woman's property, but he felt that he should not have to cut down the tree that was encroaching because it would affect the value of the neighbor's

property. At the neighbor's deposition, the woman asked the neighbor if he had ever admitted to his attorney that he was, in fact, encroaching on the woman's property. The neighbor objected. The issue was brought to court for a ruling on the neighbor's objection. How should the court rule?

A. The objection should be overruled because the woman was entitled to any exculpatory evidence.

B. The objection should be overruled because the statements were relevant.

C. The objection should be sustained because the statements were irrelevant.

D. The objection should be sustained because the neighbor's statements were privileged.

65. A woman who was a citizen of North Dakota sued a man who was a citizen of Tennessee for injuries she received following an automobile accident involving the man. She brought her lawsuit in federal district court and alleged $75,000 in damages. The man moved to dismiss the lawsuit for lack of subject matter jurisdiction. Will his motion be successful?

A. Yes because there was no in rem jurisdiction.

B. Yes because there was no subject matter jurisdiction.

C. No because automobile accidents are always federal issues, and there was thus subject matter jurisdiction.

D. No because there was subject matter jurisdiction here.

66. A woman was beheaded in an automobile accident while she was driving. Her automobile had been struck by an automobile driven by a man who worked for a delivery company. The woman was a citizen of Wyoming. The man was a citizen of Idaho, and the company was also a citizen of Idaho. The woman's estate brought a lawsuit in federal district court against both the man and the company, alleging $90,000 in damages. The company moved to dismiss for lack of subject matter jurisdiction. Will the company's motion be successful?

A. Yes because there was quasi in rem jurisdiction.

B. Yes because there was no subject matter jurisdiction.

C. No because subject matter was not required here.

D. No because there was subject matter jurisdiction.

67. A woman sued the U.S. Government in federal district court under Federal Tort

Claims Act, alleging $50,000 in property damage allegedly caused by a U.S. postal worker making his rounds on a Post Office mail delivery truck when he drove his truck onto the woman's property at a high rate of speed. The woman was a citizen of Michigan. The U.S. Government denied that the accident was caused by the postal worker but alleged that it was caused by a defect in either the brakes, the tires, the rubber in the tires or the metal the truck body. The woman subsequently brought different but related state law claims as part of the same lawsuit against the manufacturer of the truck, the manufacturer of the truck tires, the manufacturer of the rubber of which the tires were composed, and the manufacturer of the metal of which the truck body was composed. Each of these manufacturers was a citizen of Michigan. The woman alleged $200,000 in damages against the manufacturers. As a group, the manufacturers moved to dismiss the woman's claims against them. How should the court rule?

A. The court should deny the motion to dismiss because the claims against the manufacturers would not predominate over the woman's original claim against the man.

B. The court may deny the motion to dismiss because adding these defendants would not destroy subject matter jurisdiction.

C. The court may grant the motion to dismiss because the claims against the manufacturers would predominate over the woman's original claim against the man.

D. The court should grant the motion to dismiss because adding these defendants would destroy subject matter jurisdiction.

68. A man who was a citizen of New York hired an architect who was also a citizen of New York to design his California vacation house. Using the architect's plans, the man then hired a builder who was a citizen of California to construct the house according to the architect's plans.

Before anyone could enter the house, the entire house suddenly collapsed. The man sued the builder in federal district court, alleging that the builder's negligence had caused the house to be built so poorly that it collapsed. The man asked for $80,000 in damages.

The builder served a timely third-party complaint and summons on the architect, claiming that the architect's defective plans had caused the house to sink. As a result, the builder had to spend $100,000 more on the project than originally anticipated, which caused the builder to go bankrupt. The builder, thus, sought $100,000 from the architect.

The architect moved to dismiss the third-party complaint. Which of the following statements is correct?

A. The court should grant the architect's motion because impleader is improper.

B. The court should grant the architect's motion because allowing the builder to take legal action against the architect, a citizen of New York, would destroy diversity.

C. The court should deny the architect's motion because impleader was proper.

D. The court should deny the architect's motion because the court could exercise supplemental jurisdiction over the builder's third-party claim against the architect.

69. A woman who was a citizen of Arizona sued a man who was a citizen of Colorado in federal district court, alleging intentional infliction of emotional distress and false imprisonment when he locked her in a "fun house" containing many oddly-shaped mirrors, which obscured the exit door and played sounds of screaming over the fun house's loudspeakers.

The woman alleged $78,000 in damages against the man. Inasmuch as the man was also the woman's former boss, the woman also brought a claim against both the man and the company where she had worked for $100,000 in back salary owed. The company was a citizen of Arkansas.

The company moved to dismiss the woman's claim for back salary owed. How should the court rule on the company's motion?

A. The court should grant the motion because the woman's claim against the man for back salary owed was unrelated to her claims against the man for intentional infliction of emotional distress and false imprisonment.

B. The court should grant the motion because the woman's claim against the company was unrelated to her original claim against the man.

C. The court should deny the motion because the woman's claim against the man for back salary owed was substantially related to her claims against the man for intentional infliction of emotional distress and false imprisonment.

D. The court should deny the motion because the woman's claim against the company was substantially related to her original claim against the man.

70. A homeowner contracted with a builder and a subcontractor to build his house in upstate New York. Both the homeowner and the subcontractor were citizens of New York. The builder was a citizen of New Jersey.

Within a day of the homeowner moving into the house, the roof of the house fell. Moments later, the remainder of the house crumbled into the ground. The homeowner, who miraculously emerged unharmed, brought a lawsuit in federal district court against the builder, and the builder, in turn, brought a claim against the subcontractor.

Two months after filing his complaint against the builder, the homeowner moved for leave to amend his complaint to add a claim against the subcontractor, alleging that the subcontractor's defective laying of the foundation contributed to the crumbling of the house. The subcontractor opposed the homeowner's motion. Which of the following statements is correct?

A. The motion should be denied because the subcontractor will be prejudiced in having to defend against two claims (the builder's and the homeowner's) instead of only one claim (the builder's).

B. The motion should be denied because the subcontractor waived his subject matter jurisdiction defense.

C. The motion should be denied, because, otherwise, diversity will be destroyed.

D. The motion should be granted because the homeowner's claim against the subcontractor arose out of the same transaction and occurrence as his claim against the builder.

71. A customer sued a store and a distributor for a defective product. The distributor cross-claimed against the store for contribution, in case a judgment was rendered in full against the distributor.

After a trial, judgment was rendered in favor of the customer.

Both the store and the distributor appealed, and their appeals were each dismissed. The customer collected the full amount of his judgment from the store. The store then sued the distributor for contribution, claiming reimbursement in proportion to the store's degree of fault for the defective product. The distributor moved to dismiss the store's lawsuit. Which of the following statements is correct?

A. The motion to dismiss should be granted because the store should have counterclaimed for contribution in the previous suit by the customer against the store and the distributor.

B. The motion to dismiss should be granted because cross-claims that arise out of the same transaction and occurrence are compulsory.

C. The motion to dismiss should be denied because, when the store failed to assert its contribution

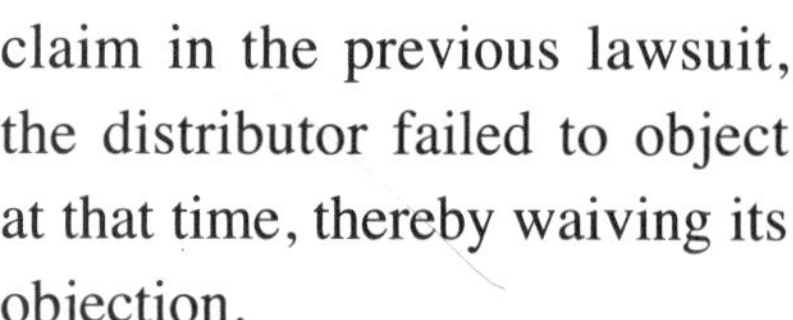

claim in the previous lawsuit, the distributor failed to object at that time, thereby waiving its objection.

D. The motion to dismiss should be denied because cross-claims that arise out of the same transaction and occurrence are never compulsory.

72. A woman sued a man in federal district court in New York, alleging a violation of the Sherman Antitrust Act. Both the woman and the man were citizens of New York. The woman alleged $75,000 in damages. The man moved to dismiss the woman's claim on the grounds that the federal court lacked subject matter jurisdiction. Which of the following statements is correct?

A. The court has no subject matter jurisdiction because there is no personal jurisdiction over the man.

B. The court has no subject matter jurisdiction because both the woman and the man are New York citizens.

C. The court has subject matter jurisdiction because the amount in controversy has been met.

D. The court has subject matter jurisdiction because the claims arise under federal law.

73. A number of Iranian immigrants were denied asylum by a particularly harsh immigration judge. Of those denied asylum, 98% were women. By contrast, almost 79% of the Iranian men who appeared before this particular immigration judge and applied for asylum had their cases granted.

The women who had been denied asylum, as a class, sued the immigration judge in federal district court, alleging a total of $10,000 in damages. Will the court certify the class?

A. Yes.

B. Yes because federal courts are granted unlimited discretion as to which classes to certify.

C. No because the amount in controversy was inadequate.

D. No because the women were all from Iran.

74. A class in a class action lawsuit in federal district court was certified because requiring each class member to sue individually would result in inconsistent or varying adjudications with respect to individual class members that would establish incompatible standards of conduct for the party opposing the class.

The court directed notice to the class. Did the court exceed its statutory authority?

A. Yes because the named plaintiff must always give notice to the class.

B. Yes because the defendant must always give notice to the class.

C. No because it followed the proper procedure as outlined in the Federal Rules of Civil Procedure.

D. No because it followed the proper procedure as outlined in the Federal Rules of Evidence.

75. An attorney represented a class in a class action lawsuit in which the attorney was also the named plaintiff. Which of the following statements is correct?

A. The court will find that the attorney's status as class attorney made him an inadequate class representative.

B. The court will find that the attorney's status as named plaintiff made him an adequate class representative because it gave him an even greater stake in the successful outcome of the suit than he would have if he were not also the class attorney.

C. The court will find that the attorney's status as class attorney made him an adequate class representative because it saved the class the cost of hiring a separate lawyer.

D. The court will find the attorney's status as class attorney to be irrelevant as to whether or not he could adequately represent the class.

76. A woman brought a lawsuit in federal district court against a corporation for a faulty product. Because 10,000 others were damaged by the same product, the woman brought her lawsuit as the class representative in a class action lawsuit.

Because she wanted the strongest possible claim against the corporation, the woman included a statement in her notice to the 10,000 class members that it was mandatory that each of these 10,000 people be a part of the class. Was this adequate notice?

A. Yes because judicial economy disfavors allowing each of these individuals the ability to sue individually.

B. Yes because the woman's notice used the proper language, as required by the Federal Rules of Civil Procedure.

C. No because it violated one of the Federal Rules of Civil Procedure.

D. No because 10,000 exceeds the maximum number of people who can be required to be part of a class under the Federal Rules of Civil Procedure.

77. A woman was in a car accident and was severely injured. The other driver died at the scene. The woman then sued the dead man's estate in federal district court for her injuries. As it happens, a year before he had died, the other driver had thought it would be prudent to draft a will. The other driver had asked his accountant to review the other driver's assets and draft a report so that the other driver would know the extent, nature and worth of his estate.

The woman served a request to produce that report. The executor of the other driver's estate objected. Which of the following is the strongest objection that the executor could make?

A. The report is irrelevant.

B. The report contains confidential information.

C. The report is protected by the work product immunity.

D. The report is protected by Rule 26(b)(4) of the Federal Rules of Civil Procedure [facts and opinions of experts].

78. A woman sued a doctor, in federal district court, for medical malpractice. The doctor sought to depose an expert in medical malpractice who had been identified by the woman pursuant to disclosure requirements, as a witness who the woman had retained to provide expert testimony in the case. The doctor served upon the expert a notice of deposition. The doctor had not yet served any interrogatories on the woman, nor had the woman received any reports prepared by the expert on the expert's proposed trial testimony.

The woman moved for a protective order to prevent the doctor from proceeding with the expert's deposition. Which of the following statements is correct?

A. The protective order should be granted because the doctor had not yet received any reports prepared by the expert regarding the expert's proposed trial testimony.

B. The protective order should be granted because the doctor had not yet served and received answers to interrogatories regarding the expert's proposed trial testimony.

C. The protective order should be granted because the facts and opinions held by an expert who has been retained or specially employed in preparation for trial can only be discovered upon a showing of exceptional circumstances.

D. The protective order should be denied.

79. A plaintiff sued a defendant in federal district court for damages that were

brought about in a vehicle collision in which both parties had been driving their respective automobiles.

At trial, the plaintiff's only evidence on liability was the testimony of an expert who testified that, based upon the circumstantial evidence that he had viewed at the scene of the accident, including skid marks, the position of the automobiles and the condition of the wreckage, it was his opinion that the defendant's automobile could well have veered into the lane in which the plaintiff had been driving at the time of the collision in question. On cross-examination, the expert witness confirmed his findings.

The defendant then moved for judgment as a matter of law on the issue of causation. Which of the following statements is correct?

A. The defendant's motion was premature and should, therefore, be denied because the plaintiff had not yet presented her entire case.

B. The defendant's motion should be denied because the credibility of the expert witness was for the jury to determine, not the court.

C. The defendant's motion should be denied because, when there is a conflict in the evidence, the jury should resolve that conflict, not the court.

D. The defendant's motion should be denied because the court could find that there was a legally sufficient evidentiary basis for the jury to find in favor of the plaintiff under these circumstances.

80. A woman sued a man in federal district court for a battery that had allegedly occurred at night in a dark alley. The man moved under Rule 35(a) of the Federal Rules of Civil Procedure to compel an eye examination of the woman's eyewitness, submitting an affidavit from the witness' ex-wife in which she affirmed that the witness suffered from serious night blindness. Which of the following statements is correct?

A. The court should grant the motion because the affidavit from the witness' wife shows that the condition of the witness' eyes is "in controversy."

B. The court should deny the motion because the witness is not a party to the action.

C. The court should grant the motion because the condition of the witness' eyesight is relevant to the case.

D. The court should deny the motion because the witness' ex-wife is biased.

81. A woman was injured in an accident in her workplace. She sued a fellow em-

ployee in federal district court, alleging that that employee's negligence was the cause of the accident. She moved under Rule 35(a) of the Federal Rules of Civil Procedure to compel the employee to submit to a neurological and a psychological examination based upon an affidavit from the woman's attorney that the attorney's review of court files showed that the employee had been found liable for workplace negligence four times in the past. Which of the following statements is correct?

A. The court should grant the motion because the employee was a person who was under the control of the company, a party defendant.

B. The court should grant the motion because the employee's ability to safely operate the equipment at the workplace was centrally relevant to the case.

C. The court should deny the motion because the woman did not show that the employee's nervous system and mental state were "in controversy."

D. The court should deny the motion because the affidavit of the woman's attorney was not based upon personal knowledge.

82. A woman sued a man for negligence subsequent to an automobile accident in which both the woman and the man had been involved. Following discovery, the woman made a motion for summary judgment and submitted an affidavit of her best friend. In the affidavit, the best friend stated under oath that she knew that the woman would never run a red light. In response, the man only submitted his answer in which he denied that he had run the red light and alleged that the woman had run the red light.

The man then objected to the woman's motion, stating that she had used improper evidence in support of her motion.

How should the court rule on the man's objection?

A. The objection should be sustained because the woman did not meet her movant's burden.

B. The objection should be sustained because the woman only presented one affidavit in support of her motion for summary judgment.

C. The objection should be overruled because the man did not meet his respondent's burden.

D. The objection should be overruled because courts never grant offensive summary judgment motions based on affidavit testimony.

83. A woman and a man were involved in a motorcycle collision. As a result of

the accident, neither the woman nor the man could recall the circumstances leading up to the collision. The woman's only evidence to prove that the man caused the collision was a trucker, who was prepared to testify to the following: that, for 10 minutes before the collision, he had been following the man's motorcycle and that at each red light, the man had run the light. However, the trucker turned off the street prior to the intersection where the collision occurred and, thus, did not witness the collision.

The woman also presented as witnesses two bishops who swore that they saw the man run the red light.

The man's rebuttal case consisted of one witness, a twice-convicted perjurer, who swore that he saw the woman run the red light. After the jury returned a verdict in favor of the man, the woman moved for a judgment as a matter of law in her favor and, in the alternative, for a new trial. Which of the following statements is correct?

A. The woman's motion should be denied because an offensive motion for judgment as a matter of law can never be granted where the movant has offered oral testimony, since credibility is always a jury issue.

B. The woman's motion should be denied because she did not make a motion for a judgment as a matter of law before the close of all the evidence.

C. The woman's motion should be granted because she met her burden of production and the man did not.

D. The woman's motion should be granted because her case "overwhelmed" the man's case.

84. A woman sued a man in federal district court for false imprisonment. The court found in favor of the man. The woman made a motion for a new trial based upon an affidavit of a juror who swore that he had voted against the woman because he was biased against the woman based on her race. How should the court rule on the woman's motion?

A. The court should grant the woman's motion because there was juror misconduct.

B. The court should grant the woman's motion because the juror's affidavit was admissible.

C. The court should grant the woman's motion because the court may always inquire into a juror's thought processes in order to determine if bias played a role in the ultimate verdict.

D. The court should deny the woman's motion because the juror's affidavit was inadmissible.

85. Two women who were citizens of Nevada purchased identical clothing from a store located in California. Because they were both in a rush, they did not try on the clothing in the store. However, after returning home, both women did try on the clothing. Both of the women's newly-purchased clothing spontaneously burst into flames upon making contact with their skin. Both women were severely burned and together brought a lawsuit in federal district court against the store, alleging $2,000,000 in damages.

The store made a motion to dismiss for lack of subject matter jurisdiction. How should the court rule on the motion?

A. The court should deny the store's motion because there was personal jurisdiction

B. The court should deny the store's motion because there was subject matter jurisdiction.

C. The court should grant the store's motion because there was no personal jurisdiction.

D. The court should grant the store's motion because there was no subject matter jurisdiction.

86. A woman sued a man in state court in Nevada, alleging that he had violated her patent rights to an invention when the man made a business trip to Nevada for the purpose of selling the invention to a distributor in Nevada. This was the only time that the man had been in Nevada. The man made a motion to dismiss for lack of jurisdiction. How should the court rule?

A. The court should deny the man's motion.

B. The court should grant the man's motion because, while there was subject matter jurisdiction, there was no personal jurisdiction.

C. The court should grant the man's motion because, while there was personal jurisdiction, there was no subject matter jurisdiction.

D. The court should grant the man's motion because there was neither personal nor subject matter jurisdiction.

87. A woman owed $10,000 to her doctor. Her doctor sued the woman in federal district court. The woman failed to appear for trial, and a default judgment was entered in favor of the doctor for $8,000. The doctor then sued the woman for the remaining $2,000. This time, the woman appeared for the trial and made a motion to dismiss the doctor's claim. How should the court rule on the woman's motion?

A. The court should grant the woman's motion.

B. The court should grant the woman's motion because she never had a chance to defend herself against the doctor's original claim.

C. The court should deny the woman's motion because she should have appeared for the initial lawsuit.

D. The court should deny the woman's motion because the original judgment was not on the merits.

88. A man who was a citizen of California was attending a bachelor party in Nevada. He drank quite a bit of beer at the party and got into an argument with a stripper who was performing at the party and punched her in the face. Four weeks later, the man was served at his home in California. He was ordered to come back to Nevada to answer a lawsuit that the stripper had filed against him in federal district court in Nevada, alleging that the man had battered her. The man made a motion to dismiss for improper service. How should the court rule?

A. The court should deny the man's motion because the stripper's cause of action arose out of the man's actions in Nevada.

B. The court should deny the man's motion because the man was a California citizen.

C. The court should grant the man's motion because the man was a California citizen.

D. The court should grant the man's motion because he was a Nevada citizen.

89. A man who was a citizen of New Jersey went to New York to purchase a boat for fishing. The manufacturer of the boat was a citizen of the State of New York, as was the retail outfit that sold the boat to the man. The man returned to New Jersey and set out for a fishing trip. When he was in the middle of the river, the boat collapsed because of defective part, and the man drowned. The man's widow brought a lawsuit in federal district court against both the manufacturer and the retailer. She asked for $500,000 in damages. The defendants moved to dismiss for lack of subject matter jurisdiction. How should the court rule on this motion?

A. The court should deny the motion because there was personal jurisdiction

B. The court should deny the motion because there was subject matter jurisdiction.

C. The court should grant the motion because there was no personal jurisdiction.

D. The court should grant the motion because there was no subject matter jurisdiction.

90. A woman was shot one day while walking in a field. Although she survived, she suffered severe injuries. During the subsequent investigation, it was revealed that the shot had come from one of two hunters who had both fired their rifles at the same time, mistaking the woman for a deer.

The woman sued one of the hunters in federal district court. Ultimately, a judgment was entered in favor of that hunter.

The woman then sued the second hunter, again in federal district court. The second hunter moved to dismiss the woman's lawsuit against him. How should the court rule on the second hunter's motion?

A. The court should deny the second hunter's motion because neither res judicata nor any joinder rule required the woman to join both hunters as co-defendants.

B. The court should deny the second hunter's motion because the second hunter waived his res judicata defense by failing to intervene in the lawsuit against the first hunter.

C. The court should deny the second hunter's motion because the judgment against the first hunter was not "on the merits."

D. The court should grant the second hunter's motion because the woman should not be allowed to "hedge her bets" by suing a series of defendants, one-by-one, on the same claim until the supply of defendants runs out.

91. A man drank a great deal of alcohol in a bar. He subsequently drove home and, as he was driving, his vehicle collided with an automobile that was being driven by a woman. The woman was injured and subsequently brought a personal injury suit in a federal district court against the bar, alleging $105,000 in damages, including $75,000 for pain and suffering because the bar had continued to serve alcohol to the man, despite knowing that he was drunk and was, therefore, responsible for the collision and the woman's injuries. Representatives of the bar failed to appear in court, and the woman obtained a default judgment against the bar.

The woman then sued the man for her injuries in the collision. She moved for partial summary judgment based on the judgment in her favor in the first lawsuit by the woman against the bar on the issue of the man's liability for causing the collision. Which of the following statements is not correct?

A. The woman could not invoke collateral estoppel because the Due Process Clause of the United States Constitution prevented the man from being bound by the judgment in the lawsuit by the woman against the bar.

B. The woman could not invoke collateral estoppel because no facts were actually determined in the first lawsuit by the woman against the bar.

C. The woman could not invoke collateral estoppel because the judgment in the lawsuit by the woman against the bar was not "on the merits."

D. The mutuality of estoppel rule is inapplicable to resolve the issue whether the woman could invoke the benefits of collateral estoppel.

92. A woman who was a citizen of Italy came to Arkansas as a permanent resident and married a man who was a citizen of the United States and a citizen of Arkansas. After two years, the man filed for divorce in federal district court in Arkansas. The woman made a motion to dismiss for lack of jurisdiction. How should the court rule on her motion?

A. The court should grant the woman's motion because it lacked personal jurisdiction.

B. The court should grant the woman's motion because it lacked subject matter jurisdiction.

C. The court should deny the woman's motion because federal courts have exclusive jurisdiction over foreign citizens.

D. The court should deny the woman's motion because federal courts always have jurisdiction over divorce.

93. A woman who was the named plaintiff in a class action lawsuit in federal district court lived one block from the courthouse. Eight other class members lived within four miles of the courthouse. The remaining class members lived approximately 100 miles or more from the courthouse. There was a proposed settlement of the case. Each class member, except for the named plaintiff (the woman) and the eight class members who lived within four miles of the courthouse, was offered an equal amount of money to settle. The woman and the other eight class members who lived within four miles of the courthouse were offered significantly more money to settle than were the other class members because these nine individuals lived closer to the courthouse, thus, making it easier to be in contact with them.

Should the court approve this proposed settlement?

A. No because it would violate the Class Equities Protection Act.

B. No because it unfairly discriminated against the class members who lived farther from the courthouse.

C. Yes because class members are allowed to negotiate any settlement that they choose.

D. Yes because the woman and the eight others who lived near the courthouse saved the court staff a great amount of money in stamps and other fees involved in locating them.

94. A woman died when a safe fell on her. The terms of her will stated that the woman's cousin would be the executrix of the will. The woman's son contested the terms of the will. He brought his action in federal district court based on diversity of citizenship and the adequate amount in controversy.

The son had his complaint served on the first adult over the age of 18 years who answered the door when the sheriff went to the woman's house to serve the complaint. However, the rule in the forum state required service only on the executor (or executrix).

The following day, the executrix moved to quash the son's complaint based on improper service of process. How should the court rule on the executrix's motion?

A. The motion should be granted because the "Erie" doctrine required the court to apply the state rule because that rule embodied important substantive interests.

B. The motion should be granted because service of process was improper under these facts.

C. The motion should be denied because service of process was proper under these facts.

D. The motion should be denied because it was not made in a timely manner.

95. A woman, who lived near the state line, sued her neighbor, who lived across the state line, in federal district court for nuisance, alleging $80,000 in damages. Subject matter jurisdiction was established, since the neighbor and the woman were citizens of different States, and the amount in controversy was met.

They agreed to nonbinding mediation. Following the mediation, the woman dropped her lawsuit against the neighbor. A few months later, the woman changed her mind and reinstituted her nuisance lawsuit against the neighbor. The neighbor moved to dismiss based on res judicata. How should the court rule?

A. The court should deny the neighbor's motion because the mediation resulted in a judgment in favor of the woman.

B. The court should deny the neighbor's motion because res judicata does not apply here.

C. The court should grant the neighbor's motion because the mediation resulted in a judgment in favor of the neighbor.

D. The court should grant the neighbor's motion because mediation is always binding.

96. A married woman sued a man (who was not her husband) in federal district court for negligence and loss of consortium. The jury ultimately returned a verdict in favor of the man on the negligence issue, but was unable to reach a decision on the issue of loss of consortium.

The woman then sued the man in state court based on the same incident that had given rise to the lawsuit in federal district court, again for negligence and loss of consortium.

The man moved to dismiss both of the woman's claims based upon the judgment in the prior federal lawsuit. Which of the following statements is correct?

A. The woman should be collaterally estopped on the issue of negligence because the federal court "actually and necessarily determined" that the man was not negligent.

B. The woman should be collaterally estopped on the issue of loss of consortium because the federal court "actually and necessarily determined" that there was no loss of consortium here.

C. The woman should be collaterally estopped on both the issue of negligence and the issue of loss of consortium because the federal court "actually and necessarily determined" in favor of the man on both issues.

D. The woman should not be collaterally estopped on either the issue of negligence or the issue of loss of consortium because the federal court did not "actually and necessarily determine" in favor of the man on either issue.

97. A man was tried for the murder of his wife. The jury returned a verdict of not guilty. The wife's estate then sued the man for wrongful death. The man moved for summary judgment based upon the not guilty verdict in the murder case that had been brought against him. Which of the following statements is correct?

A. The court will grant the man's motion for partial summary judgment.

B. The court will grant the man's motion for summary judgment.

C. The court will deny the man's motion for summary judgment.

D. The court will deny the man's motion for partial summary judgment.

98. A woman and her best friend were shopping in a store. The best friend put a scarf in her purse. The woman and her

best friend then left the store without paying for the scarf. The storeowner then sued the woman for conversion of the scarf. The jury found the woman not liable. The storeowner then brought a lawsuit against the best friend for conversion based on the same transaction.

The best friend made a motion to dismiss based on mutuality of estoppel. How should the court rule on the best friend's motion?

A. The court should grant the motion based on res judicata.

B. The court should grant the motion based on mutuality of estoppel.

C. The court should deny the motion based on mutuality of estoppel.

D. The court should deny the motion based on res judicata.

99. A woman who was a citizen of California brought a lawsuit for negligence in federal district court against a man who was also a citizen of California, alleging $76,000 in damages. Judgment was entered in favor of the woman. The man then filed a motion to vacate the judgment based on lack of subject matter jurisdiction.

How should the court rule on the man's motion?

A. The motion should be denied because the man waived his subject matter jurisdiction defense.

B. The motion should be denied because the court had personal jurisdiction over the man.

C. The motion should be granted because the court lacked subject matter jurisdiction.

D. The motion should be granted because the court lacked personal jurisdiction

100. A woman sued a man in federal district court who had allegedly deliberately hit her with a shopping cart. After a jury trial, judgment was entered in favor of the woman. Five weeks after entry of judgment, the man made a motion for a new trial on grounds of juror misconduct. The man offered in support of his motion the affidavit of a juror, who stated that during the trial on one evening, she had visited the store where the alleged incident had occurred and in speaking with several store employees who had witnessed the incident but did not testify at the trial, the juror had learned that the man actually did not hit the woman with the shopping cart but, rather, that the woman had actually slipped and fell against the shopping cart. This information affected the juror in her deliberations. Which of the following statements is correct?

A. If the court believes the juror's affidavit, the court should grant the man's motion because evidence of extraneous prejudicial information improperly brought to a juror's attention is admissible in federal court to impeach the verdict.

B. Even if the court believes the juror's affidavit, the court should deny the man's motion because there is no showing that the juror's misconduct prejudiced the ultimate verdict.

C. If the court believes the juror's affidavit, the court should grant the man's motion because evidence of extrinsic misconduct is admissible to impeach the verdict.

D. Even if the court believes the juror's affidavit, the court should deny the man's motion because it was untimely.

END OF QUESTIONS

CIVIL PROCEDURE ANSWERS

1. D is correct. One of the traditional bases of personal jurisdiction is consent. Consent is automatic in federal court when a defendant fails to challenge personal jurisdiction either by making a pre-answer motion or, if no pre-answer motion is made, then by raising lack of personal jurisdiction as a defense in the answer. Here, the man personally appeared to answer the woman's complaint against him. Four months later, at a subsequent hearing, the man made a motion alleging that there was no personal jurisdiction over him. However, by personally appearing at the original hearing and then making the motion to dismiss four months later, the man consented to the State X court's personal jurisdiction over him. Thus, the court should deny the man's motion because he did consent to the court's personal jurisdiction over him.

   A is incorrect for the reasons discussed in D.

   B is an incorrect statement of law. Challenges to personal jurisdiction must be raised at the outset (either through a pre-answer motion or in the answer if no pre-answer motion is made) and cannot be raised at a later time, as the man is attempting to do here. However, since the man consented (as discussed in D), the challenge would fail, anyway.

   C is incorrect because, although the man may have had sufficient minimum contacts with State X (the facts state that the cause of action arose from the man's driving in State X), minimum contacts were not required because, by personally appearing to answer the woman's allegations against him without raising the defense of lack of personal jurisdiction, the man consented to the State X court's personal jurisdiction over him, as discussed in D.

2. C is correct. A traditional basis of personal jurisdiction is domicile in the state. Domicile is the person's permanent place of residence. Here, the woman had a vacation home in State X, but the facts indicate that her permanent residence (i.e., her domicile) was in State Y. Furthermore, there were no other connections to State X: the incident occurred in State Y, and both the woman and the man were domiciliaries of State Y. Although the man, as plaintiff, could choose the forum for his lawsuit, the court could not assert personal jurisdiction over a non-resident (here, the woman) absent long arm statute and minimum contacts, neither of which were given in these facts. Therefore, since there was no basis for the State X court to assert personal jurisdiction over the woman, her motion to dismiss should be granted.

   A is incorrect because the woman's vacation home in State X did not make her a citizen (domiciliary) of State X; the facts state that her permanent home was in State Y.

B is incorrect because mailing a motion challenging personal jurisdiction does not constitute consent to personal jurisdiction.

D is an incorrect statement of law, since state courts have general subject matter jurisdiction over most matters, including personal injury lawsuits (which was the case here).

3. A is correct. The jurisdiction of the federal court here appears to be based on diversity (rather than federal question) because the woman was suing for personal injuries only (not typically a federal question), and both the woman (a California plaintiff) and the fast food chain (a Florida defendant) were citizens of different states. Assuming the amount in controversy exceeds $75,000, the requirements for diversity jurisdiction are satisfied The California plaintiff did not assert a claim directly against the California third-party defendant.

   Assuming the third-party claim seeks more than $75,000, there is no need for supplemental jurisdiction to support the third-party claim because the third-party plaintiff and third-party defendant are citizens of different states.

   Thus, the woman's motion should be denied.

   B is incorrect because a plaintiff may always object to anything it wants, regardless of how the court ultimately rules on the objection.

   C is incorrect for the reasons discussed in A.

   D is incorrect because the woman was still free to sue the fast food chain as part of the distribution chain that ultimately led to her receiving the allegedly tainted meat that caused her injury, even if the meat supplier was the original source of the meat.

4. B is correct.

   Here, plaintiff was suing an additional defendant (the supervisor), and both the plaintiff and the supervisor were citizens of the same State (Wyoming), which would destroy diversity if subject matter jurisdiction were based on diversity. Here, however, the woman's lawsuit was based on gender discrimination, under a federal civil rights statute. Thus, subject matter jurisdiction was based on federal question, and diversity was thus not at issue, and it did not matter that the woman and the supervisor were citizens of the same State. Supplemental jurisdiction is not an issue here because the claims against both defendants arise under federal law so supplemental jurisdiction is not needed.

   A is incorrect because anyone can move to dismiss a lawsuit, if the basis for the motion is the destruction of (or lack of) subject matter jurisdiction, which was the case here. However, subject matter jurisdiction was not destroyed in this case, for the reasons discussed in B.

C is incorrect for the reasons discussed in B.

D is incorrect because the woman is allowed to add additional defendants, so long as doing so does not destroy subject matter jurisdiction.

5. A is correct. In federal court, subject matter jurisdiction is based upon either a federal question (28 U.S.C. §1331) or complete diversity of citizenship and an amount in controversy over $75,000 (28 U.S.C. §1332).

Here, the woman was injured in a Federal Express (FedEx) office. Despite the word "Federal" in its name, Federal Express is a private company; it is not the federal post office (the United States Postal Service). Thus, she was not injured on federal property, and there is nothing about her claim that is based on federal law. As a result, there was no federal question here. Consequently, a federal court (such as the district court in which the woman brought her lawsuit) would only have subject matter jurisdiction, if there was complete diversity of citizenship and an amount in controversy over $75,000.

Although the woman's personal injury lawsuit claim exceeded $75,000 in damages (she had $76,000 in damages), she was struck by her next-door neighbor. Unless she lived on the state line, her next door neighbor came from the same state as the woman. Thus, there was no diversity of citizenship. As a result, the man's motion to dismiss for lack of subject matter jurisdiction will be granted because there was neither federal question nor diversity of citizenship jurisdiction.

B and D are incorrect because personal jurisdiction was not at issue in these facts; the man's motion to dismiss was based on lack of subject matter jurisdiction, not lack of personal jurisdiction.

C is incorrect for the reasons discussed in A.

6. B is correct. Personal jurisdiction can be established when a person purposefully avails himself of the laws and protections of the state in question. Here, the man drove through State Y on a daily basis, and the incident in question occurred on State Y roads. As a result, the man had minimum contacts with State Y such that asserting personal jurisdiction over him would not offend traditional notions of fair play and justice. Therefore, the man's motion to dismiss the woman's lawsuit for lack of personal jurisdiction will be denied.

A is an incorrect statement of law, since state courts have general subject matter jurisdiction over most matters, including personal injury lawsuits (which was the case here). Also, subject matter jurisdiction was note an issue here because the motion to dismiss was based on lack of personal jurisdiction.

C is incorrect for the reasons discussed in B.

D is incorrect because, while inconvenience may be taken into account, there was, nonetheless, personal jurisdiction over the man for the reasons discussed in B.

7. A is correct because it applies all of the elements of the Massachusetts long arm statute as given. Here, the woman potentially caused a tortious injury to the man in Connecticut, not Massachusetts. The facts state that the woman had never been to Massachusetts. As a result, she did not derive substantial revenue from goods used or consumed or services rendered in Massachusetts. In addition, she did not regularly do or solicit business in Massachusetts.

B and C are incorrect because, while they apply traditional elements of typical long arm statutes, the fact pattern here gives an actual statute. As a result, the elements given in that particular statute must be applied. Since these elements are not present in the statute as given, they are not arguments that the woman can raise.

D is incorrect because lack of citizenship does not negate personal jurisdiction, if there is a long arm statute on point. Here, however, the woman could raise the arguments discussed in A to negate personal jurisdiction.

8. D is correct. In Shaffer v. Heitner, 433 U.S. 186 (1977), the Supreme Court set for the requirements for quasi-in-rem jurisdiction. The court said that quasi-in-rem jurisdiction may exist in situations that do not offend notions of "fair play and substantial justice." Although the Court limited the number of situations in which quasi-in-rem jurisdiction would exist, the Court did not abolish this basis of jurisdiction altogether. Today, quasi-in-rem jurisdiction may still exist even when there would otherwise be no personal jurisdiction over a particular defendant under a long arm statute.

Here, the facts are almost identical to the facts in Shaffer. In that case, quasi-in-rem jurisdiction was attempted in Delaware based on nonresident defendant's ownership of stock in a Delaware corporation. The Supreme Court held that this was not enough to satisfy the minimum contacts test set forth in International Shoe v. Washington, 326 U.S. 310 (1945) and, as a result, held that quasi-in-rem jurisdiction could not be exercised by the Delaware court.

Similarly here, the facts state that the man had no contact with California, other than his purchase of stock in a California corporation which was not the subject of the lawsuit (which was personal injury arising out of an Illinois auto accident). Thus, under the rules articulated in Shaffer and in International Shoe, the man would not be deemed to have had sufficient minimum contacts with California to enable the courts in that state to exercise either personal or quasi-in-rem jurisdiction. Thus, the man's motion should be granted.

A is incorrect because, while corporate citizenship provides a basis for personal jurisdiction over the corporation, here it is a stockholder in the corporation (the man) who is being sued personally, not the corporation itself. Thus, the fact that the corporation is a citizen of California is irrelevant to the analysis here.

B and C are incorrect for the reasons discussed in D.

9. D is correct. In federal court, subject matter jurisdiction is based upon either a federal question or complete diversity of citizenship and an amount in controversy over $75,000. When a case is originally brought in state court, a party may remove the case to federal court if the federal court has subject matter jurisdiction. However, a case is not removable where original jurisdiction is based solely on diversity and a defendant is a citizen of the forum state.

Here, the lawsuit was based on personal injury, which is generally not a federal question. Thus, the only basis for subject matter jurisdiction in the federal court would be diversity.

In this case, there was complete diversity of citizenship (the plaintiff - the woman - was a citizen of Montana, and the defendant - the man - was a citizen of Hawaii), and the amount in controversy ($76,800) exceeded $75,000.

Nonetheless, removal was improper because the man was a citizen of the forum state (Hawaii).

A is incorrect because supplemental jurisdiction only exists when the federal court is already hearing a case based on either federal question or diversity and is simply exercising jurisdiction over an additional claim. Here, however, the case could not be removed to federal court for the reasons discussed in D. Consequently, the federal court could not hear the case in the first place and would, thus, be unable to exercise supplemental jurisdiction over any additional claims. (Furthermore, the facts do not discuss any additional claims being brought that would form the basis of supplemental jurisdiction.)

B is incorrect, because, while the requirements for diversity jurisdiction were met, the case was originally brought in state court and could not be removed to federal court for the reasons discussed in D.

C is incorrect because the fact that the woman was a citizen of Montana helped form a basis for diversity jurisdiction (since the man was a citizen of a different state - Hawaii). This argued in favor of, not against, the federal court exercising jurisdiction. However, the man's motion should still be denied for the reasons discussed in D.

10. B is correct. Under Rule 12(b)(2) of the Federal Rules of Civil Procedure, a party may make a motion to dismiss for lack of personal jurisdiction. Personal jurisdiction exists either when there is a traditional basis - such as the

defendant's presence in the forum state - or when the defendant has complied with the jurisdiction's long arm statute. Assuming that this jurisdiction has a traditional long arm statute, the District Court will have personal jurisdiction over the toy store, if the toy store had enough minimum contacts with the forum jurisdiction that the exercise of jurisdiction "will not offend traditional notions of fair play and substantial justice." (See International Shoe Co. v. Washington, 326 U.S. 310 (1945).)

In order to test for minimum contacts, courts will look to the defendant's purposeful availment of the forum state, the frequency and regularity of defendant's contacts with the forum state, foreseeability of the defendant being sued in the forum state, reasonableness of the defendant being sued in the forum state, the burden on the defendant in being sued in the forum state versus the burden on the plaintiff having to bring the lawsuit elsewhere, and the forum state's interest in having the lawsuit heard there.

Here, the toy store did not purposefully avail itself of the U.S. market. In Asahi Metal Industry v Superior Court, 480 U.S. 102 (1987), Justice O'Connor's plurality opinion stated that "a defendant's awareness that the stream of commerce may or will sweep the product into the forum state does not convert the mere act of placing the product into the stream into an act purposefully directed toward the forum state." Even applying Justice Brennan's "stream of commerce" theory, purposeful availment is lacking because, in Asahi, the sales of the component parts to the manufacturer of the finished product were characterized as "regular and extensive." This is clearly not the case with the toy store here that had never sold any toys in the U.S., aside from the ten toys. The toy store just happened to sell these 10 toys to the woman, who unilaterally brought them to the U.S.

A is incorrect because, unlike Asahi, the claim arose directly out of an injury to a plaintiff in the U.S., and the plaintiff is an American. Therefore, the forum state's interest in litigating an injury to one of its citizens is not slight, as A would suggest.

C is incorrect because it states a reason to have the lawsuit heard in the U.S., which goes against the toy store's motion to dismiss. The question asks for arguments in support of the motion.

D is incorrect for the reasons discussed above.

11. A is correct. Personal jurisdiction exists either when there is a traditional basis - such as the defendant's presence in the forum state - or when the defendant has complied with the jurisdiction's long arm statute. Assuming that this jurisdiction has a traditional long arm statute, the District Court will have personal jurisdiction over the toy store, if the meat packer had enough minimum

contacts with the forum jurisdiction that the exercise of jurisdiction "will not offend traditional notions of fair play and substantial justice." (See International Shoe Co. v. Washington, 326 U.S. 310 (1945).)

In order to test for minimum contacts, courts will look to the defendant's purposeful availment of the forum state, the frequency and regularity of defendant's contacts with the forum state, foreseeability of the defendant being sued in the forum state, reasonableness of the defendant being sued in the forum state, the burden on the defendant in being sued in the forum state versus the burden on the plaintiff having to bring the lawsuit elsewhere, and the forum state's interest in having the lawsuit heard there.

Here, the meat packer sold meat to the restaurant, knowing that the restaurant was located in Oklahoma. It, therefore, purposefully availed itself of the laws of Oklahoma. The restaurant was a regular customer of the meat packer. Thus, the meat packer's contact with Oklahoma was systematic and continuous. It was also foreseeable that any injuries resulting from consumption of the meat could occur in Oklahoma, as was the case here.

Because of the meat packer's regular contacts with the restaurant in Oklahoma, the meat packer should have reasonably expected to be sued there for injuries occurring in Oklahoma as a result of consumption of the meat packer's meat. Also, Oklahoma had an interest in hearing the lawsuit there because the injury occurred there.

Lastly, despite any burden to the meat packer in having to go to Oklahoma to defend itself, the above factors weigh against any burden to the meat packer.

For all of the above reasons, the Oklahoma court had personal jurisdiction over the meat packer.

B is incorrect because personal jurisdiction over the plaintiff (here, the man) is irrelevant to a motion made by a defendant (here, the meat packer) to dismiss for lack of personal jurisdiction over the defendant.

C is incorrect for the reasons discussed in A.

D is incorrect for the reasons discussed in B.

12. D is the correct answer. Whether or not venue is improper, the man previously brought a pre-answer motion under Rule 12(b) of the Federal Rules of Civil Procedure in which he moved to dismiss the lawsuit for lack of personal jurisdiction and lack of subject matter jurisdiction. However, he omitted from that motion an objection to venue. The venue objection was, therefore, waived under Rule 12(h)(1)(A) of the Federal Rules of Civil Procedure, even if venue was improperly laid.

A is incorrect because, even though venue was proper (since the incident occurred across the street from that courthouse, in that forum state), the court will not engage in this analysis because the man waived his right to object to venue for the reasons discussed in D.

B and C are incorrect because, as discussed in the explanation to A, the court will not analyze whether or not venue was proper because the man waived his right to object to venue for the reasons discussed in D.

13. C is correct. In federal court, subject matter jurisdiction is based upon either a federal question or complete diversity of citizenship and an amount in controversy over $75,000.

Here, the woman - who was a citizen of Wyoming - was suing the man - who was a citizen of Maine - for $500,000 in damages in a personal injury lawsuit. Personal injury is typically not a federal question; it depends entirely on state law.

However because the woman and the man were citizens of different states (Wyoming and Maine, respectively), and because the amount in controversy ($500,000) exceeded $75,000, the federal court had diversity jurisdiction over this case. Consequently, the first claim should not be dismissed.

Under Rule 18(a) of the Federal Rules of Civil Procedure, "a party asserting a claim...may join, as independent or alternative claims, as many claims as it has against an opposing party." This Rule does not require that additional claims be related to the original claim.

Here, the woman's original claim against the man (for personal injury) was proper for the reasons discussed above. As a result, under Rule 18(a), the woman could then bring any additional claims against the man, even where, as here, the additional claim (intellectual property violation) was not related to the original claim (personal injury). Further, the court has federal question jurisdiction over the intellectual property claim arising under federal law.

Consequently, the second claim should not be dismissed, either.

A, B, and D are incorrect for the reasons discussed in C.

14. C is correct. In federal court, subject matter jurisdiction is based upon either a federal question (28 U.S.C. §1331) or complete diversity of citizenship and an amount in controversy over $75,000 (28 U.S.C. §1332).

Rule 24 of the Federal Rules of Civil Procedure allows a new party to intervene in an existing lawsuit in order to protect that new party's rights when the new party has an interest in subject of the existing lawsuit such that not allowing the new party to intervene would impair the new party's rights.

However, since the plaintiff and the man are both North Carolina citizens, intervention destroys diversity. There is no supplemental jurisdiction over the claim against the man because, under 28 USC §1367(b), if a new party seeks to intervene under Rule 24 of the Federal Rules of Civil Procedure and that intervention would destroy complete diversity, then the intervention will not be permitted.

Here, the man was a citizen of North Carolina, the company was headquartered in South Carolina, and the amount in controversy was $80,000 (and, thus, exceeded $75,000). As a result, at the onset of and during the lawsuit, there was complete diversity of citizenship, and the amount in controversy requirement was met as well.

However, when the owner, who was a citizen of North Carolina, attempted to intervene, such intervention, if allowed, would destroy complete diversity of citizenship because the man (the plaintiff) was also a citizen of North Carolina.

Therefore, the owner's motion to intervene will be denied.

A and B are incorrect for the reasons discussed in C.

D is incorrect because the issue in 28 USC §1367(b) is subject matter (i.e., diversity) jurisdiction, not personal jurisdiction, as discussed in C.

15. D is correct. Under 28 USC §1391(b):

A civil action may be brought in:

(1) a judicial district in which any defendant resides, if all defendants are residents of the State in which the district is located;

(2) a judicial district in which a substantial part of the events or omissions giving rise to the claim occurred, or a substantial part of property that is the subject of the action is situated; or

(3) if there is no district in which an action may otherwise be brought as provided in this section, any judicial district in which any defendant is subject to the court's personal jurisdiction with respect to such action.

Here, venue would be proper in all four judicial districts, including the southern judicial district, under 1391(b)(1), because all defendants reside in the same state, and 1391(b)(2) because the incident occurred in the southern district.

A is incorrect because it contradicts the facts (they raised the venue issue before answering the woman's complaint).

B is incorrect for the reasons discussed in C.

C is incorrect because it only discusses the jurisdiction issue, not the venue issue.

A CIVIL PROCEDURE

16. D is correct. In order for Turkey to be a non-viable alternative forum, its law must not effectively offer any remedy to the woman. Here, the facts state that the relevant Turkish laws are roughly equivalent to their U.S. counterparts. The fact that it would merely be more difficult for the woman to win under substantive Turkish law is not enough of a reason to deny the man's motion to move the case to Turkey.

    A is incorrect for the reasons discussed in D.

    B is incorrect because, while the plaintiff controls where the lawsuit is initially brought, the defendant may subsequently move to change to a different court, for example, for reasons of forum non conveniens or through removal.

    C is incorrect because the facts state that the man, while a resident of Turkey, was a citizen of the United States. U.S. courts have jurisdiction over U.S. citizens, even if they do not reside in the United States.

17. A is correct. In Shaffer v. Heitner, 433 U.S. 186 (1977), the Supreme Court set for the requirements for quasi-in-rem jurisdiction. The court said that quasi-in-rem jurisdiction may exist in situations that do not offend notions of "fair play and substantial justice" under a minimum contacts analysis. Today, quasi-in-rem jurisdiction may still exist even when there would otherwise be no personal jurisdiction over a particular defendant under a long arm statute. The Court did not abolish this basis of jurisdiction altogether but limited it to situations where the defendant placed the res in the forum state and the cause of action arises out of the res.

    Here, the woman attached the man's Rhode Island bank account for the purposes of securing quasi-in-rem jurisdiction. Because the facts indicate that the man had never been in Rhode Island except to open the bank account ten years earlier, there would be no basis for personal jurisdiction over the man. And there is no basis for quasi-in-rem jurisdiction because the plaintiff's personal injury cause of action does not arise out of the bank account.

    B, C, and D are incorrect for the reasons discussed in A.

18. C is correct. The jurisdiction of the federal court here appears to be based on diversity (rather than federal question) because the man was suing for defamation only (not typically a federal question), and both the man (plaintiff) and the woman (defendant) were citizens of different states.

    Under 28 USC §1367(a), a federal district court that has original jurisdiction over a case (such as here, where the district court had diversity jurisdiction) also has jurisdiction over all other claims that are "so related to claims in the action within such original jurisdiction that they form part of the same case or controversy under Article III of the United States Constitution. Such supplemental jurisdiction shall include claims that involve the joinder or intervention of additional parties."

However, under 28 USC §1367(b), the court will not have supplemental jurisdiction, if the supplemental claim would destroy diversity. This subsection only applies where it is the plaintiff who is suing an additional defendant. Here, the man (the plaintiff) was suing an additional defendant (the daughter), and the daughter and the man were both citizens of the same state (Maine). Thus, diversity was destroyed by adding the daughter as a defendant. The woman's motion should, therefore, be granted.

A is incorrect for the reasons discussed in C.

B is incorrect. The man was allowed to add additional defendants, so long as doing so did not destroy subject matter jurisdiction. However, adding the additional defendant (the daughter) did destroy subject matter jurisdiction in this case for the reasons discussed in C.

D is incorrect because defamation is not normally a federal question.

19. D is correct. In federal court, subject matter jurisdiction is based upon either a federal question or complete diversity of citizenship and an amount in controversy over $75,000.

Here, the woman was alleging copyright infringement. Copyright law is exclusively a federal matter. Thus, there was a federal question, which established the basis for subject matter jurisdiction.

A and B are incorrect. They both deal with elements of diversity jurisdiction, which was not required here because, as discussed in D, there was subject matter jurisdiction due to the federal question (copyright infringement).

C is incorrect because the man's motion to dismiss was based on lack of subject matter jurisdiction, not lack of personal jurisdiction.

20. D is correct. Under *Hanna v. Plumer*, 380 U.S. 460 (1965), the federal courts in diversity actions must apply all federal rules of civil procedure that are on point over conflicting state rules.

Under Rule 12(b) of the Federal Rules of Civil Procedure, a party may assert certain defenses in a motion. Under Rule 12(b)(2), one of these defenses is lack of personal jurisdiction. Under Rule 12(b)(6), another defense is failure to state a claim upon which relief can be granted.

Under Burnham v. Superior Court of California, 495 U.S. 604 (1990), personal jurisdiction exists where a person is personally served in the forum state.

Here, the cousin was served in California (the forum state) while he was there to visit his college roommate. Thus, under Burnham, service on the cousin was proper because he was personally served in the forum state.

The cousin was also properly impleaded, since the man was not trying to shift liability over to the cousin, thereby effectively making the cousin the defendant. Rather, the man was asserting that, if the man were held liable to the woman, the cousin had to pay a proportional share of whatever the man paid to the woman.

A is incorrect because the cousin's attack on personal jurisdiction was procedurally proper under Rule 12(b)(2) of the Federal Rules of Civil Procedure, as discussed above. (However, for the reasons discussed in D, the court will find that there was personal jurisdiction over the cousin.)

Further, contrary to what A states, Hanna v. Plumer requires the federal court to apply all federal rules of civil procedure that are on point over a conflicting state rule, as discussed above. Thus, the court will not apply California's "special appearance," but rather, the federal rule.

B is incorrect because the man was personally served while he was physically present in California (the forum state), as discussed in D.

C is incorrect because, as discussed in D, the man was not attempting to make his cousin a defendant; rather, the man was merely asserting that the cousin had to pay a proportional share, if the man were ultimately found liable to the woman.

21. C is correct. In federal court, subject matter jurisdiction is based upon either a federal question or complete diversity of citizenship and an amount in controversy over $75,000. Separate claims against a single defendant may be aggregated in order to meet the requirement that the amount in controversy exceed $75,000.

Furthermore, under Rule 18(a) of the Federal Rules of Civil Procedure, "a party asserting a claim...may join, as independent or alternative claims, as many claims as it has against an opposing party." This Rule does not require that additional claims be related to the original claim.

Here, the estate of the woman - who was a citizen of Hawaii - was suing the man - who was a citizen of Alaska - for $35,000 in damages, in a wrongful death lawsuit. The woman's estate brought an additional claim against the man for wrongful termination, alleging $70,000 in damages.

Neither the first claim (wrongful death) nor the second claim (wrongful termination) is typically a federal question; they both depend entirely on state law. Thus, there was no federal question jurisdiction; the only type of subject matter jurisdiction that the federal district court could exercise here would be diversity jurisdiction.

As discussed, the woman was a citizen of Hawaii, and the man was a citizen of Alaska. Thus, there was complete diversity of citizenship.

Regarding the amount in controversy, because the first claim (wrongful death) and the second claim (wrongful termination) were by the same plaintiff (the woman's estate) against the same defendant (the man), the two claims could be aggregated: since $35,000 (first claim) + $70,000 (second claim) exceeds $75,000, the amount in controversy requirement was satisfied as well.

Thus, the federal district court had diversity jurisdiction over this case. As a result, the man's first motion (to dismiss for lack of subject matter jurisdiction) should be denied.

Regarding the man's second motion (to dismiss the second claim because it was wholly unrelated to the first claim), as discussed, Rule 18(a) allows a plaintiff to assert as many claims as it has against a defendant, even if those claims are not related, as is the case here with the two claims that the woman's estate is making against the man (wrongful death and wrongful termination, respectively).

Because Rule 18(a) allows the woman's estate to assert both claims against the man, the man's second motion should be denied as well.

A, B, and D are incorrect for the reasons discussed in C.

22. A is correct. In federal court, subject matter jurisdiction is based upon either a federal question or complete diversity of citizenship and an amount in controversy over $75,000.

Here, the woman was an employee of the post office (the United States Postal Service). She was suing for actions she alleged occurred on federal property, i.e., the post office, giving a basis for federal question subject matter jurisdiction. As a result, the man's motion should be dismissed because there was subject matter jurisdiction here.

B is incorrect for two reasons: there was personal jurisdiction, since both the woman and the man were located in California, and the alleged incidents occurred in California. Secondly, the man's motion was based on lack of subject matter jurisdiction, not lack of personal jurisdiction.

C and D are incorrect for the reasons discussed in A. In addition, C is incorrect because it makes no sense: the man's motion was to dismiss for lack of subject matter jurisdiction; thus, if the court were to grant the man's motion, it would be an indication that there was no subject matter jurisdiction, while C says precisely the opposite.

23. D is correct. In federal court, subject matter jurisdiction is based upon either a federal question (28 U.S.C. §1331) or complete diversity of citizenship and an amount in controversy over $75,000 (28 U.S.C. §1332).

Rule 14(a)(3) of the Federal Rules of Civil Procedure states that a "plaintiff may assert against the third-party defendant any claim arising out of the transaction or occurrence that is the subject matter of the plaintiff's claim against the third-party plaintiff."

However, under 28 USC §1367(b), if a plaintiff asserts a claim against a third-party defendant under Rule 14 of the Federal Rules of Civil Procedure, and the assertion of that additional claim would destroy complete diversity, then the additional claim will not be permitted.

Here, the woman's lawsuit was brought in federal district court. Her claim was for negligence, which is typically not a federal question. Thus, the only basis for subject matter jurisdiction would be diversity. In this case, the woman was a citizen of Nevada, and the man (the original defendant) was a citizen of New Mexico. The amount in controversy was $500,000 (and thus exceeded $75,000). As a result, at the onset of and during the lawsuit, there was complete diversity of citizenship, and the amount in controversy requirement was met, as well.

However, when the woman attempted to add her neighbor, who was a citizen of Nevada, as an additional defendant under Rule 14(a)(3) of the Federal Rules of Civil Procedure, this would destroy diversity because both the woman (the plaintiff) and the neighbor (the new defendant) were citizens of the same state (Nevada).

Thus, the neighbor's motion should be granted because adding him as a defendant would destroy subject matter jurisdiction (diversity).

A, B, and C are incorrect for the reasons discussed in D. Furthermore, B and C are incorrect because pendent and ancillary jurisdiction no longer exist and have been replaced by supplemental jurisdiction.

24. C is correct. Under Rule 14(a) of the Federal Rules of Civil Procedure, parties whose claims are related to the original claim may be brought into the original lawsuit. This is known as the impleader rule. Here, impleading the captains was improper because the U.S. Government was not asking, in its third-party complaint, for reimbursement from the captains for whatever refund the Government had to pay to the company. Rather, the Government was asserting an independent claim against the captains based upon their alleged employment tax liability to the U.S. (if the court determined that the company did not owe that tax liability to the U.S.)

A is incorrect for the reasons discussed in C.

B is incorrect for the reasons discussed in C and because it is possible that neither the company nor the captains were liable to the Government. For example, the court might have deemed the crewmen to be self-employed.

D is incorrect because, as discussed in C, the claims against the company and against the captains were completely independent of each other. Thus, there would be no risk of inconsistencies here.

25. A is correct. Joint tortfeasors are not necessary or indispensable parties under Rule 19 of the Federal Rules of Civil Procedure. It is up to the plaintiff to determine which defendants to sue in which actions. Here, the company was, in effect, arguing that the two other joint tortfeasors should have been joined by the man in the federal court lawsuit against the company.

B is incorrect because it fails to apply the elements of Rule 19(a). It does not discuss whether the parties are "necessary" or "indispensable," as A does.

C is incorrect because the company, in the absence of the doctor and the hospital, will still be able to assert its defense that the doctor and the hospital were the cause of plaintiff's injuries.

D is incorrect for the reasons discussed in A.

26. D is correct. There is a potential conflict of interest when the same individual is both the attorney representing the class and the named class representative. Here, that was the situation because the attorney representing the class is also the named class representative.

A, B, and C are incorrect for the reasons discussed in D.

Furthermore, C is incorrect because the issue of having the amount in controversy be greater than $75,000 comes up when there is a question regarding diversity jurisdiction in federal courts, which was not raised in these facts.

27. C is correct. Under Rule 23(a) of the Federal Rules of Civil Procedure, "One or more members of a class may sue or be sued as representative parties on behalf of all members only if:

(1) the class is so numerous that joinder of all members is impracticable;

(2) there are questions of law or fact common to the class;

(3) the claims or defenses of the representative parties are typical of the claims or defenses of the class; and

(4) the representative parties will fairly and adequately protect the interests of the class.

Here, while (1) has arguably been met (since there were 5,000 individuals in the proposed class), the attempt to have all 5,000 be deemed a class will fail because of elements (2) and (3). In particular, as discussed in the facts, some individuals were allegedly injured by falling speakers, others allegedly suffered hearing loss, and others were allegedly electrocuted. These are separate and distinct claims. Thus, the questions of fact are not common to everyone in the proposed class.

Furthermore, the attempt to represent the entire class will fail on element (4) because the individuals who sought to represent the entire class only alleged that they themselves had been injured when they were crushed by the falling speakers. They could, therefore, not "fairly and adequately protect the interests of the class," since other members alleged hearing loss, and others alleged injuries through electrocution.

As a result, the court should find that these individuals cannot represent the entire class of 5,000 individuals, since there were differing claims among these 5,000 individuals.

Finally, if the court finds that this is a 23(b)(3) "damage" class action, the predominance requirement will not be satisfied because of the different factual issues among the class member's different claims.

A and B are incorrect for the reasons discussed in C.

D is incorrect because there is no such thing as the "multitude of plaintiffs" rule.

28. D is correct. Rule 33(b)(4) of the Federal Rules of Civil Procedure states, "The grounds for objecting to an interrogatory must be stated with specificity. Any ground not stated in a timely objection is waived, unless the court excuses the failure for good cause."

Here, the man merely objected to the interrogatory without stating any grounds for the objection. Therefore, the woman's motion to compel should be granted.

A is incorrect for the reasons discussed in D.

B and C are incorrect because the issue of the maximum number of interrogatories was not raised in these facts.

29. A is correct because under Rule 26(a)(1)(A)(i) of the Federal Rules of Civil Procedure, "The name and, if known, the address and telephone number of each individual likely to have discoverable information—along with the subjects of that information—that the disclosing party may use to support its claims or defenses, unless the use would be solely for impeachment" is a required initial disclosure.

B, C, and D are incorrect because under Rule 26(a)(1)(B) of the Federal Rules of Civil Procedure, all of these items are exempt from initial discovery.

30. B is correct. Under Rule 28(a)(1)(A) of the Federal Rules of Civil Procedure, a deposition may be heard by "an officer authorized to administer oaths either by federal law or by the law in the place of examination." Here, the notary public was commissioned by the state in which the deposition was being held. By getting his commission from that state, the notary public was authorized to administer oaths by that state. As a result, the defendant's objection should be overruled, and the notary public should be allowed to hear the defendant's deposition.

A, C, and D are incorrect for the reasons discussed in B.

Furthermore, A is incorrect because judges do not hear depositions.

C is also incorrect because it is not necessary for the notary public to be deputized. As discussed in B, so long as the notary public was authorized to administer oaths by the state (which was the case here), this was sufficient for the notary public to be able to hear the deposition.

31. D is correct. Under Rule 26(a)(2)(A) of the Federal Rules of Civil Procedure, the identity of expert witnesses to be used at trial must be disclosed to the other side, and under Rule 26(a)(2)(B), those expert witnesses must prepare reports, which must also be disclosed to the other side.

Here, it appears that the building owners were using the chemist's services to see whether he would be able to testify favorably for the building owners at trial. Although the chemist spent two hours investigating; wrote a five-page report; and received a $200 "honorarium," the building owners decided not to call the chemist as a witness at trial.

Therefore, Rule 26(a)(2)(A) does not apply here. Because Rule 26(a)(2)(A) does not apply here, the requirement to disclose the report under Rule 26(a),(2)(B) does not apply here, either. Consequently, the report did not have to be produced.

Further, since the chemist is a nontestifying expert, Rule 26(b)(4) applies. If the chemist is deemed to have been retained in anticipation of litigation, then discovery of his report can be compelled only if plaintiff can show "exceptional circumstances" which are not satisfied here since the facts do not indicate that plaintiff cannot hire its own expert to investigate the wreckage. Most likely, the chemist will be deemed to be a casually consulted expert, because of the honorarium and two-hour investigation. As such, his report is not discoverable.

A and C are incorrect for the reasons discussed in D.

A is also incorrect because it states the rule for overcoming the work product immunity, which was not at issue under these facts.

B is incorrect because the contents of the chemist's report were relevant to the subject matter (i.e., the cause of the explosion) and, also, the purpose of the chemist's investigation was apparently motivated by litigation. The building owners wanted to determine the chemist's suitability as a trial witness, but for the reasons discussed in D, the report did not need to be produced.

32. B is correct. Here, the man sought to depose the employee to discover facts that the employee learned as an ordinary percipient witness, i.e., what the employee discovered as he investigated the train wreckage as part of the employee's ordinary duties. The employee did not learn these particular facts in preparation for trial, but pursuant to his accident prevention duties as an employee in the train company's accident prevention department. The fact that two months later, the employee was added to the train company's legal team and was asked to re-investigate does not change the analysis, since the man was asking for the employee's initial report that had been prepared pursuant to the employee's ordinary duties before the employee became part of the legal team.

    Therefore, the train company's motion for a protective order should be denied.

    A is incorrect because it states the standard for overcoming the work product immunity. The initial report was not covered by the work product doctrine for the reasons discussed in B.

    C is incorrect because exceptional circumstances did not need to be shown here, since the employee's initial report had been prepared as part of the employee's ordinary duties before the employee became part of the train company's legal team, as discussed in B.

    D is incorrect for the reasons discussed in B and because the facts learned by the employee at the wreckage site were relevant to the cause of the crash.

33. A is correct. The mechanic's eyewitness observations of the crash were clearly relevant and not protected as work product or under the attorney-client privilege.

    The note was not work product because it was a note voluntarily written and sent to the airline by a third party (the mechanic). No effort was expended by the airline or its counsel to secure this note.

    The note was not protected under the attorney-client privilege because the mechanic was not communicating with his own attorneys. Hence, the airline's attorneys could not prevent the plaintiff from receiving the mechanic's note during discovery because there is no applicable Federal Rule of Civil Procedure to prevent this from occurring.

    B is incorrect because the mechanic did not acquire his facts and opinions in anticipation of litigation. While he did write the note to the airline's attorneys with the likelihood of a lawsuit against the airline in mind, he was not retained by the airline to observe or investigate the crash. Therefore, the mechanic was not an expert for purposes of this rule.

C is incorrect because the note is neither the work product of the airline nor its attorneys for the reasons discussed in A.

D is incorrect because the note was not protected under the attorney-client privilege for the reasons discussed in A.

34. B is correct because it is the only choice that states an incorrect answer. It is the old-fashioned, fast-eroding common law rule of "mutuality of estoppel," not the Due Process Clause, that would prevent the woman, a stranger to the federal class action suit, from invoking collateral estoppel. The Due Process Clause is inapplicable because the bus company did, in fact, have its day in court on the issue of the bus driver's negligence as the cause of the crash.

A is incorrect because it states a correct answer. The Iowa state court must give the same enforcement scope to the federal class action judgment that the federal courts give to that judgment.

C is incorrect because it, too, contains a correct answer. Federal law, under Parklane Hosiery Co. v. Shore, 439 U.S. 322 (1979), gives the federal court discretion to refuse to allow a stranger to invoke collateral estoppel, if the stranger stayed out of the earlier suit because of a "wait and see" attitude.

D is incorrect because it states a correct answer: Iowa must give the same enforcement scope to a federal court judgment as the federal courts give that judgment. Thus, if the federal courts would have prevented the woman from relying on the previous judgment in favor of the class, then the Iowa court could not grant the woman's motion, either.

35. A is correct. This version of the statute violates the Seventh Amendment because it deprives a party of his right to have all issues relating to the damage claims tried before a jury. The other versions of the statute are all constitutional; therefore, B, C and D are incorrect.

B is incorrect because the terms of the statute in B provide for jury trials in both damage and injunctive actions. Such a statute would not violate the Seventh Amendment because there is no right to a judge (or bench) trial in a formerly equitable claim.

C is incorrect because the terms of the statute C do not address the jury trial issue, but a court would apply the Seventh Amendment to require a jury trial of all issues pertaining to the damage claim (if a jury trial were timely demanded).

D is incorrect because the statute in D provides for a judge, not a jury, to try issues in suits brought by the federal government for the imposition of fines to vindicate public rights. Such suits, tried before an administrative tribunal before an administrative law judge, have been held not to require juries under the Seventh Amendment.

36. B is correct. Although the debtor was "in default" for having failed to answer or otherwise defend against the suit, his act of engaging in settlement negotiations throughout the six-week period indicates that he did not intend to write-off the creditor's lawsuit. Therefore, the debtor's settlement activities would be deemed an "appearance" entitling him to notice before default judgment was entered. He will, thus, be able to set aside the default judgment.

    A is incorrect because, although the debtor did not timely answer or otherwise defend (which made him "in default"), for the reasons discussed in B, he did make "an appearance" and would, therefore, be entitled to have the default judgment against him be set aside.

    C and D are incorrect for the reasons discussed in B.

37. C is correct. Under Rule 41(a) of the Federal Rules of Civil Procedure, the plaintiff has a right to voluntarily dismiss his own suit in federal court until the defendant answers the complaint or moves for summary judgment, whichever occurs first.

    Here, the woman (the plaintiff) filed her notice of dismissal after the man (the defendant) served his answer. Hence, the man's motion to quash the notice should be granted.

    A is incorrect because it ignores the fact that the man served his answer before the woman filed her notice of dismissal. Because the man had served his answer, it was not necessary for him to file a motion for summary judgment before his motion to quash the notice of dismissal could be granted, as discussed in C.

    B is incorrect for the reasons discussed in C.

    D is incorrect because it contains an incorrect statement of law. Plaintiffs do have a limited - but not an absolute - right to voluntarily dismiss their actions under Rule 41(a), as discussed in C.

38. B is correct. The movant's burden in a summary judgment motion is to show that there is no material issue of fact to be resolved by the jury.

    Here, the doctor did not meet his movant's burden because, from his moving papers, there was still a material issue of fact for the jury to resolve, i.e., whether the sponges had been left inside the woman during the surgery in question or if they had been left inside the woman during previous surgeries.

Thus, the doctor's motion for summary judgment should be denied.

A is incorrect because, even with res ipsa loquitur, there are still issues regarding causation and damages that need to be resolved (here, whether the sponge had been left inside the woman during the surgery in question or during a previous surgery and also the damage amount).

C is incorrect because the woman did not have a respondent's burden, since the doctor failed to satisfy his movant's burden, as discussed in B.

D is incorrect because whether or not the sponges had been left inside the woman during the surgery in question or during a previous surgery was a material issue of fact for the jury to resolve at trial.

39. D is correct because it is the only choice that correctly states the law under Rule 16(e) of the Federal Rules of Civil Procedure, namely, that, "The order following a final pretrial conference shall be modified only to prevent manifest injustice."

Here, there were no facts to indicate that the woman needed to amend the pre-trial order to add the state common law cause of action in order to prevent manifest injustice. Therefore, D is a correct statement.

A, B, and C are incorrect for the reasons discussed in D.

40. D is correct. Rule 50(a)(1)(A) of the Federal Rules of Civil Procedure states, "If a party has been fully heard on an issue during a jury trial and the court finds that a reasonable jury would not have a legally sufficient evidentiary basis to find for the party on that issue, the court may...resolve the issue against the party."

Here, the client was fully heard (he gave testimony before the jury). The client argued that the lawyer had not filed the lawsuit before the statute of limitations had run and that the client would have won his case had the lawyer filed the lawsuit prior to the running of the statute of limitations. By contrast, the lawyer and his four witnesses all argued that the lawsuit had been filed prior to the running of the statute of limitations. There is, thus, a clear conflict in the evidence that the jury must be allowed to resolve, namely, the client's assertion that the lawsuit had not been filed prior to the running of the statute of limitations, versus the lawyer's assertion that the case had been filed prior to the running of the statute of limitations.

Thus, the credibility of the client's testimony had to be evaluated by the jury to determine whether or not there was a basis to find for the client. As such, the court could not find for the lawyer without the jury evaluating the credibility of the client's testimony. Consequently, it was up to the jury, not the court, to resolve the issue in favor of one of the parties and against the other party.

A and B are incorrect for the reasons discussed in D.

C is incorrect because Rule 50(b)(2) states that "motions for judgment as a matter of law may be made at any time before submission of the case to the jury."

41. C is correct. The two observations of the man's behavior in the courtroom were relevant to his credibility, which was a crucial issue in the case and was an issue for the jury to resolve. Therefore, the jury did nothing improper in basing its credibility determination on their observations of the man in the courtroom. As a result, the motion should be denied.

    A, B, and D are incorrect for the reasons discussed in C.

42. A is correct. To be reviewable by an appellate court, an error by the court must be objected to at the trial court level. Otherwise, that objection is waived. Here, the woman did not raise her hearsay objection until after a verdict was rendered; the first time that she raised the hearsay issue was on appeal.

    Therefore, the objection was not reviewable.

    B is incorrect. The term "interlocutory" refers to an order, sentence, decree, or judgment that is given after the commencement but before the termination of a cause of action. An interlocutory order, sentence, decree, or judgment is used to provide a temporary or provisional decision on an issue. As a result, an interlocutory order, sentence, decree, or judgment is not final and is usually not subject to appeal.

    Here, the issue was not a provisional or temporary order given by the judge. Rather, the issue was a supposed error in allowing hearsay to be admitted. However, as discussed in A, the woman's failure to object to the hearsay at the trial court level meant that she waived this objection and could not raise it for the first time at the appellate level.

    C is incorrect for the reasons discussed in A. Even if the admission of the hearsay would have prejudiced the verdict, the woman's failure to raise the objection to the admission of the hearsay while the case was still at the trial level means that she waived this objection and could not raise it for the first time at the appellate level.

    D is incorrect because there is nothing exceptional about a failure to raise a hearsay objection; it is simply a matter of poor lawyering, which does not undo the rule discussed in A that such issues cannot be raised for the first time at the appellate level.

43. C is correct because of the terminology. The verdict was rendered in the man's favor, so he was obviously not appealing the verdict itself. This is what the woman was appealing.

The man's appeal was based on the fact that his motion for attorney's fees was denied. As a result, the man should have cross-appealed as part of the woman's appeal; he should not have done a separate appeal solely on the issue of his motion for attorney's fees because this was not the kind of attack that he could make on the trial court's rulings.

A, B, and D are incorrect for the reasons discussed in C.

44. D is correct. Under Rule 13(a)(1) of the Federal Rules of Civil Procedure, a defendant must state as a counterclaim any claims that arise out of the same transaction or occurrence as the plaintiff's claim, as long as this would not require adding additional parties over whom the court does not have jurisdiction.

Here, the woman originally sued the man for battery in the incident involving the taking of the fountain pen from her purse.

The man's subsequent lawsuit against the woman for battery (i.e., for spitting in his face) also involved the incident in which the fountain pen had been taken from the woman's purse.

Because the man's battery lawsuit arose out of the same transaction/occurrence as the woman's claim (namely, the incident involving the taking of the fountain pen from the woman's purse), and because no additional parties were involved here, the man's claim should have been raised as a compulsory counterclaim during the woman's original lawsuit.

Since the man failed to raise his battery claim during the woman's lawsuit, he was barred from raising it in a later lawsuit under Rule 13(a)(1).

As a result, the court should grant the woman's motion.

A, B, and C are incorrect for the reasons discussed in D.

A and C are also incorrect because once the woman's judgment had been rendered and her case closed, that judgment would not be disturbed without an order from a higher appellate court, which was not the case here.

45. A is correct. Under Rule 56(e)(2) of the Federal Rules of Civil Procedure, " When one party moves for summary judgment or partial summary judgment, if the nonmoving party "fails to... properly address...[the moving] party's assertion of fact..., the court may...consider the fact undisputed for purposes of the motion."

Here, the nonmoving party (here, the man) failed to respond to the woman's allegation that she had not known that her alleged breach of contract would negatively affect the man's other business. Thus, under Rule 56(e)(2), the court may consider this fact to be undisputed for purposes of the woman's motion.

A CIVIL PROCEDURE

As a result, the court may grant the woman's motion for partial summary judgment on the issue of interference with perspective commercial advantage.

B is incorrect because, while it is a true statement, it is not relevant because partial summary judgment is allowed to limit the issues that will be litigated at trial, even if the trial itself can proceed.

C is incorrect because it is an incorrect statement of law.

D is incorrect because the Hadley v. Baxendale rule is a rule regarding consequential damages, and it only becomes relevant once contractual liability has been found. Here, the woman moved for partial summary judgment on the issue of interference with perspective commercial advantage. The issue of breach of contract had yet to be decided for or against the woman.

46. B is correct. The woman chose to assert her property damage and personal injury claims, which arose out of the same transaction (the automobile collision) separately. This is known as splitting the cause of action and is not allowed in federal district court (or in most state courts). Unlike California, which adopts the primary rights test to define the scope of the cause of action, the federal courts follow the Restatement's "same transaction" test.

Therefore, the man's motion for summary judgment should be granted.

A is incorrect because the Double Jeopardy Clause only applies in criminal cases. Here, the woman's two lawsuits were civil cases.

C is incorrect because it contradicts the facts, as discussed in B.

D is incorrect for the reasons discussed in B.

47. D is correct. In federal district court under Rule 4(k)(1)(A) of the Federal Rules of Civil Procedure, personal jurisdiction follows the rules of the forum state. However, subject matter jurisdiction is based upon either a federal question (28 U.S.C. §1331) or complete diversity of citizenship and an amount in controversy over $75,000 (28 U.S.C. §1332).

Here, the incident in question took place in Los Angeles, California, which was also the location of the court in which the woman's lawsuit was brought. Thus, the court had personal jurisdiction over the man.

Regarding subject matter jurisdiction, the woman's lawsuit was for negligence, which is almost never a federal question. Consequently, the only type of subject matter jurisdiction that could exist here would be diversity jurisdiction.

In this case, the amount in controversy was $500,000. Thus, the amount in controversy was over $75,000.

Regarding complete diversity of citizenship, 28 U.S.C. §1332(a)(2) provides for "alienage jurisdiction" in that it considers the citizenship of the plaintiff and the defendant to be diverse, if one is a United States citizen and the other is a citizen of a foreign country.

However, 28 U.S.C. §1332(a)(2) goes on to state, as an exception to alienage jurisdiction, that "the [federal] district courts shall not have original jurisdiction under this subsection of an action between citizens of a state and citizens or subjects of a foreign state who are lawfully admitted for permanent residence in the United States and are domiciled in the same state."

Here, the woman was a citizen of California. The man was a citizen of a foreign country (Germany). However, he was a lawful permanent resident of the United States and was domiciled in California.

Consequently, for purposes of diversity jurisdiction, both the woman and the man were considered citizens of California. As a result, there was no diversity jurisdiction here.

The man's motion should, thus, be granted because the district lacked jurisdiction under these facts (in this case, subject matter jurisdiction).

A and B are incorrect for the reasons discussed in D.

C is incorrect because federal district courts can have jurisdiction over negligence actions in diversity cases or if the incident in question takes place on federal property (such as in a national park or in a post office).

48. D is the correct answer. Under the doctrine of res judicata, a prior judgment on the merits will prevent relitigation on the same issue between the same parties and privies from the original law lawsuit. However, a dismissal on personal jurisdiction grounds is not deemed to be "on the merits" and will, therefore, not have any res judicata effect on subsequent lawsuits between the same parties or privies.

Here, the Nevada action was dismissed solely based on lack of personal jurisdiction; the Nevada court made no decision as to whether or not the man had, in fact, trespassed. Thus, it was not a decision "on the merits," and it had no res judicata effect that would preclude the woman from refiling the lawsuit in Wyoming.

A is incorrect for the reasons discussed in D.

B is incorrect because, although the man was physically present in Nevada (at the Hoover Dam) when he was personally served in Nevada (not in Wyoming), the court in Wyoming had personal jurisdiction over him because he was a citizen of Wyoming, even though he was not served in Wyoming.

C is an incorrect statement of law. Trespass actions may only be brought in a state that has personal jurisdiction over the parties.

49. A is the correct answer. Under the doctrine of res judicata, a prior judgment on the merits will prevent relitigation on the same issue between the same parties and privies from the original law lawsuit.

The test for determining whether the man split his "cause of action" is the "same transaction" test (since the man brought his previous defamation lawsuit against the woman in a federal district court) and the allegedly false statements occurred at the same time as the allegedly defamatory statements, and one would (for the sake of judicial economy) expect to try both the defamation and false light invasion of privacy claims in the same lawsuit.

Therefore, the woman's motion to dismiss should be granted on res judicata grounds.

B and C are incorrect for the reasons discussed in A.

D is incorrect both because this would be a reason to grant (rather than deny) the woman's motion and because, as discussed in A, res judicata precludes the entire claim, not merely a single issue (which is what collateral estoppel is).

50. C is the correct answer. Under the doctrine of res judicata, a prior judgment on the merits will prevent relitigation on the same cause of action between the same parties and privies from the original law lawsuit.

Here, the woman initially sued the lumberjack for trespass, and the court determined that the lumberjack had not trespassed. (This was a prior judgment on the merits.) However, when the man (a different party) then attempted to sue the lumberjack for trespass, the lumberjack brought a motion for summary judgment based on res judicata. The court should deny this motion because the man was not a party to the original lawsuit between the woman and the lumberjack. Therefore, the concept of res judicata would not apply because the claim of trespass was not being relitigated between the same parties or privies.

A is incorrect for the reasons discussed in C.

B is incorrect both because the lumberjack's motion was based on res judicata, not double jeopardy, and because double jeopardy may only be raised in criminal cases, not in civil lawsuits such as the one here.

D is incorrect both because it contradicts

the facts (since the jury in the lawsuit by the woman against the lumberjack had determined that the lumberjack had not trespassed) and for the reasons discussed in C.

51. A is the correct answer because it states the correct standard under the U.S. Supreme Court's opinions in *Bell Atlantic Corporation v. Twombly*, 550 U.S. 544 (2007) and *Iqbal v. Ashcroft*, 556 U.S. 662 (2009) for evaluating the sufficiency of the pleadings. Although Rule 8 of the Federal Rules of Civil Procedure requires only a short and plain statement of the claim showing the pleader is entitled to relief, the Supreme Court in *Twombly* and *Iqbal* stated a two-part test: first, the court should ignore all conclusory allegations (these are not entitled to the assumption of truth) and, second, the court should evaluate the factual allegations to determine whether they plausibly suggest that the plaintiff is entitled to relief. Particularized facts are not required. Here, the court should disregard the conclusory allegations regarding the defects.

    Thus, the manufacturer's motion to dismiss will be granted.

    B is incorrect for the reasons discussed in A.

    C is incorrect because Rule 12(b)(6) of the Federal Rules of Civil Procedure permits the manufacturer to attack the sufficiency of the complaint in its answer, if it had not previously made a pre-answer motion.

    D is incorrect because, unlike "special appearance" practice in many state courts, Rule 12 of the Federal Rules of Civil Procedure allows a defendant to assert the insufficiency of the complaint as a defense in the answer (along with denials).

52. C is correct. Rule 26 (a)(1) no longer requires that disputed facts be alleged with particularity in order to trigger disclosure obligations. Here, however, the bicycle manufacturer's refusal to disclose was based upon its argument that the man's complaint did not allege with particularity the parts of the man's bicycle that were defective. C correctly states the bicycle manufacturer's initial disclosure obligation.

    A, B, and D are incorrect for the reasons discussed in C.

    B is also incorrect because the bicycle manufacturer's obligations were not limited to individuals with discoverable information relevant to the case. Rather, the bicycle manufacturer had a duty to disclose to the man the identity of each individual likely to have discoverable information that the bicycle manufacturer could use to support its defenses to the man's action.

53. D is the correct answer. Rule 26(b)(4)(A) of the Federal Rules of Civil Procedure provides that all experts who will be testifying witnesses at trial may be deposed. There is no requirement that the discovering party serve interrogato-

ries beforehand. These former preliminary requirements were eliminated by amendments to Rule 26(b)(4) effective in December 1993.

Therefore, the hair dye manufacturer's motion for a protective order to bar the deposition of the expert should be denied.

A is incorrect because Rule 26(b)(4) recognizes the woman's legitimate need to depose the expert in order to prepare for the cross-examination of the expert at trial.

B is incorrect for the reasons discussed in D.

C is incorrect because the question of the protection of the facts and opinions of an expert witnesses is covered by Rule 26(a)(2) (Disclosure of Expert Testimony, not a 26(b)(3) (work product) issue. The work product rule of Rule 26(b)(3) does not cover "facts."

54. A is the correct answer. Rule 26(a)(1)(A)(ii) states that with only a few exceptions, " a party must, without awaiting a discovery request, provide to the other parties...a copy—or a description by category and location—of all documents, electronically stored information, and tangible things that the disclosing party has in its possession, custody, or control and may use to support its claims or defenses, unless the use would be solely for impeachment."

Here, the blowtorch manufacturer sent the woman a list identifying all of the manufacturer's employees with knowledge of the design of the blowtorch in question that the blowtorch manufacturer could use in support of its defense and describing by category and location all documents in the possession, custody and control of the blowtorch manufacturer relating to the design of that blowtorch that the blowtorch manufacturer could use in support of its defense.

In providing these descriptions, the blowtorch manufacturer complied with Rule 26(a)(1)(A)(ii). As discussed, the blowtorch manufacturer was not required to provide the woman with actual copies of those documents.

B is incorrect because, as discussed in A, Rule 26(a)(1)(A)(ii) allowed the blowtorch manufacturer to provide either copies of the documents or a description of the documents. Furthermore, the Rule did not require the woman to make a formal request, as discussed above.

C is incorrect because Rule 26(a)(1)(A)(ii) says no such thing.

D is incorrect for the reasons discussed in A.

55. D is the correct answer. Rules 26(a)(3)(A) and 26(a)(3)(B) required the woman to disclose her trial witnesses at least 30 days before trial without the need for the man to serve a discovery request.

Here, she failed to make this disclosure. Thus, the man's motion for sanctions against the woman should be granted.

B is incorrect for the reasons discussed In D.

A and C are incorrect because the issue here is not one of discovery under Rule 26(b), but of automatic required disclosure under Rule 26(a).

56. A is the correct answer. Under Rule 56(a) of the Federal Rules of Civil Procedure, if the movant shows that there is no genuine dispute as to any material fact and the movant is entitled to judgment as a matter of law.

Here, the woman was suing the man for false imprisonment. However, both she and the man acknowledged that the woman had been free to leave at any time at the time of the alleged incident. Since one of the elements of false imprisonment is a determination that the plaintiff had not been free to leave and both the woman and the man agreed that that had not been the case here, there was no genuine dispute as to any material fact. As a result, the movant (the man) was entitled to judgment as a matter of law.

B and D are incorrect statements of law.

C is incorrect for the reasons discussed in A.

57. C is the correct answer. Under the doctrine of res judicata, a prior judgment on the merits will prevent relitigation on the same issue between the same parties and privies from the original law lawsuit.

The test for determining whether the landlord split his "cause of action" is the "same transaction" test (since the landlord brought his previous lawsuit against the tenant in a federal district court) and at the time of the original lawsuit, the tenant was already in arrears on his January, February, and March rent. Therefore, one would (for the sake of judicial economy) expect to try the claims for all three months in the same lawsuit.

Therefore, when the landlord sued the tenant for only January and February in one lawsuit and sued the tenant for March in a separate lawsuit, the landlord split his cause of action, and the tenant's motion to dismiss the second lawsuit will, thus, be granted.

A and D are incorrect because rent arrearage can usually be collected. However, there are some circumstances in which it cannot be collected. Therefore, the terms "always" and "never" are incorrect statements of law. A and D are also incorrect because, the landlord in this case only sued for January and February. For the reasons discussed in C, he will be unable to sue the same tenant for the March rent.

B is incorrect for the reasons discussed in C.

58. A is the correct answer. Under the doctrine of collateral estoppel, a prior judgment on the merits will prevent relitigation on the same issue between the same parties and privies from the original law lawsuit. However, most jurisdictions have abandoned the mutuality rule, so that a nonparty can invoke collateral estoppel on an issue determined by a prior judgment.

Here, the prior judgment in the lawsuit by the landlord against the tenant was a final judgment on the merits. The issue of whether rent was in arrears was decided in favor of the Tenant in the previous action. If the jurisdiction that entered the judgment does not follow the mutuality rule, the girlfriend will be able to preclude the Landlord from attempting to prove again that the rent was in arrears. Thus the girlfriend's motion for summary judgment will be granted.

B, C, and D are incorrect for the reasons discussed in A.

Furthermore, B contradicts the facts because there was a final judgment rendered in the lawsuit between the landlord and the tenant.

59. B is the correct answer. Under the doctrine of res judicata, a prior judgment on the merits precludes a second action on the same cause of action between the same parties or their privies. Under the doctrine of collateral estoppel, a prior judgment on the merits will prevent relitigation on the same issue between the same parties and privies from the original law lawsuit.

Here, the woman previously sued the man for intentional infliction of emotional distress, and a final judgment was entered on this issue in favor of the man. The woman then brought a lawsuit against the man for both intentional infliction of emotional distress and defamation. Here, the parties were the same (the woman and the man), and both the cause of action and the issue of intentional infliction of emotional distress had previously been litigated but not defamation. Therefore, under the doctrine of res judicata and collateral estoppel, the woman will be prevented from asserting her intentional infliction of emotional distress claim again and from relitigating the issue of intentional infliction of emotional distress.

Thus, the court should grant partial summary judgment on this issue, but allow the issue of defamation to be litigated.

A, C, and D are incorrect for the reasons discussed in B.

60. B is the correct answer. A non-party (here, the friend) has an unqualified right to get a copy of his own witness statement, and a party (here, the woman) has an unqualified right to get a copy

of his own witness statement. Here, the woman should ask her friend to demand a copy of the friend's statement. Thus, the woman's motion to compel should not be granted.

A, C, and D are incorrect for the reasons discussed in B.

Furthermore, C is incorrect because here the woman was in pro per (representing herself). As such, she was entitled to document requests and the ability to make motions to compel, if the man failed to comply with her document requests. She was not required to be a lawyer to do so because she was representing herself.

61. B is correct because the woman obtained the witness statement to assist in her defense to the man's lawsuit. Therefore, the statement was presumably prepared in anticipation of litigation and is, thus, protected under the work product doctrine.

A is incorrect because the attorney-client privilege does not apply to the witness' statement because the witness was not the client of the woman's lawyer.

C is incorrect because the witness was an eyewitness to the incident. Therefore, the witness' statement was relevant.

D is incorrect because the witness' statement, while relevant as discussed in C, is still not discoverable for the reasons discussed in B.

62. C is the correct answer. Under Rule 407 of the Federal Rules of Evidence, subsequent remedial measures - i.e., those measures taken to correct the problem that gave rise to the lawsuit - are not admissible at trial. However, this does not prevent their discovery for purposes of pre-trial preparation under Rule 26(b)(1) of the Federal Rules of Civil Procedure, which states, "For good cause, the court may order discovery of any matter relevant to the subject matter involved in the action. Relevant information need not be admissible at the trial, if the discovery appears reasonably calculated to lead to the discovery of admissible evidence."

Thus, even if the materials dealing with repairs to subsequent blenders were not admissible at trial under the Federal Rules of Evidence, they were still discoverable under the Federal Rules of Civil Procedure. Therefore, the materials were discoverable.

A is incorrect because there is no indication that the materials contained the impressions of any experts. Furthermore, the materials were not prepared in anticipation of future litigation; they were prepared to fix the problem with the blenders.

B is incorrect for the reasons discussed in C.

D is incorrect because the materials were relevant, since they help to demonstrate that there was a problem with the blender the woman used, which needed correcting.

63. D is the correct answer because (1) the presence of fruit on the floor of this particular supermarket location was relevant to the cause of the woman's accident; and (2) the dominant purpose behind the report's preparation was to record the results of a health investigation.

While it is true that there is a dual purpose here, i.e., to promote sanitary conditions (the mission of the Health Department) and to prepare for a possible suit by the Health Dept. against the supermarket for possible violations of the Health Code, the question is: what was the dominant purpose? If the former, the report is not protected. In any event, the report is not protected as work product, even if the latter purpose was dominant because the report was not prepared by any of the parties to the lawsuit by the woman against the supermarket for use in litigating that lawsuit. Thus, the report was discoverable.

A and C are incorrect for the reasons discussed in D.

B is incorrect both for the reasons discussed in D and because there was nothing in the facts to suggest that the Health Dept. report was confidential.

64. D is the correct answer. The attorney-client privilege applies whenever a person contacts an attorney for legal advice. The privilege protects any confidential communication that the client or a potential client divulges to an attorney. This information is not discoverable.

Here, the neighbor admitted to his attorney that he was encroaching on the woman's property. Presumably, such an admission would be made in confidence. It would, therefore, be protected from discovery under the attorney-client privilege.

A is incorrect for the reasons discussed in D. Furthermore, this was a civil, not a criminal case. The exculpatory evidence rule only applies in criminal cases.

B is incorrect because the statements, while relevant (since the neighbor admitted to encroaching, which was the subject of the woman's lawsuit), the statements were, nonetheless, not discoverable for the reasons discussed in D.

C is incorrect because the statements were relevant, as discussed in B. However, as discussed in D, they were still not discoverable.

65. B is correct. In federal court, subject matter jurisdiction is based upon either a federal question (28 U.S.C. §1331) or complete diversity of citizenship and an amount in controversy over $75,000 (28 U.S.C. §1332).

Here, while the woman and the man were citizens of different states (North Dakota and Tennessee, respectively), the woman alleged precisely $75,000 in damages. As discussed above, 28 U.S.C. §1332 will only grant a federal district court diversity jurisdiction, if the amount in controversy exceeds $75,000.

Thus, the man's motion to dismiss the lawsuit for lack of subject matter jurisdiction will be successful.

A is incorrect because this lawsuit does not deal with in rem jurisdiction (i.e., jurisdiction involving a piece of property).

C is incorrect because automobile accidents are usually not federal issues (unless they occur in a National Park or other federal land or there are other unusual circumstances making them federal issues). Lawsuits involving automobile accidents may generally be brought in federal court only if there is complete diversity of citizenship and an amount in controversy exceeding $75,000.

D is incorrect for the reasons discussed in B.

66. D is correct. In federal court, subject matter jurisdiction is based upon either a federal question (28 U.S.C. §1331) or complete diversity of citizenship and an amount in controversy over $75,000 (28 U.S.C. §1332).

Here, the woman was a citizen of Wyoming, and both the man and the company were citizens of Idaho. The amount in controversy was $90,000, which exceeded the $75,000 minimum. Thus, there was complete diversity of citizenship, and the amount in controversy exceeded $75,000.

It is true that both the man and the company were citizens of the same State (Idaho), but this does not destroy diversity jurisdiction because the man and the company were both defendants, and 28 U.S.C. §1332 requires only that no plaintiff be a citizen of the same State as any defendant, which was the case here.

Thus, the company's motion will not be successful.

A is incorrect quasi in rem jurisdiction deals with jurisdiction over a piece of property, which is irrelevant to these facts.

B is incorrect for the reasons discussed in D.

C is an incorrect statement of law. Subject matter jurisdiction is always required.

67. C is the correct answer. In federal court, subject matter jurisdiction is based upon either a federal question (28 U.S.C. §1331), complete diversity of citizenship and an amount in controversy over $75,000 (28 U.S.C. §1332), or supple-

mental jurisdiction over related state claims.

Rule 20(a) of the Federal Rules of Civil Procedure states that "Persons * * * may be joined in one action as defendants if: (A) any right to relief is asserted against them jointly, severally, or in the alternative with respect to or arising out of the same transaction, occurrence, or series of transactions or occurrences; and (B) any question of law or fact common to all defendants will arise in the action. Here, the defendants are properly joined because there exists a common question of fact, i.e., who or what caused the accident, and arise out of the same occurrence, i.e., the accident.

28 USC §1367(a) states that: "the district courts shall have supplemental jurisdiction over all other claims that are so related to claims in the action within such original jurisdiction that they form part of the same case or controversy under Article III of the United States Constitution." However, 28 USC §1367(c)(2) states that "The district courts may decline to exercise supplemental jurisdiction over a claim... if...the claim substantially predominates over the claim or claims over which the district court has original jurisdiction."

Here, although the court does not have original jurisdiction over the state law claims because the plaintiff and the other defendants are Michigan citizens (hence, no diversity), the court does have original federal question subject matter jurisdiction over the federal claim against the U.S. Government and the state claims against the other defendants are related to the federal claim. Hence, the court has the power to exercise supplemental jurisdiction over the state claims. However, the state claims seek for times the damages as the federal claim. As a result, the claims against the manufacturers would predominate over the woman's claim against the original defendant (the U.S. Government). Consequently, the court may exercise its discretion to decline to hear the woman's claims against the manufacturers.

The court may, thus, grant the manufacturers' motion.

A, B, and D are incorrect for the reasons discussed in C.

68. A is the correct answer.

In federal court, subject matter jurisdiction is based upon either a federal question or complete diversity of citizenship and an amount in controversy over $75,000.

Here, the claim appears to be based on diversity, since negligence with regard to home building is generally an issue of state law rather than federal law. In this case, the man, who was a citizen of New York, sued the builder, who was a citizen of California. There was, thus, diversity of citizenship. The amount of controversy was $80,000; consequently, the amount in controversy exceeded $75,000.

As a result, the federal district court had diversity jurisdiction here.

In this case, impleader was improper because the builder's third-party complaint asserted an "independent" instead of a "derivative" claim against the architect. The claim was not derivative because the builder could not be held liable under the law for the misdeeds of the architect because the man, not the builder, hired the architect.

The builder's third-party claim was independent of the man's main claim because the builder was not seeking indemnity from the architect in the event that the builder were found liable to the man. Instead, the builder was seeking to be compensated for damage to its business (i.e., bankruptcy).

Thus, even if the builder were found not liable to the man, the builder could still recover against the architect for destroying the builder's business.

C is incorrect for the reasons discussed in A.

B is incorrect because, as discussed in A, the builder could take legal action against the architect in the form of an independent lawsuit rather than impleader.

Here, the builder was a citizen of California, and the architect was a citizen of New York. The amount in controversy - $100,000 - exceeded $75,000.

As a result, an action by the builder against the architect would not destroy diversity.

For the reasons discussed in A, however, the builder's actions against the architect had to be in the form of an independent claim against the architect rather than impleader.

D is incorrect because there is no supplemental jurisdiction issue, since the third-party claim was independently supported by diversity jurisdiction, as discussed in B.

69. B is the correct answer. Under Rule 18(a) of the Federal Rules of Civil Procedure, "A party asserting a claim, counterclaim, crossclaim, or third-party claim may join as independent or alternative claims, as many claims as it has against an opposing party." Under Rule 20, a plaintiff may join claims against two or more defendants if the claims arise out of the same transaction or occurrence and share a common question of law or fact.

Here, the woman's original claim against the man was for intentional infliction of emotional distress and false imprisonment. Her new claim against both the man and the company were for back salary owed, which does not appear to have any relation to the original claim against the man for intentional infliction of emotional distress and false imprisonment.

Under Rule 18(a), the woman could nonetheless bring this claim against the man because this rule allows for even unrelated claims to be brought against someone who is already an "opposing party," which the man, as the original defendant, is.

However, under Rule 24, she could not bring the claim for back salary against the company because it was unrelated to her original claim against the man, and the company was not an original "opposing party" (as the man was).

Thus, the court should grant the company's motion.

A is incorrect for the reasons discussed in B.

C and D are incorrect because, as discussed above, the woman's claim for back salary was unrelated to her original claim for intentional infliction of emotional distress and false imprisonment.

70. C is the correct answer. Under 28 USC §1367(a), a federal district court that has original jurisdiction over a case (such as here, where the district court had diversity jurisdiction) also shall have supplemental jurisdiction over all other claims that are "so related to claims in the action within such original jurisdiction that they form part of the same case or controversy under Article III of the United States Constitution. Such supplemental jurisdiction shall include claims that involve the joinder or intervention of additional parties."

However, supplemental jurisdiction is limited by 28 USC §1367(b), which states that federal courts may not exercise supplemental jurisdiction over a claim by a plaintiff against a person made a party under Rule 14 of the Federal Rules of Civil Procedure (claims against third party defendants) where subject matter jurisdiction is dependent based solely on diversity jurisdiction, and where the exercise of supplemental jurisdiction would undermine (or be inconsistent with) the requirements of complete diversity.

Here, the homeowner could not have initially sued both the builder and the subcontractor in his original complaint because complete diversity would have been destroyed (since the homeowner and the subcontractor were both citizens of New York).

Thus, the homeowner's motion should be denied because allowing the homeowner's claim against the subcontractor - a third party defendant, initially made part of this lawsuit by virtue of the builder's claim against the subcontractor - to proceed would destroy complete diversity.

A is incorrect because this is not a legal basis to deny the man's motion.

B is incorrect because subject matter jurisdiction can be challenged at any time during the litigation and even on appeal.

D is incorrect because it only addresses the joinder issue and not the jurisdictional. Because the homeowner's claim against the subcontractor did, indeed, arise out of the same transaction and occurrence as the builder's claim against the subcontractor, that fact merely permitted the homeowner, as a joinder issue, to also assert a claim directly against the subcontractor as a third-party defendant brought in by the builder.

Despite proper joinder under Rule 14(a) of the Federal Rules of Civil Procedure, however, 28 USC §1367(b) does not permit the court to assert supplemental jurisdiction over this claim, as discussed above.

71. A is the correct answer. When the distributor cross-claimed against the store for contribution in the previous lawsuit, the store's claim for contribution should have been asserted and joined by means of a compulsory counterclaim.

B is incorrect because the store's contribution claim would have been asserted against the distributor as an "opposing party" (not merely a "co-party") and, therefore, should be characterized as a "counterclaim," not a "cross-claim."

C is incorrect because no rule requires the distributor to have objected to the store's failure to assert its compulsory counterclaim.

D is incorrect because, while it is true that cross-claims are never compulsory, the store's contribution claim should have been characterized as a "counterclaim," not a "cross-claim," as discussed in B.

72. D is correct. In federal court, subject matter jurisdiction is based upon either a federal question or complete diversity of citizenship and an amount in controversy over $75,000.

Here, the woman was alleging a violation of the Sherman Antitrust Act (a federal law). Since a federal law was involved, there was a federal question that established the basis for subject matter jurisdiction. Even though the woman and the man were from the same state (New York), which would destroy diversity, diversity is irrelevant where a federal question serves as a basis for subject matter jurisdiction. In addition, the fact that the amount in controversy did not exceed the $75,000 requirement is also irrelevant where subject matter jurisdiction is established through a federal question.

A is incorrect because, as discussed in D, there was subject matter jurisdiction here. In addition, there was personal jurisdiction because the court was located in New York, and the man was a citizen of the forum state (New York).

B and C are incorrect for the reasons discussed in D. In addition, C is incorrect because, if this were a diversity question, the amount in controversy would not be met because it is precisely $75,000; it does not exceed $75,000, as would be required for diversity jurisdiction.

73. A is the correct answer. Subject matter jurisdiction in class action lawsuits in federal court must be based on either diversity of citizenship and at least $5,000,000 in controversy under 28 USC §1332 or federal question under 28 USC §1331.

    Here, the plaintiffs were suing an immigration judge for gender discrimination in the adjudication of their asylum claims. Immigration is exclusively a federal matter. Thus, this was a federal question. As such, no amount in controversy was required. Therefore, the fact that the plaintiffs alleged $10,000 damages did not prevent the court from certifying the class for the purposes of this lawsuit.

    B is an incorrect statement of law.

    C and D are incorrect because they discuss issues related to diversity jurisdiction. For the reasons discussed in A, diversity is not the basis of the subject matter jurisdiction of the lawsuit.

74. C is the correct answer. Under Rule 23(b)(1)(A) of the Federal Rules of Civil Procedure, a class may be maintained if requiring each class member to sue individually would result in inconsistent or varying adjudications with respect to individual class members that would establish incompatible standards of conduct for the party opposing the class."

    Under Rule 23(c)(2)(A) of the Federal Rules of Civil Procedure, "For any class certified under Rule 23(b)(1)..., the court may direct appropriate notice to the class."

    Here, the class was certified under Rule 23(b)(1) because the precise language given in the facts as the reason for class certification is exactly the same as the language in Rule 23(b)(1)(A). Therefore, under Rule 23(c)(2)(A), the court may direct appropriate notice to the class, which is what it did here. The court, thus, complied with the Federal Rules of Civil Procedure. As a result, it did not exceed its discretion.

    A and B are incorrect for the reasons discussed in C. In addition, the defendant is not the person who gives notice to the plaintiffs in class action lawsuits; the defendant is not responsible for notifying the plaintiffs that they are suing him.

    D is incorrect because, as discussed above, the notice rules come from the Federal Rules of Civil Procedure, not the Federal Rules of Evidence.

75. A is the correct answer. The attorney's dual status as class representative and

as attorney for the class posed a potential conflict of interest. If a settlement were offered, the attorney's interest in maximizing his fees could interfere in his judgment as to whether or not to accept the settlement offer because the class members would not be receiving fees and would, thus, have more of an interest in settling than would the attorney.

B, C and D are incorrect for the reasons discussed in A.

76. C is the correct answer. Rule 23(c)(2)(B)(v) of the Federal Rules of Civil Procedure states that notice must clearly state, "that the court will exclude from the class any member who requests exclusion."

Here, the woman sent a notice that indicated that no member could opt out of the class. (It was mandatory that all 10,000 individuals be part of the class.) Therefore, the woman's notice was not adequate.

A is incorrect because, although judicial economy does disfavor allowing each of these 10,000 people to sue individually, the rule discussed in C still requires that they be given the opportunity to opt out of the class.

B is incorrect for the reasons discussed in C.

D is incorrect because there is neither a minimum nor a maximum number of people who can be mandated to be part of a class. As discussed in C, all class members - no matter the size of the class - must be allowed to opt out of the class should they so choose.

77. A is the correct answer. Under Rule 26(b)(1) of the Federal Rules of Civil Procedure, "Parties may obtain discovery regarding any nonprivileged matter that is relevant to any party's claim or defense—including the existence, description, nature, custody, condition, and location of any documents or other tangible things and the identity and location of persons who know of any discoverable matter. For good cause, the court may order discovery of any matter relevant to the subject matter involved in the action. Relevant information need not be admissible at the trial if the discovery appears reasonably calculated to lead to the discovery of admissible evidence."

Here however, the other driver's wealth is not relevant to the subject matter of the lawsuit because it has no bearing on the issue of liability or the amount of damages that will be assessed, if the other driver were to be found liable for the woman's injuries.

Of course, the other driver's wealth will be important to show whether or not the woman will be able to ultimately recover any money, but this issue only will only come into play if the other driver were to first be found liable for the woman's injuries.

B, C, and D are incorrect both for the reasons discussed in A and because the report was prepared to assist the other driver in drafting his will, not in anticipation of litigation.

78. A is the correct answer. Rule 26(a)(2)(B) of the Federal Rules of Civil Procedure, regarding automatic required "disclosure" obligations of parties, requires that an expert who has been retained by a party to provide expert testimony at trial prepare a detailed report regarding that proposed trial testimony. Rule 26(b)(4)(A) unconditionally permits the deposition of experts who are designated to provide trial testimony, but requires that such deposition not take place before the report [required by Rule 26(a)(2)(B)] is received by the deposing party.

Here, the protective order sought by the woman should be granted because the doctor had not yet received any reports prepared by the expert regarding the expert's proposed trial testimony.

B is incorrect because Rule 26(b)(4)(A) no longer requires the service of special interrogatories as a pre-condition to a motion to depose the expert witness.

C is incorrect because the rule it cites applies only to retained or specially employed non-testifying experts. Here, the facts state that the woman had retained the expert to testify at trial. Thus, the expert was not "non-testifying." Consequently, this rule does not apply to these facts.

D is incorrect for the reasons discussed in A.

79. D is the correct answer. Under Rule 50(a) of the Federal Rules of Civil Procedure, "If a party has been fully heard on an issue during a jury trial and the court finds that a reasonable jury would not have a legally sufficient evidentiary basis to find for the party on that issue, the court may: (A) resolve the issue against the party; and (B) grant a motion for judgment as a matter of law against the party on a claim or defense that, under the controlling law, can be maintained or defeated only with a favorable finding on that issue."

Here, the plaintiff presented only one witness on the issue of causation who testified that the defendant had been at fault in the collision in question, and the plaintiff's witness confirmed his findings on cross-examination.

In accordance with Rule 50(a) of the Federal Rules of Civil Procedure discussed above, the plaintiff had been fully heard on the issue of causation during a jury trial, and the court could find that a reasonable jury, if it found the expert's testimony credible, would have a legally sufficient evidentiary basis to find for the plaintiffon the issue of causation. In fact, the evidence from the expert witness strongly suggested that the defendant had been at fault in the collision in question.

In addition, the defendant had had an opportunity on cross-examination to contradict the expert witness' testimony, but failed to do so.

Thus, the court should deny the defendant's motion for judgment as a matter of law.

A is incorrect because a motion for judgment as a matter of law can be made at any time.

B is incorrect because, while the jury can weigh the credibility of an expert witness in general, the motion for judgment as a matter of law will be denied for the reasons discussed in D.

C is incorrect both because it contradicts the facts (inasmuch as there was no conflict in the evidence) and for the reasons discussed in D.

80. B is the correct answer. Under Rule 35(a) of the Federal Rules of Civil Procedure, "The court where the action is pending may order a party whose mental or physical condition—including blood group—is in controversy to submit to a physical or mental examination by a suitably licensed or certified examiner."

Here, although the affidavit of the witness' ex-wife indicates that the condition of the witness' eyes are "in controversy," the witness cannot be compelled to submit to an eye examination because he is only a non-party witness.

A, C, and D are incorrect for the reasons discussed in B.

Furthermore, C is incorrect because, while the condition of the witness' eyesight is relevant to the witness' ability to accurately describe what he saw the night of the alleged battery (the subject of the lawsuit), relevance is not enough to compel an eye examination for the reasons discussed in B.

81. C is the correct answer. Under Rule 35(a) of the Federal Rules of Civil Procedure, "The court where the action is pending may order a party whose mental or physical condition—including blood group—is in controversy to submit to a physical or mental examination by a suitably licensed or certified examiner."

Here, the employee, as the defendant, was a party to the woman's lawsuit. As such, if his physical or mental condition were in controversy, the woman would be able to compel him to submit to a mental or physical examination.

Here however, the employee's record of negligence in the past could have been the result of any number of reasons and did not point specifically to poor reflexes or some form of mental illness. Therefore, the woman did not met the "in controversy" requirement of Rule 35(a), and the court should deny her motion.

A is incorrect because, while it is a correct statement of law, it is irrelevant here because the company was not being sued; the woman was only suing the employee.

B is incorrect because, while the employee's ability to safely operate the equipment at the workplace was relevant, this needed to also be "in controversy," which it was not for the reasons discussed in C.

D is incorrect because the affidavit of the woman's attorney was based upon personal knowledge of the contents of the court files. However, the motion should still be denied for the reasons discussed in C.

82. A is the correct answer. Under Rule 56(c)(2) of the Federal Rules of Civil Procedure, "A party may object that the material cited to support or dispute a fact [in a motion for summary judgment] cannot be presented in a form that would be admissible in evidence."

Here, the woman's best friend was a witness whose affidavit would not be admissible in evidence because it contains the speculation of a non-expert (namely, that the woman could not have possibly run the red light to cause the accident). There is no way to present this affidavit "in a form that would be admissible in evidence."

Therefore, the man's objection to the evidence supporting the woman's motion for summary judgment should be sustained because the woman did not meet her movant's burden, since she was trying to present inadmissible evidence in support of her motion for summary judgment.

B is incorrect because there is no minimum number of affidavits that can be presented in favor of a motion for summary judgment.

C is incorrect because the burden of proof did not shift to the man, since the woman did not meet her movant's burden, as discussed in A.

D is an incorrect statement of law.

83. B is the correct answer. As a prerequisite for a renewed motion for judgment as a matter of law, the movant must have previously made a motion for a judgment as a matter of law by before the close of all the evidence.

Here, the woman made her motion for judgment as a matter of law after the verdict had been rendered in favor of the man (and thus, by definition, after the close of all the evidence). Even if she had so moved, her renewed motion would still have been denied because the jury has the right to believe the twice-convicted perjurer over the two bishops. However, this was not one of the choices given in the question.

A is an incorrect statement of the law.

C is incorrect because, in order for the woman to win her motion, she had to show that she did more than merely meet her burden of production, but rather, that she had proven her case conclusively. Only then would the burden of production have shifted to the man.

D is incorrect (1) because the term "overwhelmed" is properly used only to describe the situation where plaintiff has barely met her burden of production and the defendant's evidence is so strong that it "overwhelms" plaintiff's case entitling defendant to a defensive motion for judgment as a matter of law; and (2) because there was a conflict in the evidence, thus, creating a two-sided credibility issue for the jury.

84. D is the correct answer. Federal Rule of Evidence 606(b) bars any inquiry into the thought processes of jurors (which would include "bias").

Here, the woman made a motion for a new trial based upon the affidavit of a juror, which stated that he had voted against the woman based upon her race (bias). Thus, according to the Federal Rules of Evidence, the juror's affidavit would be inadmissible because it would be an inquiry into the thought process of jurors.

Thus, the court should deny the woman's motion for a new trial.

A, B, and C are incorrect for the reasons discussed in D.

85. B is correct. In federal court, subject matter jurisdiction is based upon either a federal question or complete diversity of citizenship and an amount in controversy over $75,000. Complete diversity of citizenship is achieved, if plaintiffs and defendants are citizens of different states.

Here, there were two plaintiffs (the two women) who were both citizens of Nevada. The store was located in California and was, thus, a citizen of California. Therefore, plaintiffs and defendants were from separate states. The fact that there were two plaintiffs who were citizens of the same state (Nevada) would not destroy diversity of citizenship because diversity is only concerned that no plaintiff and no defendant be a citizen of the same state.

In addition, the women alleged $2,000,000 in damages, which exceeded $75,000. Thus, the amount in controversy requirement was also met.

Therefore, the store's motion to dismiss should be denied.

A and C are incorrect because the store's motion was based on lack of subject matter (rather than personal) jurisdiction.

D is incorrect for the reasons discussed in B.

86. C is correct. In state court, personal jurisdiction arises from, among other things, the defendant's presence in the

state. State courts have subject matter jurisdiction over most matters, except for those that are exclusively federal. Patent law is one such area of law in which federal courts have exclusive jurisdiction.

Here, the alleged violation occurred in Nevada. Thus, even though the man had never been in Nevada before this incident, his presence in the forum state for the purpose of selling the invention to the distributor formed the basis for personal jurisdiction over him. However, the woman was alleging a violation of her patent rights. Because patent law is an area in which the federal courts have exclusive jurisdiction; it constitutes a rare case in which state courts lack subject jurisdiction. Thus, there was no subject matter jurisdiction here.

A, B, and D are incorrect for the reasons discussed in C.

87. A is the correct answer. Under the doctrine of res judicata, a prior judgment on the merits will prevent relitigation on the same issue between the same parties and privies from the original law lawsuit.

Res judicata precludes the doctor from asserting his claim for the remaining $2,000 against the woman in a second lawsuit because the default judgment against the woman was a valid final judgment "on the merits" (a default judgment is deemed to operate as though it were "on the merits"). Therefore, the doctor's second lawsuit against the woman was precluded by res judicata, and the woman's motion to dismiss should be granted.

B is incorrect because, although it is a true factual statement, it states the wrong reasons to grant the woman's motion. The motion should be granted based on the res judicata effects of the doctor's original lawsuit, as discussed in A.

C is incorrect because the court will not deny the woman's motion in the second lawsuit as a way to punish her for her failure to appear in the first lawsuit.

D is incorrect for the reasons discussed in A.

88. A is the correct answer. Under Rule 12(b)(2) of the Federal Rules of Civil Procedure, a party may make a motion to dismiss for lack of personal jurisdiction. Personal jurisdiction exists either when there is a traditional basis - such as the defendant's presence in the forum state - or when the defendant has complied with the jurisdiction's long arm statute. Assuming that this jurisdiction has a traditional long arm statute, the district court will have personal jurisdiction over the defendant, if the defendant had sufficient minimum contacts with the forum jurisdiction that the exercise of jurisdiction "will not offend traditional notions of fair play and substantial justice." (See International Shoe Co. v. Washington, 326 U.S. 310 (1945).)

In order to test for minimum contacts, courts will look to the defendant's purposeful availment of the forum state, the frequency and regularity of the defendant's contacts with the forum state, foreseeability of the defendant being sued in the forum state, defendant's reasonable expectation of being sued in the forum state, the burden on the defendant in being sued in the forum state versus the burden on the plaintiff having to bring the lawsuit elsewhere, and the forum state's interest in having the lawsuit heard there.

Here, the alleged battery occurred in Nevada (the forum state). It was, therefore, it should reasonably be expected that the man would be sued in Nevada, rather than elsewhere. Furthermore, any witnesses to the act would presumably be in Nevada, and all other connection to the case was in Nevada. Consequently, under the rule articulated in International Shoe, the man had sufficient minimum contacts with Nevada such that suing him there would not offend traditional notions of fair play and substantial justice. Once minimum contacts were established with Nevada, the man could be served outside Nevada, as was the case here. Consequently, the court should deny the man's motion.

B is incorrect because, even though the man was a California citizen, he still had sufficient minimum contacts with Nevada for the lawsuit to be heard in Nevada, as discussed in A.

C and D are incorrect for the reasons discussed in A. Furthermore, D is also incorrect because the man was a California citizen, not a Nevada citizen.

89. B is correct. In federal court, subject matter jurisdiction is based upon either a federal question or complete diversity of citizenship and an amount in controversy over $75,000. Complete diversity of citizenship is achieved if plaintiffs and defendants are citizens of different states.

Here, there were two defendants who were both citizens of New York. The deceased man (on whose behalf the lawsuit was brought) was a citizen of New Jersey. Therefore, plaintiffs and defendants were from separate states. The fact that there were two defendants who were citizens of the same state (New York) would not destroy diversity of citizenship because diversity is only concerned that no plaintiff and no defendant be a citizen of the same state.

In addition, the widow alleged $500,000 in damages, which exceeded $75,000. Thus, the amount in controversy requirement was also met.

Therefore, the motion to dismiss should be denied.

A and C are incorrect because the motion was based on lack of subject matter (rather than personal) jurisdiction.

D is incorrect for the reasons discussed in B.

90. A is the correct answer. Under the doctrine of res judicata, a prior judgment on the merits will prevent relitigation on the same issue between the same parties and privies from the original law lawsuit.

The res judicata issue presented here is whether the woman should have asserted a claim for her damages against both hunters at the same time. Res judicata does not require a plaintiff to join every tortfeasor against her in the same lawsuit.

As a result, she was allowed to sue the second hunter in a subsequent lawsuit, and the second hunter's motion to dismiss based on res judicata should be denied.

B is incorrect because it was not mandatory that the second hunter intervene in the lawsuit against the first hunter.

C is incorrect because the judgment in the lawsuit against the first hunter was "on the merits." However, it had nothing to do with the second hunter and will, therefore, not serve as a basis to rule on the second hunter's motion to dismiss.

D is incorrect for the reasons discussed in A.

91. C is the correct answer because it is the only choice that is not a correct statement, since a default judgment is deemed to operate as though it were "on the merits."

A is a correct statement because the man was not a party nor in privity with a party in the lawsuit by the woman against the bar.

B is a correct statement because, since the judgment in the lawsuit by the woman against the bar was a default judgment, no facts were determined in that lawsuit.

D is a correct statement because mutuality only applies to the assertion of collateral estoppel by a stranger. Here, the woman was no stranger to her previous lawsuit against the bar.

92. B is correct. In federal court, subject matter jurisdiction is based upon either a federal question or complete diversity of citizenship and an amount in controversy over $75,000.

Here, the subject matter of the man's lawsuit was divorce (not a federal question). In addition, both the woman and the man were citizens of Arkansas. Thus, there was no diversity of citizenship, either. (The fact that the woman was not a U.S. citizen does not change this; by becoming a resident of Arkansas, she became a citizen of Arkansas.) For both reasons, the federal court lacked subject matter jurisdiction, and the woman's motion should be granted.

A is incorrect because, as discussed in B, the woman was a citizen of Arkansas. Thus, courts in Arkansas (state or federal) had personal jurisdiction over her.

C is an incorrect statement of law.

D is incorrect for the reasons discussed in B.

93. B is the correct answer. Under 28 USC §1714, "The court may not approve a proposed settlement that provides for the payment of greater sums to some class members than to others solely on the basis that the class members to whom the greater sums are to be paid are located in closer geographic proximity to the court."

Here, the woman and eight other class members lived in closer geographic proximity to the court (within four miles) than the other class members (who lived within 100 miles of the court). The facts state that their greater geographic proximity to the court was the reason why they were offered a greater amount of money in settlement. Thus, the court should not approve this proposed settlement.

A is incorrect because the Class Equities Protection Act does not exist.

C and D are incorrect for the reasons discussed in B.

94. C is the correct answer. In *Erie Railroad Co. v. Tompkins*, 304 U.S. 64 (1938), the Supreme Court held that, in diversity cases, federal courts are to apply state substantive law and federal procedural rules.

In Hanna v. Plumer, 380 U.S. 460 (1965), the Court was faced with facts almost identical to the fact pattern in this question. In Hanna, a State rule required service of process only on the executor (or executrix) of a will in will contests. By contrast, the Federal Rules of Civil Procedure (in the current version, Rule 4(e)(2)(B)) allow for service of process on any competent adult in the household. The Court held that the rules for service of process are procedural, not substantive, and that under the Erie doctrine, the federal rules for service of process were to be followed instead of the state rules.

Here, like in Hanna, service of process was made on a competent adult who was not the executrix. While this may have violated the state rule on the subject, since this case was being heard in federal district court, the federal rules were to be applied for the reasons discussed above. As discussed, the Federal Rules of Civil Procedure allow for service of process on any competent adult in the household. Thus, service of process was proper here.

As a result, the executrix's motion to quash will be denied.

A and B are incorrect for the reasons discussed in C. Furthermore, as discussed in C, the state rule did not encompass important substantive interests; it was merely procedural.

D is incorrect because it contradicts the facts. The executrix made her motion the following day. It was, thus, timely.

95. B is the correct answer. Under the doctrine of res judicata, a prior judgment on the merits will prevent relitigation on the same issue between the same parties and privies from the original law lawsuit.

Here, although the same parties (the woman and the neighbor) were involved when the woman reinstituted her lawsuit, there was never a judgment on the merits because the woman simply dropped her original lawsuit following the mediation.

A and C are incorrect because, as discussed in B, there was no judgment on the merits in favor of either party, since the original lawsuit was simply dropped.

D is an incorrect statement of law.

96. A is the correct answer. Collateral estoppel ("issue preclusion") occurs when one issue is "fully and fairly litigated" in a prior lawsuit. It prevents the same issue from being relitigated in a subsequent lawsuit.

Here, the woman initially sued the man in federal district court for both negligence and loss of consortium. A verdict was returned in favor of the man in that lawsuit on the issue of negligence. However, the jury did not reach a decision on the issue of loss of consortium.

Subsequently, the woman sued the man in state court based on the same transaction that had given rise to the federal district court lawsuit (negligence and loss of consortium issues).

The man then moved to dismiss both of the woman's state court claims. As discussed, the issue of negligence had been decided in the prior federal lawsuit, while no decision had been reached on the issue of loss of consortium. Thus, the man's motion to dismiss will not be granted because the issue of loss of consortium still needs to be litigated.

However because the issue of negligence had been "fully and fairly litigated" in the federal district court, the woman was collaterally estopped from raising the negligence issue in state court.

B, C, and D are incorrect for the reasons discussed in A.

97. C is the correct answer. The movant's burden in a summary judgment motion is to show that there is no material issue of fact to be resolved by the jury.

Here, the man was the moving party. He has failed to show that there was no material issue to be resolved by the jury because an acquittal in criminal court only means that there was no showing "beyond a reasonable doubt" (the burden of proof in a criminal case) that the defendant had committed the crime in question.

In a civil lawsuit, however, the burden of proof is only "preponderance of the evidence," which is not as heavy a burden as the "beyond a reasonable doubt" burden of proof. Consequently, the man's acquittal in the criminal case does not necessarily resolve the issue based on the "preponderance of the evidence" standard.

Also, the wife's estate was not a party to the prior criminal proceeding.

Therefore, since there were material issues of fact to be resolved in the civil lawsuit, the man failed to meet his burden for summary judgment, and his motion will be denied.

A, B, and D are incorrect for the reasons discussed in C.

A and D are also incorrect because they contradict the facts, since the man never made a motion for partial summary judgment.

98. C is the correct answer. Under the doctrine of res judicata, a prior judgment on the merits will prevent relitigation on the same issue between the same parties and privies from the original law lawsuit.

Mutuality of estoppel prevents the use of collateral estoppel by a stranger to the previous suit.

Here, the parties in the original lawsuit were the storeowner (plaintiff) and the woman (the defendant). The parties in the second lawsuit were the storeowner (plaintiff) and the woman's best friend (defendant). Thus, the best friend was a stranger to the original lawsuit.

As a result, she could not use mutuality of estoppel. In addition, the parties (the store owner and the woman versus the store owner and the best friend) were different in the two lawsuits, and the issues were also different in the two lawsuits. Specifically, the first lawsuit dealt with whether or not the woman had converted the scarf to her own use, while the issue in the second lawsuit was whether or not the best friend had converted the scarf.

Consequently, the best friend could not use either the doctrine of res judicata or mutuality of estoppel for the reasons discussed above.

A, B, and D are incorrect for the reasons discussed in C.

99. C is the correct answer. In federal court, subject matter jurisdiction must be based on either a federal question or

complete diversity of citizenship with an amount in controversy exceeding $75,000. Subject matter jurisdiction may be raised at any time and is never considered waived within the original action.

Here the woman's lawsuit was based on diversity of citizenship as a basis for subject matter jurisdiction. The amount in controversy exceeded $75,000. However, since complete diversity of citizenship is required for subject matter jurisdiction and both the woman (plaintiff) and the man (defendant) were citizens of the same state (California), there was no diversity of citizenship. As such the court lacked subject matter jurisdiction. Thus, any judgment the court rendered could be overturned, since subject matter jurisdiction can be raised at any time.

A is incorrect for the reasons discussed in C.

B and D are incorrect because the court will not reach the issue of personal jurisdiction, unless it has subject matter jurisdiction, and the court lacked subject matter jurisdiction for the reasons discussed in C.

100. D is the correct answer. Rule 606(b) of the Federal Rule of Evidence states that, upon a motion by the nonprevailing party for a new trial, a former juror "may testify about (1) whether extraneous prejudicial information was improperly brought to the jury's attention, [and] (2) whether any outside influence was improperly brought to bear upon any juror."

Here, the juror was influenced by the information that he had received from the store employees. This extraneous information, obtained outside of court, affected the juror's decision in the case. It was thus, "improperly brought" to this juror's attention and constituted an "outside influence" that "was improperly brought to bear" upon this juror.

However, Rule 59(b) of the Federal Rules of Civil Procedure provides that "A motion for a new trial must be filed no later than 28 days after the entry of judgment."

Here, the man filed his motion five weeks after the entry of judgment. Consequently, regardless of the merits of his motion, it will be denied because it was untimely.

A and C are incorrect for the reasons discussed in D.

B is incorrect because it contradicts the facts. The juror's improper receipt of extraneous information directly affected that juror's decision in the case.

END OF ANSWERS

CONSTITUTIONAL LAW

CONSTITUTIONAL LAW - QUESTION BREAKDOWN

1. Fourteenth Amendment Due Process
2. Establishment Clause – Religion
3. Establishment Clause – Religion
4. Freedom of Religion
5. Freedom of Speech
6. Procedural Issues
7. Freedom of Speech – Standard Review
8. Freedom of Speech – Standard Review
9. Procedural Issues – Ripeness
10. Procedural Issues – Mootness
11. Commerce Clause
12. Freedom of Speech
13. Freedom of Speech – Prior Restraint
14. Freedom of Speech – Time, Place, and Manner Restrictions
15. §1983 U.S. Code
16. Due Process
17. Commerce Clause
18. Fifth Amendment Takings Clause
19. Freedom of Speech – Public Forum
20. Third Amendment
21. Twenty-First Amendment/Dormant Commerce Clause
22. Nineteenth Amendment
23. Freedom of Speech (Expression) – Non-Public Forum
24. Eleventh Amendment
25. Eleventh Amendment
26. Tenth Amendment
27. Pre-Emption Doctrine
28. Procedural Issues – U.S. Supreme Court (original jurisdiction)
29. Procedural Issue – U.S. Supreme Court Review
30. Freedom of Association – Standard of Review
31. Substantive Due Process – Abortion Rights
32. Substantive Due Process – Abortion Rights

33. Substantive Due Process – Abortion – Informed Consent

34. Substantive Due Process – Abortion – Notice to Husband

35. Substantive Due Process – Minors' Right to an Abortion

36. Mootness

37. Commerce Clause

38. Overbreadth Doctrine

39. Overbreadth Doctrine/Obscenity

40. Thirteenth Amendment - State Action

41. First Amendment – Free Speech and Press Clause

42. Freedom of Speech - Commercial Speech

43. Legislative Branch

44. Equal Protection

45. Equal Protection

46. Procedural Issues – Standing

47. Procedural Issues – Ripeness

48. Takings Clause

49. First Amendment – Right to an Open Trial

50. First Amendment – Right to an Open Trial

51. First Amendment – Pretrial Hearing

52. Freedom of Press

53. Fourteenth Amendment Due Process Clause (incorporation)

54. Freedom of Religion – Protected Conduct

55. Freedom of Religion

56. Substantive Due Process

57. Freedom of Speech

58. Substantive Due Process – Right to Privacy

59. Establishment Clause – Secular Purpose

60. Establishment Clause – Secular Purpose

61. Free Speech

62. Free Exercise of Religion

63. Political Speech

64. Free Exercise Clause

65. Free Exercise – Teachings in Private Schools

66. Free Exercise Clause

67. Symbolic Speech

68. Unprotected Speech – Clear and Present Danger

69. Unprotected Speech – Fighting Words

70. Freedom of Speech – Obscenity

71. Freedom of Speech – Content

72. Symbolic Speech

73. Free Exercise Clause

74. Separation of Powers – Congressional Power

75. Judicial Appointment

76. Speech and Debate Clause

77. Speech and Debate Clause Extraordinary Acts

78. Executive Powers – Pardons

79. Executive Powers – Pardons

80. Judicial Jurisdiction – Foreign Ambassadors

81. Sovereign Immunity/10th/11th Amendment

82. Congressional Power

83. Substantive Due Process

84. Substantive Due Process

85. Equal Protection

86. 1st Amendment/4th Amendment/5th Amendment

87. Commercial Speech

88. Treaties

89. Commercial Speech

90. Congressional Power

91. Procedural Issues

92. Procedural Due Process

93. Procedural Due Process

94. State Action

95. Equal Protection – Illegitimacy

96. Equal Protection – Standard of Review

97. Due Process/Takings Clause

98. Title of Nobility

99. Freedom of Association

100. Freedom of Association

101. Freedom of Speech – Defamation

CONSTITUTIONAL LAW QUESTIONS

1. During the Christmas season, a city in the United States of America displayed a depiction of the various scenes of the birth of Jesus, the central figure of Christianity and of the Christmas holiday. A resident of the city brought a lawsuit against the city to enjoin the city from displaying the scenes. On which provision of the U.S. Constitution will his lawsuit be based?

   A. First Amendment non-establishment of religion.

   B. First Amendment freedom of speech.

   C. Fourteenth Amendment due process.

   D. Fifth Amendment due process.

2. A town was located inside a larger school district. The town consisted entirely of members of a particular religious sect. In order to save money that parents would otherwise have to spend on private parochial schools, the town decided to set up a brand new school district within the town to exclusively serve the needs of the town. A person from a neighboring town located in the original school district brought a lawsuit, alleging that the arrangement was unconstitutional because the new school district would only serve members of a particular religious sect and would result in a loss of revenue to the original school district. Will the lawsuit be successful?

   A. Yes, under the Establishment Clause of the First Amendment to the United States Constitution.

   B. Yes, under the Free Exercise Clause of the First Amendment to the United States Constitution.

   C. No because the person from the neighboring town lacked standing to bring this lawsuit.

   D. No because new school districts can be set up anywhere for any reason, under the Taxing and Spending Clause to the United States Constitution.

3. A boy attended a public high school that was known for its innovative course offerings. Among the courses offered at the school were Eastern Philosophy, Comparative Religion, and Comparative Philosophy. In order to facilitate understanding between all people and to integrate the school's offerings into all aspects of the school, each year an official of one of the world's major religions was asked to lead a prayer/affirmation before the season's first football game. The boy filed suit to enjoin this practice. Will his lawsuit prevail?

A. Yes because the prayer excessively entangled a religion with public schooling.

B. Yes because the use of officials from the world's major religions interfered with the boy's ability to practice his own religion (or no religion).

C. No because all religions were being treated equally.

D. No because the boy's claim was not in earnest.

4. The city council of an American city offers prayers before its weekly meetings, in order to set the serious tone for the meetings and remind each council member of the gravity of their decisions. One council member happens to be against all religion and brings a lawsuit against the president of the city council to enjoin these prayers. Will he prevail?

   A. Yes because an opening prayer at city council meetings violates the Religion Clause of the U.S. Constitution.

   B. Yes because an opening prayer at city council meetings violates the Speech Clause of the U.S. Constitution.

   C. No because an opening prayer at city council meetings does not violate the Free Exercise Clause of the First Amendment to the U.S. Constitution.

   D. No because an opening prayer at city council meetings does not violate the Establishment Clause of the First Amendment to the U.S. Constitution.

5. A woman in the District of Columbia was enthusiastic about a particular candidate for mayor in an upcoming election to the point of almost religious fervor. She, therefore, went into the local courthouse to speak on behalf of that candidate because she knew that she would reach many potential voters there. She was arrested for violating a city ordinance banning all speeches in courthouse lobbies. At trial, she challenged her arrest on constitutional grounds. What would be her best challenge to her arrest under the United States Constitution?

   A. First Amendment freedom of religion.

   B. Fifth Amendment due process.

   C. First Amendment freedom of speech.

   D. Fourteenth Amendment due process.

6. A women's organization in a U.S. state whose members believed in abortion brought a lawsuit against the governor of their state, following the passage of a state law that prohibited abortions. Some of the members of the organization were pregnant and attempted to get abortions, but were prohibited because of the new law. Will the court hear the lawsuit by the organization?

   A. No because the women must have their husbands' consent prior to bringing the lawsuit.

   B. No because only the women seeking abortions may bring the lawsuit.

   C. Yes because abortions can never be prohibited by U.S. states.

   D. Yes because the organization can bring the lawsuit.

7. A U.S. state has made it a misdemeanor for anyone to give political speeches during Election Day hours within 75 feet of polling places. A supporter of a particular presidential candidate approached voters within 50 feet of a polling place in that state on Election Day. The supporter approached people entering the polls with the following soliloquy: "Would you like to know what our candidate stands for?" If the response was positive, the supporter gave a five-minute description. If the response was negative, the supporter offered a flyer.

   An undercover policeman arrested the supporter while the supporter was in the process of offering a pamphlet. At trial, the supporter claimed that the arrest and the law on which it was based violated the supporter's rights under the United States Constitution.

   Which standard of review will the court utilize to analyze the supporter's constitutional claim?

   A. Time, place, and manner test.

   B. Reasonable basis.

   C. Polling place principle.

   D. State basis.

8. A law professor was terminated from her employment at a law school. The professor believed that the termination was based on her age, and she brought an age discrimination lawsuit against the law school. What standard of review should the court apply in deciding her case?

   A. Rational basis.

   B. Intermediate scrutiny.

   C. Strict scrutiny.

   D. Reasonable scrutiny.

9. A U.S. state had a law on its books for 50 years. However, the law has yet to be enforced. A man was gravely concerned that he might become the first victim of this law and, thus, brought a preemptive lawsuit in federal court to have the law overturned because the law was unconstitutional. If this suit is dismissed, what will be the likely reason?

   A. Mootness.

   B. The man's bad faith.

   C. Ripeness.

   D. Independent state grounds.

10. The school board had a program that made it mandatory for pregnant high school girls to be removed from their regular classrooms and forced to take courses in prenatal care. A high school student became pregnant during her junior year of high school. She had no desire to leave her regular classroom. Thus, when the school board tried to force her to take the mandatory prenatal care courses, she instituted a lawsuit, alleging that the policy of forcing pregnant high school girls to take prenatal care classes was a violation of their constitutional rights. Before the case was heard, she had a miscarriage. The school board moved for immediate dismissal of the lawsuit. The high school girl's best defense against the school board's motion is:

   A. The school has no important public policy regarding prenatal care.

   B. The school board had no compelling interest in ensuring that pregnant high school girls learn about prenatal care.

   C. The school board has no rational basis in ensuring that pregnant high school girls learn about prenatal care.

   D. The case is still ripe for review.

11. Due to the world's and nation's dwindling supply of oil, a state has encouraged in-state businesses to embark on the production of nuclear energy, which also produces toxic nuclear waste. The state offers a 20% discount to in-state corporations to dispose of their nuclear waste in a non-toxic manner.

    A corporation in a bordering state is in the business of producing nuclear energy. Much of the energy it produces is sold to the citizens and businesses in the first state.

    If the corporation challenges the state for not giving it a 20% discount on disposal, its challenge will:

   A. Prevail because of the Commerce Clause.

B. Prevail because of the Due Process Clause.

C. Prevail because of the Equal Protection Clause.

D. Fail because of the sovereignty of state regulation.

12. A man strongly disagreed with the concept of an income tax. In order to attract media attention to his campaign against the income tax, he ran naked down a public street carrying a sign saying, "F...k the Income Tax!" The man was arrested for public indecency. At trial, the man, now fully clothed, challenged his arrest under the United States Constitution. On what basis was the challenge most likely based?

A. Freedom of association.

B. Freedom of speech.

C. Equal protection.

D. Due process.

13. A U.S. state created a censorship board. The members of the censorship board were allowed to pre-screen certain movies before they were released into the community. The director of a movie that was sent to the censorship board prior to its public release took the censorship board to court to challenge the state law on U.S. constitutional grounds. The court will most likely hold that the actions of the censorship board were:

A. A prior restraint.

B. A reasonable time, place and manner restriction.

C. Not "state action."

D. A violation of the Contracts Clause.

14. A U.S. city passed an ordinance requiring all of those who wished to give speeches in the public square to apply for a permit and pay a fee based on the approximate costs to the city (regarding extra police, clean-up, etc.). The city ordinance created a special board whose job was to make an accurate tabulation of these costs.

A politically motivated group applied for a permit to give a speech in the public square. The permit was granted, but a $500 fee "to cover costs" was levied. The group never gave its speech, but instead, requested a state court to restrain and enjoin the city's procedure.

If the city's procedure is declared unconstitutional, what would be the most likely reason?

A. The procedure was not narrowly tailored to meet the city's interest, and it vested too much power in the board.

B. It was not rationally related to a legitimate city interest.

C. It was not substantially related to an important city interest.

D. It was not compelling.

15. A city, because of its many, naturally-occurring rivers, is always building bridges. Unfortunately, the city failed to either train or warn its employees about the dangers of building bridges. A city worker died in a bridge-related accident. His widow then sued the city based on §1983 U.S. Code.

For a §1983 claim to succeed, there must be:

A. A tort on the part of the city.

B. A crime on the part of the city.

C. A violation of constitutional rights by the city.

D. The widow must first make a claim through worker's compensation.

16. A woman received a parking ticket. She called the city parking administration and was told that she had to pay the ticket before she could have her case heard and that if she prevailed, her money would be refunded.

The woman immediately appealed to a state court, alleging a constitutional violation of her procedural due process rights in that she was being deprived of her property (her money she had to pay for the parking ticket) before she could argue her case. Will her constitutional argument be successful?

A. Yes because she did not have an opportunity to argue that she did not violate the parking laws.

B. Yes because she was not given adequate notice and an opportunity to be heard.

C. No because she violated the parking laws.

D. No because she was given adequate notice and an opportunity to be heard.

17. A state has prohibited all restaurants in the state from accepting meat produced out-of-state. There is no evidence that the refused meat is toxic. A restaurant in the state has found a great deal on out-of-state meat and wishes to purchase it, but is prevented from doing so by the regulation. It, therefore, brings a challenge against the regulation. Will the restaurant prevail?

A. No because a state can refuse to allow out-of-state meat from coming into the state because the meat might be toxic.

B. Yes because of the Commerce Clause.

C. Yes because the restaurant could serve only in-state meat.

D. No because of the Contracts Clause.

18. A U.S. city was in financial trouble and desperately needed new sources of income. A developer proposed to build a luxury hotel in that city. The hotel would include several stores and other sources of sales tax revenue for the city. However, the proposed site of the hotel was already occupied by several private residences.

The owners of many of the residences agreed to be bought out for the fair market value of their homes. The owners of nine of the residences, however, refused to sell their homes. The city, therefore, forced these owners to sell their homes for fair market value, citing its eminent domain power. The owners of these nine residences brought a lawsuit against the city to enjoin the sale of their homes. Will they be successful in their lawsuit?

A. No, under the Third Amendment to the United States Constitution.

B. No because this was a valid taking.

C. Yes because this was an invalid taking.

D. Yes because the government can never force people to sell their homes.

19. Are the public areas in commercial airports considered "public forums?"

A. Yes because the public is allowed.

B. Yes because airports have, by common custom, become a forum for the marketplace of ideas.

C. No because many airports are privately-owned.

D. No because there is a difference between an airport and a public park, street, or sidewalk.

20. A group of anti-war hippies fell in love and married. Over the ensuing years, their anti-war views did not abate and, in fact, got stronger. The hippies had one son who, as he grew up, developed political views that were diametrically opposed to those of his parents. On his eighteenth birthday, he joined the military over his parents' objections, even though it was peacetime.

Two months later, he was allowed to come home on leave. His parents, however, refused to let him into the house. The son then obtained an order from his base commander that required the parents to let their son into the home. The parents sued the base commander, citing their rights under U.S. Constitution. What would be the parents' best constitutional argument against being forced to let their son into their home?

A. The Third Amendment.

B. The Second Amendment.

C. The First Amendment.

D. The Thirteenth Amendment.

21. A U.S. state passed a law permitting in-state wineries to make direct sales to buyers, but requiring out-of-state wineries to use wholesalers and retailers, which greatly increased their costs. An out-of-state winery sold directly to in-state customers and was fined by the State Commissioner of Alcohol Sales, who cited the state law above.

    The out-of-state winery sued the commissioner, saying that its rights under the U.S. Constitution had been violated. What is the winery's best argument in support of its lawsuit?

    A. The Commerce Clause.

    B. The Taxing and Spending Clause.

    C. The Twenty-First Amendment.

    D. The Eighteenth Amendment.

22. A U.S. state placed a proposition on its ballots that totally prohibited abortions in that state. Knowing that a large percentage of female voters would vote against this proposition, the state passed a law prohibiting any female from voting in that state. On Election Day, a twenty-five-year-old female U.S. citizen voter who lived in that state went to the polls to vote and was prohibited from voting under this law. The voter sued the state's Secretary of State. On which U.S. constitutional provision should her lawsuit be based?

    A. The Eighth Amendment's prohibition against cruel and unusual punishment.

    B. The Fifteenth Amendment.

    C. The Due Process Clause of the Fifth Amendment.

    D. The Nineteenth Amendment.

23. A group of college students went to a local military base in the U.S. to distribute anti-war literature. They were arrested for violating a federal law that prohibited distribution of political literature on military bases because such activities would disrupt the smooth functioning of the military. At trial, they defended on U.S. constitutional grounds. What will be the government's best argument in support of the arrest?

    A. The law was valid under the Third Amendment to the U.S. Constitution.

    B. The law was valid under the Second Amendment to the U.S. Constitution.

C. The law applied, regardless of the content of the political literature.

D. The law applied, regardless of the viewpoint expressed in the political literature.

24. Two men applied to be jailers at a county jail for women in a U.S. state. The county refused to hire the men because of their gender. The men sued the county for gender discrimination. Will the court hear the case?

A. Yes because men are always allowed to work in womens' jails and prisons.

B. Yes because the county is not immune from lawsuit.

C. No because the county is immune from lawsuits.

D. No because the county had valid reasons not to hire the men.

25. The United States Congress passed and the President signed a labor law dealing with fair labor standards. The law gave employees the right to sue their employers for violations of the new law. Eight years later, a probation officer who was employed by a U.S. state believed that his employer (the state) was violating the federal labor law. He, therefore, brought a lawsuit against his employer. The court should:

A. Hear the case and find in favor of the probation officer.

B. Hear the case and find in favor of the employer.

C. Dismiss the lawsuit because the United States government cannot be sued.

D. Dismiss his lawsuit.

26. Congress enacted a new law containing the following three clauses:

1) States will receive federal monetary incentives for providing for waste disposal;

2) States providing for such disposal can surcharge states that do not; and

3) If there are no waste programs developed, states must take title to their own waste and must pay all "damages" if they do not take title to their own waste.

One U.S. state has challenged the constitutionality of the new law.

On what grounds will they most likely base this challenge?

A. Commerce Clause.

B. Tenth Amendment.

C. Ninth Amendment.

D. Just compensation.

27. A U.S. state provided for the growing and selling of a certain medicinal herb throughout the state due to the beneficial effects of smoking that herb, particularly for people who were terminally ill.

The federal government, however, strongly believed that that herb had no beneficial values whatsoever and that it was, in fact, a dangerous narcotic. The federal government, therefore, declared the growing, selling, and ingesting of this herb to violate federal law.

Citing the federal law, federal law enforcement officers raided a dispensary in the state that was selling the herb, pursuant to the state law that allowed it to do so. The owner of the dispensary was arrested and charged with violating the federal law. The owner stated that his arrest was unconstitutional because state law allowed him to grow and sell this herb within this particular state.

When the owner is brought to trial in federal criminal court, the most likely outcome will be:

A. The owner's challenge will be rejected because the federal law was a valid exercise of the narcotic substances clause.

B. The owner's challenge will be rejected because the state law was preempted by the federal law.

C. The owner's challenge will be upheld because he was operating his dispensary pursuant to a state law.

D. The owner's challenge will be upheld because the federal law was preempted by the state law.

28. A national monument was located on an island in between two U.S. states. For years, it was believed that the island was located in the state on the eastern side of the island. However, the people from the state on the western side of the island fervently believed that the island was actually located in their state.

The western state brought a lawsuit against the eastern state to determine once and for all in which state the island was actually located. Which is the appropriate court to initially hear this lawsuit?

A. The United States District Court.

B. The United States Supreme Court.

C. The western state's highest court.

D. The eastern state's highest court.

29. A man challenged a state law on U.S. constitutional grounds. He lost his case on the trial court level and then appealed all the way to the state's highest court, where he lost, as well. He now wishes to appeal to the U.S. Supreme Court. Must the U.S. Supreme Court accept review of his case?

A. Yes because the challenge involves the U.S. Constitution.

B. Yes because there is a "case or controversy."

C. No because the issue is moot.

D. No because the U.S. Supreme Court is not required to accept appeals of this type.

30. A U.S. state required, for a new political party to be placed on the electoral ballot, a showing of "significant" public support. This was interpreted by the state's highest court to require for statewide election either petitions signed by no more than 1% of the voters, or a 5% showing in a previous election.

However, a city within that state had a more stringent requirement: 5% of the eligible voters had to first sign a petition before a new political party could be placed on that city's ballots.

A new political party received signatures from 4% of eligible voters. Consequently, the mayor of the city refused to add that political party's candidates to the city's ballots.

The candidates sued the mayor to have their names placed on the ballots.

Will they prevail?

A. Yes, if the mayor cannot prove that the rules on new political parties are necessary to serve a compelling government interest.

B. Yes, if the mayor can show that the rules on new political parties are rationally related to a permissible government interest.

C. No because of the Tenth Amendment to the U.S. Constitution.

D. No because of the Eleventh Amendment to the U.S. Constitution.

31. A U.S. state enacted a law that stated, "An abortion is generally not to be allowed when the fetus is viable." A woman in that state wanted to get an abortion during the eighth month of her pregnancy. The state prevented her from doing so, citing this law. The woman appealed. Will the court uphold the law?

A. Yes because of Roe v. Wade.

B. Yes because a fetus is considered

to be a viable human being at all stages of the pregnancy.

C. No because the state may never interfere with a woman's privacy right.

D. No because the right to an abortion is sacrosanct.

32. A U.S. state enacted a law that stated, "A woman must receive information at least 24 hours prior to the abortion regarding alternatives to abortion, including adoption." A woman wished to have an abortion immediately, but was prevented from doing so because her doctor told her that, under the state law, she had to first be given information regarding alternatives to abortions and then wait 24 hours prior to having the abortion.

The woman brought a lawsuit to have the law declared unconstitutional. Will she prevail?

A. Yes because it is a pre-viability regulation contrary to Roe v. Wade.

B. Yes because abortion is a fundamental privacy right.

C. No because a U.S. state may not regulate abortion in any way.

D. No because the regulation does not place an undue burden on the right to abortion.

33. A U.S. state enacted a law that stated, "A woman must give informed consent to an abortion 24 hours prior to the abortion unless her health is imminently in danger." The law was challenged in court by an individual who had standing to do so. Will the law be upheld?

A. Yes, but only as to the "medical-emergency" provision.

B. Yes, but only as to the "informed" provision.

C. Yes, but only as to the "consent" provision.

D. Yes.

34. A U.S. territory enacted a law that stated, "A married woman must furnish proof at least 24 hours prior to the abortion that her husband has been informed."

The law was challenged in court by a married, but separated pregnant woman who did not wish to inform her husband that she was pregnant. Will the law be upheld?

A. Yes because the U.S. Constitution does not apply in U.S. territories.

B. Yes because requiring the husband to consent does not place an undue burden on the husband.

C. Yes because requiring the husband's consent does not place an undue burden on the woman who seeks to have an abortion.

D. No because requiring the husband's consent is an undue burden on the woman.

35. Under the law of one U.S. state, "An unmarried minor must either furnish proof of one of her parent's consent to the abortion or judicial-approval of her abortion." An unmarried minor in that state wished to have an abortion without first informing her parents, but was prevented from doing so because of this law.

She challenged this law in court. Will the law be upheld?

A. Yes because the minor should not be insulated from those who may wish to counsel her against the abortion.

B. Yes, but only if the abortion occurs in the second trimester of pregnancy.

C. No, if the abortion occurs in the first trimester of pregnancy.

D. This is an open issue under present jurisprudence.

36. A teenage girl became pregnant during her junior year of high school. The school board had a regulation that all pregnant high school students had to be dismissed from their classes and be home schooled until the birth of their child. During the summer between the girl's junior and senior years of high school, she suffered a miscarriage. Although she was allowed to return to her regular classes in the fall, she sued through a guardian ad litem to have the school board regulation declared unconstitutional. Will she prevail?

A. No because the issue is now moot, since she is no longer pregnant.

B. No because the issue is not ripe for adjudication.

C. Yes, other girls can become pregnant.

D. Yes because the law continues to apply to her.

37. A mail order business is located in a U.S. state. It has targeted a mailing to all grocery stores in a neighboring state. The neighboring state has decided to impose a use tax on the property sold by a company from the first state. The company's only contact with the neighboring state is via the mailings and subsequent sales. Is the neighboring state's tax constitutional?

A. No because there are no minimum contacts.

B. No because there is a Commerce Clause violation.

C. Yes because there is a substantial nexus.

D. No because the federal government regulates the mail.

38. A man built a cross and burned it in the yard of a member of an ethnic minority group. The man was apprehended shortly thereafter. He was prosecuted under his state's "Hate Crime Law." The law, in pertinent part, read as follows:

"It is a class 1 misdemeanor to burn a cross, display a swastika, or state any racial epithet for the purpose of expressing racial or ethnic hatred in a public place or on private property that is not in the lawful possession of the suspect."

Will the man's burning of the cross suffice to find him guilty under the state's Hate Crime Law?

A. Yes because all of the elements of the crime appear to have been met.

B. Yes because the man's acts were constitutionally unprotected.

C. No because there was no mens rea in the crime.

D. No because the law was overbroad.

39. A U.S. state passed the following law:

"It shall be a misdemeanor to display the female breasts anywhere in public."

A group representing an entity dedicated to curing cancer posted a billboard on a public highway displaying a woman who was naked from the waist up doing a breast self-examination to show women how to examine their breasts to look for lumps that could be cancerous. The president of the group was arrested under the above-referenced law. Can she be convicted under this law?

A. Yes because all of the elements of the crime appear to have been met.

B. Yes because the billboard was obscene.

C. No because there was no mens rea in the crime.

D. No because the law was facially unconstitutional.

40. In order to save money, a businessman decided to import laborers from another country and threaten them with deportation if they did not work for him for free. One of the businessman's competitors discovered this arrangement and reported the businessman to the authorities, who promptly arrested the man and charged him with violating the Thirteenth Amendment's prohibition against involuntary servitude. Will the prosecutors be successful?

13TH – NO STATE ACTOR REQUIRED

A. Yes because the man was forcing the laborers to work for him involuntarily.

B. Yes because the work in which the laborers were engaged constituted servitude.

C. No because the workers were working for the man voluntarily.

D. No because the man was not an arm of the government.

41. A U.S. state has enacted the following law:

1) An individual is permitted to write about his/her life. But, if the writing describes crimes for which the individual has been convicted, or crimes for which the individual is formally charged, or crimes to which the individual admits, but for which he/she has not been formally charged, all proceeds, profits and royalties shall be turned over to the state's Victim's Fund.

2) A publisher, co-author or lawyer, who participates in the publishing of material delineated in Clause 1 above, must furnish all proceeds, profits, and royalties that would have been payable to the author directly to the state's Victim's Fund.

A man has been convicted of several "contract killings." A writer decided to write the man's story. The writer interviewed the man and wrote a manuscript, which the writer sent off to his publisher. Before the manuscript could be published, the writer was arrested and charged with violating the above law. At trial, the state will:

A. Win because the writer profited from crime.

B. Win because the writer wrote about crime.

C. Win because the writer profited from another's crime.

D. Lose because the writer was not guilty.

42. An attorney put out large billboards all over a city in the U.S. state where he was licensed to practice law. The billboards said:

I will take any personal injury case for only 10% contingency.

In fact, the attorney took a 33½ % contingency fee for all personal injury cases. He was arrested under a state law that prohibited all commercial advertising on billboards in that state. The attorney defended on free speech grounds. Will his defense be successful?

A. Yes because there was nothing wrong with the attorney's advertisement as written.

B. Yes because the law in question was invalid.

C. No because the attorney lied on the billboard.

D. No because attorney advertising is illegal.

43. Over the years, some states have experienced a decrease in their populations, while others have experienced a population increase. In order to facilitate proportional representation in the U.S. House of Representatives, Congress has increased the seats available in the growing states and decreased the seats available in the declining states, but not beyond that accounted for by increased or decreased population. If one of the declining states challenges this reduction, it will:

A. Succeed, since states must be given equal representation.

B. Fail because states must be given equal representation.

C. Fail because the facts seem to indicate an equal apportionment method was used.

D. Fail because Congress has complete power over apportionment.

44. In Brown v. Board of Education, 347 U.S. 483 (1954), the landmark U.S. Supreme Court decision through which public schools were desegregated under court supervision, federal jurisdiction was established under which of the following reasons and/or theories?

A. Separate but equal schools segregated by race are inherently unequal, as well as a privileges and immunities violation.

B. Separate but equal schools segregated by race are inherently unequal, as well as an equal protection violation.

C. Separate but equal schools segregated by race are inherently unequal, as well as a due process violation.

D. Separate but equal schools segregated by race are inherently unequal, a privileges and immunities violation, an equal protection violation, and a due process violation.

45. In the landmark decision of Brown v. Board of Education, 347 U.S. 483 (1954), the U.S. Supreme Court held that public schools must be desegregated under federal court supervision.

A U.S. state had its primary, secondary and post-secondary schools under the supervision of the local federal district court, pursuant to the Brown decision. The supervision was based on that state's former pattern of de jure segregation. In that era, that state assigned students to school solely depending on the race of the student.

Many years later, all enrollments in that state were open at all schools, regardless of race. However, of the five state-run universities, three remained overwhelmingly Caucasian and two remain overwhelmingly of African descent.

If the state's school administrators are presently found to be in good faith, are the U.S. Supreme Court and its lower federal courts discharged from supervising desegregation?

A. Yes, provided admission policies are race-neutral.

B. Yes because there is no more that can be accomplished.

C. Yes because of state's rights.

D. No because all five state-run universities remain predominantly segregated.

46. A man filed suit in federal court to enjoin enforcement of a federal law that required all sex offenders to register with the federal government because he strongly believed that this was strictly a state issue. What is (or are) the best reason(s) for the court to refuse to hear this case?

A. The man lacks standing and the case is not ripe for review.

B. The man lacks standing, the case is not ripe for review, and there is no case or controversy.

C. The man lacks standing, the case is not ripe for review, there is no case or controversy, and there is no federal question.

D. There is no diversity of citizenship, nor has the proper amount in controversy been alleged.

47. The United States Congress passed a law that made it a federal crime to buy any type of fireworks. The law was to take effect on August 1. A woman was concerned that under this law, she would not be able to purchase fireworks for future Fourth of July celebrations. Consequently, she brought suit in federal court on July 1 to have this law declared unconstitutional. What will be the most likely result?

A. The court will dismiss the case because it is not ripe for review.

B. The court will find that the law brings about an unconstitutional government taking.

C. The court will dismiss the case because the woman lacks standing.

D. The court will dismiss the suit because it is moot.

48. A city in a U.S. state enacted a rent-control ordinance. The ordinance was specifically aimed at controlling the rent in mobile home parks. The ordinance at issue not only "froze" the rent for current tenants, but also set a maximum rent per site.

If the owner of a mobile home park in that city, who could substantiate that she was prevented from raising rent in her park, filed a federal suit to overturn the ordinance based on an abrogation of the Takings Clause, this suit will:

A. Fail because there was no "taking."

B. Fail because the Takings Clause is not applicable to the states.

C. Fail because the case is not ripe.

D. Succeed.

49. A celebrity was accused of killing his wife. If both the celebrity and the prosecution consent to precluding the press and public from the trial, can the judge exclude the press and public from the trial?

A. Yes, since both parties consented.

B. Yes, since trials never need be public.

1st Amend reqs crim trials be open

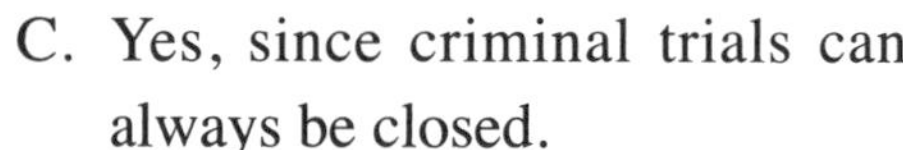
C. Yes, since criminal trials can always be closed.

D. No.

50. A woman was on trial for shoplifting. Although she consented to excluding the press and the public from the trial, the prosecution did not consent. Can the judge preclude the press and public from the trial?

A. No, since both parties must consent.

B. Yes, since trials never need be public.

C. Yes, since criminal trials can always be closed.

D. No.

51. A public official was charged with sexual abuse of his wife's minor daughter (by another marriage). There was a pre-trial admissibility hearing regarding the introduction of certain nude photographs allegedly showing the public official with the daughter. Can the judge close this pretrial admissibility hearing?

A. No because the press and public have a right to be there.

B. Yes because the press and public may always be excluded from pretrial hearings.

C. Yes because there is a compelling reason to exclude the press and the public, so long as the press and public are allowed to see a transcript of the hearing soon after its completion.

D. No because the public may never be excluded from pretrial hearings.

52. Which provision of the Constitution guarantees freedom of the press?

A. First Amendment.

B. Sixth Amendment.

C. Fifth Amendment.

D. Eighth Amendment.

53. Which clause of the Constitution prevents states from establishing an official religion?

A. First Amendment Establishment Clause.

B. First Amendment Free Exercise Clause.

C. Fourteenth Amendment Due Process Clause.

D. Fourteenth Amendment Equal Protection Clause.

54. A woman was the high priestess of a religion that required all church members to pay dues of $100 per month and also to engage in both oral sex and sexual intercourse with the high priestess. The high priestess was arrested and charged under a state statute that said, "It is a misdemeanor to offer sexual intercourse or non-intercourse sexual relations for hire." She offers as her defense the Free Exercise Clause of the First Amendment to the United States Constitution. She will most likely:

A. Succeed because she was exercising a religion.

B. Fail because the Free Exercise Clause does not protect against prosecution for prostitution.

C. Succeed because the adults consented.

D. Fail because her religion was bogus.

55. A church operated a homeless shelter. Among other things, the church permitted homeless prostitutes to safely operate their prostitution businesses within the shelter. The church was prosecuted under a state statute that made it a felony to operate a house of prostitution. The church's best defense will be:

A. There were other religious activities that the church offered in the homeless shelter besides sexual intercourse.

B. Taking prostitutes off the streets a public health service.

C. The church, as a religious institution, is completely immune from prosecution.

D. The church is protected under the Free Exercise Clause of the First Amendment to the United States Constitution.

56. During the Gay Pride parade in a U.S. city, a homosexual couple engaged in fellatio in the privacy of their home just before leaving to go to the parade. While they were performing fellatio, two policemen knocked down the door and arrested both men for violation of a state statute that made cunnilingus and fellatio misdemeanors. If the couple is prosecuted, the state will most likely:

A. Succeed because there is no right to extra-marital sexual privacy.

B. Fail because the acts were private and consensual.

C. Fail because there was no fellatio being performed.

D. Fail because there was no genital penetration.

57. A woman worked as a high-priced escort. She wrote a book describing her life as a high-priced escort. The book, which became a bestseller, glamorized this lifestyle and, after reading the book, many other women became high-priced escorts. The woman was prosecuted for violation of a state statute under which, "Solicitation occurs when one person induces another to participate in a crime, intending that this person so participate." Her best defense will be:

A. The Necessary and Proper Clause.

B. Freedom of speech.

C. The penumbra right to privacy.

D. Freedom of association.

58. A married couple was engaging in sexual relations, including cunnilingus and fellatio in their bedroom in their home. There was a knock on their door because the next-door neighbors had called the police to report noise coming from the couple's home. The husband answered the door naked, and the policeman asked if he and his wife were engaging in cunnilingus and fellatio. When the husband said yes, he and his wife were arrested. If the couple is prosecuted under a state statute that makes it a misdemeanor to engage in cunnilingus and fellatio, which defense will be the most likely to succeed?

A. Right to privacy.

B. Right to marry.

C. Freedom of religion.

D. Freedom of expression.

59. A law student attended a private law school affiliated with a religious group. Because he did not have a lot of income, he received federal financial aid to attend the law school. A wealthy law student, who did not qualify for federal financial aid, brought a lawsuit to challenge the constitutionality of federal financial aid being given to students at the religiously-affiliated law school. He will:

A. Succeed because of the Free Exercise Clause.

B. Succeed because of the Commerce Clause.

C. Succeed because of the Establishment Clause.

D. Not succeed because of the Establishment Clause.

60. A U.S. state required all businesses in that state to close on Sundays. An exemption was given to health care providers. A kosher store was required under Jewish religious law to close on Saturdays (the Jewish Sabbath). They believed that being required to also close on Sundays (the Christian Sabbath) would pose an unreasonable economic detriment to them and that the law essentially required them to observe the Christian Sabbath in addition to the Jewish Sabbath that they already observed. They, therefore, brought a lawsuit to challenge this law on First Amendment Establishment Clause grounds. They will:

A. Succeed because the law is for the purpose of enforcing the Christian Sabbath.

B. Succeed because it impedes their free exercise of religion.

C. Succeed because it is a taking without just compensation.

D. Not succeed.

61. A U.S. state changed the state motto on its license plates to "JUST SAY NO." A citizen of that state was offended by this because he believed it was wrong to demand others behave in a certain way. So, he altered his plate to read, "JUST SAY NOT." The state police arrested him for defacing public property (since the plates technically belong to the state). He was convicted.

What is the likely ground of the man's appeal suggested by the closest Supreme Court precedent?

A. First Amendment free speech.

B. First Amendment freedom of religion.

C. Fourth Amendment search and seizure.

D. First Amendment freedom of association.

62. Due to the problem of rising unemployment in the District of Columbia, the government of the District of Columbia enacted a law that stated that if a person refused to work on Saturdays for any reason and was fired from his job because of his refusal to work on Saturdays, he could not claim unemployment benefits.

A religious Jewish resident of the District of Columbia was fired from his job because he refused to work on Saturday, which is the Jewish Sabbath. He applied for and was refused unemployment benefits. After exhausting all of his administrative remedies, he brought suit in federal district court, alleging that the law was unconstitutional. Will he prevail in his lawsuit?

A. No because rising unemployment is an important government issue.

B. Yes because almost 2,000 years ago, the church moved the Sabbath day to Sunday.

C. Yes because the law was an unconstitutional violation of his freedom of speech.

D. Yes because the law was an unconstitutional violation of his freedom of religion.

63. A public school student refused to salute the flag in his second grade class. He was disciplined by his teacher and sent to the principal to serve two hours of detention. The student had refused to salute the flag based on his religious upbringing, which taught that one's allegiance is owed only to God. His mother, on his behalf, sued the school board, seeking to enjoin forced flag-saluting and also seeking unspecified damages. Will the student's lawsuit prevail?

A. No because this was not truly prejudicial to his religious practices.

B. No because the Constitution protects family values, such as saluting the flag.

C. Yes because the Constitution protects family values such as a person's right not to be forced to appear to support state-sponsored political views.

D. Yes because the teaching of the student's religion was essentially correct.

64. The parents of a 14-year-old girl recently converted to a religion that required that parents home school their children. The parents immediately withdrew the girl from public school and began home schooling her. The school district mandated that all students attend public or private schools until the age of 18.

The parents then received a fine for not sending their daughter to either a public or private school, along with a letter requiring that the parents send their daughter to either a public or private school.

The parents sued the school district, alleging that the requirement to send children to either public or private school until age 18 is unconstitutional. Will they prevail?

A. No because the daughter will miss out on school experiences if she does not attend a public or private school.

B. Yes, based on the Free Exercise Clause and privacy.

C. No because there is a compelling interest in the education of minors.

D. Yes because the school district lacks jurisdiction.

65. In response to a law requiring all students to attend a school until age 17, the followers of a particular religion form their own private religious school, which teaches the basic subjects taught in the public school (reading, writing, science, arithmetic, etc.), as well as religious studies. If the school district enacts a new rule to the effect that all students must only attend public school until the age of 17 and the followers of the religion challenge this rule, they will:

A. Prevail because of the parental right to privacy and because, in effect, the district was violating the Establishment Clause of the First Amendment.

B. Prevail because, in effect, the district was violating the Establishment Clause of the First Amendment, and because the school district was violating the Free Exercise Clause of the First Amendment.

C. Prevail because of the parental right to privacy and because the school district was violating the Free Exercise Clause of the First Amendment.

D. Prevail because of the parental right to privacy, because, in effect, the district was violating the Establishment Clause of the First Amendment, and because the school district was violating the Free Exercise Clause of the First Amendment.

66. A religion that has existed for fifty years has fallen on hard times. One congregant believes that the present president of the religion has allowed the assets and membership of the religion to drastically fall, but the president will not give up his presidency. Thus, the congregant files suit in the state court to order the president of the religion to stand for a democratic election. Will the congregant prevail?

A. No because of the Free Exercise Clause.

B. No because of the Establishment Clause.

C. No because there is no case or controversy.

D. Yes, if the facts establish the congregant's claim to be true.

67. A man in a U.S. state was very upset because he had learned that certain states allowed medical marijuana, but neither his state nor the federal government allowed it. He had the following words embroidered on his jacket:

"F..k my state and the federal government for not allowing medical marijuana."

The man was arrested for wearing the jacket on a public street and prosecuted under a state law that made it a misdemeanor to maliciously disturb the peace of any person or neighborhood by offensive conduct.

The man's defense was that the statute was unconstitutional.

Will his defense be successful?

A. No because conduct can always be regulated.

B. No because the jacket contained offensive language.

C. Yes because conduct can never be regulated.

D. Yes because the statute as written violates the U.S. Constitution.

68. During the screening of a popular movie, a woman in the audience was disgusted with the movie and yelled, "Fire," for the purpose of getting the audience members to leave the theater, so that the film would be less successful. There was, in fact, no fire and the woman knew this.

The theater patrons panicked, and someone was almost trampled by the stampede of people.

The woman was arrested under a state law that stated, "It is a misdemeanor to knowingly make any false statements in a public place that are likely to cause panic."

At trial, the woman, in her defense, claimed that the statute under which she had been arrested was unconstitutional. Will her defense be successful?

A. Yes because the state may never prohibit any type of speech.

B. Yes because the statute as written is unconstitutional.

C. No because the statute as written is constitutional.

D. No because the woman thought that there was a fire.

69. A man thoroughly despised the mayor of his town. One day, the man went to a public park where people often gave political speeches on a whole range of topics. The man began to speak about all of the mayor's shortcomings. As the man spoke, he began to draw a crowd. Finally, when the crowd had reached approximately fifty individuals, the man concluded his speech by saying, "For all of these reasons, I think we would even be better off if someone just went and killed the mayor. In fact, the mayor is coming down the street at this very moment and will be here in about five minutes."

One of the people who had attended the speech was working at the park, cutting trees with a chainsaw. When the mayor arrived, the person took the chainsaw and beheaded the mayor.

The man who had given the speech was immediately arrested under a law that made it illegal to advocate killing public officials. In his defense, the man said that he had a right to give his political opinions and that was all he had been doing. Will he be convicted?

A. Yes because he was a conspirator to the murder of the mayor.

B. Yes because speech of this type can be regulated.

C. No because his acts were in public.

D. No because he did not actually kill the mayor.

70. A club catering to adult females offered erotic dancing by men. In the dances, the men did a "strip tease," in which they removed all of their clothing, except for a tight bikini-type bottom.

The club and several of the male dancers were prosecuted under the state's indecent exposure statute, which stated:

"It shall be a misdemeanor to display any parts of the human genitalia anywhere in public."

Will the prosecution be successful?

A. Yes because they were guilty of displaying human genitalia.

B. Yes because the club's action were clearly contrary to the state's community standards.

C. No because the display of genitalia could not be proven.

D. No because the human genitalia were not exposed.

71. A woman worked as a hot dog vender. In order to attract business, she wore a thong bikini while selling her hot dogs. She was arrested for violating a state statute that banned hot dog venders from wearing bikinis. Will the woman's First Amendment "symbolic speech" argument succeed?

A. Yes because she was doing nothing unlawful.

B. Yes because her sales approach had artistic First Amendment content.

C. No because there was no speech content to her acts or to the city's prosecution of her.

D. No because the state had a right to ban hot dog venders from wearing bikinis.

72. A U.S. state pictured on its flag a western gunslinger. Because a woman found not only guns, but the whole gunslinger mentality patently offensive, she called a press conference and publicly burned the state flag. In this state, it was a misdemeanor to: "Purposely burn, destroy, mutilate, defile, desecrate or dirty the state or federal flag." The woman was prosecuted and convicted in state court and appealed to the U.S. Supreme Court on U.S. constitutional grounds. The U.S. Supreme Court granted certiorari.

Will her appeal succeed?

A. Yes because the crime was strict liability and, thus, overbroad.

B. Yes because the state infringed her First Amendment rights.

C. No because the flag she burned was a state flag.

D. No because she lacked the mens rea to be prosecuted under this law.

73. A state passed a law completely banning a particular drug throughout that state. A particular religion, however, used that drug as part of its sacred rituals.

A priest of that religion used the drug as part of a religious ritual and was prosecuted under the state law banning the use of the drug. If he challenges the law based on First Amendment grounds, he will:

A. Succeed because of the Free Exercise Clause.

B. Succeed because there is no compelling state interest.

C. Fail because of the Freedom of Association Clause.

D. Fail because of the Free Exercise Clause.

74. What majority of Congress is necessary to overturn a presidential veto?

A. Two-thirds of either house.

B. Two-thirds of the Senate.

C. Two-thirds of the House of Representatives.

D. Two-thirds of both houses.

75. Sick and tired of the poor quality of appointees to the U.S. Supreme Court, both houses of Congress pass a law whereby the power to appoint U.S. Supreme Court judges is stripped from the President and resides solely in the houses. The so-called "Supreme Judiciary Act" is vetoed by the President; but the veto is overturned. The President challenges Congress' power to enact this act. The Court will likely find that:

   A. The Act is unconstitutional, and federal judicial selection is solely a presidential decision.

   B. Federal judicial selection is solely a presidential decision.

   C. The Act is unconstitutional.

   D. The Act is constitutional.

76. During a debate in the United States Senate about whether or not to fund a particular university, a United States Senator argued that the scientific work produced by that university "is not up to the standards of grammar school – let alone fit for a $150,000 federal grant."

   If the university sues the Senator for defamation, his best defense will be:

   A. First Amendment freedom of speech.

   B. Article I Speech and Debate Clause.

   C. The university was a public entity.

   D. Sovereign immunity.

77. During a debate about public funding of health care, a member of the United States House of Representatives made disparaging remarks about a particular private insurance company. Soon afterward, it was discovered that the Representative had received a bribe from a competing insurance company, for the purpose of convincing the Representative to make the disparaging remarks. The disparaged insurance company sued the Representative for defamation. Will the insurance company prevail?

   A. No, since there was sovereign immunity.

   B. No because of the Speech and Debate Clause.

   C. Yes because public funding of health care is a vital matter.

   D. Yes because under these facts the representative will have no adequate defense from lawsuit.

78. A woman was convicted of robbing a neighborhood convenience store in a U.S. state. She appealed to the President of the United States for a pardon, and the President subsequently pardoned her for that crime. If the Attorney General of that state challenges this pardon, the Attorney General's challenge will:

A. Fail because pardoning crimes is one of the enumerated presidential powers.

B. Fail because the President's power is limited to pardon for political crimes.

C. Succeed because the President's power is limited to federal crimes. NOT STATE

D. Succeed because pardoning minor crimes is not one of the President's powers.

79. The President of the United States pardoned a man for "any and all federal crimes that the man committed during the man's lifetime, up to and including those committed as of this date."

Two years after the President left office, the man was convicted of a federal crime. Will the President's pardon bar federal prosecution?

A. No because the President's pardon power does not apply to state crimes.

B. No because the President's pardon power does not extend to crimes committed after the President leaves office.

C. Yes, if the President who issued the pardon was still alive at the time the man was convicted.

D. Yes, unless the crime was infamous.

80. A foreign ambassador was arrested by the police in a U.S. state for driving while intoxicated. In fact, the ambassador was not legally drunk and was unaware of the state prohibition of driving while intoxicated. The local district attorney decides to prosecute. What is the ambassador's best defense?

A. The state does not have jurisdiction.

B. The ambassador was not drunk.

C. The ambassador was ignorant of the law.

D. The state does not have jurisdiction over foreigners in that state.

81. The Attorney General of a U.S. state had a pattern of convening grand juries to investigate his political rivals and extort "gifts" for his immediate relatives in violation of a federal statute on abuse of office. One such individual targeted for investigation sued the Attorney General of that state. Will his lawsuit be heard?

A. No because of the doctrine of sovereign immunity.

B. No because of the Eleventh Amendment.

C. No because of the Tenth Amendment.

D. Yes.

82. A presidential candidate was subpoenaed by Congress regarding an investigation into political corruption. The subpoena required him to furnish lists of all "party affiliates." The candidate refused to furnish the lists and was held in contempt of Congress. The candidate brought a lawsuit to challenge his contempt citation. What will be his best argument?

A. Voting rights power.

B. Impeachment power.

C. Subpoena power.

D. Taxing and spending power.

83. Two men had been in a monogamous homosexual relationship for ten years. They decided to get married and applied to the county for a marriage license, but the license was denied because the U.S. state in which they resided prohibited homosexual marriages. They brought a lawsuit under the U.S. Constitution against the county clerk who had denied them the marriage license.

What is the clerk's best argument why the denial should be upheld?

A. There is no constitutional right to engage in consensual homosexuality.

B. There is no constitutional right to marry.

C. There is no constitutional right to privacy.

D. Marriage regulations are within a state's jurisdiction.

84. The dean of a state university denied a man admission because he was white, and the university preferred to admit black students. The man brought a lawsuit against the dean of that university. What would be the man's best argument in support of his lawsuit?

A. The dean had no discretion in denying admission to otherwise acceptable applicants.

B. The dean's denial was a Due Process Clause violation.

C. The dean's denial served no rational basis.

D. The dean had no compelling interest in denying the man admission.

85. Immigrants to the U.S. from a particular country were very concerned about maintaining their culture. They, therefore, formed a town in a U.S. state and set up public schools that prohibited students whose ancestry was not from that country from attending the public schools. One student who was prohibited from attending the public

schools due to his ancestry brought a lawsuit against the school district. Will he prevail?

A. No because there was no denial of equal protection.

B. No because there was a rational basis for the ban.

C. Yes because there was a denial of equal protection.

D. Yes because the state had a substantial interest for the ban.

86. In the privacy of his home, a man read an advertisement describing a video containing "an array of 13-year-old girls, performing all imaginable sexual acts." The man sent away for the video. The video was lawfully intercepted by the Post Office and then delivered to the man. A proper warrant to search the man's apartment for the video was obtained. The video was found, and the man was then prosecuted in his state for the "knowing possession of obscene materials involving minors." Which of the following propositions is or are correct?

A. The warrant was overbroad, and the Post Office search was in violation of the Fourth Amendment.

B. The warrant was overbroad.

C. The First Amendment protects the right to possess obscenity that involves children in the home.

D. The First Amendment does not protect the right to possess obscenity that involves children in the home.

87. A series of advertisements on billboards in a U.S. state purported to offer the lowest prices. The ads indicated that the prices were so low because the goods were imported and "Not Made in America." Incensed by the ads, the state legislature made it a misdemeanor to advertise clothing in the state.

A clothing company that advertised on billboards in the state challenged the outright ban. Will they succeed?

A. No because regulations of this type are part of the state's police powers.

B. No because there was a legitimate state interest shown.

C. Yes because the ad was protected under the First Amendment.

D. Yes because of the Commerce Clause.

88. The United States ratified a treaty with a foreign country to allow for free entry into the United States for anyone from that country for the purpose of working with no visa required. A U.S. state

passed a law prohibiting anyone from that country from working in that state. A person from the foreign country came into the state and started working. A police officer from that state arrested the foreigner for violation of the state law. The foreigner sued the police officer. Will he prevail?

A. Yes because of the Supremacy Clause.

B. Yes because of the Privileges and Immunities Clause.

C. No because states may not pass any laws dealing with immigration.

D. No because of the Tenth Amendment.

89. A U.S state passed a law banning all legal and medical advertising because they were "unprofessional and have decreased the quality of services." A law firm and a health maintenance organization (HMO) brought a lawsuit challenging the constitutionality of this ban under the U.S. Constitution. What would be their best constitutional argument?

A. Vagueness Doctrine.

B. Ripeness Doctrine.

C. Commercial Speech Doctrine.

D. Takings Clause.

90. A U.S. state requires all of its attorneys to pass a moral fitness exam in order to be licensed there. The burden is on the applicant to show good moral character. Ten years earlier, an applicant had declared bankruptcy. In the last eight years, however, he has established a fine credit rating and has held a steady job. The applicant, after passing the bar examination, is denied a law license by the state Supreme Court due to his prior bankruptcy. The applicant appeals his license denial to a federal court. What will be his best argument on federal appeal?

A. He is now morally fit.

B. Significant time has passed.

C. The state's ruling is contrary to Congress's intent to allow bankrupt persons to start over.

D. By definition, lawyers have no moral fitness. Therefore, this requirement is unrealistic.

91. Procedural due process differs from substantive due process in that:

A. Procedural due process concerns state regulation, while substantive due process concerns federal regulation.

B. There is no difference.

C. Procedural due process concerns the right to notice and hearing,

while substantive due process deals with fundamental rights and standards of review.

D. Procedural due process is an actual legal concept, while substantive due process does not exist.

92. One day, a school bully arrived at his public school and was told that he had been suspended from public school for six months in the hopes that this would protect the other students from his bullying. The student brought a lawsuit in federal court, alleging that his constitutional rights had been violated. Will he prevail?

A. Yes because he was not given a prior hearing.

B. Yes because school bullying was the way the student expressed himself, which is a fundamental right that he had under the U.S. Constitution.

C. No because school bullies can be suspended from public school at any time.

D. No because the school board has an interest in protecting the other students.

93. A boy attended a public junior high school in a U.S. state. Despite his young age, the boy was a political activist. Having kept up on the latest and most important United States Supreme Court pronouncements, the boy believed that it was his constitutional right to burn a U.S. flag in political protest. Attempting to exercise this right, the boy burned his U.S. flag in the main auditorium of the school in the middle of the entering class's ceremony. The boy was immediately suspended from school because he had burned the flag.

Was his suspension constitutional?

A. Yes because he burned the flag in an unreasonable time, place, and manner.

B. Yes because flag burning is never permitted in a public school.

C. No because the boy was not given a hearing.

D. No because he burned the flag in a reasonable time, place, and manner.

94. A privately owned shopping mall had lights installed in each parking space for the convenience of its shoppers. The lights turned red when the space was occupied and green when the space was vacant. A color blind individual brought a lawsuit against the mall owners, alleging that his constitutional rights were violated because he (and other color blind individuals) could not distinguish between the red and green lights in the parking spaces. What is the shopping mall's best defense against the lawsuit?

A. Procedural due process.

B. Substantive due process.

C. First Amendment.

D. State action.

95. Intent on restoring family values, a U.S. state has enacted a statute whereby illegitimate children cannot sue in tort for the wrongful death of their parents. Is this a lawful state regulation?

A. Yes under the Tenth Amendment.

B. Yes because the state has a permissible interest in so legislating.

C. Yes because the state has a rational basis in so legislating.

D. No because the statute violates the U.S. Constitution.

96. A U.S. state precludes all individuals who are color blind and dyslexic from working as technicians in the state's nuclear power plant because of safety concerns. It has been shown that many of these individuals are capable of performing the technical work required. Nevertheless, they are precluded. One such individual sued based on a denial of Fourteenth Amendment equal protection. Will his suit prevail?

A. Yes, if he could perform the required work.

B. Yes because in this case there was no compelling state interest.

C. Yes because there was no rational basis.

D. No because there was a rational basis.

97. A U.S. state criminalized certain real estate practices prospectively. After many years, there was public outcry against the few old landowners who had engaged in such conduct before the state made this conduct illegal. The state, therefore, produced a list of the twenty worst "offenders." It also fined them $25,000 each and declared them guilty of a "misdemeanor against the People of the State." The offenders were not sentenced, however, to any time in jail. The "offenders" brought a claim alleging that their U.S. constitutional rights were violated. Under which of the following U.S. constitutional clauses will these individuals have a successful claim?

A. The Takings and Due Process Clauses of the Fifth Amendment, the Bills of Attainder Clause, and the Ex Post Facto Clause.

B. The Bills of Attainder Clause, the Ex Post Facto Clause, and the Takings Clause.

C. The Due Process Clause of the Fifth Amendment.

D. Their claim will not succeed because no jail time was imposed.

98. The President of the United States decided to bestow upon his Chief of Staff the title of "Royal Knight." The title had no significance whatsoever, but there was an official ceremony at the White House. A private citizen challenged this action in federal court. Will the challenge succeed?

A. No because the title has no significance.

B. Yes because it is a title of nobility.

C. No because it is analogous to a Presidential medal.

D. No because the private citizen had no standing.

99. A man was found guilty of murder. At the sentencing phase and over objection of the defense, the jury was told that the man was a member of a white supremacist group. The man was sentenced to death. He appealed the conviction based on the prosecutor's allusion to his membership in the white supremacist group.

What will his best constitutional argument be?

A. He is being subjected to cruel and unusual punishment.

B. His freedom of association rights were abridged.

C. His free speech rights were abridged.

D. His free exercise rights were abridged.

100. A club had existed in a U.S. city for almost one-hundred years for the purpose of enabling businesses to come together and work out common issues that they faced (such as business taxes, availability of fire and rescue services, etc.). The club received funding from the city and the state, in addition to dues paid by members.

A businesswoman applied for membership in the club and was excluded under the club's policy that women could not be members of that club. She sued the club. What is the club's best argument?

A. Free exercise of religion.

B. Freedom of commerce.

C. Freedom of speech.

D. Freedom of association.

101. A story about a movie star appeared in a tabloid. In the story, it was alleged that the movie star was infected with genital herpes. In fact, the movie star was not infected with herpes, and the writer of the article was aware of this

fact. If the movie star sues the newspaper in tort for defamation, he will:

A. Prevail because the story was damaging.

B. Prevail because the movie star did not have genital herpes.

C. Prevail because the movie star had a right to privacy.

D. Fail because the movie star did not have a right to privacy.

END OF QUESTIONS

CONSTITUTIONAL LAW ANSWERS

1. C is the correct answer. Here, the government entity in question is a city, which is considered an arm of the state in which it is located. The First Amendment protections (including the Establishment Clause) have been incorporated to the states (and, thus, to city governments) by way of the Due Process Clause of the Fourteenth Amendment. A and B are incorrect because, while the First Amendment is technically implicated here, it is actually the Due Process Clause of the Fourteenth Amendment that is used against states and cities, as discussed in C; the First Amendment is only used directly when the lawsuit is against the federal government, which is not the case here. D is incorrect because the Due Process Clause of the Fifth Amendment is only applicable against the federal government, not against states (and cities within states).

2. A is the correct answer. In Board of Education of Kiryas Joel v. Grumet, 512 U.S. 687 (1994), the Court found a violation of the Establishment Clause of the First Amendment to the United States Constitution when a separate school district was created to exclusively serve the educational needs of one religious sect because it violated the test of Lemon v. Kurtzman, 403 U.S. 602 (1970), in that there would be excessive governmental entanglement with religion because the district was set up solely for the purpose of serving the needs of one particular religious sect.

   Here, the facts are basically the same as in the Grumet case above. Thus, there would be a violation of the Establishment Clause. The person from the neighboring town will be successful in his lawsuit.

   B is incorrect. The Free Exercise Clause is not invoked under these facts because the government is not prohibiting the exercise of any religion here. In fact, the government is making it easier for members of this religious sect to exercise their religion by setting up a new school district exclusively for them. However, because it violates the Establishment Clause (as discussed in A), the district will not be allowed to remain in its current form.

   C is incorrect because, in fact, the person from the neighboring town will have standing. Normally, people will not have standing simply because they are taxpayers. However, if a taxpayer alleges a violation of the Establishment Clause of the First Amendment to the United States Constitution, the taxpayer will have standing. Here, the person from the neighboring town is alleging a violation of the Establishment Clause of the First Amendment to the United States Constitution, and there is a sufficient nexus to the Constitution to find standing.

   D is an incorrect statement of law.

3. A is the correct answer. Here, the government entity in question is a city, which is considered an arm of the state in which it is located. The First Amendment protections (including the Establishment Clause) have been incorporated to the states (and, thus, to city governments) by way of the Due Process Clause of the Fourteenth Amendment. The First Amendment analysis applies here.

The test of Lemon v. Kurtzman, 403 U.S. 602 (1970) is controlling. The Establishment Clause is violated, unless a state practice has a secular purpose, a religiously neutral effect, and does not entangle a religion with the government. In Lee v. Weisman, 505 U.S. 577 (1992), a benediction by a rabbi before a school graduation was held to violate the Establishment Clause, not only because of the concerns expressed in Lemon, but also because "there are heightened concerns with protecting freedom of conscience from subtle coercive pressure in the elementary and secondary public schools." (Lee at 592.) Here, the prayer before high school football games is similar to the fact pattern in Lee, in that a public high school is considered a "secondary public school."

Thus, the prayer will be found to violate the Establishment Clause, both because it constitutes excessive government entanglement with religion and because of the heightened concerns discussed in Lee. Consequently, the boy will prevail in his lawsuit.

B is incorrect because no facts indicate that the boy was forbidden to practice his own religion or no religion.

C is incorrect because it does not matter if all religions are being treated equally; the government is not permitted to engage in actions that violate the Establishment Clause. Here, the prayer before the football games violates the Establishment Clause for the reasons discussed in A.

D is incorrect because the motives for a person suing are not relevant. The issue is whether he has a good cause of action.

4. D is the correct answer. Here, the government entity in question is a city, which is considered an arm of the state in which it is located. The First Amendment protections (including the Establishment Clause) have been incorporated to the states (and, thus, to city governments) by way of the Due Process Clause of the Fourteenth Amendment. Thus, First Amendment analysis applies here.

The test of Lemon v. Kurtzman, 403 U.S. 602 (1970) is controlling. The Establishment Clause is violated, unless a state practice has a secular purpose, a religiously neutral effect, and does not entangle a religion with the government. In Marsh v. Chambers, 463 U.S. 783 (1983), Nebraska's practice of allowing a prayer before legislative sessions was held to not violate the Lemon test because of America's long history of beginning legislative sessions with prayer. Here, the opening prayers at the city council meetings also had a secular purpose (setting the serious tone for the legislative sessions). Furthermore, the opening prayers neither advanced nor inhibited religion, and they also did not constitute government entanglement with religion because of America's long history of opening legislative sessions with prayer, as discussed in Marsh.

A is incorrect for the reasons discussed in D.

B is incorrect because there is no speech prohibition here. Starting city council sessions with a prayer does not prevent anyone from speaking. In fact, it involves someone speaking (the person leading the prayer). Thus, there is no violation of the Speech Clause here.

C is incorrect because starting city council sessions with a prayer does not prevent people from freely exercising their religion.

5. C is the correct answer. The woman was arrested while giving a speech on behalf of a political candidate. Political speeches are the quintessential protection given by the First Amendment to the United States Constitution. In this case, the challenge would be analyzed under the test for non-public forums because courthouse lobbies are government-owned, but have not been opened to the public for the purpose of giving speeches. The test for non-public forums is whether the law in question is viewpoint-neutral and is reasonably related to a legitimate government interest. In this case, the law against all speeches in courthouse lobbies applies to all speeches, regardless of the viewpoint. The law in question is, therefore, viewpoint-neutral. The law appears to have been set up to ensure that the litigants are not intimidated and to ensure the free flow of traffic in the courthouse. The law in question is, therefore, reasonably related to a legitimate government interest. Consequently, although First Amendment freedom of speech would be the woman's best argument, the argument will still fail.

   A is incorrect because, although the woman had almost religious fervor about the candidate, her speech still did not constitute religious worship. It was a political speech on behalf of the candidate. Thus, this would not be the woman's best constitutional argument.

   B and D are incorrect because the woman was given a trial. Therefore, her due process rights were not violated. In addition, D is incorrect because the Fourteenth Amendment only applies against the states. Here, the woman was in the District of Columbia, where even the local government is run by the federal government.

6. D is the correct answer. In order to bring a lawsuit under the U.S. Constitution, an individual must show that he has standing to sue. Standing requires an actual

injury, causation, and redressibility. An organization may sue on behalf of its members if the organization's members have standing to bring the lawsuit individually, the interests that the organization is seeking to protect are germane to the purpose of the organization, and the participation of the individual members of the organization is not required in order for the lawsuit to be heard.

Here, the individual members seeking abortions had standing in that they could show injury (being prohibited from getting abortions), which has been caused by the state law, and if the law is found unconstitutional, their injury would be able to be redressed (because they would then be able to get abortions). The issue of abortions is germane to the organization's purpose because the organization was formed around its belief in abortion, and the individual members of the organization were not required in order for the lawsuit to be heard.

A and C are legally incorrect. For example, Planned Parenthood of Southeastern Pennsylvania v. Casey, 505 U.S. 833 (1992) set out when abortions may be regulated or prohibited.

B is incorrect for the reasons discussed in D.

7. A is the correct answer. Restrictions on freedom of political speech are subjected to the most heightened degree of scrutiny, which is strict scrutiny. Here, however, the law prohibited political speeches within 75 feet of polling places and only on Election Day. Thus, the law will be analyzed based on whether this was a valid time, place, and manner restriction.

B, C, and D are incorrect both for the reasons discussed in A and because they do not exist.

8. A is the correct answer. Age-related discrimination cases receive the lowest level of scrutiny, which is rational basis. The plaintiff (here, the law professor) had the burden of showing that her termination was completely arbitrary and capricious, with no rational basis. The school must merely articulate any rational reason for the termination in order to prevail. Thus, the standard of review is rational basis.

B and C are incorrect for the reasons discussed in A.

D is incorrect because this standard of review does not exist.

9. C is the correct answer. Article III of the United States Constitution states that, when a constitutional claim is brought in court, the court will only hear an actual "case or controversy." See, e.g., Poe v. Ullman, 367 U.S. 497 (1961). As a general rule, a statute that has been on the books for some time, that is openly disobeyed, and that is not enforced indicates there is no real controversy.

Here, the law in question has yet to be enforced, even though it has been on the books for 50 years. Thus, the lawsuit will be dismissed because it is not yet ripe.

A is incorrect because, since the law is still on the books, the point being challenged has not been legally settled – therefore, it is, by definition, not "moot."

B is incorrect because the motive of the litigant in bringing a lawsuit is generally of de minimis importance.

D is incorrect because it misconstrues the meaning of the Tenth Amendment (Independent State Grounds Clause). Although a state is permitted to expand the rights of its citizens under its own constitution, it is not permitted to remove rights that are federally guaranteed. Here, the man is alleging a violation of the U.S. Constitution. If he is correct that the law violates the U.S. Constitution, then the law will not be allowed to remain on the books, even if there are "independent state grounds." However, because the case is not yet ripe, this issue will not be heard in the courts until the case becomes ripe, as discussed in C.

10. D is the correct answer. Article III of the United States Constitution states that, when a constitutional claim is brought in court, the court will only hear an actual "case or controversy." See, e.g., Poe v. Ullman, 367 U.S. 497 (1961). Here, the school board is arguing that the girl no longer has an actual "case or controversy" because she is no longer pregnant (i.e., had a miscarriage) and that the case is, therefore, moot. However, there is an exception to the mootness policy in cases where the injury (i.e., the pregnancy) is capable of repetition, but evading review. Here, the student could become pregnant again while she is in high school. Thus, her case falls under this exception. Thus, the case remains ripe for review, and this is her best defense against the school board's motion.

    A, B, and C are incorrect because this question deals with the school board's preliminary motion, and A, B, and C all deal with issues that are brought in the merits portion of the case.

11. A is the correct answer. The Dormant Commerce Clause prohibits states from restraining interstate commerce through economic protectionism. Here, the first state is offering a 20% discount to in-state companies for the purpose of disposing of their nuclear waste. This discount is not offered to similar out-of-state companies. Thus, the discount is a form of economic protectionism prohibited by the Dormant Commerce Clause and is, thus, unconstitutional. See Chemical Waste Management Inc. v. Hunt, *504 U.S. 334* (1992).

    Although Chemical Waste Management dealt with a state taxing out-of-state companies at a higher rate than in-state companies, in this case, a 20% discount to in-state companies in essence amounts to a higher payment from out-of-state companies. The court in Chemical Waste Management found the higher tax to be unconstitutional. Similarly, the 20% discount to in-state companies would also be unconstitutional.

B is incorrect because the Due Process Clause of the Fourteenth Amendment is not relevant to this question, since it has to do with the regulation of interstate commerce, which invokes the Commerce Clause, rather than the Due Process Clause.

C is incorrect because, although two groups are being treated differently (in-state and out-of-state companies), the discrimination is purely economic and, as such, is tested under the rational basis test. Under this test, the state only has to demonstrate that the discount is rationally related to a legitimate government purpose. In this case, there is a legitimate government purpose, namely, the non-toxic disposal of nuclear waste.

D is also incorrect because, while states do have a great deal of sovereignty, the Commerce Clause supersedes this sovereignty. Thus, A is correct and D is incorrect.

12. B is the correct answer. The facts here are similar to the facts in Cohen v. California, 403 U.S. 15 (1971). That case made three findings:

First, U.S. states are not allowed to censor their residents simply to make a more "civil" society. Second, it is difficult to distinguish between vulgarity and harmless heightened emotion. Third, passion is a natural part of political protest, and the free exchange of ideas may include some vulgarity as a side effect.

Here, the sign the man was carrying while running naked down the street was a form of speech by conduct known as symbolic speech. Therefore, freedom of speech would be the basis of the man's challenge.

A, C, and D are incorrect for the reasons discussed in B.

13. A is the correct answer because the censorship board was restraining the dissemination of the movie (which constitutes a form of speech) in advance of its release. This, by definition, is a prior restraint.

B and D are incorrect for the reasons discussed in A.

C is obviously incorrect because a state government's actions are considered to be state/governmental action by definition. Here, it was the state that set up the censorship board. Thus, its actions constitute "state action."

14. A is the correct answer. Under the U.S. Constitution, government entities may make reasonable time, place,

and manner restrictions on speech in public forums, if the restrictions are content-neutral, narrowly tailored to serve a significant government interest, and leave open alternative channels of communication.

Here, the speeches in question were to be given in the public square, which is a public forum. The facts here are similar to the facts in Forsyth County v. Nationalist Movement, 505 U.S. 123 (1992). In that case, the Supreme Court found that charging a fee based on the estimated cost to the city of allowing that speech was akin to charging fees based on the content of that speech and was, thus, a violation of the First Amendment Freedom of Speech Clause, as applied to the states by way of the Due Process Clause of the Fourteenth Amendment. Thus, the ordinance was an improper time, place, and manner restriction and vested too much power in the board.

B, C, and D are incorrect for the reasons discussed in A.

15. C is the correct answer. In order for there to be a §1983 claim (i.e., a claim under §1 of the Civil Rights Act of 1871), there must be a constitutional violation on the part of the city for the claimant to be successful in his lawsuit. Here, although the city may have committed a tort in not warning of the dangers, the claimant has not shown any constitutional violations on the part of the city. Therefore, the widow's claim will not succeed.

A is incorrect because it is not enough that the city committed a tort. Such tort may give rise to a successful civil suit, but not a §1983 claim. See Collins v. Harker Heights, 503 U.S. 115 (1992).

B is incorrect because whether or not the city has committed a crime is not an issue in a §1983 claim. Rather, the issue is whether there has been a constitutional violation, as discussed in C.

D is incorrect because there is no requirement under §1983 to exhaust remedies by first bringing a worker's compensation claim.

16. D is the correct answer. Procedural due process concerns the right to notice and hearing before anyone can be deprived of life, liberty, or property (Fifth Amendment for the federal government and Fourteenth Amendment for the states). Here, the woman will be deprived of her property (her money) before she has a hearing. However, the parking ticket itself served as notice, and the fact that the woman would be granted a hearing after paying the ticket (with a refund if she prevailed) constituted the woman's right to a hearing. Thus, the woman's constitutional argument will not be successful.

A and B are incorrect for the reasons discussed in D.

C is incorrect because it does not matter if the woman violated the law, if the law were unconstitutional. However, for the reasons discussed in D, the law was constitutional.

17. B is the correct answer. The Dormant Commerce Clause prohibits states from restraining interstate commerce through economic protectionism. Here, the state is prohibiting the importation of out-of-state meat, which appears to be favoring in-state meat producers. The effect of the regulation is, in fact, economic protectionism: local meat producers are afforded an advantage over out-of-state meat producers. This is prohibited under the Dormant Commerce Clause. See Fort Gratiot Sanitary Landfill v. Michigan Department of Natural Resources, *504 U.S. 353* (1992).

    A is incorrect for the reasons discussed in B. C is incorrect because an economic advantage is given to in-state meat producers, which is unconstitutional for the reasons discussed in B. Furthermore, the restaurant would be prohibited from exercising its right to get a better deal from an out-of-state meat producer, since it is being forced to only use in-state meat.

    D is incorrect because the Contracts Clause prohibits states from interfering with existing contracts. Here, the restaurant has not yet entered into a contract with the out-of-state meat producer. Thus, the Contracts Clause would not apply under these facts.

18. B is the correct answer. The facts here are similar to the facts in Kelo v. City of New London, 545 U.S. 469 (2005). In that case, the Supreme Court held that, under the Takings Clause of the Fifth Amendment (which has been incorporated to the states by way of the Due Process Clause of the Fourteenth Amendment), a city may force owners of private residences to sell their homes in order to make way for a project that will economically benefit the city, even if the new project is also privately owned.

    Here, the city was in financial distress and the facts state that the hotel development project would financially benefit the city. Therefore, so long as the owners of these homes were given the fair market value of their homes (which was the case here), they may be forced to sell their homes. This was, therefore, a valid taking.

    A is incorrect because the Third Amendment has to do with the forced quartering of soldiers in private homes. Here, there were no soldiers involved.

    C is incorrect for the reasons discussed in B.

    D is incorrect because, as shown in B, the government may often force people to sell their homes, so long as the owners of the homes are given just compensation (i.e., fair market value) for their homes, and so long as there is a valid purpose under the Fifth Amendment (as discussed above).

19. D is the correct answer. As set out in International Society for Krishna Consciousness v. Lee, 505 U.S. 672 (1992), airports are considered to be "non-public forums" for First Amendment free speech purposes. Airports are a new phenomenon and will not be given the status of, e.g., a public park. Since sidewalks outside the airport are available for exercising speech rights and due to the hurried nature of air travel, the most protective level of expression was held to be inappropriate. Therefore, there are no areas in commercial airports that are public forums.

    A is incorrect because the mere fact that the public is allowed in a place does not make that place a "public forum." For an obvious example, the public is allowed within a courtroom to watch trials, but the courtroom is not a public forum.

    B is incorrect for the reasons discussed in D.

    C is incorrect. The question asked about commercial airports, which are generally government-owned, but are not public forums for the reasons discussed in D. By contrast, privately-owned airports are "private forums," but the question did not ask about privately-owned airports.

20. A is the correct answer. Under the Third Amendment to the United States Constitution, "No soldier shall, in time of peace be quartered in any house, without the consent of the owner, nor in time of war, but in a manner to be prescribed by law."

    Here, the base commander was trying to force the parents to house their son (a soldier) during peacetime. The parents did not consent. Therefore, their best argument in support of their lawsuit against the base commander would be the Third Amendment to the United States Constitution.

    B, C, and D are incorrect for the reasons discussed in A.

21. A is the correct answer. The facts here are similar to the facts in Granholm v. Heald, 544 U.S. 460 (2005). In that case, the state tried to defend its different treatment of in-state and out-of-state wineries under Section 2 of the Twenty-First Amendment, which allows individual states to ban alcohol sales, even though Prohibition was repealed nationally (through the Twenty-First Amendment's repeal of the Eighteenth Amendment).

    However in Granholm, the Supreme Court held that even after the Twenty-First Amendment's ratification, alcohol sales were still subject to the requirement of the Dormant Commerce Clause (which is not an actual clause, but rather, an interpretation of the Commerce Clause). The Dormant Commerce Clause requires that state regulations not discriminate against out-of-state entities.

Here, like in Granholm, the state required out-of-state wineries to sell only through wholesalers or retailers, while in-state wineries were allowed to sell directly to the public, therefore, giving a major financial advantage to in-state wineries, in violation of the Dormant Commerce Clause. In Granholm, this regulation was struck down, under the Dormant Commerce Clause. Thus, the Commerce Clause would be the winery's best constitutional argument.

B, C, and D are incorrect for the reasons discussed in A.

22. D is the correct answer. Under the Nineteenth Amendment, "The right of citizens of the United States to vote shall not be denied or abridged by the United States or by any state on account of sex."

Here, the state passed a law that prohibited all females from voting, in direct violation of the Nineteenth Amendment. Therefore, this would be the voter's best constitutional argument in support of her lawsuit.

A is incorrect because, while prohibiting females from voting may be considered "cruel and unusual," it was not being done as a punishment under these facts.

B is incorrect because it forbids restrictions on voting based on race. Here, there was nothing suggesting any race-based voting restrictions, only gender-based restrictions.

C is incorrect because the Due Process Clause of the Fifth Amendment only applies to the federal government (as opposed to the Due Process Clause of the Fourteenth Amendment, which applies to the states). Here, this was a state law, not a federal law. Therefore, the Fifth Amendment's Due Process Clause is incorrect.

23. D is the correct answer. As discussed in Greer v. Spock, 424 U.S. 828 (1976), military bases are considered non-public forums, in that they are not open to the public for the purpose of disseminating speech. The test for non-public forums is whether the law in question is viewpoint-neutral and is reasonably related to a legitimate government interest.

In this case, the law was being enforced on a military base, which as discussed, was considered a non-public forum. The government's interest in ensuring the smooth functioning of the military will be considered legitimate (especially since it is similar to the justification used in Spock). The law was reasonably related to this interest because the dissemination of political speech does disrupt military exercises and goes against the smooth functioning of the military. Finally, the law was viewpoint-neutral because it applied to all political speech, regardless of the viewpoint (e.g., regardless of whether the speech in question was pro- or anti-war). Thus, this will be the government's best argument in support of the arrest.

A is incorrect because the Third Amendment has to do with the forced quartering of soldiers in private homes. Here, the soldiers were on a military base, not in private homes. Thus, the Third Amendment was not invoked in this case.

B is incorrect because the Second Amendment has to do with the right to bear arms. In this case, no one was infringing on anyone's right to bear arms. Thus, the Second Amendment was not invoked here.

C is incorrect because content-neutrality is required in public forums, while viewpoint-neutrality is required in nonpublic forums, such as military bases. In this case, the law barred the distribution of political literature on military bases. This was content-based because the law banned political literature, but not other types of literature. However, the law did not go into the viewpoint expressed in the political literature (e.g., whether the literature expressed a pro- or antiwar viewpoint). Thus, for the reasons discussed in D, the law and, thus, the arrest were valid.

24. B is the correct answer. Under the Eleventh Amendment to the United States Constitution, U.S. states are immune from lawsuit, unless they have waived their immunity.

This immunity has been held to apply against U.S. states, but not against counties. (See, e.g., Lincoln County v. Luning, 133 U.S. 529 (1890)). Here, the county refused to hire the men to work in a county women's jail. Since the county is not immune from lawsuit, the court will hear the case.

A is incorrect because it is legally incorrect.

C is incorrect for the reasons discussed in B.

D is incorrect because it addresses the merits of the lawsuit and the question asked whether or not the court will hear the case.

25. D is the correct answer. Under the Eleventh Amendment to the United States Constitution, U.S. states are immune from lawsuit, unless they have waived their immunity. Here, the probation officer is suing his employer, which is a U.S. state. There is nothing in the facts to indicate that state has waived its Eleventh Amendment immunity. The facts here are virtually identical to Alden v. Maine, 527 U.S. 706 (1999), where the U.S. Supreme Court dismissed, on Eleventh Amendment grounds, a similar lawsuit by a state probation officer against the state of Maine.

A and B are incorrect for the reasons discussed in D. (Note, B is incorrect because the lawsuit will never be heard; it will be dismissed before it is ever heard, as discussed in D.)

C is incorrect because the probation officer was suing a state, not the United States government.

26. B is the correct answer. The Tenth Amendment to the United States Constitution states, "The powers not delegated to the United States by the Constitution, nor prohibited by it to the states, are reserved to the states respectively, or to the people."

The facts of this question precisely match the facts of New York v. United States, 505 U.S. 144 (1992). In that case, the Supreme Court held that, while the first two parts of the law may have been valid exercises of federal power, the third part, which required states to "take title to their own waste and must pay all 'damages' if they do not take title to their own waste," was an invalid commandeering because it directly forced states to enforce federal law. Therefore, the Tenth Amendment would be the state's best challenge to this law.

A is incorrect because, although Article I, Section 8 of the United States Constitution provides for Congress to have power over commerce, this would be a good reason to uphold this law, and the question asks for the state's best challenge to this law. Therefore, this would be a wrong answer.

C is incorrect because the Ninth Amendment states that, "The enumeration in the Constitution, of certain rights, shall not be construed to deny or disparage others retained by the people." This is irrelevant to this fact pattern because a state is bringing the challenge here.

D is incorrect because it refers to the Takings Clause, which requires that taking of private property only occur if the government provides just compensation. This is likewise completely irrelevant to these facts because there is no private property being taken here.

27. B is the correct answer. When the federal government passes a law, no state is allowed to pass any law that contradicts the federal law. This is known as federal preemption because the Supremacy Clause of the United States Constitution mandates that federal law is the supreme law of the land.

Here, the federal government has outlawed the growing, selling, and ingesting of a particular herb. Therefore, the state law that legalized the growing, selling, and ingesting of that same herb contradicted the federal law that outlawed the growing, selling, and ingesting of the herb. As a result, under the Doctrine of Federal Preemption, the state law will be struck down in favor of the federal law, and the owner's challenge will be dismissed.

A, C, and D are incorrect for the reasons discussed in B. Furthermore, A is incorrect because there is no such thing as the narcotic substances clause.

28. B is the correct answer. Under Article

III of the United States Constitution, the U.S. Supreme Court has original jurisdiction for a limited category of cases, including lawsuits between U.S. states. Here, the lawsuit is between two U.S. states (the western state and the eastern state). Therefore, the U.S. Supreme Court is the proper court to initially hear this case. Note, the U.S. Supreme Court MUST hear this case; it is not discretionary, since this is a matter of original jurisdiction. A, C, and D are incorrect for the reasons discussed in B.

29. D is the correct answer. Review of state court decisions by the U.S. Supreme Court is discretionary. It is by petition on writ of certiorari. The writ is granted when four of the nine justices wish to hear the case. Cases may be accepted when there is confusion in constitutional law when there is a split among the federal circuits or when the justices desire to make a change in the law. The decision whether or not to review is in the hands of the judges of the high court. Here, the man is appealing a decision from his state's highest court. Thus, the U.S. Supreme Court has discretion as to whether or not to hear this case.

    A and B are incorrect for the reasons discussed in D.

    C is incorrect both because the issue is not moot and because, as discussed in D, the U.S. Supreme Court has discretion whether or not to hear this case.

30. A is the correct answer. In Illinois State Board of Education v. Socialist Worker's Party, 440 US 173 (1979), the U.S. Supreme Court indicated that the association rights implicit in the First and Fourteenth Amendments are infringed by ballot access rules. Here, the mayor must meet strict scrutiny requirements to justify his city's more stringent rules for the political party's candidates to appear on city ballots. There is nothing in the facts to indicate any compelling reason for either the mayor's decision or for the city's more stringent requirements. Thus, the candidates will prevail in their lawsuit.

    B is incorrect because it states the rational basis test. This is not the appropriate test for freedom of association because freedom of association is a fundamental right and, therefore, requires strict scrutiny, as discussed in A.

    C is incorrect because this is not a federalism question, but an infringement on fundamental federal constitutional rights. Thus, the Tenth Amendment is inapplicable.

    D is incorrect because the Eleventh Amendment is only implicated when someone sues a U.S. state. Here, the candidates are suing the mayor of a city within that state.

31. A is the correct answer. Although in Planned Parenthood of Southeastern Pennsylvania v. Casey, 505 U.S. 833 (1992), the right to an abortion was limited; this right was not completely

A CONSTITUTIONAL LAW

over-ruled. Under Roe v. Wade, 410 U.S. 113 (1973), there was no right to abortion when the fetus was viable, i.e., in the third trimester because the state's interest in protecting potential life normally outweighed the mother's right to terminate her pregnancy during that time. This aspect of Roe has, therefore, remained intact.

Here, the state law in question did little else than reiterate this aspect of Roe. Thus, the court will uphold the law.

B is incorrect because the state has an interest in protecting potential life, but under Roe and Casey, this has been defined as the third trimester of pregnancy.

C and D are incorrect for the reasons discussed in A.

32. D is the correct answer. Under Planned Parenthood of Southeastern Pennsylvania v. Casey, 505 U.S. 833 (1992), the rigid trimester test of Roe v. Wade, 410 U.S. 113 (1973) was abandoned. Under that test, the woman had a right to abortion in the first trimester. Under Roe, there could be no pre-viability regulation, since the state's interests were not compelling enough at that time. Under Casey, however, a new "undue burden" standard was created. Thus, pre-viability regulation is acceptable, if the regulation does not place an undue burden on the constitutionally-protected privacy right of abortion. A one-day notice of alternatives requirement, although a burden, is not an undue burden – and, thus, is constitutional under Casey.

Here, the woman was attempting to have an abortion immediately and sued to have the law declared unconstitutional. For the reasons discussed above, she will not prevail.

A is incorrect because the pre-viability regulation aspect of Roe was abandoned, as discussed in D.

B is incorrect for the reasons discussed in D. Although abortion is a privacy right, certain limitations are permitted, so long as they comply with the framework set forth in Casey.

C is incorrect for the reasons discussed in D.

33. D is the correct answer. Under Planned Parenthood of Southeastern Pennsylvania v. Casey, 505 U.S. 833 (1992), abortion restrictions may not place an undue burden on the woman seeking an abortion. Here, the medical emergency aspect of the state law in no way limits the abortion right. The informed and consent aspects of the state law, although imposing a burden on the abortion right, are little more than the requirement that the woman be told of other options prior to having the abortion. Thus, under the Casey test, they are acceptable.

A, B, and C are incorrect because they only deal with one aspect of the law; only D deals with all three aspects.

34. D is the correct answer. Under Planned Parenthood of Southeastern Pennsylvania v. Casey, 505 U.S. 833 (1992) and Roe v. Wade, 410 U.S. 113 (1973), abortion restrictions may not place an undue burden on the woman seeking the abortion. The Court has held that requiring women who are beyond the age of majority to get their husbands' consent prior to getting an abortion unduly burdens the women because the decision whether or not to have an abortion is the women's decision, not the husband's. Furthermore, the burden is even greater where, as in this case, the wife and the husband are separated. Since it is the woman's interest that is paramount, this law is unconstitutional.

A is an incorrect statement of law. The U.S. Constitution applies throughout the United States, even in U.S. territories.

B and C are incorrect for the reasons discussed in D. Furthermore, B is also incorrect because it is the burden on the woman, not the husband, that is paramount.

35. A is the correct answer. Under Planned Parenthood of Southeastern Pennsylvania v. Casey, 505 U.S. 833 (1992) and Roe v. Wade, 410 U.S. 113 (1973), the courts have held that minor girls may not make their decisions as intelligently as adult women. Thus, under the Casey reasoning, this limitation is constitutional. Under the Casey analysis as found by the Supreme Court, minors should not be insulated from others wishing to counsel against the abortion, such as parents.

Here, the pregnant girl was an unmarried minor. The law as applied to her will, therefore, be upheld for the reasons discussed above.

B and C are incorrect for the reasons discussed in A.

D is incorrect because the issue is no longer open.

36. D is the correct answer. There is a judicial limitation that requires that a case must be ripe for adjudication (and, thus, not moot). This limitation would generally prevent the girl from bringing the lawsuit because she is no longer pregnant and, thus, does not have an active case or controversy active for adjudication. However, there is an exception to the mootness limitation known as "capable of repetition yet evading review."

Here, the girl could become pregnant again before graduating from high school, in which case she would once again be dismissed from her regular classes under the state law in question. Thus, this would be capable of repetition. Furthermore, denying the girl the right to have her case heard on mootness grounds would prevent the law from being reviewed because there is always a chance that the girl could suffer another miscarriage prior to the case being heard.

A and B are incorrect for the reasons discussed in D.

C is incorrect because the girl only had standing to sue on her own behalf, not on behalf of other girls, except as part of a class-action lawsuit, which was not the case here.

37. B is the correct answer. The Commerce Clause is violated when a state imposes a use tax on a mail order business that lacks a substantial nexus with the state. Here, the facts do not indicate a substantial nexus between the mail order company and the neighboring state because all of the mail order company's sales in the neighboring state result from its mailings. Merely mailing to grocery stores in a state is not a substantial nexus in accordance with the Commerce Clause requirements. In fact, in Quill Corp. v. North Dakota, *504 U.S. 298* (1992), such a tax was held to violate the Commerce Clause.

A is incorrect because, although selling goods in the state is a sufficient minimum contacts for Due Process Clause analysis, it will not per se satisfy the protections required by the Commerce Clause. Since A utilized the inappropriate due process test, it is incorrect.

C is incorrect for the reasons discussed in B.

D is incorrect because, although a true statement, it is irrelevant to these facts, since the correct analysis has to do with whether there is a substantial nexus, as discussed in B.

38. D is the correct answer. Traditional and present analysis protects speech that states unpopular views – leaving it to the free market of ideas to prove it wrong. See, e.g., R.A.V. v. City of St. Paul, Minnesota, 505 U.S. 377 (1992), under the First Amendment Freedom of Speech Clause (as applied to the states by way of the Fourteenth Amendment Due Process Clause).

Here, the state's Hate Crime Law violated the First Amendment Freedom of Speech Clause because it was "overbroad" in that it went beyond the constitutional standard for punishment in substantially all of its applications. The law not only prohibited so-called fighting words, but also prohibited the stating of views, which, though unpopular, are within the traditional domain of First Amendment protection. For example, under the Hate Crime Law as written, it would be criminal to give a speech denouncing one race.

A is incorrect because the fact that all of the written elements of a crime are present does not insulate the crime from constitutional attack (or defense). B is incorrect because, although the man's acts were undoubtedly not constitutionally protected, he must be convicted under a legitimate constitutional law. Here, as discussed in D, the law was not constitutional and cannot be used as a basis to convict the man.

C is incorrect because mens rea is irrelevant when the law in question is unconstitutional. Here, the law was unconstitutional for the reasons discussed in D.

39. D is the correct answer. Under Miller v. California, 413 U.S. 15 (1973), obscene speech is not protected (including speech by expression), if it meets that case's three-prong test. However, a law that bans obscene speech cannot be overbroad and also ban protected speech.

Here, although the group did not speak directly, its billboard constituted speech by expression, depicting the partially naked woman. However, the reason the woman was shown partially naked was for health purposes, as opposed to obscenity. Such speech by expression would be protected speech. The law banning the display of "the female breasts anywhere in public" under all circumstances was facially overbroad and, thus, unconstitutional. The president of the group cannot be convicted under this law.

A is incorrect because a conviction is unconstitutional, if the crime is unconstitutional – regardless of whether the defendant was proven to commit it, and regardless of whether there is another different crime under which the defendant should have been charged.

B is incorrect for the reasons discussed in D.

C is incorrect because mens rea is irrelevant when the law in question is unconstitutional. Here, the law was unconstitutional for the reasons discussed in D.

40. A is the correct answer. Under the Thirteenth Amendment to the United States Constitution, "Neither slavery nor involuntary servitude, except as a punishment for crime whereof the party shall have been duly convicted, shall exist within the United States, or any place subject to their jurisdiction." Note, unlike the rest of the U.S. Constitution, the Thirteenth Amendment does not require state action; it is the only part of the U.S. Constitution that private individuals can violate. (See, e.g., Bailey v. Alabama, 219 U.S. 219 (1911).)

Here, although the businessman was a private employer as discussed above, the Thirteenth Amendment still applied to him. He forced the laborers to work for free, which was in violation of the Thirteenth Amendment's prohibition against involuntary servitude. Thus, the prosecutors will be successful.

B is incorrect because servitude (i.e., labor) is perfectly legal; it is only involuntary servitude that violates the Thirteenth Amendment.

C is factually incorrect. The laborers were being threatened with deportation, if they did not work for the businessman for free. Such an arrangement is not voluntary.

D is incorrect because, as discussed in A, state action is not required for the Thirteenth Amendment.

41. D is the correct answer. In this case, the state has adopted a so-called "Son of Sam" law. Writing books is a form of speech. Regulations of speech are subject to strict scrutiny analysis, under which the state must show that the regulation is necessary to achieve a compelling state interest, that the regulation is narrowly tailored to advance that interest, and that the regulation is the least restrictive alternative. The U.S. Supreme Court examined a similar law in Simon & Schuster Inc. v. Members of the New York state Crime Victim's Board, 502 U.S. 105 (1991). In broad statement, it was there held that such laws violate the First Amendment Free Speech and Press Clauses because, while they do advance a compelling state interest in compensating victims of crimes, these laws are not narrowly tailored, nor are they the least restrictive alternative because the laws did not necessarily prevent criminals from profiting from their crimes, and also because there was no provision to compensate victims.

Here, since the writer was neither the publisher, the co-author of the work, nor the man's lawyer, he did not violate the language of the statute. Therefore, the state will lose its case against the writer.

A, B, and C are incorrect for the reasons discussed in D.

42. B is the correct answer. Laws regulating commercial speech must show a substantial government interest, must directly advance that interest, and must be narrowly tailored to advance that interest. (Note, the laws do not have to be the least restrictive alternative.) Here, the law prohibited all commercial advertising on billboards in the state. No state interest was given or advanced. Thus, the law was not narrowly tailored to any state interest. Consequently, the law was an invalid regulation of commercial speech. As a result, the attorney's defense will prevail.

A is incorrect because there was something wrong with the attorney's advertisement - it contained a false statement (that he worked on a 10% contingency fee when, in fact, he worked for a much higher contingency fee). However, the facts state that the attorney was being prosecuted under the law against billboard advertising, not under a law against false advertising.

C is incorrect for the reasons discussed in A.

D is incorrect because attorney advertising is legal, as long as it is true and not misleading, under Bates v. State Bar of Arizona, 433 U.S. 350 (1977).

43. C is the correct answer. Article I, §2 of the U.S. Constitution provides certain rudimentary requirements regarding the allotment to the states of representatives (e.g., no fewer than one). However,

constitutional jurisprudence has essentially left the matter in the hands of Congress. Since the early part of the twentieth century, Congress has utilized an "equal apportionment" method. In United States Department of Commerce v. Montana, *503 U.S. 442* (1992), this method was challenged. The Court held that Congress had ample power to adopt the method of equal proportions to determine the number of seats available to each state in the House of Representatives.

Here, Congress has increased and decreased the numbers of seats allotted to the states according to proportional representation. Congress has, thus, acted in accordance with the Constitution and the case law. As a result, the state's challenge will fail.

A and B are incorrect because equal representation (two per state) is required for the Senate. The number of representatives that a state sends to the House of Representatives is determined by proportional representation, as discussed in C.

D is incorrect for the reasons discussed in C.

44. B is the correct answer. State-run (public) schooling is considered to be state action. Thus, public schools in the USA are subject to U.S. constitutional limitations. In Brown, it was reasoned that separate public schools based on race are inherently unequal. In discerning which aspect of the Fourteenth Amendment was violated, the Court logically chose the Equal Protection Clause, since similarly situated individuals were not being treated in a like manner (i.e., white students and black students were being treated differently). A, C, and D are incorrect because they include other aspects of the Fourteenth Amendment on which the Court's decision was not based.

45. D is the correct answer. As held in United States v. Fordice, 505 U.S. 717 (1992), the repercussions of *de jure* segregation are in no way alleviated by an open admissions policy (race-neutrality) that perpetuates past discrimination. Here, although the state had a race-neutral enrollment policy in its public universities and was complying with Brown in good faith, the fact that the state-run universities remained in effect segregated prevented the discharge of federal supervision.

A, B, and C are incorrect for the reasons discussed in D.

46. B is the correct answer. An individual must show that he has standing to sue. Standing requires an actual injury, causation, and redressibility. Here, man has not alleged any injury to himself that was caused by the federal law and that can be redressed. Thus, he does not have standing, and there is also no case or controversy. The case is not ripe for review because there is nothing in the facts to show that the law being challenged has yet been enforced.

A is incorrect because it does not discuss the case or controversy issue.

C is incorrect because there is a federal question here; it is a federal law that is being challenged.

D is incorrect because diversity (and amount in controversy) is not required when there is a federal question. Here, there is a federal question, for the reasons discussed in C.

47. A is the correct answer. In order for a lawsuit to be heard that alleges issues under the United States Constitution, there must be a live case or controversy, as stated in Article III. Here, the woman is bringing a lawsuit challenging the constitutionality of the federal law (which is a federal question). The facts state that the law will not take effect until August 1, and the woman has brought her suit on July 1, one month prior to the law taking effect. Thus, the case is not yet ripe for review.

B is incorrect because the court will not reach the point where it makes any findings because the suit will be dismissed prior to this point, for the reasons discussed in A.

C is incorrect because the woman has standing, since she would be potentially injured if and when the law were enforced, inasmuch as she wishes to purchase fireworks, and the law bans the purchase of fireworks.

D is incorrect because mootness only occurs when a case was once ripe, but no longer is. Here, the case is not even ripe yet, for the reasons discussed in A.

48. A is the correct answer. The Takings Clause of the Fifth Amendment to the United States Constitution has been made applicable to the states by way of the Fourteenth Amendment to the United States Constitution. As Yee v. City of Escondido, 503 U.S. 519 (1992) indicated, for there to be a governmental taking, there must be a physical occupation/trespass/invasion of the property or a regulatory taking that goes too far. Here, the rent control law under these facts does not involve a physical occupation/trespass/invasion of the property. The law was, however, regulatory in that it regulated the rent that could be charged. However, the facts here match the facts in Yee, and in that case, the U.S. Supreme Court refused to strike down the ordinance in question, despite the plaintiff's argument that there was a Takings Clause violation there. Thus, the lawsuit will fail, based on the U.S. Supreme Court's current interpretation of the Takings Clause.

B is incorrect because the Takings Clause is applicable to the states, via the Fourteenth Amendment Due Process Clause, as discussed in A.

C is incorrect because the case is ready for adjudication The owner wanted to charge higher rent and was prevented from doing so by the ordinance in question, which was already in effect.

D is incorrect for the reasons discussed in A.

49. D is the correct answer. As indicated in Richmond Newspapers, Inc. v. Virginia, 448 U.S. 555 (1980), the public and press have a First Amendment right to have criminal trials be open, unless there is an overriding state interest to the contrary. Thus, open trials are not only for the benefit of the parties – but are also for the benefit of society's perception of justice. Thus, party consent is essentially irrelevant.

Here, both the celebrity criminal defendant and the prosecution (both parties to the case) want the press and public excluded from the trial. For the reasons discussed in D, however, they may not do so.

A, B, and C are incorrect for the reasons discussed in D.

50. D is the correct answer. As indicated in Richmond Newspapers, Inc. v. Virginia, 448 U.S. 555 (1980), the public and press have a First Amendment right to have criminal trials be open, unless there is an overriding state interest to the contrary. Thus, open trials are not only for the benefit of the parties – but are also for the benefit of society's perception of justice. Thus, party consent is essentially irrelevant.

Here, the woman (the criminal defendant) wants the press and public excluded from the trial, and the prosecutor did not consent to this exclusion. For the reasons discussed in D, however, she may not do so.

A, B, and C are incorrect for the reasons discussed in D.

51. C is the correct answer. Although the Sixth Amendment guarantees the criminal defendant the right to a public trial, in some circumstances, the public and the press can be excluded.

In Gannett Co., Inc. v. DePasquale, 443 U.S. 368 (1979), it was held that in certain extenuating/prejudicial circumstances the press and public could be barred from pre-trial admissibility hearings – provided that a transcript of the hearing was made available to the press and public soon thereafter. Thus, since there is a diminished First Amendment right in the fact-pattern of pre-trial, the press and public do not have an absolute right to be there.

Here, the introduction of nude pictures off the public official with the underage daughter would be one such extenuating/pretrial circumstance. Thus, the judge may exclude both the press and the public from the pretrial hearing.

A, B, and D are incorrect for the reasons discussed in C.

52. A is the correct answer. The First Amendment states, "Congress shall make no law...abridging the freedom... of the press."

Here, the question asks which clause of the Constitution guarantees freedom of the press. Thus, the First Amendment is the correct answer.

B, C, and D are incorrect for the reasons discussed in C.

53. A is the correct answer. The First Amendment Establishment Clause by itself applies only to the federal government. Here, the question asks about states. The Establishment Clause has been incorporated to the states by way of the Due Process Clause of the Fourteenth Amendment. Therefore, the Fourteenth Amendment Due Process Clause is the correct answer.

B, C, and D are incorrect for the reasons discussed in A. B is also incorrect because, while the Sixth Amendment does guarantee criminal defendants the right to a public trial, this does not necessarily mean that the press is allowed to attend the trial.

54. B is the correct answer. Under Employment Div. Dept. of Human Resources of Ore. v. Smith, 494 U.S. 872 (1990), an infringement on a person's religious practices is constitutional, if the rule in question is generally applicable. However, the Religious Freedom Restoration Act of 1993 (RFRA), 107 Stat. 1488, as amended, 42 USC §2000bb *et seq* overruled Smith. This overruling was only vis-à-vis the federal government (See City of Boerne v. Flores, 521 U.S. 507 (1997). Here, the high priestess is being prosecuted by a state rather than the federal government. Thus, Smith is the applicable law under these facts.

In this case, the state statute is generally applicable in that it applies to anyone who charges money for sexual encounters, regardless of whether it is a requirement of a religion. Here, the religion's requirement of a $100 per month payment of dues will be construed to be a fee for the high priestess' sexual encounters. Thus, the high priestess will be found guilty of prostitution under the statute. Her defense will fail.

A is incorrect for the reasons discussed in B.

C is incorrect because consent is irrelevant to the crime of prostitution.

D is incorrect for two reasons. First, the U.S. Supreme Court is loathe to adjudge the merits or lack thereof of a religion. United States v. Ballard, 322 U.S. 78 (1944). Under the Ballard standard, all that is important under these facts is that the high priestess has a sincere belief in the religion in question. There is nothing in the facts to indicate that she did not have a sincere belief in this religion. Second, even if a religion is legitimate and traditional, the conduct of its adherents can be regulated because free exercise of religion is subject to laws that meet the Smith standard of general applicability, as discussed in B.

55. A is the correct answer. Prostitution is sex-for-hire. Here, the homeless prostitutes who lived in the church shelter continued to operate their prostitution businesses inside the shelter. However, the church homeless shelter was not a house of prostitution because other church activities were performed in the shelter. These arguments may not be accepted, but they are the best defense the church can offer.

B is incorrect. While it may be a true statement of fact, it would not prevent the church from being successfully prosecuted for operating a house of prostitution.

C is an incorrect statement of law, as discussed in D, for example.

D is incorrect because, under Employment Div. Dept. of Human Resources of Ore. v. Smith, 494 U.S. 872 (1990), an infringement on a person's religious practices is constitutional, if the rule in question is generally applicable. However, the Religious Freedom Restoration Act of 1993 (RFRA), 107 Stat. 1488, as amended, 42 USC §2000bb *et seq* overruled Smith. This overruling was only vis-à-vis the federal government (See City of Boerne v. Flores, 521 U.S. 507 (1997). Here, the church is being prosecuted by a state rather than the federal government. Thus, Smith is the applicable law under these facts.

In this case, the state statute is generally applicable in that it applies to anyone who operates a house of prostitution, regardless of whether it is being done in a church-run homeless shelter. Thus, the Free Exercise Clause would not be a good defense under these facts.

56. B is correct. The Court in Lawrence v. Texas, 539 U.S. 558 (2003) in essence held that there is a fundamental right of privacy to engage in non-marital sexual activity for all persons. In Lawrence, a state statute that criminalized homosexual sexual conduct was struck down. Here, the acts being criminalized are completely on point with Lawrence. Thus, the prosecution will fail because the acts in question were private and consensual.

A is incorrect for the reasons discussed in B.

C is incorrect because it contradicts the facts and because fellatio being performed by consenting adults in the privacy of their home cannot constitutionally be prosecuted for the reasons discussed in B.

D is incorrect because genital penetration is not required for prosecution under the law in question.

57. B is the correct answer. Although the First Amendment freedom of speech will not allow the incitement of another to imminent lawless activity, most any-

CONSTITUTIONAL LAW

thing short of that is protected. Brandenburg v. Ohio, 395 U.S. 444 (1969). Writing a book glamorizing the lifestyle of a high-priced escort is certainly First Amendment protected because the book did not directly advocate that engage in this lifestyle. Thus, the First Amendment freedom of speech protections would be the woman's best defense.

A, C, and D are incorrect because these clauses are not applicable under these facts.

58. A is the correct answer. In Griswold v. Connecticut, 381 U.S. 479 (1965), it was held that making criminal the use of contraceptives between a husband and wife was unconstitutional in that the marital right to privacy was fundamental. Thus, what the couple in this case does sexually inside their own home is constitutionally protected. Thus, the right to privacy is their best defense. B is incorrect because it misreads the facts. The couple's right to marry was not being questioned. C is incorrect because religious conduct is not at issue in this question. D is incorrect because freedom of expression is not at issue in this question.

59. D is the correct answer. The Establishment Clause of the First Amendment to the United States Constitution prohibits the government from establishing a religion. According to Lemon v. Kurtzman, 403 U.S. 602 (1970), establishing a religion occurs when the government makes regulations that do not have a secular purpose; either advance or inhibit religion; or involve excessive governmental entanglement with religion.

Here, even though federal financial aid was given to a religiously-affiliated law school, there appears to be secular purpose to giving this aid to any student who qualifies, regardless of the religious affiliation of the school that that student is attending. In addition, giving federal financial aid does not appear to advance or inhibit religion for the same reasons. Finally, when aid is given at the college or law school level, there is no excessive entanglement with religion because the financial aid is being given for the purpose of secular studies - in this case, the study of law - not for the purpose of engaging in any religious studies.

A is incorrect because there is no free exercise issue implicated here, since the giving of federal financial aid does nothing to inhibit the free exercise of religion.

B is incorrect because the Commerce Clause has been found to justify virtually any federal law that applies across state lines. In this case, federal financial aid is given throughout the United States - i.e., across state lines. Thus, under the current interpretation of the Commerce Clause, the challenge would fail.

C is incorrect for the reasons discussed in D.

60. D is the correct answer. In a long line of cases, the U.S. Supreme Court has upheld the validity of the so-called Sunday closing laws. Were the Court to have construed these laws as establishing the Christian Sabbath, then, of course, these laws would have been suspect. However, they have been upheld on secular grounds. They promote a uniform day of rest and repose in the community. This has been held to be a valid state interest. Braunfeld v. Braun, 366 U.S. 599 (1961); Gallagher v. Crown Kosher Market, 366 U.S. 617 (1960); McGowan v. Maryland, 366 U.S. 420 (1961); Two Guys v. McGinley, 366 U.S. 582 (1961).

Here, the kosher store wanted to be able to be open on Sundays because, since Jewish law requires Jewish businesses to be closed on Saturdays, if the kosher store followed the state law, it would be forced to be closed for two days (i.e., Saturdays and Sundays) and would lose a significant amount of money as a result. Thus, the kosher store had standing to challenge the law.

However, because of the case law cited above, the Sunday closure laws under these facts will be upheld as not violating the Establishment Clause. Therefore, the kosher store will not succeed in its challenge.

A is incorrect for the reasons discussed in D.

B is incorrect because the Free Exercise Clause is only implicated when one's right to freely practice religion is restrained. Here, the store can still be closed on the Jewish Sabbath (Saturday). Thus, there is no restraint on the free exercise of religion here.

C is incorrect because, although the store will lose significant money by being forced to close on Sundays (as required under this law), this is not considered a taking. Laws of this type have been held to be an allowable taking, for the reasons discussed in D.

61. A is the correct answer. Wooley v. Maynard, 430 U.S. 705 (1977), a case directly on point, held that a Jehovah's Witness had the right to cover what he believed to be the sacrilegious motto of New Hampshire's license plate: "Live Free or Die" under free speech grounds.

Here, the man similarly altered the part of his license plate quoting the state motto on free speech grounds (speech by conduct and by expression). Therefore, freedom of speech would be the most likely ground of the man's appeal.

B, C, and D are incorrect for the reasons discussed in A.

62. D is the correct answer. Under Employment Div. Dept. of Human Resources of Ore. v. Smith, 494 U.S. 872 (1990), an infringement on a person's religious practices is constitutional, if the rule

in question is generally applicable. However, the Religious Freedom Restoration Act of 1993 (RFRA), 107 Stat. 1488, as amended, 42 USC §2000bb *et seq* overruled Smith. This overruling was only vis-à-vis the federal government (See City of Boerne v. Flores, 521 U.S. 507 (1997).

Under the RFRA, it must be demonstrated "that application of the burden to the person -- (1) is in furtherance of a compelling governmental interest; and (2) is the least restrictive means of furthering that compelling governmental interest." §2000bb-1(b).

Here, the District of Columbia law stated that anyone who refused to work on a Saturday and was subsequently fired could not receive unemployment was a law of general applicability (it applied to everyone, regardless of their reason for refusing to work on Saturdays). The law amounted to an infringement on the Jewish worker's religious practices, but under Smith, such a law would still be found constitutional because of its general applicability.

However, under the RFRA, the law would be unconstitutional, if it failed to meet the above-stated rule (essentially, a strict scrutiny standard), and the law was a federal law. In this case, the law was enacted in the District of Columbia. Laws enacted in the District of Columbia are considered federal. Consequently, the RFRA, rather than Smith, applies in this case.

In this case, the government likely had a compelling interest in reducing unemployment.

However, the law may fail on the second prong (least restrictive alternative): the mere fact that unemployment was rising does not appear to justify the law because forcing people to work on Saturdays will not ensure that one who cannot work on Saturdays due to religious reasons will not become unemployed. In fact, the man in these facts did become unemployed after being fired for his refusal to work on Saturdays due to religious reasons. The man would refuse to work on Saturdays, whether or not he could get unemployment benefits because the mandates of his religion required him to do so. Therefore, he joined the ranks of the unemployed, which completely defeated the government's purpose in enacting the law in the first place. As a result, the law was not the least restrictive method of furthering the government's interest in reducing unemployment.

Consequently, the government could not meet its burden. The man will prevail in his lawsuit.

A is incorrect because, while rising unemployment is an important government issue, the law is not the least restrictive alternative, as discussed in D.

B is incorrect because it is irrelevant to these facts, since Jews and others who do not follow the church's mandates are not bound by the church's decision 2,000 years ago.

C is incorrect because there was no speech in this case. The man simply wished to practice his religion. Thus, C is incorrect, and D is correct.

63. C is the correct answer. In West Virginia Board of Education v. Barnette, 319 U.S. 624 (1943), the Court held that requiring a public school student to salute the flag, when this impinged on his ability not to be forced into supporting or appearing to support the viewpoint of the government, violated his free speech rights.

Here, the public school required all students to salute the flag and punished those who did not, such as the student in this fact pattern. This amounted to forcing the student to either support or appear to support the government's political viewpoint that the flag should be saluted.

When the government attempts to restrict political speech or enforce a particular political viewpoint, it must meet the strict scrutiny analysis. Under this analysis, it must show that the rule is necessary to achieve a compelling state interest, that the rule is narrowly tailored to achieve this interest, and that the rule is the least restrictive alternative.

Here, the government has not demonstrated any compelling reason why the flag must be saluted by all students. Furthermore, the rule is not narrowly tailored because it applies to all students, even if they personally disagree with saluting the flag. For similar reasons, the rule is not the least restrictive alternative because there are far less restrictive means of achieving the goal of having the flag saluted, such as having only students who personally support saluting the flag do so.

As a result, the rule violated the student's free speech rights, for the reasons discussed above.

A is incorrect. It is true that requiring the student to salute the flag did infringe on his freedom of religion (his religion prohibited saluting the flag or anything else other than God). However, under Employment Div. Dept. of Human Resources of Ore. v. Smith, 494 U.S. 872 (1990), an infringement on a person's religious practices is constitutional, if the rule in question is generally applicable. The Religious Freedom Restoration Act of 1993 (RFRA), 107 Stat. 1488, as amended, 42 USC §2000bb *et seq* overruled Smith. However, this overruling was only vis-à-vis the federal government (See City of Boerne v. Flores, 521 U.S. 507 (1997).

In this case, the rule is being applied in a public school. Unless the public school is located in the District of Columbia or in a U.S. territory, the public school will be an arm of the state (rather than federal) government. Consequently, the rule in Smith will apply to the school.

In this case, the rule was generally applicable, in that it required all students to salute the flag, regardless of their religious beliefs. Consequently, the fact that the rule requiring saluting the flag burdened the student's religious practices will not be the reasons why the rule is unconstitutional. Rather, the rule will be found unconstitutional for the reasons discussed in C.

B is incorrect for the reasons discussed in C.

D is incorrect because under United States v. Ballard, 322 U.S. 78 (1944), the courts may not look into the correctness (or reasonableness), or lack thereof, of a particular religious view. Rather, they look into the sincerity with which the religious belief is held.

64. B is the correct answer. Although there are certainly some limits as to when a parent can take a child out of a public school for due process privacy reasons, when this is based on religious reasons the U.S. Supreme Court has been more tolerant. Thus, in Wisconsin v. Yoder, 406 U.S. 205 (1972), a parent was allowed to cease a child's education at 14, even though the state required education until the age of 16.

Note, Yoder was reconfirmed by the Court's opinion in Employment Div. Dept. of Human Resources of Ore. v. Smith, 494 U.S. 872 (1990), even after Smith changed free exercise jurisprudence. The Religious Freedom Restoration Act of 1993 (RFRA), 107 Stat. 1488, as amended, 42 USC §2000bb *et seq* overruled Smith, but this overruling was only vis-à-vis the federal government (See City of Boerne v. Flores, 521 U.S. 507 (1997). In this case, the facts do not state whether a state or the federal government was involved, but usually public schools and school districts are arms of state governments (except in United States territories and the District of Columbia). Thus, the RFRA is likely inapplicable here, and Smith and Yoder remain the law.

The facts here are directly on point with the Yoder case because in both Yoder and under these facts, the parents did not send their children to a traditional school due to religious reasons. Since Yoder is directly on point and corresponds to the facts in this question, B is the correct answer.

A is incorrect because, although the child may "miss out" on school experiences, a principle of U.S. constitutional jurisprudence is to not adjudge different views on how religions conduct their family affairs. It is up to the family to decide whether or not to send the child to a traditional school, regardless of whether the state believes that the child would "miss out" on any school experiences by not being in a traditional school.

C is incorrect because the "compelling interest" standard is part of the RFRA, which as discussed in B, does not apply under these facts.

D is incorrect because public schools have jurisdiction over their students.

65. C is the correct answer. This issue was directly addressed in Pierce v. Society of Sisters, 268 U.S. 510 (1925). That case held that, provided that the private religious school teaches the basics (reading, writing, science), the state cannot forbid such under the Due Process Clause of the Fourteenth Amendment. The Supreme Court used privacy to decide Pierce.

Free Exercise would also be correct here under Wisconsin v. Yoder, 406 U.S. 205 (1972). In Yoder, a parent was allowed to cease a child's education at 14 even though the state required education until the age of 16.

Yoder was reconfirmed by the Court's opinion in Employment Div. Dept. of Human Resources of Ore. v. Smith, 494 U.S. 872 (1990), even after Smith changed free exercise jurisprudence. The Religious Freedom Restoration Act of 1993 (RFRA), 107 Stat. 1488, as amended, 42 USC §2000bb *et seq* overruled Smith, but this overruling was only vis-à-vis the federal government (See City of Boerne v. Flores, 521 U.S. 507 (1997). In this case, the facts do not state whether a state or the federal government was involved, but usually public schools and school districts are arms of state governments (except in United States territories and the District of Columbia). Thus, the RFRA is likely inapplicable here, and Smith and Yoder remain the law.

Here, like in Pierce, the religious school teaches the basic subjects. Therefore, the state cannot forbid parents from sending their children to these religious schools because of the Due Process Clause of the Fourteenth Amendment and the right to privacy.

Yoder held that a parent could cease a child's education at age fourteen for religious reasons, even though the state required education until age sixteen. In applying Yoder to these facts, although the facts are different (the parents here do not want to cease their children's education, but rather, want to have their children attend religious schools that teach the basic subjects), the principles of Yoder will apply because in both Yoder and these facts, the state requirement would burden the parents' free exercise of their religion.

For the above reasons the parents will prevail for the reasons discussed in C.

A is incorrect because, while the right to privacy is invoked (as discussed in C), there is no claim that this is an Establishment Clause violation, unless the state is trying to make students attend school in order to advance or inhibit religious belief. There are no facts on that point here. Thus, there is no Establishment Clause violation, so A is incorrect.

B is incorrect because, while there was a Free Exercise Clause violation (as discussed in C), there was no Establishment Clause violation (as discussed in A).

D is incorrect because, while there was a violation of the right to privacy and of the Free Exercise Clause (as discussed In C), there was no violation of the Establishment Clause (as discussed in A).

Therefore, C is correct and A, B and D are incorrect.

66. A is the correct answer. The Free Exercise Clause of the First Amendment has been interpreted to prohibit "meddling" by the state or federal governments in intra-church disputes (except those, of course, which regard crimes). Serbian Orthodox Diocese v. Milivojevich, 426 U.S. 696 (1976). State interference would compromise the free exercise of that religion. Here, the religion in question had an internal dispute regarding the belief of one congregant that the present president of the religion had allowed the assets and membership of the religion to drastically fall. This is an internal dispute in the religion. Therefore, the congregant will not prevail in his lawsuit in state court to force the president of the religion to stand for democratic election.

B is incorrect. The Establishment Clause of the First Amendment to the United States Constitution prohibits the government from establishing a religion. Establishing a religion occurs when the government makes regulations that do not have a secular purpose; either advance or inhibit religion; or involve excessive governmental entanglement with religion. This is known as the Lemon test. Here, if the government were allowed to determine how the president of the religion should be selected, this would have a secular purpose (deciding how the president of the religion - a secular position - is to be selected). Such a decision would neither advance nor inhibit religion because the presidency is a secular position. Finally, while there would be some minimal governmental entanglement if the government forces democratic elections upon this religion, this type of entanglement would not be excessive because the presidency is a secular position within the religion, as discussed above. Therefore, the Establishment Clause would not be violated, but the Free Exercise Clause would be (as discussed in A).

C is incorrect there is a case or controversy because, if the congregant were to prevail in his lawsuit, the president of the religion would be injured because he could be potentially voted out of office. However, the case or controversy requirement is only a a threshold to get the case heard in court; it does not explain why the congregant will or will not succeed in his lawsuit.

D is incorrect for the reasons discussed in A.

67. D is the correct answer. The facts here are similar to the facts in Cohen v. California, 403 U.S. 15 (1971). That case made three findings:

First, U.S. states are not allowed to censor their residents simply to make a more "civil" society. Second, it is difficult to distinguish between vulgarity and harmless heightened emotion. Third, passion is a natural part of political protest, and the free exchange of ideas may include some vulgarity as a side effect.

Here, the man's jacket was a form of speech by conduct known as symbolic speech. Under Cohen, such symbolic speech would be considered constitutional. Thus, the man's defense will be successful.

A, B, and C are incorrect for the reasons discussed in D.

68. C is the correct answer. Although the First Amendment (made applicable to the states by way of the Due Process Clause of the Fourteenth Amendment) provides a Freedom of Speech Clause, this freedom is not absolute. In Schenck v. United States, 249 U.S. 47 (1919), for example, the Court mentioned that a man would not be free to yell "Fire" in a crowded movie theater when there was, in fact, no fire because such would needlessly cause panic.

Here, the woman yelled "Fire!" in a crowded theater and caused a panic. Therefore, her arrest was valid under a valid state law that was constitutional.

A and B are incorrect for the reasons discussed in C.

D is incorrect because it contradicts the facts.

69. B is the correct answer. In Brandenburg v. Ohio, 395 U.S. 444 (1969), the U.S. Supreme Court held that certain speech constitutes "fighting words" and can be regulated if:

1. The speech in question advocates imminent lawless action;

2. The threatened action poses serious risk of harm;

3. The speaker specifically intends the lawless action to occur;

4. The illegal action is likely to occur.

Here, the man's speech advocated lawless action (killing the mayor), the action was imminent because the mayor was going to arrive in five minutes; the threatened action posed a serious risk of harm (the mayor being killed); the man specifically intended the killing (the lawless action) to occur because he had just said, "For all of these reasons, I think we would even be better off if someone just went and killed the mayor;" and the illegal action (the killing) was likely to occur (and in fact did occur). Thus, the man's defense will fail.

A and D are incorrect because there was no agreement between the man and the killer (which is required for conspiracy). Furthermore, the man was not on trial for conspiracy, nor was he on trial for murder.

C is incorrect because this alone would not be a complete constitutional defense.

70. D is the correct answer. A correct answer here requires interpreting the plain meaning of the state statute. Since the law bans the display of the human genitalia, it is apparent that the statute does not regulate the wearing of tight and shear clothing that merely outlines the human genitalia, but does not display the genitalia. Therefore, since no genitalia was exposed, the prosecution will not be successful.

A, B, and C are incorrect, for the reasons discussed in D. B is also incorrect because, although it correctly states the standard from Miller v. California, 413 U.S. 15 (1973), this standard is irrelevant under these facts because the law in question is unconstitutional, as discussed in D.

71. C is the correct answer. Although speech by expression is considered protected speech, the woman in these facts wore the bikini, not for the purposes of expressing anything, but rather, simply as a way to attract more business. Thus, any constitutional speech-related arguments she may pose are irrelevant and will fail.

A and D are irrelevant because the question only asked if her First Amendment argument would succeed.

B is incorrect for the reasons discussed in C.

72. B is the correct answer. Flag-burning, as political protest be it of a state or a federal flag, is considered to be symbolic speech, and is, thus, First Amendment protected. United States v. Eichman, 496 U.S. 310 (1990). Here, the woman burned a state flag to protest symbols on the flag that she found offensive. Thus, she will succeed on appeal.

A is incorrect because the law was not overbroad; it was quite specific as to which acts were criminalized. However because the state infringed on her First Amendment rights, her appeal will succeed, as discussed in B.

C and D are incorrect for the reasons discussed in B.

Furthermore, C is incorrect because the law banned the burning of state and federal flags. The U.S. Supreme Court had jurisdiction to hear this case, even though it involved the burning of a state flag, because the U.S. Constitution (here, the First Amendment) was implicated.

D is also incorrect because *mens rea* is irrelevant when the law in question is unconstitutional. Here, the law was unconstitutional for the reasons discussed in B.

73. D is the correct answer. Under Employment Div. Dept. of Human Resources

of Ore. v. Smith, 494 U.S. 872 (1990), an infringement on a person's religious practices is constitutional, if the rule in question is generally applicable. However, the Religious Freedom Restoration Act of 1993 (RFRA), 107 Stat. 1488, as amended, 42 USC §2000bb *et seq* overruled Smith. This overruling was only vis-à-vis the federal government (See City of Boerne v. Flores, 521 U.S. 507 (1997).

Here, the priest was being prosecuted by a state rather than the federal government. Thus, Smith is the applicable law under these facts.

In this case, the facts are virtually identical to the facts in Smith: the state law, under these facts, was generally applicable to all uses of this particular drug (religious uses or other uses). Thus, the priest will not prevail in his lawsuit.

A and B are incorrect for the reasons discussed in D.

C is incorrect because he was in no way impeded from associating with members of his religion. Thus, the Freedom of Association Clause does not apply to these facts.

74. D is the correct answer. This is a simple "black letter" question. Pursuant to Article I, §7 of the U.S. Constitution, both houses of Congress can overturn a presidential veto by two-thirds vote. Because no U.S. Supreme Court has in any way modified the interpretation of this Clause, D is correct and A, B and C are incorrect.

75. C is the correct answer. Pursuant to Article II, §2 of the U.S. Constitution, the President – not Congress – has the power of judicial appointment. Therefore, the Act in question is clearly contrary to the language of the Constitution and is, thus, unconstitutional.

A and B are incorrect because federal judicial selection is not solely a presidential power because the language of the Constitution (Article II, §7) indicates that such appointment must be with the advice and consent of the Senate. The power of appointment is, therefore, not solely a presidential decision.

D is incorrect for the reasons discussed in C.

76. B is the correct answer. Article I, §6, Clause 1 affords all U.S. Senators and Representatives immunity for their legislative functions. Here, the Senator was simply debating whether or not to give a grant. He, thus, had complete immunity from being sued for defamation as a result of what he said on the Senate floor during the Senate debate. Gravel v. United States, 408 U.S. 606 (1972). Thus, this is the Senator's best defense.

A is incorrect because the Article I Speech and Debate Clause gives complete immunity from lawsuits, while the First Amendment's Freedom of Speech

Clause is subject to standards of review. Thus, lawsuits can be brought under the Freedom of Speech Clause. As a result, this would not be the Senator's best defense.

C is incorrect because it is irrelevant here, whether or not the plaintiff (the university) is a public entity.

D is incorrect because the facts indicate it was not the government, but rather, the Senator himself who was being sued, so sovereign immunity would not apply here.

77. D is the correct answer. The Speech and Debate Clause (Article I, §6, Clause 1) does not protect a legislator from extraordinary acts, such as taking a bribe. <u>United States v. Brewster</u>, 408 U.S. 501 (1972). Here, the representative had accepted a bribe to make the disparaging comments during the debate. As discussed, this is the type of extraordinary act that is not protected by the Speech and Debate Clause.

A is incorrect, since it was the Representative, not the government itself, who was being sued. Therefore, sovereign immunity does not apply here.

B is incorrect since bribe taking is beyond the protections of the Speech and Debate Clause, as discussed in D.

C is incorrect because, whether or not it is factually true, it is irrelevant to the question.

78. C is the correct answer. The presidential power to pardon is broad. However, it does not include the right to pardon for state crimes. The language of Article II, §2 is limited to crimes against the federal government. Here, the facts state that the woman's conviction was for robbing a convenience store in a U.S. state. Robbing a convenience store in a U.S. state is a state crime. (It is only a federal crime when it occurs on federal land, such as the District of Columbia or in a national park, which was not the case here.)

A is incorrect because, even though pardoning is one of the President's enumerated powers, the power only relates to federal crimes.

B is incorrect because the power to pardon extends beyond political crimes, so long as those political crimes are federal crimes.

D is incorrect because the President's pardoning power does extend to minor crimes, so long as those crimes occur on federal land, as discussed in C.

79. B is the correct answer. The President's power to pardon is limited to pardon of federal crimes. However, the pardon is not prospective. Thus, the pardon does not cover crimes committed after the effective date of the pardon. Here, the man was convicted of a crime after the President left office. By definition, this occurred after the effective date of the pardon, since the President could not

have issued a pardon after ceasing to be the President.

A is incorrect because, while a true statement, it does not apply to these facts because the man was convicted of a federal crime.

C is an incorrect statement of law, for the reasons discussed in B.

D is incorrect because the pardon power is not limited to non-infamous crimes.

80. A is the correct answer. The U.S. Supreme Court has original and exclusive jurisdiction over foreign ambassadors, under Article III, §2. Here, the criminal defendant is a foreign ambassador. Therefore, the state does not have jurisdiction. B is incorrect because it is a far better defense to prove that the prosecuting court lacks jurisdiction than that an element of the crime was not met. C is an incorrect statement of law because ignorance of the law is never a valid defense to a crime. D is incorrect because a U.S. state, as a general rule, does have jurisdiction over foreigners in that state, with the exception of foreign diplomats.

81. D is the correct answer. The Eleventh Amendment grants immunity to states for lawsuits against that state in federal court initiated by a citizen of the state when the citizen seeks damages. However, it does not grant immunity against lawsuits for injunctive relief or against state officials in their individual capacity. Here, the plaintiff is suing the Attorney General in his individual capacity for his individual actions (investigating his political rivals and extort "gifts" for his immediate relatives, in violation of a federal statute on abuse of office). Therefore, the Eleventh Amendment would not be applicable here, and the plaintiff's case will be heard.

A and B are incorrect for the reasons discussed in D.

C is incorrect. The powers not given to the federal government are reserved to the states, under the Tenth Amendment. This is not an issue in this case.

82. C is the correct answer. Although the congressional power to subpoena is broad, it is not absolute. Thus, a subpoena cannot compel a person to incriminate herself (as per the Fifth Amendment self-incrimination clause). The subpoena must be reasonably related to the investigation. Otherwise, it is beyond the legitimate power of Congress. Gibson v. Florida Legislative Committee, 372 U.S. 539 (1963). Here, the subpoena required the candidate to furnish lists of all "party affiliates." This subpoena was too broad, and could have a potentially chilling effect on First Amendment freedom of association rights, among other things. Therefore, Congress' abuse of its subpoena power would be the candidate's best argument.

A is incorrect because the Voting Rights Act of 1965 dealt with individual

American citizens' rights to vote. This is not relevant to this fact pattern.

B is incorrect because articles of impeachment can only be brought against a sitting president. Here, the candidate had not yet been elected to office.

D is incorrect because there are no taxing and spending issues in this fact pattern.

83. D is the correct answer. There is no constitutional right for homosexuals to marry. Furthermore, under the federal Defense of Marriage Act, states are not required to legalize homosexual marriages (and the federal government will not recognize homosexual marriages from states that have legalized homosexual marriages). Thus, it remains within the state's power to decide whether or not to legalize homosexual marriages. Here, the clerk is being sued for denying homosexual couple a marriage license pursuant to a state law that makes homosexual marriages illegal. As a result, this would be the clerk's best argument.

A is incorrect. Under Lawrence v. Texas, 539 U.S. 558 (2003) state laws that outlaw consensual homosexual sodomy are unconstitutional. However, this question deals with homosexual marriage, not homosexual sodomy. As discussed in D, homosexual marriage is strictly a state issue. Thus, this would not be the clerk's best defense.

B and C are incorrect because the rights to marry (B) and privacy (C) are part of the penumbra of U.S. constitutional rights (i.e., they are not explicitly written in the United States Constitution, but have still been found to exist there).

84. D is the correct answer. Under the Fourteenth Amendment, "no state shall... deny to any person within its jurisdiction the equal protection of the law." Race-based regulations are acceptable only when there is a "compelling state interest." Race-based regulations are inherently "suspect." On the facts given, it is unconstitutional for the dean of the state university (an arm of the state) to deny admission to a white applicant solely on the basis of his race, absent a compelling interest. Here, there was no compelling interest to deny the man admission on the basis of his race. Thus, this would be the man's best argument in support of his lawsuit.

A is incorrect because university deans do have some discretion to deny otherwise acceptable applicants admission, so long as the denial is not based on race or anything else unconstitutional.

B is incorrect because the constitutional clause at issue is not the Due Process Clause, but rather the Equal Protection Clause (unequal treatment of those who are similarly situated).

C is incorrect because the correct analysis, when race is at issue, is not whether the state regulation has a rational basis, but rather, whether it is necessary to achieve a compelling state interest.

85. C is the correct answer. Under the Equal Protection Clause of the Fourteenth Amendment to the United States Constitution, no (U.S.) state can "deny to any person within its jurisdiction the equal protection of the laws." Equal protection has been held to include discrimination based on national origin. See, e.g., Yick Wo v. Hopkins, 118 U.S. 356 (1886). When distinctions are made by a state (here, the school board is an arm of the state) based on national origin, the state must show a compelling reason for the discrimination, as well as the fact that what the state is trying to accomplish is being done by the least onerous alternative.

Here, the school board refused to admit the student simply because of his ancestry. The school board did not show a compelling reason for this refusal to admit the student. (The mere fact that everyone was from one national origin was not a compelling reason.) Therefore, the student will prevail because there has been a denial of his equal protection rights.

A is incorrect for the reasons discussed in C.

B and D are incorrect because the standard of review for equal protection violations based on national origin is strict scrutiny, not rational basis (A) or intermediate scrutiny (D).

86. D is the correct answer. Obscenity is not protected speech. Furthermore, the First Amendment does not protect the right to possess obscenity involving children in the home. Osborne v. Ohio, 495 U.S. 103 (1990). Here, the man ordered the video that contained obscene materials involving children (i.e., 13-year-old girls). Even though he viewed it in the privacy of his home, such viewing is not constitutionally protected under the First Amendment freedom of speech.

A and B are incorrect because the facts stipulate that the video was lawfully intercepted, and that the warrant was proper and was specifically for the purpose of searching for the video in question.

C is incorrect for the reasons discussed in D.

87. C is the correct answer. Although commercial speech is not given the same degree of protection as political speech, it is, nevertheless, protected under First Amendment to the United States Constitution (as incorporated to the states by way of the Due Process Clause of the Fourteenth Amendment). Provided that the ad is truthful and not misleading, the state can limit the ad, only if there is a substantial interest that is narrowly tailored to meet that interest. Virginia State Board of Pharmacy v. Virginia Citizens Consumer Council, 425 U.S. 748 (1976). Here, the outright clothing ad ban in the state is not narrowly-tailored because no facts indicate the

ad to be deceptive, and the mere fact that the state was incensed by the ads was not a strong enough state interest to justify the ban. Therefore, the First Amendment Freedom of Speech Clause offers protection to this type of commercial speech.

A is incorrect because a state's police powers do not allow an unconstitutional the infringement of First Amendment rights.

B is incorrect because no legitimate state interest was shown, and because the other prongs of the commercial speech doctrine were not met (as discussed above).

D is incorrect because no facts indicate a restriction of interstate commerce.

88. A is the correct answer. The Supremacy Clause of Article IV, §2 indicates that a ratified treaty is the supreme law of the land and that a state cannot interfere with such. Nielson v. Johnson, 279 U.S. 47 (1929). Here, a treaty has been ratified that allows citizens of a particular foreign country to enter the United States for the purpose of working there. (The treaty in this fact pattern is similar to the actual Compact of Free Association between the United States and the Republic of Palau.) Since treaties are the supreme law of the land, the state law in these facts that prohibits foreigners from that country from working in that state, in direct violation of the treaty, will be found unconstitutional for this reason. Thus, the foreigner will prevail.

B is incorrect because no facts indicate that privileges or immunities of U.S. citizens are being denied. In fact, a foreigner is suing, not a U.S. citizen.

C is incorrect because, under limited circumstances, states may pass laws that indirectly deal with immigration. (See, for example, Arizona v. United States, 23 2012 U.S. LEXIS 4872 (June 25, 2012).)

D is incorrect because the Tenth Amendment only allows the states to regulate in the areas of non-enumerated federal powers. Treaties, however, are a federal power, as discussed in A.

89. C is the correct answer. As Virginia State Board of Pharmacy, 425 U.S. 748 (1976) and Bates v. State Bar Of Arizona, 433 U.S. 350 (1977) indicated, ads by professionals (be they by pharmacists, lawyers, or, inferentially, doctors) are given significant First Amendment protection, under the "Commercial Speech Doctrine." (The First Amendment has been incorporated to the states by way of the Due Process Clause of the Fourteenth Amendment.)

Provided that the ad is truthful and not misleading, the state can limit the ad only if there is a substantial interest that is narrowly tailored to meet that interest.

Here, the statute banned all legal and medical advertising simply because they were "unprofessional and have decreased the quality of services." This justification was not a substantial interest that was narrowly tailored to meet that interest. Therefore, the best constitutional argument of the law firm and the HMO would be the commercial speech doctrine.

A is incorrect because there is nothing vague about the law; it bans all legal and medical advertising.

B is incorrect because the law firm and the HMO were already injured by the law, which prevented them from advertising. Therefore, the case is ripe for adjudication.

D is incorrect because no property has been taken here.

90. C is the correct answer. Pursuant to Article I, §8, Clause 4 of the United States Constitution, Congress has exclusive jurisdiction over regarding the law of bankruptcy. Thus, since Congress has established bankruptcy laws (which allow individuals a new beginning), a state cannot contravene those laws by forever penalizing an individual for a bankruptcy. Here, the state is penalizing the applicant for a bankruptcy that occurred ten years earlier, by denying his moral fitness application. Therefore, this would be the applicant's best argument on appeal.

A, B, and D are incorrect for the reasons discussed in C.

91. C is the correct answer. Procedural due process concerns the right to notice and hearing before anyone can be deprived of life, liberty, or property (Fifth Amendment for the federal government and Fourteenth Amendment for the states), while substantive due process deals with fundamental rights and standards of review.

A, B, and D are incorrect for the reasons discussed in C. Furthermore, A is incorrect because both types of due process apply to the federal government (via the Fifth Amendment) and the state governments (via the Fourteenth Amendment).

92. A is the correct answer. Procedural due process concerns the right to notice and hearing before anyone can be deprived of life, liberty, or property (Fifth Amendment for the federal government and Fourteenth Amendment for the states). Attendance at public school has been held to be a property right. Goss v. Lopez, 419 U.S. 565 (1975). Here, the bully was suspended from public school without a hearing. Therefore, his procedural due process rights were violated. For this reason, he will prevail in his lawsuit.

B, C, and D are incorrect, for the reasons discussed in A. Furthermore, D is also incorrect because, although the school board had an interest in protecting the other students from the bully, they still needed to give the bully a hearing before suspending him, as discussed in A.

93. C is the correct answer. Procedural due process concerns the right to notice and hearing before anyone can be deprived of life, liberty, or property (Fifth Amendment for the federal government and Fourteenth Amendment for the states). Attendance at public school has been held to be a property right. Goss v. Lopez, 419 U.S. 565 (1975). Here, the boy was suspended from public school without a hearing. Therefore, his procedural due process rights were violated, and for this reason, he will prevail in his lawsuit. Even though the boy may have been constitutionally able to burn his flag if he had done so in a reasonable time, place, and manner, the fact that he was not given his notice and opportunity to be heard would make his suspension unconstitutional.

A, B, and D are incorrect for the reasons discussed in C.

94. D is the correct answer. Other than the Thirteenth Amendment (which bars slavery), the U.S. Constitution only applies to government action. This is known as the State Action Doctrine. Here, the facts stipulate that the shopping mall is privately owned, and there is nothing in the facts to indicate government involvement (such as government funding, government part ownership of the mall, etc.). Thus, the U.S. Constitution does not apply to the owners of the mall, so this would be their best defense.

A, B, and C are incorrect because they are all constitutional defenses, and, as discussed in D, the U.S. Constitution does not apply to the shopping mall owners under these facts.

95. D is the correct answer. The applicable standard of review for laws that discriminate on the basis of legitimacy, under the Fourteenth Amendment's Equal Protection Clause is intermediate scrutiny. Under intermediate scrutiny, a state government must prove that a law is substantially related to an important government interest, in order for the law to be deemed constitutional. Here, no government interest other than restoring family values has been presented in the facts. In Levy v. Louisiana, 391 U.S. 68 (1968), the Supreme Court held a highly similar state statute to be unconstitutional on these grounds. Thus, the statute in these facts will also be held to be unconstitutional.

A is incorrect because there are no Tenth Amendment independent state grounds because the state-applicable Fourteenth Amendment Equal Protection Clause is controlling.

B and C are incorrect, not only in reaching the wrong conclusion, but also because they utilize the incorrect level of scrutiny as required by the Equal Protection Clause (which in this case requires intermediate scrutiny).

96. D is the correct answer. Mental and physical impairment is not a suspect classification under Equal Protection Clause analysis, and, thus, the state regulation need only meet the rational basis test to be constitutional, under the United States Constitution. City of Cleburne v. Cleburne Living Center, 473 U.S. 432 (1985). In that case, the Court held that a housing statute that discriminated on the basis of disability was not rationally related to a legitimate government purpose. Here, by contrast, the statute involves work in a nuclear power plant. Thus, safety issues will likely be found to be a rational reason for the statute. Since it was definitely implied that some disabled individuals could not perform the work and since it is common knowledge that nuclear plants are ultra-hazardous; it is quite clear that the state would meet the minimal requirements of proving a rational basis for their legislation.

    A, B, and C are incorrect for the reasons discussed in D. Furthermore, B utilizes the wrong standard of review. As discussed in D, the correct standard of review here is rational basis, whereas B uses strict scrutiny.

97. B is the correct answer. A bill of attainder is a law that punishes an individual without the benefit of a judicial trial (Article I, §10, clause 1). An ex post facto law is a law that criminalizes conduct that occurred prior to the passage of the law that criminalized that conduct (Article I, §10, clause 1). Here, the offenders list named individuals as offenders without giving them the benefit of a judicial trial. Thus, the U.S. Constitution's prohibition against bills of attainder was violated.

    Furthermore, at the time the individuals under these facts engaged in the real estate practices in question, this conduct was not yet illegal. Thus, criminalizing that conduct after the fact - which is what has occurred here - violates the U.S. Constitution's prohibition against ex post facto laws.

    In addition, the Takings Clause was violated. As Yee v. City of Escondido, 503 U.S. 519 (1992) indicated, for there to be a governmental taking, there must be a physical occupation/trespass/invasion of the property or a regulatory taking that goes too far. Here, there was no physical occupation/trespass/invasion of any property of any of the offenders. However, there was a regulatory taking because the "offenders" were fined $25,000 for engaging in real estate practices. This interfered with their use of their property and, thus, constituted a regulatory taking that went too far.

    A is incorrect because there was no violation of the Due Process Clause of the Fifth Amendment to the United States Constitution because the Due Process Clause of the Fifth Amendment is not applicable to the states. (The Due Process Clause of the Fourteenth Amendment is applicable to the states, but it is not mentioned in this question.)

C is incorrect for the reasons discussed in A.

D is incorrect because a constitutional violation can occur, even in the absence of the imposition of jail time.

98. D is the correct answer. It is true that, under Article I, §9, Clause 8 of the United States Constitution, "No Title of Nobility shall be granted by the United States," and this is just what the President did in granting the Chief of Staff a Title of Nobility. The President's actions were clearly unconstitutional. However, in order to challenge an alleged constitutional violation, the challenger must have standing, which requires an actual stake in the action or an injury. Here, the private citizen will not be able to show any actual injury, nor does he have any stake in the action, since he is merely offended by President's actions here. Thus, his case will not be heard for lack of standing.

A, B, and C are incorrect because they all state possible results of the case being heard, and, as discussed in D, the case will not be heard for lack of standing.

99. B is the correct answer. Dawson v. Delaware, 503 U.S. 159 (1992), set out a similar fact pattern. In that case, it was held that a reference to the defendant's membership in a white supremacist organization violated the defendant's First Amendment freedom of association rights. Association was at issue because the defendant was being punished not for his criminal act, but rather for the company he kept. The facts here are virtually identical to the facts in Dawson. Thus, freedom of association rights would be the man's best argument.

A is incorrect because it is a now long-standing principle of constitutional criminal procedure that capital punishment is not per se cruel and unusual.

C is incorrect because no facts indicate symbolic speech or statements of the defendant were used against him.

D is incorrect because free exercise is only implicated when a person's rights to freely exercise his religion are abridged. There is nothing in these facts to show that the man's rights to freely exercise his religion were affected in any way.

100. D is the correct answer. Freedom of association is the club's best argument because under the First Amendment's Freedom of Association Clause, the male members of the club believed that their right to freely associate only with other males was abridged. However, this argument would fail because in Roberts v. United States Jaycees, 468 U.S. 609 (1984), the U.S. Supreme Court held that an all-male club could not discriminate against females when gender discrimination had nothing to do with the club's purpose.

In Roberts, as well as in this case, the purpose of the club was to enable businesses to come together and work out common issues that they faced. This had nothing to do with the gender of the club's members, unlike the Boy Scouts or Girl Scouts, for example (whose purpose is to enable boys to learn to become good men and girls to become good women, respectively).

A is incorrect because there are no religious rights implicated under these facts.

B is incorrect because the Commerce Clause is not implicated here, since there is nothing showing either the federal government regulating interstate commerce or the state government interfering with interstate commerce.

C is incorrect because there is nothing in these facts to show that anyone has been prevented from speaking freely.

101. B is the correct answer. Under the case of New York Times v. Sullivan, 376 U.S. 254 (1964), defamation suits are limited by the First Amendment – particularly when the allegedly defamatory remarks concern a public figure. In such an instance, the remarks must not only be false, but they must also be made knowingly or in reckless disregard of their falsity.

Here, the movie star was a public figure. Thus, for there to be defamation, the movie star must prove that the tabloid published the story with knowledge of its falsity or with reckless disregard for the truth (i.e., actual malice). Here, the movie star did not have genital herpes. Thus, the story was false. Furthermore, the writer was aware that the movie star did not have genital herpes, but published the story anyway. Therefore, the movie star will be able to show malice and will prevail.

A is incorrect because the press often damages a person – but that is the side effect of having free speech.

C and D are incorrect because the right to privacy is essentially only a limitation on governmental conduct. Here, the tabloid was a private entity.

END OF ANSWERS

A
CONSTITUTIONAL LAW

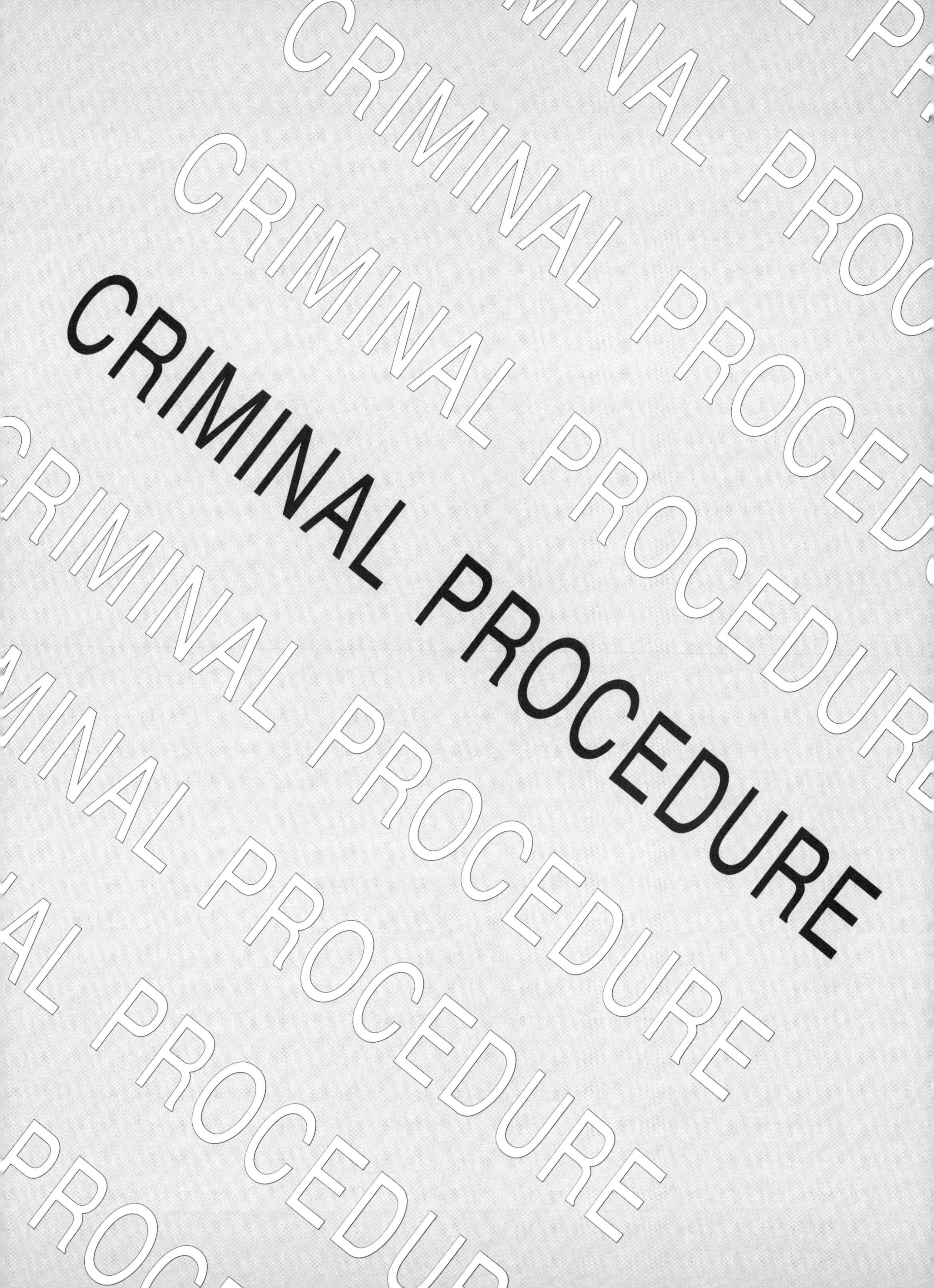
CRIMINAL PROCEDURE

CRIMINAL PROCEDURE - QUESTION BREAKDOWN

1. Fourth Amendment – Expectation of Privacy
2. Sixth Amendment Right to Speedy Trial
3. Sixth Amendment Right to Counsel
4. Fourth Amendment – Warrant Exceptions: Consent
5. Fourth Amendment – Exclusionary Rule
6. Fourth Amendment - Search – Open Fields Exception
7. Fourth Amendment – Warrant Exceptions: Automobile
8. Sixth Amendment – Right to Counsel
9. Sixth Amendment – Right to Counsel
10. Eighth Amendment - Cruel and Unusual Punishment, Victim Impact Statements
11. Eighth Amendment - Cruel and Unusual Punishment
12. Eighth Amendment - Cruel and Unusual Punishment
13. Fourth Amendment – Right to Privacy
14. Fourth Amendment – Illegally Seized Property
15. Eighth Amendment - Cruel and Unusual Punishment
16. Sixth Amendment – Right to Counsel
17. Fifth Amendment – Coercive Interrogation
18. Fifth Amendment – Coerced Confessions
19. Sixth Amendment – Right to Counsel
20. Sixth Amendment – Right to Counsel
21. Fourth Amendment – Expectation of Privacy (curtilage)
22. Fourth Amendment – Expectation of Privacy (discarded garbage)
23. Fourth Amendment – Warrant Requirements
24. Fourth Amendment – Warrant Requirements
25. Fourth Amendment – Exclusionary Rule
26. Fourth Amendment - Fruit of the Poisonous Tree
27. Fourth Amendment - Exigent Circumstances
28. Fourth Amendment – Search

29. Fourth Amendment – Search
30. Fourth Amendment – Standing
31. Fourth Amendment – Border Search
32. Fourth Amendment – Administrative Exception
33. Sixth Amendment – Right to Counsel
34. Sixth Amendment – Right to Jury Trial
35. Sixth Amendment – Right to Jury Trial
36. Fifth Amendment – Double Jeopardy
37. Fourth Amendment – Search Incident to Lawful Arrest
38. Fourth Amendment - Exclusionary Rule – Inevitable Discovery
39. Fourth Amendment – Detention of Others
40. Fourth Amendment - Warrant – Probable Cause
41. Fourth Amendment - Administrative Searches
42. Fifth Amendment - Miranda, Substantial and Injurious Effect
43. Fifth Amendment - Miranda Rights
44. Sixth Amendment – Right to Counsel - Out-of-Court Identification
45. Sixth Amendment – Right to Counsel
46. Sixth Amendment – Right to Counsel
47. Competency of Defendants to Stand Trial
48. Sixth Amendment – Confrontation Clause
49. Eighth Amendment - Cruel and Unusual Punishment
50. Habeas Corpus Petition - Miranda violation
51. Fourth Amendment – Expectation of Privacy
52. Fourth Amendment – Expectation of Privacy
53. Fourth Amendment – Search Warrant
54. Fourth Amendment – State Action
55. Fourth Amendment – Right to Privacy
56. Fourth Amendment Search – Reasonable Suspicion
57. Fourth Amendment Search – Reasonable Suspicion
58. Fourth Amendment Search – Expectation of Privacy
59. Sixth Amendment – Speedy Trial
60. Sixth Amendment – Impartial Jury

61. Sixth Amendment – Confrontation

62. Sixth Amendment – Right to Counsel

63. Fourth Amendment - Warrant Exceptions – Plain View

64. Eighth Amendment - Excessive Fines/ Incorporation to the States

65. Eighth Amendment – Cruel and Unusual Punishment

66. Eighth Amendment – Cruel and Unusual Punishment

67. Fifth Amendment – Privilege Against Self-Incrimination

68. Fifth Amendment – Double Jeopardy

69. Fourth Amendment Search - Expectation of Privacy

70. Fourth Amendment - Search and Seizure

71. Fourth Amendment Search - Expectation of Privacy

72. Fourth Amendment – Government Action

73. Fourth Amendment - Warrant Exception – Consent

74. Fourth Amendment - Expectation of Privacy – Hotel Rooms

75. Fourth Amendment - Warrant Expectation – Consent

76. Fourth Amendment Search - Automobile Exception

77. Fourth Amendment - Probationers

78. Fifth Amendment Due Process Clause and Fourteenth Amendment Due Process Clause – Coerced Confessions

79. Fourth Amendment Search - Consent

80. Fourth Amendment - Concealment

81. Fourth Amendment Search - Voluntary Consent

82. Fourth Amendment - Validity of Warrant

83. Fourth Amendment Search - Mistaken Identity

84. Fourth Amendment - Warrant Execution

85. Fourth Amendment - Warrant Execution

86. Fourth Amendment Search – Incident to Arrest

87. Inapplicability of U.S. Constitution Outside the United States

88. Fourth Amendment - Plain View

89. Fourth Amendment Search

90. Fourth Amendment Search

91. Fourth Amendment Search

92. Sixth Amendment Right to Impartial Jury of One's Peers

93. Sixth Amendment Right to Impartial Jury of One's Peers

94. Fifth Amendment - Miranda (waiver of)

95. Fifth Amendment - Custodial Interrogation, Miranda

96. Fifth Amendment - Custodial Interrogation, Miranda

97. Fourth Amendment - Terry Stop; Fifth Amendment - Custodial Interrogation, Miranda

98. Due Process - Guilty Plea

99. Due Process - Guilty Plea/Habeas Corpus

100. Due Process - Guilty Plea

CRIMINAL PROCEDURE QUESTIONS

1. A man in a U.S. state was waiting for a bus when a police officer spotted him. For no particular reason, the police officer walked up to the man and said, "Hold it right there, mister." The man immediately ran away and threw away a marijuana joint that was on his person. The man was prosecuted for illegal marijuana possession. The man filed a motion to suppress the marijuana. This motion will:

   A. Succeed because the man's rights were violated.

   B. Succeed because the police officer had no probable cause to stop the man.

   C. Fail because the man had no standing, the man abandoned the marijuana joint, and the man was not "seized."

   D. Fail because marijuana possession is not a federal crime.

2. A woman was arrested and charged with solicitation to commit prostitution. Her arrest was performed by an undercover officer who informed her that she had the right to remain silent, that anything she said could and would be used against her in a court of law, that she had the right to an attorney, and that if she could not afford an attorney, an attorney would be appointed for her. She was then brought to jail. After eighteen months had passed, the woman had still not been brought before a judge. The woman filed a writ to the State Supreme Court, demanding that she immediately be brought before a judge.

   Her best argument is:

   A. Her Sixth Amendment rights were violated.

   B. Her Fourth Amendment rights were violated.

   C. She was not Mirandized.

   D. She was entrapped.

3. An indigent (poor) man was arrested and charged with rape. At trial, the man represented himself and the judge failed to inform him that he had a right to an attorney. The man was convicted and sentenced to a jail term. On appeal, he alleged that his constitutional rights were violated. Which would be his best argument?

   A. The man's Sixth Amendment rights were violated.

   B. The man's Fifth Amendment rights were violated.

   C. The man's Fourth Amendment rights were violated.

D. The man's First Amendment rights were violated.

4. After obtaining the consent of a bus company, a police officer walked onto one of the company's buses. One by one, the police officer walked up to each passenger and asked for the passenger's consent to search that passenger's bags. One woman who was a passenger on the bus handed her closed purse to the police officer, even though the purse contained cocaine. The police officer opened the purse and saw the cocaine. The woman was immediately arrested and charged with cocaine possession. At trial, will the cocaine be admissible against the woman?

   A. No because there was no warrant to search.

   B. No because of the hot pursuit exception to the warrant requirement.

   C. Yes because of the plain view exception to the warrant requirement.

   D. Yes because no warrant was required under these facts.

5. A man was arrested for a crime under a law that was subsequently deemed unconstitutional. At the time of his arrest, 25 grams of marijuana were found on his person. Can he be prosecuted for the drug possession?

   A. Yes because they are entirely different laws.

   B. Yes because of the drug exception to the warrant requirement.

   C. Yes because the arrest was legal.

   D. No.

6. Police officers, with no warrant or probable cause, investigated and found a field containing marijuana plants one mile from a man's home. The police officers did a search and discovered that the man was the owner of the field. The man was then arrested for growing marijuana. He moved to suppress the introduction of the marijuana obtained from the man's field because the police had neither probable cause nor a warrant to obtain it. Will the marijuana be suppressed?

   A. No because the field was part of the curtilage of the man's home.

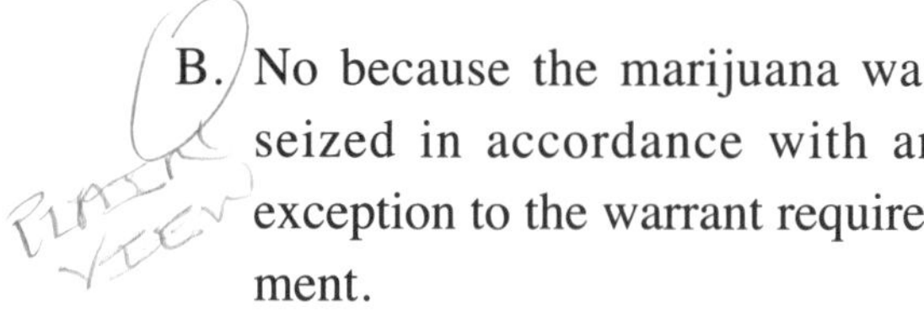

   B. No because the marijuana was seized in accordance with an exception to the warrant requirement.

   C. Yes because the field was not part of the curtilage of the man's home.

   D. Yes because the police had neither probable cause nor a warrant to seize the marijuana.

7. A woman was driving her automobile

faster than the posted speed limit. She was pulled over by a police officer. The police officer asked her if he could search the passenger area of her car. The woman said, "Yes." The officer found a closed bag in the back seat and in it was LSD (contraband). The officer then opened the trunk of the woman's automobile and found a closed suitcase. The police officer opened the closed suitcase and found $10,000 worth of LSD.

The police officer's search of the suitcase was:

A. Lawful under the automobile exception to the warrant requirement.

B. Lawful under the plain view exception to the warrant requirement.

C. Lawful under the exigency exception to the warrant requirement.

D. Lawful under the drug exception to the warrant requirement.

8. A woman was charged with forgery and retained a lawyer to represent her at trial. After the formal charging, she was released on bail. A police officer called the woman on the phone and asked her about an unrelated theft. The woman admitted to the theft. The admission is:

A. Admissible because it was given over the phone.

B. Admissible because it was voluntary.

C. Admissible because her right to counsel did not apply.

D. Inadmissible.

9. A woman was represented by a retained lawyer on a charge of manslaughter. She was found guilty. She told her attorney to appeal. However, the attorney missed the deadline. There was overwhelming evidence, however, that she was guilty. The woman sought collateral relief. She will:

A. Prevail because the attorney was ineffective.

B. Fail because there was no prejudice.

C. Fail because the attorney was privately retained.

D. Fail because collateral appeal is not allowed.

10. A man in a U.S state was tried in state court and found guilty of murder, a capital crime. During the capital sentencing phase, the prosecutor introduced evidence of the effect of the killing on the victim's children. This statement:

A. Violates due process.

B. Violates the Cruel and Unusual Punishment Clause.

C. Violates the hearsay rule.

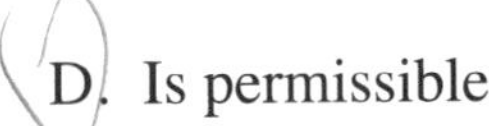

D. Is permissible.

11. A woman was convicted of grand theft and sentenced to three years in prison. While in prison, the woman was occasionally sexually molested by other female prisoners. She filed a writ of habeas corpus, arguing cruel and unusual punishment.

In order for the writ to succeed, what must the woman prove?

A. The sexual molestation was cruel and unusual.

B. The warden was "deliberately indifferent" to the woman's condition.

C. The sexual molestation was cruel and unusual and the warden was "deliberately indifferent" to the woman's condition.

D. The sexual molestation was cruel, but not necessarily unusual.

12. A man in a U.S. state was convicted of the rape of a child. Although severely injured and traumatized, the child did not die. The man was sentenced to death under a state statute. He appealed, claiming that his sentence violated the United States Constitution. Will his appeal be successful?

A. Yes because his Fifth Amendment rights were violated.

B. Yes because his Fourth Amendment rights were violated.

C. Yes because his Sixth Amendment rights were violated.

D. Yes because his Eighth Amendment rights were violated.

13. The police, with no probable cause, attached a global positioning system (GPS) device to the bottom of an automobile. For the following month, the police then tracked the movements of the automobile and, consequently, of the automobile's owner who was driving the automobile throughout that month.

Solely because of the GPS device, the police were able to track the automobile's owner to his meetings with known terrorists. The automobile's owner was subsequently arrested on suspicion of plotting acts of terrorism.

At trial, the automobile's owner moved for all charges against him to be dismissed. The automobile's owner's motion will be:

A. Granted because his Fourth Amendment rights had been violated.

B. Granted because his freedom of association rights had been violated.

C. Denied because the arrest was lawful.

D. Denied because the GPS device had given the police reliable information upon which they relied to arrest the automobile's owner.

14. A man was selling cocaine and was caught with the cocaine by the police. He was charged with the crime of selling cocaine. At trial, the man took the stand in his own defense. The cocaine, which had been illegally seized, was used to impeach him. He was convicted and sentenced to life in prison pursuant to the legislature's guidelines.

The use of the cocaine to impeach the man was:

A. Harmless error.

B. Proper.

C. Improper.

D. Harmful error.

15. A man in a U.S. state was convicted of possession of 662 grams of cocaine. A state law provided for a mandatory sentence of life in prison without the possibility of parole for possession of 650 grams or more of cocaine. As a result, the judge sentenced the man to life in prison without the possibility of parole, citing this state law. The man argued that his sentence violated the United States Constitution because it was disproportionate to the crime. Will he be successful?

A. Yes because the punishment was disproportionate to the crime.

B. Yes because cocaine possession is not a serious crime.

C. No because punishments do not have to be proportionate to the underlying crime.

D. No because cocaine possession is a serious crime.

16. A man was charged with transportation for sale of marijuana. He obtained a criminal attorney to represent him. On the advice of the criminal attorney, he pled guilty and expected to receive a light sentence. Instead, he found himself in immigration proceedings and facing deportation from the United States because the man was not a United States citizen, but the criminal attorney had failed to advise the man that pleading guilty to this charge would render him deportable.

The man sought to reopen and vacate his criminal conviction because of the criminal attorney's failure to advise him about the immigration consequences of the guilty plea. The man's efforts to reopen and vacate the criminal conviction will:

A. Fail because deportation is a mere collateral consequence of a criminal conviction.

B. Fail because criminal attorneys cannot be expected to know immigration law.

C. Succeed because his Sixth Amendment right to counsel was violated.

D. Succeed because his Eighth Amendment right to not be subjected to cruel and unusual punishment was violated.

17. An investigator worked for the police. He believed a man to have raped a woman. However, the investigator needed to gather evidence. One night, he found the man in a bar. He approached the man and proceeded to repeatedly punch the man. The investigator said to the man, "You know, this will all stop if you just admit that you raped the woman." The man then admitted to the rape and the investigator immediately stopped punching him. At trial, evidence of the man's confession was admitted without objection. The man was convicted and appealed on the ground that his confession should not have been admitted. Will he be successful in his appeal?

A. Yes because the investigator worked for the police.

B. Yes because the methods used to obtain the confession were coercive.

C. No because the methods used to obtain the confession were necessary under the public safety exception.

D. No because the confession was given voluntarily.

18. A woman was found murdered by the side of the road. A police investigation revealed traces of DNA from only the victim and one man, who became the prime suspect. In addition, only two sets of fingerprints were found: the victim's fingerprints and the man's fingerprints at the scene of the crime. Furthermore, a gun registered to the man was found fifty feet from the scene of the crime. The man was subsequently arrested.

During the police interrogation, the man refused to confess to the murder of the woman. The police interrogator beat the man repeatedly on the head and told the man that the beatings would stop if the man confessed to the murder of the woman. The man confessed to the murder and was subsequently convicted of that murder.

On appeal, the man argued that his conviction should be overturned. Will the appeal be successful?

A. No because there was a lot of evidence besides the confession

SUFF EVID TO CONVICT w/o COERCED CONFESSION

that the man had committed the murder.

B. No because it was necessary to beat the man in order to obtain his confession, since murder is such a serious crime.

C. Yes because the man's confession was coerced.

D. Yes because it is never permissible to beat a confession out of someone.

19. A man was arrested for robbing a liquor store. The police questioned him for hours, refused to allow him to make a telephone call, and did not give him any food or drink. Finally, exhausted and hungry, the man confessed to robbing the liquor store. Counsel was appointed for the man and, at trial, the man's counsel failed to object to the prosecutor's introduction of the confession. The man was subsequently convicted. The man's counsel's failure to object to the admission of the confession:

A. Violated the man's right to patronize the liquor store and freely assemble there under the First Amendment.

B. Per se violated the Equal Protection Clause.

C. May violate the Equal Protection Clause.

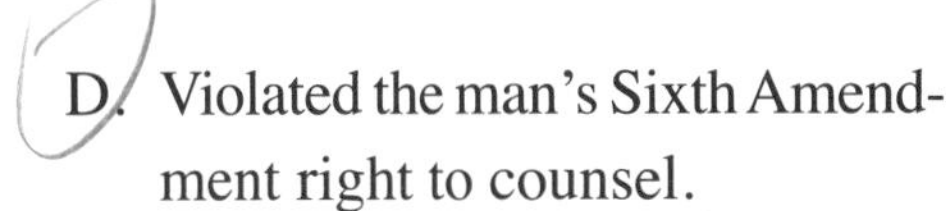

D. Violated the man's Sixth Amendment right to counsel.

20. A man was arrested on suspicion of being under the influence of marijuana. At the police station, the man's urine was analyzed by a trained expert without first allowing the man to consult with the man's attorney. Marijuana was found in the man's urine. At a suppression hearing, the man argued that performing the urine analysis without first allowing him to consult with his attorney was a violation of his rights under the Sixth Amendment to the United States Constitution. Will his argument be successful?

A. No because the urine analysis was cruel and unusual punishment.

B. No because the man did not personally say anything when his urine was analyzed.

C. Yes because the urine analysis was the equivalent of the man making a statement.

D. Yes because the man's right to an attorney present was violated.

21. A police officer, while on routine patrol, walked into an unused barn that was located far away from the nearest residence. The barn was, in fact, owned by a man who lived forty miles away from the barn. The police officer saw several machine guns inside the barn.

The police officer's discovery of the machine guns was lawful because:

A. Of the exigency exception.

B. Of the good faith exception.

C. Of the administrative exception.

D. The barn was not part of the curtilage of the man's home.

22. A police officer opened a dumpster located on a public sidewalk outside a man's home. Inside the dumpster, the police officer discovered expended hand grenades.

The discovery of the expended hand grenades was lawful because:

A. Of the exigency exception.

B. Of the good faith exception.

C. Of the administrative exception.

D. They were in a public dumpster.

23. A police officer suspected that a man had committed eight beheadings and other acts of mayhem and went to a magistrate to obtain a warrant to search the man's home. However, the warrant failed to include the magistrate's signature.

The warrant was:

A. Defective because it lacked a signature.

B. Defective because warrants can only be used to search individuals personally, not to search their homes.

C. Not defective because warrants do not need judicial approval.

D. Not defective because of the good faith exception.

24. A woman was suspected of murdering her husband by electrocuting him in the bathtub. A police officer wished to search the woman's home for evidence of the murder. However, the officer could not find a proper warrant application to fit murders committed in bathtubs, so he used a warrant application from a nearby district that was for controlled substances rather than murder. The police officer neglected to delete the references to controlled substances from the warrant application and submitted the warrant application to a judge for signature. The judge should find the warrant application:

A. Was unconstitutional because it came from a nearby district.

B. Was unconstitutional because it did not conform to the Fourth Amendment's warrant requirements.

C. Was constitutional because it conformed to the Fourth Amendment's warrant requirements.

D. Was constitutional because judges must always sign warrants to search the homes of suspected murderers.

25. A police officer wished to search the home of a prominent businessman suspected of fraud. He made an application to a judge for a search warrant. The warrant, however, was constitutionally defective. Nonetheless, the judge erroneously told the police officer that the warrant was valid and signed the warrant. The police officer then took the warrant to the businessman's home, knocked on the front door, and when the businessman opened the door, the police officer showed the businessman the warrant and demanded to be let into the home to search it in accordance with the terms of the warrant.

    Did the businessman have to allow the police officer to search his home?

    A. No because the police officer acted in bad faith.

    B. No because, despite what the judge told the police officer, the warrant was constitutionally defective and could, therefore, not be used to search the businessman's home.

    C. Yes because a warrant signed by a judge is always valid.

    D. Yes because the judge told the police officer that the warrant was valid, and the police officer had no reason to think otherwise.

26. A police officer towed a woman's car to the local impound lot because of a good faith belief that her car had been illegally parked. A routine inventory revealed marijuana in the car. In fact, the woman's car had been legally parked. The woman was prosecuted for the misdemeanor of marijuana possession. She moved to suppress the introduction of the marijuana. Her motion to suppress will:

    A. Succeed because of the fruit of the poisonous tree doctrine.

    B. Fail because this was a misdemeanor.

    C. Fail because of the inventory exception.

    D. Fail because of the good faith exception.

27. A police officer entered a woman's house after hearing screams. When he entered, he found the woman with a man. The woman ordered the police officer out of her house immediately. She said, "I was just fooling around with my boyfriend. Everything's okay."

The police officer believed her and immediately left the house.

The police officer's entry into the woman's house was:

A. Lawful because of his good faith.

B. Lawful because of the exigency exception.

C. Lawful under a doctrine of assumption of the risk.

D. Not lawful.

28. A police officer entered a woman's home with the woman's consent to investigate the woman's claim that someone had broken into her home earlier that day. While inside the home, the police officer noticed a bong on her kitchen table. The police officer knew that bongs usually contain hashish or other unlawful substances. He, therefore, seized the bong. Was the seizure lawful?

A. Yes because of the exigency exception.

B. Yes because of the doctrine of assumption of the risk.

C. Yes because of the plain view exception.

D. Yes because it was not a search.

29. A police officer went into a donut shop to buy breakfast. While making his purchase, he noticed that the cashier had a brass case behind the glass counter. His expertise indicated that such cases could be used to hold cocaine. The police officer opened the case without the cashier's consent and found cocaine in it.

If the cashier is prosecuted for cocaine possession, he will likely be:

A. Acquitted because the cocaine was in the donut shop where the cashier worked.

B. Acquitted because the cocaine was illegally discovered.

C. Convicted because of the police officer's good faith.

D. Convicted because the cocaine would have inevitably been discovered.

30. A woman invited her boyfriend to stay the night at her house. That night, a police officer, who was passing by the house, thought that he heard a gunshot coming from inside the house. The police officer immediately kicked down the front door and discovered that the "gunshot" had actually been a cork being removed from a champagne bottle.

As the police officer turned to leave the house, he spotted the boyfriend's briefcase. The briefcase appeared very expensive, although the boyfriend did not appear to be wealthy. This aroused the police officer's suspicions, so he immediately opened the boyfriend's briefcase and discovered a severed human head inside.

The boyfriend was arrested on suspicion of murder. At trial, the boyfriend moved to exclude evidence of anything taken from the briefcase. Does the boyfriend have standing to make this motion?

A. No because he was merely an overnight guest.

B. No because the police officer had probable cause.

C. Yes because he was an overnight guest.

D. Yes because of the LaFave doctrine.

31. A woman returned from a trip to an island. Her pupils were dilated, and she appeared to be in an impaired state. When she approached the U.S. customs officer, she was directed to a private room where her luggage was searched. She was also subjected to a full body search by a female officer. The officer found and removed traces of marijuana from under the woman's fingernails. The woman was immediately arrested for possession of marijuana. At trial, the woman moved to exclude the marijuana because it had been obtained without a warrant. Will the woman's motion be granted?

A. Yes because a warrant was required under these circumstances.

B. Yes because the marijuana was not in plain view.

C. No because no warrant was required under these circumstances. BORDER

D. No because the marijuana was in plain view.

32. A city enacted a policy whereby all police officers in that city's police department were subjected to random drug testing. The city made this policy because of the widespread drug problem. If an officer was found to be using drugs, rehabilitation was offered unless other factors indicate significant involvement with organized crime. The policy is likely:

A. Lawful under the drug exception to the warrant requirement.

B. Lawful under the administrative exception.

C. Lawful under the exigency exception.

D. Lawful because examination of breath, blood, and urine are not searches.

33. A woman was tried on a charge of prostitution. She requested counsel because she was indigent. Her request was denied. She was tried and sentenced to one month in jail.

The judge's denial of counsel was:

A. Not erroneous because this was a petty offense.

B. Not erroneous because the offense was punishable by six months jail.

C. Not erroneous because the woman was not indigent.

D. Erroneous.

34. A man in a U.S. state was charged with driving an automobile while the man was under the influence of alcohol. The relevant state statute imposed a maximum penalty of five months in county jail along with a ninety-day driver's license suspension, community service, and a $1,000 fine. The man requested a jury trial. The judge denied the man's request. The judge's denial of a jury trial was:

A. Plain error.

B. Harmless error.

C. Correct.

D. Gross negligence.

35. A man was arrested and charged with bestiality, a crime that carried a potential jail term of eight months. As per his request, a jury was empanelled for his trial. However, the jury consisted of only seven people. The man objected that he was not given a jury of twelve. The judge overruled the man's objection. The judge's overruling of the man's objection was:

A. Improper because the man had a right to a jury consisting of at least twelve people.

B. Improper because there were no animals on the jury.

C. Proper because there were more than three people on the jury.

D. Proper because the man did not have a right to a jury consisting of at least twelve people.

36. A woman and a man agreed to commit a bank robbery. Upon entering the bank, they pulled out their guns and fled with $7,000 of cash. Two days later, they were captured by a bounty hunter who brought them to the nearest police station. They were prosecuted in the state for conspiracy and robbery and subsequently convicted. On appeal, they argued that their convictions violated the Double Jeopardy Clause of the United States Constitution. Assuming that the prosecutor had proven each element of each crime beyond a reasonable doubt, will their convictions of both crimes stand?

A. Yes because of the separate sovereign limitation on double jeopardy protection.

B. Yes because conspiracy and robbery are distinct offenses under double jeopardy analysis.

C. No because each offense does not require proof of an additional fact.

D. No because robbery is a lesser-included offense of conspiracy to commit robbery.

37. A police officer apprehended a fleeing felon who had just robbed a convenience store. The officer placed the felon under arrest and conducted a search of the felon's body. The officer discovered cocaine in the pocket of the felon's jacket, which he was then wearing. The felon moved to suppress the cocaine as a fruit of an illegal search and seizure. Will the motion be granted?

A. Yes because the felon was under arrest.

B. Yes because there were exigent circumstances.

C. No because the felon was under arrest.

D. No because there were exigent circumstances.

38. A policeman suspected a man of possessing marijuana. The policeman then took out his brass knuckles and beat the suspect to a pulp. Finally, the suspect admitted to having a half-pound of marijuana. Unknown to the policeman, a policewoman was on the verge of linking the suspect to the drug trade in that city. The suspect was prosecuted for possession of a controlled substance. The policeman's testimony and the half-pound of marijuana found by the policeman were introduced into evidence. The suspect's attorney made all appropriate motions to suppress. These motions were denied. The suspect was convicted and appealed within the statutory time limit. The prosecution's best argument regarding sustaining the conviction, is:

A. The good faith exception.

B. There was an independent source.

C. This was a state case.

D. Inevitable discovery.

39. A search warrant was issued to search a woman's home for illegal ammunition and guns. The warrant was based on probable cause, properly sworn out before a neutral judge and was specific as to the woman's address. The warrant was executed at 1:00 p.m. on a Thursday afternoon, the day after it was issued. The woman was detained for 45 minutes, while her house was searched for illegal ammunition and guns. Two

of the woman's friends who were also at the woman's home were detained as well.

After the discovery of the illegal weaponry, the woman was arrested. The officers also arrested the woman's two friends. After the arrest, the two friends were found to be concealing on their persons small amounts of crack cocaine. Which of the following propositions is correct?

A. The woman's detention was unlawful and, thus, the evidence will be suppressed.

B. The detention of the woman's two friends was unlawful and, thus, the evidence against the woman will be suppressed.

C. The detention of the woman's two friends was unlawful and, thus, all evidence against the friends will be suppressed.

D. The detention of the woman was lawful, but all of the evidence against the two friends will be admitted as well.

40. A police officer swore out an affidavit before a neutral judge. His information was based on the confidential tip of a personally-known informant that a man was illegally storing toxic waste in his barn. The warrant was issued. In executing the warrant, the police officer looked through all large containers in the barn. Inside the containers, the police officer found not only toxic waste, but also several bales of marijuana. Which of the following propositions are correct?

A. The search warrant had to be based on probable cause.

B. The search warrant had to be based on probable cause, and the test for probable cause was whether the informant was reliable and had a basis for his knowledge.

C. The search warrant had to be based on probable cause and the seizure of the marijuana, though outside the scope of the warrant, was probably lawful.

D. The test for probable cause was whether the informant was reliable and had a basis for his knowledge.

41. Pawnshops in a U.S. city were closely regulated. The reason for the ordinances was that pawnshops were often used to "fence" stolen property, that illegal guns were often sold through pawnshops, and that the city had received hundreds of complaints regarding the shops.

Among the city ordinances was the requirement that, in order to do business, the pawnshop had to keep complete records of all chattels received and from whom, and also keep records of all chattels sold and to whom these chattels were sold. In addition, in applying for a business license, pawnshop owners also consent to inspection of their pawnshops by the police in order to verify the pawnshop owners' compliance with these ordinances.

A pawnshop in the city was inspected by a police officer. He found several violations, including a weapon violation that subjected the owner of the pawnshop to criminal liability. Will a motion to suppress this evidence succeed?

A. No because of the good faith exception to the warrant requirement.

B. No because of the administrative exception.

C. Yes because a warrant was required.

D. Yes because of the bad faith of the police officer.

42. Over defense objection, a defendant's confession was introduced. The confession had been taken after police interrogation in violation of Miranda. The defendant was subsequently convicted in state court, and the defendant appealed to federal court on habeas corpus grounds. What must the prosecution show in order to preserve the conviction?

A. That the error was harmless beyond a reasonable doubt.

B. That the error was harmless by a preponderance of the evidence.

C. That the error had neither a substantial nor an injurious effect.

D. That the error was harmless by clear and convincing evidence.

43. A woman was placed under arrest for extortion. After being given the Miranda warnings she said, "I don't want to talk." Two hours later, the woman was taken to another police station. After the routine booking, a different officer came into the interrogation room and proceeded to question the woman about a murder that the police had still not solved. Ultimately, after 45 minutes, the woman confessed to the murder. Is the confession admissible in a subsequent criminal trial for murder?

A. No because extortion is a theft offense.

B. No because extortion is a particularly serious crime.

C. Yes because murder is a serious crime, so Miranda is inapplicable in cases such as this one.

D. Yes because the woman's request to remain silent had been scrupulously honored by the police.

44. A woman was arrested for assault. It was stipulated that there was probable cause that she had committed the assault. The arrest was made in public. Assault is considered a misdemeanor in this jurisdiction. The alleged victim of the assault, within five minutes of act, was asked whether the woman was the perpetrator. The alleged victim responded, "She is definitely the one!" Was this out-of-court identification admissible?

A. Yes because the Sixth Amendment right to counsel had not attached.

NOT UNTIL FORMALLY CHARGED

B. No because the Sixth Amendment right to counsel had attached.

C. No because this was misleading and overly suggestive.

D. No because due process was denied.

45. A man was charged with racketeering and hired a criminal defense attorney to represent him for that charge. In order to help bolster its case, the prosecution sent out an undercover investigator to befriend the man and, thereby, hopefully learn inculpatory facts regarding the racketeering charge. The investigator learned several pieces of information from actively questioning the man, some of which were relevant to the racketeering charge and some of which were relevant to the man's other crimes for which he had not been charged. Which of the following propositions is the most accurate?

A. The use of the investigator was unconstitutional.

B. No information found by the investigator via dialogue with the man is admissible.

C. Only that information discovered by the investigator regarding crimes unrelated to the racketeering is admissible.

D. All information discovered by the investigator is admissible.

46. A woman was charged with petty theft. Under state law, the maximum sentence for this crime could not exceed six months in jail for first-time offenders. The woman was a first-time offender. She was indigent and could not afford counsel. Her request to have counsel was denied on the grounds that she would likely not serve any jail time, even if convicted. In fact, she was convicted. No jail time was given. Have the woman's rights under the United States Constitution been denied?

A. No because the potential for jail must be over six months in order for the right to counsel to attach.

B. Yes because the conviction might potentially be used if she were later charged with another crime.

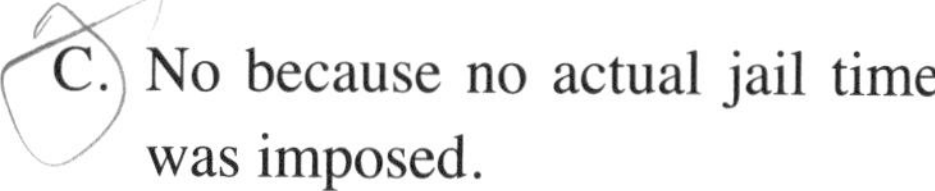

C. No because no actual jail time was imposed.

D. Yes because indigents have an absolute right to the appointment of counsel at "critical stages," such as this.

47. A woman in a U.S. state went on a wild killing spree, evidently initiated by the romantic rejection of a man she loved. The woman committed five gruesome and bloody murders. She openly admitted to the killing and claimed that it was "the devil's hand that led" her to commit the murders. The woman's attorney, pre-trial, moved that the woman not be tried and would be furnished with a psychiatric examination. Under prevailing U.S. constitutional rules, must the trial judge make such an inquiry?

A. No, this claim should be heard on appeal.

B. Yes because insane defendants cannot be tried.

C. No because no facts indicate disorientation or inability to participate in her own defense.

D. Yes because incompetent defendants cannot be tried.

48. A woman and a man were tried on a charge of conspiracy to distribute controlled substances. They were tried together. The woman voluntarily took the stand and argued that the man had used duress in order to obtain her participation. The woman and the man were represented by different defense attorneys. The man's attorney began his cross-examination of the woman. The woman's attorney at once objected, arguing that if this cross-examination proceeded, the woman's self-incrimination rights would be abrogated. How should the trial judge rule?

A. For the woman because she cannot be compelled to incriminate herself.

B. For the man because he has the right to confront adverse witnesses.

C. A mistrial should be declared because two constitutional rights are in direct opposition.

D. For the man's attorney because the attorney had a right to do his job.

49. By legislative enactment, a U.S. state has deemed all those convicted of capital crimes and duly sentenced to death be executed by dismemberment. A man was convicted of a capital crime in that state and was sentenced to execution by dismemberment under this state statute. He challenged his sentence under the United States Constitution. In his challenge, what will he need to prove?

A. Only that other states do not have similar statutes.

B. Only that this method of execution is more painful than other methods of execution.

C. Other states do not have similar statutes and also that this method of execution is more painful than other methods of execution.

D. That this punishment is disproportionate to the crime for which he was sentenced.

50. A woman in a U.S. state beheaded, dismembered, and incinerated her boyfriend. She was subsequently arrested and charged with murder. The arresting officer interrogated her without first giving her the Miranda warnings. The woman confessed to the murder. Her attorney did not move to suppress the confession. The woman was ultimately convicted of murder. She did not file an appeal to the State Appellate Court, nor did she file an appeal to the State Supreme Court. Two years later, while in prison, she filed a habeas corpus petition to the State Supreme Court. The petition was summarily dismissed. The woman then filed a habeas corpus petition to the federal district court, arguing that her Fifth Amendment, Fourteenth Amendment, and Miranda rights had been denied. Will this petition be successful?

A. Yes because there was plain error.

B. Yes because there was a stipulated violation of Miranda.

C. Yes because her counsel was ineffective.

D. No because there was inadequate cause for not moving to suppress the confession at the pre-trial, trial phase, or at the direct appeal phase.

51. A teacher at a public high school discovered a female student smoking in the girl's bathroom. Since the girl was violating the school rules, the teacher took the girl to the principal's office where the girl met with the vice-principal. The girl denied that she had been smoking.

The vice-principal led the girl into his private office and demanded to see her purse. He opened the purse, found cigarettes inside, and accused the girl of lying. While reaching into the purse, the vice-principal noticed a small glass vial containing a white powdery substance. Thinking it was probably cocaine, he further searched the purse and found three more vials full of the same white substance, a glass straw, and a mirror. The girl admitted to having a drug problem.

The vice-principal notified the girl's mother and turned the purse over to the police. The white powdery substance proved to be cocaine. The girl was prosecuted for illegal possession of cocaine with the intent to sell. Her attorney filed a motion to suppress the cocaine and cocaine paraphernalia. This motion will fail because:

A. The girl had no standing.

B. The vice-principal's search did not violate the Fourth Amendment.

C. The search was conducted by a school official.

D. The vice-principal's search resulting in the discovery of the evidence of cocaine was "reasonable."

52. A prisoner in a state penitentiary was sound asleep in his prison cell. While the prisoner was asleep, a prison guard snuck into the prisoner's prison cell and proceeded to search through the prisoner's belongings. The guard woke the prisoner up when the guard found three small balloons of heroin stuck underneath the prisoner's bed. The prisoner denied any knowledge of the heroin. The guard notified the prison's warden. The prisoner was charged with possession of heroin. At trial, the prisoner filed a motion to suppress the heroin. Are the balloons of heroin admissible against the prisoner?

A. No because the guard had no warrant to conduct such a search.

B. No because there was no exigent circumstances.

C. Yes, if the guard was acting on a tip from a reliable informant.

D. Yes because the prisoner was incarcerated in a state penitentiary.

53. A man was arrested by the United States Postal Police without a warrant at his place of employment. At the same time, other officers of the United States Postal Police were searching the man's home, having been let in by a neighbor who knew where the key was kept. Inside, the officers found and confiscated various incriminating papers and articles.

The man was charged with use of the mails for the purpose of transporting certain coupons or tickets representing chances or shares in a lottery or gift enterprise. At trial, the man moved for the court to order the return of his property on the grounds that the papers had been obtained without a search warrant and by breaking into his home in violation of the Fourth Amendment.

Should the court grant the man's motion for the return of his property?

A. No because the police were merely trying to bring proof to the aid of the government and were acting under the color of their office.

B. No because the circumstances did not dictate that the police needed to secure a warrant.

C. Yes because the police acted without sanction of law.

D. Yes because the man made a seasonal application for the return of his property.

54. A woman used a private shipper to send a package to a man. In route, the package got damaged. The shipper opened the package and discovered a mysterious white powder inside. The shipper immediately called the United States Drug Enforcement Administration (DEA). The DEA agents took a small sample of the powder and discovered it to be cocaine. The woman was arrested for shipping cocaine. At trial, she moved to suppress the cocaine because it had been illegally seized. Will her motion succeed?

A. Yes because there was no probable cause for the shipper to have opened the package.

B. Yes because the DEA agents lacked a warrant.

C. No because DEA agents do not need a warrant to conduct searches.

D. No because a warrant was not required under the circumstances.

55. Police officers in a U.S. state had reason to believe that a woman in their city had child pornography in her home. One night, without obtaining a warrant, the police officers forcibly broke down the woman's front door and, despite the woman's protests, they entered and searched her house. Child pornography was subsequently discovered during the search. The woman was charged with possession of child pornography. At trial, the prosecution did not produce a search warrant, nor did they account for their failure to do so. Can the child pornography found at the woman's residence be used against her at trial?

A. Yes because in a prosecution in a state court for a state crime the Fourteenth Amendment does not forbid the admission of evidence obtained by an unreasonable search and seizure.

B. Yes because, even if the officers' search was unreasonable, they were legitimately on the premises.

C. Yes because child pornography is inherently evil.

D. No because the right to privacy is enforceable against the states.

56. A woman was driving her automobile at 50 mph in a residential district in a U.S. state. A police officer, noticing the excessive speed, pulled her over. When the woman rolled down her window, the police officer was overwhelmed by the smell of breath mints. The woman was asked to step out of the car and perform a field sobriety test. She passed the

test, but the officer felt that the woman was probably an alcoholic who was able to perform most daily functions while intoxicated and was sure that the strong smell of breath mints was for the purpose of covering up the smell of alcohol.

Believing there was probably a bottle of alcohol somewhere, the police officer searched the woman's entire car. Under the driver's seat, he found a baggy containing an 1/8 ounce of cocaine. The woman was arrested and taken immediately to the police station. The woman filed a motion to suppress the cocaine.

This motion will likely:

A. Fail because the overwhelming smell of breath mints gave the police officer all the reason he needed to search the woman's car.

B. Fail because cocaine was found.

C. Fail because of the inventory exception.

D. Succeed.

57. A police officer in a U.S. state pulled over a driver because the rear of his car was very low to the ground. Suspecting that something illegal might be in the trunk, the police officer searched the car and found 12 cases of cigarettes not bearing tax seals from that state. The car and cigarettes were seized and the driver was arrested and charged with violation of state law. The police officer had neither a search nor an arrest warrant. Pursuant to a state statute, a petition for forfeiture of the automobile was filed. The driver, by timely objection, sought dismissal of the forfeiture petition claiming that the evidence had been illegally obtained. Will the forfeiture petition be dismissed?

A. Yes because the seizure was founded upon evidence illegally obtained since, under the particular circumstances, the police officer acted without probable cause.

B. No because the inventory search exception allowed the police officer to act as he did.

C. No because the exclusionary rule does not apply to civil forfeitures.

D. No because contraband once seized cannot be returned to its owner.

58. An off-duty police officer was walking his dog when he noticed some leaves in a field he was passing. The leaves looked like marijuana to him, so he went home and came back to the same sidewalk with his binoculars. Using the binoculars and still standing on the sidewalk, the officer looked into a greenhouse that was located on the

same field, but approximately one mile from the house of the owner of the field. The officer saw more marijuana. The officer waited for the owner of the property to return, and at that time, the officer arrested the owner for possession of marijuana. Was the officer's discovery of the greenhouse marijuana lawful?

A. No because the officer was off-duty at the time.

B. No because he had no probable cause to look inside the greenhouse with his binoculars.

C. No because he only had license look at the property with his naked eye, not with his binoculars.

D. Yes because no significant privacy expectation was invaded.

59. A woman was charged with prostitution in a U.S. state. The woman represented herself at arraignment where bail was denied. As a result, while awaiting trial, she remained in jail. Throughout this period, she interviewed several lawyers, but was unable to settle upon one that she liked. She asked the judge for several continuances in order to find an attorney she liked. Finally after six months, she found an attorney she liked and the trial proceeded. The first thing the lawyer did was make a motion for the charges to be dismissed because the woman had been in jail for six months, while awaiting trial. The motion will likely be:

A. Granted because the woman's right to a speedy trial was denied.

B. Granted because the woman should not have represented herself at arraignment.

C. Denied because there was no prejudice to the woman.

D. Denied because the woman asked for the continuances.

60. Under pressure from a pregnant women's advocacy group, a county in a U.S. state exempted pregnant women from jury duty, unless these women specifically requested to be included as potential jurors. A woman in this county was later arrested and charged with felony-murder for a death that occurred as she was stealing baby formula in preparation for the birth of her baby. She requested a jury trial. The jury panel consisted of all men and non-pregnant women. The woman challenged the composition of the jury panel. Will she be successful?

A. No because the county specifically exempted pregnant women from jury service, unless they requested to be included as potential jurors.

B. No because the hormones present in a pregnant woman may

prevent her from making the rational decisions necessary to serve as a juror.

C. Yes because there were no pregnant women on the jury.

D. Yes because no pregnant woman asked to be on this jury.

61. A man in a U.S. state was arrested on suspicion of driving while intoxicated. A sample of the man's blood was taken and tested by a particular analyst. At trial, however, the analyst's results were made available to the man, but a different analyst testified as to the results of the blood-alcohol test. The man moved to exclude the testimony of the analyst. Will his motion be successful?

A. Yes because the man's Eighth Amendment and Fourteenth Amendment rights were violated.

B. Yes because the man's Sixth Amendment and Fourteenth Amendment rights were violated.

C. No because the man's Sixth Amendment and Fourteenth Amendment rights were not violated.

D. No because the man's Eighth Amendment and Fourteenth Amendment rights were not violated.

62. A man in a U.S. state was arrested for bestiality. At trial, the man, who was not a licensed attorney, asked to represent himself. The judge was concerned the man would not be adequately able to represent himself. Because the man was indigent, the judge insisted that the man accept the services of a public defender. The man was ultimately convicted. Rather than bring an action for ineffective assistance of counsel, the man argued on appeal that the public defender had been forced upon him, even though he had said that he wished to represent himself. Will his appeal be successful?

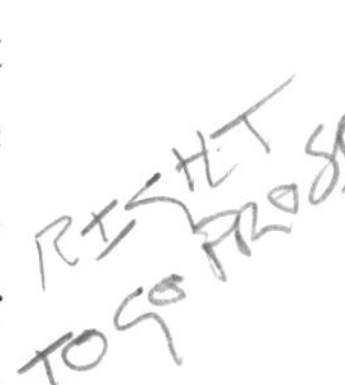

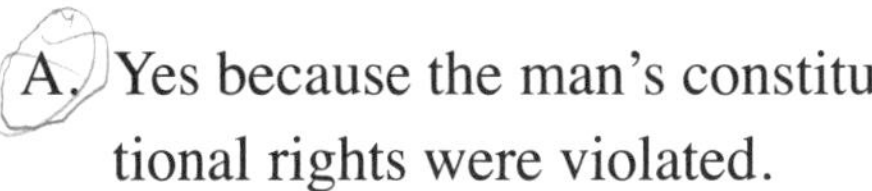

A. Yes because the man's constitutional rights were violated.

B. Yes because public defenders generally lose cases.

C. No because only licensed attorneys can represent people in court.

D. No because the man's constitutional rights were not violated.

63. A man was walking to his girlfriend's home in a U.S. state, planning to ask the girlfriend to marry him. He was very nervous. He passed a police officer who noticed that the man was behaving strangely. The officer stopped the man and did a pat-down search. The officer found nothing but the ring that the man was intending to give to his girlfriend. The officer believed that the ring was

likely stolen and confiscated the ring. The man was charged with possession of stolen goods.

At trial, the man moved to suppress introduction of the ring as evidence against him. Will his motion be successful?

A. No because the pat down was necessary for the safety of the police officer.

B. Yes because the ring was not stolen.

C. Yes because the police officer had no reasonable suspicion to stop and frisk the man.

D. Yes because the police officer had no probable cause to stop and frisk the man.

64. A man in a U.S. state was charged with shoplifting a $200 leather jacket. For this, he was tried in state court, found guilty, and fined $10,000. On appeal, he challenged the fine as excessive in violation of his rights under the United States Constitution. Will he prevail?

A. Yes.

B. Yes because this fine was a violation of his rights under the U.S. Constitution.

C. No because this fine was not excessive as defined under the U.S. Constitution.

D. No.

65. A U.S. citizen soldier in the United States Army was court-martialed and convicted of desertion. Because desertion was found to be reprehensible and disruptive to the smooth functioning of the Army, the soldier was not only given a dishonorable discharge from the Army, but was also stripped of his U.S. citizenship.

He appealed his case and it eventually ended up at the U.S. Supreme Court. On appeal, he alleged that stripping him of his citizenship violated his U.S. constitutional rights. Will his appeal be successful?

A. No because the U.S. Constitution does not apply to military courts.

B. No because a person cannot appeal a military decision to the U.S. Supreme Court.

C. Yes because his Eighth Amendment rights were violated.

D. Yes because his Fourth Amendment rights were violated.

66. A mildly mentally retarded man was convicted in a U.S. state court of mayhem and felony-murder after he cut off his mother's hand, causing her to bleed to death. He was sentenced to death by painless lethal injection. On appeal, he challenged his death sentence as a violation of his rights under the U.S. Constitution. Will he be successful in his appeal?

A. Yes because execution by lethal injection is always cruel and unusual punishment.

B. Yes because, under these facts, execution was cruel and unusual punishment.

C. No because the Eighth Amendment only applies to cases in federal court.

D. No because the man was only mildly (as opposed to severely) mentally retarded.

67. A woman and a man were arrested for robbery of a bank insured by the Federal Deposit and Insurance Corporation (FDIC). They were tried in federal court. Invoking her right to remain silent, the woman refused to take the stand.

During his closing argument, the prosecutor stated that the woman's failure to take the stand probably indicated her guilt.

Both the woman and the man were convicted. The woman appealed alleging a violation of her constitutional rights. Will her appeal be successful?

A. No under the Fifth Amendment.

B. No under the Fourteenth Amendment.

C. Yes under the Fifth Amendment.

D. Yes under the Fourteenth Amendment.

68. A man was tried in a U.S. state court for murder that occurred inside a post office. He was acquitted. However, he was then immediately arrested by the United States Postal Police and ultimately tried for the same murder in federal court where he was convicted and sentenced to death. He appealed his conviction, alleging that his rights under the U.S. Constitution had been violated. Will his appeal be successful?

A. Yes because there was a double jeopardy violation here.

B. Yes because a person who was acquitted of a crime cannot be retried for that crime.

C. No because postal crimes are not covered by the double jeopardy clause.

D. No because there was no double jeopardy violation here.

69. A man cheated on his taxes and shredded the incriminating documents. He threw the shredded paper into a trash can that was located on the sidewalk outside his home. The man's tax return had been red-flagged by the Internal Revenue Service (IRS) computer and two IRS agents were sent to the man's house to investigate. The agents searched through that trash can and found it full of the shredded documents. The agents took the shredded documents with them back to their headquarters and proceeded to painstakingly piece them together. Based upon the pieced-together documents, the IRS was able to make a case of tax fraud against the man. The man was arrested for tax fraud. At trial, he made a motion to suppress the evidence obtained from the trash can. His motion will:

A. Succeed because the man shredded the documents so no one could read them.

B. Succeed because the documents in their shredded state were in no way incriminating.

C. Fail.

D. Succeed because the IRS agents did not have a search warrant to search the trash can.

70. During their examination of a damaged package, employees of a private shipping company observed a white powdery substance, originally concealed within eight layers of brown paper and tape. A federal agent who was summoned removed a trace amount of the white substance, subjected it to a test, and determined that it was cocaine. Did the federal agent's field test constitute an unlawful search or seizure within the meaning of the Fourth Amendment?

A. No because no warrant was required.

B. Yes because a protected possessory interest was infringed.

C. Yes because the field test likely destroyed some of the evidence.

D. Yes because there was no search warrant to search the package.

71. A woman mistakenly received a package containing apparently pornographic videos. Since there were people engaged in sexual acts on the video boxes, the woman turned the videos over to agents of the Federal Bureau of Investigation (FBI). The agents watched the videos and were able to ascertain that they were, in fact, pornographic. Did the FBI agents need a warrant to view the pornographic videos sent to the woman by mistake?

A. No because the woman, who was a private party, opened the videos that revealed the pornographic video boxes.

B. No because the video boxes were obviously pornographic as depicted by the pictures of sexual acts on the outside of them.

C. Yes because watching pornographic videos is not part of the agents' job description and a warrant was, thus, required to go beyond their job description and watch the videos.

D. Yes because the woman did not watch the videos.

72. An employee of the United States Postal Service opened a suspicious-looking package with a return address from a neighborhood that was known to have a high population of hashish users. The employee was hoping the package would contain some black-tar hashish due to the return address and the fact it was to be delivered to a nearby fraternity house. The employee took the package home with him and discovered 12 grams of blonde hashish instead of black-tar. A little disappointed, the employee smoked some of the hashish in order to get in a better mood. Unfortunately, he became extremely paranoid, realized what he had done was wrong, and turned the hashish over to the Federal Bureau of Investigation (FBI) the next morning. The agents brought a prosecution action against the sender. Were the employee's actions governed by the Fourth Amendment?

A. No because he procured the hashish for his personal use.

B. Yes because he was is a postal employee.

C. Yes because he discovered the hashish during the course and scope of his employment.

D. Yes because the employee's search and seizure was done to further a governmental objective.

73. The police in a U.S. city were looking for a bookmaking kingpin. Two officers drove to the kingpin's house, thinking that he might be home, to ask him some questions concerning the recent murder of a jockey. They knocked on the door, and the kingpin's butler answered the door. "May we come in?" one of the officers asked. "Yes, you may," the butler said. Did the officers obtain voluntary consent?

A. No because butlers cannot give consent, since they do not own the home in question.

B. No because only the kingpin (i.e., the homeowner) could give consent.

C. Yes because the police did not use any intimidation and the butler had the authority to consent.

D. Yes, unless the police officers were drunk at the time.

74. While cleaning a hotel room after check-out time, a housekeeper at the hotel discovered a sizeable amount of cocaine on the night stand. She quickly walked to the hotel's donut shop where she told a police officer about the cocaine. He followed her to the hotel room and the housekeeper let the police officer inside the room. The police officer further searched the room and found more cocaine and cocaine paraphernalia. The police officer waited in the room until the guest currently staying in that room returned. The police officer immediately and arrested the guest and charged him with possession of cocaine. Was the consent to search given by the housekeeper valid?

A. Yes because it was after check-out time.

B. Yes because hotel staff can give consent to a search of a hotel room at any time.

C. No because a third party cannot give consent.

D. No because only hotel management can give consent to a search of a hotel room.

75. One night, there was a knock at the door of a college student's apartment located in a U.S. state. "Who is it?" the college student asked. "The police! Open up!" The college student peered through the peep-hole and saw three police officers in uniform. "Sorry, but I can't let you in." "You'd better! We have a search warrant!" Flustered, she let the police inside. Three of them bolted through the door and thoroughly searched the apartment. The police found two pounds of marijuana, scales, and other items indicating drug use and drug dealing.

During the search, the student asked, "May I see the search warrant, please?" The officers all started laughing. One of them said, "We have no search warrant, you dumb broad!" Shocked, the student screamed, "But that's the only reason I let you in!" "Oh well," one of the officers shrugged. Did the officers obtain valid consent to enter and search her apartment?

A. Yes because the search incriminated the college student.

B. Yes because securing a search warrant is a mere formality when the officers have probable cause.

C. No because the Fourth Amendment requires warrants to be obtained in all situations.

D. No because there was no valid consent given.

76. A woman was driving her vehicle in a U.S. state one night when police officers motioned for her to stop her vehicle on the side of the road. She did so. The police officers asked to see her driver's license, which she produced. The officers confirmed that the license was suspended and arrested the woman for driving with a suspended license. She was handcuffed and placed in the back of the police car. The police officers then searched the woman's vehicle and discovered cocaine under the driver's seat. Was the search of the vehicle lawful?

A. No because, under the circumstances, a warrant was required to search the vehicle.

B. No because the woman cooperated with the police and they were, therefore, required to first obtain her consent before searching her vehicle.

C. Yes because once the woman was under arrest and inside the police car, the police could search her vehicle even without a warrant.

D. Yes because the police officers had a reasonable suspicion that they might be in danger.

77. A criminal was sentenced to five years of probation. During the probation period, officers obtained information that he was fencing stolen goods. They went to his home and searched it without a warrant while he was out of town and found large amounts of stolen goods. Will the police officer's search of the criminal's home be upheld?

A. No because the police entered his home without a search warrant.

B. No because he was out of town and could not consent to the search.

C. Yes because, under these particular circumstances, the search was valid. CONDITIONAL LIBERTY

D. Yes because warrants are never required to search the homes of convicted criminals.

78. A woman was arrested on suspicion shoplifting. The police took her to an interrogation room equipped with high-powered electric lights, cameras, and several other pieces of equipment and interrogated her for 36 hours continuously. The woman ultimately confessed to having committed the shoplifting for which she had been arrested.

At trial, the woman made a motion to exclude her confession. Her motion will:

A. Succeed because the confession was coerced.

B. Succeed because the police lacked a warrant to interrogate the woman.

C. Fail because the confession was not coerced.

D. Fail because the police can never interrogate a person once an arrest has taken place. After the arrest, the suspect can only be interrogated by the prosecutor in a courtroom.

79. A police officer posed as a drug purchaser and gained entry into the home of a known drug dealer in a U.S. state for the express purpose of purchasing illegal drugs. When inside the home and while the drug dealer was in the bathroom, the officer took the opportunity to look into closed drawers and envelopes, finding cocaine and cocaine paraphernalia. The drug dealer was arrested for possession of cocaine. At trial, the drug dealer made a motion to suppress the evidence of the cocaine. The motion will:

A. Fail because the police officer posed as a drug purchaser.

B. Fail because the drug dealer left the room, thus, giving the police officer implied consent to search the closed drawers and envelopes.

C. Succeed because the police officer concealed his status as a law enforcement officer.

D. Succeed because the police officer looked into closed drawers and envelopes while the drug dealer was in the bathroom.

80. A police officer gained entry into a woman's home in a U.S. state by pretending to be a telephone technician. Once the police officer was inside, the police officer witnessed the woman performing acts of necrophilia (sexual intercourse with dead bodies). The woman was arrested and charged with necrophilia. At trial, the woman made a motion to suppress the evidence. The motion will:

A. Succeed because the police officer did not represent himself as having an illegal purpose.

B. Succeed because necrophilia is not illegal.

C. Fail because the police officer did not make any additional intrusions into the woman's home.

D. Fail because the police officer posed as a telephone technician.

81. A police officer gained entry into a chef's home in a U.S. state by telling the chef that he was looking for an escaped convict who had broken out of the nearby state penitentiary. Actually, the police officer was looking to bust the chef for baking desserts filled with marijuana. Once inside, the officer saw a sizeable amount of marijuana leaves

on a mirror on the chef's kitchen table. The chef was arrested. At trial, he made a motion to suppress the evidence because the police officer had used deceptive practices to gain entry into the chef's home. The motion will:

A. Succeed because the police officer misrepresented his purpose.

B. Succeed because the police officer did not represent himself as having an illegal purpose.

C. Fail because the chef's consent was voluntary.

D. Fail because baking with marijuana is a crime.

82. Two policemen had secured a warrant to search a man personally, as well as the man's place of residence known as "8709 Portapotty Place, fifth floor apartment." Both the man and his apartment were located in a U.S. state. The policemen reasonably believed that there was only one fifth floor apartment at 8709 Portapotty Place. In fact, there were two apartments located on the fifth floor of that address, one belonging to the man and the other to a woman. Before the policemen realized that there were two fifth floor apartments, they had entered the woman's apartment through an unlocked door because they thought it was the man's apartment. The policemen found two kilos of hashish on the dining room table next to a drug scale. The woman was subsequently arrested for possession of narcotics with intent to sell. She filed a motion to suppress the evidence because the officers had entered the premises without a search warrant. The motion will:

A. Succeed because the warrant will be found defective.

B. Succeed because the officers searched the wrong residence.

C. Fail because warrants are not required to search apartments, only stand-alone houses.

D. Fail because, at the time that they obtained the warrant, the policemen had a reasonable belief that there was only one apartment on the fifth floor of this building.

83. A police officer was searching for a robbery suspect who was wearing blue jeans and a lime-green t-shirt. As he was driving, the officer spotted a man wearing blue jeans and a lime-green t-shirt walking briskly down the boulevard. With his gun drawn, the officer instructed the man to put his hands over his head. "What's this all about?" the man asked. "You know what it's all about," the police officer replied. "Don't tell me you don't know anything about the coin shop you just robbed." "I did not rob any shops." "Yeah, right," replied the officer. The officer saw something suspicious in the man's pants pocket. The police officer searched through the

pocket and found that the hard object was a brick of hashish. However, the police officer did not find a gun, nor did he find any coins or any items sold in a coin shop.

"Where'd you stash the coins?" "I already told you, I did not rob any shop." The police officer demanded that the man produce his driver's license. The driver's license revealed that the man was not the individual for whom the police officer had been searching. Nonetheless, the police officer handcuffed the man and drove him to the coin shop, hopefully to be identified by the coin shop's owner.

"No, that's not the guy," said the owner of the coin shop. "Wearing similar clothes, but that's not he." The police officer then seized the hashish and arrested the man for possession of hashish. At trial, the man made a motion to suppress the hashish. The motion will:

A. Fail because the hashish was obtained based on a pat down search of the man conducted pursuant to the police officer's reasonable belief that the man had robbed the shop and the police officer feared for his safety.

B. Fail because police officers may always conduct pat-down searches of pedestrians for any reason. Warrants are only required inside buildings.

C. Succeed because the police officer had no reason to search the man's pockets.

D. Succeed because the owner of the coin shop proved the man's innocence.

84. On June 1, two police officers in a U.S. state secured a warrant to search a man's house. However, inundated with paperwork and other law enforcement matters, the officers were unable to act on the warrant until July 7. Once they did execute the warrant, they were able to seize the anticipated cocaine from the man's apartment. The man was arrested for possession of cocaine. At trial, the man filed a motion to suppress the cocaine. The motion will:

A. Succeed because warrants always expire ten days after they are secured.

B. Succeed, unless the warrant was executed in daytime hours.

C. Fail because the officers acted on the warrant on July 7.

D. Fail, if the warrant had not expired.

85. A police officer received a credible tip that the resident of a particular house in a U.S. state was "armed and dangerous." He quietly approached the house and busted down the front door without giving notice or warning to the resident

or anyone else inside the house. He bolted through the house and found large amounts of drugs and illegal assault rifles. The resident was arrested for possession of narcotic and illegal assault rifles. At trial, the resident made a motion to suppress the evidence.

The motion will:

A. Succeed because the officer did not give notice of his authority and purpose for entering the resident's home.

B. Succeed because the officer unnecessarily broke down the front door to gain entry.

C. Fail under the narcotics exception to the warrant requirement.

D. Fail because this was deemed a legitimate exigency.

86. A police officer received a reliable tip that a parolee in a U.S. state was engaging in illegal activities within his home. The police officer went to the home and arrested and handcuffed the parolee without incident. Knowing that the parolee had extremely dangerous associates and fearing that these associates might be present in the home, the police officer looked through large mahogany cabinets in the living room as well as closets in an immediately adjoining hallway, fearing that attackers could likely be present. During his search, they found large amounts of cocaine. At trial, the parolee made a motion to suppress the cocaine. The motion will:

A. Succeed because the officer did not have probable cause to search the cabinets and closets.

B. Succeed because the officer did not have reasonable suspicion to search the cabinets and closets.

C. Fail because there was an actual threat to the officer.

D. Fail because the officer felt threatened.

87. An American citizen was about to return to the USA from Europe. While waiting to board the airplane, local police officers grabbed his carry-on bag and search it, discovering cocaine inside. The man was immediately arrested and sentenced to spend the rest of his life in prison. On appeal, the man alleged that his Fourth Amendment rights had been violated and that his sentence constituted cruel and unusual punishment in violation of his Eighth Amendment rights.

The appellate court will hold that:

A. Both the Fourth and the Eighth Amendment were violated.

B. The Eighth Amendment was violated, but the Fourth Amendment was not violated.

C. The Fourth Amendment was violated, but the Eighth Amendment was not violated.

D. Neither the Fourth nor the Eighth Amendment applies in this case.

88. Believing that a woman's house in a U.S. state contained both illegal weapons and stolen property, a police officer applied for a warrant to search her house for both weapons and stolen property. However, the warrant as signed by the magistrate authorized only to search for stolen property. The officer executing the warrant did not find any stolen property, but found the weapons in plain view. The woman was arrested for illegal possession of weapons. At trial, the woman made a motion to suppress the weapons. The motion will:

A. Succeed because the officer knew about the weapons, given the fact he applied for a warrant indicating weapons.

B. Succeed because the officer hoped to find the weapons, given the fact he applied for a warrant indicating weapons.

C. Succeed because the weapons were not discovered "inadvertently" for the plain view doctrine to apply, given the fact the officer applied for a warrant indicating weapons.

D. Fail because it was a valid search.

89. Three officers in a U.S. state executed a valid warrant to search for drugs in a neighborhood bar known for drug use. Once lawfully inside the bar, the officers arrested and handcuffed individual customers who appeared suspicious and then searched their pockets, purses, and wallets for any indicia of drugs. The search of the customers was:

A. Lawful because people who frequent a bar known for drug use are likely to have drugs on their person.

B. Lawful because the officers searched pockets, purses, and wallets.

C. Unlawful because the officers had no probable cause to arrest the customers.

D. Unlawful because the search warrant only allowed the officers to search the bar, not the personal effects of the customers.

90. Police officers in a U.S. state assumed that most graduate students in public universities either bought or sold illegal drugs. One day, the officers came to a student's classroom and, without a warrant, proceeded to frisk that student. Drugs were discovered in his pockets. He was arrested and charged with possession of illegal drugs with intent to

sell. At trial, he moved to suppress the drugs. His motion will:

A. Succeed because the student's Fourth Amendment rights were violated and because there was an invasion of his privacy.

B. Succeed because the student was humiliated in front of his classmates.

C. Fail because the police officers' actions were reasonable.

D. Fail because the Fourth Amendment does not apply in public universities.

91. A U.S. government office inside the United States exploded and a bomb was the suspected cause. In addition, experts believed that the bomb was likely detonated from inside the building. As people started to run out of the building, agents from the Federal Bureau of Investigation (who also had offices in the building) detained them and would not let them leave the building until they could be ruled out as suspects in the bombing. Was this detention lawful?

A. No because the agents had no reason to suspect other people in the building.

B. No because the agents had no probable cause to detain the people in the building.

C. Yes because Federal Bureau of Investigation agents can detain anyone they wish for as long as they wish.

D. Yes because, under the circumstances, temporary detention of the people in the building was warranted.

92. A man was arrested for the murder of a doctor who performed abortions. He requested a jury trial. During voir dire, the prosecutor excluded for cause any potential jurors who supported the motives of the individual who killed the doctor. The man was found guilty and sentenced to death. Before he was executed, he executed a writ of habeas corpus, alleging that he had not been given an impartial jury of his peers and that people who had supported his motives in killing the doctors had been specifically excluded from his jury. Will the man's writ be successful?

A. No because the jurors were properly excluded.

B. No because murder is illegal.

C. Yes because the jurors were improperly excluded.

D. Yes because man was justified in his actions in killing the doctor under the Unborn Infant Protection Act.

93. A man was arrested for murdering, dismembering, and eating his wife. He requested a jury trial. During voir dire, the prosecutor excluded for cause any potential jurors who opposed the death penalty (which the prosecutor planned to seek if the man was found guilty). The man was found guilty and sentenced to death by firing squad. Before he was executed, he executed a writ of habeas corpus, alleging that he had not been given an impartial jury of his peers because opponents of the death penalty had been specifically excluded from his jury. Will the man's writ be successful?

    A. Yes because the jurors were improperly excluded.

    B. Yes because the death penalty violates the Eighth Amendment.

    C. No because the jurors were properly excluded.

    D. No because the death penalty is the law of the land.

94. A man in a U.S. state ran a red light late one night and was pulled over by a police officer. The police officer asked the man to step out of the car because the man's pupils were dilated and he was talking extremely fast. The police officer suspected cocaine use. The man failed a field sobriety test and was taken back to the police station. There, the man agreed to waive his Miranda rights and talk to the police officer. The man, however, insisted that nothing be put in writing and requested that all tape recorders be turned off. The man also indicated that he would not make a written statement outside the presence of counsel. The man proceeded to make incriminating statements.

    Should the man's incriminating statements be suppressed?

    A. No because the questioning was consistent with the Fifth Amendment to the United States Constitution.

    B. Yes because when the man requested that none of his statements be put in writing or tape-recorded, the officers should have realized that the man did not understand that his statements could be used as evidence even if not written down or recorded.

    C. Yes because the man's waiver of his Miranda rights was conditional.

    D. Yes because the man indicated he would not make a written statement outside the presence of counsel.

95. Nine police officers lawfully entered the house of a female suspect in a crime at 3:00 a.m. and questioned her in her own bedroom without reading her the Miranda warnings. During this

questioning session, she made several incriminating statements. Should the officers have read the woman her Miranda rights prior to questioning her?

A. No because she was not being questioned at the police station.

B. No because a suspect cannot be in custody in his own home.

C. Yes because there were nine officers in the woman's bedroom.

D. Yes because the woman voluntarily waived her Miranda rights.

96. A graduate student who was a "person of interest" in a police investigation accepted an invitation from a police officer to come down to the police station for questioning, but was not under arrest. Would the student be deemed to be in custody?

A. Yes because the questioning took place at the police station.

B. Yes because the student was invited by a police officer.

C. No, unless the invitation appeared to be a kind of offer that could not be reasonably refused.

D. No because the student was not under arrest.

97. A waitress was pulled over by a police officer under suspicion of drunk driving. The officer proceeded to ask the waitress a series of questions, trying to ascertain whether the waitress had been drinking, how much she had been drinking, and when she had had her last drink. Would the police officer's questioning of the waitress be considered custodial interrogation?

A. Yes because the person doing the questioning was a police officer.

B. Yes because the police officer detained the waitress.

C. No because the waitress had not been arrested.

D. No, unless the police officer knew that the waitress had been drinking alcohol.

98. A man in a U.S. state was on trial for murder. Before the matter came to trial, the court determined that he was indigent. He was provided with a public defender. A week later at his arraignment, the man pleaded guilty to the offense. The judge did not ask the man any questions concerning his plea and the man did not in any way address the court. He was found guilty based on the plea and sentenced to death by guillotine.

Will his conviction be reversed on appeal?

A. Yes because he was denied due process of law.

B. No because this was no reversible error, since he was found guilty based on credible eyewitness testimony.

C. No because he pled guilty.

D. No because there cannot be reversible error when the defendant admits guilt as was the case here.

99. A man pled guilty to two criminal charges in a U.S. state. The man's attorney successfully negotiated a plea bargain with the state where the man would plead guilty to both charges if the state would impose concurrent prison sentences totaling 25 years in prison. The attorney also advised the man that the man would be required to serve at least one-third of the sentence before he would be eligible for parole.

The man signed a plea agreement, indicating that he understood the charges against him and the consequences of pleading guilty and that his pleas had not been induced by "force, fear, threat, promise or intimidation."

Almost three years later, the man filed a federal habeas corpus petition, alleging that his guilty plea had been involuntary because his attorney had informed him that the man would be eligible for parole after serving one-third of the sentence. In fact, because the man had been convicted of a separate felony more than five years prior to the two offenses discussed above, he was classified as a "second offender" and, under state law, he would be required to serve one-half of the sentence before being eligible for parole. The man asked the State Appellate Court to reduce his sentence to a term of years that would result in his becoming eligible for parole in conformance with his original plea-bargain expectations. Will the man be granted relief?

A. No, if the man did not allege in his habeas petition that he would have pled not guilty and insisted on going to trial had he been correctly informed about his parole eligibility date.

B. Yes because the court-appointed attorney's constitutionally ineffective performance affected the outcome of the plea bargaining process.

C. Yes because the man guilty plea was not voluntary, intelligent, and knowing.

D. Yes because the man had a mistaken belief as to when he would become eligible for parole.

100. A man was indicted on two felony counts of bookmaking. After negotiations, the man's attorney was able to persuade the district attorney to allow

the man to plead to a lesser-included offense, which carried a maximum sentence of one year in prison upon conviction. The district attorney also agreed to make no recommendations as to length of sentence.

The man subsequently entered his plea of guilty to the lesser offense. The man explained to the sentencing judge that his plea was voluntary, intelligent, and knowing and that he understood all implications of pleading guilty. The man's plea was accepted and a date for sentencing was set.

At the sentencing hearing, a new and different prosecutor recommended that the man be given the maximum one-year sentence. The man's attorney immediately objected to this because the man had been promised that no sentencing recommendations would be made. The sentencing judge proceeded to impose the maximum one-year sentence claiming that the prosecutor's recommendation had no influence whatsoever on his decision. Should the man be allowed to withdraw his guilty plea?

A. Yes because the earlier plea did not irrevocably waive the man's federal constitutional right to a trial.

B. No because the judge was not influenced by the prosecutor's recommendation.

C. No because a plea cannot rest on a promise or agreement of the prosecutor.

D. No because there was a different prosecutor at the sentencing phase of the trial.

END OF QUESTIONS

Q
CRIMINAL
PROCEDURE

CRIMINAL PROCEDURE ANSWERS

1. C is the correct answer. The Fourth Amendment protection against unreasonable and warrantless searches and seizures has been incorporated to the states by way of the Due Process Clause of the Fourteenth Amendment to the United States Constitution as stated in Wolf v. Colorado, 338 U.S. 25 (1949). However, Wolf had said that, while the protection against unreasonable searches and seizures was incorporated to the states, the "fruit of the poisonous tree" doctrine - by which evidence seized in violation of the Fourth Amendment is deemed inadmissible in court - was not incorporated to the states. This aspect of Wolf was overruled by Mapp v. Ohio, 367 U.S. 643 (1961). As a result, any evidence obtained in violation of the Fourth Amendment is now inadmissible in either state or federal proceedings.

   Here, however, the man had no reasonable expectation of privacy in the area searched, here a public place because he abandoned the marijuana joint. Had the man been seized, the answer would have been different. That is, his abandonment of the marijuana would have been the "fruit" of the illegal seizure. But, in California v. Hodari D, 499 U.S. 621 (1991), the Court held that there is no seizure unless there is actual restraint or a submission to police authority. There was no seizure here because the man ran away before the police officer could restrain him.

   Thus, the motion to suppress will fail.

   A and B are incorrect for the reasons discussed in C.

   D is an incorrect statement of law; marijuana possession is a federal crime.

2. A is the correct answer. The Sixth Amendment right to a speedy trial has been incorporated to the states by way of the Due Process Clause of the Fourteenth Amendment to the United States Constitution as stated in Klopfer v. North Carolina, 386 U.S. 213 (1967). In Klopfer, the defendant had to wait eighteen months for a trial, which the U.S. Supreme Court said violated the Sixth Amendment right to a speedy trial. Similarly, in these facts, the woman has had to wait for eighteen months before seeing a judge. Therefore, this would be her best argument.

   B is incorrect because the woman was charged with solicitation to commit prostitution. Under these circumstances, if the arresting officer had been in uniform, the woman would likely not have solicited him for prostitution. Therefore, her reasonable expectation of privacy would not have been violated. Since being undercover would be the only way the police officer could catch someone in the act of solicitation to commit prostitution, there was no violation of the woman's Fourth Amendment rights under these facts.

A CRIMINAL PROCEDURE

C is incorrect because it contradicts the facts, which state that the woman was informed of her rights as required under *Miranda*.

D is incorrect because an entrapment defense requires that the defendant not be criminally predisposed to commit the crime. Here, the woman actively and voluntarily solicited the undercover police officer for prostitution. Thus, she was predisposed to commit the crime. In addition, the police officer did nothing to encourage the woman to solicit him; the woman did so on her own, again confirming that she was predisposed to commit the crime.

3. A is the correct answer. Under Gideon v. Wainwright, 372 U.S. 335 (1963), the Sixth Amendment right to counsel was incorporated to the states by way of the Due Process Clause of the Fourteenth Amendment to the United States Constitution. Note, in Scott v. Illinois, 440 U.S. 367 (1979), the Gideon holding was limited to cases that resulted in incarceration. Here, the man was not told by the judge that he had a right to counsel; he represented himself and he was convicted and sentenced to jail. Therefore, his Sixth Amendment right to counsel was violated, and this would be his best argument on appeal.

B is incorrect because there is nothing in the facts to indicate that his Fifth Amendment right against self-incrimination was violated.

C is incorrect because there is nothing in the facts to indicate that the man's Fourth Amendment right against unreasonable search and seizure was violated.

D is incorrect because there is nothing in the facts to indicate that the man's First Amendment rights (speech, assembly, religion) were violated.

4. D is the correct answer. The Fourth Amendment protection against unreasonable and warrantless searches and seizures has been incorporated to the states by way of the Due Process Clause of the Fourteenth Amendment to the United States Constitution as stated in Wolf v. Colorado, 338 U.S. 25 (1949). However, Wolf had said that, while the protection against unreasonable searches and seizures was incorporated to the states, the "fruit of the poisonous tree" doctrine - by which evidence seized in violation of the Fourth Amendment is deemed inadmissible in court - was not incorporated to the states. This aspect of Wolf was overruled by Mapp v. Ohio, 367 U.S. 643 (1961). As a result, any evidence obtained in violation of the Fourth Amendment is now inadmissible in either state or federal proceedings.

However, while a person has the right to refuse a warrantless search by a police officer, an individual need not be told of his right to refuse a search, provided that there was no police coercion. The test for consent is simply voluntariness under the totality of the circumstances. Florida v. Bostick, 501 U.S. 429 (1991).

Here, the woman voluntarily handed over her purse to the police officer. There is nothing in the facts to indicate any coercion by the police officer. Therefore, the cocaine will be admissible against the woman because the police officer was not required to have a warrant under the circumstances, since the woman voluntarily handed over her purse to be searched (consent exception to the warrant requirement).

A is incorrect for the reasons discussed in D.

B is incorrect because there was no hot pursuit here, since the police officer was already on the bus, so the police officer and the bus' contents were going to the same place at the same time.

C is incorrect because the plain view exception requires that the seized item or items to be in the police officer's plain view. Here, the woman's purse was closed. Thus, the cocaine inside the purse was not in the police officer's plain view.

5. D is the correct answer. The Fourth Amendment protection against unreasonable and warrantless searches and seizures has been incorporated to the states by way of the Due Process Clause of the Fourteenth Amendment to the United States Constitution as stated in Wolf v. Colorado, 338 U.S. 25 (1949). However, Wolf had said that, while the protection against unreasonable searches and seizures was incorporated to the states, the "fruit of the poisonous tree" doctrine - by which evidence seized in violation of the Fourth Amendment is deemed inadmissible in court - was not incorporated to the states. This aspect of Wolf was overruled by Mapp v. Ohio, 367 U.S. 643 (1961). As a result, any evidence obtained in violation of the Fourth Amendment is now inadmissible in either state or federal proceedings.

Under the Exclusionary Rule of the Fourth Amendment, if there was unlawful governmental activity and illegal evidence is discovered as a result of that activity, that evidence is generally to be suppressed. See Wong Sun v. United States, 371 U.S. 471 (1963).

Here, it is stipulated in the facts that the law that was the basis for the arrest was deemed unconstitutional. Since the arrest and follow-up search were the fruit of that arrest, the evidence obtained in the arrest (the marijuana) must be suppressed under the Exclusionary Rule.

A and C are incorrect for the reasons discussed in D.

B is incorrect because there is no drug exception to the warrant requirement.

6. B is the correct answer. The Fourth Amendment protection against unreasonable and warrantless searches and seizures has been incorporated to the states by way of the Due Process Clause of the Fourteenth Amendment to the United States Constitution as stated in

Wolf v. Colorado, 338 U.S. 25 (1949). However, Wolf had said that, while the protection against unreasonable searches and seizures was incorporated to the states, the "fruit of the poisonous tree" doctrine - by which evidence seized in violation of the Fourth Amendment is deemed inadmissible in court - was not incorporated to the states. This aspect of Wolf was overruled by Mapp v. Ohio, 367 U.S. 643 (1961). As a result, any evidence obtained in violation of the Fourth Amendment is now inadmissible in either state or federal proceedings.

Here, the marijuana was located in an open field and was readily visible to anyone passing by. Thus, neither probable cause nor a warrant was needed to seize it under the open fields exception to the warrant requirement. Oliver v. United States, 466 U.S. 170 (1984).

A is incorrect because the field was not part of the curtilage of the man's home; it was located one mile away from the man's home, and the police did not know that the field belonged to the man until they conducted a search to discover who the owner of the field was.

C and D are incorrect for the reasons discussed in B.

7. A is the correct answer. The Fourth Amendment protection against unreasonable and warrantless searches and seizures has been incorporated to the states by way of the Due Process Clause of the Fourteenth Amendment to the United States Constitution as stated in Wolf v. Colorado, 338 U.S. 25 (1949). However, Wolf had said that, while the protection against unreasonable searches and seizures was incorporated to the states, the "fruit of the poisonous tree" doctrine - by which evidence seized in violation of the Fourth Amendment is deemed inadmissible in court - was not incorporated to the states. This aspect of Wolf was overruled by Mapp v. Ohio, 367 U.S. 643 (1961). As a result, any evidence obtained in violation of the Fourth Amendment is now inadmissible in either state or federal proceedings.

Once there is probable cause of contraband in a car, the whole car can be searched – including the search of closed containers. See California v. Acevedo 500 U.S. 565 (1991).

Here, the woman was driving her automobile faster than the posted speed limit. The police officer, thus, had probable cause to pull her over. The police officer then asked the woman if he could search the passenger area of the woman's automobile. The woman consented when she said, "Yes." The police officer then found the closed bag in the back seat and in it was LSD (contraband).

This, in turn, gave the police officer probable cause to search the rest of the automobile, including the trunk. Because the police officer had probable cause to search the trunk, he had probable cause to open the suitcase that he found inside the trunk where the $10,000 worth of LSD was found.

His search was, therefore, lawful under the automobile exception to the warrant requirement.

B is incorrect because the LSD was inside the trunk of the woman's automobile and inside a closed suitcase. The LSD was thus not in plain view - i.e., it could not be seen without opening or moving something.

C is incorrect because there was no immediate danger or hot pursuit.

D is incorrect because there is no recognized drug exception to the warrant requirement.

8. C is the correct answer. Once an individual is formally charged, he possesses the Sixth Amendment right to counsel. If he invokes the right to counsel, the police can neither directly nor indirectly (via use of an informant) interrogate him on the charged crime. Massiah v. United States, 377 U.S. 201 (1964). However, unlike the Fifth Amendment Miranda protection, the Sixth Amendment protection extends only to interrogation regarding the indicted/arraigned crime. It is "offense-specific." McNeil v. Wisconsin, 501 U.S. 171 (1991). (This can easily be remembered by the phrase, "The Sixth Amendment is specific; the Fifth Amendment is full.")

Here, the woman was formally charged with the crime of forgery and retained an attorney to represent her. The police officer then called the woman on the telephone and asked her about an unrelated crime. Because the crime was unrelated to the forgery charge, the woman's Sixth Amendment right to counsel was not violated. (Note, the woman had been released on bail and was, thus, not in custody at the time. As a result, Miranda rights did not apply here.)

A is incorrect because it is irrelevant whether the confession was given over the telephone or in person.

B is incorrect because it is irrelevant whether the confession was given voluntarily if the woman had had a right to counsel at the time of the confession. However for the reasons discussed in C, she did not have a right to counsel at the time of the confession.

D is incorrect for the reasons discussed in C.

9. A is the correct answer. Under the Sixth Amendment to the United States Constitution, which has been incorporated to the states by way of the Due Process Clause of the Fourteenth Amendment to the United States Constitution, all criminal defendants have a right to counsel, which is presumed to include the right to effective counsel. When an attorney misses the filing deadline of an appeal of right, ineffective counsel

is presumed. Lozada v. Deeds, 498 U.S. 430 (1991). Here, the attorney missed the filing deadline for the appeal. Thus, ineffective counsel would be presumed. As a result, the woman's Sixth Amendment right to counsel has been violated, so her collateral challenge will succeed.

B is incorrect because, although Strickland v. Washington, 466 U.S. 668 (1984) ordinarily required prejudice to the verdict, prejudice is not necessary when the attorney misses a filing deadline under Lozada. Here even though the facts state that there was overwhelming evidence that the woman was guilty (thus, no prejudice to her), prejudice is not a factor in determining whether or not there was ineffective assistance of counsel when a filing deadline has been missed as was the case here.

C is incorrect because, since all attorneys are state-licensed, it is irrelevant that the attorney was privately retained.

D is incorrect because a collateral appeal is allowed on this issue. See Strickland.

10. D is the correct answer. The prohibition against cruel and unusual punishment from the Eighth Amendment to the United States Constitution has been incorporated to the states by way of the Due Process Clause of the Fourteenth Amendment. Robinson v. California, 370 U.S. 660 (1962). The U.S. Supreme Court has ruled that the introduction of "victim impact" statements at capital sentencing hearings does not violate the prohibition against cruel and unusual punishment. Payne v. Tennessee, 501 U.S. 808 (1991).

Here, the man was found guilty of murder, a capital crime. The prosecutor introduced the victim impact statements at this time, thereby complying with Payne. Consequently, the victim impact statements were admissible.

A, B and C are incorrect for the reasons discussed in D.

11. C is the correct answer. The prohibition against cruel and unusual punishment from the Eighth Amendment to the United States Constitution has been incorporated to the states by way of the Due Process Clause of the Fourteenth Amendment. Robinson v. California, 370 U.S. 660 (1962). To satisfy an Eighth Amendment claim of cruel and unusual punishment by a prisoner, it must be shown that the punishment was cruel and unusual and that the warden was intentionally indifferent to the condition of the prisoner in question. See, e.g., Wilson v. Seiter, 501 U.S. 294 (1991).

Here, the woman asserted a claim that she had been sexually molested while in prison and that this was cruel and unusual punishment. For the reasons discussed above, in order to prevail, the woman will need to show that the molestation constituted cruel and unusual punishment and that the warden was intentionally indifferent to the molestation.

A, B, and D are incorrect for the reasons discussed in C because A, B, and D each only discuss part of what is required for a prisoner to prevail on a claim of cruel and unusual punishment, while C discusses everything that a prisoner must show in order to prevail on such a claim.

12. D is the correct answer. The prohibition against cruel and unusual punishment from the Eighth Amendment to the United States Constitution has been incorporated to the states by way of the Due Process Clause of the Fourteenth Amendment. Robinson v. California, 370 U.S. 660 (1962).

    In Kennedy v. Louisiana, 554 U.S. 407 (2008), it was held that the death penalty as a punishment for child rape where the child victim did not die violated the Eighth Amendment.

    Here as in Kennedy, the man was convicted of child rape, and the child did not die. Consequently, sentencing him to death violated the Eighth Amendment and the man will, thus, prevail in his appeal.

    A is incorrect because none of the Fifth Amendment rights have been invoked under these facts.

    B is incorrect because none of the Fourth Amendment rights have been invoked under these facts.

    C is incorrect because none of the Sixth Amendment rights have been invoked under these facts.

13. A is the correct answer. The Fourth Amendment protection against unreasonable and warrantless searches and seizures has been incorporated to the states by way of the Due Process Clause of the Fourteenth Amendment to the United States Constitution as stated in Wolf v. Colorado, 338 U.S. 25 (1949). However, Wolf had said that, while the protection against unreasonable searches and seizures was incorporated to the states, the "fruit of the poisonous tree" doctrine - by which evidence seized in violation of the Fourth Amendment is deemed inadmissible in court - was not incorporated to the states. This aspect of Wolf was overruled by Mapp v. Ohio, 367 U.S. 643 (1961). As a result, any evidence obtained in violation of the Fourth Amendment is now inadmissible in either state or federal proceedings.

    In United States v. Jones, 132 S. Ct. 945 (2012), the Supreme Court found that the installation of a global positioning system (GPS) device under an automobile violated the reasonable expectation of privacy of the husband of the automobile's owner, who regularly drove that automobile.

    Here, the reasonable expectation of

privacy was even higher than in Jones because it was the actual owner of the automobile, rather than a spouse, who was arrested. The facts stipulate that throughout the month that the police monitored the automobile's activity, the automobile's owner regular drove the automobile. The facts further stipulate that the police discovered the automobile's owner's meetings with the terrorists solely because of the use of the GPS device.

Since the automobile's owner had a reasonable expectation of privacy and because the facts stipulate that the police had no probable cause to install the GPS device in the first place, the installation of the GPS device under the automobile violated the reasonable expectation of privacy of the automobile's owner.

Therefore, the automobile's owner motion will be granted because the charges against him were based solely upon the information obtained from the police's unconstitutional use of the GPS device.

B is incorrect because the man was not arrested for associating with the known terrorists; he was arrested because his meetings with the known terrorists led the police to believe that the automobile's owner was plotting an act of terrorism.

C and D are incorrect for the reasons discussed in A.

14. B is the correct answer. The Fourth Amendment protection against unreasonable and warrantless searches and seizures has been incorporated to the states by way of the Due Process Clause of the Fourteenth Amendment to the United States Constitution as stated in Wolf v. Colorado, 338 U.S. 25 (1949). However, Wolf had said that, while the protection against unreasonable searches and seizures was incorporated to the states, the "fruit of the poisonous tree" doctrine - by which evidence seized in violation of the Fourth Amendment is deemed inadmissible in court - was not incorporated to the states. This aspect of Wolf was overruled by Mapp v. Ohio, 367 U.S. 643 (1961). As a result, any evidence obtained in violation of the Fourth Amendment is now inadmissible in either state or federal proceedings

Although the Fourth Amendment prevents illegally seized evidence from being used in the case-in-chief, illegally seized evidence can be used to impeach. United States v. Havens, 446 U.S. 620 (1980).

Here, the facts indicate that the cocaine was illegally seized, and that it was introduced to impeach the testimony of the man, who had taken the stand in his own defense. Therefore, it was proper to introduce the cocaine into evidence to impeach the man's testimony.

A and D are incorrect because the introduction of the cocaine was not an error, whether harmless or harmful as discussed in B.

C is incorrect for the reasons discussed in B.

15. C is the correct answer. The prohibition against cruel and unusual punishment from the Eighth Amendment to the United States Constitution has been incorporated to the states by way of the Due Process Clause of the Fourteenth Amendment. Robinson v. California, 370 U.S. 660 (1962).

In Harmelin v. Michigan, 501 U.S. 957 (1991), the U.S. Supreme Court held that a state law mandating a sentence of life in prison without the possibility of parole for a conviction of possession of 650 or more grams of cocaine may have been cruel, but was not unusual. Because the Eighth Amendment only prohibits punishments that are both cruel and unusual, the Supreme Court held that the sentence did not violate the Eighth Amendment because such a sentence, while possibly cruel, was not unusual. The case also held that there is no requirement under the Eighth Amendment that the punishment be proportionate to the crime.

Here as is Harmelin, the man was sentenced to a mandatory sentence of life in prison without the possibility of parole under a state law mandating such a sentence for a conviction of possession of over 650 grams of cocaine. Thus, the man's constitutional challenge will not be successful.

A is incorrect for the reasons discussed in C.

B and D are incorrect because it is irrelevant whether cocaine possession is a serious crime.

16. C is the correct answer. Under the Sixth Amendment to the United States Constitution, which has been incorporated to the states by way of the Due Process Clause of the Fourteenth Amendment to the United States Constitution, all criminal defendants have a right to counsel, which is presumed to include the right to effective counsel.

Under Padilla v. Kentucky, 130 S. Ct. 1473 (2010), criminal attorneys must advise their clients of the immigration consequences of guilty pleas. Failure to do so violates the clients' right to effective counsel under the Sixth Amendment.

Here as in Padilla, the man was charged with transportation of marijuana for sale, but the criminal attorney failed to advise him of the immigration consequences of a guilty plea. Thus, the man's Sixth Amendment right to effective counsel was violated. As a result, he will be able to successfully reopen and vacate his conviction.

A is incorrect because the Padilla Court expressly rejected the argument that deportation is a mere collateral consequence of a guilty plea. Rather, Padilla said as discussed in C, that criminal attorneys have an affirmative duty to effectively advise their clients of the immigration consequences of guilty pleas under the Sixth Amendment.

B is incorrect for the reasons discussed in C.

D is incorrect because deportation has been held to not be punishment but rather, an administrative action taken against certain non-U.S. citizens, nor is it cruel or unusual. See, e.g., Wong Wing v. United States, 163 U.S. 228 (1896).

17. B is the correct answer. The privilege against self-incrimination under the Fifth Amendment to the United States Constitution has been incorporated to the states by way of the Due Process Clause of the Fourteenth Amendment. Brown v. Mississippi, 297 U.S. 278 (1936), Malloy v. Hogan, 378 U.S. 1 (1964).

In Brown, the United States Supreme Court held that confessions extracted through the use of force or violence violated both the Due Process Clause of the Fourteenth Amendment and the privilege against self-incrimination under the Fifth Amendment.

Here as in Brown, the man's confession was obtained through force. (The man was punched repeatedly until he confessed to the rape.) As a result, the man will be successful in his appeal because the methods used to obtain his confession were coercive.

A is incorrect because if the investigator worked for the police and he questioned the man, the man should have been given his Miranda rights. However, a non-Mirandized confession as was the case here, can be admitted under certain circumstances, but a coerced confession can never be admitted. Therefore, whether or not the investigator worked for the police is only relevant if the investigator used force to obtain the confession. However, A does not address the issue of force. It is, thus, a wrong answer.

C is incorrect for the reasons discussed in B.

D is incorrect because a confession obtained through coercion is by definition not voluntary.

18. A is the correct answer. The privilege against self-incrimination under the Fifth Amendment to the United States Constitution has been incorporated to the states by way of the Due Process Clause of the Fourteenth Amendment. Brown v. Mississippi, 297 U.S. 278 (1936), Malloy v. Hogan, 378 U.S. 1 (1964).

In Brown, the United States Supreme Court held that confessions extracted through the use of force or violence violated both the Due Process Clause of the Fourteenth Amendment and the privilege against self-incrimination under the Fifth Amendment.

However, in Arizona v. Fulminante, 499 U.S. 279 (1991), the Supreme Court held that even confessions that are coerced can be subject to harmless error analysis. In other words, if the individual would have been convicted even absent the coerced confession, the conviction will not be overturned merely because the confession had been coerced.

Here, only the victim's DNA and the man's DNA were found at the scene of the crime, only the victim's fingerprints and the man's fingerprints were found at the scene of the crime, and a gun registered to the man was found near the scene of the crime. These pieces of evidence alone would have been sufficient to convict the man even absent his confession (which had clearly been coerced due to the police interrogator's beating of the man).

B is incorrect because it is never considered necessary to beat a confession out of a suspect for a crime that has already occurred. However, because the beaten confession under these facts was harmless error as discussed in A, the conviction will not be overturned.

C is incorrect for the reasons discussed in A.

D is incorrect for the reasons discussed in B.

19. D is the correct answer. Under the Sixth Amendment to the United States Constitution, which has been incorporated to the states by way of the Due Process Clause of the Fourteenth Amendment to the United States Constitution, all criminal defendants have a right to counsel, which is presumed to include the right to effective counsel.

In order for there to be a violation of the right to effective counsel, there must be attorney error and prejudice. Strickland v. Washington, 466 U.S. 668 (1984). Here, the man's confession was involuntary. (The police questioned him for hours, refused to allow him to make a telephone call, and did not give him any food or drink. Finally, exhausted and hungry, the man confessed to robbing the liquor store.) Involuntary confessions may not be used for any purpose. (See, e.g., Dickerson v. United States, 530 U.S. 428 (2000).) Therefore, when the prosecutor sought to introduce the man's involuntary confession,and the man's attorney failed to object, this was a per se violation of the man's Sixth Amendment right to effective counsel because there was attorney error (failure to object to the prosecution's introduction of the man's involuntary confession), and there was prejudice (but for the introduction of the man's involuntary confession, the man would likely have not been convicted).

A is incorrect because the First Amendment does not give a person the right to rob a store.

B and C are incorrect because there are

no facts here that indicate an issue of suspect class, nor is there any indication that the man has been treated differently from anyone else similarly situated.

20. B is the correct answer. Under the Sixth Amendment to the United States Constitution, which has been incorporated to the states by way of the Due Process Clause of the Fourteenth Amendment to the United States Constitution, all criminal defendants have a right to counsel.

However, the right to counsel only attaches when the criminal defendant actually says something. In Schmerber v. California, 384 U.S. 757 (1966), the defendant unsuccessfully argued that he should have been able to consult with an attorney prior to submitting to a blood analysis. However, the Supreme Court held that the man did not actually say anything and that the man was, in fact, completely irrelevant to the analysis (other than being the donor of the blood) and that there was, thus, nothing about which he needed to consult an attorney prior to the blood test.

Here, the man's urine was analyzed without the man first being allowed to consult with his attorney. However, like the defendant in Schmerber, the man here was irrelevant to the analysis (other than being the donor of the urine) and did not actually say anything. Thus, his Sixth Amendment right to counsel did not attach here. As a result, his argument will fail.

A is incorrect because there is nothing in these facts to suggest that the man's urine was taken in a cruel or unusual manner.

C and D incorrect for the reasons discussed in B.

21. D is the correct answer. The Fourth Amendment protection against unreasonable and warrantless searches and seizures has been incorporated to the states by way of the Due Process Clause of the Fourteenth Amendment to the United States Constitution as stated in Wolf v. Colorado, 338 U.S. 25 (1949). However, Wolf had said that, while the protection against unreasonable searches and seizures was incorporated to the states, the "fruit of the poisonous tree" doctrine - by which evidence seized in violation of the Fourth Amendment is deemed inadmissible in court - was not incorporated to the states. This aspect of Wolf was overruled by Mapp v. Ohio, 367 U.S. 643 (1961). As a result, any evidence obtained in violation of the Fourth Amendment is now inadmissible in either state or federal proceedings.

There is no Fourth Amendment protection if there was no expectation of privacy. In United States v. Dunn 480 U.S. 294 (1987), the Supreme Court held that there was no expectation of privacy in a barn that was not part of the curtilage of the owner's home.

Here, the barn was located forty miles away from the man's home and was unused. Thus, the man had no significant expectation of privacy vis-à-vis his barn even though the man owned the barn, since the barn was not part of the curtilage of the man's home.

A is incorrect because there was no emergency.

B is incorrect because no warrant was obtained initially. Thus, the good faith exception does not apply here.

C is incorrect because the police officer's "search" was not related to public safety.

22. D is the best answer. The Fourth Amendment protection against unreasonable and warrantless searches and seizures has been incorporated to the states by way of the Due Process Clause of the Fourteenth Amendment to the United States Constitution as stated in Wolf v. Colorado, 338 U.S. 25 (1949). However, Wolf had said that, while the protection against unreasonable searches and seizures was incorporated to the states, the "fruit of the poisonous tree" doctrine - by which evidence seized in violation of the Fourth Amendment is deemed inadmissible in court - was not incorporated to the states. This aspect of Wolf was overruled by Mapp v. Ohio, 367 U.S. 643 (1961). As a result, any evidence obtained in violation of the Fourth Amendment is now inadmissible in either state or federal proceedings.

In California v. Greenwood, 486 U.S. 35 (1988), the Supreme Court held that there was no expectation of privacy for searches of garbage that had been left outside for the purpose of being taken by strangers (i.e., garbage collectors). Thus, there was no Fourth Amendment violation when the garbage was searched by different strangers (police officers).

Here, the facts indicate that the dumpster was outside of the home, on a public sidewalk. Thus, the contents of the dumpster, like the garbage in Greenwood, had been left in a public area for the purpose of being taken by strangers (i.e., garbage collectors). Thus, there was no Fourth Amendment violation when the garbage was searched by a different stranger (the police officer) because the man had no expectation of privacy with regard to this discarded garbage.

A is incorrect because there was no emergency.

B is incorrect because no warrant was obtained initially. Thus, the good faith exception does not apply here.

C is incorrect because the police officer's "search" was not related to public safety.

23. A is the correct answer. The Fourth Amendment protection against unreasonable and warrantless searches and seizures has been incorporated to the states by way of the Due Process Clause

of the Fourteenth Amendment to the United States Constitution as stated in Wolf v. Colorado, 338 U.S. 25 (1949). However, Wolf had said that, while the protection against unreasonable searches and seizures was incorporated to the states, the "fruit of the poisonous tree" doctrine - by which evidence seized in violation of the Fourth Amendment is deemed inadmissible in court - was not incorporated to the states. This aspect of Wolf was overruled by Mapp v. Ohio, 367 U.S. 643 (1961). As a result, any evidence obtained in violation of the Fourth Amendment is now inadmissible in either state or federal proceedings.

Warrants require judicial/magistrate approval and such is either by signature or seal. Here, the facts indicate that the warrant had not been signed by the magistrate. Thus, the warrant was defective.

B is an incorrect statement of law. Arrest warrants may be used against people personally, but search warrants may be used against people personally (e.g., to search the contents of their pockets) as well as against their homes.

C is incorrect because warrants definitely need judicial approval.

D is incorrect because, although the fruits of a search performed in good faith reliance on a warrant later deemed defective does not necessarily require suppression of that evidence, the warrant, itself, is nevertheless still defective.

24. B is the correct answer. The Fourth Amendment protection against unreasonable and warrantless searches and seizures has been incorporated to the states by way of the Due Process Clause of the Fourteenth Amendment to the United States Constitution as stated in Wolf v. Colorado, 338 U.S. 25 (1949). However, Wolf had said that, while the protection against unreasonable searches and seizures was incorporated to the states, the "fruit of the poisonous tree" doctrine - by which evidence seized in violation of the Fourth Amendment is deemed inadmissible in court - was not incorporated to the states. This aspect of Wolf was overruled by Mapp v. Ohio, 367 U.S. 643 (1961). As a result, any evidence obtained in violation of the Fourth Amendment is now inadmissible in either state or federal proceedings.

In order to conform to the Fourth Amendment's warrant requirements, search warrants must state with particularity the items to be seized, and the items to be seized must be related to the crime in question. Massachusetts v. Sheppard 468 U.S. 981 (1984).

Here, the woman was suspected of murder. However, the warrant that the police officer submitted to the judge dealt with controlled substances, which had nothing to do with the crime of which the woman was suspected (murder). Therefore, the warrant did not conform to the Fourth Amendment's warrant requirements, and the judge should find it unconstitutional.

A is incorrect because it does not matter that the warrant came from a nearby district, so long as it conformed to the Fourth Amendment's warrant requirements.

C is incorrect for the reasons discussed in B.

D is an incorrect statement of law.

25. D is the correct answer. The Fourth Amendment protection against unreasonable and warrantless searches and seizures has been incorporated to the states by way of the Due Process Clause of the Fourteenth Amendment to the United States Constitution as stated in Wolf v. Colorado, 338 U.S. 25 (1949). However, Wolf had said that, while the protection against unreasonable searches and seizures was incorporated to the states, the "fruit of the poisonous tree" doctrine - by which evidence seized in violation of the Fourth Amendment is deemed inadmissible in court - was not incorporated to the states. This aspect of Wolf was overruled by Mapp v. Ohio, 367 U.S. 643 (1961). As a result, any evidence obtained in violation of the Fourth Amendment is now inadmissible in either state or federal proceedings.

A police officer is not required to second-guess a judge and if a judge erroneously tells a police officer that a search warrant is constitutionally valid, the police officer may utilize that search warrant to execute the search in question, so long as the police officer had a good faith belief that the judge had correctly stated that the warrant was constitutionally valid. Massachusetts v. Sheppard 468 U.S. 981 (1984).

Here, the judge erroneously told the police officer that the search warrant was constitutionally valid. There is nothing in the facts to show that the police officer had any reason to think that the judge had incorrectly stated that the warrant was valid. Therefore, the police officer was acting in good faith and may utilize the warrant to execute the search in question. As a result, the businessman had to allow the police officer into his home to execute the search.

A and B are incorrect for the reasons discussed in D.

C is an incorrect statement of law.

26. A is the correct answer. The Fourth Amendment protection against unreasonable and warrantless searches and seizures has been incorporated to the states by way of the Due Process Clause of the Fourteenth Amendment to the United States Constitution as stated in Wolf v. Colorado, 338 U.S. 25 (1949). However, Wolf had said that, while the protection against unreasonable searches and seizures was incorporated to the states, the "fruit of the poisonous tree" doctrine - by which evidence seized in violation of the Fourth Amendment is deemed inadmissible in court - was not incorporated to the states. This aspect of

Wolf was overruled by Mapp v. Ohio, 367 U.S. 643 (1961). As a result, any evidence obtained in violation of the Fourth Amendment is now inadmissible in either state or federal proceedings.

Under the fruit of the poisonous tree doctrine, evidence that is illegally seized must be suppressed. Nardone v. United States, 308 U.S. 338 (1939).

Here, the facts state the police officer had a good faith belief that the car had been illegally parked. However, the seizure of the car was still unlawful because the car had, in fact, been legally parked. Under the fruit of the poisonous tree doctrine, since the seizure of the car was unlawful, the evidence so discovered is to be suppressed. Thus, the woman's motion will be successful.

B is incorrect because the exclusionary rule is applicable to misdemeanors.

C is incorrect because the inventory exception requires lawful police possession of the property. Here as discussed in A, the police did not have lawful possession of the property (the car) because it had been legally parked, despite the police officer's belief to the contrary.

D is incorrect because the good faith exception requires there to be a warrant. Here, there was no warrant.

27. B is correct. The Fourth Amendment protection against unreasonable and warrantless searches and seizures has been incorporated to the states by way of the Due Process Clause of the Fourteenth Amendment to the United States Constitution as stated in Wolf v. Colorado, 338 U.S. 25 (1949). However, Wolf had said that, while the protection against unreasonable searches and seizures was incorporated to the states, the "fruit of the poisonous tree" doctrine - by which evidence seized in violation of the Fourth Amendment is deemed inadmissible in court - was not incorporated to the states. This aspect of Wolf was overruled by Mapp v. Ohio, 367 U.S. 643 (1961). As a result, any evidence obtained in violation of the Fourth Amendment is now inadmissible in either state or federal proceedings.

A police officer can enter a dwelling if he has probable cause that there is an emergency. A scream furnishes such probable cause. This is called the exigency exception to the warrant requirement. For example, in Brigham City v. Stuart, 547 U.S. 398 (2006), exigency was found where the police entered a dwelling after hearing screams from a loud party when the screams caused the police to believe that someone might be in immediate danger.

Here, similar to what happened in Brigham, the police officer heard the woman screaming, providing him with probable cause to enter her home. Thus, he did not require a warrant, under the exigency exception.

A is incorrect because good faith alone,

without a warrant, is not a recognized exception to the warrant requirement.

C is incorrect because in no way did the woman or her boyfriend consent to the officer's entry. In fact, the woman immediately ordered the police officer to leave her home.

D is incorrect for the reasons discussed in B.

28. D is the correct answer. The Fourth Amendment protection against unreasonable and warrantless searches and seizures has been incorporated to the states by way of the Due Process Clause of the Fourteenth Amendment to the United States Constitution as stated in Wolf v. Colorado, 338 U.S. 25 (1949). However, Wolf had said that, while the protection against unreasonable searches and seizures was incorporated to the states, the "fruit of the poisonous tree" doctrine - by which evidence seized in violation of the Fourth Amendment is deemed inadmissible in court - was not incorporated to the states. This aspect of Wolf was overruled by Mapp v. Ohio, 367 U.S. 643 (1961). As a result, any evidence obtained in violation of the Fourth Amendment is now inadmissible in either state or federal proceedings.

Naked eye surveillance when the officer is lawfully positioned is not a search for Fourth Amendment purposes. California v. Ciraolo, 476 U.S. 207 (1986).

Here, the woman had consented to the officer entering her home, so that the officer could investigate a break-in that had occurred earlier that day. Thus, the officer was legally in the home when he saw the bong. Therefore, his seizure of the bong was not the result of a Fourth Amendment search.

A is incorrect because the observation was not related to the apparent exigency. In other words, there was no concern that the bong might disappear in the immediate future.

B is incorrect because there was no risk assumed here; the police officer was merely in the home to investigate an apparent break-in.

C is incorrect because the plain view exception applies to items that are incriminating. Here, the bong in and of itself was not incriminating, since the bong could have contained lawful substances.

29. B is the correct answer. The Fourth Amendment protection against unreasonable and warrantless searches and seizures has been incorporated to the states by way of the Due Process Clause of the Fourteenth Amendment to the United States Constitution as stated in Wolf v. Colorado, 338 U.S. 25 (1949). However, Wolf had said that, while the protection against unreasonable searches and seizures was incorporated to the states, the "fruit of the poisonous tree" doctrine - by which evidence seized in violation of the Fourth Amendment is

deemed inadmissible in court - was not incorporated to the states. This aspect of Wolf was overruled by Mapp v. Ohio, 367 U.S. 643 (1961). As a result, any evidence obtained in violation of the Fourth Amendment is now inadmissible in either state or federal proceedings.

Here, although the police officer was lawfully in the donut shop, there was no probable cause that the brass case contained cocaine. Thus, the plain view exception to the warrant requirement is unavailable, and the evidence was illegally discovered.

A is incorrect because the mere fact that the case was in the donut shop where the cashier worked does not invalidate the search and seizure provided there was a recognized warrant exception. However as discussed in B, there was no recognized warrant exception in this case.

C is incorrect because good faith alone, without a warrant, is not a recognized exception to the warrant requirement.

D is incorrect because no facts indicate that the cocaine would have inevitably been discovered.

30. C is the correct answer. The Fourth Amendment protection against unreasonable and warrantless searches and seizures has been incorporated to the states by way of the Due Process Clause of the Fourteenth Amendment to the United States Constitution as stated in Wolf v. Colorado, 338 U.S. 25 (1949). However, Wolf had said that, while the protection against unreasonable searches and seizures was incorporated to the states, the "fruit of the poisonous tree" doctrine - by which evidence seized in violation of the Fourth Amendment is deemed inadmissible in court - was not incorporated to the states. This aspect of Wolf was overruled by Mapp v. Ohio, 367 U.S. 643 (1961). As a result, any evidence obtained in violation of the Fourth Amendment is now inadmissible in either state or federal proceedings.

An invited overnight guest has standing to object to the search of his property in the premises and to later move to exclude anything found in a search of his property. Minnesota v. Olson, 495 U.S. 91 (1990).

Here, the police officer had a probable cause to enter the house without a warrant because he thought that he heard a gun shot.

The problem, however, arose when, on the way out of the house, the police officer spotted and then opened the boyfriend's briefcase and found the severed human head inside. The facts state that the boyfriend was an overnight guest. He, therefore had standing to object to this warrantless search of his property for the reasons discussed in Olson.

A is incorrect for the reasons discussed in C.

B is incorrect because, although the police officer had probable cause to enter the home (he thought he heard gunshots), he did not have probable cause to search the boyfriend's briefcase, since the only thing about the briefcase that aroused the police officer's suspicions was the fact that the briefcase appeared expensive.

D is incorrect because LaFave is the name of a hornbook; there is no LaFave doctrine.

31. C is the correct answer. The Fourth Amendment protection against unreasonable and warrantless searches and seizures has been incorporated to the states by way of the Due Process Clause of the Fourteenth Amendment to the United States Constitution as stated in Wolf v. Colorado, 338 U.S. 25 (1949). However, Wolf had said that, while the protection against unreasonable searches and seizures was incorporated to the states, the "fruit of the poisonous tree" doctrine - by which evidence seized in violation of the Fourth Amendment is deemed inadmissible in court - was not incorporated to the states. This aspect of Wolf was overruled by Mapp v. Ohio, 367 U.S. 643 (1961). As a result, any evidence obtained in violation of the Fourth Amendment is now inadmissible in either state or federal proceedings.

    Border searches are an exception to the Fourth Amendment's warrant requirement. In United States v. Montoya De Hernandez, 473 U.S. 531 (1985), the Supreme Court held that officers at a border may engage in a body search when they have reasonable suspicion to do so.

    Here, the woman's pupils were dilated and she appeared impaired. These two facts put together would give rise to a reasonable suspicion that she was under the influence of marijuana. Furthermore, she was at a U.S. border. Consequently, the officers at the border had reasonable suspicion to perform the full body search on the woman without the need to first obtain a warrant. As a result, the woman's motion will not be granted.

    A and B are incorrect for the reasons discussed in C and D.

    D is incorrect because the marijuana was not in plain view; it was under the woman's fingernails. However, the full body search could still be performed for the reasons discussed in C.

32. B is the correct answer. The Fourth Amendment protection against unreasonable and warrantless searches and seizures has been incorporated to the states by way of the Due Process Clause of the Fourteenth Amendment to the United States Constitution as stated in Wolf v. Colorado, 338 U.S. 25 (1949). However, Wolf had said that, while the protection against unreasonable searches and seizures was incorporated to the states, the "fruit of the poisonous tree" doctrine - by which evidence seized in

violation of the Fourth Amendment is deemed inadmissible in court - was not incorporated to the states. This aspect of Wolf was overruled by Mapp v. Ohio, 367 U.S. 643 (1961). As a result, any evidence obtained in violation of the Fourth Amendment is now inadmissible in either state or federal proceedings.

The Skinner v. Railway Labor Executives Association, 489 U.S. 602 (1989) and National Treasury Employees Union v. Von Raab, 489 U.S. 656 (1989) cases indicate that because of the widespread drug problem and public safety, drug testing of railroad employees associated with an accident and customs agents seeking promotion to be lawful under the administrative exception.

Here, the facts indicate that there was a widespread drug problem, which necessitated the city enacting a law that required drug testing here for the same reasons that the drug testing was found necessary in Skinner and in Von Raab. Since drug testing of railroad employees was found to be acceptable even in the absence of a warrant, by logical analogy, police officer drug testing is most probably acceptable as well, since it likewise involves a government agency drug testing its own employees.

A is incorrect because there is no drug exception to the warrant requirement.

C is incorrect because there was no emergency.

D is incorrect because examination of bodily fluids is both a search and a seizure. However, no warrant was required for the reasons discussed in B.

33. D is the correct answer. Under the Sixth Amendment to the United States Constitution, which has been incorporated to the states by way of the Due Process Clause of the Fourteenth Amendment to the United States Constitution, all criminal defendants have a right to counsel and if any jail time is to be served, counsel must be provided to the indigent. Scott v. Illinois, 440 U.S. 367 (1979).

    Here, the facts clearly state that the woman was indigent and she was sentenced to one month in jail after a trial in which she was denied counsel. Therefore, the judge's denial of her request for counsel was erroneous.

    A and B are incorrect for the reasons discussed in D. C is incorrect because it contradicts the facts.

34. C is the correct answer. Under the Sixth Amendment to the United States Constitution, which has been incorporated to the states by way of the Due Process Clause of the Fourteenth Amendment to the United States Constitution, all criminal defendants have a right to a jury trial when the sentence is potentially over six months or when there are additional penalties to demonstrate that the state legislature considers the offense to be serious. Blanton v. North Las Vegas 489 U.S. 538 (1989).

Here, the maximum sentence was five months, which was less than six months. Furthermore, the additional penalties were not sufficiently serious enough to show that the state legislature considered this offense to be serious enough for the right to a jury trial to attach. (In fact, the additional penalties here were identical to the additional penalties in Blanton where a right to a jury trial was not found.) Thus, there was no right to a jury trial here, and the judge's denial was correct.

A and B are incorrect for the reasons discussed in C. D is incorrect because this is not a torts case.

35. D is the correct answer. Under the Sixth Amendment to the United States Constitution, which has been incorporated to the states by way of the Due Process Clause of the Fourteenth Amendment to the United States Constitution, all criminal defendants have a right to a jury trial when the sentence is potentially over six months.

In Williams v. Florida, 399 U.S. 78 (1970), the U.S. Supreme Court held that, while historically juries have consisted of twelve people, there is no actual right to juries of twelve and that a jury of six fulfilled the Sixth Amendment right to a jury.

Here, the crime with which the man was charged carried a potential jail term of eight months. Because eight months is more than six months, the man had a right to a jury trial. Although the jury in this case consisted of seven people, rather than twelve, this was not a violation of the man's Sixth Amendment right to a jury because, while less than twelve people, the jury consisted of more than six people (which was the case in Williams). Thus, the judge's overruling of the man's objection was proper for this reason.

A is incorrect for the reasons discussed in D.

B is incorrect because animals do not sit on juries.

C is incorrect because in Ballew v. Georgia, 435 U.S. 223 (1978), the U.S. Supreme Court held that a jury of five people was too few to satisfy the Sixth Amendment right to a jury. Thus, having a jury of three people would also be too few.

36. B is the correct answer. The protection against double jeopardy from the Fifth Amendment to the United States Constitution has been incorporated to the states by way of the Due Process Clause of the Fourteenth Amendment to the United States Constitution. Benton v. Maryland, 395 U.S. 784 (1969). The protection against double jeopardy protects a person against being tried twice for the same crime.

As a matter of law, conspiracy and its target offense are distinct offenses for double jeopardy purposes. United

States v. Felix, 503 U.S. 378 (1992).

Here, the woman and the man were tried for robbery and for conspiracy to commit robbery. Because conspiracy and the target offense (here, robbery) are separate offenses under Felix, their conviction for both offenses did not violate the Double Jeopardy Clause. Therefore, their convictions will stand.

A is incorrect because the crimes were not prosecuted in separate jurisdictions; they were prosecuted in the same court. Thus, the separate sovereign limitation on double jeopardy protection is inapplicable here.

C is incorrect because conspiracy requires proof of the additional fact that there was an agreement and robbery requires proof of an additional fact that the crime was completed (not just agreed to). Thus, utilizing the traditional analysis from Blockburger v. United States, 284 U.S. 299 (1932), these are separate offenses and, consequently, the convictions for both offenses does not violate double jeopardy.

D is an incorrect statement of law; robbery is not a lesser-included offense of conspiracy to commit robbery. As discussed above, they are separate crimes.

37. C is the correct answer. The Fourth Amendment protection against unreasonable and warrantless searches and seizures has been incorporated to the states by way of the Due Process Clause of the Fourteenth Amendment to the United States Constitution as stated in Wolf v. Colorado, 338 U.S. 25 (1949). However, Wolf had said that, while the protection against unreasonable searches and seizures was incorporated to the states, the "fruit of the poisonous tree" doctrine - by which evidence seized in violation of the Fourth Amendment is deemed inadmissible in court - was not incorporated to the states. This aspect of Wolf was overruled by Mapp v. Ohio, 367 U.S. 643 (1961). As a result, any evidence obtained in violation of the Fourth Amendment is now inadmissible in either state or federal proceedings.

Under Chimel v. California, 395 U.S. 752 (1969) and its progeny, once a person is lawfully placed under arrest, anything within that person's immediate "wingspan" (i.e., the area immediately adjacent to the person from which the person may destroy evidence) may be searched without the need to first obtain a warrant as a search incident to a lawful arrest.

Here, the fleeing felon was lawfully arrested because he had just fled from a robbery that he had committed. The police officer, after placing the felon under arrest, discovered the cocaine inside the felon's jacket pocket, which the felon was then wearing. This was within the felon's "wingspan" and, therefore, the police officer did not require a warrant to search this area and discover the cocaine.

Therefore, the felon's motion will be denied.

A is incorrect for the reasons discussed in C.

B and D are incorrect because there were no exigent circumstances. The felon had been placed under arrest, so there was no danger that he would immediately dispose of the cocaine, since he was not free to do so.

38. D is the correct answer. The Fourth Amendment protection against unreasonable and warrantless searches and seizures has been incorporated to the states by way of the Due Process Clause of the Fourteenth Amendment to the United States Constitution as stated in Wolf v. Colorado, 338 U.S. 25 (1949). However, Wolf had said that, while the protection against unreasonable searches and seizures was incorporated to the states, the "fruit of the poisonous tree" doctrine - by which evidence seized in violation of the Fourth Amendment is deemed inadmissible in court - was not incorporated to the states. This aspect of Wolf was overruled by Mapp v. Ohio, 367 U.S. 643 (1961). As a result, any evidence obtained in violation of the Fourth Amendment is now inadmissible in either state or federal proceedings.

However, an exception to this Exclusionary Rule allows introduction of illegally seized evidence if the prosecution shows by a preponderance that the evidence would inevitably have been discovered. Nix v. Williams, 467 U.S. 431 (1984).

Here, the question asked what was the prosecutor's best argument for allowing in the evidence of the suspect's marijuana possession. At first blush, the evidence about the marijuana appears to have been illegally obtained because the policeman only elicited the confession after beating the suspect to a pulp.

However, since it was stipulated that the policewoman was on the verge of independently discovering the marijuana, the prosecutor's best argument is "inevitable discovery."

Although the facts did not utilize the precise legal standard above, nevertheless, the stipulation indicates the likely applicability of this exception.

A is incorrect because the good faith exception to the Exclusionary Rule requires there to be a warrant. There are no facts that indicate that there was a warrant here.

B is incorrect because, in fact, there was no independent source. The policewoman had not yet discovered the drugs. There was only a hypothetical independent source. This is "inevitable discovery," rather than an independent source. Thus, B is incorrect for the reasons that D is correct.

C is incorrect because as discussed above, the Fourth Amendment has been incorporated to the states by way of the Due Process Clause of the Fourteenth Amendment. Thus, the fact that this was a state case is not a correct answer.

39. C is the correct answer. The Fourth Amendment protection against unreasonable and warrantless searches and seizures has been incorporated to the states by way of the Due Process Clause of the Fourteenth Amendment to the United States Constitution as stated in Wolf v. Colorado, 338 U.S. 25 (1949). However, Wolf had said that, while the protection against unreasonable searches and seizures was incorporated to the states, the "fruit of the poisonous tree" doctrine - by which evidence seized in violation of the Fourth Amendment is deemed inadmissible in court - was not incorporated to the states. This aspect of Wolf was overruled by Mapp v. Ohio, 367 U.S. 643 (1961). As a result, any evidence obtained in violation of the Fourth Amendment is now inadmissible in either state or federal proceedings.

    Although a search warrant allows the detention of the lawful possessor of the premises to be searched, it does not allow the detention of those merely present at the situs of the search. Ybarra v. Illinois, 444 U.S. 85 (1979).

    Here, similar to Ybarra, the woman's two friends were merely at the situs (the woman's home). Therefore, the detention of the two friends was in violation of the Fourth Amendment, and evidence discovered as a result must be suppressed.

    A is incorrect because the lawful possessor of premises to be searched can be detained. This is an inherent power of a search warrant. Michigan v. Summers, 452 U. S. 692 (1981).

    B is incorrect because, although the detention of the woman's friends was unlawful (as discussed in C), this did not aid the woman in any way. "Mere" police illegality, not directly related to evidence discovered against the defendant (here the woman), in no way mandated suppression of evidence against the defendant. Fourth Amendment rights are personal.

    D is incorrect for the reasons discussed in C.

40. C is the correct answer. The Fourth Amendment protection against unreasonable and warrantless searches and seizures has been incorporated to the states by way of the Due Process Clause of the Fourteenth Amendment to the United States Constitution as stated in Wolf v. Colorado, 338 U.S. 25 (1949). However, Wolf had said that, while the protection against unreasonable searches and seizures was incorporated to the states, the "fruit of the poisonous tree" doctrine - by which evidence seized in violation of the Fourth Amendment is deemed inadmissible in court - was not incorporated to the states. This aspect of Wolf was overruled by Mapp v. Ohio, 367 U.S. 643 (1961). As a result, any evidence obtained in violation of the Fourth Amendment is now inadmissible

in either state or federal proceedings.

The language of the Fourth Amendment itself requires probable cause in order for a warrant to be issued. In addition, items observed in "plain view," while lawfully executing a warrant, can be seized. This is a traditional exception to the warrant requirement, and the facts meet the requirements of this exception (probable cause and object was obviously incriminating). See generally Horton v. California, 496 U.S. 128 (1990).

Here, the police officer had a warrant to search the containers in the barn. Once the police officer was looking inside the containers, he found the marijuana. Because the police officer was within his rights to look inside the containers (because of the warrant), anything that he saw inside the containers will be admissible under the "plain view" exception and, thus, no separate warrant was required for the marijuana.

A is incorrect because it only discusses the issue of probable cause for a search warrant and not the seizure of the marijuana under the "plain view" exception (discussed in C, above).

B and D are incorrect because the test for whether there was probable cause, via a confidential informant's tip, is no longer the two-pronged Aguilar-Spinelli test from Aguilar v. Texas, 378 U.S. 108 (1964) and Spinelli v. United States, 393 U.S. 410 (1969), but is simply whether the totality of the circumstances indicate there to be probable cause of crime, contraband, or evidence of crime under Illinois v. Gates, 462 U.S. 213 (1983). Here, under the totality of the circumstances test, there was evidence of a crime (the storing of toxic waste).

41. B is the correct answer. The Fourth Amendment protection against unreasonable and warrantless searches and seizures has been incorporated to the states by way of the Due Process Clause of the Fourteenth Amendment to the United States Constitution as stated in Wolf v. Colorado, 338 U.S. 25 (1949). However, Wolf had said that, while the protection against unreasonable searches and seizures was incorporated to the states, the "fruit of the poisonous tree" doctrine - by which evidence seized in violation of the Fourth Amendment is deemed inadmissible in court - was not incorporated to the states. This aspect of Wolf was overruled by Mapp v. Ohio, 367 U.S. 643 (1961). As a result, any evidence obtained in violation of the Fourth Amendment is now inadmissible in either state or federal proceedings.

Administrative searches are acceptable even without an administrative ("area") warrant, when these searches are based on a valid public policy, there is a regulation allowing such and the area to be searched is considered to be a "closely regulated" business.

The facts of New York v. Burger, 482

U.S. 691 (1987) are directly analogous to the facts of this case. In Burger, junkyards were considered closely regulated, there was an ordinance allowing these regulations, the search was by a police officer and criminal prosecution resulted. It was held to be no Fourth Amendment violation because this was a valid administrative search. Under the facts in this question, there was also a valid ordinance (in this case for pawnshops), and the police officer was searching the pawnshop in order to verify the pawnshop owner's compliance with the ordinance, similar to the police officer in Burger. Thus, the motion to suppress will be denied because there was a valid administrative exception to the warrant requirement in this case.

A is incorrect because no warrant was issued under the given facts, and a warrant is a requirement in order to utilize the good faith exception. In addition, A is also incorrect because the good-faith exception is to the Exclusionary Rule, it is not an exception to the warrant requirement.

C is incorrect for the reasons discussed in B.

D is incorrect for two reasons: First, no facts indicate the police officer to have acted in bad faith. Second, the bad faith of the involved officer is not relevant to the acceptability of an administrative search. The elements required of a proper administrative search were set out above in C and do not include good faith.

42. C is the correct answer. The privilege against self-incrimination under the Fifth Amendment to the United States Constitution has been incorporated to the states by way of the Due Process Clause of the Fourteenth Amendment. Brown v. Mississippi, 297 U.S. 278 (1936), Malloy v. Hogan, 378 U.S. 1 (1964). Miranda interprets the Fifth Amendment's self-incrimination clause.

Here, although it was stipulated in the facts that there was a Miranda violation, the U.S. Supreme Court has indicated that in a federal habeas court (as was the case here), the error must be analyzed under the "substantial and injurious effect" standard. Fry v. Pliler, 551 U.S. 112 (2007). Thus, this is the standard that the prosecution must use to preserve the conviction.

A is incorrect because the "harmless, beyond a reasonable doubt" standard is the standard that must be followed in state court, not federal habeas court as discussed in Fry. Here, the court was a federal habeas court. Thus, the court must follow the "substantial and injurious effect" standard, not the "harmless, beyond a reasonable doubt" standard.

B and D are incorrect for the reasons discussed in C.

43. D is the correct answer. The privilege against self-incrimination under the Fifth Amendment to the United States Constitution has been incorporated to the states by way of the Due Process Clause of the Fourteenth Amendment. Brown v. Mississippi, 297 U.S. 278 (1936), Malloy v. Hogan, 378 U.S. 1 (1964). Miranda interprets the Fifth Amendment's self-incrimination clause. The privilege against self-incrimination includes the right to remain silent.

The Supreme Court has held that the right to remain silent has been scrupulously honored when a defendant invokes the right to remain silent and is then transferred to a different police station, and following a prolonged period without questioning, a different officer questions the defendant about a different crime. Michigan v. Mosley, 423 U.S. 96 (1975).

Here, the woman was arrested for extortion, given her Miranda rights, and invoked the right to remain silent. After a prolonged period (two hours), and after a transfer to a different police station, the woman was interrogated by a different police officer about a murder (which is a different crime from the extortion for which she had invoked her right to remain silent). Consequently, under Mosley, the police had scrupulously honored the woman's right to remain silent and her confession to the murder is, therefore, admissible in the subsequent murder trial.

A and B are incorrect for the reasons discussed in D.

C is an incorrect statement of law.

44. A is the correct answer. Under Gideon v. Wainwright, 372 U.S. 335 (1963), the Sixth Amendment right to counsel was incorporated to the states by way of the Due Process Clause of the Fourteenth Amendment to the United States Constitution.

However, the Sixth Amendment right to counsel only attaches when a suspect has been formally charged with a crime (not just arrested). If the Sixth Amendment right to counsel attaches, an attorney must be present during the post-charging, live identification procedure. If the attorney has not been invited, the out-of-court identification will be suppressed. United States v. Wade 388 *U.S.* 218 (1967).

Here, since there was no formal charging here, the identification is likely admissible.

B is incorrect for the reasons discussed in A.

C and D are incorrect because only extraordinarily unfair or "suggestive" visual identification procedures violate due process. Although a one-on-one identification (known as a "showup") is somewhat suggestive, it is extraordinarily rare for a one-on-one identification is deemed to be a constitutional violation. On the facts of this case, the proximity of the identification with the alleged crime (just five minutes later) and the sureness of the alleged victim undoubtedly indicate the identification to be admissible. Neil v. Biggers 409 U.S. 188 (1972).

45. C is the correct answer. Once an individual is formally charged, he possesses the Sixth Amendment right to counsel. If he invokes the right to counsel, the police can neither directly nor indirectly (via use of an informant) interrogate him on the charged crime. Massiah v. United States, 377 U.S. 201 (1964). However, unlike the Fifth Amendment Miranda protection, the Sixth Amendment protection extends only to interrogation regarding the indicted/arraigned crime. It is "offense specific". McNeil v. Wisconsin, 501 U.S. 171 (1991). (This can easily be remembered by the phrase, "The Sixth Amendment is specific; the Fifth Amendment is full.")

Here, the man was formally charged with racketeering and obtained counsel to represent him on that charge. Therefore, any statements that the man made to the undercover investigator regarding racketeering are inadmissible, while statements that he made regarding other crimes are admissible.

B and D are incorrect for the reasons discussed in C.

A is incorrect because the use of an investigator is constitutional as discussed in C.

46. C is the correct answer. Under Gideon v. Wainwright, 372 U.S. 335 (1963), the Sixth Amendment right to counsel was incorporated to the states by way of the Due Process Clause of the Fourteenth Amendment to the United States Constitution. Note, in Scott v. Illinois, 440 U.S. 367 (1979), the Gideon holding was limited to cases that resulted in incarceration. Here, no jail time was imposed upon the woman. Thus, there was no constitutional violation.

A is incorrect because, while the right to a jury trial attaches when the potential jail time is over six months, the right to counsel attaches if jail time is actually imposed as discussed in C.

B is an incorrect statement of law. Prior convictions may be used to enhance a sentence even if the person was not represented by counsel at the time of the prior conviction. Nichols v. U.S., 511 U.S. 738 (1994).

D is incorrect for the reasons discussed in C.

47. D is the correct answer. Pate v. Robinson, 383 U.S. 375 (1966) indicated that trial judges on their own motion must insure that unless the defendant is mentally competent, he cannot be criminally tried. On the facts given, such an inquiry is clearly warranted. Delusions, such

as the woman's claim that it was "the devil's hand that led" her to commit the murders, indicate a substantial possibility of incompetence, i.e., the inability to aid in the defense and disorientation as to the facts of the crime and reality (see Dusky v. United States, 362 U.S. 402 (1960)). Thus, on the facts given, it was an unconstitutional violation of Fourteenth Amendment due process to not require psychiatric evaluation regarding competency prior to the trial and the woman cannot be tried absent a psychiatric finding of competency.

A is incorrect for the reasons discussed in D.

B is incorrect because the issue at hand is not whether the defendant is insane. Insanity is an affirmative defense. It has a different test from competency. That is, a defendant may be sufficiently oriented and possess sufficient ability to aid in his own defense and still not know what he was doing was wrong. Furthermore, insanity looks into what was the defendant's state of mind at the time of the crime, itself. Competency looks into what was the defendant's state of mind at the time of trial, which was the issue here.

C is factually incorrect because there were sufficient facts indicating extreme mental disorder and, thus, a real possibility of incompetence as discussed in D. The inquiry must be made via a pre-trial psychiatric examination.

48. B is the correct answer. With few exceptions, the Sixth Amendment Confrontation Clause as applied to the states by the Fourteenth Amendment Due Process Clause, mandates that defendants be allowed to confront (cross-examine) adverse witnesses. Pointer v. Texas, 380 U.S. 400 (1965).

Here, the woman was on the stand and testified that the man had used duress in forcing her to participate in the crime. Thus, she was an adverse witness and under the Sixth Amendment Confrontation Clause, the man had a right to confront her by cross-examining her as discussed above.

A is incorrect because a defendant waives his Fifth and Fourteenth Amendment self-incrimination protection by voluntarily taking the stand at the trial. Here, the woman voluntarily took the stand and is, thus, subject to cross-examination even if it would tend to incriminate her. She cannot take the stand, testify on her own behalf and then refuse to answer questions on cross-examination that are reasonably related as here, to her testimony on direct. Brown v. United States, 356 U.S. 148 (1958).

C is incorrect for the reasons discussed in A and B. Although two constitutional rights do conflict here (confrontation and self incrimination), the Supreme Court has struck a reasonable balance, via the above rulings.

D is incorrect because the attorney's rights are not in question under these facts.

49. C is the correct answer. The prohibition against cruel and unusual punishment from the Eighth Amendment to the United States Constitution has been incorporated to the states by way of the Due Process Clause of the Fourteenth Amendment. Robinson v. California, 370 U.S. 660 (1962).

In Harmelin v. Michigan, 501 U.S. 957 (1991), it was held that the Eighth Amendment prohibits punishments that are both cruel and unusual. Here, the man will need to show that death by dismemberment is more painful than other methods of execution in order to meet the "cruel" requirement, and he will need to show that no other states have such laws in order to show that this punishment is also unusual. By showing both, he will meet the standard of "cruel and unusual."

A and B are incorrect because they each only discuss part of what the man must prove. B discusses the "cruel" requirement, and A discusses the "unusual" requirement. As discussed in C, however, the man must prove both in order to prevail.

D is incorrect because in Harmelin, the U.S. Supreme Court also held that there is no requirement under the Eighth Amendment that the punishment be proportionate to the crime.

50. D is the correct answer. When a habeas corpus petitioner does not object to the admissibility of certain evidence at the appropriate time (usually this is pre-trial, but it could be at trial depending on the state's rules), then he is deemed to have "procedurally defaulted" (by failing to contemporaneously object). In such instance, in order for this defaulted claim to be heard on habeas (collateral appeal), he must show good cause why the objection was not brought up at the appropriate time and also must show prejudice to his case. Wainwright v. Sykes, 433 U.S. 72 (1977).

Here, the woman failed to object to the admission of her confession, which had been obtained without the woman being advised of her Miranda rights, at several stages: she did not move for a suppression hearing at pre-trial, she (through her attorney) did not object at trial, she did not appeal to the State Appellate Court, nor did she appeal to the State Supreme Court. Finally, after two years, she did appeal to the State Supreme Court, but by then she had exhausted her chances to object to the admission of the confession, so the State Supreme Court properly dismissed her appeal. Thus, her habeas corpus petition to the U.S. District Court will similarly be unsuccessful, since Miranda is and has been settled law, and the woman will be unable to show "cause" why she did not bring up this claim at the appropriate time.

A is incorrect for the reasons discussed in D.

B is incorrect because it contradicts the facts. In fact, neither the woman nor her attorney said anything about Miranda. Thus, it was not stipulated that Miranda had been given.

C is incorrect because this is not what the woman claimed in her habeas corpus petition; all the woman claimed was that her Miranda rights had been violated, which for the reasons discussed in D, will be unsuccessful. Although the woman's counsel seems to have been ineffective, the court will not *sua sponte* address issues that are not brought up by the petitioner (here, the woman).

51. D is the correct answer. The Fourth Amendment protection against unreasonable and warrantless searches and seizures has been incorporated to the states by way of the Due Process Clause of the Fourteenth Amendment to the United States Constitution as stated in Wolf v. Colorado, 338 U.S. 25 (1949). However, Wolf had said that, while the protection against unreasonable searches and seizures was incorporated to the states, the "fruit of the poisonous tree" doctrine - by which evidence seized in violation of the Fourth Amendment is deemed inadmissible in court - was not incorporated to the states. This aspect of Wolf was overruled by Mapp v. Ohio, 367 U.S. 643 (1961). As a result, any evidence obtained in violation of the Fourth Amendment is now inadmissible in either state or federal proceedings.

In New Jersey v. T.L.O., 469 U.S. 325 (1985), the Supreme Court held that a school official's intrusion into the privacy of a student was "reasonable," since it was necessary to achieve the legitimate end of preserving order in the schools. Here, since the vice-principal was merely investigating whether a school rule had been violated (namely, the rule against smoking cigarettes), his searching of the purse for cigarettes would be deemed "reasonable."

A is incorrect because the girl, a student, had no reasonable expectation of privacy (an element of standing) because the vice-principal, a school official, was merely investigating whether a violation of a school infraction has occurred. B and C are incorrect because they do not specifically discuss the concept of "reasonableness," which is a necessary element for the reasons discussed in D.

52. D is the correct answer. The Fourth Amendment protection against unreasonable and warrantless searches and seizures has been incorporated to the states by way of the Due Process Clause of the Fourteenth Amendment to the United States Constitution as stated in Wolf v. Colorado, 338 U.S. 25 (1949). However, Wolf had said that, while the protection against unreasonable searches and seizures was incorporated to the states, the "fruit of the poisonous tree" doctrine - by which evidence seized in violation of the Fourth Amendment is deemed inadmissible in court - was not incorporated to the states. This aspect of

Wolf was overruled by Mapp v. Ohio, 367 U.S. 643 (1961). As a result, any evidence obtained in violation of the Fourth Amendment is now inadmissible in either state or federal proceedings.

In Hudson v. Palmer, 468 U.S. 517 (1984), the Supreme Court concluded that the requirements of prison security make it unreasonable for prisoners to expect protection for their privacy.

Here as in Hudson, the prisoner was incarcerated. Thus, he had no reasonable expectation of privacy. The heroin could thus be obtained without any warrant. As a result, the balloons of heroin will be admissible against the prisoner.

A is incorrect for the reasons discussed in D.

B is incorrect because there were no exigent circumstances. Since the prisoner was in a cell asleep at the time of the search, it was unlikely that he would be able to quickly dispose of the heroin balloons.

C is incorrect because a tip was not required, since a warrant was not required as discussed in D.

53. C is the correct answer. The Fourth Amendment to the United States Constitution states, "The right of the people to be secure in their persons, houses, papers, and effects, against unreasonable searches and seizures, shall not be violated, and no warrants shall issue, but upon probable cause, supported by oath or affirmation, and particularly describing the place to be searched, and the persons or things to be seized."

Here, the United States Postal Police should have secured a search warrant upon sworn information, describing with reasonable particularity the thing for which the search was to be made. By not doing so, the police acted "without sanction of law" in direct violation of the Fourth Amendment. (See Weeks v. United States, 232 U.S. 383 (1914)).

A and B are incorrect for the reasons discussed in C.

D is incorrect because a defendant is not necessarily entitled to the return of his property merely because his application for its return was seasonal.

54. D is the best answer. The Fourth Amendment to the United States Constitution states, "The right of the people to be secure in their persons, houses, papers, and effects, against unreasonable searches and seizures, shall not be violated, and no warrants shall issue, but upon probable cause, supported by oath or affirmation, and particularly describing the place to be searched, and the persons or things to be seized."

However, the Fourth Amendment, like the rest of the United States Constitution (other than the Thirteenth Amendment), only applies to government entities. This is known as the "state action" requirement.

The facts here are similar to the facts in United States v. Jacobsen, 466 U.S. 109 (1984). In that case as here, the initial search was conducted by a private shipper. As a result, the Fourth Amendment did not apply. The DEA agents were, of course, government agents. However, by the time the agents searched the package, it had already been opened by an entity to which the Fourth Amendment did not apply (the private shipper).

As stated in Jacobsen, "the federal agents did not infringe any constitutionally protected privacy interest that had not already been frustrated as the result of private conduct [here, the action of the private shipper in opening the package]. To the extent that a protected possessory interest was infringed [by taking and testing a small amount of the powder], the infringement was *de minimis* and constitutionally reasonable." (Jacobsen at 126.)

A and B are incorrect for the reasons discussed in D.

C is an incorrect statement of law. However, although DEA agents generally do require a warrant, no warrant was required under these facts for the reasons discussed in D.

55. D is the correct answer. The Fourth Amendment protection against unreasonable and warrantless searches and seizures has been incorporated to the states by way of the Due Process Clause of the Fourteenth Amendment to the United States Constitution as stated in Wolf v. Colorado, 338 U.S. 25 (1949). However, Wolf had said that, while the protection against unreasonable searches and seizures was incorporated to the states, the "fruit of the poisonous tree" doctrine - by which evidence seized in violation of the Fourth Amendment is deemed inadmissible in court - was not incorporated to the states. This aspect of Wolf was overruled by Mapp v. Ohio, 367 U.S. 643 (1961). As a result, any evidence obtained in violation of the Fourth Amendment is now inadmissible in either state or federal proceedings.

Here, the police officers entered the woman's home forcibly without a warrant in violation of the Fourth Amendment's requirement that a warrant be obtained prior to the police entering a person's home. In addition, the woman certainly did not consent to the search, both because she protested and because the police officers forcibly entered her home. Thus, the woman's right to be free of an unreasonable search and seizure (right to privacy) was violated, and as such, the child pornography that was obtained from her home was not admissible against her at trial.

A and B are incorrect statements of law.

C is incorrect because it is irrelevant.

56. D is the correct answer. The Fourth Amendment protection against unreasonable and warrantless searches and seizures has been incorporated to the states by way of the Due Process Clause of the Fourteenth Amendment to the United States Constitution as stated in Wolf v. Colorado, 338 U.S. 25 (1949). However, Wolf had said that, while the protection against unreasonable searches and seizures was incorporated to the states, the "fruit of the poisonous tree" doctrine - by which evidence seized in violation of the Fourth Amendment is deemed inadmissible in court - was not incorporated to the states. This aspect of Wolf was overruled by Mapp v. Ohio, 367 U.S. 643 (1961). As a result, any evidence obtained in violation of the Fourth Amendment is now inadmissible in either state or federal proceedings.

D is correct because, absent other facts, the mere smell of breath mints does not mean the driver is intoxicated. For that reason, the police officer did not have probable cause to search the automobile. As a result, the woman's motion to suppress the cocaine will succeed.

A is incorrect for the reasons discussed in D.

B is incorrect because it is irrelevant what was found in the face of an unlawful search.

C is incorrect because there are no facts that give rise to this exception. Moreover, the inventory exception requires lawful police possession of the property.

57. A is the correct answer. The Fourth Amendment protection against unreasonable and warrantless searches and seizures has been incorporated to the states by way of the Due Process Clause of the Fourteenth Amendment to the United States Constitution as stated in Wolf v. Colorado, 338 U.S. 25 (1949). However, Wolf had said that, while the protection against unreasonable searches and seizures was incorporated to the states, the "fruit of the poisonous tree" doctrine - by which evidence seized in violation of the Fourth Amendment is deemed inadmissible in court - was not incorporated to the states. This aspect of Wolf was overruled by Mapp v. Ohio, 367 U.S. 643 (1961). As a result, any evidence obtained in violation of the Fourth Amendment is now inadmissible in either state or federal proceedings.

The facts here are similar to the facts in One 1958 Plymouth Sedan v. Commonwealth of Pennsylvania, 380 U.S. 693 (1965). In that case as here, the police officer had no probable cause to search the car. The rear of the car could have been low because he was transporting bags of fertilizer home to do gardening work, or for any number of other legal reasons. Thus, a low rear-end does not necessarily speak of illegal activity. As a result, the forfeiture must be reversed.

B is incorrect because there are no facts that give rise to this exception.

Moreover, the inventory exception requires lawful police possession of the property.

C is an incorrect statement of law.

D is irrelevant because the automobile is not contraband. The driver was not asking for the return of the contraband (the cigarettes).

58. D is the correct answer. The Fourth Amendment protection against unreasonable and warrantless searches and seizures has been incorporated to the states by way of the Due Process Clause of the Fourteenth Amendment to the United States Constitution as stated in Wolf v. Colorado, 338 U.S. 25 (1949). However, Wolf had said that, while the protection against unreasonable searches and seizures was incorporated to the states, the "fruit of the poisonous tree" doctrine - by which evidence seized in violation of the Fourth Amendment is deemed inadmissible in court - was not incorporated to the states. This aspect of Wolf was overruled by Mapp v. Ohio, 367 U.S. 643 (1961). As a result, any evidence obtained in violation of the Fourth Amendment is now inadmissible in either state or federal proceedings.

There is no Fourth Amendment protection if there was no expectation of privacy. In United States v. Dunn 480 U.S. 294 (1987), the Supreme Court held that there was no expectation of privacy in a barn that was not part of the curtilage of the owner's home.

Similarly here, the greenhouse was located approximately one mile from the owner's house and was, therefore, not part of the curtilage of the house. As a result, the owner had no expectation of privacy under Dunn. Thus, the discovery of the greenhouse marijuana was lawful.

A is incorrect because off-duty police officers remain police officers and have the same rights and responsibilities that they have when they are on-duty. Furthermore, this would not affect the discovery of the greenhouse marijuana, which was lawful for the reasons discussed in D.

B is incorrect because there was probable cause, since the leaves that the officer noticed as he was initially walking past the field looked like marijuana to him.

C is an incorrect statement of law. A person is permitted to use naked eyes or binoculars to view anything while standing on a public sidewalk as the officer was here.

59. D is the correct answer. Under the Sixth Amendment to the United States Constitution, which has been incorporated to the states by way of the Due Process Clause of the Fourteenth Amendment to the United States Constitution, all criminal defendants have a right to a speedy trial.

However, in Barker v. Wingo, 407 U.S.

514 (1972), the Court held that the right to a speedy trial was waived when the defendant caused the delay.

Here, the six-month delay was caused by the woman (the defendant) asking for several continuances. Because she caused the delay, she waived her right to a speedy trial.

A is incorrect for the reasons discussed in D.

B is incorrect because people have the right to represent themselves under Faretta v. California, 422 U.S. 806 (1975).

C is incorrect because the delay likely caused the woman prejudice. However, the delay was caused by the woman herself as discussed in D.

60. C is the correct answer. Under the Sixth Amendment to the United States Constitution, which has been incorporated to the states by way of the Due Process Clause of the Fourteenth Amendment to the United States Constitution, all criminal defendants have a right to a trial by jury of their peers.

In Taylor v. Louisiana, 419 U.S. 522 (1975), the Court invalidated a state statute that exempted women from jury duty unless the women specifically requested to be included as potential jurors.

Similarly here, the county ordinance in question exempted pregnant women from jury duty unless they specifically requested to be included as potential jurors. This violates the Sixth Amendment right of criminal defendants to be judged by an impartial jury of their peers because it prevents a cross-section of the population from being included as potential jurors, namely, pregnant women. Thus, the woman's challenge will be successful.

A and D are incorrect for the reasons discussed in C.

B is incorrect because this is not a consideration that can legally be taken into account.

61. B is the correct answer. Under the Sixth Amendment to the United States Constitution, which has been incorporated to the states by way of the Due Process Clause of the Fourteenth Amendment to the United States Constitution, all criminal defendants have a right to confront witnesses against them.

In Bullcoming v. New Mexico, 131 S. Ct. 2705 (2011), the Court held that a defendant's Sixth Amendment right to confront witnesses against him was violated when a blood-alcohol test was performed on a sample of the defendant's blood, but an analyst other than the one who had performed the test testified at trial.

Similarly here, the analyst who performed the blood-alcohol test did not testify at trial. Rather, a different analyst testified. This violated the man's right to confront the analyst who performed the test. Therefore, the man's motion to exclude the testimony of the analyst who did testify will be successful.

A and D are incorrect because there are no Eighth Amendment issues arising under this fact pattern.

C is incorrect for the reasons discussed in B.

62. A is the correct answer. Under the Sixth Amendment to the United States Constitution, which has been incorporated to the states by way of the Due Process Clause of the Fourteenth Amendment to the United States Constitution, all criminal defendants have a right to effective assistance of counsel. In Faretta v. California, 422 U.S. 806 (1975), the Court held that the Sixth Amendment right to effective assistance of counsel includes the right to represent oneself.

Here, the man insisted on representing himself, but the court forced him to accept representation by a lawyer (a public defender). This violated the man's constitutional right to represent himself as discussed in Faretta. Consequently, his appeal will be successful for this reason.

B is not a legally valid argument.

C and D are incorrect for the reasons discussed in A.

63. C is the correct answer. The Fourth Amendment protection against unreasonable and warrantless searches and seizures has been incorporated to the states by way of the Due Process Clause of the Fourteenth Amendment to the United States Constitution as stated in Wolf v. Colorado, 338 U.S. 25 (1949). However, Wolf had said that, while the protection against unreasonable searches and seizures was incorporated to the states, the "fruit of the poisonous tree" doctrine - by which evidence seized in violation of the Fourth Amendment is deemed inadmissible in court - was not incorporated to the states. This aspect of Wolf was overruled by Mapp v. Ohio, 367 U.S. 643 (1961). As a result, any evidence obtained in violation of the Fourth Amendment is now inadmissible in either state or federal proceedings.

In Terry v. Ohio, 392 U.S. 1 (1968), the Court held that a police officer may conduct a warrantless pat down of pedestrians if the police officer has a reasonable suspicion that criminal activity is afoot. In the facts here, the officer simply saw the man behaving strangely. This did not rise to the level of reasonable suspicion that criminal activity was afoot. Therefore, the pat down was a violation of the man's Fourth Amendment rights. As a result, the man's motion to suppress introduction of the ring that was obtained as a result of the pat down will succeed.

A is incorrect for the reasons discussed in C.

B is incorrect because it is irrelevant whether or not the ring was stolen. This may be used later as a reason to find the man not guilty, but the question is about whether the ring can be introduced as evidence at trial, not about the man's ultimate guilt or innocence.

D is incorrect because a police officer does not need to have probable cause to pat down pedestrians. The police officer only needs to have reasonable suspicion as discussed in C.

64. D is the correct answer. The Eighth Amendment to the U.S. Constitution states, "Excessive bail shall not be required, nor excessive fines imposed, nor cruel and unusual punishments inflicted."

The excessive fines provision has not been incorporated to the states.

Here, the man was charged and tried in state court and fined $10,000 for stealing a leather jacket worth $200. On appeal, he challenged the amount of the fine as excessive based on the U.S. Constitution. However, since the excessive fines provision has not been incorporated to the states, the man's argument on appeal will not be successful.

A and B are incorrect for the reasons discussed in D.

C is incorrect. While the fine may have been excessive, since the excessive fines provision has not been incorporated to the states, the appellate court will not make this decision based on the U.S. Constitution as C states. (They may decide that the fine was excessive based on some other source, such as the State Constitution, but since C states "as defined under the U.S. Constitution," it is an incorrect answer.)

65. C is the correct answer. The Eighth Amendment to the U.S. Constitution states, "Excessive bail shall not be required, nor excessive fines imposed, nor cruel and unusual punishments inflicted."

In Trop v. Dulles, 356 U.S. 86 (1958), the U.S. Supreme Court held that depriving a soldier of his U.S. citizenship violated the Eighth Amendment's prohibition against cruel and unusual punishment.

The facts here are similar to the facts in Trop. As a result, the soldier's appeal will be successful based on the Eighth Amendment.

A and B are incorrect statements of law.

D is incorrect because nothing in this fact pattern dealt with a violation of the soldier's Fourth Amendment rights.

66. B is the correct answer. The Eighth Amendment to the U.S. Constitution states, "Excessive bail shall not be required, nor excessive fines imposed,

nor cruel and unusual punishments inflicted." In Robinson v. California, 370 U.S. 660 (1962), the Supreme Court held that the "cruel and unusual punishment" provision of the Eighth Amendment has been incorporated to the states.

In Atkins v. Virginia, 536 U.S. 304 (2002), the Court held that executing a mentally retarded man, even one who only had mild mental retardation, constituted unusual punishment and, thus, violated the Eighth Amendment prohibition against cruel and unusual punishment.

Similarly here, the man was mildly mentally retarded. As a result, executing him would be a violation of his Eighth Amendment protection against cruel and unusual punishment. Therefore, his appeal will be successful.

A is an incorrect statement of law.

C is incorrect for the reasons discussed in B.

D is incorrect because even in Atkins, the defendant was only mildly mentally retarded, yet the Supreme Court still held that he could not be executed because executing the mentally handicapped (regardless of the degree of this handicap) was found to violate the Eighth Amendment.

67. C is the correct answer. In Griffin v. California, 380 U.S. 609 (1965), the Court held that the Fifth Amendment privilege against self-incrimination, which includes the right to not testify against oneself, also meant that when a defendant refused to take the stand, the prosecutor could not tell the jury to make any inference about the defendant's guilt when the defendant invoked his right to not testify against himself.

Similarly here, the woman invoked her Fifth Amendment privilege to not take the stand against herself. The prosecutor, thus, violated her Fifth Amendment rights when he told the jury that they could make an inference about the woman's guilt based on her refusal to take the stand.

Thus, her appeal will be successful for this reason.

A and B are incorrect for the reasons discussed in C.

In addition, B is incorrect because this case was in federal court, not state court. Therefore, the Fifth Amendment, rather than the Fourteenth Amendment, is the basis of the woman's rights here.

D is incorrect for the reasons discussed in B.

68. D is the correct answer. The protection against double jeopardy from the Fifth Amendment to the United States Constitution has been incorporated to the states by way of the Due Process Clause of the Fourteenth Amendment to

the United States Constitution. Benton v. Maryland, 395 U.S. 784 (1969). The protection against double jeopardy protects a person against being tried twice for the same crime.

In United States v. Lanza, 260 U.S. 377 (1922), the Supreme Court held that there was no double jeopardy violation when there were overlapping jurisdictions. In that case, a person was tried twice for the same act, first under a state law and then under a federal law. Because there were overlapping jurisdictions in that case, there was no double jeopardy violation.

Similarly here, the man was first tried for and acquitted of the state crime of murder occurring within that state. He was next tried for and convicted of the federal crime of murder occurring inside federal property (in this case, a post office). Because there were overlapping jurisdictions here (state and federal), there was no double jeopardy violation.

Thus, the man's appeal will not be successful.

A and B are incorrect for the reasons discussed in D.

C is an incorrect statement of law.

69. C is the correct answer. In California v. Greenwood, 486 U.S. 35 (1988), the Supreme Court held that there was no expectation of privacy for searches of garbage that had been left outside for the purpose of being taken by strangers (i.e., garbage collectors). Thus, there was no Fourth Amendment violation when the garbage was searched by different strangers (e.g., police officers, or IRS agents as in the case here).

Here, the trash can was located on the sidewalk outside the man's home. It could, therefore, be searched by the IRS agents without a warrant because the man had no expectation of privacy. Consequently, his motion will fail.

A, B, and D are incorrect for the reasons discussed in C.

70. A is the correct answer. The Fourth Amendment to the United States Constitution states, "The right of the people to be secure in their persons, houses, papers, and effects, against unreasonable searches and seizures, shall not be violated, and no warrants shall issue, but upon probable cause, supported by oath or affirmation, and particularly describing the place to be searched and the persons or things to be seized."

However, the Fourth Amendment, like the rest of the United States Constitution (other than the Thirteenth Amendment), only applies to government entities. This is known as the "state action" requirement.

The facts here are similar to the facts in United States v. Jacobsen, 466 U.S. 109 (1984). In that case as here, the initial search was conducted by a private shipper. As a result, the Fourth Amendment did not apply. The federal agents were, of course, government agents. However, by the time the agents searched the package, it had already been opened by an entity to which the Fourth Amendment did not apply (the private shipper).

As stated in Jacobsen, "the federal agents did not infringe any constitutionally protected privacy interest that had not already been frustrated as the result of private conduct [here, the action of the private shipper in opening the package]. To the extent that a protected possessory interest was infringed [by taking and testing a small amount of the powder], the infringement was *de minimis* and constitutionally reasonable." (Jacobsen at 126.)

B is incorrect because the federal agent did not infringe any constitutionally protected privacy interest that had not already been frustrated as the result of private conduct (the employees of the private shipping company).

C is incorrect because a field test can destroy some of the evidence, not all of it, and still render the search and seizure valid. The facts do not indicate all of the evidence was destroyed. As such, the seizure was not unreasonable.

D is incorrect for the reasons discussed in A.

71. D is the correct answer. The Fourth Amendment to the United States Constitution states, "The right of the people to be secure in their persons, houses, papers, and effects, against unreasonable searches and seizures, shall not be violated, and no warrants shall issue, but upon probable cause, supported by oath or affirmation, and particularly describing the place to be searched and the persons or things to be seized."

However, the Fourth Amendment, like the rest of the United States Constitution (other than the Thirteenth Amendment), only applies to government entities. This is known as the "state action" requirement.

In United States v. Jacobsen, 466 U.S. 109 (1984), a private entity viewed the item in question before the government agents did so. As a result, the government agents in that case did not require a warrant to view the item because it had already been opened by a private party.

Here, however, the facts here are similar to the facts in Walter v. United States, 447 U.S. 649 (1980). In that case, videos depicting homosexual activity were sent to a private party who had not ordered those videos. FBI agents were called and the agents viewed the tapes. The Court held that the FBI agents' viewing of the tapes constituted a governmental search and, thus, required a warrant.

Similarly here, the woman (a private party) received tapes that she had not ordered. She did not view them or open them, but instead called the FBI and, like in Walter, the FBI agents viewed the tapes. Thus for the reasons discussed in Walter, the FBI agents engaged in a governmental search when they viewed the tapes and, thus, required a warrant to do so because, unlike the case in Jacobsen, the private party (here, the woman) was not the first party to actually view the items (here, the tapes). Rather, the government agents (the FBI agents) were the first ones to do so.

A and B are incorrect because the woman did not actually view the tapes as discussed in D.

C is incorrect because the agents' job description is irrelevant as to whether or not a warrant is required. A warrant is required whenever government agents conduct a search unless an exception applies. This is true even when the search is part of the agents' job description.

72. A is the correct answer. The Fourth Amendment to the United States Constitution states, "The right of the people to be secure in their persons, houses, papers, and effects, against unreasonable searches and seizures, shall not be violated, and no warrants shall issue, but upon probable cause, supported by oath or affirmation, and particularly describing the place to be searched and the persons or things to be seized."

However here even though the postal employee was by definition a government worker, by taking the hashish home and putting it to personal use by smoking it "to get in a better mood," the employee was not furthering a governmental objective. Thus, his actions were not governed by the Fourth Amendment. (See, e.g., United States v. Smith, 810 F.2d 996 (10th Cir. 1987)).

B, C, and D are incorrect for the reasons discussed in A.

73. C is the correct answer. The Fourth Amendment protection against unreasonable and warrantless searches and seizures has been incorporated to the states by way of the Due Process Clause of the Fourteenth Amendment to the United States Constitution as stated in Wolf v. Colorado, 338 U.S. 25 (1949). However, Wolf had said that, while the protection against unreasonable searches and seizures was incorporated to the states, the "fruit of the poisonous tree" doctrine - by which evidence seized in violation of the Fourth Amendment is deemed inadmissible in court - was not incorporated to the states. This aspect of Wolf was overruled by Mapp v. Ohio, 367 U.S. 643 (1961). As a result, any evidence obtained in violation of the Fourth Amendment is now inadmissible in either state or federal proceedings.

In Illiinois v. Rodriguez, 497 U.S. 177 (1990), the Court said that the police may enter a home as long as consent is given by someone who is apparently in a position to grant that consent. In Rodriguez, that person was the defendant's roommate. Here, consent was given by the kingpin's butler. In both cases, consent was given by someone in an apparent position to give such consent, since both a roommate (who resides there as well) and a butler (whose job includes answering the door and letting people into the home) have apparent authority to grant entry.

In Florida v. Bostick, 501 U.S. 429 (1991). the Court found evidence inadmissible when it had been obtained through intimidation. Here, by contrast, there are no facts to show that the butler was in any intimidated by the police.

A and B are incorrect for the reasons discussed in C.

D is an incorrect statement of law.

74. A is the correct answer. The Fourth Amendment protection against unreasonable and warrantless searches and seizures has been incorporated to the states by way of the Due Process Clause of the Fourteenth Amendment to the United States Constitution as stated in Wolf v. Colorado, 338 U.S. 25 (1949). However, Wolf had said that, while the protection against unreasonable searches and seizures was incorporated to the states, the "fruit of the poisonous tree" doctrine - by which evidence seized in violation of the Fourth Amendment is deemed inadmissible in court - was not incorporated to the states. This aspect of Wolf was overruled by Mapp v. Ohio, 367 U.S. 643 (1961). As a result, any evidence obtained in violation of the Fourth Amendment is now inadmissible in either state or federal proceedings.

As discussed in Stoner v. California, 376 U.S. 483 (1964), a hotel guest, not the staff of the hotel, has standing to give or deny consent to the police to enter and search that guest's hotel room. Here, however, hotel management or staff was entitled to retake possession of a room because it was after check-out time. At this time, the hotel guest no longer had standing to challenge a warrantless search of the hotel room.

B, C, and D are incorrect for the reasons discussed in A.

75. D is the correct answer. The Fourth Amendment protection against unreasonable and warrantless searches and seizures has been incorporated to the states by way of the Due Process Clause of the Fourteenth Amendment to the United States Constitution as stated in Wolf v. Colorado, 338 U.S. 25 (1949). However, Wolf had said that, while the protection against unreasonable searches and seizures was incorporated to the states, the "fruit of the poisonous tree" doctrine - by which evidence seized in violation of the Fourth Amendment is deemed inadmissible in court - was not incorporated to the states. This aspect of Wolf was overruled by Mapp v. Ohio, 367 U.S. 643 (1961). As a result, any evidence obtained in violation of the

Fourth Amendment is now inadmissible in either state or federal proceedings.

In Bumper v. North Carolina, 391 U.S. 543 (1968), the Court held that there is no valid consent given when police officers announce that they have a warrant but, in fact, do not have one.

Here as in Bumper, the police announced that they had a warrant and the college student then opened the door. When she asked them to see the warrant, they laughed and admitted that they did not actually have one. Therefore, there was no valid consent given and the search was, thus, invalid.

In addition, the facts state that the college student refused to let the police officers into her apartment until they made the statement about possessing a warrant, which further shows that she would not have allowed them into her apartment, but for her belief that they possessed a warrant.

A and B are incorrect for the reasons discussed in D.

B and C are incorrect statements of law. (Regarding C, there are exceptions to the warrant requirement, making C an incorrect statement of law.)

76. A is the correct answer. The Fourth Amendment protection against unreasonable and warrantless searches and seizures has been incorporated to the states by way of the Due Process Clause of the Fourteenth Amendment to the United States Constitution as stated in Wolf v. Colorado, 338 U.S. 25 (1949). However, Wolf had said that, while the protection against unreasonable searches and seizures was incorporated to the states, the "fruit of the poisonous tree" doctrine - by which evidence seized in violation of the Fourth Amendment is deemed inadmissible in court - was not incorporated to the states. This aspect of Wolf was overruled by Mapp v. Ohio, 367 U.S. 643 (1961). As a result, any evidence obtained in violation of the Fourth Amendment is now inadmissible in either state or federal proceedings.

In Arizona v. Gant, 556 U.S. 332 (2009), a man was arrested for driving with a suspended license, handcuffed, and placed in the back of the police car. As a result, the police officers required a warrant to search his vehicle because driving with a suspended license is an offense for which the police officers could not expect to find evidence inside the vehicle; either the license was suspended or it was not. Furthermore, the police officers had no special safety concerns that would enable them to search the vehicle without a warrant because the man was handcuffed and in the back of the police car, and because the offense of driving with a suspended license does not present special safety concerns.

Similarly here, the woman was arrested merely for driving with a suspended license and was handcuffed and placed in the back of the police car. As a result, the police officers could not search her vehicle without obtaining a warrant (unless one of the warrant exceptions applied, which they did not in this case).

B is incorrect because warrantless searches may be conducted without the consent of the driver of a vehicle even when the driver cooperates with the police if a warrant exception applies. However, no warrant exception applied in this case for the reasons discussed in A.

C and D are incorrect for the reasons discussed in A.

77. C is the correct answer. The Fourth Amendment protection against unreasonable and warrantless searches and seizures has been incorporated to the states by way of the Due Process Clause of the Fourteenth Amendment to the United States Constitution as stated in Wolf v. Colorado, 338 U.S. 25 (1949). However, Wolf had said that, while the protection against unreasonable searches and seizures was incorporated to the states, the "fruit of the poisonous tree" doctrine - by which evidence seized in violation of the Fourth Amendment is deemed inadmissible in court - was not incorporated to the states. This aspect of Wolf was overruled by Mapp v. Ohio, 367 U.S. 643 (1961). As a result, any evidence obtained in violation of the Fourth Amendment is now inadmissible in either state or federal proceedings.

In Griffin v. Wisconsin, 483 U.S. 868 (1987), the Court held that people on probation only had a conditional liberty and as a result could have their homes searched with less than probable cause and without a warrant.

Here, the police searched the criminal's home when he was out of town because they had obtained information that there might be stolen goods inside the home. As discussed in Griffin, this information was sufficient for them to search his home, whether or not the information constituted probable cause, and even if the officers lacked a warrant because the criminal was on probation at the time.

Therefore, the search will be upheld.

A and B are incorrect for the reasons discussed in C.

D is incorrect because warrants are required to search the homes of convicted criminals even if they are neither in prison nor on probation (unless one of the warrant exceptions apply).

78. A is the correct answer. The Due Process Clause of the Fifth Amendment (as applied to the federal government) and the Due Process Clause of the Fourteenth Amendment (as applied to state governments) have been held to be violated when confessions are obtained through coercion.

In Ashcraft v. Tennessee, 322 U.S. 143 (1944), the defendant was interrogated for 36 hours without a break in a room filled with heavy electric lights, cameras, and other equipment. The defendant ultimately confessed to the crime in question. The Supreme Court held that the defendant's due process rights had been violated by this line of questioning, and that his confession had been coerced by such prolonged questioning in such a stressful environment.

The facts here are similar to the facts in Ashcraft. The woman, like the defendant in Ashcraft, was interrogated for 36 hours without a break in a room filled with cameras, electric lights, and other equipment. Thus, her confession will be deemed to have been coerced in violation of the Due Process Clause. As a result, her motion to suppress the confession will succeed.

B is incorrect because a warrant is not required to interrogate a suspect.

C is incorrect for the reasons discussed in A.

D is an incorrect statement of law.

79. D is the correct answer. The Fourth Amendment protection against unreasonable and warrantless searches and seizures has been incorporated to the states by way of the Due Process Clause of the Fourteenth Amendment to the United States Constitution as stated in Wolf v. Colorado, 338 U.S. 25 (1949). However, Wolf had said that, while the protection against unreasonable searches and seizures was incorporated to the states, the "fruit of the poisonous tree" doctrine - by which evidence seized in violation of the Fourth Amendment is deemed inadmissible in court - was not incorporated to the states. This aspect of Wolf was overruled by Mapp v. Ohio, 367 U.S. 643 (1961). As a result, any evidence obtained in violation of the Fourth Amendment is now inadmissible in either state or federal proceedings.

In Lewis v. United States, 385 U.S. 206 (1966), the Court held that there is no illegal entry when a police officer conceals his identity to gain entry into a home for the purpose of conducting an illegal transaction (such as by posing as a drug purchaser to gain consensual entry to the home of a drug dealer in order to purchase drugs).

Here as in Lewis, the police officer posed as a drug purchaser in order to gain consensual entry into the home of the drug dealer to purchase drugs. However, the officer's additional intrusions into the drawers and envelopes while the drug dealer was in the bathroom could not be justified on the basis of consent, since the drug dealer only consented to let the police officer inside his home, not his drawers and envelopes.

Thus, the drug dealer's motion to suppress will succeed.

A, B, and C are incorrect for the reasons discussed in D.

80. A is the correct answer. The Fourth Amendment protection against unreasonable and warrantless searches and seizures has been incorporated to the states by way of the Due Process Clause of the Fourteenth Amendment to the United States Constitution as stated in Wolf v. Colorado, 338 U.S. 25 (1949). However, Wolf had said that, while the protection against unreasonable searches and seizures was incorporated to the states, the "fruit of the poisonous tree" doctrine - by which evidence seized in violation of the Fourth Amendment is deemed inadmissible in court - was not incorporated to the states. This aspect of Wolf was overruled by Mapp v. Ohio, 367 U.S. 643 (1961). As a result, any evidence obtained in violation of the Fourth Amendment is now inadmissible in either state or federal proceedings.

In Lewis v. United States, 385 U.S. 206 (1966), the Court held that there is no illegal entry when a police officer conceals his identity to gain entry into a home for the purpose of conducting an illegal transaction (such as by posing as a drug purchaser to gain consensual entry to the home of a drug dealer in order to purchase drugs).

However, the result would likely be different if, as here, the police officer gained entry by pretending to be a telephone technician, a gas-meter reader, or some other individual who was entering the home for a lawful purpose. In this scenario, there would be no understanding that an illegal transaction is about to take place, since the defendant would believe the officer to be a telephone technician and not a person there to buy drugs or to engage in some other illegal purpose.

As a result, the woman's motion will succeed.

B is an incorrect statement of law. Necrophilia is a crime in the majority of U.S. states.

C and D are incorrect for the reasons discussed in A.

81. C is the correct answer. The Fourth Amendment protection against unreasonable and warrantless searches and seizures has been incorporated to the states by way of the Due Process Clause of the Fourteenth Amendment to the United States Constitution as stated in Wolf v. Colorado, 338 U.S. 25 (1949). However, Wolf had said that, while the protection against unreasonable searches and seizures was incorporated to the states, the "fruit of the poisonous tree" doctrine - by which evidence seized in violation of the Fourth Amendment is deemed inadmissible in court - was not incorporated to the states. This aspect of Wolf was overruled by Mapp v. Ohio, 367 U.S. 643 (1961). As a result, any evidence obtained in violation of the Fourth Amendment is now inadmissible in either state or federal proceedings.

In Bumper v. North Carolina, 391 U.S. 543 (1968), the Court "upheld the voluntariness of consent despite the deceptive practices by government agents." In short, officers can disclose their identity but misrepresent their purpose. Here because the officer's behavior was not threatening or coercive and the chef was willing to let the officer enter for the purpose of searching for an escaped convict, and since the officer did not exceed the scope of the consent, the evidence would be admissible.

Thus, the chef's motion will fail.

A and B are incorrect for the reasons discussed in C.

D is incorrect because even though baking with marijuana is a crime under the laws of most U.S. states and is also a crime under federal law, the motion would still succeed if the officer's entry were unlawful. However for the reasons discussed in C, the officer's entry was lawful here.

82. D is the correct answer. The Fourth Amendment protection against unreasonable and warrantless searches and seizures has been incorporated to the states by way of the Due Process Clause of the Fourteenth Amendment to the United States Constitution as stated in Wolf v. Colorado, 338 U.S. 25 (1949). However, Wolf had said that, while the protection against unreasonable searches and seizures was incorporated to the states, the "fruit of the poisonous tree" doctrine - by which evidence seized in violation of the Fourth Amendment is deemed inadmissible in court - was not incorporated to the states. This aspect of Wolf was overruled by Mapp v. Ohio, 367 U.S. 643 (1961). As a result, any evidence obtained in violation of the Fourth Amendment is now inadmissible in either state or federal proceedings.

The facts here are virtually identical to the facts in Maryland v. Garrison, 480 U.S. 79 (1987). In that case, the police officers reasonably believed that there was only one apartment located on the third floor of a particular building when, in fact, there was more than one. In Garrison, the police officers used the warrant to mistakenly search the wrong apartment on the third floor of that building. The Court found the warrant to be valid because it was based on the officers' reasonable belief that there was only one apartment on that floor.

Similarly here, the policemen reasonably believed that there was only one apartment on the fifth floor of the building. Because they based their warrant on this reasonable belief, the woman's motion will fail and the evidence obtained when they mistakenly searched the wrong apartment on the fifth floor of the building (here, the woman's apartment) will be admissible.

A and B are incorrect for the reasons discussed in D.

C is an incorrect statement of law.

83. A is the correct answer. The Fourth

Amendment protection against unreasonable and warrantless searches and seizures has been incorporated to the states by way of the Due Process Clause of the Fourteenth Amendment to the United States Constitution as stated in Wolf v. Colorado, 338 U.S. 25 (1949). However, Wolf had said that, while the protection against unreasonable searches and seizures was incorporated to the states, the "fruit of the poisonous tree" doctrine - by which evidence seized in violation of the Fourth Amendment is deemed inadmissible in court - was not incorporated to the states. This aspect of Wolf was overruled by Mapp v. Ohio, 367 U.S. 643 (1961). As a result, any evidence obtained in violation of the Fourth Amendment is now inadmissible in either state or federal proceedings.

Hill v. California, 401 U.S. 797 (1971), upheld the lawfulness of an arrest that turned out to be a case of mistaken identity. Similarly here, the police officer had a reasonable belief that the man was the robbery suspect at the time the search was made. Consequently, the police officer feared for his safety, since a gun may have been used in the robbery. Thus, the police officer's pat down search for the gun (as well as the coins) will be deemed lawful even though his reasonable belief about the identity of the man turned out to be mistaken. Consequently, the man's motion to suppress the hashish will fail.

B is an incorrect statement of law.

C and D are incorrect for the reasons discussed in A.

84. D is the correct answer. The Fourth Amendment protection against unreasonable and warrantless searches and seizures has been incorporated to the states by way of the Due Process Clause of the Fourteenth Amendment to the United States Constitution as stated in Wolf v. Colorado, 338 U.S. 25 (1949). However, Wolf had said that, while the protection against unreasonable searches and seizures was incorporated to the states, the "fruit of the poisonous tree" doctrine - by which evidence seized in violation of the Fourth Amendment is deemed inadmissible in court - was not incorporated to the states. This aspect of Wolf was overruled by Mapp v. Ohio, 367 U.S. 643 (1961). As a result, any evidence obtained in violation of the Fourth Amendment is now inadmissible in either state or federal proceedings.

In some jurisdictions, unreasonable delay in acting upon a warrant may make the arrest unlawful. Since in this case approximately five weeks had passed before the police officers executed the warrant, it could be possible that the information the warrant was based on had become stale. Typically, warrants have to be acted upon within ten days. However, if the warrant here was still valid, then the search would have been lawful, despite the almost five-week delay in executing the warrant. Thus, if the warrant was still valid, the motion to suppress the cocaine will fail.

A is incorrect for the reasons discussed in D, since the ten-day rule is not an absolute rule followed in all jurisdictions.

B is incorrect because the facts do not state if this particular jurisdiction required that a search warrant be executed during daytime hours.

C is incorrect because it is not enough that the officers ultimately executed the warrant. The warrant must be executed before it expires.

85. D is the correct answer. The Fourth Amendment protection against unreasonable and warrantless searches and seizures has been incorporated to the states by way of the Due Process Clause of the Fourteenth Amendment to the United States Constitution as stated in Wolf v. Colorado, 338 U.S. 25 (1949). However, Wolf had said that, while the protection against unreasonable searches and seizures was incorporated to the states, the "fruit of the poisonous tree" doctrine - by which evidence seized in violation of the Fourth Amendment is deemed inadmissible in court - was not incorporated to the states. This aspect of Wolf was overruled by Mapp v. Ohio, 367 U.S. 643 (1961). As a result, any evidence obtained in violation of the Fourth Amendment is now inadmissible in either state or federal proceedings.

Most U.S. jurisdictions have held that if an officer knows that the occupant of a particular building is armed and dangerous, the officer may enter the building without giving advance notice of his authority and purpose. Here, the police officer received a reliable tip that the resident was "armed and dangerous." As a result, the police officer did not require a warrant in order to enter the resident's home. In addition, the police officer's actions in breaking down the door were reasonable under the circumstances because, if the police officer had identified himself before breaking down the door, the resident may have injured the police officer and/or destroyed evidence.

As a result, the resident's motion will fail.

A and B are incorrect for the reasons discussed in D.

C is incorrect because there is no such exception to the warrant requirement.

86. D is the correct answer. The Fourth Amendment protection against unreasonable and warrantless searches and seizures has been incorporated to the states by way of the Due Process Clause of the Fourteenth Amendment to the United States Constitution as stated in Wolf v. Colorado, 338 U.S. 25 (1949). However, Wolf had said that, while the protection against unreasonable searches and seizures was incorporated to the states, the "fruit of the poisonous tree" doctrine - by which evidence seized in violation of the Fourth Amendment is deemed inadmissible in court - was not

incorporated to the states. This aspect of Wolf was overruled by Mapp v. Ohio, 367 U.S. 643 (1961). As a result, any evidence obtained in violation of the Fourth Amendment is now inadmissible in either state or federal proceedings.

In Maryland v. Buie, 494 U.S. 325 (1990), the Court held that police officers are allowed to "look in closets and other spaces immediately adjoining the place of arrest from which an attack could immediately be launched."

Here, since the parolee was known to the officer to have extremely dangerous associates, it was reasonable for the officer to believe that one of the parolee's associates could indeed be armed and dangerous and could be hiding somewhere in the home. As a result, the officer's search, limited to the living room and an adjoining hallway, was valid.

A and B are incorrect because, under such circumstances, the arresting officer did not need probable cause or reasonable suspicion for the reasons discussed in D.

C is incorrect both because it is an incorrect statement of fact (there was no actual threat to the police officer) and because it is not important if there was actually a threat to the officer; the standard is whether or not the police officer legitimately felt threatened, which he did here as discussed in D.

87. D is the correct answer. The United States Constitution only applies in the United States and its territories. Here, the man was in Europe, about to board an airplane back to the United States. He was, thus, outside the United States at the time of the incident. Therefore, neither the Fourth nor the Eighth Amendment applied here.

A, B, and C are incorrect for the reasons discussed in D.

88. D is the correct answer. The Fourth Amendment protection against unreasonable and warrantless searches and seizures has been incorporated to the states by way of the Due Process Clause of the Fourteenth Amendment to the United States Constitution as stated in Wolf v. Colorado, 338 U.S. 25 (1949). However, Wolf had said that, while the protection against unreasonable searches and seizures was incorporated to the states, the "fruit of the poisonous tree" doctrine - by which evidence seized in violation of the Fourth Amendment is deemed inadmissible in court - was not incorporated to the states. This aspect of Wolf was overruled by Mapp v. Ohio, 367 U.S. 643 (1961). As a result, any evidence obtained in violation of the Fourth Amendment is now inadmissible in either state or federal proceedings.

The language of the Fourth Amendment itself requires probable cause in order for a warrant to be issued. In addition, items observed in "plain view," while lawfully executing a warrant, can be seized. This is a traditional exception to the warrant requirement, and the facts meet the requirements of this exception (probable cause and object was obviously incriminating). See generally Horton v. California, 496 U.S. 128 (1990).

Here, the warrant mentioned only stolen property, not illegal weapons. Nonetheless, the motion will fail because the search would not be invalidated merely because the officer knew about the weapons and hoped to find them during the search, since the officer entered the home with a valid warrant (since the officer also believed that there was stolen property in the home for which the warrant authorized him to search) and the weapons were in plain view.

A and B are in correct for the reasons discussed in D.

C is incorrect because evidence does not need to be discovered "inadvertently" for the plain view doctrine to apply.

89. C is the correct answer. The Fourth Amendment protection against unreasonable and warrantless searches and seizures has been incorporated to the states by way of the Due Process Clause of the Fourteenth Amendment to the United States Constitution as stated in Wolf v. Colorado, 338 U.S. 25 (1949). However, Wolf had said that, while the protection against unreasonable searches and seizures was incorporated to the states, the "fruit of the poisonous tree" doctrine - by which evidence seized in violation of the Fourth Amendment is deemed inadmissible in court - was not incorporated to the states. This aspect of Wolf was overruled by Mapp v. Ohio, 367 U.S. 643 (1961). As a result, any evidence obtained in violation of the Fourth Amendment is now inadmissible in either state or federal proceedings.

Here, there is nothing in the facts to indicate that the officers had probable cause to arrest any of the customers. (See Ybarra v. Illinois, 444 U.S. 85 (1979)). Consequently, the searches of the customers' pockets, purses and wallets was not lawful because the initial arrests of the customers were not lawful.

A and B are incorrect for the reasons discussed in C.

D is incorrect because the searches of the customers' pockets, purses and wallets would have been valid if the customers had been lawfully arrested. However, the unlawfulness of the customers' arrests invalidated these searches as discussed in C.

90. A is the correct answer. The Fourth Amendment protection against unreasonable and warrantless searches and seizures has been incorporated to the states by way of the Due Process Clause of the Fourteenth Amendment to the United States Constitution as stated in Wolf v. Colorado, 338 U.S. 25 (1949). However, Wolf had said that, while the protection against unreasonable search-

es and seizures was incorporated to the states, the "fruit of the poisonous tree" doctrine - by which evidence seized in violation of the Fourth Amendment is deemed inadmissible in court - was not incorporated to the states. This aspect of Wolf was overruled by Mapp v. Ohio, 367 U.S. 643 (1961). As a result, any evidence obtained in violation of the Fourth Amendment is now inadmissible in either state or federal proceedings.

In New Jersey v. T.L.O., 469 U.S. 325 (1985), the Supreme Court held that a school official's intrusion into the privacy of a student was "reasonable," since it was necessary to achieve the legitimate end of preserving order in the schools. However, this case did not apply to public universities where the students are mostly adults and have full constitutional protections.

Here, the police officers had neither probable cause nor reasonable suspicion to frisk the student. In addition, the frisk was not necessary for the protection of the officers. (See Ybarra v. Illinois, 444 U.S. 85 (1979).)

Thus, the student's motion will succeed because his Fourth Amendment rights and his right to privacy were violated.

B is incorrect because this is not a legally valid reason to invalidate a search.

C is incorrect for the reasons discussed in A.

D is an incorrect statement of law.

91. D is the correct answer. In Michigan v. Summers, 452 U.S. 692 (1981), the Court held that temporary detention is warranted, if it is necessary to prevent the culprit from fleeing in case grounds for arrest are found in the search, minimize the risk of harm to the officers, and facilitate the orderly completion of the search.

Here, the Federal Bureau of Investigation agents needed to temporarily detain everyone in the building because as indicated in the fact pattern, one of them was likely the culprit (because the bomb was likely detonated from inside the building) and if they had not detained everyone inside the building, the culprit would have been able to escape.

A and B are incorrect for the reasons discussed in D.

C is an incorrect statement of law.

92. A is the correct answer. In Duncan v. Louisiana, 391 U.S. 145 (1968), the Court held that the Sixth Amendment right to trial by an impartial jury of one's peers has been incorporated to the states by way of the Due Process Clause of the Fourteenth Amendment.

In Lockhart v. McCree, 476 U.S. 162 (1986), the Court held that the right to an impartial jury of ones peers means that a jury should be selected from a cross-section of society based on diversity of race and other characteristics, but not necessarily diversity of views on such subjects as the death penalty. Specifically, the Court held that individuals whose beliefs would prevent them from applying the rule of law (such as refusing to find people guilty because of agreement with the defendant's criminal actions) could properly be excluded.

Here, potential jurors who supported the defendant's motives in killing the abortion doctor were categorically excluded. As discussed in Lockhart, this was a proper basis to exclude potential jurors. Thus, the writ will fail for this reason.

B is incorrect because it is irrelevant to the question that murder is illegal. The question deals with the exclusion of potential jurors, not the illegality of murder.

C is incorrect for the reasons discussed in A.

D is incorrect because there is no such law.

93. C is the correct answer. In Duncan v. Louisiana, 391 U.S. 145 (1968), the Court held that the Sixth Amendment right to trial by an impartial jury of one's peers has been incorporated to the states by way of the Due Process Clause of the Fourteenth Amendment.

In addition, the prohibition against cruel and unusual punishment from the Eighth Amendment to the United States Constitution has been incorporated to the states by way of the Due Process Clause of the Fourteenth Amendment. Robinson v. California, 370 U.S. 660 (1962).

In Lockhart v. McCree, 476 U.S. 162 (1986), the Court held that the right to an impartial jury of one's peers means that a jury should be selected from a cross-section of society based on diversity of race and other characteristics, but not necessarily diversity of views on such subjects as the death penalty. Specifically, the Court held that individuals whose beliefs would prevent them from applying the rule of law (such as the imposition of the death penalty where warranted) could properly be excluded.

Here, potential jurors who were opposed to the death penalty were categorically excluded. As discussed in Lockhart, this was a proper basis to exclude potential jurors. Thus, the writ will fail for this reason.

A is incorrect for the reasons discussed in C.

B is incorrect because in Gregg v. Georgia, 428 U.S. 153 (1976), the Court held that the death penalty does not necessarily violate the Eighth Amendment's prohibition against cruel and unusual punishment.

D is incorrect both because the death penalty is not "the law of the land" (it is only the law in the individual states that provide for it and in federal criminal court) and because this is irrelevant to whether or not the potential jurors were properly excluded.

94. A is the correct answer. The privilege against self-incrimination under the Fifth Amendment to the United States Constitution has been incorporated to the states by way of the Due Process Clause of the Fourteenth Amendment. Brown v. Mississippi, 297 U.S. 278 (1936), Malloy v. Hogan, 378 U.S. 1 (1964).

Miranda interprets the Fifth Amendment's self-incrimination clause. Under Miranda, the police must make a person aware of the enumerated Miranda rights when that person is in custody and being interrogated. In Connecticut v. Barrett, 479 U.S. 523 (1987), the Supreme Court held that Miranda is satisfied when the police provide a person who is in custody and being interrogated with his Miranda rights and that person voluntarily chooses to waive these rights.

In this case, the man was given his Miranda rights when he was in police custody and being interrogated. and the man then waived his Miranda rights. It is irrelevant that the man later tried to put conditions on this waiver. ("The man, however, insisted that nothing be put in writing and requested that all tape recorders be turned off. The man also indicated that he would not make a written statement outside the presence of counsel.") Once the man voluntarily chose to waive his Miranda rights after these rights were explained to him (as was the case here), that waiver applied to all incriminating statements that the man proceeded to give; he could not condition his waiver of his Miranda rights.

B, C, and D are incorrect for the reasons discussed in A.

95. C is the correct answer. The privilege against self-incrimination under the Fifth Amendment to the United States Constitution has been incorporated to the states by way of the Due Process Clause of the Fourteenth Amendment. Brown v. Mississippi, 297 U.S. 278 (1936), Malloy v. Hogan, 378 U.S. 1 (1964).

Miranda interprets the Fifth Amendment's self-incrimination clause. Under Miranda, the police must make a person aware of the enumerated Miranda rights when that person is in custody and being interrogated. One does not need to be in a police station or under arrest to be considered "in custody." Rather, the "totality of the circumstances" can be considered. Haynes v. Washington, 373 U.S. 503, 514 (1963).

Here, the woman was being interrogated in her home by nine police officers. Having nine police officers in her home questioning the woman would have likely caused the woman to feel that she was not free to leave. She would, therefore, be considered to have been in custody. (See, e.g., United States v. Craighead, 539 F.3d 1073 (9th Cir. 2008)). Thus, the police should have read the woman her Miranda rights prior to questioning her.

A is incorrect because individuals can be in custody outside the police station as discussed in C.

B is incorrect because a suspect can be in custody in his own home as discussed in C.

D is incorrect because the woman did not voluntarily waive her Miranda rights, since she was never read these rights. A person cannot waive his Miranda rights if these rights are not read to that person.

96. C is the correct answer. The privilege against self-incrimination under the Fifth Amendment to the United States Constitution has been incorporated to the states by way of the Due Process Clause of the Fourteenth Amendment. Brown v. Mississippi, 297 U.S. 278 (1936), Malloy v. Hogan, 378 U.S. 1 (1964).

Miranda interprets the Fifth Amendment's self-incrimination clause. Under Miranda, the police must make a person aware of the enumerated Miranda rights when that person is in custody and being interrogated.

In this case, if the invitation was the kind that could not be refused, coercion would likely be found present. If so, then a finding of custody is likely. The mere fact that the student was being questioned by the police at the police station while not under arrest would normally not be considered to be "in custody." However, if there were implied coercion here, then the person would still be considered to be "in custody" nonetheless.

A is incorrect because an individual is not necessarily "in custody" just because he is at the police station as discussed in C.

B is incorrect because it would depend on what kind of invitation was extended to the student.

D is incorrect because an individual does not have to be under arrest to be "in custody," as discussed in C.

97. C is the correct answer. The privilege against unreasonable searches and seizures under the Fourth Amendment to the United States Constitution has been incorporated to the states by way of the Due Process Clause of the Fourteenth Amendment. Mapp v. Ohio, 367 U.S. 643 (1961).

In addition, the privilege against self-incrimination under the Fifth Amendment to the United States Constitution has been incorporated to the states by way of the Due Process Clause of the

Fourteenth Amendment. Brown v. Mississippi, 297 U.S. 278 (1936), Malloy v. Hogan, 378 U.S. 1 (1964).

Miranda interprets the Fifth Amendment's self-incrimination clause. Under Miranda, the police must make a person aware of the enumerated Miranda rights when that person is in custody and being interrogated.

An officer can investigate suspicious circumstances without triggering the need to give Miranda warnings. Such roadside questioning would likely be deemed a Terry stop and would not require a warrant under the Fourth Amendment. (See Berkemer v. Mc Carty, 468 U.S. 420 (1984)).

Here, the officer suspected that the waitress had been drinking alcohol. The officer could, therefore, question her without a warrant and without the need for Miranda warnings because his questioning would not be considered to have been custodial interrogation.

A is incorrect because questioning by a police officer is not always custodial interrogation as discussed in C.

B is incorrect because as discussed in C, the waitress could be detained for suspicion of drunk driving.

D is incorrect because the officer only needed a good-faith belief that the waitress was drunk.

98. A is the correct answer. According to Rule 11(c) of the Federal Rules of Criminal Procedure and Brady v. United States, 397 U.S. 742 (1970), the Due Process Clause of the Fourteenth Amendment to the United States Constitution requires that state courts take certain precautions in order to ensure the validity of guilty pleas.

Here, the man pled guilty, but the record indicates that the man was not asked any questions by the judge concerning his guilty plea, nor did the man address the court. As such, the judge accepted the man's guilty plea without any affirmative showing that the guilty plea was voluntary, intelligent, and knowing, since the judge did not question the man in regard to his plea. Thus, his conviction will be reversed.

B is incorrect because reversible error can occur even if a defendant's conviction is based on credible eyewitness testimony. Furthermore, there is nothing in the facts to indicate that there was any credible eyewitness testimony in this case, particularly because the case did not go to trial, since the man pled guilty.

C and D are incorrect for the reasons discussed in A.

99. A is the correct answer. Under Hill v. Lockhart, 474 U.S. 52 (1985), a defendant (here, the man), must demonstrate in his habeas petition that there was a reasonable probability that, but for the

attorney's errors, he would not have pleaded guilty and would have insisted on going to trial. Thus, if this was not alleged, no relief will be granted.

B is incorrect for the reasons discussed in A.

C is incorrect because the United States Supreme Court has never held that the United States Constitution requires the state to furnish a defendant with information about parole eligibility in order for the defendant's plea of guilty to be voluntary. (See, e.g., Fed. Rule Crim. Proc. 11(c); Advisory Committee's Notes on 1974 Amendment to Fed. Rule Crim. Proc. 11, 18 U.S.C.App., p. 22).

D is incorrect because as discussed in A, the man's mistaken belief will have no bearing on whether he is granted relief absent a showing that he would have acted otherwise had he had the correct information at his disposal.

100. A is the correct answer. In Santobello v. New York, 404 U.S. 257 (1971), the Supreme Court found that the state was required to abide by its commitments concerning sentence recommendations on a guilty pleas that the defendant entered as part of a plea bargain.

Here, the plea bargain was for the district attorney to allow the man to plead to a lesser-included offense, in exchange for the district attorney's agreement to make no recommendations as to length of sentence. However, the district attorney (a different prosecutor from the one who had made the agreement, but from the same district attorney's office and, thus, bound by the same agreement) recommended that the maximum one-year sentence be imposed. This violates the principle articulated in Santobello as discussed above.

Therefore, the man should be allowed to withdraw his guilty plea.

B, C, and D are incorrect for the reasons discussed in A.

END OF ANSWERS

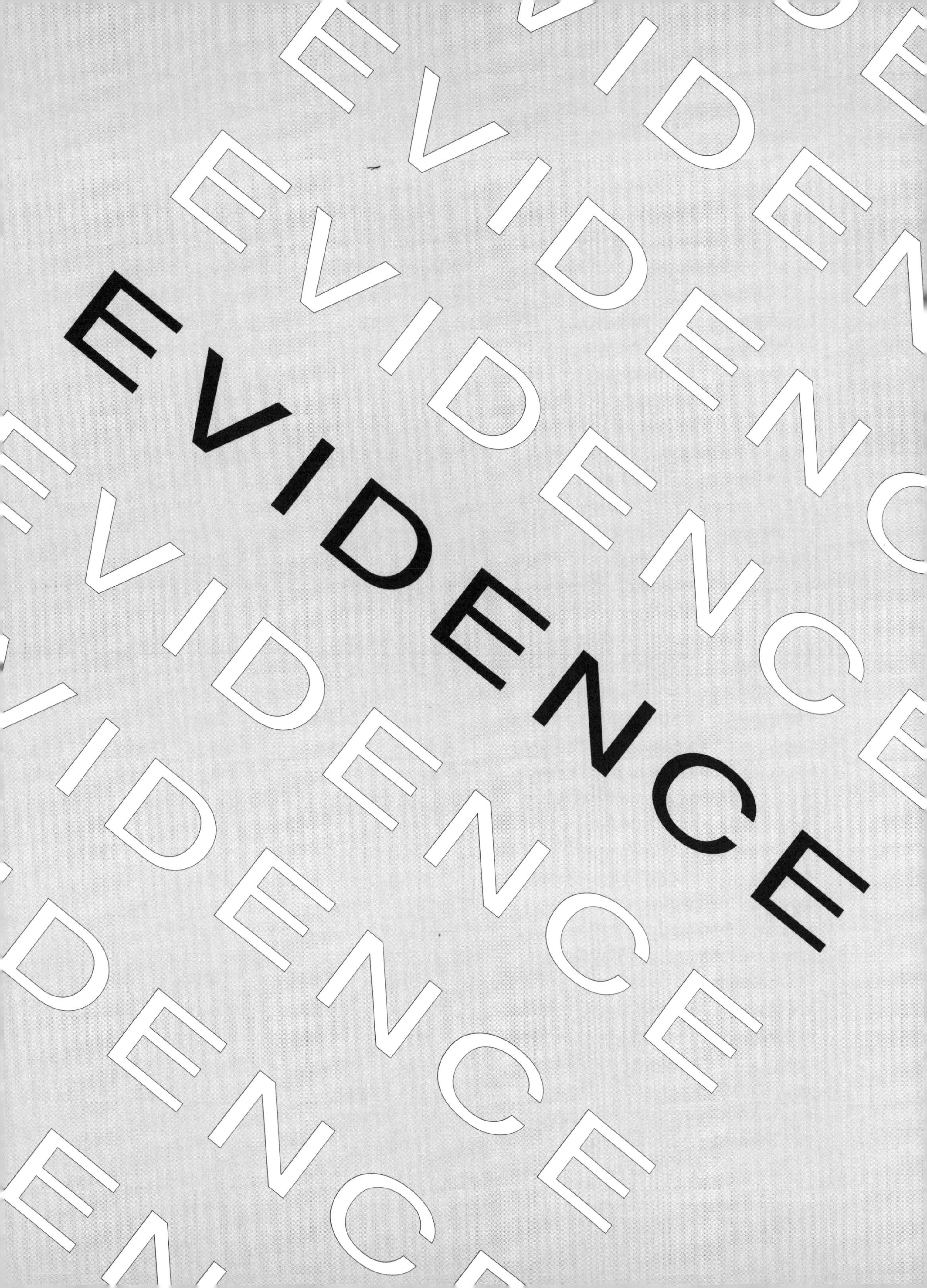
EVIDENCE

EVIDENCE - QUESTION BREAKDOWN

1. Foundation – Admissibility of Photographs
2. Character Evidence
3. Present State of Mind
4. Bias
5. Legal Relevancy
6. Character Evidence
7. Hearsay/Exception – Present Sense Impression
8. Impeachment – Prior Inconsistent Statements
9. Subsequent Remedial Measures
10. Payment of – Medical and Similar Expenses
11. Privileges – Physician/Patient
12. Authentication and Best Evidence Rule
13. Privileges – Attorney/Client
14. Privileges – Attorney/Client
15. Hearsay Exception – Present Sense Impression
16. Character Evidence
17. Voice Identification
18. Character Evidence – Civil Cases
19. Relevancy – Impeachment
20. Impeachment – Collateral Issue
21. Hearsay Exception – Excited Utterance
22. Hearsay Exemption - Admission
23. Hearsay Exception – Physical Condition
24. Admissibility – Settlement Offers
25. Present Recollection Refreshed
26. Character Evidence – Defamation
27. Marital Communication Privilege
28. Impeachment – Extrinsic Evidence
29. Hearsay Exception or Exemption - Admission
30. Character Evidence
31. Privilege – Doctor/Patient
32. Expert Testimony
33. Subsequent Remedial Measures
34. Subsequent Remedial Measures

35. Competency to Testify
36. Settlement or Compromise Offers
37. Subsequent Remedial Measures
38. Hearsay Exemption - Vicarious Admission
39. Hearsay Exemption - Party Admission
40. Judicial Notice
41. Judicial Notice
42. Self-Incrimination
43. Impeachment
44. Hearsay
45. Hearsay Exception or Exemption - Admission
46. Hearsay Exception – Business Records
47. Hearsay
48. Hearsay Exception - Present Physical Condition
49. Hearsay Exception – Statement Made for Diagnosis
50. Impeachment – Prior Inconsistent
51. Admissibility of Medical Expenses
52. Admissibility of Medical Expenses
53. Hearsay Exception – Present Sense Impression
54. Personal knowledge
55. Privilege – Attorney/Client
56. Impeachment
57. Character Evidence
58. Character Evidence
59. Hearsay Rule
60. Authentication
61. Personal Knowledge
62. Expert Testimony
63. Opinion Testimony
64. Subsequent Remedial Measures
65. Impeachment
66. Judicial Notice
67. Lay Opinion
68. Privileges – Attorney/Client
69. Best Evidence Rule – Collateral Matter
70. Witness credibility
71. Character Evidence – Specific Acts
72. Character Evidence – Specific Acts

73. Admissibility – Settlement Offers
74. Privilege – Attorney/Client
75. Subsequent Remedial Measures
76. Subsequent Remedial Measures
77. Expert Testimony
78. Character Evidence – Prior Bad Acts
79. Character Evidence
80. Expert Testimony
81. Character Evidence
82. Privilege – Attorney/Client
83. Character Evidence
84. Character Evidence – Civil Cases
85. Hearsay Exception – Present Sense Impression
86. Hearsay Exception – Present Sense Impression
87. Logical Relevancy
88. Impeachment – Collateral Matters
89. Nonhearsay
90. Not Hearsay – Command and Questions
91. Not Hearsay – Machine or Animals
92. Hearsay
93. Impeachment – Extrinsic Evidence
94. Hearsay
95. Character – Wrongful Death Action
96. Character – Specific Instances of Conduct
97. Best Evidence
98. Impeachment
99. Hearsay
100. Authentication – Opinion Testimony
101. Non-Hearsay
102. Hearsay Exception Physical Condition
103. Character Evidence
104. Payment of Medical and Similar Expenses
105. Privilege – Husband/Wife
106. Privilege – Marital Communication
107. Privilege – Attorney/Client
108. Hearsay
109. Hearsay
110. Habit Evidence

EVIDENCE QUESTIONS

1. A woman is suing a man for injuries that she suffered when the man's bicycle collided with hers. The issue in the lawsuit is whether the man was riding his bicycle on the correct side of the roadway. The woman seeks to introduce a photograph that shows that the man was riding his bicycle on the wrong side of the road. The man objects to the introduction of the photograph. The court will rule that the photograph is:

   A. Admissible, if there is testimony offered showing the photograph to be an accurate representation of the scene of the accident.

   B. Admissible because the man can cross-examine the woman as to the accuracy of the photograph.

   C. Inadmissible, unless the photographer testifies to the accuracy of the photograph.

   D. Inadmissible, unless the photograph was taken by an investigative agent at the accident scene.

2. A woman was keeping a man as a prisoner. When the man refused to eat his breakfast, it is alleged that the woman took a carving knife and beheaded him. The woman was tried for the murder of the man. The woman called her first witness to testify to her reputation in the community as a "peaceful woman." The court will rule the testimony:

   A. Admissible, as it tends to prove that the woman is believable.

   B. Admissible, as it tends to prove that the woman is innocent.

   C. Inadmissible because the woman herself has not yet testified.

   D. Inadmissible because reputation evidence is inadmissible to prove one's character.

3. A man was on trial for robbery of a bank. He called a witness to testify that the day before the bank robbery, the man had told the witness that he had been selected to be sent up into space that same day. The court will rule the testimony:

   A. Inadmissible hearsay not falling within any exception.

   B. Inadmissible because it is irrelevant.

   C. Admissible because it is relevant.

   D. Admissible because it is a declaration of the man's present state of mind.

4. A man was on trial for the murder of a transient. The man calls his mother as a witness to testify as to his alibi that he

was out of the state at the time that the transient was murdered. On cross-examination, the prosecutor asks, "Aren't you the man's mother?" The court will rule the question:

A. Improper because the question goes beyond the scope of direct examination.

B. Improper because the question is irrelevant.

C. Proper, as it tends to prove bias.

D. Proper because a relative cannot testify as to another relative's reputation.

5. A man was on trial for murder. He called a witness to testify as to his alibi. On cross-examination the prosecutor asked the witness, "Isn't it true that you were on a jury that acquitted the man of a criminal charge?" If the court sustained the man's objection, it will be because:

A. The question went beyond the scope of direct examination.

B. The probative value was outweighed by the prejudicial effect.

C. It was a leading question.

D. Prior jury service rendered the witness incompetent to testify here.

6. A woman was robbed by someone carrying an unusual psychedelic-painted gun. A robber was arrested and charged with armed robbery. At trial, the prosecution seeks to offer evidence that the robber, who had been arrested, had previously robbed a man with the same gun. The court will rule the evidence:

A. Inadmissible because the robber's good character is at issue.

B. Inadmissible because this evidence will unduly prejudice the robber.

C. Admissible because it shows that the robber is capable of committing armed robbery.

D. Admissible because it tends to show that this was a "signature crime."

7. A man was drinking heavily in a bar. When the man left the bar and began to drive home, his vehicle struck a pedestrian crossing the street. The pedestrian was injured and brought a lawsuit against the man.

At trial, the pedestrian presented an eyewitness against the man. The pedestrian testified that he had noticed that the man's vehicle had been swerving in and out of traffic immediately before the accident, and the man had appeared to be drunk. The man objected. The eyewitness' testimony is:

A. Admissible as an excited utterance.

B. Admissible as a present sense impression.

C. Admissible as a prior consistent statement.

D. Inadmissible because the eyewitness had no expertise in determining whether one is drunk.

8. A woman sued a man for defamation. At trial, the woman called a witness, expecting him to testify that he had heard the man call the woman a prostitute. Instead, to her surprise, the witness testified that he had heard the man state that the woman was a devout church-goer and that she had never been a prostitute in her entire life. The woman now wants to confront the witness with a statement that he had made at his deposition that he had heard the man call the woman a prostitute. The man objected. Which of the following is the most likely ruling by the court regarding the witness' statement in his deposition?

A. It is inadmissible because one cannot impeach his own witness.

B. It is inadmissible because it is hearsay.

C. It may be used only to impeach the witness.

D. It is admissible to impeach the witness and as evidence that the man had called the woman a prostitute.

9. A man was drinking heavily in a bar. On his drive home, his vehicle struck and beheaded a pedestrian. The pedestrian died as a result. The pedestrian's estate sued the man for wrongful death. At trial, the man offered evidence that, after the accident, the owner of the bar where he had been drinking put into effect a rule limiting all patrons to two drinks per hour. The court will rule that this evidence is:

A. Admissible to show that the bar was negligent on previous occasions.

B. Admissible to show that the bar knew precautionary measures were needed.

C. Admissible because subsequent remedial repairs are discouraged due to public policy.

D. Inadmissible because subsequent remedial measures are not admissible to prove culpable conduct.

10. A pedestrian was severely injured when an automobile collided with him. The pedestrian sues the driver of the automobile. The pedestrian offers evidence that the driver came to see him in the hospital after the accident, and offered to pay all of his medical expenses. The driver

then stated, "That's the least I can do after hitting you with my vehicle, since the whole accident was my fault." The statement made by the driver is:

A. Admissible as an admission in connection with an offer to compromise.

B. Admissible as a party admission by the driver that the driver was at fault.

C. Inadmissible as hearsay not within any exception.

D. Inadmissible as an admission made in connection with an offer to pay medical expenses.

11. A hit man stabbed a gang member to death. The hit man was supposed to collect his fee for killing the gang member the day after he did the killing. However, shortly after the hit man stabbed the gang member, the hit man noticed that the hand that had done the stabbing was swollen. The hit man went to a hospital and was told that he would have to stay at the hospital for a couple of days to have surgery on his hand because the hand was broken. The hit man refused and said, "I have to leave because I have to meet the mob boss, who is going to pay me for killing the gang member." The head nurse, who was also in the room, heard the statement. The hit man and the mob boss were subsequently charged with conspiracy.

The prosecution offers the doctor's testimony of the hit man's statement into evidence. The hit man objects. The court will find the doctor's testimony:

A. Inadmissible because of the physician-patient privilege.

B Admissible because the head nurse heard the statement.

C. Admissible because it is not protected by the physician-patient privilege.

D. Admissible because the statement that the hit man made was not made in confidence.

12. A woman contracted with a man to paint her home. The man did not paint the home, so the woman sued the man for breach of contract. The man claimed that the woman actually prevented him from performing his duties under the contract. In his defense, the man sought to introduce a letter that he received from the woman indicating that she no longer needed his services because she had sold her home.

In order for the letter to be admissible the man must:

A. Only provide the court with the original letter.

B. Show evidence of the authenticity of the letter and provide the court with the original letter.

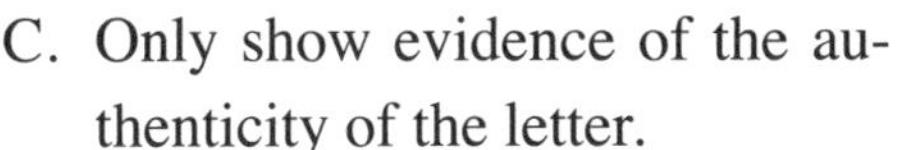

C. Only show evidence of the authenticity of the letter.

D. Have an expert witness testify that the woman had written the letter.

13. An employee of a trucking company got into an automobile collision with a vehicle driven by a woman. The woman brought suit against the trucking company and the employee, as joint defendants. The trucking company and the employee consulted an attorney about the suit. The attorney called his investigator into the conference. The investigator made notes as to the discussion of what happened.

The woman called the employee to testify to admissions made by the trucking company in the conference. The trucking company objected. The court should rule that the employee's testimony is:

A. Inadmissible because the best evidence was the investigator's notes.

B. Inadmissible because of the attorney-client privilege.

C. Admissible because others were present at the conference other than the trucking company and the attorney.

D. Admissible because the employee was an adverse party.

14. A man sued a railroad company for injuries sustained when the man's ~~vehicle~~ truck collided with one of the railroad company's trains. The railroad company's manager prepared a report of the accident, at the request of the company's attorney. During discovery, the man demanded that the report be produced. Will the court rule for the production of the report?

A. No because it is a privileged communication.

B. No because the report contains hearsay.

C. No because the report is self-serving.

D. Yes because business reports are not privileged.

15. A woman sued a man for damage to the woman's home. The damage resulted from a chemical explosion from an experiment that the man was conducting in the garage. A relevant fact in the woman's lawsuit was the magnitude of the explosion. On direct examination, the woman was asked if she remembered the explosion. She stated, "I recall my daughter running out from her bedroom and screaming that the bedroom windows had just shattered." The daughter was 14-years-old.

The woman objected. The court will rule the woman's testimony:

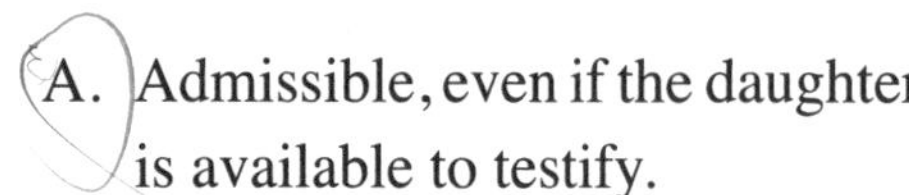

A. Admissible, even if the daughter is available to testify.

B. Inadmissible because the daughter is available to testify.

C. Inadmissible as hearsay not within any exception.

D. Inadmissible because the daughter is a child.

16. A defendant is on trial for fraud. He is charged with selling "phony" leases to a condominium timeshare. In his opening statement, the defendant's attorney states that the defendant did not know that the leases were phony. At trial, the prosecution seeks to introduce evidence that the defendant had, on five other occasions, set up phony condo deals. The defendant's attorney objected. The court will rule that the evidence is:

A. Inadmissible because it is not relevant.

B. Inadmissible because character cannot be proven by instances of misconduct.

C. Admissible to show his intent to defraud.

D. Admissible because past crimes are always admissible.

17. A woman sues a man for damages done to the woman's crops by the man's cow. The woman offers testimony that she looked up the man's telephone number on the internet. The woman proceeded to call that number and a voice answered saying, "This is the man." The woman then asked, "Was it your cow that trampled my sweet peas?" The voice replied, "Yes." The court should rule the testimony:

A. Admissible because the man identified himself as the speaker, coupled with the accuracy of the internet, and the phone transmission system, furnishes sufficient authentication.

B. Admissible because anyone can identify another's voice.

C. Inadmissible, unless the woman can prove she is familiar with the man's voice.

D. Inadmissible, unless the man has been given the opportunity to admit or deny whether or not the conversation took place.

18. A woman sues a man for injuries she received in a motorcycle accident on a public highway involving the woman and the man. The woman alleges that the man was speeding, driving recklessly, and performing dangerous stunts on the public highway. The woman calls a witness to testify that the man has the reputation in the community of being a "dare devil" rider and frequently performs dangerous stunts on public highways. The court will rule that the witness' testimony is:

A. Admissible because it shows the man is a negligent motorcycle rider.

B. Admissible because it is habit evidence.

C. Inadmissible to show negligence.

D. Inadmissible because the man has not offered testimony of his good character.

19. A man sued a woman for personal injuries resulting from a car accident. The man alleged that the collision was caused by the woman running a red light. The man called a witness to testify that the woman's car in which he was riding ran the red light. The witness, however, testified that the woman's car did not run the red light.

The man then called a bystander who had observed the accident to testify that the woman's car did run the red light. The court should rule that the bystander's testimony is:

A. Admissible because the bystander's testimony is relevant to material issues.

B. Admissible because the man was surprised by the witness' testimony.

C. Inadmissible because the man is bound by the witness' testimony.

D. Inadmissible because the man cannot impeach his own witness.

20. A woman sued grocery store for injuries sustained when she fell on a slippery floor in an aisle inside the store. She alleged that the store negligently failed to mop up some water on the floor of the aisle, causing her to slip and fall when she walked on top of the water. She called a witness who testified that there was water in the middle of the grocery store aisle on the day of the incident.

On cross-examination the witness was asked by the grocery store's attorney if the witness was "high" at the time he witnessed the incident. The witness replied, "No, I have never touched alcohol or drugs in my life." The grocery store's attorney now seeks to introduce testimony of a drug dealer that the witness had been high from a joint that the drug dealer had sold the witness and had watched the witness smoke at a party eighteen months before. The court will rule the drug dealer's testimony:

A. Inadmissible because a witness cannot be impeached by specific acts.

B. Inadmissible because the question of whether the witness was high or not is a collateral matter.

C. Admissible to show the witness is not truthful.

D. Admissible to impeach the witness as to his lack of memory.

21. A woman was injured by a falling box in a warehouse. There were several eyewitnesses at the scene of the incident. She sued the warehouse. At trial she called an eyewitness, who intended to testify that at time of the incident the eyewitness had screamed, "Look out! That box is about to fall and hit you!" The court will rule this testimony:

A. Inadmissible because the statement preceded the accident.

B. Inadmissible because the eyewitness is available as a witness.

C. Inadmissible as hearsay not within any exception.

D. Admissible as an excited utterance.

22. A driver's automobile hit and injured a jogger while the jogger was jogging across a marked crosswalk. There were several witnesses at the scene of the accident. The jogger sued the driver for the jogger's injuries. At trial, the jogger called the policeman who had investigated the accident. The policeman testified, "The passenger in the driver's automobile, said, 'Our car hit the jogger while he was in the crosswalk.' The driver was present but remained silent." The court will rule this testimony:

A. Admissible because the passenger's statement is imputed to the driver.

B. Admissible as a party admission.

C. Inadmissible because the driver probably was just experiencing shock.

D. Inadmissible, unless the driver has already testified.

23. A driver drove his automobile into a jogger, who was jogging on the side of the road. The jogger then sued the driver for the jogger's personal injuries.

In court, the jogger wanted to introduce his wife's testimony that the day after the accident the jogger had said to his wife, "My hip must be fractured, it really hurts." The court will rule the testimony:

A. Inadmissible because it is self-serving.

B. Inadmissible as hearsay not within any exception.

C. Admissible as a statement de-

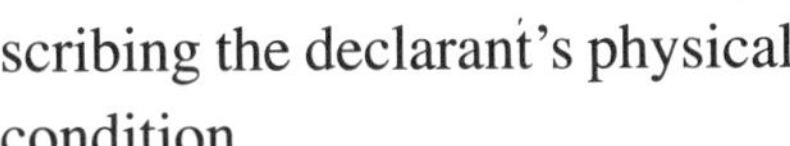

scribing the declarant's physical condition.

D. Admissible to prove that the jogger's hip was fractured.

24. A woman went to a hair salon to have her hair dyed red. The hair stylist used the wrong solution on the woman's hair, and woman's hair turned green. The woman sued the hair stylist. At the trial, the woman sought to introduce into evidence that the hair stylist offered to redo the woman's hair dye and to pay the woman $1,000. The court will rule this evidence:

A. Inadmissible because of public policy.

B. Inadmissible because it is not relevant to the question of damages.

C. Admissible as a party admission.

D. Admissible against the hair stylist's pecuniary interests.

25. A woman was a passenger in a driver's automobile. While riding in the driver's automobile, the automobile was struck in the rear by another vehicle. Both the driver and the passenger brought a lawsuit against the driver of the other vehicle.

On the day after the accident, the passenger wrote a letter to her uncle, describing the details of the accident. At trial, the passenger was unable to remember some details of the accident. The driver wanted to show the passenger her letter over the objection of the driver of the other vehicle. The court should:

A. Allow the letter under past recollection recorded.

B. Allow the letter under present recollection refreshed.

C. Disallow the letter because it was written one day after the accident.

D. Disallow the letter because the letter is self-serving.

26. A woman is suing a man for defamation. She alleges that he has told all of the woman's friends and her employer that she once was a "call girl." At trial, the man calls a policeman to testify that eight years ago she was arrested for prostitution. The court will rule that the policeman's testimony is:

A. Admissible because it is relevant.

B. Admissible because character itself is at issue.

C. Inadmissible as hearsay.

D. Inadmissible because the prejudicial effect outweighs any probative value.

27. A divorcee who despises her ex-husband reads in the paper that he is being tried for fraudulent stock transactions. She remembers that while she was married to her ex-husband, he had explained to her the scheme that he had committed. She wants to testify for the prosecution. The ex-husband objected. Will the court allow the divorcee to testify?

    A. Yes because once the marriage is dissolved, the privilege no longer exists.

    B. Yes because the ex-husband committed a crime.

    C. No because it was a confidential communication made during marriage.

    D. No because the divorcee is only doing it out of spite for the ex-husband.

28. A woman sued a man for injuries sustained in an automobile accident. The woman called an eyewitness as a witness. The eyewitness testified that the man was wearing a red jacket at the time of the accident. The man then called to the stand a bystander who had also been present at the time of the accident. The bystander was to testify that the man's jacket was green. The bystander's testimony is:

    A. Admissible as tending to prove a material fact.

    B. Admissible as bearing on the eyewitness' truthfulness.

    C. Inadmissible because the eyewitness' capacity to observe is not at issue.

    D. Inadmissible because the jacket color is not a significant issue here.

29. A woman sued her doctor for malpractice following a surgery on her leg. The doctor testified on his own behalf that he had followed all the proper medical procedures during the surgery. The woman then called a nurse to testify that shortly after the surgery, the doctor had told her, "I wish I had not left that sponge inside the woman prior to closing her up. I hope she doesn't notice." The court will find the nurse's testimony:

    A. Inadmissible because it is hearsay not within any exception.

    B. Inadmissible because no foundation was laid.

    C. Admissible as a prior inconsistent statement.

    D. Admissible as an admission.

30. A woman is on trial for the murder of her boyfriend. She does not plan on taking the stand. However, she calls a man to testify that she has a reputation for non-violence. Will the court allow the man's testimony?

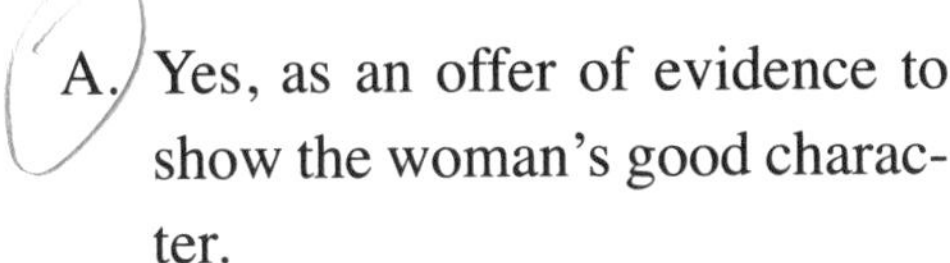

A. Yes, as an offer of evidence to show the woman's good character.

B. No because character evidence is not admissible to support a defendant's claim she is innocent of the crime.

C. No because the woman has not yet taken the stand.

D. Yes, so long as the man is an expert witness on nonviolence.

31. A physician was called as a witness by the defendant in a lawsuit involving an automobile accident. The physician was asked to testify to statements made by a person who had been a passenger in one of the cars at the time of the accident (and who was not a party to the lawsuit), for the purpose of obtaining treatment from the physician. The passenger was still in the hospital and could not personally attend the trial. Which of the following is the correct basis for excluding evidence of the passenger's statement?

A. An objection by the physician asserting the passenger's privilege against disclosure of confidential communications made by the passenger to the physician, for purposes of treatment.

B. An objection by the passenger's attorney, on the ground of doctor-patient privilege.

C. A finding by the trial judge that the patient did not actually receive treatment.

D. The assertion of a privilege by the passenger's attorney, present at trial as a spectator at the passenger's request, and allowed by the trial judge.

32. A client was injured in an automobile accident when her vehicle was struck another vehicle. The client retained a law firm to pursue a personal injury case against the operator of the other vehicle. The client retained the law firm six weeks prior to the running of the statute of limitations on her claim. The complaint was never prepared, nor filed. The statute of limitations on the client's claim has run.

The client then sued the law firm for negligence. This case is on trial with a jury.

In order to establish a breach of standard of care owed to her by the law firm, the client:

A. Must have a legal expert from the same locality testify that defendant's conduct was a breach.

B. Must have a legal expert from the same state testify that the law firm's conduct was a breach.

C. Can rely on the application of the jurors' common knowledge as to whether there was a breach.

D. Can rely on the judge, as an expert in law, to advise the jury whether there was a breach.

33. A woman was injured when the steering wheel on the car she was driving locked. The woman sued the manufacturer of the steering wheel. The woman learned and testified that just after her accident, the steering wheel manufacturer had begun to install steering wheels that do not lock while a person is driving the vehicle in which the steering wheel is installed. The steering wheel manufacturer objected to the woman's testimony. The objection will be:

A. Overruled because fault is not at issue.

B. Sustained because the evidence is irrelevant.

C. Sustained because of the public policy to encourage safety.

D. Overruled because it shows that the steering wheel manufacturer has a consciousness of guilt.

34. A woman sued a hotel for injuries she sustained in a fall in the hotel lobby. The lobby floor was covered with tile. The evidence was that the lobby floor had been waxed approximately an hour before the woman slipped on it and, although the wax had dried, there appeared to be excessive dried wax caked on several tiles. The hotel denied the woman's claim that it was negligent. The hotel offered proof that the week before the woman's fall, at least 11,000 people had walked across the lobby floor without incident. The trial judge should rule the evidence:

A. Admissible because it tends to prove that the woman did not use reasonable care.

B. Admissible because it tends to prove that the hotel was careful in maintaining the floors.

C. Admissible because it proves that no dangerous condition existed.

D. Inadmissible because it does not bear on the issue of the hotel's exercise of due care on this occasion.

35. A man was on trial for murder. The only eyewitness to the crime was a woman, whose testimony was largely uncorroborated by other evidence. The woman was called by the prosecution to testify to what she saw on the night in question. The man's counsel objected to the woman testifying on the ground that the woman was incompetent to testify by reason of a long history of mental illness. The man's counsel offered documentary evidence to the court that the woman had recently been in a mental institution, and moved to have

the court order the woman to submit to a psychiatric examination. The court denied the motion. Did the court make an error in permitting the woman to testify?

A. No because a person who has a mental illness or defect is not per se incompetent to testify.

B. No because the woman was the only witness to the crime.

C. Yes because a mentally ill person is disqualified from testifying.

D. Yes, unless the woman was insane.

36. A woman sued a man for injuries suffered by the woman when their automobiles collided. At trial, the woman offers into evidence a properly authenticated letter from the man that says, "Your claim seems too high, but because I might be found at fault, I'm prepared to offer you half of what you ask." The letter is:

A. Admissible as an admission.

B. Admissible as a statement against the man's pecuniary interest.

C. Inadmissible as hearsay.

D. Inadmissible because the man's statement was made in an effort to settle a claim.

37. A woman purchased a blender from a retail store. The first time she attempted to use the blender, following the instructions in the manual, it sucked in her hand and pulverized it. The woman sues the manufacturer of the blender. The woman seeks to introduce evidence that as soon as the manufacturer was served with her complaint, it recalled all of the blenders of that model. The attorney for the manufacturer objects to the admission of this evidence. The court should rule that the evidence is:

A. Admissible as an admission.

B. Admissible as a declaration against interest.

C. Inadmissible as a subsequent remedial repair.

D. Inadmissible because manufacturers always recall defective products.

38. A woman was injured when her car was struck by a truck owned by a corporation. The truck was driven by an employee of the corporation. Another corporation employee had been a passenger in the truck at the time of the accident. The woman sued the corporation for negligence, alleging that the driver of the truck had failed to yield the right-of-way.

The woman sought to introduce the written statement of the passenger that the driver of the truck had left his

glasses (which he is required to wear while operating a motor vehicle) at the restaurant where they had had lunch just before the accident. The statement is admissible against the corporation, if:

A. The woman first proves that the passenger was an employee of the corporation at the time she had written her statement, and that the statement concerned a matter within the scope of her employment.

B. The woman produces independent evidence that the driver of the truck had not been wearing his glasses at the time of the accident.

C. The passenger is shown to be beyond the court's subpoena power.

D. The statement was made under oath in an affidavit form.

39. A man was on trial for beheading a woman. At trial, the woman's husband testified that a week after the incident, the man had telephoned the husband and had said, "I'm so sorry I beheaded your wife." The man objected. The statement is:

A. Admissible, since it is exempted from the hearsay rule.

B. Admissible as an exception to the hearsay rule.

C. Admissible as a declaration against interest.

D. Inadmissible, since it is hearsay not within any exception.

40. A man was arrested and charged with illegally driving a stolen vehicle across the state line. Evidence was presented that he drove the car from New York to Chicago. The judge took judicial notice of the fact that it was impossible to drive from New York to Chicago without crossing the state line. The judge's taking of judicial notice:

A. Meant that the prosecution did not have to produce further evidence that driving from New York to Chicago involves the crossing of state lines.

B. Shifted the burden to the man to present evidence in rebuttal.

C. Shifted the burden on the man to prove that he did not drive from New York to Chicago.

D. Conclusively proved the point that to drive from New York to Chicago, state lines were crossed.

41. A woman sued a man for fraud, claiming that the man had sold her a defective parrot because the parrot would not speak, even though the woman had not trained the parrot to do so. At trial, the woman requested that the judge take

judicial notice that all parrots speak. The judge also owned a parrot and stated that he would not take judicial notice of the fact that the woman's parrot was defective because it did not speak, since the judge's own parrot did not speak until the judge had trained the parrot to do so. The judge's refusal to take judicial notice that the parrot was defective was:

A. Correct because the judge knew that parrots need to be trained to speak, since his own parrot had to be trained to speak.

B. Correct because it is common knowledge that parrots must be trained to speak.

C. Correct because the decision whether or not to take judicial notice is completely within the judge's discretion.

D. Incorrect because a judge must always take judicial notice when requested to do so.

42. At the trial of a woman for a murder, the prosecution called a witness, who testified that he saw the woman kill the victim. The woman believed that, at the time of the alleged murder, the witness was 200 miles away, engaged in a narcotics deal. On cross-examination by the woman, the witness was asked whether he was, in fact, 200 miles away, purchasing narcotics on the date of the alleged murder. The witness refused to answer the question on self-incrimination grounds.

The judge ordered the witness to answer the question. The judge's order was:

A. Correct because the witness had not been charged with any crime and, thus, could claim no privilege.

B. Incorrect because the witness properly invoked the privilege.

C. Correct because the public interest in allowing an accused to defend himself outweighs the interest of a non-party witness in the privilege.

D. Correct because the trial record did not establish that the witness' answer could be incriminating.

43. A man was being prosecuted for burglary. At trial, the man testified on his own behalf, denying that he had committed the burglary. On cross-examination, the prosecution asked the man whether he had been convicted ten years ago for burglary. The question of the earlier burglary conviction is:

A. Proper, if the court determined that its probative value outweighed its prejudicial effect.

B. Proper because a defendant's character may always be attacked by the prosecution.

EVIDENCE

C. Improper because it is character evidence.

D. Improper because the conviction is ten years old, and the defense must have been given notice of its use prior to trial.

44. In a lawsuit attacking the validity of a trust executed ten years ago, the plaintiff alleged the mental incompetency of the settlor and offered into evidence a properly authenticated affidavit of the settlor's brother. The affidavit stated that the brother had observed the settlor closely over a period of a month, that the settlor had engaged in instances of unusual behavior (which were described), and that the settlor's appearance had changed from being neat, alert and aware, to disordered and absent-minded. The judge should rule the brother's affidavit:

A. Inadmissible as opinion.

B. Inadmissible as hearsay not within any exception.

C. Admissible, since the declaration was the best evidence that the statement was made.

D. Admissible, as an official statement.

45. A woman and a man were arrested for armed robbery. They were taken to the police station and placed in an interrogation room. After the police officer gave them their Miranda warnings, the woman said, "Look, the man planned the whole thing, we robbed the place, and I was dumb enough to follow along." The man said nothing. The man was then taken to another room, and a full confession was obtained from the woman.

If the man is brought to trial for armed robbery, the fact that he failed to object to the woman's statement and remained silent, is:

A. Admissible as an admission.

B. Admissible because a statement of a participant in a crime is admissible against another participant.

C. Inadmissible because it is hearsay.

D. Inadmissible because, under the circumstances, there was no duty for the man to respond.

46. A case of whiskey was stolen from a liquor truck when it was parked outside a bar. At trial, to prove that the whiskey was on the truck, the shipping manager for the company that owned the liquor truck was called by the prosecution to testify. The shipping manager testified that he did not have first-hand knowledge that the whiskey was aboard the truck at the time of the theft. Thereupon, the prosecution asked the shipping manager, "Did you receive a shipping

invoice listing the contents on that truck for that particular day?" The shipping manager replied, "Yes, I did receive from the shipping clerk an invoice listing the merchandise, as customary." The shipping manager then produced the invoice. If the prosecuting attorney offers the invoice into evidence, the trial judge should:

A. Admit the invoice, only because it is a record of regularly conducted business activity.

B. Admit the invoice, only because it is recorded recollection.

C. Admit the invoice because it would qualify as a business record and as a record of recollection.

D. Exclude the invoice as hearsay not within any exception.

47. While crossing the street, a pedestrian was hit by a red car driven by a woman. The pedestrian sued the woman for his injuries.

At trial, the pedestrian called a policeman to testify that an hour after the accident, a bus driver had stopped and said to him, "Officer, an hour ago I saw a hit and run accident involving a red car and a pedestrian." The policeman's testimony should be:

A. Admissible as a present sense impression.

B. Admissible as a statement of perception.

C. Inadmissible as hearsay not within any exception.

D. Inadmissible because it is irrelevant.

48. A man was injured while operating a lawnmower. The man went straight inside his house and told his wife, "Take me to the hospital. I am bleeding." The man recovered and sued the manufacturer of the lawn mower. At trial, the man sought to introduce his wife's testimony regarding the statement he had made to her immediately after he was injured by the lawn mower. The wife's testimony should be:

A. Admitted as a statement of present physical condition.

B. Admitted as evidence of liability against the manufacturer of the lawn mower.

C. Excluded because the statement was not made to a treating doctor.

D. Excluded because the man was not qualified as an expert to determine his own medical condition.

49. A man went to the doctor to get a vasectomy. Instead, the doctor castrated him. The man sued the doctor for mal-

practice. At trial, he called as a witness another physician to whom the man had complained of pain from the castration. The physician was to testify that the man had said to him, "I am in severe pain from the castration." The physician's testimony regarding the man's statements to him is:

A. Inadmissible because the statement is not reliable.

B. Inadmissible because the statement relates to a condition perceivable by a lay person.

C. Admissible because the man may give an opinion as to his own diagnosis and required treatment.

D. Admissible for the purpose of diagnosis and treatment.

50. After checking into a hotel, a hotel guest went to the elevator on the lobby level floor to proceed to his room. When the elevator doors opened, he stepped into the elevator shaft, unaware that the elevator car itself had not descended to the lobby. The guest fell two feet to the floor below. The elevator actually was out of service because it was being repaired that day. The guest sued the hotel, claiming he suffers from permanent knee injuries as a result of the incident and that he had had no knee injuries prior to the incident.

The hotel sought to introduce certain statements the guest had made to his general physician three years before the incident. On that occasion, the guest had told the physician, "I awoke this morning with severe knee pain, after I helped a college buddy with moving yesterday." The guest objected. The statement is:

A. Admissible because statements made more than two years prior to the lawsuit are admissible.

B. Admissible because the statement relates to the guest's medical condition, which is in issue.

C. Inadmissible because the statement is protected from disclosure by the physician-patient privilege.

D. Inadmissible.

51. A woman sued a man for personal injuries that she sustained when she was struck by the man's bicycle when the woman was walking in a crosswalk. Immediately after the accident, the man ran over to the woman and said, "I know I was not watching where I was going when my bicycle stuck you, but if you're hurt, I'll pay your medical bills."

At trial, the woman called an eyewitness to the accident, as her first witness. The eyewitness proposed to testify that he had heard the man tell the woman, "I know I was not watching where I was going when my bicycle stuck you,

but if you're hurt, I'll pay your medical bills." The man objected. If the eyewitness' testimony is admitted, it will most likely be admitted because the proffered evidence is:

A. Admissible as an opinion.

B. Admissible as a party admission.

C. Admissible as a present sense impression.

D. Admissible as a declaration against interest.

52. A woman had a pool party at their home. A young child jumped into the pool and started to drown. The woman retrieved the child from the pool and gave him CPR, and the child survived. The woman told the child's father that she would pay any medical expenses the father incurred for the child. The woman's statement was overheard by a neighbor, who was attending the party. Later, however, the woman refused to pay the child's medical expenses. The child's parents sue the woman, on the child's behalf.

The parents (on behalf of the child) call the neighbor to testify. The neighbor begins to testify about the woman's offer to pay the child's medical expenses. The woman objected. The trial judge should:

A. Sustain the objection because the police report is the best evidence of the woman's statement.

B. Sustain the objection in the interest of humanitarian considerations.

C. Sustain the objection because offers to pay medical expenses are inadmissible.

D. Overrule the objection because the statement is an admission.

53. A man was charged with vehicular battery after driving through a red light and crashing his car into a woman's truck. The woman suffered massive internal injuries and lapsed into a coma until several hours after she reached the hospital. The woman's best friend had been a passenger in the truck. The best friend miraculously received only a few minor bruises. After the collision, the best friend stayed with the woman, trying to comfort her until the ambulance arrived.

At trial, the best friend was called to the stand by the district attorney, who asked the best friend if the woman had said anything to her before being taken to the hospital. The best friend answered affirmatively, and testified that the woman had been conscious for a few brief moments after the accident when she had stated, "He never stopped for that red light."

Upon the man's objection, the court should rule the testimony concerning the woman's statement to the best friend:

A. Inadmissible because the woman's statement was hearsay.

B. Inadmissible because the woman's statement lacked trustworthiness.

C. Admissible as a present sense impression by the woman.

D. Admissible as an admission.

54. A tall woman with red hair robbed a liquor store. Later, she was arrested and charged with the armed robbery. At her trial, several eyewitnesses testified they had seen a tall red-haired woman pull out a gun and rob the store's owner. The woman appeared at trial with a shaved head. The prosecution called the sheriff's deputy who had processed the woman when she had initially arrived at the jail to testify that the woman had red hair when she was first got to the jail. The woman's objected. The trial judge should rule the deputy's testimony is:

A. Admissible as a prior identification.

B. Admissible because the deputy had personal knowledge of the woman's hair color.

C. Inadmissible as hearsay not within any exception.

D. Inadmissible because it is opinion.

55. A woman sued a man for injuries sustained in an automobile accident. The man consulted an attorney to represent him in his defense. During the consultation, the attorney's secretary took notes. A month later, the secretary quit her job. The man decided not to hire the attorney, but to act in pro per instead. During the man's trial, the prosecution called the secretary to testify to what was said at the initial conference. The proposed testimony is:

A. Admissible because the man did not hire the attorney.

B. Admissible because the secretary's presence at the conference destroyed the privilege.

C. Inadmissible because of the attorney-client privilege.

D. Inadmissible because the secretary is no longer working for the attorney.

56. A woman sued a man for battery. The woman called a witness to testify that the incident occurred on December 23. Although the witness was not questioned about a deposition he made before trial, the witness had previously testified at his deposition that the in-

cident occurred on December 14. On cross-examination, the man offered the witness' deposition into evidence. The trial judge should rule the deposition:

A. Admissible as substantive evidence the incident occurred on December 14.

B. Inadmissible because the witness was available to testify at the trial.

C. Inadmissible as hearsay not within any exception.

D. Inadmissible because there were no facts showing that the witness was intentionally untruthful.

57. One morning, a man telephoned his friend and asked the friend if the man could borrow his car. The man promised the friend that the car would be returned later that afternoon. The friend agreed to allow the man to borrow the car. While driving the friend's car, the man was involved in an automobile accident with a woman. She sues the friend for negligence.

In her case in chief, the woman calls a witness to testify that the witness saw the man driving carelessly on three prior occasions. The trial judge should rule the testimony:

A. Inadmissible because it is irrelevant.

B. Inadmissible because a non-driving vehicle owner can never be sued for the negligence of a driver.

C. Admissible against the friend, as evidence of the man's lack of fitness.

D. Inadmissible as hearsay not within any exception.

58. A woman and a man were studying together for the Bar Examination. A heated argument ensued regarding the true meaning of the Rule in Dumpor's case. The woman became so enraged that she hit the man in the head with her Fleming's outline. The man sued the woman for battery. The woman raised self-defense as a defense. In the man's case in chief, the man presented a witness to testify to that on four previous occasions, the woman had hit her study partners with books. The court should find the witness' testimony:

A. Admissible as evidence of habit.

B. Inadmissible because it is more prejudicial than probative.

C. Admissible because it is proper character evidence.

D. Inadmissible because of bias.

59. A woman was charged with murder for shooting a man with her gun. She

testified at trial that she had honestly believed that the man had already died from a heart attack before he was shot. In rebuttal, the district attorney called a witness to testify that, just before she saw the woman shoot the man, she had heard the man shout, "I'm going to die."

The woman objected to the witness' proposed testimony on grounds that it was inadmissible hearsay. If the trial court judge overrules the objection, the reason will most likely be that:

A. Although hearsay, the man's statement was made in the belief of impending death.

B. Although hearsay, the man's statement related to his present physical condition.

C. It was not hearsay because the man's statement was admissible to show "notice or knowledge" by the woman that the man was still alive.

D. It was not hearsay because the witness had firsthand knowledge of the events as they transpired.

60. A woman sued an artist for defamation. The artist had painted a picture portraying a female engaging in sexual conduct, and the woman's complaint alleged that the female in the picture was easily recognizable as the woman. The artist signed the picture and displayed it in a gallery. At trial, the woman called a witness who had seen the picture at the gallery. The witness intended to state that he had observed the picture hanging in the gallery and had noticed that the artist's name was signed on the picture in the lower right corner. Upon proper objection the court should rule the witness' testimony:

A. Inadmissible because the witness' testimony is not the best evidence.

B. Inadmissible because the witness' description of the picture is insufficiently authenticated.

C. Admissible because the witness properly authenticated the painting by identifying the artist who signed the painting.

D. Admissible because the witness had personal knowledge of the facts to which he was testifying.

61. A woman sued a murderer for the wrongful death of the woman's husband. As part of her lawsuit for damages, the woman had to demonstrate how much money her husband would have earned if the murderer had not murdered him. At trial, the woman offered the testimony of her husband's former business partner, who stated that the average net profit from the business of each partner over the preceding five years was $100,000. Further, evidence was

presented showing that the partnership books were in the former business partner's possession and that the former business partner was willing to allow for their inspection.

The testimony of the former business partner is:

A. Admissible, since the information is relevant and the books are available for inspection.

B. Admissible, since the facts sought demonstrated the earnings of the partnership and the former business partner had personal knowledge of those facts.

C. Inadmissible as hearsay not falling within any exception.

D. Inadmissible because the former business partner's testimony is not the best evidence.

62. Two young men were on trial for murder. The cousin of one of the young men was an attorney, and he represented both men. The men both claimed that they did not commit the murder. Several witnesses claimed that they saw the two men leaving the scene of the crime in a vehicle that matched the description of the vehicle that the two men were driving. The cousin called his girlfriend to testify that the tire marks left by the murderer's vehicle could not have been made by the two young men's vehicle. The girlfriend had worked in her father's mechanic shop while growing up and knew about virtually every type of tire in existence and the tire marks they leave behind. Upon objection, the court should rule the girlfriend's testimony:

A. Admissible because the girlfriend was a qualified expert in tire marks.

B. Inadmissible because of the best evidence rule.

C. Inadmissible because the girlfriend did not have personal knowledge of the facts to which she was testifying.

D. Inadmissible as hearsay not falling within any exception.

63. A man dies, leaving a will by which he bequeaths his entire estate to his friend. The man's only heir at law brings a lawsuit to contest the will on grounds of incapacity. At the trial, the friend calls a doctor and the man's former housekeeper as witnesses, both of whom offer to testify affirmatively when asked whether the man knew enough about "the nature and extent of his property, and the natural objects of his bounty" at the time of the man's execution of the will. Other evidence has shown: (1) that the former housekeeper had seen the man daily for over 25 years, until the date of his death; and (2) that the doctor is a psychiatrist, stipulated by the parties to be qualified, who had occasion to examine the man the week before he

executed his will. Upon objection, the court should:

A. Exclude the testimony of both witnesses because both are attempting to testify to their opinions on an ultimate issue in the case.

B. Admit the doctor's testimony, and exclude the former housekeeper's testimony.

C. Admit the former housekeeper's testimony, and exclude the doctor's testimony.

D. Admit the testimony of both witnesses.

64. A woman sued a man for damages for injuries that the woman incurred when a badly rotted limb fell from a tree in front of the man's home and hit the woman. The man claimed that the tree was on city property; thus, he was not liable to the woman for her injuries. At trial, the woman offered testimony that a week after the accident, the man had the tree cut down. The evidence is:

A. Inadmissible, since such is against public policy so as to further safety precautions.

B. Inadmissible, since it is irrelevant.

C. Admissible to show that the tree was on the man's property.

D. Admissible to show that the tree was in rotten condition.

65. A man was prosecuted for the murder of a woman. At trial, a witness testified against the man. On cross-examination, the man asked the witness the following question, "Isn't it true that charges against you as an accomplice in the woman's murder are being dropped in exchange for your testimony against the man?" The question is:

A. Proper impeachment because it shows that the witness has a self-interest in testifying against the man.

B. Proper impeachment on cross-examination, even though extrinsic proof will not be allowed if the question is answered in the negative.

C. Improper impeachment.

D. Improper because specific instances of misconduct may not be used to impeach.

66. A woman sued a car manufacturer for fraud because the manufacturer had stated that the car was "Made in the USA." At trial, the manufacturer brought evidence that the car had been made in New Mexico and asked the court to take judicial notice of the fact that New Mexico is located in the United States. May the court take judicial notice of this fact?

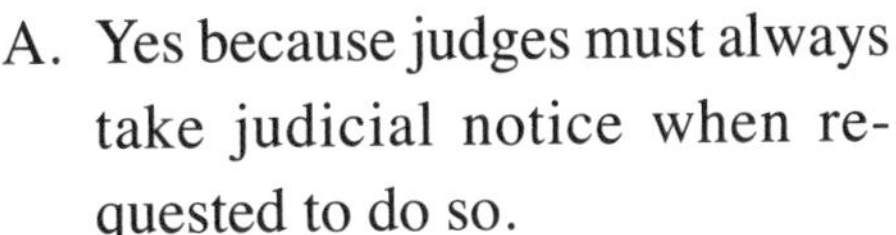

A. Yes because judges must always take judicial notice when requested to do so.

B. Yes because New Mexico's location in the United States is a matter of common knowledge.

C. No because New Mexico, like the rest of Mexico, is not part of the United States.

D. No because no foundation has been laid to demonstrate that New Mexico is part of the United States.

67. A victim was injured in an automobile accident and rushed to the emergency room at a hospital. A victim subsequently brought an action against the hospital for malpractice, claiming that the hospital delayed in giving her prompt medical attention, which resulted in a delay in her recovery period.

At trial, the nurse who had attended to the victim proposed to testify that when the victim was brought into the emergency room, the victim was unconscious and would, thus, not have been aware of any alleged delay in treatment. The victim's attorney objects. The trial judge should:

A. Sustain the objection because the nurse is not a qualified expert.

B. Sustain the objection because it goes to an ultimate issue of fact.

C. Overrule the objection on the grounds of nurse-patient privilege.

D. Overrule the objection because the nurse had observed the victim when she was brought into the hospital.

68. A man was driving his sports car when the car struck a 6-year-old boy, who was crossing the street on the way to school. The boy was permanently paralyzed as a result of this encounter.

The boy and his father visited an attorney in regard to bringing a case against the man for the injuries that the boy sustained. The father did not retain the attorney to represent the boy in the lawsuit. Instead, the father hired another lawyer to handle the case.

At trial, the man's lawyer calls the first attorney to testify as to what the boy had said to him in regard to his physical condition during the consultation that that attorney had had with the boy and the boy's father. The attorney's testimony is:

A. Admissible because no attorney-client relationship existed.

B. Admissible because the element of confidentiality is not satisfied when a third person is present with the attorney and client.

C. Inadmissible because it was a statement of physical condition.

D. Inadmissible because of the attorney-client privilege.

69. A man was being sued for breach of employment contract by an employer. The employer had hired the man to obtain a patent on all his inventions within 30 days of their finalization stage. The day of the finalization of a particular invention was in question. The employer claimed that the finalization date was May 1. The man claimed that it was June 1.

At trial, the man was called to testify. His counsel asked him if he was certain about the date, June 1, on which the invention was finalized. The man replied, "Yes, it was June 1 because I remember reading a story in that day's newspaper about the 8.0 earthquake in Los Angeles, which destroyed most of downtown." The employer's counsel objected to the reference of the newspaper and made a motion to strike. The judge should:

A. Grant the motion on the grounds that the best evidence rule requires production of the newspaper.

B. Grant the motion because the reference to the newspaper story does not fit within any exception to the hearsay rule.

C. Deny the motion on the grounds that the court can take judicial notice of the local newspaper.

D. Deny the motion because a witness may refer to a collateral document without providing the document.

70. In a lawsuit between a woman and a man arising out of an automobile accident, a bystander who had observed the accident was called to the stand by the woman to testify that the man had driven his automobile through a red light, which caused the accident. On cross-examination, the bystander was asked if he had ever been convicted for false pretenses, which the bystander denied. The prosecutor then offered a certified copy of the criminal conviction into evidence. The woman objected. The court should:

A. Overrule the objection because it bears on the bystander's credibility.

B. Overrule the objection because it does not prove whether or not the bystander was telling the truth.

C. Sustain the objection because it is irrelevant.

D. Sustain the objection because the bystander's character is not in issue.

71. A man was arrested and charged with raping a woman. He claimed that he did not rape her because she had consented to his advances. At trial, the man was prepared to testify that he had engaged in sexual intercourse with the woman on many occasions with the woman's consent during the previous month before the rape allegedly occurred. The man's testimony is:

A. Admissible as evidence of specific acts to show consent.

B. Admissible as evidence of habit.

C. Inadmissible character evidence.

D. Inadmissible because reputation or opinion evidence of past sexual behavior of the victim is not permitted.

72. A man was on trial for burglary. He testified on his own behalf, denying that he committed the burglary. On cross-examination, the prosecution asked him if in sixteen years earlier he had been convicted of robbery. The prosecution had never given any notice to the defense that it was going to bring up the conviction from sixteen years earlier. The man's attorney objected. The court should:

A. Overrule the objection because the prosecutor may test the credibility of the witness.

B. Overrule the objection because the testimony is immaterial.

C. Sustain the objection because the crime is too old.

D. Sustain the objection because the adverse party was not given written notice.

73. A woman sued a man for injuries suffered by her when the man collided his motorcycle into the woman. The woman prayed for $1 million in her lawsuit. At trial, the woman offered into evidence a properly authenticated letter from the man that stated, "Your claim of damage seems too high, but because I have no insurance and I was at fault, I'm prepared to pay the amount you have asked." The letter is:

A. Admissible under public policy reasons.

B. Admissible because it is a party admission.

C. Inadmissible because the man's statement is opinion.

D. Inadmissible because the statement was made during an effort to settle a claim.

74. A woman was sued by a man for the sale of her 80% interest of the stock of a closely held corporation. The woman consulted an attorney regarding this sale. She explained to the attorney the

reason for the sale and disclosed the financial condition of the corporation. The attorney determined that the transaction was too complex and in violation of a shareholder agreement. The attorney decided to decline the case. The woman then hired another lawyer to represent her.

At trial, the man calls the first attorney to testify to the contents of the conversation between him and the woman. The woman objected. The court should:

A. Sustain the objection because of the attorney-client relationship.

B. Sustain the objection because the conversation is not relevant to the sale of the stock.

C. Overrule the objection because the attorney was not retained by the woman.

D. Overrule the objection because the attorney-client privilege did not attach.

75. A man owned a house that he rented to a woman. The lease stated that the woman would maintain the house and yard in its present condition. While walking home one day, a child was hit on the head when a tree limb fell from the man's property, seriously injuring her. It is agreed between the parties that the tree fell because of dry rot. The man hired a contractor the next day to have the whole tree removed from the property. The child now brings suit against the man in Superior Court. At trial, the man testified that he rented out the house to the woman, who he claimed was responsible for the maintenance of the yard under the terms of the lease. The child introduces into evidence that the man had the contractor remove the tree from the property the next day. The evidence is:

A. Admissible because the evidence is not being used to prove negligence or culpable conduct.

B. Admissible because the man was at fault.

C. Inadmissible because the man's acts were subsequent remedial measures.

D. Inadmissible because the probative value substantially outweighed its prejudicial effect.

76. A man was employed at a soda can manufacturer as a quality control tester of the "flip-top" openers on 12-ounce beverage cans produced by the manufacturer for soda cans. One day while at work, the man was injured when one of the "flip-tops" fell unnoticed into the can he was testing, only to be swallowed by the man on his next sip of soda. The man died as a result.

The man's wife brought a wrongful death action against the manufacturer. At trial, the wife sought to introduce the manufacturer's offer to pay funeral expenses. The manufacturer objected. The court should:

A. Sustain the objection, since offering to pay funeral expenses is not admissible to prove liability.

B. Overrule the objection because offering to pay funeral expenses is admissible to prove liability.

C. Overrule the objection, since the manufacturer's statement is a party admission.

D. Overrule the objection, since the manufacturer's statement is a declaration against their interest.

77. A man was on trial for killing the cashier at a local convenience store. One of his defenses is that he is innocent by reason of a mental disease or defect such that he could not appreciate the wrongfulness of his acts. The defense presented expert testimony through a psychiatrist who was properly qualified as an expert. The psychiatrist testified that the man suffered a mental disease or defect at the time of his acts, as to the characteristics of that mental disease or defect, and his diagnosis of the man. Over objection of the district attorney, the defense then offered the psychiatrist's opinion that the man did not know his acts were wrong when committed. How will the court rule on the prosecution's objection?

A. Overruled because the psychiatrist was properly qualified as an expert before testifying.

B. Overruled because the psychiatrist's expert opinion that the man suffered from a mental disease or defect was uncontroverted.

C. Sustained because an expert cannot testify on whether the defendant had the mental condition constituting an element of a defense to the crime charged.

D. Sustained because the psychiatrist's testimony was biased in favor of the man.

78. A woman was driving down the street and failed to stop her vehicle at a stop sign. Her vehicle collided with a motorcycle. The motorcycle driver was severely injured. He subsequently sued the woman for his personal injuries. At trial, the woman wished to present testimony from her best friend that the previous week, the best friend was a passenger in the woman's vehicle, and that the woman stopped her vehicle at every stop sign and red traffic signal that they encountered throughout that particular drive. The motorcycle driver objects to the best friend's testimony. The court should:

A. Sustain the objection because the testimony pertains to an impermissible character trait.

B. Sustain the objection because it is improper opinion testimony.

C. Overrule the objection because the best friend had personal knowledge of the woman's character.

D. Overrule the objection because it tends to disprove the motorcycle driver's claim that the woman drove negligently when her vehicle collided with the motorcycle.

79. A woman left a department store without paying for a blouse. She was stopped after exiting and was charged with shoplifting. At trial, the prosecution introduced into evidence that the woman exited from the department store without paying for the blouse, which was found on her baby stroller. She testified that she had walked out of the store with the blouse hanging on the outside of her baby's stroller and that she had forgotten that she had placed it there while she looked for a matching skirt.

The woman's attorney called to the stand a cashier at a nearby jewelry store to testify as follows: two hours before she was charged with shoplifting at the department store, the woman had shopped at the jewelry store and, after paying for a $2,000 diamond ring she had purchased, walked out of the store leaving the diamond ring on a store counter. The prosecution objects to the testimony of the cashier. The court should:

A. Sustain the objection because the testimony pertains to an impermissible character trait.

B. Sustain the objection because it is improper opinion testimony.

C. Overrule the objection because the cashier had first-hand knowledge of the woman's conduct in the store on the occasion in question.

D. Overrule the objection because the cashier's testimony tends to disprove the woman's intent to commit the crime of shoplifting at the department store.

80. A woman left a department store without paying for a blouse. She was stopped after exiting and was charged with shoplifting. At trial, the prosecution introduced into evidence that the woman had exited from the department store without paying for the blouse, which was found on her baby stroller. The woman testified that she had walked out of the store with the blouse hanging on the outside of her stroller and that she had forgotten that she had placed it there while she looked for a matching skirt.

The woman also called a psychologist to testify that he had treated the woman and, in his opinion, the woman was suffering from a psychological condition that impaired her memory and caused her to be forgetful. The prosecution objects to the testimony of the psychologist. The court should:

A. Sustain the objection because the testimony pertains to an impermissible character trait.

B. Sustain the objection because it is improper opinion testimony.

C. Sustain the objection because the psychologist was not a qualified expert.

D. Overrule the objection because the psychologist's testimony is consistent with a finding of innocence.

81. A defendant was charged with the sale of heroin. He denied making the alleged sale. The defendant called his friend, who testified that for six years he had known the defendant socially and had lived in the same neighborhood as the defendant. The defendant then asked the friend whether the defendant had a character trait for non-violence. The prosecution objected. The court should:

A. Sustain the objection because evidence of a defendant's non-violent character is always admissible in a criminal case.

B. Sustain the objection because the evidence of the character trait of non-violence is irrelevant to the issue of selling narcotics.

C. Overrule the objection because the testimony is permissible character evidence.

D. Overrule the objection because once character evidence is admitted into evidence, the door is opened for further character evidence.

82. A man was charged with murder. He pled not guilty. At the request of the man's lawyer, the trial judge appointed two psychiatrists to examine the man and advise the man's lawyer as to whether the man should rely upon the defense of mental defect. At trial, the man's defense was diminished capacity. The man's lawyer called one of the two psychiatrists who had examined the man. The psychiatrist gave an opinion in support of the man's defense. The man's lawyer rested her case. In rebuttal, the prosecution called the second psychiatrist to give an opinion contrary to that of the first psychiatrist. The man's lawyer objected. The court should:

A. Sustain the objection because of the attorney-client privilege.

ATTY/PSYCH PRIV

B. Sustain the objection because of the psychiatrist-patient privilege.

C. Overrule the objection because as the man's expert medical provider, she is not permitted to testify adverse to the man's interest.

D. Overrule the objection because the second psychiatrist was never listed as the prosecution's expert prior to trial.

83. A man is charged with the murder of his mistress. As part of the prosecution's case in chief, the prosecutor offers a certified copy of the man's prior conviction for murdering his boss. The man objected. The evidence is:

A. Admissible because it tends to prove the man's plan.

B. Admissible because it shows the man's intent.

C. Inadmissible because it is improper character evidence.

D. Inadmissible because the prior murder is irrelevant.

84. A woman is suing a man for damages arising out of an automobile accident. She claims that the man was negligent. At trial, the woman calls a witness to the stand. The witness testifies that he is a member of the same church that the man attends, and that the man has a reputation for being a "careless" driver. The man's attorney objected to the testimony. The trial court should:

A. Allow the testimony because it is trustworthy.

B. Allow the testimony because it is relevant to the issue of whether the man was negligent.

C. Not allow the testimony because it is improper character evidence.

D. Not allow the testimony because the man has not testified.

85. A woman sued a man for injuries suffered by her when the man collided his blue truck into her automobile. At trial, the woman called to the stand the person who had been driving the woman's automobile at the time of the accident. The driver testified that he had been driving the woman's automobile when the accident happened and that the woman had been a passenger in the automobile at the time. He further testified that when he pulled onto the freeway, the woman said to him, "Watch out for that blue truck - it looks like the driver has been drinking, and he can't seem to keep control over his car." The man objected. The testimony is:

A. Admissible for public policy reasons.

B. Admissible as a present sense impression.

C. Inadmissible as hearsay.

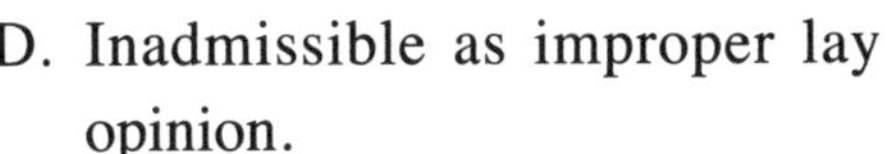

D. Inadmissible as improper lay opinion.

86. While driving within the scope of employment for an oil company, a man ran his truck over a woman. An eyewitness had observed the accident from across the street, while standing on her front lawn. Immediately after the accident, the eyewitness walked over to the injured woman, and stated, "It's too bad that truck never slowed down."

In an action by the woman against the oil company, evidence of the eyewitness' statement is:

A. Inadmissible because it was not authorized by the man's employer.

B. Inadmissible because the eyewitness was not under a state of excitement when the statement was made.

C. Admissible because the oil company certified the man's conduct when it hired him as an employee.

D. Admissible as a present sense impression.

87. While riding her bike home from school, a girl was struck by a car driven by a drunkard. The drunkard was arrested at the scene for driving while under the influence of alcohol. When the drunkard was booked at the police station, he was videotaped in his intoxicated state.

At trial, the prosecution offers the tape into evidence. The tape shows the drunkard answering questions by police officers while slurring his words and acting in an unsteady manner. The drunkard objects to the introduction of the tape. The court should:

A. Admit the tape because its probative value is not substantially outweighed by the danger of unfair prejudice.

B. Admit the tape because it is a party admission.

C. Not admit the tape because it is hearsay not within any exception.

D. Not admit the tape because its probative value is substantially outweighed by the danger of unfair prejudice

88. One day, a driver struck a pedestrian in a crosswalk. The pedestrian was seriously injured. The pedestrian sued the driver for the injuries the pedestrian had received in the auto accident. The pedestrian claimed that the driver was negligent because he had been driving his automobile over the speed limit.

At trial, the pedestrian called a woman to testify that she had seen the accident from across the street and that the driver was wearing a hat at the time of the accident. The driver then called a man who had observed the accident to testify

that the driver was not wearing a hat at the time of the accident.

The man's testimony is:

A. Admissible because it is relevant to the issue of who was negligent.

B. Admissible because it tends to test the credibility of the woman.

C. Inadmissible because it is extrinsic evidence on a collateral matter.

D. Inadmissible because it is irrelevant.

89. A man sued a woman for injuries he received when her vehicle collided with his vehicle. The man alleged that the woman was speeding at the time of the accident. The woman testified that at the time of the accident, she was driving her vehicle at a speed of 25 miles per hour in a 35 mile-per-hour zone. The man did not cross-examine the woman. Instead, the man called the police officer who had investigated the accident to testify that, at the time of the accident, the woman had told the officer that her vehicle had been traveling at 40 miles per hour. The officer's testimony is:

A. Admissible as a declaration against interest.

B. Admissible because it is not hearsay.

C. Inadmissible because it is hearsay not within any exception.

D. Inadmissible because it lacks foundation.

90. While driving home from work, a man stopped at a bar for a drink. After having a few drinks, he asked the bartender for another drink. The bartender, worried about the man's intoxicated state, told the man that he had already had enough to drink. The man then became very angry, and said to the bartender, "Get me a drink or else." The bartender again refused.

Angered by the bartender's response, the man jumped off his bar stool and hit the bartender. The bartender brought a lawsuit against the man for battery. At trial, the bartender took the stand. The bartender's proposed testimony was that the man had stated to him, "Get me a drink or else." The man objected to the testimony. The court should:

A. Overrule the objection because it was not hearsay.

B. Overrule the objection because it was probative of the declarant's state of mind.

C. Sustain the objection because it was hearsay not within any exception.

D. Sustain the objection because the man could not form the intent to commit a battery while intoxicated.

91. While out on patrol, a policeman pulled over a car, alleging that its driver was driving faster than the posted speed limit of 30 MPH. The policeman issued the driver a speeding ticket. At the man's trial for speeding, after laying a foundation for admitting the radar reading, the policeman testified that he was stopped at the corner of 5th and Golden and pointed his radar gun at the driver's car. The gun rated the car's speed to be 45 MPH. The man objected to the testimony. The trial court should:

A. Not allow the testimony because the evidentiary foundation was insufficient to establish all elements of a speeding violation.

B. Not allow the testimony because it was hearsay.

C. Allow the testimony because radar readings are an exception to the hearsay rule.

D. Allow the testimony because it is not hearsay.

92. A woman sued a man for fraud, alleging that a Rolls Royce that the man had sold to her was really a Bentley. In order to prove the Rolls Royce was genuine, the man introduced the bill of sale he had received at a car auction when he had purchased the car. The woman objected. The bill of sale was:

A. Admissible because documents of title are conclusive of rightful ownership.

B. Admissible because it was a party admission.

C. Inadmissible because it was hearsay not within any exception.

D. Inadmissible because it was not the best evidence.

93. A man was arrested and charged with burglary. At trial, a witness testified that the man was watching television at the witness' home at the time of the burglary. On cross-examination of the witness, the prosecutor asked him, "Don't you certify art reproductions as antique originals in order to sell them at a higher price at your antique store?" The prosecutor was informed of this by the witness' employee. Certifying art reproductions as originals is punishable as a misdemeanor. If the man objects, the objection will be:

A. Sustained because it relates to a collateral matter.

B. Sustained, unless the witness has been convicted for certifying reproduction art works as originals.

C. Overruled within the discretion of the court because certifying reproductions as originals bears on the witness' truthfulness.

D. Overruled within the discretion of the court because certifying reproductions of art works as originals is punishable as a misdemeanor.

94. A man was charged with battery on a policeman growing out of his arrest by that policeman. The man's defense was self-defense against excessive force used by the policeman. Through discovery proceedings, the man secured the policeman's disciplinary records, which contained written complaints by three citizens stating that that policeman had used excessive force on each of them within six months prior to the man's incident with the policeman. The man offered the records in evidence. The prosecution objected. The court should rule the disciplinary reports were:

A. Not allowed because they were hearsay.

B. Allowed because it was proper character evidence under the "victim's exception."

C. Allowed because of the business record exception.

D. Allowed because the report was permissible to prove this character trait of the policeman.

95. A widow sues her cousin for the wrongful death of the widow's late husband. On the issue of damages, the widow testifies that she and her late husband had a happy and affectionate marital relationship during their entire marriage. In defense, the cousin seeks to introduce evidence of the fact that a decade earlier, the late husband had separated from the widow and had lived with another woman. The widow objected. The court should:

A. Sustain the objection, since the evidence is self-serving.

B. Sustain the objection because of the dead man's statute.

C. Overrule the objection because it is proper character evidence.

D. Overrule the objection because the evidence is relevant.

96. A defendant is charged with the rape of a minor girl. At trial, the prosecution seeks to establish that the defendant and another man had picked up the minor and offered her a ride to a party and then took her to a secluded area and raped her.

The prosecution then calls a witness to testify that six weeks earlier, when the witness was with a girlfriend, the defendant and another male had picked them up and offered to take them to a party, but instead drove them to a secluded area where the defendant and his friend forced the witness and her girlfriend to submit to sexual intercourse. The witness and her girlfriend escaped when the men were momentarily distracted.

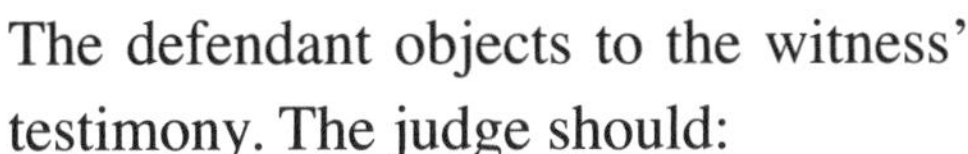

The defendant objects to the witness' testimony. The judge should:

A. Overrule the objection because it is permissible character evidence.

B. Overrule the objection because the testimony is relevant to the defendant's state of mind.

C. Sustain the objection because it is impermissible character evidence.

D. Sustain the objection because it is too prejudicial.

97. A man was fired from his job for drunkenness and incompetency. His supervisor had warned him about his conduct, but was fed up when the man failed to show up for work for three straight days. The man retaliated by suing for back wages, claiming that his employment contract provided wages at below the minimum wage and set forth a "waiver" of overtime wages at any rate higher than the regular hourly rate. His employer disputed the man's allegations as to the contractual terms. The man intended to testify as to the alleged wage rates set forth in his employment contract with his employer. The employer objected. The court should:

A. Admit the testimony because the man had personal knowledge of the contents of the contract.

B. Admit the testimony because it is a material issue in the action.

C. Not admit the testimony because it is hearsay not within any exception.

D. Not admit the testimony because the contract is the best evidence.

98. A man was charged with assault with a deadly weapon upon a woman. The woman testified that the man struck her with an iron pipe without cause. The prosecution then called a witness to the stand, who testified that he had known and lived next door to the woman for ten years. The prosecution then asked the witness, "What is the reputation as to whether the woman is an honest and a truthful person?" The man objected. The court should:

A. Sustain the objection because opinion evidence of a witness' character is never allowed to attack or support the credibility of the witness.

B. Sustain the objection because the woman's character for truthfulness has not yet been attacked.

C. Overrule the objection because it is relevant.

D. Overrule the objection because it is a collateral matter.

99. A woman and a man were arrested for robbing a jewelry store. The woman made a plea bargain with the district attorney to turn state's evidence against a defendant in another case for an unrelated crime.

The man was now on trial for the robbery. His roommate was the sole defense witness. The man called the roommate to the stand to testify that the man had told the roommate that the woman alone had robbed the jewelry store. The prosecution objected to the roommate's testimony. The testimony was:

A. Admissible as a co-conspirator party admission.

B. Admissible because it was direct proof that the man had not committed the robbery.

C. Inadmissible as hearsay not within any recognized exception.

D. Inadmissible because the roommate's testimony was biased.

100. A woman sued a man for damages for personal injuries arising out of a rear-end automobile accident. While testifying, the woman produced a printed letter that stated, "My foot slipped off the brake. Don't worry, I will see that all your damages are paid." The letter was signed "Man" but contained no return address. The woman was asked by her counsel if the woman was familiar with the man's signature. The woman answered, "No, but I received the letter in the mail two weeks after the accident." The woman offered the letter into evidence.

The man objected on the grounds of authentication. The letter will be deemed:

A. Admissible because the contents of the letter lay the foundation for authentication.

B. Admissible because it is direct proof that the man was at fault.

C. Inadmissible because the woman was not familiar with the man's signature.

D. Inadmissible because the letter is self-serving.

101. A woman sued her hairdresser, alleging that the hairdresser used the wrong formula when dying her hair, which caused the woman's hair to turn blue instead of red. At trial, the woman produced a letter that she had received from the hairdresser. In the letter, the hairdresser stated, "I am so sorry for using the wrong hair dye. Please come back to the salon so that I can correct my mistake. Sincerely, hair dresser." The hairdresser objects to the production of the letter on the grounds of hearsay. The letter is:

A. Admissible because it is not-hearsay.

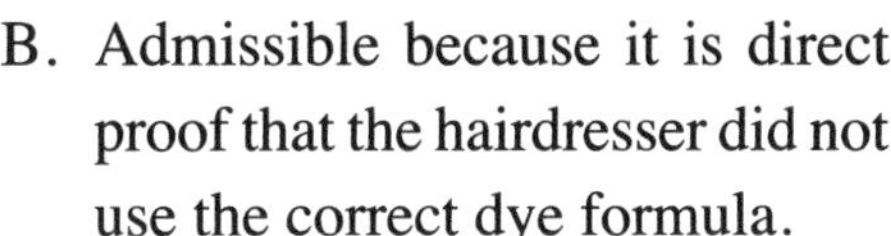

B. Admissible because it is direct proof that the hairdresser did not use the correct dye formula.

C. Inadmissible as hearsay not within any recognized exception.

D. Admissible as hearsay that falls within a recognized exception.

102. After being admitted to a movie theater, a man slipped on a loose piece of carpeting in the theater lobby. He sustained injuries to his back and sued the theater for his injuries. At trial, the theater called a witness to testify that a week before the accident the man had told the witness, "I cannot finish our golf game because of pains in my back." The man objected to the testimony. The court should rule the testimony:

A. Admissible.

B. Admissible under the sports injuries exception to the hearsay rule.

C. Inadmissible as hearsay.

D. Inadmissible as an improper lay opinion.

103. A defendant was charged with armed robbery of a convenience store. At trial, the defendant took the stand and denied that he was the person who had robbed the convenience store. The prosecution seeks to enter into evidence that the defendant had robbed two gas stations in the past two months. The defendant objects to this evidence. The evidence is:

A. Admissible to prove that the defendant robbed the convenience store.

B. Admissible to prove a pertinent trait of the defendant's character.

C. Inadmissible because character evidence may not be used to prove that the defendant acted in conformity therewith.

D. Inadmissible because character evidence must be proven by reputation or opinion evidence.

104. When a girl was driving her car home from school, her vehicle crashed into a pedestrian, completely paralyzing him. The pedestrian sued the girl for the personal injuries he sustained. At trial, the pedestrian testifies that immediately after the accident, the girl got out of her car, raced over to the pedestrian, and said, "Don't worry, I'll pay all your medical bills." The girl objects to the pedestrian's testimony. The testimony is:

A. Admissible because it is an admission of liability.

B. Admissible because she would

not have offered to pay medical expenses if she were not at fault.

C. Inadmissible because it is hearsay not within any recognized exception.

D. Inadmissible because it is an offer to pay medical bills.

105. A married couple, both musicians, performed music together in a nightclub. One night, the husband had taken drugs and punched a club patron. The wife observed the incident. The prosecutor filed battery charges against the husband and called the wife as a witness to testify about the incident. The wife objected.

Must the wife testify at trial?

A. Yes because the wife's testimony would be considered a confidential marital communication.

B. Yes because she had personal knowledge of the incident.

C. No because she would be testifying against the husband.

D. Yes because the husband's conduct is not considered a marital communication.

106. A man has been arrested for cocaine trafficking. After his arrest, he privately speaks to his wife, saying that he was in fact guilty, but that he would "beat the rap." The wife was angry at the husband for his drug use, and she obtained a marital dissolution. She has now been called to testify at the man's trial concerning the man's statement to her. Upon objection by the man's attorney, the court should:

A. Exclude the evidence because the statement was a confidential communication.

B. Admit the evidence because the testimonial privilege terminates upon dissolution of marriage.

C. Admit the evidence because the marital privilege is inapplicable to admissions.

D. Admit the evidence because the wife will testify voluntarily.

107. A private detective is well-known for his ability to solve difficult crimes. The detective has been unable to capture one suspected criminal during his career. The criminal is a master of disguise.

Intent on turning the tables and putting the detective in jail, the criminal posed as a criminal defense attorney after he found out that the detective was in trouble with the law. The detective was stopped for a traffic violation and was found to have cocaine in his possession. When the detective visited the criminal's "law" office, the detective admitted to the criminal that the detective possessed the cocaine for his personal use on the date in question. It was unknown to the detective that the criminal was not an attorney.

After the visit, the detective did not hire the criminal to represent him. Armed with the detective's confession, the criminal called the district attorney and "cut a deal" in exchange for evidence of the detective's guilt. The prosecutor sought to have the criminal testify at the detective's drug possession trial. The detective's attorney objected. The testimony of the detective's confession will be deemed:

A. Inadmissible because the criminal obtained the evidence through clandestine means.

B. Inadmissible because of the attorney-client privilege.

C. Admissible as a statement against interest.

D. Admissible because the criminal was merely pretending to be an attorney.

108. A train was involved in a serious collision with a man. As a result of that collision, the train's engineer was slightly injured and the man was crushed to death by the train. The man's heirs brought a wrongful death suit against the railroad company that owned the train.

At trial, the company sought to introduce its accident report filed by the engineer at the time of the accident. The accident report said that the engineer had been driving carefully at the time of the accident. The man had been sleeping on the railroad tracks, and there was no way to avoid crushing him with the train.

The engineer was no longer an employee of the company and had moved to an unknown location. The man's heirs objected to introduction of the accident report. The report was:

A. Admissible because it was a business record.

B. Admissible because the engineer was unavailable to testify.

C. Inadmissible because it was hearsay, without an exception.

D. Inadmissible because it was not the best evidence.

109. A man was charged with the murder of his wife. At trial, the prosecution called to the stand the woman who had been the maid of the man and his wife. The maid's proposed testimony was that the wife had come to her late one night and said, "The man has poisoned me." The wife died shortly thereafter. The man objected to the introduction of the wife's statement to the maid. The trial court should:

A. Permit the testimony because it was a dying declaration.

B. Permit the testimony because it was relevant to the wife's state of mind.

C. Exclude the testimony because it was hearsay.

D. Exclude the testimony because of the dead man's statute.

110. While shopping at a grocery store, a woman slipped and fell on a piece of candy on the floor of an aisle. The woman sustained serious back injuries and now brings suit against the grocery store for her injuries.

At trial, the grocery store calls the store janitor to the stand. The janitor testifies that he regularly sweeps the floor every half hour and that he never leaves anything on the floor. He further testifies that if there had been anything on the floor when he swept, including a piece of candy, he would have seen it. The woman objects to the janitor's testimony. The court should:

A. Admit the testimony because it is relevant.

B. Admit the testimony because it is proper habit evidence.

C. Exclude the testimony as speculative.

D. Exclude the testimony as prejudicial.

END OF QUESTIONS

EVIDENCE ANSWERS

1. A is the correct answer. If a proper foundation is laid, the photograph is admissible into evidence. This requires that there be someone who can testify that the photograph is a true and accurate representation of the accident scene. Since anyone who was present at the scene when the photograph was taken can testify to the accuracy of the photograph, the photographer does not have to be present. B is incorrect because the burden is on the woman (the plaintiff), not the man (the defendant), to lay the foundation showing that the photograph is a true and accurate representation of the accident scene. C is incorrect because the photographer does not have to be present. D is incorrect because the photo could be taken by anyone; it does not have to be an investigative agent.

2. B is the correct answer. A defendant in a criminal case may introduce evidence of her good character to show that she is not the type of person likely to murder someone. Here, the witness is going to testify about the woman's peaceful character, which tends to show that the woman is unlikely to have murdered the man.

   A is incorrect because the woman has not taken the stand and put her credibility into issue. Therefore, credibility is not at issue here.

   C is incorrect because, under the Fifth Amendment to the Constitution (which has been incorporated to the states via the Due Process Clause of the 14th Amendment), a criminal defendant is not required to take the stand. Nevertheless, the witness' testimony may be brought in for the reasons discussed in B.

   D is an incorrect statement of law. Under certain circumstances, reputation evidence is a permissible way to prove character.

3. D is the correct answer. Under Rule 803(3), "The following are not excluded by the rule against hearsay, regardless of whether the declarant is available as a witness... A statement of the declarant's then-existing state of mind (such as motive, intent, or plan)." Here, the witness was testifying as to the man's then-existing state of mind (his imminent departure into space, which would have prevented him from being on the same planet as the bank on the day it was robbed).

   A is incorrect because under the Federal Rules of Evidence, present state of mind is nonhearsay.

   B is incorrect because the defendant's mental state is certainly probative, i.e., relevant - it may establish his alibi.

   C is incorrect because relevance is not a controlling issue as to whether or not evidence can be admitted; it is merely an initial inquiry.

A

EVIDENCE

4. C is the correct answer. Questions that point to possible prejudice or bias are always considered relevant and admissible. Here, the man has called his mother as an alibi witness, and she will testify that he was out of the state when the transient was murdered. The fact that the witness is the man's mother would indicate bias (i.e. that the mother might lie to protect her son). Therefore, the prosecutor's question will be deemed proper.

   A is incorrect since, as a matter of law, bias and prejudice do not go beyond the scope of direct examination. B is incorrect for the reasons discussed in C. D is incorrect because it is an incorrect statement of law. A relative can testify, but questions as to bias will be allowed, as discussed in C.

5. B is the correct answer. Under Rule 403,

   "The court may exclude relevant evidence, if its probative value is substantially outweighed by a danger of one or more of the following: unfair prejudice, confusing the issues, misleading the jury, undue delay, wasting time, or needlessly presenting cumulative evidence."

   Here, the prosecutor's question ("Isn't it true that you were on a jury that acquitted the man of a criminal charge?") would have a great prejudicial effect on the jury because it would tend to confuse the issues, mislead the jury, and cause unfair prejudice in favor of the prosecution. Therefore, the judge had the discretion to decide that the probative value is substantially outweighed by the potential prejudice.

   A is incorrect because a question tending to prove bias is never beyond the scope of direct examination. C is incorrect because leading questions are permitted on cross-examination. D is an incorrect statement of law.

6. D is the correct answer. The general rule is that other crimes or wrongs are not admissible to prove a person's character (i.e., propensity to act a certain way) to show action that the person acted in conformity with his character (i.e., propensity). However, under Rule 404(b)(2), character evidence may be brought in to demonstrate "motive, opportunity, intent, preparation, plan, knowledge, identity, absence of mistake, or lack of accident." This may be easily remembered using the "MIMIC" mneumonic: motive, intent, mistake (lack thereof), identity, or common scheme or plan.

   Here, a woman was robbed by a person using a psychedelic-painted gun. A man had been previously robbed by a person using an identical psychedelic-painted gun. The use of a psychedelic-painted gun in both robberies indicates that this is the robber's "signature" crime because the psychedelic-painted gun is unique enough to be relevant, in a non-character way, to establish the robber's modus operandi (common scheme or plan, i.e., that the accused tends to operate in this manner).

A is incorrect because, in this fact pattern, the robber's character is not "in issue." B is incorrect because, although the evidence may be prejudicial, the risk of causing unfair prejudice to the robber (by showing his propensity to rob) does not substantially outweigh the evidence's strong probative value (to show the robber's modus operandi, as discussed in D). C is incorrect because mere possession of the gun would not show the robber is capable of armed robbery.

7. B is the correct answer. Under the Rule 803(1), "The following are not excluded by the rule against hearsay, regardless of whether the declarant is available as a witness...present sense impression, [which is defined as] a statement describing or explaining an event or condition made while or immediately after the declarant perceived it." This is an exception to the hearsay rule.

   Here, the eyewitness made an observation about a condition she observed while she was observing it (that the man's vehicle had been swerving in and out of traffic just before the accident, and the man had appeared to be drunk). The eyewitness' statement would, thus, qualify as a present sense impression.

   A is incorrect because, under Rule 803(2), the excited utterance exception requires that the statement was made under the stress of an exciting event. This is not the case here because the eyewitness was not personally involved in the accident and was, therefore, not under any stress at that time.

   C is incorrect because a prior consistent statement is used to rebut a charge of recent fabrication. Here, the eyewitness' credibility as a witness has not been attacked (i.e., impeached) as a recent fabrication. There is nothing in the facts to indicate that the eyewitness had made any inconsistent statements, prior or otherwise.

   D is incorrect because the state of drunkenness is the type of subject on which a layperson may give an opinion.

8. D is the correct answer. The Federal Rules of Evidence allow a prior inconsistent statement to be used for impeachment purposes as well as substantive evidence of the fact in question, if the statement was made under oath at a proceeding (including a deposition), and the declarant is available to testify concerning the statement. Here, the witness' statement that the he had heard the man call the woman a prostitute was made at a deposition, and the witness is testifying at trial and is, thus, available. Therefore, the deposition statement is admissible to impeach the witness and as substantive evidence of the fact in question, namely that the man in fact had called the woman a prostitute.

   A is incorrect because, under the Federal Rules of Evidence, one may impeach his own witness.

B is incorrect because a prior inconsistent statement, made under oath, is not hearsay under the Federal Rules of Evidence.

C is incorrect for the reasons discussed in D.

9. D is the correct answer. Under Rule 407, "When measures are taken that would have made an earlier injury or harm less likely to occur, evidence of the subsequent measures is not admissible to prove negligence, culpable conduct, a defect in a product or its design, or a need for a warning or instruction."

The rationale falls under public policy. If such evidence could be used to establish the prior existence of a dangerous condition or practice, the person liable would be reluctant to take corrective action. A, B and C are incorrect for the reasons discussed in D.

10. B is the correct answer. Under Rule 409, "Evidence of furnishing, promising to pay, or offering to pay medical, hospital, or similar expenses resulting from an injury is not admissible to prove liability for the injury." An out-of-court statement made by a party, offered to prove the truth of the matter asserted, is called a party admission.

Under the Federal Rules of Evidence, party admissions are considered to be nonhearsay and are, therefore, admissible.

This question turns on the fact that there were two separate statements made by the driver: (1) the offer to pay medical expenses; and (2) the statement that the whole accident was the driver's fault. Consequently, each statement gets a separate analysis.

Here, the driver offered to pay the pedestrian's medical expenses. This offer is not admissible under Rule 409. However, the driver then said, "That's the least I can do after hitting you with my vehicle, since the whole accident was my fault." This statement was made out of court (at the hospital), by a party (the driver) and is being offered to prove the truth of the matter asserted (that the accident was the driver's fault). Therefore, the second statement (that the whole accident was the driver's fault) is admissible, nonhearsay.

A is incorrect because, under an offer to compromise accompanying the admission, it would most likely be inadmissible. Here, there was no offer to compromise, just an offer to pay medical expenses.

C and D are incorrect for the reasons discussed in B.

11. C is the correct answer. For the physician-patient privilege to attach, the information obtained from the patient must be necessary to enable the physician to treat the patient. Here, the hit man's statement to the doctor about having to meet the mob boss to get

paid for killing the gang member does not relate to treatment and is, thus, not protected by the privilege.

A is incorrect for the reasons discussed in C. B is an incorrect statement of law. Confidentiality, which is an essential element to the formation of the privilege, would not be impaired by the fact that the head nurse overheard the hit man's communication to the doctor because the head nurse is a necessary party to a transaction between a patient and a doctor. D is incorrect because, whether or not the hit man intended this statement to be confidential the privilege would not apply, for the reasons discussed in A.

12. B is the correct answer. Under Rule 901, "To satisfy the requirement of authenticating or identifying an item of evidence, the proponent must produce evidence sufficient to support a finding that the item is what the proponent claims it is."

Under the Best Evidence Rule, which is Rule 1002, "An original writing, recording, or photograph is required in order to prove its content, unless these rules or a federal statute provides otherwise." However, under Rule 1004(d), "An original is not required and other evidence of the content of a writing, recording, or photograph is admissible if… the writing, recording, or photograph is not closely related to a controlling issue."

Here, the man was attempting to introduce a letter from the woman. This letter must first be authenticated, under Rule 901. In addition, the letter related closely to a controlling issue in this case (the fact that the woman prevented the man from performing his duties under the contract, and the man is being sued for breach of contract). Therefore, the man must also introduce the original letter, as required under Rule 1002. The exception in Rule 1004(d) does not apply here because the letter is closely related to a controlling issue, as discussed above.

A and C are incorrect because they are incomplete, for the reasons discussed in B. D is incorrect because the letter does not need to be authenticated by an expert. The letter can be authenticated by any person who is familiar with the woman's signature and, presumably, because the man and the woman signed the contract, the man had seen the woman's signature before.

13. B is the correct answer. Attorney-client communications remain privileged, even when made in the presence of joint clients or others, if the others are "reasonably necessary" to the consultation. Here, an attorney's investigator is a "reasonably necessary" party to the consultation. Thus, the attorney-client privilege is not waived because of the presence of the investigator at the conference. Therefore, the content of the conference is protected under the attorney-client privilege and is not admissible.

A is incorrect because the testimony is not offered to prove the contents of the investigator's notes - thus, the best evidence rule is inapplicable. C is incorrect because the other persons present were reasonably necessary to the consultation, as discussed in B. Thus, the privilege attaches. D is incorrect because the employee and the trucking company were joint clients, so the attorney-client privilege would attach.

14. A is the correct answer. A business report prepared as a communication from client to attorney is protected by the attorney-client privilege and is, thus, inadmissible. B and C are incorrect because even though a report contains hearsay or is self-serving, it does not prevent its discovery by the opponent. However, it is inadmissible because it is privileged, as discussed in A. D is incorrect for the reasons discussed in A.

15. A is the correct answer. Under the Rule 803(1), "The following are not excluded by the rule against hearsay, regardless of whether the declarant is available as a witness...present sense impression. A statement describing or explaining an event or condition, made while or immediately after the declarant perceived it." This is an exception to the hearsay rule.

    Here, the woman testified that she had heard her daughter state that the bedroom windows had shattered. This statement was relevant to the magnitude of the explosion in the garage (since it had caused the bedroom windows to shatter). The daughter's statement that the woman had heard was made while the daughter was perceiving the event (the shattering of the windows). Thus, the statement would qualify as a present sense impression. The fact that the daughter could be available would not render the woman's testimony inadmissible, as stated in the rule.

    B is incorrect because the declarant, the daughter, does not have to be unavailable, as discussed in A.

    C is incorrect because, although the statement is hearsay, it falls within the present sense impression exception, as discussed in A.

    D is an incorrect statement of law. Although the daughter is not a legal adult (18 years of age), she is still able to perceive and communicate.

16. C is the correct answer. The general rule is that other crimes or wrongs are not admissible to prove a person's character (i.e., propensity to act a certain way) to show action that the person acted in conformity with his character (i.e., propensity). However, under Rule 404(b)(2), character evidence may be brought in to demonstrate "motive, opportunity, intent, preparation, plan, knowledge, identity, absence of mistake, or lack of accident.." This may be easily remembered using the "MIMIC" mneumonic: motive, intent, mistake (lack thereof), identity, or common scheme or plan.

Here, this evidence may be used to show the defendant's intent because, in the past, he had intentionally defrauded five other people using phony leases, and he did the same thing in this case. In addition, the use of phony leases in five other instances also indicates the defendant's common scheme or plan, so long as the previous phony condo leases were clearly a "signature crime" of the defendant.

A is incorrect because the defendant's prior use of phony leases is highly relevant because the defendant is being tried for use of phony leases in this case. Therefore, the evidence would not be inadmissible as irrelevant as stated in A.

B is incorrect, for the reasons discussed in C. D is incorrect because it is an incorrect statement of law.

17. A is the correct answer. A voice may be identified in several ways, so long as they are reliable. Here, the woman looked up the man's telephone number on the internet (which contains an updated list of telephone numbers and may, thus, be considered reliable), and the man identified himself (which is also reliable). Since there were two reliable means of identifying the man's voice, his voice was reliably and properly identified.

B is incorrect, for the reasons discussed in A. C is incorrect because the woman does not have to be familiar with the man's voice for authentication. D is an incorrect statement of law.

18. C is the correct answer. Under Rule 404, "Evidence of a person's character or character trait is not admissible to prove that on a particular occasion the person acted in accordance with the character or trait." There are exceptions to this general rule in civil cases, if character is at issue in the case, such as in defamation, assault, and battery cases. Here, this is a civil negligence case, not an assault, battery, or defamation case. Consequently, the exceptions do not apply in this case. Therefore, the defendant's character as a "daredevil" driver is not admissible.

A is incorrect, for the reasons discussed in C. B is incorrect because under Rule 406, "Evidence of a person's habit or an organization's routine practice may be admitted to prove that on a particular occasion the person or organization acted in accordance with the habit or routine practice." However, habit is a specific and unvarying response to a specific situation. Being a "daredevil" rider is too general to be classified as "habit." D is incorrect because this answer states the rule for criminal cases, not civil.

19. A is the correct answer. The bystander's testimony is relevant in two ways: first, it is substantive evidence that tends to establish a consequential proposition, i.e., that the woman, in fact, ran the red light and, second, it impeaches the

witness' testimony by contradicting him (i.e., by showing that the witness' testimony — that the woman's car did not run the red light — was false). B is incorrect because the mere fact that the man was surprised does not give him the right to impeach. C and D are both incorrect. Under Rule 607, "Any party, including the party that called the witness, may attack the witness's credibility."

20. B is the correct answer. A witness may not be impeached on a matter not directly relevant to the issues in the case. Here, the question as to whether the witness was high 18 months prior to the incident is collateral to the issue of whether there was water in the middle of the grocery store aisle.

    A is incorrect because the Federal Rules of Evidence allow for the impeachment of a witness by specific acts of conduct. C is incorrect because the witness' use of marijuana is not logically relevant to show that the witness has an untruthful character. D is incorrect because the witness' use of marijuana 18 months prior to the event to which he testified in court is not logically relevant to show an impaired memory of that event.

21. D is the correct answer. Under Rule 803(2), "The following are not excluded by the rule against hearsay, regardless of whether the declarant is available as a witness...excited utterance, [which is defined as] a statement relating to a startling event or condition, made while the declarant was under the stress of excitement that it caused."

    Here, the eyewitness made the statement while under the stress of the excitement of the possibility of the box falling on top of the woman, as indicated by the fact that the eyewitness had screamed her warning statement to the woman immediately prior to the box actually falling on top of the woman. Thus, the eyewitness' statement is admissible under the excited utterance exception to the hearsay rule.

    A is incorrect because, although the statement preceded the incident, it was still made relating to a startling event.

    B is incorrect because unavailability is not a requirement, as discussed in D.

    C is incorrect because, although it is hearsay, it falls within an exception, as discussed in D.

22. B is the correct answer. An out-of-court statement made by a party and used against that party is an admission and exempted from the hearsay rule. Under Rule 801(d)(2)(B), an admission includes a statement that a party to a lawsuit "manifested that it adopted or believed to be true." Here, the passenger's statement, "Our car hit the jogger while he was in the crosswalk," was made to the police officer who has testified to that statement. By remaining silent and failing to deny the passenger's statement, the driver has manifested that he

adopted the statement or believed it to be true, as discussed in Rule 801(d)(2)(B). Thus, the statement is admissible as an admission.

A is incorrect because the passenger's statement was not imputed to the driver, but rather, constituted an admission by silence, as discussed in B.

C and D are incorrect for the reasons discussed in B.

23. C is the correct answer. Under Rule 801(c), hearsay is an out-of-court statement offered to prove the truth of the matter asserted. However, under Rule 803(3), "A statement of the declarant's then-existing state of mind (such as motive, intent, or plan) or emotional, sensory, or physical condition (such as mental feeling, pain, or bodily health)" is admissible as an exception to the hearsay rule.

Here, the jogger made the statement to his wife out of court, and he is offering the statement to show that his knee was, in fact, hurting the day after he was struck by the driver's automobile. However, the jogger's statement is a statement about his physical condition, and under Rule 803(3), this statement would qualify as an exception to the hearsay rule and would, thus, be admissible.

A is incorrect because self-serving evidence may be admissible. B is incorrect because it falls within the Rule 803(3) exception for physical condition, as discussed in C. D is incorrect because only an expert could testify to whether or not the hip was fractured.

24. A is the correct answer. Under Rule 408, evidence that one party offered to settle or compromise the claim against another is generally inadmissible to show liability.

Here, the hairstylist made an offer to re-dye the woman's hair and pay her $1,000. This statement is inadmissible under Rule 408 for the public policy reason that people should be encouraged to settle lawsuits out of court.

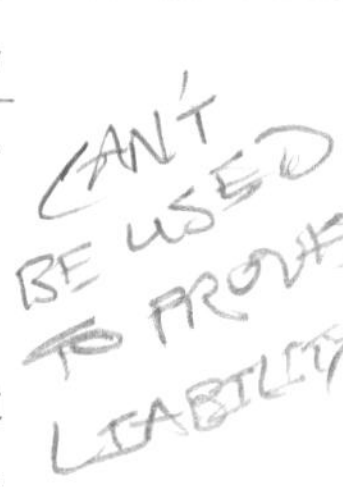

B is incorrect because the settlement offer is relevant to the issue of damages because it tends to show that the hair stylist was at fault, since she would not have offered to re-do the hair dye and pay the $1,000 if she were not at fault. However, for the reasons discussed in A, the hairstylist's offer is inadmissible.

C is incorrect because an admission is an out-of-court statement made by a party, offered to prove the truth of the matter asserted. Under the Federal Rules of Evidence, party admissions are considered to be nonhearsay and are, therefore, admissible. However, here, the hair stylist merely offered to re-dye the hair and pay $1,000; she did not admit to any fault or liability. Thus, the offer was not an admission.

D is incorrect because, even though the statement may be against the hair stylist's pecuniary interest, it is inadmissible because it is an offer to compromise, as discussed in A.

25. B is the correct answer. Under the doctrine of present recollection refreshed, a witness may be shown anything that may reasonably refresh his recollection. Here, the passenger could not remember some of the details about the accident. The letter that she had written to her uncle was then shown to her to help her remember these details. Therefore, the letter may be used to refresh her recollection of these facts.

A is incorrect because past recollection recorded introduces the contents of a writing into evidence and requires the laying of a foundation. Here, neither the contents of the letter nor the letter itself is being introduced into evidence; the passenger was merely being shown the letter to refresh her recollection.

C is incorrect because the time lapse factor here is not enough to prevent use of the letter, since it was only one day.

D is incorrect because evidence may not be excluded merely because it is self-serving.

26. B is the correct answer. Under Rule 404, "Evidence of a person's character or character trait is not admissible to prove that on a particular occasion the person acted in accordance with the character or trait." There are exceptions to this general rule in civil cases, if character is at issue in the case, such as in defamation, assault, and battery cases. Here, the woman is suing the man for defamation. Thus, the policeman's testimony regarding her prior arrest for prostitution is relevant because her character is at issue in a defamation suit, regarding whether or not she was a "call girl" (i.e., a prostitute). In addition, the evidence is admissible as an exception to Rule 404, as discussed above.

A is incorrect because, although evidence may be relevant, it is not always admissible. Here, the evidence is admissible as an exception to Rule 404, as discussed in B above.

C is incorrect because the statement is not hearsay. Under Rule 801(c), hearsay is an out-of-court statement offered to prove the truth of the matter asserted. Here, the policeman is testifying directly. The statement is, therefore, not an out-of-court statement.

D is incorrect because character is directly at issue in a defamation case, i.e., it is highly probative.

27. C is the correct answer. A confidential marital communication ("pillow talk") made during the marriage remains privileged, even after the marriage has ended. Either spouse may assert the privilege to bar the other from testifying. Here, the divorcee wants to testify against her ex-husband. Her

testimony concerns a statement that the ex-husband had made to her during the marriage in which he explained the scheme to her. The facts suggest that the ex-husband intended this information to remain confidential because the statement would be an admission by the ex-husband that he had committed a crime.

A is incorrect for the reasons discussed in C. B is incorrect because the confidential marital communication privilege may be asserted in both civil and criminal proceedings. D is incorrect because "spite" has nothing to do with whether or not the divorcee will be allowed to testify.

28. D is the correct answer. Extrinsic evidence is inadmissible to impeach a witness on a collateral matter. Here, the color of the man's jacket is a collateral (i.e., insignificant) issue as to whether or not the man was at fault in the accident. Thus, the court will not allow its time to be wasted on such triviality, so the bystander's testimony will be inadmissible.

A is incorrect for the reasons discussed in D.

B is incorrect because the bystander's testimony is not relevant to show the eyewitness' untruthful character. Rather, the bystander's testimony is relevant to contradict the eyewitness on the color of the man's jacket, which tends to undermine the eyewitness' credibility as a witness by casting doubt on how attentive he was in observing the event in question. However, the color of the man's jacket is a collateral matter for the reasons discussed in D.

C is incorrect because the eyewitness' capacity to observe is a relevant issue. However, as discussed in D, the color of the man's jacket is a collateral issue, so the bystander's testimony will be inadmissible.

29. D is the correct answer. Under the Federal Rules of Evidence, an admission is an out-of-court statement made by a party that is offered at trial against that party by the opposing party for the truth of the matter asserted. Here, the nurse is going to testify that the doctor had told her shortly after the surgery (out-of-court) that he had left a sponge inside the woman (an admission of negligence). This statement is being offered against the doctor to show that he had, in fact, left the sponge inside the woman (i.e., it is being offered for its truth). It is, thus, an admission and is admissible under the Federal Rules of Evidence.

A is incorrect because an admission is admissible as nonhearsay under the Federal Rules of Evidence.

B is incorrect because, under the Federal Rules of Evidence, an admission requires no foundation to be admissible in court.

C is incorrect because a prior inconsistent statement requires that the declarant be unavailable to testify. Here, the declarant is the doctor. As a party to this lawsuit, the doctor is available to testify. Thus, the doctor's statement to the nurse is not admissible as a prior inconsistent statement.

30. A is the correct answer. Under Rule 404(a)(2)(A), "A defendant may offer evidence of the defendant's pertinent trait, and if the evidence is admitted, the prosecutor may offer evidence to rebut it." Here, the woman is the defendant in this criminal case. She may always offer evidence of her good character to show that she was unlikely to commit the crime charged.

    B is incorrect, for the reasons discussed in A. C is incorrect because the woman does not have to take the stand for the man's testimony to be admissible. D is incorrect because this is a matter of the man's personal knowledge about the woman and, thus, does not require him to be an expert.

31. A is the correct answer. The doctor-patient privilege protects any communication that was intended to be confidential and was made for the purpose of medical diagnosis and treatment. This privilege protects any information obtained by verbal statements, examination, and any diagnosis and treatment. The patient is the holder of the privilege, but if the patient is not present at trial, the physician is ethically obligated to assert the privilege on the patient's behalf. The facts state that the physician was called in to testify as a defense witness regarding statements made by the passenger to the physician for the purpose of obtaining medical treatment. Since the passenger was not present, the physician must assert the privilege on the passenger's behalf. B, C and D are incorrect for the reasons discussed in A.

32. C is the correct answer. As a general rule, expert testimony is required when a conclusion cannot be reached using common knowledge. Here, the failure of the law firm to timely file the client's claim before the statute of limitations prohibited the filing of the claim is a matter from which an average juror is competent to draw a conclusion. This is merely an issue of time, which does not require expert testimony. A and B are incorrect for the reason discussed in C. D is an incorrect statement of law because the judge is not allowed in a jury case to resolve the issue of the existence of negligence in the action before him.

33. C is the correct answer. Under Rule 407, "When measures are taken that would have made an earlier injury or harm less likely to occur, evidence of the subsequent measures is not admissible to prove negligence, culpable conduct, a defect in a product or its design, or a need for a warning or instruction."

    The rationale falls under public policy; if such evidence could be used to establish the prior existence of a dangerous condition or practice, the person liable would be reluctant to take corrective action.

Here, the facts indicate that the woman had learned about and was testifying regarding the steering wheel manufacturer's use of steering wheels that do not lock while a vehicle is being driven, a practice that the steering wheel manufacturer had begun to implement after the woman's accident and injuries. Thus, the steering wheel manufacturer's corrective measure would be inadmissible, under Rule 407.

A is incorrect because the fault of the steering wheel manufacturer is not only at issue here; it is a central issue in this case.

B is incorrect because it is relevant that the steering wheel manufacturer changed its policies regarding steering wheels following the woman's accident. It tends to show that the steering wheel was the cause of the woman's accident. However, the evidence will be inadmissible for the reasons discussed in C.

D is incorrect. While it is a true factual statement, the evidence will be inadmissible for the reasons discussed in C.

34. D is the correct answer. Under Rule 407, "When measures are taken that would have made an earlier injury or harm less likely to occur, evidence of the subsequent measures is not admissible to prove negligence, culpable conduct, a defect in a product or its design, or a need for a warning or instruction."

The rationale falls under public policy; if such evidence could be used to establish the prior existence of a dangerous condition or practice, the person liable would be reluctant to take corrective action.

Here, however, the facts state that the hallway had been waxed approximately one hour before the accident. Thus, there was no substantial identity of material circumstances between the freshly waxed condition of the floor, and the floor that was used by 11,000 other people without incident over the prior one-week period.

A and B are incorrect, for the reasons discussed in D.

C is incorrect because evidence of the absence of prior accidents to show the nonexistence of a dangerous condition or causation is subject to the "substantial similarity" requirement. Under the stated facts, the hallway floor had just been waxed an hour before the woman walked on it. The hotel did not lay a foundation showing that the floor was in substantially similar condition (i.e., excessively waxed) the previous week when the 11,000 people walked on it. Because the substantial similarity requirement was not met, D is the correct answer.

35. A is the correct answer. There is no rule that disqualifies a person with mental illness or defect from testifying on account of those mental illnesses or defects. The test of competency to testify is not insanity, but only whether a witness can appreciate the obligation to tell the truth and have sufficient ability to perceive and communicate perceptions. Here, there is nothing in the facts to indicate that the woman lacked the ability to appreciate the obligation to tell the truth, nor is there anything to show that she lacked sufficient ability to perceive and communicate perceptions. Thus, the judge was correct in permitting the woman to testify. B, C and D are incorrect, for the reasons discussed in answer A.

36. D is the correct answer. Under Rule 408:

"Evidence of the following is not admissible — on behalf of any party — either to prove or disprove the validity or amount of a disputed claim or to impeach by a prior inconsistent statement or a contradiction: furnishing, promising, or offering — or accepting, promising to accept, or offering to accept — a valuable consideration in compromising or attempting to compromise the claim; and conduct or a statement made during compromise negotiations about the claim — except when offered in a criminal case and when the negotiations related to a claim by a public office in the exercise of its regulatory, investigative, or enforcement authority."

Here, the man wrote, "Your claim seems too high, but because I might be found at fault, I'm prepared to offer you half of what you ask." This is an offer to settle the woman's lawsuit. As such, it would not be admissible under Rule 408.

A is incorrect because an admission is an out-of-court statement made by a party, offered to prove the truth of the matter asserted. Under the Federal Rules of Evidence, party admissions are considered to be nonhearsay and are, therefore, admissible. However here, the man wrote in his letter that he might be at fault. This could not be construed as an admission because it was not a definite statement that he was at fault.

B is incorrect because, even though the statement may be against the man's pecuniary interest, it is inadmissible because it is an offer to compromise, as discussed in D.

C is incorrect for the reasons discussed in D.

37. C is the correct answer. Under Rule 407, "When measures are taken that would have made an earlier injury or harm less likely to occur, evidence of the subsequent measures is not admissible to prove negligence, culpable conduct, a defect in a product or its design, or a need for a warning or instruction."

The rationale falls under public policy; if such evidence could be used to establish the prior existence of a dangerous condition or practice, the person liable would be reluctant to take corrective action.

Here, the manufacturer recalled the defective blenders, which was an appropriate subsequent corrective action that would not be likely to have happened if the admission of such actions were allowed to show antecedent negligence on the part of the manufacturer.

A and B are incorrect, for the reasons discussed in C. D is incorrect because it is irrelevant.

38. A is the correct answer. Under Rule 801(d)(2)(D), a statement that "was made by the party's agent or employee on a matter within the scope of that relationship and while it existed" may be offered against the party." No authority to speak is required.

Here, the passenger was an employee of the corporation at the time of the accident. Her statement that the driver had left his glasses (which he was required to wear while driving) at the restaurant where she and the driver had eaten just before the accident is being offered against the corporation. The statement is relevant because the fact that the driver had not been wearing his glasses as required may have contributed to his failure to yield the right-of-way and, thus, caused the accident to occur.

Consequently, the statement is admissible under Rule 801(d)(2)(D).

C is incorrect because an admission does not require proof of unavailability to be admissible. B and D are incorrect for the reasons discussed in A.

39. A is the correct answer. An admission is an out-of-court statement made by a party and offered against that party. Admissions are considered nonhearsay or hearsay exemptions. Under Rule 801(d)(2)(A), an admission includes a statement that "was made by the party in an individual or representative capacity" and is being offered against that party.

Here, the man (the defendant and, thus, a party) made a statement that he had beheaded the woman. The woman's husband testified to the statement that the man had made to the husband. Thus, it is being used against the man and is, thus, admissible as an admission. B is incorrect because admissions are hearsay exemptions, as discussed in A; they are not exceptions to the hearsay rule. C and D are incorrect for the reasons discussed in answer A.

40. A is the correct answer. Under Rule 201(f), "In a civil case, the court must instruct the jury to accept the noticed fact as conclusive. In a criminal case, the court must instruct the jury that it may or may not accept the noticed fact as conclusive."

Here, the trial is a criminal trial. Thus, by the judge taking judicial notice, this merely allowed the jury to accept the fact as true or not that the man drove across state lines (an element in the crime charged). B, C, and D are incorrect, for the reasons discussed in A. B and C are also incorrect because in a criminal trial the burden of proof as to each element of a crime always remains with the prosecution.

41. B is the correct answer because judicial notice may be taken of any matter that is within common knowledge. Here, it is common knowledge that parrots must be trained to speak. Thus, the judge may take judicial notice of this fact. The fact that the judge refused to take judicial notice the woman's untrained parrot was defective because it did not speak was, thus, correct because common knowledge says that parrots must be trained before they will speak.

A is incorrect because judicial notice must be based on common knowledge, not on the judge's personal experience.

C is incorrect because the decision whether or not to take judicial notice is not completely within the judge's discretion. Rather, it must be based on common knowledge, as discussed in B.

D is incorrect because a judge may only take judicial notice of matters that are within common knowledge, as discussed in B.

42. B is the correct answer. Under the Fifth Amendment, which is incorporated to the states by way of the Due Process Clause of the Fourteenth Amendment, a person cannot be compelled to testify against himself in court. If a witness' testimony concerning a crime could lead to a criminal conviction, the privilege against self-incrimination can be claimed. Here, the witness' testimony could lead to a criminal conviction for the crime of purchasing narcotics (a controlled substance). Therefore, the judge's order was incorrect.

A is incorrect because there need not be a charge pending in order to invoke the privilege against self-incrimination.

C is incorrect for the reasons discussed in B.

D is incorrect because under the privilege against self-incrimination, the possibility of self-incrimination is sufficient for the privilege to be invoked; the self-incrimination does not need to be established in the record (because putting it in the record would defeat the purpose of the privilege in the first place, since the incriminating evidence would then become part of the record).

43. A is the correct answer. Under Rule 609(a)(1)(B), evidence of a crime that "was punishable by death or by imprisonment for more than one year...must be admitted in a criminal case in which the witness is a defendant, if the probative value of the evidence outweighs its prejudicial effect to that defendant."

Here, the witness is defendant, who is on trial for burglary. The admission of the defendant's previous burglary conviction is, thus, highly prejudicial. However, the probative prejudicial concerns are within the discretion of the judge. If the judge determines that the probative value of the previous burglary conviction does outweigh the prejudice to the defendant, then the evidence of the previous burglary conviction must be admitted under Rule 609(a)(1)(B).

B is an incorrect statement of law. C is incorrect because the defendant's character may not be introduced by the prosecution, unless it falls under the MIMIC rule (motive, identity, mistake, intent, common scheme or plan). Here, one prior burglary conviction is not evidence of a common scheme or plan. Thus, it is improper character evidence. D is incorrect because Rule 609 provides that notice must be given for crimes more than ten years old. Here, the crime took place exactly ten years ago, thus, requiring no notice.

44. B is the correct answer. Under Rule 801(c), hearsay is an out-of-court statement being offered to prove the truth of the matter asserted and is inadmissible, unless there is a recognized exception. Here, the affidavit is being offered in evidence to prove the settlor's incompetency (i.e., offered for the truth), and is an out-of-court statement by the declarant, the settlor's brother. The affidavit is inadmissible hearsay, unless there is an exception. Based upon the facts, there is no exception that will apply. A is incorrect because lay opinion as to common perceptions is permitted. C and D are incorrect for the reasons discussed in B.

45. D is the correct answer because a criminal defendant, after being read his Miranda rights, has a right to remain silent. Although an adoptive admission by silence can generally be used against a party who manifested his adoption or belief in its truth by conduct or silence, here it cannot, since the man was exercising a constitutional right. A, B and C are incorrect for the reasons stated in answer D.

46. A is the correct answer. Under Rule 801(c), hearsay is an out-of-court statement being offered to prove the truth of the matter asserted and is inadmissible, unless there is a recognized exception. Under the business records exception, hearsay evidence may be admitted if the evidence was part of the regularly conducted business. Here, the shipping manager received the invoice from the shipping clerk as part of his regular-conducted business responsibilities. His testimony merely authenticated the invoice and is, thus, sufficient to lay a foundation in order to allow the shipping invoice into evidence. Consequently, the invoice will be admissible under the business records exception to the hearsay rule.

B is incorrect because the shipping manager had no personal knowledge of

A

EVIDENCE

the merchandise listed upon the invoice. C is incorrect for the reasons discussed in A and B. D is incorrect because the invoice qualifies as a business record, an exception to the hearsay rule, as discussed in A.

47. C is the correct answer. Under Rule 801(c), hearsay is an out-of-court statement being offered to prove the truth of the matter asserted and is inadmissible, unless there is a recognized exception. Here, the statement is offered to prove that the woman's car had collided with the pedestrian (the truth of the matter asserted). The statement was made by a bus driver outside of court. The facts do not indicate that there is any exception to the hearsay rule here. Therefore, the testimony will be inadmissible.

    A is incorrect because a present sense impression is a statement describing or explaining an event or condition made at the time of the event or immediately thereafter. Here, a one-hour time lapse between the accident and the statement made allowed time for fabrication. Thus, the statement is not trustworthy and does not qualify as a present sense impression. B is incorrect for the reason discussed in C. D is an incorrect statement. The testimony is relevant because it describes the accident in question. However, it is in admissible as hearsay, as discussed in C.

48. A is the correct answer. Under Rule 803(3), "The following are not excluded by the rule against hearsay, regardless of whether the declarant is available as a witness... A statement of the declarant's then-existing...emotional, sensory, or physical condition (such as mental feeling, pain, or bodily health)."

    Here, the man's statement to his wife that he was bleeding is relevant because he had made the statement shortly after he was injured by the lawn mower. His statement that he was bleeding and needed to be taken to the hospital was a statement of his then-existing physical condition. The wife's testimony should, thus, be admitted under the hearsay exception for a description of present physical condition, discussed above.

    B is incorrect because the statement merely described the man's physical condition. It was not conclusive evidence as to whether or not the lawn mower company was negligent.

    C is incorrect because there is no requirement that the declarant's statement be made to a treating doctor. D is incorrect because the man, as a layperson, is permitted to describe his own condition.

49. D is the correct answer. Under Rule 801(c), hearsay is an out-of-court statement offered for the truth of the matter asserted. However, under Rule 803(4), a statement made for the purpose of medical diagnosis or treatment and describing medical history, or past or present symptoms, pain or sensations, or the inception or general character

of the cause or external source thereof insofar as reasonably pertinent to diagnosis or treatment, is admissible as an exception to the hearsay rule.

Here, the man's statement to the physician about his pain after the castration was made for the purpose of getting diagnosis and treatment from the physician. The man's statement is, therefore, admissible, under Rule 803(4) as a hearsay exception.

A is incorrect because the man's statement to the physician was reliable, since the man needed to accurately describe his condition in order to receive the proper diagnosis and treatment.

B is incorrect because it describes the reason why the man's statement would be admissible, since one's own physical condition is perceivable by that person, even if he is a layperson.

C is incorrect because the man was not giving an opinion about his diagnosis and treatment. Rather, he was merely telling the physician how he felt in order to enable the physician to diagnose and treat him.

50. B is the correct answer. Under Rule 801(c), hearsay is an out-of-court statement offered for the truth of the matter asserted. However, under Rule 803(4), a statement made for the purpose of medical diagnosis or treatment and describing medical history, or past or present symptoms, pain or sensations, or the inception or general character of the cause or external source thereof insofar as reasonably pertinent to diagnosis or treatment, is admissible as an exception to the hearsay rule.

Here, the guest's statement to the physician is hearsay, since it is being offered to prove the truth of the guest's assertion, i.e., that he suffered knee pain after helping a college buddy move. However, the statement is admissible under Rule 803(4) because the statement was made so that the guest could obtain a medical diagnosis from the physician. Therefore, the statement is admissible as an exception to the hearsay rule.

A is incorrect because there is no such rule.

C is incorrect because, under the physician-patient privilege (a statutory privilege), the privilege cannot be claimed in a personal injury lawsuit where the patient relies on a physical condition as an element of his claim or defense. Here, the guest is suing the hotel for personal injuries and is claiming that the hotel is responsible for his knee injury (i.e., the guest's physical condition). Thus, the physician-patient privilege will not prevent the admission of the statement here.

D is incorrect for the reasons discussed in B.

51. B is the correct answer. Under Rule 409, "Evidence of furnishing, promising to

pay, or offering to pay medical, hospital, or similar expenses resulting from an injury is not admissible to prove liability for the injury." However, an admission is admissible. An admission is an out-of-court statement made by a party and used for the truth of the matter asserted against that party in court.

Here, the statement is compound. There was an admission (""I know I was not watching where I was going when my bicycle stuck you."), and there was also an offer to pay medical expenses ("but if you're hurt, I'll pay your medical bills.")

Thus, under the Federal Rules of Evidence, the part of the statement that was an admission will be admissible, while the part of the statement that was an offer to pay medical expenses will be inadmissible.

A is incorrect because there is no opinion being offered, merely a statement that the man "was not watching where I was going when my bicycle struck you" that is being offered to prove the truth of the matter asserted.

C is incorrect because a present sense impression is an exception to the hearsay rule. Here, as discussed in B, the statement was nonhearsay.

D is incorrect because a declaration against interest requires the declarant to be unavailable. Here, as a party to the lawsuit, the man (the declarant) was available. Thus, the statement was not admissible as a declaration against interest.

52. C is the correct answer. Under Rule 409, "Evidence of furnishing, promising to pay, or offering to pay medical, hospital, or similar expenses resulting from an injury is not admissible to prove liability for the injury."

Here, the woman made an offer to pay medical expenses for the child. This statement is inadmissible under Rule 409. The fact that the statement was overheard by the neighbor does not alter its inadmissibility under Rule 409. Therefore, the woman's objection should be sustained.

A is incorrect because it assumes facts not contained in the fact pattern (i.e., that there was a police report) and, furthermore, the best evidence rule is inapplicable here because the neighbor's testimony is not being offered to prove the contents of a writing (the neighbor testified to what he overheard the woman say to the child's father).

B is incorrect because this is not a legally recognized reason to allow a statement to be admitted or excluded.

D is incorrect because an admission is an out-of-court statement made by a party, offered to prove the truth of the matter asserted. Under the Federal Rules of Evidence, party admissions are considered to be nonhearsay and are, therefore, admissible. However, here, the woman merely offered to pay the child's medical expenses; she did not admit to any fault or liability. Thus, the statement cannot be offered as an admission.

53. C is the correct answer. Under the Rule 803(1), "The following are not excluded by the rule against hearsay, regardless of whether the declarant is available as a witness...Present Sense Impression, [which is defined as] a statement describing or explaining an event or condition made while or immediately after the declarant perceived it." This is an exception to the hearsay rule.

    Here, the best friend's testimony about the woman's statement concerning the man's failure to stop for the red light described the incident immediately after the accident. Because the woman was conscious for only a few moments after the accident, her statement was necessarily made immediately after the accident occurred. Therefore, her statement is a present sense impression. A, B and D are incorrect for the reasons discussed in C.

54. B is the correct answer. A witness may testify to things of which he has personal knowledge. Here, the sheriff's deputy had processed the woman when she had first arrived at the jail. He, thus, had personal knowledge of her hair color at the time she checked into jail.

    A is incorrect because a prior identification requires the witness to have made a statement of identification prior to trial, which the deputy did not do here.

    C is incorrect because under Rule 801(c), hearsay is an out-of-court statement being offered for the truth of the matter asserted. Here, there is no out-of-court statement being offered. Rather, the deputy is merely testifying as to the woman's hair color at the time he processed her into jail.

    D is incorrect because the deputy is not giving an opinion about the woman's hair color, but is merely stating what he observed.

55. C is the correct answer. The attorney-client privilege protects those communications that the client either expressly made confidential or would reasonably be assumed, under the circumstances, to be confidential. Attorney-client communications remain privileged, even when made in the presence of joint clients or others, if the others are "reasonably necessary" to the consultation. Here, an attorney's secretary was a "reasonably necessary" party to the consultation. In the case where a lawyer has a clerk or secretary present, the privilege is still in effect, even if the client does not retain that attorney, as was the case here. A, B, and D are incorrect for the reasons discussed in C.

56. A is the correct answer. Under the Federal Rules of Evidence, a prior inconsistent statement in a deposition may

be used as substantive evidence. Comment to Rule 613(b) says that, although foundation must be laid for extrinsic proof of a prior inconsistent statement, the witness does not have to be shown the prior inconsistent statement before introducing the intrinsic evidence, as long as the witness, at some time during trial, has the opportunity to explain.

Here, although the witness was not questioned about the deposition, on direct examination, the deposition was introduced on cross-examination. Since the witness is still on the stand, the witness will, therefore, have the opportunity to explain.

B is incorrect because unavailability to testify is not a requirement, as discussed in A. C is incorrect for the reasons discussed in A. D is incorrect because intentional untruthfulness is not a requirement for admissibility of deposition testimony, as discussed in A.

57. C is the correct answer. Under Rule 405, " When a person's character or character trait is an essential element of a charge, claim, or defense, the character or trait may also be proved by relevant specific instances of the person's conduct."

Here, the woman sued the friend for negligently allowing the man to use the car ("negligent entrustment"). The man's propensity to drive carelessly is an element of the cause of action for negligent entrustment. Therefore, the evidence of the man's careless driving on three prior occasions is admissible as a relevant specific instances of the man's conduct.

A is incorrect because in a negligent entrustment suit regarding the entrustment of the owner's vehicle to a driver, the driver's prior driving record is highly relevant. B is an incorrect statement of law. D is incorrect because, under Rule 801(c), hearsay is an out-of-court statement offered to prove the truth of the matter asserted. Here, the witness is being called to testify about the man's prior careless driving, not about any statement. There is, thus, no hearsay here.

58. C is the correct answer. Under Rule 405(b), "When a person's character or character trait is an essential element of a charge, claim, or defense, the character or trait may also be proved by relevant specific instances of the person's conduct." Here, the man is suing the woman for battery, and woman is claiming self-defense. The woman's character is an essential element of her defense because, if she has a violent character, it is less likely that she acted in self-defense in this case. Therefore, the witness' testimony about relevant specific incidents of the woman's violent character (that on four previous occasions, the woman had hit her study partners with books) is admissible as property character evidence.

A is incorrect because habit refers to a

routine, activity, or response frequently repeated over a protracted period of time. Here, the witness is merely testifying to four prior incidents of the woman's violence. B is incorrect because the witness' testimony about the woman's prior violence is highly probative for the reasons discussed in C. D is incorrect because there is nothing in the facts to indicate bias.

59. C is the correct answer. The statement is not hearsay because it is being used to circumstantially show the woman's knowledge that the man was, in fact, still alive when he was shot. It is not being offered for its truth, and it is irrelevant what the man actually said; the statement is merely being used to show that the man said something before being shot and was, thus, not dead at the time.

A and B are incorrect because the statement was not hearsay - it was not being used to prove whether the man "was going to die." D is incorrect because firsthand knowledge is not the test as to whether a particular statement is hearsay or not.

60. A is the correct answer. The best evidence rule provides that, where a document contains terms that are material, the original document must be produced, unless reasons are shown as to why that original document is unavailable or unless the document pertains to a collateral matter. Here, the picture would qualify as a document. Therefore, the picture itself must be presented into evidence because its terms are material (whether or not the female portrayed in the picture was the woman). As a result, under the Best Evidence Rule, the picture must be presented, unless the picture has been lost or destroyed through no fault of the woman. The facts do not indicate that the picture was lost or destroyed, and, thus, the witness' testimony would not be allowed as secondary evidence.

B is incorrect because the witness' description, whether or not the description is authenticated, will not be allowed in, for the reasons discussed in A.

C is incorrect because there are no facts indicating that the witness is competent to testify whether or not it was the artist's signature on the painting. In addition, the document (the picture) had to not only be authenticated, but actually brought into court, as discussed in A.

D is incorrect for the reasons discussed in A.

61. B is the correct answer because the testimony of former business partner demonstrated the earnings of the partnership in which the former business partner had personal knowledge. It was also relevant because the woman needed to prove loss of potential earnings as part of her wrongful death lawsuit.

A is incorrect because it is immaterial whether the books can be inspected to decide whether the former business partner's testimony was permissible or not.

C is incorrect because, under Rule 801(c), hearsay is an out-of-court statement offered to prove the truth of the matter asserted. Here, the former business partner was testifying to facts of which he had personal knowledge (namely, the partnership's earnings). He was not testifying as to what the books said; rather, he merely stated that the books would be made available to corroborate what he had said about the partnership's earnings.

D is incorrect because the former business partner was not testifying to the contents of a writing, i.e., the books, as discussed in C.

62. A is the correct answer. As a general rule, expert testimony is required when a conclusion cannot be reached using common knowledge. Rule 702 defines an expert as "A witness who is qualified as an expert by knowledge, skill, experience, training, or education." Here, the girlfriend had skill, experience, and training from working in her father's mechanic shop, as well as specific knowledge about tires and the marks they leave behind. She was, thus, qualified as an expert and could testify as to whether the tire marks left by the murderer's vehicle could have been left by the vehicle driven by the two young men.

B is incorrect because the Best Evidence Rule has to do with writings. Here, there are no writings being discussed.

C is incorrect because an expert does not have to have personal knowledge. Experts may testify as to a hypothetical.

D is incorrect because, under Rule 801(c), hearsay is an out-of-court statement being offered to prove the truth of the matter asserted. Here, there is no out-of-court statement being discussed, only tire marks. Thus, there is no hearsay issue here.

63. D is the correct answer. Rule 704(a) abolished the "ultimate issue" objection that once prevented lay and expert witnesses from giving testimony phrased in terms of the ultimate facts that the jury must determine. Modernly, opinion testimony is admissible, if it would be helpful to the jury under Rules 701 (lay testimony) and 702 (expert testimony).

With respect to the question of the man's capacity to make a will (an ultimate issue in a will contest based on the man's capacity to make a will), a lay or expert witness may render a conclusion as to a legal opinion, whether or not the man had the legal capacity to make a will. Here, the opinions of the former housekeeper and doctor were based on their personal observations of the man. Therefore, this testimony will assist the jury in determining the legal issue of the man's capacity to make a will.

A, B and C are incorrect for the reasons discussed in D.

64. C is the correct answer. Under Rule 407, "When measures are taken that would have made an earlier injury or harm less likely to occur, evidence of the subsequent measures is not admissible to prove negligence, culpable conduct, a defect in a product or its design, or a need for a warning or instruction."

The rationale falls under public policy; if such evidence could be used to establish the prior existence of a dangerous condition or practice, the person liable would be reluctant to take corrective action.

However, Rule 407 goes on to state, "But the court may admit this evidence for another purpose, such as...proving ownership [or] control."

Here, it is the man's ownership of the tree that is in dispute. The fact that he later had the tree cut down demonstrates his ownership of the tree, since he would not have had the power to have the tree cut down if it were on city property, as the man claimed. A, B and D are incorrect for the reasons discussed in C.

65. A is the correct answer. In a criminal case, self-interest may be shown when the witness testifies for the state and it is shown that a criminal indictment against that witness has been forgiven or lessened in exchange for the witness' testimony. Here, the witness is being asked, "Isn't it true that charges against you as an accomplice in the woman's murder are being dropped in exchange for your testimony against the man?" If the witness is an accomplice in the murder for which the man is being prosecuted, then the witness clearly has a self-interest in testifying against the man in exchange for the criminal indictment against the witness being dropped. B, C and D are incorrect for the reasons discussed in A.

In addition, B and D are incorrect because the comment to Rule 613(b) says that, although a foundation must be laid for extrinsic proof of a prior inconsistent statement, the witness does not have to be shown the prior inconsistent statement before introducing the intrinsic evidence, as long as the witness, at some time during trial, has the opportunity to explain. Here, the witness is on the stand and, thus, has the opportunity to explain.

66. B is the correct answer because judicial notice may be taken of any matter that is within common knowledge. Here, it is common knowledge that New Mexico is part of the United States and is easily verifiable by searching on the Internet, using an atlas or checking any other reliable source. Thus, the judge may take judicial notice of this fact.

A is an incorrect statement of law. C is an incorrect statement of fact. New Mexico has been a U.S. state since January 6, 1912.

D is incorrect because no foundation is needed to admit evidence that is a matter of common knowledge by having the judge take judicial notice.

67. D is the correct answer. A lay witness may testify in the form of opinions and inferences that are rationally based on the perception of the witness and helpful to a clear understanding of either his testimony or a fact in issue. Here, the victim is suing the hospital for malpractice and alleging that she was not given prompt medical attention, which resulted in her recovery being delayed. Therefore, the nurse's testimony that the victim was unconscious when the victim came into the hospital is rationally based on her perception of the victim and will be helpful to a clear understanding of a fact in issue. (If the victim were unconscious, she would not know whether there was a delay in treatment.) A, B and C are incorrect for the reasons discussed in D.

68. D is the correct answer. A confidential communication between an attorney and his client pertaining to their relationship is privileged from disclosure. Any communications made in the course of preliminary discussions with a view of employing the lawyer are privileged, even though the employment is not accepted. In addition, the presence of the boy's father did not remove the element of "confidentiality." Since the boy was 6 years old, his father's presence was necessary for the attorney to render legal service to the boy. A and B are incorrect, for the reasons discussed in D. C is incorrect because there is no such privilege.

69. D is the correct answer. The best evidence rule provides that, where a document contains terms that are material, the original document must be produced, unless reasons are shown as to why that original document is unavailable or unless the document pertains to a collateral matter. Here, the reference to the newspaper is collateral to the issue of the finalization date. Therefore, the original newspaper article did not need to be produced. As a result, the court was correct in denying the employer's motion to strike because a witness may refer to a collateral document without providing the document.

A is incorrect for the reasons discussed in D.

B is incorrect because, under Rule 801(c), hearsay is an out-of-court statement being offered for the truth of the matter asserted. Here, the out-of-court statement in the newspaper (i.e., that there was an earthquake) is not being offered for the truth of the matter asserted (i.e., that the earthquake actually happened), but rather, simply to show which newspaper the man had seen in order to know the date.

C is incorrect because it is not necessary for the court to take judicial notice of the newspaper because what is important is the date of the newspaper, not the newspaper itself.

70. A is the correct answer. Under Rule 609(a)(2), "The following rules apply to attacking a witness's character for truthfulness by evidence of a criminal conviction…for any crime regardless of the punishment, the evidence must be admitted if the court can readily determine that establishing the elements of the crime required proving — or the witness's admitting — a dishonest act or false statement."

Here, false pretenses is a crime of truth of veracity. Therefore, the bystander's prior conviction of false pretenses is admissible under Rule 609(a)(2).

B and D are incorrect for the reasons discussed in A. C is incorrect because a witness' credibility is always relevant.

71. A is the correct answer. Rule 412(b)(1)(B) permits the introduction of "evidence of specific instances of a victim's sexual behavior with respect to the person accused of the sexual misconduct, if offered by the defendant to prove consent." Here, the man is on trial for rape and wishes to prove that the woman consented to sexual intercourse with him (and was, thus, not raped). Under Rule 412(b)(1)(B), he is permitted to introduce evidence of his past consensual sexual intercourse with the woman.

B is incorrect because habit evidence must be routine, regular, and always the same. Here, the man was merely bringing in some previous consensual sexual intercourse experience with the woman. This does not qualify as habit evidence.

C and D are incorrect for the reasons discussed in A.

72. D is the correct answer. Under Rule 609(a), evidence that an accused was convicted of a crime can be used to attack the credibility of the accused who testifies as a witness, if the crime was punishable by death or imprisonment in excess of one year and the probative value of the conviction outweighs its prejudicial effect, or the crime involves "dishonesty or false statement" (whether a felony or a misdemeanor). Under Rule 609(b), a criminal conviction over 10 years old may be admitted within the court's discretion, if it is found that the probative value substantially outweighs the prejudicial effect and the adverse party was given written notice that the conviction was to be used. Here, the conviction in question was sixteen years old and was, thus, a criminal conviction over ten years old.

Since no written notice was given to the defense before trial, even if the court finds that the probative value substantially outweighs the prejudicial effect, the objection must be sustained.

A and B are incorrect, for the reasons stated for answer D.

C is incorrect because, although the crime is more than ten years old, the prosecution may still introduce that crime if it gives written notice, as discussed in D. Here, the facts indicate that no notice - written or otherwise - was given. Thus, C is incorrect and D is correct.

73. D is the correct answer. Under Rule 408, evidence that one party offered to settle or compromise the claim against another is inadmissible to show liability, unless it is offered to prove bias, or prejudice, or to negate the contentions of undue delay, or to obstruct a criminal conviction. Here, in the man's letter, he wrote, "Your claim of damage seems too high, but because I have no insurance, and I was at fault, I'm prepared to pay the amount you have asked."

This statement contained an offer to settle the woman's lawsuit against the man, but the statement also included an admission of fault by the man. Any statements made by the parties when trying to settle are inadmissible. The Federal Rules of Evidence do not permit severance of admissions of liability from compromise discussions. Therefore, the entire statement is inadmissible.

A, B and C are incorrect, for the reasons discussed in D.

74. A is the correct answer. A confidential communication between an attorney and a prospective client, made in anticipation of potentially retaining that attorney, is privileged from disclosure, whether or not the attorney is ultimately retained by the client. Here, the woman discussed the sale of her shares of stock with the first attorney in anticipation of potentially retaining that attorney to represent her in the lawsuit. The fact that the attorney was not ultimately retained by the woman does not alter the confidential nature of the communication. Therefore, it is privileged and inadmissible.

B is factually incorrect. The facts state, "She explained to the attorney the reason for the sale and disclosed the financial condition of the corporation." The statement, therefore, was relevant to the sale.

C and D are incorrect for the reasons discussed in A.

75. A is the correct answer. Under Rule 407, "When measures are taken that would have made an earlier injury or harm less likely to occur, evidence of the subsequent measures is not admissible to prove negligence, culpable conduct, a defect in a product or its design, or a need for a warning or instruction."

The rationale falls under public policy; if such evidence could be used to establish the prior existence of a dangerous condition or practice, the person liable would be reluctant to take corrective action.

However, Rule 407 goes on to state, "But the court may admit this evidence for another purpose, such as...proving ownership [or] control."

Here, the man denied responsibility (claiming that the woman was responsible), but then went ahead and hired the contractor to remove the tree. The evidence is admissible to show the man's control in making the repairs. B, C and D are incorrect for the reason discussed in A.

76. A is the correct answer. Under Rule 409, "Evidence of furnishing, promising to pay, or offering to pay medical, hospital, or similar expenses resulting from an injury is not admissible to prove liability for the injury." Funeral expenses are considered to be "similar expenses" by the court under this rule. B is incorrect for the reasons discussed in A. C and D are incorrect because, even though the offer to pay funeral expenses could be construed as a party admission or a declaration against interest, it would not be admissible for the reasons discussed in A.

77. C is the correct answer. Under Rule 704, testimony in the form of an expert opinion is generally not objectionable because it embraces the ultimate issue or issues to be decided by the trier of fact. However, under Rule 704(b), "In a criminal case, an expert witness must not state an opinion about whether the defendant did or did not have a mental state or condition that constitutes an element of the crime charged or of a defense. Those matters are for the trier of fact [i.e., the jury] alone." Here, the psychiatrist may not give his opinion as to whether or not this criminal defendant (the man) had a mental state or condition that constitutes an element of this crime. Thus, the district attorney's objection should be sustained and the jury will be permitted to draw its own conclusions on the issue.

A is incorrect because, even if an expert is properly qualified to testify on matters of mental state or condition, he may not give an opinion on an ultimate matter of law in a criminal case, as discussed in C.

B is incorrect because the evidence is improper, even if it were uncontroverted, for the reasons discussed in C. Furthermore, there is nothing in the facts to indicate that the evidence was uncontroverted.

D is incorrect because bias in favor of one party is not a reason to exclude an expert.

78. A is the correct answer. In a civil case (such as personal injury), the plaintiff may not bring in her character for careful driving, unless the character trait is actually habitual (routine). Here, the best friend is about to testify to one incident of the plaintiff's careful driving. Thus, the friend's testimony would not be habit evidence and would be an impermissible character trait.

A

EVIDENCE

B is incorrect because the best friend's testimony is not opinion testimony, but rather, a factual recitation of events that she had observed.

C is incorrect because, although the best friend had first-hand knowledge of the woman's conduct, personal knowledge is not sufficient to overrule an objection.

D is incorrect for the reasons discussed in A.

79. D is the correct answer. This question is testing the character trait of forgetfulness because only two hours before the incident at the department store (where the woman was charged with shoplifting), the woman forgot and left a $2,000 diamond ring behind, even though she had already paid for the ring. The cashier's testimony, thus, tends to support the woman's assertion that she had similarly forgotten that she had placed the blouse on the baby carriage as she left the department store.

A is incorrect because the character trait of forgetfulness is permissible and highly relevant here where the woman was charged with shoplifting and asserted that she had no intent to do so because she had forgotten that she had put the blouse on her baby's stroller.

B is incorrect because the cashier's testimony is not opinion testimony, but rather, a factual recitation of events that he had observed.

C is incorrect because, although the cashier had first-hand knowledge of the woman's conduct in the store, personal knowledge is not sufficient to overrule an objection.

80. B is the correct answer. Under Rule 704, testimony in the form of an expert opinion is generally not objectionable because it embraces the ultimate issue or issues to be decided by the trier of fact. However, under Rule 704(b), "In a criminal case, an expert witness must not state an opinion about whether the defendant did or did not have a mental state or condition that constitutes an element of the crime charged or of a defense. Those matters are for the trier of fact [i.e., the jury] alone." Here, even though the psychologist's testimony will assist the trier of fact to determine whether or not the woman was forgetful, the woman is charged with shoplifting, which is a criminal charge. The exception in Rule 704(b) applies.

A is incorrect, for the reasons discussed in B.

C is incorrect because the facts state that the psychologist was qualified as an expert.

D is incorrect because it is an incorrect statement of law.

81. B is the correct answer. Under Rule 404(a)(2)(A), "[A] defendant may offer evidence of the defendant's pertinent trait, and if the evidence is admitted,

the prosecutor may offer evidence to rebut it." Here, non-violence is irrelevant to the issue of innocence of the crime of selling narcotics. Therefore, non-violence is not a pertinent trait in this case. As a result, the objection will be sustained. A and C are incorrect, for the reasons discussed in answer B. D is incorrect because, while it is a true statement, the evidence of the defendant's non-violent character cannot be admitted in this case, for the reasons discussed in B.

82. A is the correct answer. Where a doctor examines a party to enable the client to communicate his or her condition to the attorney, the attorney-client privilege applies. Note that where an attorney employs a physician to examine the client, the physician's report may not be privileged under the physician-patient privilege (or psychiatrist-patient privilege) because no treatment is contemplated. Therefore, the second psychiatrist's opinions, which are based on communications from the man, are protected from disclosure because the doctor was an agent of the man's lawyer when the doctor examined the man. B, C and D are incorrect for the reasons discussed in A.

83. C is the correct answer. Rule 404(b)(1), "Evidence of a crime, wrong, or other act is not admissible to prove a person's character in order to show that on a particular occasion the person acted in accordance with the character." Here, the man's murder of his boss (a crime) is not proper character evidence to show that on this occasion he acted in accordance with his character and murdered his mistress.

A is incorrect because there are not enough facts in the hypothetical to evidence a plan. A plan requires something specific; here, the facts only discuss one prior murder without anything specific about that prior murder that is also present in the murder of the mistress.

B is incorrect because the man's intent in murdering his boss does not show his intent regarding the mistress. D is incorrect because the prior murder is relevant, since the current trial is also for murder.

84. C is the correct answer. Under Rule 404, "Evidence of a person's character or character trait is not admissible to prove that on a particular occasion the person acted in accordance with the character or trait." There are exceptions to this general rule in civil cases, if character is at issue in the case, such as in defamation, assault, and battery cases. Here, this is a civil negligence case, not an assault, battery, or defamation case. Consequently, the exceptions do not apply in this case. Therefore, the testimony about the man's reputation for being a careless driver will be inadmissible as improper character evidence. A, B and D are incorrect for the reason stated in answer C.

A

EVIDENCE

85. B is the correct answer. Under the Rule 803(1), "The following are not excluded by the rule against hearsay, regardless of whether the declarant is available as a witness...Present Sense Impression, [which is defined as] a statement describing or explaining an event or condition, made while or immediately after the declarant perceived it." This is an exception to the hearsay rule.

Here, the woman's statement ("it looks like the driver has been drinking, and he can't seem to keep control over his car") is admissible because she made it while observing the man's driving manner, and her statement describes the man's driving manner. The fact that the woman is available to testify would not prevent the driver's testimony from being admissible.

A is incorrect statement because the statement is admissible under the present sense impression to the hearsay rule, as discussed in B.

C and D are incorrect for the reasons discussed in B.

86. D is the correct answer. Under the Rule 803(1), "The following are not excluded by the rule against hearsay, regardless of whether the declarant is available as a witness...present sense impression, [which is defined as] a statement describing or explaining an event or condition made while or immediately after the declarant perceived it." This is an exception to the hearsay rule.

Here, the eyewitness' statement was made immediately after she had observed the accident. Thus, the eyewitness' statement qualifies under the present sense impression exception to the hearsay rule.

A is incorrect because the declarant was the eyewitness, not the man (the employee).

B is incorrect because it states the standard for an excited utterance, not a present sense impression.

C is incorrect because whether or not the oil company negligently entrusted the driving of its truck to the man would not prevent the admission of the eyewitness' testimony.

87. A is the correct answer. Under Rule 401:

Evidence is relevant if: (a) it has any tendency to make a fact more or less probable than it would be without the evidence; and (b) the fact is of consequence in determining the action.

Relevant evidence is admissible, unless its probative value is substantially outweighed by the danger of unfair prejudice. Under these facts, the videotape is relevant to show the drunkard's intoxication. Although the tape is prejudicial, its probative value substantially outweighs its prejudice to the drunkard. Thus, it is admissible.

B is incorrect because an admission is an out-of-court statement made by a party. Here, the prosecution is introducing conduct (slurred words, not the actual words themselves). Thus, there is no admission here.

C is incorrect because, under rule 801(c), hearsay is an out-of-court statement offered to prove the truth of the matter asserted. Here, for the reasons discussed in B, the prosecution is introducing conduct, not a statement. Thus, there is no hearsay here.

D is incorrect for the reasons discussed in A.

88. C is the correct answer. Extrinsic evidence is inadmissible to impeach a witness on a collateral matter. The man's testimony of what the driver was wearing on the day of the incident is extrinsic evidence of a collateral matter because its sole relevance is to contradict the woman's testimony regarding what the driver was wearing. The man's testimony does not tend to prove or disprove what caused the accident. Therefore, the man's testimony is inadmissible because it is extrinsic evidence on a collateral matter.

A is incorrect for the reasons discussed in C.

B is incorrect because, while it may have some bearing on the woman's credibility, the issue is a collateral matter, as discussed in C.

D is incorrect because, while what a driver is wearing at the time of the accident may be relevant (such as whether the driver was wearing glasses and may have had vision issues), whether the driver was wearing a hat (which was the issue here) is not such an instance. Therefore, the testimony would be inadmissible as discussed in C.

89. B is the correct answer. Under Rule 801(d)(2)(A), "[A statement that meets the following conditions is not hearsay...an opposing party's statement. The statement is offered against an opposing party and...] was made by the party in an individual...capacity." Here, the woman is a party to the lawsuit. The officer is testifying that the woman admitted to him that she was driving at a speed of 40 mph in a 35 mph zone. Thus, the woman's out-of-court statement would qualify as an admission and would be nonhearsay under the Federal Rules of Evidence. A is incorrect because a declaration against interest requires that the declarant be unavailable to testify. Here, the woman is the declarant and, as a party to the lawsuit, is available to testify. Thus, the statement will not be admissible as a declaration against interest. C and D are incorrect for the reasons discussed in B.

90. A is the correct answer. Under Rule 801(c), hearsay is an out-of-court statement being offered to prove the truth of the matter asserted. Statements of commands and questions have no assertive

content; therefore, they cannot be hearsay. Here, the man had said, "Get me a drink or else," which is a command. The statement is not being offered to prove the truth of the matter asserted (i.e., that the bartender had gotten the man a drink), but rather, that the man had uttered this command. Therefore, it is admissible because it is not hearsay. B, C and D are incorrect for the reason discussed in A.

91. D is the correct answer. Any "statement" made by a machine or animal is not hearsay. The rationale is that statements from machines and animals are trustworthy. Here, the "statement" in question (that the driver's car was traveling at 45 MPH in a 30 MPH zone) was from a radar gun, which is a machine. It was, therefore, admissible because it was not hearsay. A, B and C are incorrect for the reasons discussed in D.

92. C is the correct answer. Under Rule 801(c), hearsay is an out-of-court statement offered to prove the truth of the matter asserted. Here, the bill of sale was being introduced to prove the truth of the man's representation that the car in question was a Rolls Royce. Thus, it was an out-of-court statement (that the car was a Rolls Royce) made in a document (a bill of sale), being offered to prove the truth of the matter asserted (that the car was indeed a Rolls Royce). Consequently, it was hearsay and was inadmissible without an exception. Here, there were no exceptions that applied.

A is an incorrect statement of law. Furthermore, rightful ownership was not the issue here; rather, the issue was whether or not the car was a Rolls Royce.

B is incorrect because an admission is an out-of-court statement made by a party. Here, the statement was made by whoever sold the Rolls Royce to the man; that person was not a party to this lawsuit. Thus, the statement was not an admission.

D is incorrect because the best evidence rule requires that the original document be brought in, rather than a copy. Here, the original bill of sale was brought in, thus, fulfilling the requirements of this rule. However, it was not admissible for the reasons discussed in C.

93. C is the correct answer. Under Rule 608(b)(1), "Except for a criminal conviction under Rule 609, extrinsic evidence is not admissible to prove specific instances of a witness's conduct in order to attack or support the witness's character for truthfulness. But the court may, on cross-examination, allow them to be inquired into, if they are probative of the character for truthfulness or untruthfulness of…the witness."

Here, the question asked on cross-examination as to whether or not the witness certified art reproductions as originals (a fraud or a falsehood) went to the witness' character for truthfulness. Therefore, such a question may be admissible, if the court determined in its discretion that the question may be asked to impeach the witness' credibility.

A is incorrect because, although the witness certifying reproductions as originals was a collateral matter, the court still has discretion, as discussed in C.

B is incorrect because, under 608(b)(1), it is not required that the witness be convicted of a crime involving untruthfulness in order for the specific instance of conduct to be admitted.

D is incorrect for the reasons discussed in B and C.

94. A is the correct answer. Under Rule 801(c), hearsay is an out-of-court statement offered to prove the truth of the matter asserted. It is not allowed in court, unless there is an exception. Here, there was no exception to allow the disciplinary reports to be admitted. They did not qualify as business records because a written complaint by a citizen is not a business record.

B is incorrect because, under the Federal Rules of Evidence, specific instance evidence of character is inadmissible under the "victim's exception" (i.e., to prove the policeman's propensity to use excessive force to show that he used excessive force against the defendant, the man). C is incorrect, for the reasons discussed in A. D is incorrect, for the reasons discussed in B.

95. C is the correct answer. Under Rule 405(b), "When a person's character or character trait is an essential element of a charge, claim, or defense, the character or trait may also be proved by relevant specific instances of the person's conduct."

In a wrongful death action, the surviving spouse is allowed to recover damages. The survivor is entitled to prove that the decedent had a character trait for being loving and affectionate to demonstrate the extent of the loss of companionship. Therefore, the decedent's character trait becomes a disputed issue. Here because the character of the decedent (the late husband) is at issue, the cousin is entitled to rebut the widow's testimony that she and her husband were happily married throughout their entire marriage by introducing evidence that the late husband had separated from the widow a decade earlier and lived with another woman during the separation.

A and B are incorrect, for the reasons stated in answer C. D is incorrect because relevance alone cannot form the basis to admit the rebuttal evidence.

96. A is the correct answer. In most U.S. jurisdictions, in a criminal case in which the defendant is accused of sexual assault, evidence of a prior rape is admissible for any relevant purpose. Here, the witness' testimony about the manner in which she was raped by the defendant (taken to a secluded area after being told that she was being given a ride to a party)

is relevant because in the current case, the minor was also driven to a secluded area and raped. B, C, and D are incorrect for the reasons discussed in A.

97. D is the correct answer. Under Rule 1002, "An original writing, recording, or photograph is required in order to prove its content, unless these rules or a federal statute provides otherwise."

Here, the man sought to prove the terms of the contract with which the employer had not complied. The man must, therefore, produce the contract, since the terms of the contract are in dispute.

A and B are incorrect, for the reasons discussed in D. C is incorrect because, under Rule 801(c), hearsay is an out-of-court statement being offered to prove truth of the matter asserted. Here, once the contract is brought in (as discussed in D), any statements made in the contract will not be out of court statements, but rather, statements made in a document in the court.

98. B is the correct answer. Under Rule 608(a), evidence offered to support the truthfulness of a witness is inadmissible, until evidence has been admitted to attack the witness' credibility. Here, the prosecution seeks to support the woman's credibility as a witness by bringing in the second witness' (neighbor's) testimony that he had lived next door to the woman for ten years and knew of her reputation for truthfulness. However, there is nothing in the facts to indicate that the woman's credibility has been attacked. Therefore, the witness' (neighbor's) testimony is inadmissible. A, C and D are incorrect for the reasons discussed in B.

99. C is the correct answer. Under Rule 801(c), hearsay is an out-of-court statement offered to prove the truth of the matter asserted and is not allowed in court, unless there is an exception. Here, the roommate's testimony contained an out-of-court statement (the statement by the man to his roommate that the woman had committed the robbery alone) and was being offered to prove the matter asserted (i.e., that that the woman had committed the robbery alone). Thus, the statement was hearsay testimony, and there were no hearsay exceptions applicable here.

A is incorrect because a co-conspirator party admission, like any admission, is an out-of-court statement made by a party and being offered against that party. Here, although the statement was made out of court by a party (the man), it was being offered in the man's defense, not against the man. Therefore, it was not a co-conspirator party admission or an admission of any kind.

B is incorrect because the statement could only be used as direct proof of the matter asserted (i.e., that the woman, not the man, had committed the robbery) if it were admissible. However, here the statement was inadmissible, for the reasons discussed in C.

D is incorrect because this is not a reason to not admit a statement, but, rather, for the prosecution to later attempt to impeach the roommate. However, this did not become an issue because the statement was inadmissible for the reasons discussed in C.

100. A is the correct answer. Rule 901(b)(4) states that one way to authenticate a document is through "the appearance, contents, substance, internal patterns, or other distinctive characteristics of the item taken together with all the circumstances." Here, the woman testified that the letter was mailed to her two weeks after the accident. This fact, together with the contents of the letter ("My foot slipped off the brake. Don't worry, I will see that all your damages are paid.") and the signature ("Man") suggest that the letter was, indeed, signed by the man and that he was using the letter to admit his fault in the accident and offer to pay the woman's damages. These circumstances make it highly unlikely that anyone else would have sent such a letter to the woman so soon after the accident. Therefore, the authentication was proper. The letter can be admitted so that the jury can determine whether, based upon the contents, they believe the letter was written by the man.

B, C and D are incorrect, for the reasons discussed in A. Furthermore, B is incorrect because, as discussed in A, authentication does not create an irrefutable presumption that the letter was, in fact, written by the man. Rather, it merely satisfies the authentication requirement such that the letter can be presented to the jury, who will make the final determination whether or not man wrote the letter. Only if the jury decides that the man wrote the letter could the letter be direct proof of his fault.

101. A is the correct answer. Under Rule 801(d)(2)(A), "[A statement that meets the following conditions is not hearsay...an opposing party's statement. The statement is offered against an opposing party and...] was made by the party in an individual...capacity." Here, the hairdresser admitted that she did not use the correct hair dye. Since the hairdresser is a party to the lawsuit (the defendant), the statements in the letter from the hairdresser qualify as an admission and are, thus, admissible as nonhearsay.

B is factually incorrect. C and D are incorrect for the reasons discussed in A.

102. A is the correct answer. Under Rule 801(c), hearsay is an out-of-court statement offered to prove the truth of the matter asserted and is not allowed in court, unless there is an exception. Under Rule 803(3), a declaration of a then-existing physical condition is an exception to the hearsay rule.

Here, the declaration made by the man, indicating his present existing bodily condition ("I cannot finish our golf game because of pains in my back") was made outside of court and was being offered to prove the truth of the matter asserted (i.e., that the man had pains in his back at the time he uttered the statement a week before the incident in the movie theater). The statement was, therefore, admissible under Rule 803(3).

B is incorrect because there is no such exception to the hearsay rule.

C and D are incorrect for the same reasons discussed in A.

103. C is the correct answer. Under Rule 404(a)(1), "Evidence of a person's character or character trait is not admissible to prove that on a particular occasion the person acted in accordance with the character or trait." There are exceptions to this general rule, but they are not applicable in this case. Here, the defendant is on trial for the robbery of a convenience store. The prosecution is attempting to introduce evidence that the defendant had previously robbed two gas stations. There are no facts to indicate that there were any unique aspects about the gas station robberies that were also present in the convenience store robbery. Thus, the gas station robberies were not "signature crimes." As a result, evidence of these robberies is inadmissible.

A and B are incorrect for the reasons discussed in C. D is incorrect because, even if character evidence in the form of reputation or opinion were offered, it is not the type of evidence that makes the evidence inadmissible, but that defendant has not "opened the door" by offering evidence of his good character.

104. D is the correct answer. Under Rule 409, "Evidence of furnishing, promising to pay, or offering to pay medical, hospital, or similar expenses resulting from an injury is not admissible to prove liability for the injury."

Here, the girl offered to pay pedestrian's medical expenses. Therefore, this offer is inadmissible under Rule 409.

A is incorrect because an admission is an out-of-court statement made by a party offered to prove the truth of the matter asserted. Under the Federal Rules of Evidence, party admissions are considered to be nonhearsay and are, therefore, admissible. However here, the girl merely offered to pay the pedestrian's medical expenses; she did not admit to any fault or liability. Thus, the statement cannot be offered as an admission

B and C are incorrect for the reasons discussed in D.

105. C is the correct answer. Under Trammel v. U.S., 445 U.S. 40 (1980), the witness-spouse alone has the power to choose whether or not to testify against the other spouse, with or without the other spouse's consent. Thus, the wife may properly refuse to testify against the husband at his battery trial.

A is incorrect because there was no communication here; the wife is merely being asked to testify as to what she witnessed, not as to any statement she was told by her husband in confidence.

B is in correct because, although the wife had personal knowledge of the incident, she could still refuse to testify for the reasons discussed in C. D is incorrect because, even though the wife's testimony would not be regarding a confidential marital communication for the reasons discussed in A, she may still refuse to testify, for the reasons discussed in C.

106. A is the correct answer. A confidential marital communication ("pillow talk") made during the marriage, remains privileged even after the marriage has ended. Either spouse may assert the privilege to bar the other from testifying. The facts indicate the man "privately speaks to his wife" and that he admits his guilt to the drug trafficking charge. Because this statement is made in confidence from the man to the wife during the marriage, the statement is a confidential marital communication, even though the wife has subsequently obtained a dissolution. Thus, even if the wife wanted to testify, the man can prevent her from disclosing the confidential statement. B, C and D are incorrect for the reasons discussed in A.

107. B is the correct answer. Although the criminal was not an attorney, the evidence will be deemed inadmissible where the client has a reasonable belief that he is seeking advice from an attorney at the time of his communication. Here, the detective had a reasonable belief that the criminal was an attorney. Even though he did not hire the criminal to represent him, the communication will be deemed privileged because it was made in contemplation of hiring the criminal to represent the detective. A, C and D are incorrect for the reasons discussed in B.

108. C is the correct answer. Under Rule 801(c), hearsay is an out-of-court statement offered to prove the truth of the matter asserted and is not allowed in court, unless there is an exception. Here, the accident report was made out of court and was being offered to prove the truth of the matter asserted in the accident report (that the accident was unavoidable). The report was, thus, hearsay and was inadmissible without an applicable exception. The only possible exception would be the business records exception. However, the report was prepared for litigation, not to record regular conduct of the business. Also, the source of the information, the engineer, indicated a "lack of trustworthiness," since the engineer could potentially be sued. Therefore, has an interest in being self-serving and making the report favorable to himself and to the railroad company.

A is incorrect, for the reasons discussed in C.

B is incorrect, for the same reasons discussed in C.

D is incorrect because the best evidence rule requires that the original, rather than a copy, be brought to court. Here, the original accident report was being brought to court, thereby satisfying the best evidence rule. However, it was inadmissible for the reasons discussed in C.

109. C is the correct answer. Under Rule 801(c), hearsay is an out-of-court statement offered to prove the truth of the matter asserted and is not allowed in court, unless there is an exception. Here, the wife's statement to the maid that the man (her husband) had poisoned her was made outside of court and was being offered to prove the truth of the matter asserted (that the man had poisoned the wife). It was, therefore, hearsay.

It was not admissible under the dying declaration exception to the hearsay rule because a dying declaration must be made under sense of impending death. Here, the wife merely said that she had been poisoned. There was nothing in her statement to indicate that she realized she was dying. The fact that she did die shortly thereafter does not alter the fact that at the time the wife made the statement, she was not apparently under a sense of impending death. Therefore, this exception does not apply here.

It was also not admissible under Rule 803(3)'s state of mind exception to the hearsay rule because the United States Supreme Court has held that the belief of the declarant does not qualify as state of mind.

A and B are incorrect, for the reasons discussed in C.

D is incorrect because the dead man's statute prohibits a party-witness from testifying about communications with a person who is now dead and using those communications against the decedent's estate. The dead man's statute is only applicable in civil cases. Here, this is a criminal case. Thus, it is not applicable here.

110. B is the correct answer. Under Rule 406, "Evidence of a person's habit... may be admitted to prove that on a particular occasion the person...acted in accordance with the habit" on a given occasion. Here, the janitor's testimony is relevant to rebut the woman's allegations that the grocery store was negligent in permitting the candy to be present on the floor because the janitor has testified that he routinely sweeps every half hour and never misses anything on the floor. The fact that the janitor is testifying about something he routinely does (i.e., every half hour and never missing anything on the floor) makes his testimony permissible habit evidence, under Rule 406.

A is incorrect because even relevant

evidence may be excluded under certain circumstances.

C is incorrect because the testimony is not speculative; it is a declaration of actual fact (i.e., that the janitor regularly sweeps the floor every half hour and that he never leaves anything on the floor).

D is incorrect because, if evidence is more probative than prejudicial, it will be admitted, as is the case here.

END OF ANSWERS

PROPERTY

PROPERTY - QUESTION BREAKDOWN

1. Future Interest
2. Assignment
3. Rule Against Perpetuities
4. Grantor – Grantee Index
5. Fee Simple Absolute
6. Adverse Possession
7. Deed Delivery
8. Defeasible – Removal Rights
9. Statute of Frauds
10. Covenants
11. Covenants
12. Life Tenant – Mortgage Principal
13. Lease/Subsequent Conveyance
14. Retaliatory Eviction
15. Tenancy by the Entirety
16. Easement by Prescription
17. Joint Tenancy
18. Statute of Frauds
19. License
20. Covenants – Running With The Land
21. Implied Reciprocal Negative Easement/Common Scheme or Plan
22. Breach of Condition
23. Deeds
24. Rule Against Perpetuities
25. Joint Tenancies
26. Vested Remainder Subject To Divestment
27. Equitable Conversion
28. Equitable Conversion
29. Deeds – Delivery
30. Deeds – Acreage Discrepancy
31. Lateral and Subjacent Support
32. Contingent Remainders
33. Express Easement

34. Negative Easements
35. Deeds – Grantor Retaining Possession
36. Deed – Acceptance by Grantee
37. Remainders – Duty Owed To Future Interest
38. Warranty Deed
39. Tenancy by the Entirety
40. Recording Act – Race – Race Notice
41. Recording Act – Bona Fide Purchase
42. Executory Interest
43. Recording Act – Notice Statute
44. Recording Act – Chain of Title
45. Recording Act – Donee
46. Recording Act – Race Statute
47. Assignment of Lease
48. Rule Against Perpetuities
49. Fixtures
50. Ameliorative Waste
51. Ameliorative Waste
52. Rule Against Perpetuities
53. Executory Interest
54. Profits a Prendre
55. Covenants – Running with the Land
56. Covenants – Benefit Running With The Land
57. Covenants – Writing Requirement
58. Covenants – Privity
59. Subjacent Support
60. Executory Interest
61. Tenants In Common
62. Tenants In Common – Co-Tenant Rights
63. Rule Against Perpetuities
64. Vested Remainder Subject to Open
65. Adverse Possession
66. Rule In Dumpor's Case
67. Covenants
68. Privity Of Contract / Privity Of Estate
69. Adverse Possession
70. Covenant of Seisin
71. Title Insurance
72. Warranty Deed

73. Quitclaim Deed – Warranties

74. Adverse Possession

75. Adverse Possession – Statute of Limitations

76. Riparian Rights

77. Statute of Frauds

78. Easements

79. Dower Rights

80. Statute of Frauds – Exception

81. Reversion

82. Life Estate

83. Fee Estate – Fee Tail

84. Reversions

85. Riparian Rights

86. Zoning

87. Easements

88. Express Easements

89. License

90. Fee Simple Absolute

91. Possibility of Reverter

92. Tenancy for Years

93. Landlord Duties

94. Easements

95. Easements – By Implication

96. Running of the Burden and Benefit Covenants

97. Covenants – Horizontal Privity

98. Equitable Servitudes – Specific Enforcement

99. Equitable Servitudes

100. Tenancy at Sufferance

101. Mortgage/Deed of Trust

102. Installment Contract

103. Mortgage Liability

104. Mortgage Transferability

105. Mortgage Liability

106. Mortgage – Assumption

107. Mortgage – Assumption

108. Mortgage – Foreclosure

109. Mortgage – Foreclosure

110. Mortgage – Foreclosure

111. Mortgage – Foreclosure

112. Mortgage – Lenders Interest

113. Mortgage – Proceed Distribution

114. Mortgage – Recording Act

115. Mortgage – Recording Act

116. Mortgage – Covenants

117. Mortgage – Recording Act

118. Mortgage – Priority of Title

119. Mortgage – Estoppel by Deed

120. Mortgage – Recording Act

121. Mortgage – Transferability

122. Mortgage – Joint Tenancy

123. Mortgage – Transferability

124. Mortgage – Interest Extinguished

125. Mortgage – Interest Extinguished

PROPERTY QUESTIONS

1. A woman conveyed her house and land to a man by a validly executed and delivered warranty deed, which stated:

   "To have and to hold the above-described tract of land in fee simple absolute, subject to the understanding that said grantee shall construct and maintain a facility for the preservation of wild horses on said property."

   The man did, in fact, construct and maintain a facility for the preservation of wild horses on the property, which he operated for ten years after the grant from the woman. However, at the end of ten years, the man converted the property to a dude ranch. All parties agree that a dude ranch is not a facility for the preservation of wild horses.

   The woman seeks a court declaration that the change in the property's use means that the land and house has reverted to her. In this lawsuit, the woman will:

   A. Lose because an equitable charge is enforceable only in equity.

   B. Win because the language of the deed created a fee simple determinable, which leaves a possibility of reverter in the grantor.

   C. Lose because the language of the deed created only a contractual obligation and did not create a reversionary interest in the grantor.

   D. Win because the language of the deed created a fee simple subject to condition subsequent, which leaves a power of termination or right of entry in the grantor.

2. A brother and a sister leased a house from a landlord. The lease was in proper form and contained the following language:

   "Any assignment, subletting or transfer of any rights under this lease without the express written consent of the landlord, shall be null and void and is prohibited."

   Despite this clause, after the brother and sister moved into the house, the sister verbally invited her boyfriend to share the house with her brother and herself. The boyfriend agreed to pay his portion of the rent to the landlord who did not object to this arrangement. The brother, however, objected to the boyfriend sharing the dwelling, even if the boyfriend paid a fair share of the rent.

   As soon as the boyfriend moved into the house, the brother sued the boyfriend, the sister, and the landlord for a declaratory judgment that the sister was without rights to assign to the boyfriend. The sister answered that she and the brother were tenants in common for the estate of a term of years, and that she had the right to assign a part interest in her undivided 1/2 interest in the leasehold. The court should award judgment in favor of:

A. The brother because a co-tenant has no right to assign any part or all of a leasehold without the consent of all relevant parties.

B. The brother because the lease contained a "non-assignment" clause.

C. The sister because the brother is not the beneficiary of the "no assignment" clause in the lease.

D. The sister because the brother's claim is essentially a restraint on alienation and is disfavored.

3. A man owned a piece of property in fee simple absolute. In 2000, a man executed his will in which he left the property:

"To my surviving widow for life, and then to such of my children who shall reach 30 years of age; however, if any such child should die under the age of 30 and such child shall be survived by a child or children, that child or children shall step up and take his or her parents' share being that share which would have gone to that parent had he or she attained the age of 30 years."

In 2000, at the time of the will, the man was married, and he and his wife had two adult children, a male and a female. The female adult child had one child of her own (the man's granddaughter). In 2011, the man's wife died and he remarried. In 2012, the man and his new wife had a son. Later that year, the man died, survived by the new wife, the two adult children, the new son, and the man's granddaughter.

In a state that applies the common law Rule Against Perpetuities unmodified by statute, the result of applying the Rule to the interests under the will is that:

A. The remainder to the man's children and grandchildren is void because the man could have married a person not yet in being at the time the man's will was executed.

B. The remainder to the children is valid, and the substitute gift to the grandchildren is also valid.

C. The remainder to the adult children is valid, but the remainder to the granddaughter is void, as is any gift to the granddaughter's future children.

D. The remainder to the children is valid, but the substitute gift to the grandchildren is void because the man could have married a person not yet in being at the time his will was executed.

4. In 2000, a woman was the owner of a piece of property. However, that same year, a man gave a warranty deed to that same property to his niece. The niece promptly recorded that deed. In 2001, the woman conveyed the same property by warranty deed to the man, who promptly recorded his deed. In 2002, the man gave a warranty deed to the property to his son, who promptly recorded his deed. The son paid fair market value for the property and was unaware of any prior conveyances of the property. Both the son and the niece claim title to the property. The court should award judgment to:

   A. The niece because her deed is prior in time to the son's.

   B. The son because he was a purchaser for value without notice of the niece's claim.

   C. Either the son or the niece, if neither one did a title search.

   D. Either the son or the niece, depending on whether the niece's deed is deemed to be recorded within the son's chain of title.

5. In 1990, a man owned a piece of property in fee simple absolute. Unbeknownst to the man, in 1991, a squatter entered the property under color of title and began to use a square of land on the eastern side of the property to cut fodder for food for the squatter's sheep. After 14 years of possession of the property, the squatter gave possession of the property to a woman. The squatter also sold the woman all his sheep and purported to transfer to the woman the squatter's interests in the fodder and fodder area by means of a document that was adequate to transfer personal property (the sheep), but inadequate to transfer real property.

   In 2006, the squatter leased the property from the man for a term of five years. At the end of the five-year term, the squatter remained on the property for two more years before he quit the property. In 2014, the man conveyed the property by quitclaim deed to his cousin. The property is located in a state where the statute of limitations for adverse possession is ten years.

   After the man's 2014 conveyance to his cousin, title to the fodder area was in:

   A. The woman, as the purchaser of the fodder area under the document selling the squatter's sheep to the woman.

   B. The person who owned fodder rights as a necessary incident to the fodder.

   C. The squatter as first taker of the fodder.

   D. The person who then held title to the property in fee simple absolute.

6. In 1985, a man moved onto a piece of property without permission. In 1990, the man's job required him to move out of the country, and he asked his niece to live on the property while he was gone. The man never returned. Instead, the niece continued to live on the property until 2006, when she got married and moved out of the state. Nevertheless, the niece commenced an action to quiet title to the property, so that she could use it as a rental property. This jurisdiction follows the common law. Will she be successful?

   A. Yes because she was related to the man.

   B. Yes because she intended to use the property as a rental property, which is allowed under the common law.

   C. No because the man needed to be in continuous possession.

   D. No because she intended to use the property as a rental property, which is not allowed under the common law.

7. A father executed and promptly recorded a deed in the proper form to his property to his daughter. When the father told the daughter about the deed, the daughter said, "Father, I don't want your ugly, over-taxed property. You take that deed right back. It's yours." Before any other relevant events, the daughter died, and her will left her entire estate to her boyfriend. The father then sued the boyfriend to quiet title in the property. If the father wins, it will be because:

   A. The presumption of delivery arising from recordation is invalid, unless the grantee has knowledge of the deed at the time of recording.

   B. There was no effective acceptance of the delivery of the deed.

   C. The daughter's renunciation of the property was a constructive conveyance to the father.

   D. The court will impose a constructive trust to carry out the daughter's intent.

8. A man conveyed a piece of property to "my son and his heirs, but if my son dies survived by children who attain the age of 30, then to my daughter and her heirs." Once the son began possessing the property, he began to cut the valuable timber on the property without giving the daughter any notice of his actions. The son is married, but has no children. If the daughter sues for an accounting for the value of the cut timber and for an injunction to prevent future logging, and the court gives judgment against the daughter and in favor of the son, it will be because:

   A. The daughter has no interest in the property.

B. The right to log and remove timber is an incident to possession.

C. The right to log and remove timber is an incident to a fee.

D. There is no showing that the son acted in bad faith.

9. A woman and a man, an unmarried couple, owned a piece of property as tenants in common. After five years, they orally agreed that there was no need for them to make wills, since the survivor of either of them would own the property solely and outright per this agreement. Three years later, the man died intestate. One day later, the woman died, also intestate. The man's sole heir is his father; the woman's sole heir is her mother. The father claims an interest in the property; the mother claims all of the property. The property is located in a state with the Statute of Frauds, but no other applicable statute. That state does not recognize common law marriages.

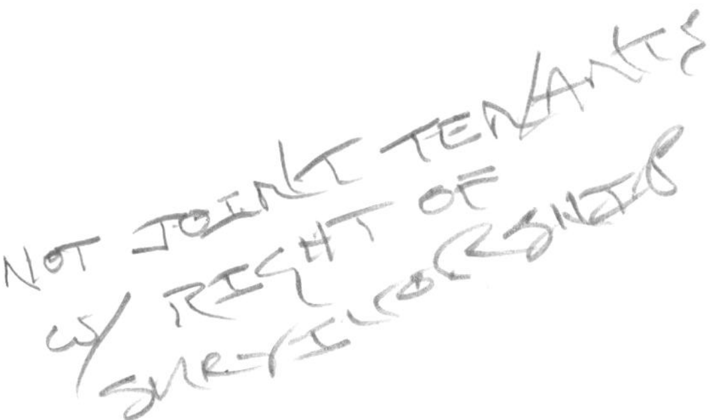

The mother sues the father to determine ownership of the property. The court should find that:

A. The mother and the father each own an undivided interest in the property because the deaths of the woman and the man were essentially simultaneous.

B. The mother and the father each own an undivided interest in the property because the Statute of Frauds applies.

C. The mother owns the property solely because the woman and the man did not make wills in detrimental reliance on the oral agreement.

D. The mother owns the property solely because she is entitled to equitable reformation of the title to reflect the oral agreement.

10. A man owns a 1,000-acre tract of land. He wishes to develop the land into a planned residential community surrounding a man-made lake and marina. He wishes to ensure that prospective purchasers of lots on the land are guaranteed the following 3 things:

1) Apart from the lake and marina, no non-residential use will be made of any of the lots.

2) Residents of lots on the land will have clear access to and use of the marina and lake, and that access and use will be capable of being transferred to subsequent purchasers of those lots.

3) Residents of lots on the land must be obligated to pay a prorated share for the maintenance of the lake and marina, regardless of their actual use of the facilities.

In the context of the entire scheme of development, which of the following will offer the best method of implementing the man's plans discussed above?

A. An easement.

B. A covenant.

C. A mortgage.

D. A personal contractual obligation by each purchaser.

11. A woman conveyed a piece of property to her adult son. In the deed, the woman stated that her adult son should keep house painted properly, take in the newspapers each day, and feed the woman's elderly father, who lived nearby. The adult son never recorded the deed.

Soon thereafter, the adult son conveyed the property to a man. The deed from the adult son to the man did not contain the restrictions found in the deed from the woman to the adult son. The adult son learned that the house was badly in need of a paint job, newspapers were piled up for weeks, and the woman's elderly father died of starvation because the man had not fed him.

The woman, the adult son, and the elderly father's estate sued the man for breach of the covenants in the son's deed. Who will prevail in this lawsuit?

A. The woman.

B. The elderly father's estate.

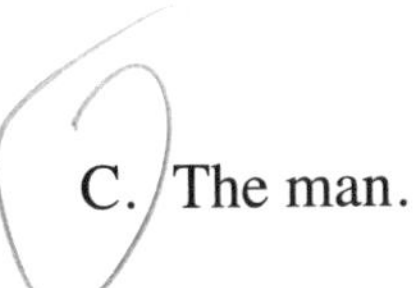

C. The man.

D. The adult son.

12. A house was owned by a woman as a life tenant and a man as remainderman in fee simple. The woman and the man were conveyed the house subject to a mortgage of $100,000, payable in $10,000 installments of the principal over ten years at ten percent interest per year payable with each installment of the principal. The house produces $50,000 in net income per year after paying all expenses, except the mortgage. The woman and the man each dispute who should pay the mortgage principal. This jurisdiction follows the common law. If the man seeks legal advice as to his obligations for the mortgage principal of the house, he should be told that:

    A. He could compel the woman to pay the mortgage principal because the income from the house is more than adequate to meet this obligation.

    B. The woman could compel the man to pay his share of the principal because the discharge of the mortgage enhances his remainder.

    C. The man is responsible for paying the principal, and the woman is responsible for paying the interest.

    D. His only protection lies in instituting an action for partition to compel the sale of the woman's life estate to obtain the value of his remainder.

13. A brother and a sister occupied a house and a lot rent-free with the owner's signed and written permission. Both the brother and the sister were 21-year-old actors looking for acting work in show business. The owner conveyed a properly executed and recorded a warranty deed to the house and the lot as follows:

    "To the brother and his heirs, upon condition that he obtain an acting role in a Hollywood movie by the time he reaches the age of 35. However, if he does not do so, then the house and the lot is to pass to my daughter, for life, and then to my daughter's two children."

    At the time of the conveyance, neither the brother nor the sister had ever acted in a Hollywood movie. One month after the conveyance to the brother, the brother informed the sister that he was now her landlord and expected a fair rental each month, payable to him. The sister refused. The house and lot are located in a jurisdiction with no statute applicable to this situation. In a properly filed action for ejectment of the sister by the brother, the court should award judgment for:

A. The brother because the owner's conveyance created a fee simple subject to executory limitation.

B. The brother because the owner's conveyance terminated the sister's tenancy.

C. The sister because the owner's permission to occupy pre-dated the owner's conveyance.

D. The sister because the owner is the sister's landlord, not the brother.

14. A tenant moved into and began paying a monthly rental for an apartment in a ten-unit apartment building. The hallways and stairwells of the building needed repair. The landlord refused to undertake those repairs, even after the tenant requested the landlord do so. Therefore, the tenant met with the other tenants and discussed with them the tenants' legal options against the landlord for failure to make repairs. When the tenant paid the next month's rent, the landlord notified the tenant that beginning the following month, the tenant's rent would be increased by $200 per month. When the tenant protested that all of the other tenants did not receive a rent increase, the landlord gave the tenant the statutorily-required 30-day notice to vacate the apartment. If the tenant prevails in a lawsuit contesting the termination of her tenancy, the most likely reason for her victory is that:

A. Her payment of monthly rental implies the existence of a periodic tenancy.

B. The $200 rent increase is unconscionable and will shock the conscience of the court.

C. The fact that the tenant would have to pay more than other tenants violates the implied agreement that rentals for similar apartments be comparable.

D. The doctrine of retaliatory eviction is part of the law of this jurisdiction.

15. Two men were married in a jurisdiction that allows same-sex marriage. They purchased a piece of property there by deed. The title to the deed stated that they owned the property as a married couple with equal rights of possession, equal shares in interest, and a gift of survivorship. One man conveyed his one-half interest to his mother. He then fell to his death while cleaning a balcony. His will left all of his property to his nieces. The surviving man sued the mother, alleging that he was sole owner of the property. This jurisdiction follows the common law with regard to joint ownership of property. Who will the court find is the owner of this property?

A. The surviving man alone.

B. The mother alone.

C. The nieces.

D. The mother and the surviving man.

16. A man owned a piece of property in fee simple absolute. However, a woman was in adverse possession of the property. During her adverse possession, the man gave his brother oral permission to use the south forty feet along the property as a road to reach the brother's own property, which was directly adjacent to the man's property. During all times relevant to this question, the brother regularly used the man's property as a road to reach the brother's property.

A few years later, the woman quit possession of the man's property without gaining title by adverse possession. The brother continued to use the south forty feet along the man's property from the time of his original use for a sufficiently long period of time to gain an easement by prescription. All of this use was accomplished without further communication between the man and the brother. The man then blocked the road on the south forty feet along his property and has refused to permit the brother's further use. The brother then sued to determine his continued use of the road. In that lawsuit, the brother should:

A. Win because his use was adverse to the woman and once adversely begun, it continued in that manner until some affirmative showing of a change.

B. Win because the brother made no attempt to renew the man's permission after the woman quit possession of the man's property.

C. Lose because the brother's use was permissive.

D. Lose because there is no evidence that the brother continued to adversely use the man's property for the required period after the woman quit the man's property.

17. A sister and a brother held a piece of property together as joint tenants. Five years after the original purchase, the sister proposed that they develop the property as a retail shopping center. The brother did not want to do so, but he orally agreed with his sister that she could alone develop the western half of the property as she wished and that he would do whatever he wanted with the eastern half of the property.

The sister then built the shopping center. Soon afterward she died, leaving her entire estate, by will, to her son.

In an appropriate lawsuit to determine the son's and the brother's respective interests in the property, if the son is adjudicated to be the owner of the western half of the property, the most likely reason for the judgment will be that:

A. The brother's actions during the sister's life have estopped him from asserting title to the half of the property.

B. The joint tenancy was terminated by the oral agreement of the sister and the brother at the time it was made.

C. The son because the law prefers that property be used for commercial purposes, rather than residential purposes.

D. The close blood relationship between the sister and the brother removes the necessity to comply with the Statute of Frauds.

18. A man orally agreed to sell a piece of property to his mother. His mother went onto the property and began making improvements. The man then told his mother that he had changed his mind and that he wanted the property back. The mother then sued the man for specific performance. Who is the rightful owner of the land?

A. The mother because daughters and sons have fiduciary duties to not violate their promises to their parents.

B. The mother because she made improvements to the land.

C. The man because he owed his mother no duties because he was no longer a minor.

D. The man because the contract violated the Statute of Frauds.

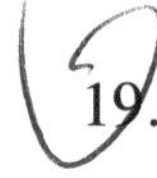

19. An aunt and a nephew entered into a valid, enforceable written contract in which the nephew agreed to buy and the aunt agreed to sell a piece of property, the aunt's residence. The contract contained a provision allowing the aunt the right to remain in residence on the property for 30 days before relinquishing possession.

Thirty days after closing, the aunt refused to leave the property. Instead, she tendered to the nephew a monthly rental payment in excess of the fair rental value of the property. The nephew refused the rent and sued to gain immediate possession of the property. There is no law of this jurisdiction dealing with this situation and the contract is similarly silent. The landlord-tenant law of this jurisdiction requires a 30-day notice by the landlord before he can evict a tenant. The nephew did not give the 30-day statutory notice. The nephew's best legal argument in support of his action for immediate possession is that the aunt is a:

A. Licensee.

B. Tenant at sufferance.

C. Tenant from month to month.

D. Trespasser ab initio.

20. A man owned a tract of land, which he subdivided into several lots. He recorded his development plan. He conveyed one of the lots to his brother. The deed from the man to the brother stated, "To brother and his heirs and assigns for residential purposes only." The man conveyed the neighboring plot to a woman. The deed from the man to the woman stated, "To the woman and her heirs and assigns for residential purposes only." The woman built a place of residence on the property and then moved onto the property to live there. Four years later, the woman transferred the property to her niece. The deed from the woman to the niece did not contain any restrictions. The niece plans to build an office building on the property. The brother sued the niece for violation of the covenant. Who will prevail in this lawsuit?

A. The brother because the restrictive covenant in the deed runs with the land.

B. The brother because the office building will lower the brother's land value.

C. The niece because she is a remote grantee – not a direct grantee of the man.

D. The niece because she did not receive a deed containing a restrictive covenant.

21. A man owned a 100-acre tract of land, prepared properly and recorded a subdivision plan that contained 40 two-acre lots and a 20-acre tract in the southeast corner. He sold 20 of the lots to individual purchasers. Those deeds all referred to the recorded plan and contained the following clause, "No multi-family dwellings shall be erected on this property."

A woman purchased one of these original lots from the man. Eight years later, the man sold the remaining land (20 lots and 20 acre parcel) to his son by a deed that referred to the plan and contained the same clause prohibiting multi-family dwellings. The son then resold the 20 lots to individual purchasers and the 20-acre parcel to his girlfriend. None of the son's deeds to the girlfriend referred to the plan or contained the multi-family dwelling restriction.

The girlfriend has announced her intention to build a multi-family condominium complex on the 20-acre parcel. The woman has sued to prevent its construction. If the girlfriend wins, it will be because:

A. The girlfriend's proposed use will allow a sufficient diversity in economic classes in the vicinity to satisfy the requirements of the Equal Protection clause of the Constitution.

B. Restrictions in deeds are to be construed in favor of free alienation of land and against the grantor.

C. There has been an insufficient showing that the common development scheme applied to the entire subdivision.

D. Restrictive equitable servitudes bind only those in privity with the original covenanting parties.

22. In 1990, the owner of a fee simple absolute in a piece of property conveyed that property to a school. The operative words of conveyance were "to the school for the life of my daughter, and then at that time to all of my grandchildren and their heirs in equal shares; provided, however, that the school shall use the property for school purposes only." After the conveyance, the school began holding classes on the property and has continued to do so for all relevant times.

In 2010, the school granted a man a right to mine and remove minerals from the northwest portion of the property. The man began to remove minerals under this grant.

All three of the original owner's present grandchildren, as well as a guardian ad litem appointed to represent the unborn grandchildren, have sued the school and the man for damages and injunction for the mining operations on the property. The daughter is still alive. There is no applicable statute. Which of the following best describes the probable outcome of the litigation?

A. The judge should not grant an injunction, nor should the judge award damages.

B. The judge should grant the injunction, but not award damages, since the original owner and the daughter are not parties to the lawsuit.

C. The judge should award damages, but not the injunction.

D. The judge should grant the injunction and impound the damages to be awarded.

23. A woman owned three condominiums in a condominium complex, numbers 6, 7 and 21. The price and fair market value of condominiums 6 and 7 was $50,000, and number 21, $75,000. A man was interested in purchasing a condominium in the complex, but could not decide between #6 or #7. Therefore, the man gave the woman $50,000, and the woman prepared and executed a deed to the man for a condominium in that complex, complete in every way except that the unit number was left blank. The woman told the man to fill in unit #6 or #7 as he wished and then the man should record the deed. The next day, the man went to the complex, filled

in unit #21 in the deed, and recorded the deed. In an action by the woman to rescind the transaction, if the woman loses, the most likely reason for that judgment is that:

A. The necessity for certainty in land title records controls.

B. The agency implied to complete the deed cannot be restricted by the oral understanding.

C. The recordation of the deed precludes any questioning of the deed in its recorded form.

D. The woman's casual business practices caused her loss.

24. In 2000, a man willed a parcel of land as follows:

"To my daughter and at her death to those of her children who survive her, provided however, that no such child of my daughter shall have the power to convey, sell or mortgage such child's interest prior to attaining the age of 30 years; and if any such child of my daughter shall not comply with this provision then that child's interest shall determine and pass to the remaining children of my daughter alive at that time, share and share alike."

The residuary clause in the 2000 will gave the residual estate to the man's daughter and son equally. In 2010, the man died, survived by his daughter and son and their two children each. In 2012, the daughter had one additional child.

In an action to determine the property rights in the parcel, the court should decide that:

A. The attempted gifts to the grandchildren are void as restraints on alienation.

B. The attempted gifts to the grandchildren are void under the Rule Against Perpetuities.

C. The attempted gifts to the grandchildren are valid, except for the provisions against sale, conveyance or mortgage.

D. The attempted gifts to the grandchildren are entirely valid and will be enforced as written.

25. A man and a woman lived together for ten years. They never formally married, although they always referred to each other as husband and wife. During this time, they decided to purchase a home. The deed was in proper form and identified the grantees "As husband and wife, and their heirs forever, as tenants by the entirety." One year later, the woman abandoned the man and the house and moved to another state. The man sued for partition. The suit for partition should be:

A. Denied, since no single tenant by the entirety has a right to sue for partition.

B. Denied, since the woman has sole title to the property.

C. Granted because the tenancy by the entirety that was created by the deed was destroyed when the woman abandoned the man.

D. Granted because the deed never created a tenancy by the entirety.

26. In 2012, a woman conveyed her home as follows:

"To my friend for life and then to my friend's two children and their heirs, provided that should any of them move to California, then that child's interest to pass to my church."

In 2012, the friend was alive and had two children. In an appropriate action to determine the interests in the home, the gift to the friend's children shall be held to be:

A. An executory interest.

B. A vested remainder subject to complete divestment.

C. An indefeasible vested remainder.

D. A contingent remainder.

27. A man owned a piece of property. In January 2012, he contracted to sell a piece of property to a woman in a fully executed, written agreement that called for the woman to pay him a $500,000 cash for the property on or before March 1, 2012. On February 29, 2012, the man died of a heart attack while taking the Bar Examination. The property had not yet closed. The man's will left his real property to his daughter and his personal property to his son.

Which statement is correct?

A. The daughter is entitled to the $500,000 on closing, since equitable conversion is inapplicable here.

B. The son is entitled to the $500,000 on closing since equitable conversion applies here.

C. Since the land sale contract could have provided for the contingency of death of one of the parties, but did not do so, death terminates the contract.

D. The death of the seller renders title to the property unmarketable.

28. A man owned a farm. In April 2012, he contracted to sell the farm to a farmer for $1,000,000 with closing to occur on May 1, 2012. On April 15, 2012, the farmer was distraught from the amount of taxes he had to pay and killed himself. The farmer's will left all of his

real property to his son and all of his personal property to his daughter. The contract is otherwise fully performed. Which statement is most correct?

A. The son has the right to specifically perform the contract.

B. The man has the right to cancel the contract and refuse the $1,000,000.

C. Since the land sale contract could have provided for the contingency of death of one of the parties, but did not do so, death terminates the contract.

D. The death of the buyer renders title to the farm unmarketable.

29. In 2011, a woman granted a piece of property to her nephew. At the time, her nephew lived in another country and was not aware that the woman had granted the property to him. In 2012, the nephew returned from his trip and learned about the deed. However, the woman had decided to, instead, grant the property to her niece. The niece promptly recorded the deed. Who is the owner of the property?

A. The nephew because the property was granted to him first.

B. The nephew because the grant to the niece was improper, since the woman no longer owned the property.

C. The niece because the deed from the woman to the niece met all of the requirements of deed delivery.

D. The niece because she recorded her deed first.

30. A woman granted a piece of property to a man. The deed stated that the property consisted of a home and land that was 40 acres and a mule. The man recorded his deed and later discovered that the property was only 39.5 acres, and the mule was dead. The man tries to rescind the deed. Will he be successful?

A. Yes because the deed description was insufficient, since it contained no description by metes and bounds.

B. Yes because the deed description was insufficient, since the acreage given was inaccurate.

C. Yes because the deed description was insufficient, since a grantor cannot convey more than she owns.

D. No because the deed description was sufficient, since the discrepancy in the description of the acreage was not fatal.

31. A woman was the fee simple owner of a vacant tract of land. The woman's land was located adjacent to a man's tract of land that had had a house and

barn located on it since 2012, and he owned that land in fee simple absolute. A month after the house and barn were built, the woman began digging a foundation for a building on her land to be located near the property line with the man's land. The woman's digging caused the barn and land on the man's land to collapse due to earth movement. This jurisdiction follows the common law. In a lawsuit by the man against the woman for damages to his barn and land, due to the woman's excavation, the prevailing party should be:

A. The man because he has an absolute right to lateral support of his land.

B. The man, unless the weight of the barn contributed to the damage.

C. The woman, if she was only negligent in her excavation.

D. The woman, unless her excavation would have caused the same damage to unimproved land, or she was negligent.

32. A farmer owned a tract of land in fee simple absolute. He conveyed it to his son "for life, and then to the children of the farmer's daughter in fee simple." At the time of the conveyance, both the son and the daughter were alive; neither had any children. What interest, if any, was created in the daughter's unborn children at the time of the conveyance?

A. A vested remainder, subject to partial divestment.

B. A contingent remainder.

C. An executory interest.

D. None.

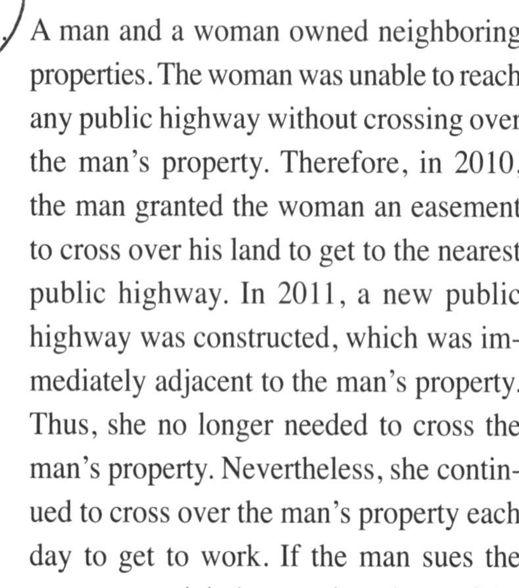

33. A man and a woman owned neighboring properties. The woman was unable to reach any public highway without crossing over the man's property. Therefore, in 2010, the man granted the woman an easement to cross over his land to get to the nearest public highway. In 2011, a new public highway was constructed, which was immediately adjacent to the man's property. Thus, she no longer needed to cross the man's property. Nevertheless, she continued to cross over the man's property each day to get to work. If the man sues the woman to enjoin her continued use of the easement, who will prevail?

A. The man because the termination of the necessity for the easement terminated the easement.

B. The man because the continued use of the easement after a material change in circumstances would diminish the fair market value of the lots without a corresponding and commensurate increase in value.

C. The woman because an incorporeal hereditament lies in grant and cannot be terminated without a writing.

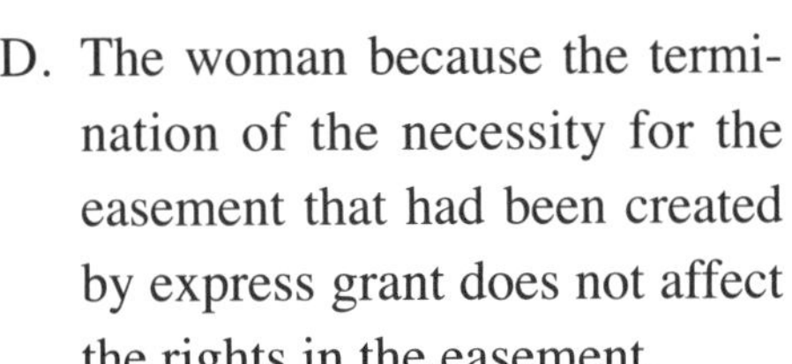

D. The woman because the termination of the necessity for the easement that had been created by express grant does not affect the rights in the easement.

34. A woman and a man were adjoining property owners. The woman had a swimming pool on her property, and she frequently sunbathed in the afternoons. The man informed the woman that he intended to erect a high-rise condominium on his property. The woman feared that the condominium would block her sunlight as she was attempting to sunbathe by her pool. If the woman sues the man to enjoin him from erecting the high-rise condominium in such a way to shade her swimming pool, the prevailing party will be:

A. The woman because the man knew that she had a pool on her property and that she sunbathed there.

B. The woman because the man's building would be an unreasonable obstruction with her natural right to an easement for light, air or view.

C. The man because the woman has no natural right to an easement for air, light or view.

D. The man because a high-rise condominium adds more property value than a swimming pool.

35. A woman was the fee simple owner of a piece of property. On January 1, 2012, she went to the house of her adult son. In her son's presence, the woman executed a warranty deed to the property and said, "Here is a deed to the property, which I am giving you as a gift." The son thanked the woman (his mother), and he took the deed and subsequently placed it in the woman's safe deposit box. In February 2012, the son received an offer to purchase the property. The recording act in this jurisdiction states that, unless a conveyance or other transfer of land is duly recorded, every deed or other conveyance of an interest in land is void as to a subsequent purchaser for value in good faith who records.

In a lawsuit by the woman against the son to establish that the woman still has title to the property, who will be successful?

A. The son because the events of January 1, 2012, were a conditional delivery to a grantee without an escrow.

B. The son because he is a donee and not a bona fide purchaser under the recording act.

C. The woman because the events of January 1, 2012, were insufficient to constitute a valid delivery.

D. The woman because the son did

not record the deed as required by the recording act.

36. A man owned a piece of property in fee simple absolute. By written deed, the man conveyed the property to his girlfriend, who accepted the deed and promptly recorded it. The following year, the man and his girlfriend broke up. The girlfriend ripped the deed in half and said, "I don't want anything that you owned, including this property!" The next day, she changed her mind and taped the deed back together. The man attempted to sell the property, and the buyer refused to close on the deal, alleging that the man no longer owned the property. As between the man and the girlfriend, who is the owner of the property?

    A. The man because the girlfriend said that she did not want the property.

    B. The man because the girlfriend ripped the deed in half.

    C. The girlfriend because she was a valid grantee to whom the property was properly conveyed.

    D. The girlfriend because she recorded the deed.

37. A woman conveyed a house and tract of land "to a man for life, remainder to the man's son and the man's son's heirs, subject to a first mortgage in favor of the bank for $100,000." The mortgage had an unpaid balance of $100,000, payable in monthly installments of $1,000 plus interest at 8% on the balance. The next payment of principal and interest is due May 1. The reasonable rental value of the property is greater than the sum necessary to meet all current charges. The man is currently living on the property. Assume that the common law rules governing contributions between life tenants and remaindermen apply in this state. How should the burden for repayment of the first mortgage to the bank be allocated between the man and the man's son?

    A. The man must pay both the principal and interest.

    B. The man's son must pay both principal and interest.

    C. The man must pay the principal, and the man's son must pay the interest.

    D. The man's son must pay the principal, and the man must pay the interest.

38. A woman and her sister lived next door to each other. The woman conveyed her property to a man by general warranty deed. Prior to this conveyance, the woman had granted an easement to her sister to cross over her property to get to a nearby lake. The man immediately brought lawsuit against the woman for breach of covenants in the general warranty deed. The court will find in the man's favor because:

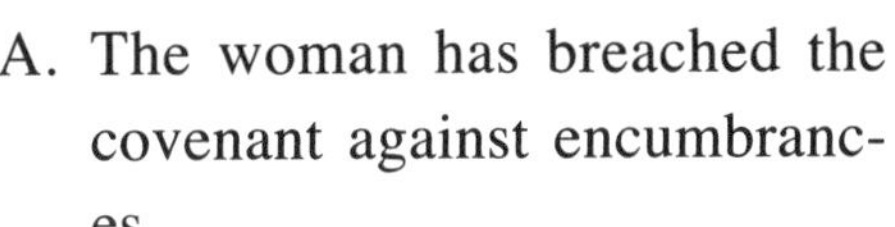

A. The woman has breached the covenant against encumbrances.

B. The woman has breached the covenant of quiet enjoyment.

C. The woman has breached the covenant of further assurances.

D. The woman has breached the covenant of seisin.

39. A man owned a tract of land in fee simple absolute. He conveyed the land to a man and a woman "as wife and husband." In this jurisdiction, this conveyance would be sufficient to create a tenancy by the entirety. Thereafter, the wife unilaterally conveyed by a deed in valid form and delivery "my undivided one-half interest in the land" to her sister. The wife died one year later when a piano fell on her head while she was out walking. The husband refused to share ownership of the property with the sister. If the sister sues the husband to quiet title in himself and herself as co-owners of the land, who will prevail?

A. The husband because the conveyance to the sister was invalid.

B. The husband because he refused to share ownership of the property with the sister.

C. The sister because the conveyance to her was valid.

D. The sister because tenancy by the entirety is no longer followed in any jurisdiction.

40. The provisions of the recording statute in a particular jurisdiction require that a junior claimant must have provided value in good faith in order to claim protection of the recording act.

What type of recording act does this jurisdiction have?

A. Race.

B. Notice.

C. Race or Race-Notice.

D. None of the above.

41. A woman was the fee simple owner of a piece of property. In 2000, the woman conveyed the property to her niece as a gift for the niece's 21st birthday. The niece recorded the deed, but she did not move onto the property. The woman began an affair with her neighbor and in 2012, conveyed the property to the neighbor. The neighbor paid the woman the fair market value of the property and promptly recorded the deed. The neighbor had no notice of the conveyance to the niece in 2000. When the niece learned of the conveyance to the neighbor, she brought an action to quiet title against him. This jurisdiction has a race-notice recording statute. Who will be successful?

A. The niece because she was the first grantee of the property.

B. The niece because she recorded her deed first.

C. The neighbor.

D. The woman.

42. A man was the owner of a tract of land in fee simple absolute. In 1990, he conveyed the property "to a woman and her heirs as long as the property is used for residential purposes, but if it is ever used for non-residential purposes prior to 2010, then to a charity." In 2004, the man died, leaving a valid will that devised all of the man's real property to his nephew. The will had no residuary clause, and the man was survived by his nephew and his son. Assume that the common law Rule Against Perpetuities applies and that all future interests are alienable, devisable, and descendible in the same manner as possessory interests in land. In 1991, the interest in the man's property held by the charity could have best been described as a (an):

A. Valid contingent remainder.

B. Invalid contingent remainder.

C. Valid executory interest.

D. Invalid executory interest.

43. A woman owned a tract of vacant land in fee simple absolute. The recording act for this jurisdiction states that, unless a conveyance or other transfer of land is duly recorded, every deed or other conveyance of an interest in land is void as to a subsequent purchaser for value in good faith. In 2010, she sold the land in fee simple for fair market value to a man by general warranty deed. The man neither recorded his deed nor moved onto the property. In 2011, the woman signed a mortgage to the land in favor of the bank in return for money that the bank had lent her. The bank had no notice of the prior deed to the man. The bank recorded its mortgage immediately.

In 2012, the man sued the bank, claiming that he owned the property and that the bank did not. Who will prevail?

A. The man because a mortgagee cannot be a subsequent purchaser within the meaning of the statute.

B. The man because a mortgagee cannot be deemed to have paid value within the meaning of the statute.

C. The bank because it recorded first.

D. The bank because it lent money without notice of the man's interest in the land.

44. In 1990, a woman sold her property for fair market value to a man by general warranty deed. The man recorded his deed in 1995. In 2000, the woman gratuitously gave her boyfriend a fee simple, general warranty deed to the same property. The boyfriend promptly recorded his deed. In 2005, the boyfriend conveyed a fee simple to the property at full fair market value by general warranty deed to his cousin. The cousin had no actual knowledge of any of the prior transactions regarding the property. The cousin promptly recorded his deed.

The recording act for this jurisdiction states that, unless a conveyance or other transfer of land is duly recorded, every deed or other conveyance of an interest in land is void as to a subsequent purchaser for value in good faith.

In 2006, the man sued the cousin, claiming that the man owned the property and that the cousin did not. If the cousin prevails, it will be because:

A. As between two warranty deeds, the subsequent one controls.

B. The boyfriend, the cousin's grantor, had no notice of the man's interest in the property.

C. The man's prior recorded deed is outside the cousin's chain of title.

D. The boyfriend, the cousin's grantor, recorded before the man.

45. A man was the fee simple owner of a piece of property. On May 1, 2011, he went to the house of his minor daughter. In the daughter's presence, the man executed a warranty deed to the property and said, "Here is a deed to the property, which I am giving you as a gift." The daughter thanked the man (her father), and she promptly recorded the deed, but never lived on the property. In January 2012, the man decided to convey the property to his girlfriend for fair market value, and did so by warranty deed. The girlfriend promptly recorded the deed. Claiming that the property was hers, the daughter brought a lawsuit against the girlfriend to quiet title. Who will be successful in the lawsuit?

A. The girlfriend because the daughter was a donee.

B. The girlfriend because the daughter was still a minor.

C. The daughter because familial gifts are preferred over purchases.

D. The daughter because her deed was the first recorded.

46. A woman owned a plantation in fee simple absolute. The recording act for this jurisdiction states that a duly recorded deed has priority over any

PROPERTY

subsequent recorded deeds in the same property. In 2010, she gave the plantation in fee simple to her brother, free of charge by quitclaim deed. The brother immediately recorded his deed. In 2011, the woman conveyed the plantation by general warranty deed to her sister, in fee simple. The sister promptly recorded her deed. In 2012, the brother brought a lawsuit to quiet title against the sister, claiming that he owned the plantation. The prevailing party will be:

A. The sister because her deed was the first recorded.

B. The sister because the brother was not a purchaser for value under the statute.

C. The sister because the brother received a quitclaim deed.

D. The brother because his was the first conveyance from the woman.

47. A woman leased her house and surrounding yard to her gardener for fifteen years. The lease contained a clause prohibiting the gardener from assigning his interest in the lease. A man has approached the gardener about assigning the house and yard to him. May the gardener do so?

A. Yes because all leases are freely alienable without any consequences under either contract or property law.

B. Yes because a lease term prohibiting assignments is strictly construed.

C. No because covenants in leases are strictly construed.

D. No because a tenant can never assign or sublease without the landlord's permission, since to do so would be to impair the landlord's security interest in the property.

48. A rancher owned a tract of land in fee simple absolute. He conveyed it "to a woman, her heirs and assigns for ranch purposes only; then to a man and his heirs forever." Assume the common law Rule Against Perpetuities applies to this conveyance. The man's interest in the tract of land as a result of this conveyance is best described as:

A. A possibility of reverter.

B. A right of entry (or power of termination).

C. An executory interest.

D. Nothing.

49. A tenant leased a single-family residence from a landlord for a term of four years. Without the landlord's knowledge, the tenant, a skilled carpenter, installed three beautiful, hand-crafted floor-to-ceiling oak bookcases, which he securely bolted to the wall next to

the fireplace. At the end of his lease, the tenant removed the bookcases, leaving several deep holes and other damage to the wall. In an action for damages to the house brought by the landlord against the tenant for the removal of the bookcases, the prevailing party will be:

A. The tenant, but only if the bookcases were used in his trade or business.

B. The tenant, but only if the jurisdiction follows the modern trend in the law of fixtures.

C. The tenant because the bookcases are considered personal property.

D. The landlord because the bookcases are considered real property.

50. During his lease, a tenant replaced the old wooden steps leading to his front door with a new, larger and more efficient set of stone steps, and he added a banister. At the end of the lease, the tenant brought a lawsuit against the landlord to recover the cost of replacing the old front door steps. This jurisdiction follows the common law. The tenant will:

A. Win because he has created an improvement to the landlord's freehold interest in the property.

B. Win because the added value of the improvement will last beyond the term of the tenant lease.

C. Lose, under the doctrine of permissive waste.

D. Lose, under the doctrine of ameliorative waste.

51. A tenant leased and moved into an apartment in an old apartment building. The apartment contained a bathroom sink that was broken, and there was no room for the tenant to put her toiletries on the counter space next to the sink. The tenant replaced the sink with a new and improved sink that made the apartment far more valuable than it had been before. At the end of the lease, the tenant left the sink when she moved out. The landlord sued the tenant regarding the sink. This jurisdiction follows the common law. The prevailing party will be:

A. The tenant because she has created an improvement to the landlord's freehold interest in the property.

B. The tenant because the added value of the improvement will last beyond the term of her lease.

C. The landlord, under the doctrine of permissive waste.

D. The landlord, under the doctrine of ameliorative waste.

52. In 2000, a woman owned a tract of land in fee simple absolute. She conveyed the property "to a man and his heirs as long as the property is used for residential purposes, but if it is ever used for non-residential purposes, then to my favorite charity." In 2005 the woman died, leaving a valid will that devised all of her real property to her niece. The will had no residuary clause, and the woman was survived by her niece and the woman's son, her sole heir. Assume that the common law Rule Against Perpetuities applies and that all future interests are alienable, devisable and descendible in the same manner as possessory interests in land.

In 2010, the woman's son and the man contracted with an investor to sell the tract of land to the investor in fee simple absolute. After a title examination, the investor refused to perform the contract because he claimed the man and the woman's son could not convey good title in fee simple absolute. In a lawsuit for specific performance by the woman's son and the man against the investor, specific performance will be:

A. Granted because the woman's son and the man together own the tract of land in fee simple absolute.

B. Granted because the man alone owns the tract of land in fee simple absolute.

C. Denied because the charity has a valid interest in the tract of land.

D. Denied because the niece has a valid interest in the tract of land.

53. In 2011, a person conveyed a tract of land "to my neighbor, but if the land is ever used as a campground, then to a soup kitchen." In 2012, the soup kitchen's interest in the land could have best been described as:

A. A valid contingent remainder.

B. An invalid contingent remainder.

C. A valid executory interest.

D. An invalid executory interest.

54. A man was the fee simple owner of a tract of land planted with a yearly, seasonal wheat crop. He made an agreement with his neighbor that in exchange for an annual payment of $1000 after the man had harvested his wheat crop, the neighbor had the privilege to take and use the leftover wheat from the man's fields to feed the neighbor's animals. That arrangement was formalized in a written document, duly signed and recorded. By its terms,

the neighbor's privilege was exclusive against all others except the man, who reserved the right to use the property for any purpose whatsoever, including harvesting all the wheat from his fields. Two years later, the state condemned the man's property by eminent domain for use as a municipal golf course. In an action by the neighbor against the state for a portion of the condemnation award for the man's property, the court will find that:

A. The neighbor has a profit a prendre, which is a property right protected by the Due Process Clause of the federal Constitution.

B. The neighbor has a license, which is a property right protected by the Due Process Clause of the federal Constitution.

C. The neighbor has a profit a prendre, which is not a property right protected by the Due Process Clause of the federal Constitution.

D. The neighbor has a license, which is not a property right protected by the Due Process Clause of the federal Constitution.

55. A man owned a tract of land in fee simple absolute. In 2000, he deeded the land to a woman in return for a promise in that same document that she would not construct anything other than a single-family dwelling on the land. If the land is used for anything other than a single family dwelling, the adjacent property that the man also owns would be worth $60,000. If the land is used only for a single-family dwelling, the adjacent property would be worth $100,000. In 2010, the woman built a multiple-family apartment house on the land. In a lawsuit for $40,000 (damages to compensate the man for the fact that the woman did not honor the 2000 agreement), the man should:

A. Win because the woman broke the 2000 promise.

B. Win, but only if the burden of the covenant touches and concerns land.

C. Win, but only if the benefit of the covenant touches and concerns land.

D. Win, but only if the benefit and the burden of the covenant touch and concern land.

56. A man owned two adjacent properties in fee simple absolute. The first property contained a single-family dwelling, and the second property contained a schoolhouse. In 2000, he deeded the property containing the single-family dwelling to his sister in return for a promise in that same document that she would not construct anything other than a single-family dwelling on the property. In 2005, he sold the property containing

the farmhouse to a teacher. In 2008, the sister built a multiple-family apartment house on her property.

With the original promise for the sister to not construct anything other than a single-family dwelling on her property, the property containing the schoolhouse is worth $200,000. If the sister's property is used for anything other than a single family dwelling, the property containing the schoolhouse would be worth $160,000.

In a lawsuit for $40,000 (damages to compensate the teacher for the fact that the sister did not honor the 2000 agreement), the teacher should:

A. Lose, even though the sister broke the 2000 promise.

B. Win because the burden of the covenant runs with the land to heirs, successors, and assigns.

C. Win because the benefit of the covenant runs with the land to heirs, successors, and assigns.

D. Win because the benefit and the burden of the covenant run with the land.

57. In 2000, a man made a promise to his next-door neighbor that he would only construct a single-family dwelling on his property because the next-door neighbor only had a single-family dwelling on his property. This promise was made in a written, notarized document executed, delivered and recorded one month later for which the man paid the neighbor $1,000. In 2005, the neighbor planned to build a multi-family dwelling house on his property. The man sued the neighbor, seeking an injunction. Will he prevail?

A. Yes because the neighbor planned to break the 2000 promise.

B. Win because the benefit and the burden of the covenant touch and concern land.

C. Lose because the man and the neighbor are not in horizontal privity with each other.

D. Lose because the man should have sought damages, not an injunction.

58. A man owned a piece of property, which he divided into separate lots for sale. The man sold a lot to a woman and another lot to his brother. The brother then sold his lot to his daughter. All the deeds contained a restriction that the properties could only be used as single-family dwellings, even though the surrounding properties were all zoned for multi-family dwellings. The daughter proceeded to construct a multi-family apartment complex on her lot. The woman then sued the daughter for damages for loss of the woman's property value, due to the multi-family apartment complex on the daughter's lot. Who will prevail?

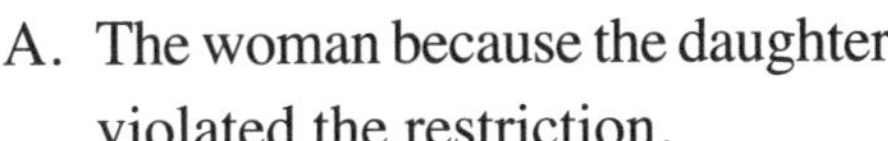

A. The woman because the daughter violated the restriction.

B. The woman because the benefit and the burden of the covenant touch and concern the land.

C. The daughter because the woman and the daughter are not in horizontal privity with each other.

D. The daughter because the surrounding properties were zoned for multi-family dwellings so as to make the daughter's restriction an economically inefficient use of the land.

59. A woman was the fee simple owner of a tract of land. In 1990, the woman built a house on the land and began occupying the property. In 2002, because she had never had a place to park her car before, the woman built a garage on the land. In 2001, she conveyed the mineral rights to the land beneath the property to a man, who immediately began mining the minerals. He enlarged his mining operations under the land, in 2003, until his excavation caused subsidence damage to the woman's house and garage. In a lawsuit by the woman against the man for subsidence damage to her house and garage on the property, if the woman cannot prove that the man negligently excavated beneath the property, she will recover:

A. Nothing.

B. Damages for the house, but not for the garage.

C. Damages for the garage, but not for the house.

D. Damages for the house and garage.

60. A man owned a tract of land in fee simple absolute. He conveyed it "to my daughter, her heirs and assigns; provided that if my sister should ever have a son, then to that son, his heirs and assigns." The limitation to the sister's "son, his heirs and assigns" is:

A. Valid because the sister's son's interest is vested subject to complete divestment.

B. Valid because the Rule Against Perpetuities does not apply to the sister's son's interest.

C. Valid because the sister's son's interest will vest, if at all, within a life in being at the creation of the interest.

D. Invalid.

61. A person conveyed a piece of property, which that person owned in fee simple absolute, "to woman and a man, jointly and forever." Ten years later, the man died, willing the property to his brother. The woman, believing she herself to be the sole owner of the property, lived on the property and paid all property taxes.

Immediately upon the man's death, the title to the property is held:

A. By the woman only.

B. By the brother only.

C. By the woman and the brother as joint tenants.

D. By the woman and the brother as tenants in common.

62. A sister and a brother held a piece of property as tenants in common. The brother lived on the property and paid all of the property taxes. The sister lived elsewhere. After two years, the brother sued the sister, demanding that she pay her fair share of the property taxes. The sister countersued for an offset for the fair market rental value of the brother's use of the property. The sister will:

A. Owe 1/2 of the property taxes paid by the brother, but receive an offset for the fair market rental value of the brother's use of the property.

B. Owe 1/2 of the property taxes paid by the brother, but not receive an offset for the fair market rental value of the brother's use of the property.

C. Not owe 1/2 of the property taxes paid by the brother, but receive an offset for the fair market rental value of the brother's use of the property.

D. Not owe 1/2 of the property taxes paid by the brother, and not receive an offset for the fair market rental value of the brother's use of the property.

63. A woman owned a tract of land in fee simple absolute. In 1980, she conveyed the land as follows: "to my boyfriend for life, and then to my boyfriend's children for life, and then to my boyfriend's grandchildren." In 1980, the boyfriend was 40-years-old and had two living sons, but no grandchildren. In 1990, the boyfriend fathered a daughter, but the daughter only lived until 2012. Which of the boyfriend's grandchildren may receive an interest under the woman's 1980 conveyance?

A. The children, if any, of the boyfriend's two sons and of the boyfriend's daughter, since the "all or nothing" rule applies.

B. The children, if any, of the boyfriend's two sons, but not the boyfriend's daughter, since the boyfriend's daughter was born after the date of the conveyance.

C. The children, if any, of the boyfriend's daughter only, since in a per stirpes distribution, each child will receive his or her deceased parent's share.

D. None, since the "all or nothing" rule applies.

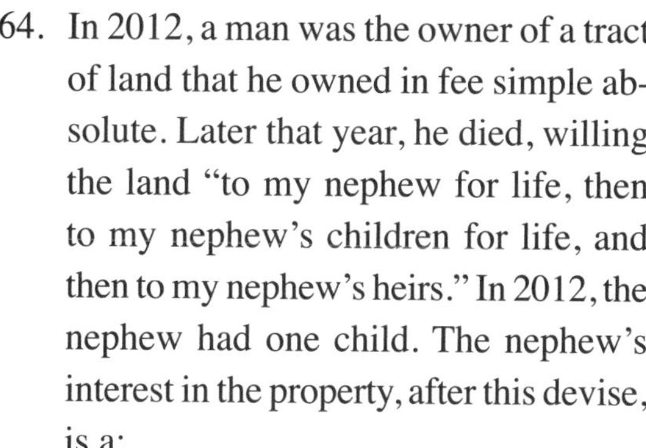

64. In 2012, a man was the owner of a tract of land that he owned in fee simple absolute. Later that year, he died, willing the land "to my nephew for life, then to my nephew's children for life, and then to my nephew's heirs." In 2012, the nephew had one child. The nephew's interest in the property, after this devise, is a:

    A. Life estate per autre vie.

    B. Fee simple absolute.

    C. Life estate and a vested remainder.

    D. None of the above.

65. A young man is the fee simple absolute owner of a piece of property. In 1980, he was 18 and lived with his parents 100 miles away from the property. In 1980, a woman illegally moved into the house on the property, planted a vegetable garden, paid all taxes and assessments on the property, and received mail and telephone service at that address. The age of majority in this jurisdiction is 21. Since 1980, the woman has continuously lived on the property. Assuming that this jurisdiction follows the common law of real property, when, if ever, does the woman gain title to the property?

    A. The year 2000, if she files an action to quiet title against the young man.

    B. The year 2003, if she files an action to quiet title against the young man.

    C. 2004 because she could not file an action to quiet title quickly against the young man.

    D. 2000, if she files an action to quiet title against the parents.

66. A landlord leased to a tenant office space. The lease prohibited assignments and/or subleases without the prior permission of the landlord. One year into his lease, the tenant transferred his interest in the office space to a woman. The landlord wrote a letter to the woman, stating that the landlord accepted the woman as an assignee under the lease. After nine months, however, the woman moved out and transferred her interest in the office space to a man, who moved into the property. The landlord refused to accept the man as a tenant and accepted no money from him. If the man sues the landlord to force the landlord to accept him as a tenant, the man's best argument would be that:

    A. Lease covenants are strictly construed against the landlord.

    B. A covenant prohibiting assignments does not prohibit subleases, and vice versa.

    C. The Rule in Dumpor's case requires the landlord to accept this assignment.

D. The Rule in Spencer's case requires the landlord to accept this assignment.

67. A landlord leased to a man 400 square feet of office space and four parking spaces in a parking garage to be constructed next door to the leased office building. That lease contained a covenant to paint and maintain the parking spaces in conformance with city codes. Six months after the man signed the lease, the parking garage was completed and the man began the rental term and moved into the office. One year into his lease, the man transferred his interest in the office and parking spaces to a woman. The woman refused to maintain the parking spaces according to the city code. If the landlord sues the woman for damages under the lease provision regarding the maintenance of the parking spaces and the landlord loses, it will most likely be because:

A. A covenant concerning a thing not yet in existence must expressly mention assignees in order to bind them.

B. There is no horizontal privity for the covenant.

C. The benefit of the covenant does not increase or enhance the value of the land or the landlord's estate therein.

D. The burden of the covenant does not curtail the use of the land or diminish the value of the tenant's estate therein.

68. A landlord rented to a tenant a luxury apartment overlooking the beach. The rental agreement contained a covenant by the tenant to pay the landlord $3,000 per month for a term of three years. Six months later, the tenant assigned his interest in the apartment to his girlfriend, who began paying rent on a timely basis. Three months later, the girlfriend moved out and transferred her interest in the apartment to her mother, who moved into the apartment. The mother never paid any rent. The landlord may collect rent from:

A. The girlfriend, under privity of contract.

B. The girlfriend, under privity of estate.

C. The mother or the tenant because both are in privity with the landlord.

D. Neither the mother nor the tenant.

69. In 1990, a man was the fee simple absolute owner of a ski cabin. In 1990, a woman moved into the ski cabin and lived there only during the winter months every year for twenty years without the man's permission. She held several parties there, paid all taxes and assessments on the property, and received mail and telephone service

at that address. Assuming that this jurisdiction follows the common law of real property and, assuming that the woman files an action to quiet title after a twenty-year period has elapsed, who holds title to the ski cabin?

A. The woman because intermittent use prevents the statute of limitations from running for purposes of adverse possession.

B. The woman because intermittent use is consistent with the nature of the property.

C. The man because intermittent use is consistent with the nature of the property.

D. The man because he never gave the woman permission to live in the ski cabin.

70. A woman was the fee simple absolute owner of a piece of property. She contracted to sell the property to a man in fee simple absolute for $40,000 by warranty deed. After the close of escrow and delivery of the warranty deed to the man in fee simple absolute, the man discovered that the woman was not the sole owner of the property; she was a tenant in common with one other person. The value of that land as a sole interest was $40,000; the value of that land as an undivided 1/4, as tenant in common, was $15,000.

The man sued the woman in a timely manner for breach of the covenant of seisin. If he prevails, his damages will be:

A. $15,000 plus interest.

B. $10,000 plus interest.

C. $25,000 plus interest.

D. $40,000 plus interest.

71. A man contracted to sell a piece of property to his brother for $30,000. The brother purchased a title insurance policy for $50,000 on the property, but the title insurance company did not disclose to the brother the fact that there was an easement on the property, and the value of the property with the easement was only $20,000. That fact was discovered by the title insurance company during its title search. If the brother sues the title insurance company and prevails, his damages will be:

A. $20,000.

B. $10,000.

C. $40,000.

D. $50,000.

72. A woman owned a piece of property. She sold and delivered the property to the man. At the time of the transfer of the property, the property was encumbered by an easement that was held by a person who was living in another

country. The person returned and began using the easement. If the man sues the woman for a breach of a covenant in the warranty deed, under which theory is he most likely to recover?

A. Breach of the covenant against encumbrances.

B. Breach of the covenant of quiet enjoyment.

C. Breach of the covenant of seisin.

D. Breach of the covenant of right to convey.

73. A man owned a piece of property worth $50,000. He conveyed it by quitclaim deed to his sister for $60,000. The sister moved onto the property. Unbeknownst to the sister, there was an easement on the property that was used almost twice a month. When the sister discovered the easement, she sued her brother for breach of the warranties in the quitclaim deed. How much can she recover?

A. $50,000.

B. $0.

C. $60,000.

D. $10,000.

74. In 1950, a man moved into a privately-owned forest. He set up a shack in an area that was totally covered by woods. He lived for the next thirty years, until a bear ate him. He left behind one heir, a sister, who immediately filed an action to quiet title against the owner of the forest. This jurisdiction follows the common law. Will she be successful?

A. Yes because the man met all of elements of adverse possession.

B. Yes because in the common law, an heir is always preferred over a stranger.

C. No because the shack was set up in an area that was totally covered by woods.

D. No because death by wild animal attack tolls the statutory period under the common law.

75. In 1949, a woman moved onto a piece of property without permission and used the property as her own. In 1950, that property was conveyed "to a man for life, then to his son in fee simple." The man never moved onto the property. In 1966, the man died. The son never moved onto the property, and the woman continued to live there. Assuming that this jurisdiction follows the common law of real property, when, if ever, does the woman become the owner of the property?

A. The year 1969.

B. The year 1971.

C. The year 1986.

D. The year 1970.

76. A man owned a one-acre tract of land. That land was located five miles away from a river, which was the nearest source of fresh water. If the man wants to transport water from the river to use to irrigate his crops, which system of water rights will best allow him to do so?

A. Natural Flow Riparian Rights and Reasonable Use Riparian Rights only.

B. Reasonable Use Riparian Rights only.

C. Prior Appropriation Rights only.

D. None of the above.

77. A man orally agreed to sell his land to a woman for $100,000. That agreement was reduced to a writing, which complied with all the formalities for the Statute of Frauds. It stated that the man would transfer by marketable title, via a warranty deed, a fee simple absolute in the land to the woman on July 1. The man contracted in writing for his agent to sign the man-woman agreement as the man's agent. The woman orally arranged to have her agent sign that same agreement for her as her agent. The agreement described above was signed by "the man's agent as agent for the man, the seller" and by the woman's agent, "as agent for the woman, the buyer." The woman later refused to complete the purchase of the man's land. If the man sues the woman, and the woman pleads the Statute of Frauds as a defense, the man will:

A. Win because the land sales contract was in writing.

B. Win because the contract between the man and his agent was in writing.

C. Lose because the contract between the woman and her agent was not in writing.

D. Lose because the land sales contract was not personally signed by the parties to be charged.

78. A teenager got written permission from a property owner to walk across the property owner's property to get to his school. The following year, the property owner sold his property to a woman. One day the woman noticed the teenager walking across the yard. She brought out a shotgun and threatened to shoot the teenager if he did not stop trespassing on her property. The teenager was scared but, nevertheless, sued for an injunction against the woman for her efforts to prevent him from walking across the property to get to school. Will he be successful?

A. No because the sale to the woman

terminated the teenager's right to walk across the property.

B. No because the teenager could take a different route to school.

C. Yes because the teenager was granted written permission to walk across the property.

D. Yes because the teenager was scared when the woman brought out a shotgun.

79. In 1940, the fee simple absolute owner of a piece of property conveyed that property to "a man, as long as California requires attorneys to pass the California Bar Examination." In 1950, the fee simple absolute owner of another piece of property conveyed to the same man "forever." In 1960, the man married a woman. In 1970, the man died, willing all his real property to his cousin. The three pieces of property are all located in a jurisdiction that retains the law pertaining to dower.

If the woman sues to receive her dower interest in the man's real property, the interest she will receive is:

A. A fee simple absolute in all seised lands.

B. A life estate in all seised lands.

C. A 1/2 interest in all seised lands.

D. A 1/3 interest in all seised lands.

80. A woman orally agreed to purchase, and her sister agreed to sell, a tract of land for $100,000. The parties reduced the agreement to a writing that contained all of the elements required by the Statute of Frauds, except that there was no mention of the $100,000 purchase price (upon which the woman and her sister orally agreed.) The sister has refused to consummate the transaction and deliver a deed to the land. In an action for specific performance by the woman against her sister, the sister has claimed the Statute of Frauds as a defense. If the woman offers into evidence the above described written agreement, and also credible evidence that the parties discussed and agreed upon the $100,000 purchase price, the woman's lawsuit for specific performance will:

A. Succeed because the law will imply that the reasonable market value of the land was discussed and agreed upon by the contracting parties – even if the fair market value was not the purchase price orally agreed upon.

B. Succeed because, if the price agreed upon is a fair and equitable one, the seller is estopped from pleading the Statute of Frauds as a defense and that term may be implied into the written memorandum.

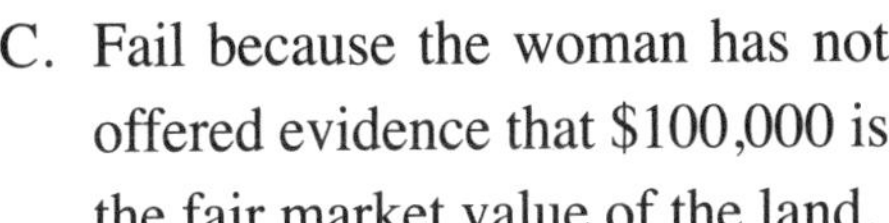

C. Fail because the woman has not offered evidence that $100,000 is the fair market value of the land.

D. Fail because price is an essential element of a written memorandum necessary to satisfy the Statute of Frauds.

81. A man owned a house in fee simple. He conveyed the house "to my daughter and the heirs of her body." What was the interest that the man had in the house immediately after the conveyance of the house to the daughter?

A. A possibility of reverter.

B. A right of entry.

C. A reversion.

D. A remainder.

82. A man was the fee simple owner of a piece of property. In 2000, he conveyed the property "to my wife and the heirs of her body." In 2012, the wife conveyed the property "to my uncle for life." Immediately after the wife's conveyance to the uncle, what was the interest that uncle had in the property?

A. A life estate for the life of the wife or the uncle, whomever dies first.

B. A life estate for the life of the wife or the uncle, whomever dies last.

C. A life estate for the life of the wife only.

D. A life estate for the life of the uncle only.

83. A woman was the fee simple owner of a farm. In 2000, she conveyed the farm "to my husband and the heirs of his body." In 2005, the husband conveyed the farm "to a farmer for life." In 2012, the husband died, survived by the woman, the farmer, and the son of the husband and the woman. In 2012, after the husband's death, what is the interest that the son had in the farm?

A. A life estate.

B. A fee simple absolute.

C. A remainder after the farmer's life estate.

D. A fee tail.

84. In 2005, a husband who owned a parcel of land in fee simple absolute conveyed the parcel "to my wife and the heirs of her body." In 2012, the wife died, survived by the husband and the child of the wife and the husband. In 2012, after the wife's death, what was the interest that the husband had in the parcel?

A. A possibility of reverter.

B. A right of entry.

C. A reversion.

D. Fee simple absolute.

85. In 2000, a woman owned a tract of land adjacent to a river that was downstream from land owned by a man and each used the river equally and in a reasonable amount for their personal needs. In 2012, the woman continued receiving the same amount of water for her needs as she had previously, but the man increased his use of the water, thereby reducing the flow of water past the woman's land. If the woman seeks to enjoin the man's additional diversion of water for his use, she will prevail if the jurisdiction follows:

A. Natural flow riparian rights theory only.

B. Reasonable use riparian rights theory only.

C. Either natural flow riparian rights theory or reasonable use riparian rights theory.

D. Neither natural flow riparian rights theory nor reasonable use riparian rights theory.

86. A state has a zoning ordinance that classifies property uses into four types: single-family residential; multi-family residential; commercial; and industrial. Single-family residential is considered the highest use of a property, next multi-family, then commercial, and industrial is the lowest use. The zoning ordinances are cumulative. Which uses are permitted in the multi-family residential zone?

A. Single-family residential and industrial.

B. Multi-family residential only.

C. Single-family residential and multi-family residential.

D. Multi-family residential, commercial, and industrial.

87. In 2000, a man was the fee simple owner of a tract of land with a house on it. In 2005, the telephone company requested and received a written agreement from the man, giving the company the right to install and maintain telephone poles and wires across the tract of land. The telephone company did, in fact, install poles and wires across the tract of land. If in 2012, the man sued to remove the telephone wires from the tract of land and he lost, it will probably be because:

A. The telephone company has a license.

B. The telephone company has an easement.

C. The telephone company has gained title to the tract of land by prescription.

D. The telephone company has an easement by necessity, since phone service is necessary in today's society.

88. In 2005, a woman gave the electric company a written grant to enter her land and install and maintain electric poles and lines. In 2010, the electric company permitted an internet service provider to lay cables on the electric poles. If the woman sues to prevent the internet service provider from entering and using her land, her best argument would be:

A. The electric company had a non-exclusive easement.

B. The electric company had an exclusive easement.

C. The electric company had an easement in gross.

D. The electric company had an easement by prescription.

89. In 2006, a man gave the city oral permission to enter his land in order to maintain the sewers that ran below the land and under his home on the land. In 2010, the man, in an attempt to sell his home, requested that the city remove the sewer lines that ran below his home. If the man sues the city to force it to remove the sewer lines and the man loses, it will most likely be because:

A. The city has a permanent easement.

B. The city has a revocable license.

C. The city has a prescriptive easement.

D. The city has an irrevocable license.

90. A man owned a tract of land in fee simple absolute. In 2000, he conveyed the tract "to the school board to be used for school purposes only." The school board accepted the gift and constructed a school on the property in 2001. The school board continued to use the property as a school until 2011, when due to a population shift in the community, the school board decided to level the school building and construct a gas station/ mini-market on the tract. All parties concede that the property has not been used for school purposes since 2011. In 2012, the school board sought to quiet title to the tract in itself. A court will most likely quiet title to the tract in:

A. The school board, in fee simple absolute.

B. The school board, but only until the man retakes the property.

C. The man, in fee simple absolute.

D. The man because it is not economically efficient to continue to use the tract as a school.

91. A woman wants to give her property to her local church, but ensure that she will automatically get the property back if the land ceases to be used as a church. If this jurisdiction follows the common law, how should the conveyance to the church be worded to satisfy the woman's wishes?

    A. "To my church, provided that the property is used as a church."

    B. "To my church, if and only if it is used as a church."

    C. "To my church, so long as the property is used as a church."

    D. "To my church, upon condition that the property is used as a church."

92. A man leased an apartment to a woman for twenty-four months, beginning January 1, 2010. The lease was in writing and provided for an annual rental of $4,800, payable in 12 monthly installments. On January 1, 2010, the man handed the keys to the apartment to the woman.

    The type of tenancy created in the woman by the lease agreement was a:

    A. Periodic tenancy whose term is month-to-month because of the monthly rental installments.

    B. Periodic tenancy whose term is year-to-year because the lease states an annual rental term of $4,800.

    C. Tenancy at will, which is turned into a periodic tenancy by the acceptance of rent.

    D. Tenancy for years because a definite ending date is provided in the lease.

93. A landlord leased an apartment to a tenant. The landlord was supposed to deliver possession to the tenant on January 1, 2012. The landlord gave the keys to the tenant on January 1, 2012. To the tenant's surprise, she found the former tenant still living in the apartment. The new tenant sued the landlord. This jurisdiction follows the modern law. Who will prevail?

    A. The new tenant because she is entitled to actual possession of the estate promised by the landlord.

    B. The new tenant because the landlord's lease with the new tenant is an election by the landlord to treat the former tenant as a tenant at sufferance or trespasser.

    C. The landlord because the new tenant, as the owner of the nonfreehold estate, is entitled to possession of the apartment and, therefore, is the only one entitled to sue the former tenant in ejectment.

D. The landlord because the landlord has fully delivered the legal right to possession to the new tenant.

94. In 2000, a man owned twenty acres with a house on the south half of the property. The man cleared a dirt road from the house to the only public road, which ran along the north frontage of the property. In 2010, the man gave, by warranty deed, the north half of the property to a woman and kept for himself the south half with the house. The man continued to use the dirt road to reach the public highway. In 2011, if the man is able to use the dirt road access the woman's property over her objections, it is because he has an:

A. Easement by implication and an easement by necessity.

B. Easement by necessity and an easement by prescription.

C. Easement by implication and an easement by prescription.

D. Easement by implication, an easement by necessity, and an easement by prescription.

95. In 2000, a man and a woman owned adjoining properties. The only way the woman could reach the only public road was to cross over the man's property. The man orally gave her permission to do so. In 2005, another public road was built. The woman could reach the new public road without having to cross over the man's property. However, it was more convenient for the woman to continue crossing over the man's property. In 2006, the woman had:

A. An easement by prescription.

B. An easement by implication.

C. An easement by necessity.

D. An express easement.

96. A man and a woman were owners of adjoining land. In 2008, the man promised the woman that he would maintain his land forever, as a single-family residence, only. That promise was made in writing and was recorded with the county recorder's office. In 2010, the woman conveyed her property to her uncle, who did not have actual knowledge of the promise.

In 2012, the man developed his land as a multiple-family apartment complex. If the uncle sues the man for damages for breaching the 2008 promise between the man and the woman, the uncle will:

A. Win because the covenant runs with the land.

B. Lose because there is no vertical privity.

C. Lose because there is no horizontal privity.

D. Lose because the covenant does not touch and concern land.

97. A man and a woman were the owners of adjoining farms. In 2005, the following written promise was made:

We, the man and the woman, for our lives and for the lives of any of our heirs and assigns, promise that our farms shall always be used as farms.

The promise was promptly recorded.

In 2006, the woman conveyed her farm to her father. In 2008, the father began to develop a luxury hotel and golf course on his property. The man immediately sued the father for breaching the 2005 promise that the man and the woman had made. The man will:

A. Win because the covenant runs with the land.

B. Lose because there is no vertical privity.

C. Lose because there is no horizontal privity.

D. Lose because the covenant does not touch and concern land.

98. A man and a woman were owners of adjoining parcels of land. In 2007, both the man and the woman promised each other that the two parcels of land would remain forever undeveloped, as wetlands. The promise was never recorded.

In 2009, the man conveyed his land to his brother. In 2010, the woman conveyed her land to her sister. Neither the sister nor the brother had actual knowledge of the promise made between the man and the woman in 2007. In 2011, the brother wishes to build a house on his land. If the sister sues the brother to specifically enforce the 2007 promise between the man and the woman, the sister will:

A. Win because the man and the woman had an interest in the same land at the same time in 2007.

B. Lose because the promise does not touch and concern land.

C. Lose because there is no vertical privity.

D. Win because the notice was sufficient.

99. A man and a woman were adjoining property owners. Last year, the man went on an extended trip to Europe. The man asked the woman to take in his newspapers until he returned. The woman orally agreed to do so.

Before the man returned, the woman conveyed her property to her mother. The mother did not take in the man's newspapers. The man's driveway ended up being piled with newspapers.

The man's sister informed him that

the mother had not been honoring the promise made between the man and the woman. The man sues the mother for specific performance of the promise. The man will:

A. Win because the man and the woman had an interest in the same land at the same time at the time the promise was made.

B. Lose because the promise did not touch and concern the land.

C. Lose because the promise was not in writing.

D. Lose because the promise violates the Thirteenth Amendment against involuntary servitude.

100. A landlord leased a piece of property to a tenant for a period of three years, beginning November 1, 2000. On November 5, 2003, the tenant was still in possession of the property without obtaining the landlord's prior consent to her continued presence on the property. As of that date, she had not paid the landlord any money for her possession of the property after October 31, 2003. Before the landlord decides what legal action to take with respect to the tenant's continued presence on the property, the tenant may best be described as a:

A. Periodic tenant.

B. Tenant for years.

C. Tenant at sufferance.

D. Trespasser.

101. One of the principal differences between a mortgage and a deed of trust is:

A. A mortgage can be foreclosed by a judicial sale, a deed of trust cannot.

B. A deed of trust can be foreclosed by a judicial sale, a mortgage cannot.

C. A mortgage can be foreclosed by a private sale, a deed of trust cannot.

D. A deed of trust can be foreclosed by a private sale, a mortgage cannot.

102. A woman agreed in writing to buy a man's land. Since the woman did not have enough cash to pay the purchase price immediately, they entered into the following land security device agreement. Their agreement stated that the woman would pay the man a monthly percentage of the total purchase price, plus interest each month, until the total price and accrued interest was paid. The woman had the legal right to possession of the property and the obligation to pay taxes, etc. on it. As security for the money owed, the man would transfer legal title to the woman when the total price was paid.

If, at any time, the woman defaulted on her payments, the man could cancel the agreement, retain all moneys paid, and retake possession. This land security device is most properly described as:

A. A deed of trust.

B. An installment land contract.

C. A mortgage.

D. A present transfer of a leasehold coupled with a future interest in fee simple absolute when the woman pays the full purchase price.

103. A man borrowed $100,000 from a woman to purchase a piece of property. In return, he gave the woman a mortgage on the property for 30 years. After 15 years, the man sold the property to his brother, who moved to the property and began paying the mortgage debt to the woman. However, after 5 years of payments, the brother moved from the property and stopped paying rent. Which of the following people are personally liable on the mortgage to the woman?

A. The man.

B. The brother.

C. The man and the brother.

D. Neither the man nor the brother.

104. A man bought a piece of property from a woman, who took a mortgage from him in return for lending him the money for the purchase price. The woman then transferred her interest in the mortgage to her cousin. The agreement from the woman to the cousin was silent as to whether the cousin assumed the mortgage along with the woman's interest in it. After the transfer from the woman to the cousin, the mortgagee's rights and responsibilities lie with:

A. The woman. If a transfer is silent, it is presumed to be taken "subject to" the mortgage.

B. The cousin. If a transfer is silent, the transferee is presumed to be "assuming" the mortgage.

C. Both the woman and the cousin. Even after the transfer, unless there is a novation, the woman is still personally liable on the mortgage.

D. The cousin. He is substituted for the woman with respect to the mortgage.

105. A man sold his property to his sister, who gave him a 30-year mortgage as security for the purchase price. Fifteen years later, the sister sold the property to her boyfriend, who assumed the mortgage. The boyfriend defaulted, and the property was sold at a judicial sale for less than the remaining debt.

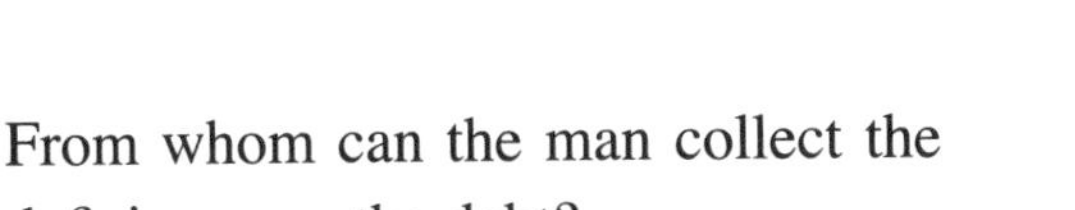

From whom can the man collect the deficiency on the debt?

A. The sister.

B. The boyfriend.

C. The sister and the boyfriend.

D. Neither the sister nor the boyfriend.

106. A man sold his house to a woman, who gave him a 30-year mortgage as security for the purchase price. Fifteen years later, the woman sold the house to her sister, who assumed the mortgage. As a result of the transfer, the man agreed to release the woman from the debt, since the property was worth more than the outstanding mortgage. However, property values fell, and the mortgage exceeded the value of the land. The sister defaulted, and the house was sold at a judicial sale for less than the remaining debt. From whom can the man collect the deficiency on the debt?

A. The woman.

B. The sister.

C. The woman and the sister.

D. Neither the woman nor the sister.

107. In 1990, a man owned a house, which he mortgaged to a woman for 30 years in order to borrow $150,000 from her. In 2000, he sold the house to his brother for $200,000. The brother did not agree to assume the mortgage, and he moved onto the property. In 2010, the man defaulted on the mortgage. The woman now wishes to sell the property at a judicial sale without the brother's consent. May she do so?

A. Yes because the brother took the property subject to the mortgage and cannot prevent the sale, even though he is not liable on the debt.

B. No because the brother took the property subject to the mortgage, and he is not liable on the debt. The property cannot be foreclosed upon without his consent.

C. Yes because the man did not pay the woman in 2000 when he received $200,000 from his brother.

D. No because the brother paid $200,000 to the original mortgagor, more money than the outstanding debt, therefore, he has been equitably discharged from the mortgage.

108. In 2000, a woman mortgaged her home to a man for $100,000. In 2005, she borrowed $35,000 from her sister and gave another mortgage on the home to her sister. The sister was aware of the

man's mortgage. In 2010, the woman defaulted on the man's loan on which there was an outstanding balance of $80,000, although she did not default on her loan from her sister. After giving notice to all relevant parties, the man foreclosed and had the property sold at a judicial sale for $120,000 after court costs, etc. The proper distribution of the foreclosure proceeds is:

A. $80,000 to the man first, then $40,000 to the woman, since she is not in default to her sister.

B. $35,000 to the sister first because she has had the security for her mortgage taken away without any action on her part, then $80,000 to the man, and last $5,000 to the woman.

C. $80,000 to the man by first in time, first in right, then $35,000 to the sister, and the last $5,000 to the woman.

D. $80,000 to the man by first in time, first in right, then $35,000 to the sister, and the remaining $5,000 to be divided by the man and the sister according to their mortgage percentages because the woman is the person in default and cannot profit from her wrongdoing.

109. In 2000, a woman mortgaged her home to a man for $100,000. In 2010, the woman borrowed $45,000 from her sister and gave another mortgage on her home to her sister. The sister was aware of the man's mortgage. In 2012, the woman defaulted on the man's loan on which there was an outstanding balance of $80,000, and she also defaulted on her loan from her sister, owing $40,000. After giving notice to all relevant parties, the man foreclosed and had the property sold at a judicial sale for $90,000 after court costs, etc. The proper distribution of the foreclosure proceeds is:

A. $60,000 to the man (2/3 of $90,000), $30,000 to the sister (1/3 of $90,000) – since the man is owed twice as much as the sister by the woman.

B. $60,000 to the man (75% of $80,000), $30,000 to the sister (75% of 40,000) – since $90,000 is 75% of $120,000 the total amount owed.

C. $50,000 to the man, $40,000 to the sister, since she is the junior mortgagee.

D. $80,000 to the man, $10,000 to the sister, since she is the junior mortgagee.

110. In 2000, a woman mortgaged her house to the bank for $100,000. In 2005, she borrowed $50,000 from her sister and gave the sister a mortgage on the house, which the sister promptly recorded. The sister was aware of the

bank's mortgage. In 2010, the woman defaulted on her loan to the bank, owing it $80,000. She did not default on her loan to her sister, of which $40,000 remained. The bank foreclosed on its mortgage, but did not give the sister notice of the foreclosure or the resulting sale. That sale netted $80,000. The new buyer was unaware that the sister was not given notice of the sale. The sister's rights in her mortgage after the bank's foreclosure:

A. Are extinguished; she was the junior claimant and there is no money left from the sale.

B. Are extinguished because the buyer at the foreclosure sale was unaware that the sister was not given notice of the sale.

C. Are not extinguished. Since she was not given notice, the property remains subject to the sister's mortgage, and the woman is still liable to her sister personally.

D. Are not extinguished. Since she was not given notice, she is entitled to be fully paid before the bank.

111. In 2000, a woman mortgaged her home to a man for $100,000. In 2010, the woman borrowed $45,000 from her sister and gave another mortgage on the home to her sister. The sister was aware of the man's mortgage. In 2012, the woman defaulted on the man's loan on which there was an outstanding balance of $90,000, but she was not in default on the second mortgage to her sister. After giving notice to all relevant parties, the man foreclosed and had the property sold to his brother at a judicial sale for $90,000 after court costs, etc. What is the state of the title to the home after the judicial sale to the man's brother?

A. Title is free and clear in the brother.

B. Title is in the brother, subject to the sister's mortgage.

C. Title is free and clear in the brother, but only if he pays the balance on the sister's mortgage.

D. Title is in the sister, but held in trust for the brother.

112. In 2000, a woman mortgaged her home to a man. In 2005, she borrowed additional money from her cousin and gave another mortgage on the home. The cousin was aware of the man's mortgage. In 2012, the woman defaulted on the cousin's loan on which there was an outstanding balance, but she was not in default on the first mortgage to the man on which there was still money owing, as well. After giving notice to all relevant parties, the cousin foreclosed and had the property sold to an investor at a judicial sale.

What is the state of the title to the home after the judicial sale to the investor?

A. Title is free and clear in the investor.

B. Title is in the investor, subject to the man's mortgage.

C. Title would be free and clear in the investor, but only if the proceeds had been enough to pay the balance on the man's mortgage.

D. Title is in the man, but held in trust for the investor.

113. In 2000, a woman mortgaged her home to a man for $100,000. In 2005, the woman borrowed $45,000 from her sister and gave another mortgage on the home. The sister was aware of the man's mortgage. In 2010, the woman defaulted on the loan from her sister on which there was an outstanding balance of $40,000, but the woman was not in default on the first mortgage from the man, on which there was still $85,000 owing. After giving notice to all relevant parties, the sister foreclosed and had the property sold to a purchaser at a judicial sale for $90,000 after court costs, etc. How should the proceeds of the judicial sale be distributed?

A. $85,000 to the man, $5,000 to the sister.

B. $40,000 to the sister, $50,000 to the man.

C. $40,000 to the sister, $50,000 to the woman.

D. All $90,000 to the sister.

114. In 2000, a woman mortgaged her home to a man for $100,000. He did not record his mortgage, although he was permitted to do so by the state's recording act. The man did not move into the home. In 2005, the woman sold the home by warranty deed to her cousin for $150,000. The cousin had no actual knowledge of the man's mortgage. What is the state of the title to the home in 2006?

A. Free and clear in the cousin.

B. In the cousin, subject to the man's mortgage.

C. In the cousin, who has a claim for breach of the covenant of seisin against the woman.

D. In the cousin, who has a claim of breach of the covenant against encumbrances against the woman.

115. In 2010, a man mortgaged his land to a woman for $100,000. The woman did not record her mortgage, since the state's recording act did not encompass property liens. In 2011, the man sold his land by warranty deed to his brother for $150,000. The brother had no actual

knowledge of the woman's mortgage. What is the state of the title in 2012?

A. Free and clear in the brother.

B. In the brother, subject to the woman's mortgage.

C. In the brother, who has a claim for breach of the covenant of seisin against the man.

D. In the brother, who has a claim of breach of the covenant of warranty against the man.

116. In 2011, a woman mortgaged a piece of property to a man for $100,000. The man did not record his mortgage, since the state's recording act did not encompass property liens. In 2012, the woman sold the same piece of property by warranty deed to her mother for $150,000. The mother had no actual knowledge of the man's mortgage. Shortly after escrow closed, the mother discovered the man's mortgage. She can now sue the woman:

A. For breach of the covenant of quiet use and enjoyment.

B. For breach of the covenant against encumbrances.

C. For breach of the covenant of seisin against the woman.

D. For breach of the covenant of warranty against the woman.

117. In 2011, a man mortgaged his home to a woman. She did not record the mortgage, although the state's recording act permitted the recording of liens. In 2012, the man transferred his mortgage to his father, who assumed that mortgage. In 2013, the mortgage went into default, and the home was sold for less than the outstanding balance on the mortgage. What are the woman's rights?

A. She may sue the man, but not the father, since the mortgage was not recorded.

B. She may sue the father, but not the man, since the father assumed the mortgage.

C. She may sue both the father and the man.

D. She may not sue either the father or the man, since she did not record her mortgage.

118. In 2010, a woman mortgaged her house to a man for $100,000. The man did not record, although the state's recording act permitted the recording of liens. In 2011, the man transferred his interest in the mortgage to his father. The father recorded that transfer. In January 2012, the woman gave a second mortgage to her cousin for $75,000. The cousin was unaware of the prior mortgage, and she recorded her mortgage. In December 2012, the woman defaulted on both mortgages with $90,000 remaining

to the father and $70,000 remaining to the cousin. The property was sold at a foreclosure sale for $80,000 after expenses. How should the court award the proceeds?

A. $80,000 to the father, since his is the senior mortgage.

B. $70,000 to the cousin, $10,000 to the father, since the cousin is the junior interest.

C. $80,000 to the father, since his is the first document to be recorded.

D. $70,000 to the cousin, $10,000 to the father, since the father's mortgage is not within the cousin's chain of title.

119. In 1990, a man sold a building to a woman for $80,000. She immediately recorded her warranty deed. In 1990, however, the building was actually owned by the man's uncle. In 2000, the uncle sold the building to the man for $90,000. That deed was promptly recorded. In 2010, the man gave a mortgage on the building to a mortgagee for $70,000. That mortgage was recorded. What is the state of the title after 2010?

A. Title is in the woman, free and clear.

B. Title is in the woman, subject to the mortgagee's mortgage.

C. Title is in the man, subject to the mortgagee's mortgage.

D. Title is in the man, free and clear.

120. In 2010, a man gave a mortgage on a piece of property to a woman for $75,000. That document was not recorded, although the state's recording act permitted the recording of liens. In 2011, the man gave another mortgage on the same property to his cousin for $75,000. The cousin did not have actual knowledge of the prior mortgage to the woman. The cousin recorded her mortgage. In 2012, the man defaulted on both mortgages, owing $65,000 on each. Both the woman and the cousin discovered and gave notice to the other, and both foreclosed on the property. The property was sold for $65,000 after expenses. Under which types of recording acts will the cousin get the $65,000 from the foreclosure?

A. Race and race-notice.

B. Race-notice and notice.

C. Race and notice.

D. Race, race-notice, and notice.

121. A brother and a sister owned a home as joint tenants in 2000. In 2005, the brother gave a mortgage on the home to the bank. In 2010, the brother died, willing the home to a beneficiary. What is the state of the title after the brother's death?

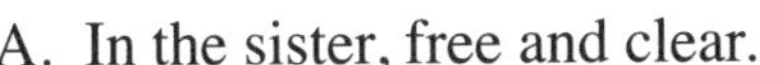

A. In the sister, free and clear.

B. In the sister, subject to the bank's mortgage.

C. In the sister and the beneficiary, as tenants in common.

D. In the sister and the beneficiary, as tenants in common, subject to the bank's mortgage on the beneficiary's share.

122. A mother, a daughter and a son all owned a piece of property as joint tenants in 2005. In 2006, the mother sold her undivided 1/3 to a woman. In 2009, the daughter mortgaged her share to a bank. In 2010, the son died, willing his share to a beneficiary. If the property is located in a state following the title theory of secured land devices, what is the state of the title to the property in 2011?

A. In the daughter, free and clear.

B. In the daughter for 2/3 subject to the bank's mortgage, and the woman for 1/3 as tenants in common.

C. In the daughter for 2/3, 1/3 subject to the bank's mortgage, and the woman for 1/3 as tenants in common.

D. In the daughter for 1/3 subject to the bank's mortgage, in the woman for 1/3, and in the beneficiary for 1/3 – all tenants in common.

123. A husband and wife owned a home as concurrent owners in 2005. In 2010, the wife secretly gave a mortgage on her share in the property to the bank in exchange for $100,000. In 2011, the wife died, leaving the mortgage in default. If the bank wishes to sell the home at a judicial foreclosure sale, it will most likely:

A. Be able to foreclose on the wife's heirs who own her former tenancy in common interest.

B. Be able to foreclose on the husband who owns his former joint tenancy interest subject to the wife's mortgage.

C. Not be able to foreclose on the husband because the wife's interest passed to him by right of survivorship.

D. Not be able to foreclose on the husband because a tenancy by the entirety cannot be severed unilaterally by one member of a married couple.

124. In 1990, a woman gave a deed of trust to her home to a man for $150,000. In 2000, she borrowed $75,000 from her cousin and gave the cousin a deed of trust on the home. The cousin was aware of the man's deed of trust. In 2010, the woman defaulted on her

loan to the man, owing him $130,000. She also defaulted on her loan to her cousin, of which $60,000 remained. The man foreclosed on his deed of trust, but did not give the cousin notice of the foreclosure or the resulting sale. The cousin did not foreclose. The judicial sale at the man's foreclosure netted $100,000. What are the cousin's rights in her deed of trust after the man's foreclosure?

A. They are not extinguished. Since she was not given notice, the property remains subject to her deed of trust, and the woman is still liable to her personally.

B. They are extinguished. The cousin was the junior claimant, and there was no money left from the sale.

C. They are not extinguished. Since the cousin was not given notice, she is entitled to be fully paid before the man.

D. They are extinguished, but only if the buyer at the foreclosure sale was unaware that the cousin was not given notice of the sale.

125. In 2000, a woman mortgaged her home to a man for $250,000. That mortgage was recorded. In 2005, the woman borrowed $175,000 from her brother and gave the brother a mortgage on the home. The brother recorded his mortgage. In 2010, the woman defaulted on her loan to the man, owing him $200,000. She did not default on her loan to her brother, of which $160,000 remained. The man foreclosed on his mortgage, but did not give the brother notice of the foreclosure or the resulting sale. The property was sold at foreclosure to an investor for $200,000. Since the foreclosure sale, the woman has not paid anything on her mortgage to her brother. If the brother seeks to force a judicial foreclosure sale of the home out from under the investor, he will:

A. Prevail because the investor had actual knowledge of the brother's mortgage.

B. Not prevail. Once a senior interest forecloses at a judicial sale, all unpaid junior claims are extinguished.

C. Prevail because he was not given notice or joined in the man's foreclosure sale.

D. Not prevail because the investor was a bona fide purchaser who purchased at a judicial sale without the brother present and without notice of the brother's interest.

END OF QUESTIONS

PROPERTY ANSWERS

1. C is the correct answer. The deed states that it is "subject to the understanding that...," which states a contractual obligation and not a limitation on the estate granted. A possibility of reverter follows a fee simple determinable and is created, if the deed contains language such as "so long as," "until," or "while." When there is a fee simple determinable, the grantor AUTOMATICALLY gets the property back when the condition occurs. A right of reentry follows a fee simple subject to condition subsequent and is created, if the deed contains language such as "but if," "upon," "provided," and "however." When there is a fee simple on condition subsequent, the grantor does NOT get the property back when the condition occurs; rather, the grantor must ELECT to take the property back by taking an affirmative action to reclaim the property. Here, the deed said, "subject to the understanding that..," which is not the language of a possibility of reverter nor of a right of reentry, for the reasons discussed above. Thus, C is the correct answer. A is incorrect because an equitable charge is created when property is expressly or constructively made liable or specially appropriated to the discharge of a debt without there being any intention to transfer ownership of the property. In the event of non-payment of the debt, the creditor's right of realization is by judicial process, i.e., by the appointment of a receiver or an order for sale. There is nothing in the facts to indicate that a debt was involved. Consequently, there was no equitable charge here. B and D are incorrect because the deed created neither a fee simple determinable nor a fee simple subject to condition subsequent, for the reasons discussed in Answer C.

2. C is the correct answer because it is really the only correct statement of law. A non-assignment clause in a lease between a landlord and tenant operates for the benefit of the landlord, not the tenants. Therefore, the brother, who was a tenant, will not be successful in his lawsuit against the sister for her bringing her boyfriend in as another tenant, in violation of the non-assignment clause.

Note, even though the landlord did not object to the boyfriend becoming another tenant, the non-assignment clause required the landlord to give express written consent. Here, while the landlord did not object, he did not give his consent in writing. Therefore, the non-assignment clause was violated. However, as discussed, it is the landlord who must bring the lawsuit, not the brother.

A is incorrect because a co-tenant may freely assign his share of the tenancy without the consent of any of the co-tenants, unless there is a contract that says otherwise. Here, there are no facts indicating that such a contract existed between the co-tenants (the sister and the brother).

B is incorrect because a "non-assignment" clause grants rights to the landlord, but not to the co-tenant (i.e., the brother), as discussed in C, above.

D is incorrect because, although it is a factually correct answer, a non-assignment clause is legal, if all parties to the clause agree to be bound by it. Here, the brother agreed to be bound by the non-assignment clause when he initially entered into the lease. Restraints on alienation are disfavored. They are sometimes upheld when public policy dictates, and "non-assignment" clauses are examples of this policy choice.

3. B is the correct answer. The Rule Against Perpetuities is not violated. The Rule Against Perpetuities forbids future interests that will not vest within a life in being plus twenty-one years. A life in being is any person who is in existence at the time the conveyance takes effect. Since a will takes effect at death, it is irrelevant who is in existence at the time the will is executed; it only matters who is in existence at the time the grantor dies.

   Here, the man granted his property through a will. At his death, we will know who all of his surviving children are, regardless of age. Since those children are lives in being, we must know, at each child's life, whether or not that child attained age 30. Thus, A, C, and D are incorrect for the reasons discussed in B.

4. D is the correct answer. This problem depends on whether the jurisdiction requires that a title searcher look in the entire grantor-grantee index for all conveyances made by a grantor, even those beyond the years the record shows title in that person. If so, then the wild deed (meaning it was outside the normal chain of title because it was conveyed before the man owned the property) from the man to the niece will be within the son's chain of title, and he is bound by constructive notice of it.

   A and B are incorrect for the reasons discussed in D. C is incorrect because failure to conduct a title search is not a valid excuse for either the niece or the son. Also, as discussed in D, not only is a title search required, but the answer to the question will depend on whether the title searcher is required to search the entire grantor-grantee index.

5. D is the correct answer. The question asks for legal title to the fodder area (land). The facts indicate that the squatter purported to sell the woman his interests in the fodder and fodder area by means of a document that was adequate to transfer personal property (the sheep), but inadequate to transfer real property. Therefore, the woman got no title to the property by virtue of this document. A and B are incorrect, for the reasons discussed in D. C is incorrect because the squatter had no legal interest in the property.

6. A is the correct answer. To gain title to a piece of property through adverse possession, a person must hold the property hostilely, openly, actually and continuously for the statutory period and file an action to quiet title after the statutory period has run. Furthermore, for purposes of continuous possession, if someone in privity with the possessor moves onto the property, the statutory period continues to run. This is known as tacking. Here, the man lived on the property for five years. Then, the man's niece moved onto the property at the man's request and lived there for sixteen more years (from 1990 to 2006). Because the niece was a relative of the man and moved onto the property at his request, she was in privity with the man. Thus, because the niece's period of possession was tacked onto man's period of possession, the statutory period will have been met (5 years + 16 years = 21 years). As a result, the niece will be successful in her action to quiet title.

   B and D are incorrect because there are no such rules under the common law. C is incorrect for the reasons discussed in A.

7. B is the correct answer. Delivery of the deed requires acceptance by the grantee. Here, the daughter (the grantee) was unaware of her father's deed when he made and recorded it. When she became aware of the deed's existence, she did not accept it. Rather, she immediately said, "Father, I don't want your ugly, over-taxed property. You take that deed right back. It's yours." Therefore, the deed never became part of the daughter's estate. Her bequest in her will of her entire estate to her boyfriend, therefore, did not include the father's property. The father will, thus, be successful in his suit to quiet title.

   A is incorrect because, even if a grantee was unaware of the deed at the time of recording, the grantee's subsequent actions at the time of learning of the existence of the deed may constitute valid delivery. Here, as discussed in B, the actions of the daughter (the grantee) upon learning of the deed indicated that she did not accept delivery of the deed, since she did not want the property.

   C is incorrect because, as discussed in B, the property never passed from the father to the daughter in the first place. Therefore, it did not need to be conveyed back to the father.

   D is incorrect because, as discussed in B, the property never became part of the daughter's estate. Therefore, her intent is irrelevant with regard to this property, since the daughter had no power to bequeath it to anyone.

8. C is the correct answer. The right to remove timber is incident to a fee, and the son has a defeasible fee. A is incorrect because the daughter does have a future interest in the property. B is incorrect because mere possession does not give one the right to log and remove timber. However, such a right is incident to a

fee interest. D is incorrect because bad faith is irrelevant to the right to take timber.

9. B is the correct answer. The Statute of Frauds requires that for interests in land to be transferred, there must be a writing. A right of survivorship must be created in the deed with the appropriate language of a joint tenancy with rights of survivorship. Here, the facts state that the woman and the man owned the property as tenants in common, not as joint tenants. Tenants in common do not have rights of survivorship. Thus, upon the deaths of the woman and the man, each of their interests will pass by will or intestacy. The facts state that neither of them had a will. They made an oral agreement that the survivor of either of them would own the property outright.

However, this oral agreement is unenforceable for two reasons: (1) It did not comply with the Statute of Frauds; and (2) it contradicted the laws of intestacy and descent (because an agreement about disposal of property upon death must comply with the laws of intestacy and descent). Thus, under the laws of intestacy, the father (as the man's heir) became the owner of the man's interest upon the man's death, and the mother (as the woman's heir) became the owner of the woman's interest upon the woman's death. Therefore, both the mother and the father own an undivided interest in the property.

A is incorrect because the woman and the man did not die simultaneously; they died one day apart, as per the facts. (There is no such thing as "essentially simultaneously.") C and D are wrong because the Statute of Frauds controls the result, as discussed in B.

10. B is the correct answer. In order to be valid, the covenant must have an intent to run with the land to subsequent successors and assigns; the covenant must touch and concern the land; the subsequent purchasers must have notice of the covenant; and horizontal and vertical privity. If these elements are met, the covenant will run with the land to bind successive owners of the property, regardless of their use of the facilities. Here, the facts indicate that the man intended for the covenants of residential user only, access to the lake and the marina, and an obligation to pay for their upkeep and maintenance to run to subsequent purchasers and assigns. These restrictions and obligations touch and concern the land because they directly affect the uses of the land.

Since the man had a common development plan for the land, all subsequent purchasers would see a record of this development plan and would, thus, receive record or constructive notice of the development plan. As a result, the notice requirement will have been met here.

Both the horizontal and vertical privity requirements will have been met, as well, because all subsequent purchasers will purchase either directly from the man or from someone else who purchased from the man or from a person who purchased from someone who purchased from the man.

As a result, a covenant would be the man's best way of ensuring that his plan is implemented.

A is incorrect because an easement grants a person the right to use someone's property and does not pertain to the payment of money. Most importantly, easements, unlike covenants, do not run with the land. As a result, an easement would only ensure that the initial purchasers are bound by the man's plans and do not bind subsequent purchasers.

Likewise, answers C and D are incorrect because both a mortgage and a personal obligation are personal to the individual who signed the promise and do not automatically pass to successor owners.

11. C is the correct answer. In order to be valid, the covenant must have an intent to run with the land to subsequent successors and assigns; the covenant must touch and concern the land; the subsequent purchasers must have notice of the covenant; and horizontal and vertical privity. If these elements are met, the covenant will run with the land to bind successive owners of the property, regardless of their use of the facilities. Here, there is nothing in the facts to indicate that the adult son intended that the man perform the duties of painting the house, taking in the groceries, and perform the duties of feeding the woman's elderly father in the rest home.

The deed from the adult son to the man did not recite the restrictions that were in the deed from the woman to the adult son, and the adult son never recorded the deed from the woman. Additionally, the adult son never told the man about the restrictions, and they were not the kind of restrictions that could be discovered through inquiry notice. As a result, the man had no notice of the restrictions.

The types of restrictions are merely personal contractual restrictions that do not touch and concern the land.

Consequently, the man will prevail in this lawsuit. A, B, and D are incorrect for the reasons discussed in C.

12. C is the correct answer. A life tenant (the woman) is responsible for the interest, and the remainderman (the man) is responsible for the principal. Here, although the mortgage was only for ten years, the life tenant (the woman) could possibly die within the ten-year period. Therefore, the general rule should be applied.

A, B, and D are incorrect for the reasons discussed in C.

A

PROPERTY

13. D is the correct answer. The owner entered into a written lease with the sister, even if it was rent-free. The subsequent conveyance by the owner to the brother only gave the brother rights in the property, if he obtained a role in a Hollywood movie by age 35, something he had not done. Thus, the owner is still the sister's landlord. A is incorrect because the brother had not yet obtained a role in a Hollywood movie and, therefore, did not yet have an interest in the property. B is incorrect as a matter of law. C is incorrect because, even after leasing the property to the brother and the sister, the owner was the fee simple owner and was free to convey the property.

14. D is the correct answer. Retaliatory eviction would prevent a landlord from raising rent in response to the assertion of a tenant's legal rights. Here, the tenant protested the landlord's failure to repair the stairwells and hallways. It was within the tenant's legal rights to protest these failures by the landlord. Thus, the tenant will prevail. A is incorrect because, although factually accurate, it is irrelevant, since the statutorily required thirty-day notice was given.

    B is incorrect because, as discussed in D, the tenant will be successful due to the doctrine of retaliatory eviction, and a $200 rent increase does not necessarily shock the conscience. C is incorrect because it states a rule of law that does not exist.

15. D is the correct answer. The facts state that this jurisdiction follows the common law with regard to joint ownership of property. At common law, a piece of property that was granted to more than one person could be held by those people in one of three ways. If it was held by people who were validly married, it was known as a tenancy by the entirety. In a tenancy by the entirety, both spouses owned the entire property as a whole, and the property could not be severed, unless there was a divorce, an agreement by both the man and the woman, or death of either. In a joint tenancy, the parties hold the property both by the whole and by the part. The tenancy could be severed unilaterally during the lifetime of either party. In a tenancy in common, each tenant only held by the part, and they could sever the tenancy by inter vivos deed or by will.

    Here, although the two men were married in a jurisdiction that allows same-sex marriage (which did not exist under the common law), this jurisdiction also follows the common law with regard to joint ownership of property. The deed recited that the man held the property as a married couple, which would indicate a tenancy by the entirety. This type of tenancy, if it were held by a married man and a woman, could only be severed by a joint agreement or divorce, and if it were not severed during the lifetime of the parties, then it would pass to the surviving spouse upon the death of one of the parties.

Here, one of the men transferred his interest in the property to his mother during his lifetime. This action severed the tenancy that had been created because, at common law, two men could not hold a piece of property in a tenancy by the entirety. The title, thus, appears to have granted the two men a joint tenancy with rights of survivorship. Such tenancy can be severed unilaterally during the lifetime of one of the joint tenants. When there are only two joint tenants, the new party to whom the portion of the property is transferred receives a tenancy in common with the remaining individual of the two original parties.

Therefore, the mother and the surviving man own the property together (as tenants in common).

A and B are incorrect for the reasons discussed in D.

C is incorrect because a will only takes effect upon the testator's death, and by the time the man died here, he had already transferred his interest in this property to his mother. As a result, he had no interest in this property to transfer to the nieces. Furthermore, a joint tenancy interest with rights of survivorship cannot be transferred by will because at the death of one of the joint tenants, the decedent's interest automatically passes to the surviving joint tenant. Thus, the nieces received no interest in this property under these facts.

16. C is the correct answer. An easement can be acquired by prescription, implication, grant, or strict necessity. An easement by prescription is acquired if the property is used hostilely, openly, actually and continuously for the statutory period, and the person using the easement files an action to quiet title after the statutory period has run. Here, the brother used the property openly and continuously for the required statutory period. However, since the man had given the brother permission to use the easement, and that permission was never taken away, the brother's usage was permissive and was, therefore, not hostile.

    A, B and D are incorrect because the woman's use of the property is irrelevant, since she never gained any legal title to the property, and the brother's usage of the property could not have been adverse to the woman. The only relationship that matters here is the one between the brother and the man, which is discussed in C.

17. A is the correct answer. A joint tenancy with right of survivorship includes four unities: time (joint tenants all acquire their interest at the same time), title (joint tenants have the same title), interest (the interest is divided equally: for example, if there are two tenants, each one holds a 50% interest; if there are three tenants, each one holds a 1/3 interest, etc.), and possession (each tenant has an equal right to possess the whole property).

A

PROPERTY

A joint tenancy may be severed unilaterally during the lifetime of the joint tenants. Here, the brother agreed to allow the sister to develop the western half of the property and agreed that he could do whatever he wanted with the eastern half of the property, and the sister then proceeded to build the shopping center. This was tantamount to a severance of the joint tenancy. Thus, upon the death of the sister, the brother would not receive her 1/2 interest by right of survivorship because of their agreement to sever the tenancy.

As a result, he is estopped from asserting title to the western half of the property. Rather, the sister's interest in the western half passed by will to her son.

B is not a correct statement of law. A joint tenancy cannot be severed by an oral agreement alone. The oral agreement must be accompanied by actions, which was the case here, where the sister built the shopping center.

C is incorrect because there is no such preference.

D is also not correct, as there is no exception for the Statute of Frauds for close family relationships.

18. B is the correct answer. In accordance with the Statute of Frauds, a contract for a sale of an interest in property must normally be in writing to be enforceable. However, when one goes onto the property to make improvements, this is a form of part performance, which allows the contract to be enforced, even in the absence of a writing. Here, the mother went onto the property and began making improvements. Consequently, under the part performance exception to the Statute of Frauds, her oral agreement with the man will be held to be enforceable. As a result, the mother is now the rightful owner of the property.

A and C are incorrect because there are no such fiduciary duties under the law, either for minors or for adults.

D is incorrect because the exception to the Statute of Frauds applies here, for the reasons discussed in B.

19. A is the correct answer. A license is a limited right to use the land of another. Upon termination of the time period stated in the license, the licensor can immediately eject the licensee.

Here, the nephew granted a license to the aunt to stay on the property for thirty days after closing. At the end of the thirty days, the aunt refused to leave and attempted to make monthly rental payments to the nephew, which the nephew refused. Since the license had expired, the nephew had an automatic right to terminate the aunt's tenancy on the property. Thus, this would be his best legal argument to gain full possession of the property.

B is incorrect because, if the aunt is a tenant at sufferance, the nephew would have the option of ejecting her, but he would still have to terminate the tenancy. This is far more time-consuming than simply calling her a licensee.

C is incorrect for two reasons: the nephew refused to accept monthly rental payments from the aunt and, even if he had accepted the money, he would need to give thirty days notice before evicting the aunt. This is far more time-consuming than simply calling the aunt a licensee.

D is incorrect because trespasser ab insio means a trespasser from the beginning, and here, since the aunt initially entered the property as per her agreement with her nephew, she was never a trespasser.

20. A is the correct answer. In order to be valid, the covenant must have an intent to run with the land to subsequent successors and assigns; the covenant must touch and concern the land; the subsequent purchasers must have notice of the covenant; and horizontal and vertical privity. If these elements are met, the covenant will run with the land to bind successive owners of the property, regardless of their use of the facilities.

    Here, the restrictive covenant in the deed from the man to the woman runs with the land to the niece, even if the deed from woman to the niece did not physically contain that covenant because the deed from the man to the woman indicated that the conveyance was "To the woman and her heirs and assigns [showing intent for the covenant to run with the land] for residential purposes only." The residential restriction touches and concerns the property.

    The privity requirements have been met, as well, because of the contractual relationships between the parties in question. The deed from the woman to the niece did not recite the restriction (no constructive notice, except for the man's recorded development plan), and the facts do not indicate that the woman told the niece about the restrictions (no actual notice). However, the niece had inquiry notice of the restriction because the woman had built a residence on the property.

    Thus, the restrictive covenant runs with the land to the niece, and she is bound by the restrictions and cannot build an office building on the property. As a result, the brother will be successful in the lawsuit.

    B is incorrect because lowering the property value is irrelevant to whether or not the niece is bound by the covenant to only use the property for residential purposes. C is incorrect because, as discussed in A, the covenant runs with the land, so the niece does not have to be a direct grantee. D is incorrect because, even though the niece's deed did not contain the restrictive covenant, she had inquiry notice of the restriction, as discussed in A.

21. C is the correct answer. In order to be valid, the covenant must have an intent to run with the land to subsequent successors and assigns; the covenant must touch and concern the land; the subsequent purchasers must have notice of the covenant; and horizontal and vertical privity. If these elements are met, the covenant will run with the land to bind successive owners of the property, regardless of their use of the facilities.

    Here, there were no restrictions in the girlfriend's deeds, and the facts do not indicate that the son told the girlfriend about the restrictions. Thus, she had neither actual nor constructive notice of the restrictions. However, notice can be found in a common development plan. Here, the only way that the girlfriend would be successful in the lawsuit is if there were an insufficient showing that the common development plan applied to the entire subdivision.

    A is incorrect for the reasons discussed in C and because the Equal Protection Clause only binds governmental entities, not private individuals. B is incorrect because, although it is true as an abstract statement of principle, it has little to do with this question, which specifically depends on whether the woman can say that it was originally contemplated that the man intended to develop the 20-acre parcel in the same manner as the 40 lots, as discussed in C. D is an incorrect statement of law. Equitable servitudes do not require privity with the original covenanting parties.

22. D is the correct answer. The owner conveyed the property "to the school for the life of my daughter, and then at that time to all of my grandchildren and their heirs in equal shares; provided, however, that the school shall use the property for school purposes only." Thus, the school has a life estate per autre vie, namely, a life estate measured by someone else's life (in this case "the life of my daughter"), and when the daughter dies, the school will no longer have rights to possess the property.

    The facts state that during the daughter's lifetime (and, thus, during the time that the school lawfully possessed the property), the school allowed a man to mine on a piece of the property. This was a breach of the condition that the school shall use the property for school purposes only." Thus, damages and an injunction are proper. A, B and C are, therefore, incorrect. Furthermore, B is also incorrect because the original owner is no longer an interested party, since he has conveyed the property away. The daughter only serves as a measuring life for the life estate per autre vie, as discussed in D; she has no other interest in the property.

23. B is the correct answer because of the parol evidence rule. Under the parol evidence rule, where there is a fully integrated written document, prior or contemporaneous oral agreements cannot be introduced to contradict the words of the written document.

Here, when the woman told the man to fill in the number of the condominium that he wanted, she in essence made him her agent. The man and the woman had an oral understanding that the man should either fill in unit #6 or unit #7, since both were valued at $50,000. Both the man and the woman understood that unit #21 was worth $75,000. Therefore, when the man wrote unit #21 on the deed and recorded it, this action was in direct conflict with the oral understanding between the man and the woman.

However, the woman will be unsuccessful in rescinding the transaction because the deed is a fully integrated written document, which cannot be contradicted by prior oral understandings under the parol evidence rule.

A is incorrect because the deed was certain on its fact, but did not reflect the oral agreement of the parties and, but for the parol evidence rule, the deed would be invalid.

C is an incorrect statement of law. D calls upon a general equitable principle that the most innocent person should not bear the loss, but that principle cannot control over legal reasons, such as agency and the parol evidence rule.

24. C is the correct answer. Using the daughter as the measuring life, we must know who her surviving children are within 21 years of her death. Only the restrictions on mortgage or sale are invalid as restraints on alienation. A, B, and D are incorrect for the reasons discussed in C.

25. D is the correct answer. At common law, a piece of property that was granted to more than one person could be held by those people in one of three ways. If it was held by a man and a woman who were validly married, it was known as a tenancy by the entirety. In a tenancy by the entirety, both the man and the woman owned the entire property as a whole, and the property could not be severed, unless there was a divorce, an agreement by both the man and the woman, or death of either. In a joint tenancy, the parties hold the property both by the whole and by the part. The tenancy could be severed unilaterally during the lifetime of either party. In a tenancy in common, each tenant only held by the part, and they could sever the tenancy by inter vivos deed or by will.

Here, although the woman and the man had a deed that stated that this was a tenancy by the entirety, since they were never validly married, a tenancy by the entirety was never created by this title. Therefore, when the woman abandoned the man, since the man and the woman were actually tenants in common (they were not joint tenants, since the deed did not say "joint tenants with right of survivorship"), the man could freely partition for sale of the property.

A and C are incorrect because, as discussed in D, there was no tenancy by the entirety here. B is incorrect because, as discussed in D, the woman and the man were tenants in common and, thus, both of them had title to the property.

26. B is the correct answer. At the end of the friend's life estate, the gift to his children takes immediate effect. It is, therefore, a vested remainder and not an executory interest. Here, the remainder to the friend's children is subject to complete divestment because the remainder will divest if any of them move to California, and that child's interest will pass to the woman's church. A is incorrect because, as discussed in B, the gift is a vested remainder rather than an executory interest. C is incorrect because the gift is vested subject to divestment ("provided that..."), as discussed in B; it is, therefore, not indefeasibly vested. D is incorrect because the gift is vested subject to divestment, as discussed in B; it is, therefore, not contingent.

27. B is the correct answer. Under the doctrine of equitable conversion, if a seller of a piece of property dies after the contract for conveyance is signed, the seller's interest in the property will be treated as personal property (a right to payment of money, rather than a right to the property itself). Here, since the man has willed his personal property to his son, the son is entitled to the $500,000 at closing. A is incorrect because equitable conversion is applicable in this situation, as discussed in B. C and D are incorrect, for the reasons discussed in B.

28. A is the correct answer. Under the doctrine of equitable conversion, the purchase price in a land sale contract is treated as personal property of the seller and title to the land is treated as the real property of the buyer. Therefore, when the farmer died, the title to the land was in him and passed to his son, his heir, who can demand specific performance of the contract. B, C, and D are incorrect for the reasons discussed in A.

29. C is the correct answer. In order to effectuate a delivery of the deed, the grantor must relinquish all dominion and control over the property; there must be a physical delivery of the deed; and the grantee must accept delivery of the deed. Here, the woman initially granted the property to the nephew. However, because the nephew did not know about the grant, he did not accept delivery of the deed. Thus, delivery to the nephew was invalid.

Before the nephew could accept delivery, the woman granted the property to the niece and delivered the deed to the niece (indicating that the woman, the grantor, had relinquished all dominion and control and had physically delivered the deed to the niece), and the niece accepted delivery of the deed.

Therefore, there has been a proper delivery, and the niece is the owner of the property.

A is incorrect because the nephew did not accept delivery of the deed, as discussed in C. Therefore, he did not meet the elements of delivery and cannot be the owner of the property.

B is incorrect because the grant to the niece was proper. As discussed in C, the woman was still the owner of the property at the time of the grant to the niece, since the nephew did not accept delivery of the deed. Therefore, the woman had the power to grant the property to the niece.

D is incorrect because the recording statutes protect subsequent bona fide purchasers (those who give value without notice). Here, the grants to both the niece and the nephew were gratuitous (no value given), so the fact that the niece recorded first is not the proper reason why she is the owner of the property. Her ownership rights are discussed in C above.

30. D is the correct answer. Although there was a discrepancy in acreage (40 acres, as opposed to 39.5 acres), the legal description of land given was sufficient to adequately identify the property, especially where, as here, the discrepancy was minor.

A is incorrect because there is no requirement that the deed contain a metes and bounds description. B is incorrect for the reasons discussed in D. C is incorrect because, although a grantor cannot convey more than she owns, the problem here is with the land description in the deed, not the amount of the property conveyed.

31. D is the correct answer. At common law, a landowner is entitled to lateral and subjacent support of his property in its natural condition. Here, the man had a house and a barn located on his property. These structures were damaged when the woman in the adjacent property began excavation. Since common law controls this question, the woman will be successful in this lawsuit because the man is suing for damage to his house and barn (both of which are manmade structures), rather than damage to his land in its natural condition. Note, the neighbor may be strictly liable for damage to buildings, if the man could show that the weight of the house and barn did not contribute to the earth movement that caused the collapse. However, here, the house and the barn were built only one month before the woman's excavation, so the man will be unable to demonstrate that the weight of the house and the barn did not contribute to the collapse.

A is incorrect because a landowner has an absolute right to lateral support for unimproved land. B is incorrect because, even if the weight of the barn contributed to the damage, he may still recover, if he can prove that the woman was negligent in her excavation. C is incorrect, for the reasons given for A and B: even if the woman were only negligent, the man would have an absolute right to lateral support for unimproved land. However, here he is suing for damage to manmade structures on his land, as discussed in D. Therefore, D correctly states the full legal principle.

32. B is the correct answer. The interest in the daughter's unborn children immediately follows the preceding life estate in the son, who is still alive. Thus, it is a remainder. Moreover, since there is no child of the daughter alive at the time of the conveyance, the remainder is contingent upon her having children before the son's death. Therefore, A and C are incorrect. D is incorrect because the daughter is the measuring life. Thus, the Rule Against Perpetuities is not violated, since the daughter (the measuring life) is still alive.

33. D is the correct answer. An easement can be acquired by prescription, implication, express grant, or strict necessity. An easement created by express grant is not dependent on continued necessity for its continuation. Here, the woman received her easement by way of an express grant from the man. At the time, the woman was completely landlocked (unable to get to a public road without crossing over the man's property), even though the new public highway was constructed, and the woman was no longer landlocked because her easement had been created by express grant. The termination of the necessity has no effect on her easement and she may, therefore, continue to use the easement. Thus, A is incorrect. B is incorrect because a diminution in value has no effect on easements. C is incorrect because this is an easement and not an incorporeal hereditament (which is an interest in land incapable of being possessed and only consisting of a right to use something). This easement was not only used but possessed by the parties.

34. C is the correct answer. There is no natural right to an easement for light, air or view. A and D are both irrelevant. B incorrect for the reasons discussed in C.

35. C is the correct answer. In order to effectuate a delivery of the deed, the grantor must relinquish all dominion and control over the property; there must be a physical delivery of the deed; and the grantee must accept delivery of the deed. The fact that the grantor retains possession of the deed creates a rebuttable presumption of an invalid delivery. Here, although the woman gave the deed to her son, showing her intent to relinquish dominion and control over the property, the son put the deed in the woman's safe deposit box. Thus, the woman could access the deed at any time. Therefore, she has retained possession, which is a rebuttable presumption of an invalid delivery. As a result, the woman is still the owner of the property.

A is factually incorrect. There were no conditions regarding the delivery of the deed, and an escrow is not required. Thus, the son would not be the owner of the property.

B is incorrect because, even though the son was a donee, there was an invalid delivery, since the grantor retained possession of the deed (as discussed in C). In addition, the son would not be protected by the recording statute because recording statutes protect bona fide purchasers and not donees. Thus, the son would not be the owner of the property.

D is incorrect because there was nothing to record. Since the delivery was invalid (as discussed in C), the woman remained the owner of the property.

36. C is the correct answer. In order to effectuate a delivery of the deed, the grantor must relinquish all dominion and control over the property; there must be a physical delivery of the deed; and the grantee must accept delivery of the deed. Here, all of the elements of a valid delivery were met. The grantor (the man) relinquished all dominion and control over the property and made a physical delivery of the deed to the grantee (the girlfriend), who accepted the deed. Her subsequent actions (such as ripping up the deed and saying that she no longer wanted the property) occurred too late because, by then, she was the owner of the property. The only way she could relinquish ownership of the property would be by deeding it back to the man, which she did not do. Therefore, the girlfriend is the lawful owner of the property.

    A and B are incorrect because, as discussed in C, both the girlfriend's statement that she did not want the property and her ripping of the deed occurred after the deed was validly delivered to and accepted by her. Thus, her statement and her ripping of the deed had no legal significance because they occurred too late. Therefore, the man is no longer the lawful owner of the property.

    D is incorrect because is acceptance of a deed, not recording, that makes one the lawful owner of a piece of property. While recording creates a presumption of acceptance, the facts already state that the girlfriend accepted the deed prior to recording it, so it is the girlfriend's acceptance of the deed, not her recording, that makes her the lawful owner of the property.

37. D is the correct answer. Repayment of the principal goes to protect the future value of the remainderman's fee. The interest represents the current use of the money borrowed and is, therefore, payable by the current user of the property (the man) Here, the man's son, who is the remainderman, is responsible for paying the principal. The man, who is the current user of the house, is responsible for paying the interest. A, B, and C are incorrect for the reasons discussed in D.

38. A is the correct answer. In a general warranty deed, the grantor makes six covenants of title. These covenants are seisin, right to convey, covenant against encumbrances, quiet enjoyment, war-

ranty, and further assurances. If there is a breach of the covenants of seisin, right to convey, and against encumbrances, this breach occurs immediately. If there is a breach of the covenants of quiet enjoyment, warranty, and further assurances, this breach occurs in the future, after the property has been conveyed to the new owner. Here, property that the woman conveyed by a general warranty deed was already encumbered by an easement to her sister. Therefore, there was an immediate breach of the covenant against encumbrances, and this is the reason why the man will be successful in his lawsuit against the woman.

B and C are incorrect because they are both covenants that are breached in the future and, here, the man brought suit immediately.

D is incorrect because the covenant of seisin states merely that the original grantor (here, the woman) is the rightful owner of the property, and there is nothing in the facts to indicate that the woman was not the rightful owner of the property.

39. A is the correct answer. At common law, a piece of property that was granted to more than one person could be held by those people in one of three ways. If it was held by people who were validly married, it was known as a tenancy by the entirety. In a tenancy by the entirety, both spouses owned the entire property as a whole, and the property could not be severed, unless there was a divorce, an agreement by both the man and the woman, or death of either. In a joint tenancy, the parties hold the property both by the whole and by the part. The tenancy could be severed unilaterally during the lifetime of either party. In a tenancy in common, each tenant only held by the part, and they could sever the tenancy by inter vivos deed or by will.

Here, the wife and the husband were legally married at the time of the conveyance and remained so when the wife attempted to convey to her sister. The title was held by the wife and the husband as tenants by the entirety, and was inalienable (not transferable) by either of them without the other spouse's consent. The facts state that the attempted conveyance to the sister was done by the wife unilaterally. It was, therefore, without the husband's consent and as a result was invalid. Thus, the husband is the sole owner of the property upon the death of his wife.

B is incorrect because, if the tenancy that the wife and husband held were either a joint tenancy or a tenancy in common, the husband would have to share ownership with the sister as a co-tenant, whether he liked it or not. However, for the reasons discussed in A, there was a tenancy by the entirety here.

C is incorrect for the reasons discussed in A. D is incorrect because there are some jurisdictions that still have tenancy by the entirety, and the facts state that this is such a jurisdiction.

40. B is the correct answer. The question states that this jurisdiction has a recording statute that provides that a junior claimant must be in good faith. Therefore, the junior claimant must be without notice. As a result, a race or a race-notice statute is inapplicable. A, C, and D are, therefore, incorrect.

41. C is the correct answer. Recording statutes are for the protection of bona fide purchasers. A bona fide purchaser is one who gives value for the property without any notice of any prior conveyance of the property. Notice can be actual (the person is told of the prior conveyance), constructive (because the prior conveyance is recorded), or inquiry (the one who receives the prior conveyance is physically occupying the property).

    Here, the neighbor had no actual knowledge of the conveyance to the niece. Since the niece was not occupying the property, he also had no inquiry notice. Regarding constructive notice, although the niece recorded her deed prior to the neighbor's recording of his deed, the niece would not be protected by the recording statutes because she did not give value. (The facts state that she received her conveyance as a gift.)

    A and B are incorrect for the reasons discussed in C. D is incorrect because the woman no longer had any interest in the property, since she had conveyed it.

42. C is the correct answer. An executory interest is a future interest in someone other than the grantor that is not a remainder. A defeasible fee is a fee simple that may be cut short by the occurrence of a condition. Here, the interest, if any, in the charity followed a defeasible fee in the woman. Therefore, it could not have been a remainder of any sort because if the property were always used for residential purposes, the charity would get nothing.

    The interest does not violate the Rule Against Perpetuities because the residential-purposes condition only applies until 2010. Therefore, using anyone alive in 1990 as the measuring life, at their death plus 21 years, we must know whether the property has been used for residential purposes by 2010 (which is only twenty years later). Thus, the executory interest does not violate the Rule Against Perpetuities and is, therefore, valid.

    A, B, and D are incorrect for the reasons discussed in C.

43. D is the correct answer. This is a notice statute, giving priority to purchasers for value who take without notice. Here, the bank gave a loan (value) to the woman. Therefore, the notice statute would apply because the facts indicate that the bank had no notice of the conveyance to the man. A and B are incorrect because a mortgagee pays consideration (the loan proceeds) for the interest in land received (mortgage) and would qualify

under the statute as an "interest in land." C is incorrect because this is not a race statute; under a notice statute, priority in recording is not required to prevail.

44. C is the correct answer. This jurisdiction has a notice statute, giving priority to purchasers for value who take without notice. When a piece of property is conveyed to a grantee, and the grantee does not record immediately, the grantee's deed is considered outside the chain of title, and any subsequent grantees would not be able to find the original grantee's deed through a traditional (pre-Internet) title search. Here, the man received his deed in 1990, but did not record until 1995. Since the man did not record his deed until 1995, his deed is, therefore, outside of the cousin's chain of title because it cannot be found under the traditional method of searching title. Therefore, the cousin is without notice of the man's interest in the property and entitled to prevail under a notice statute, such as the one in this jurisdiction.

    A is incorrect because it is an erroneous statement of law. B and D are incorrect because the cousin's rights derive from his being without notice and are not dependent on the equities regarding his grantor, the boyfriend.

45. A is the correct answer. Recording statutes protect bona fide purchasers. A bona fide purchaser is one who gives value without notice. Here, the daughter was a donee (the deed was a gift) and not a purchaser for value. Furthermore, she never lived on the property. Thus, the girlfriend would have no inquiry notice of the deed to the daughter. Nothing in the facts indicates that the girlfriend knew of the conveyance to the daughter, so there was no actual notice, either. The daughter recorded her deed before the girlfriend recorded hers. Thus, the girlfriend had record-notice of the deed to the daughter. However, the girlfriend would still win the lawsuit because the recording statutes protect bona fide purchasers and not donees.

    B is incorrect because it is irrelevant; minors can and do hold title to property. C is an incorrect and nonsensical statement of law. D is incorrect for the reasons discussed in A.

46. D is the correct answer. Here, the recording statute states, "a duly recorded deed has priority over any subsequent recorded deeds in the same property." This statute codifies the common law rule of "first in time, first in right." Here, the brother recorded his deed before the sister recorded her deed. Thus, the brother will prevail in this lawsuit. A, B, and D are incorrect for the reasons discussed in D.

47. B is the correct answer. Covenants in a lease against assignment or subletting are strictly construed against the landlord because such covenants are restraints on alienation and land interests should be freely alienable. Here, the lease from the woman to the gardener contained a covenant prohibiting the

gardener from assigning the lease. Construing this covenant strictly against the landlord (here, the woman), the tenant (here, the gardener) should be allowed to freely assign his lease. However, note that due to the non-assignment clause in the lease, if the gardener leases to the man, the gardener will be contractually liable to the landlord for breach of contract because a lease is both a contract and an interest in land. A, C, and D are incorrect for the reasons discussed in B.

48. D is the correct answer. The man's interest would have been an executory interest, since it follows a fee – had it not violated the Rule Against Perpetuities. It violates the Rule since there is no life in being such that at that person's death, we must know whether or not the property will cease being used for ranch purposes within 21 years of a life in being. For instance, the property could be used for other than ranch purposes during the lifetime of an unknown future heir or assign of the woman. It is not a fee simple determinable because it does not contain the language "so long as," "until," or "while." It is not a fee simple on condition subsequent because it does not contain the language "but if," "upon," "provided," or "however." Thus, A and B are wrong, even before the application of the Rule, because a possibility of reverter follows a fee simple determinable, and a right of reentry follows a fee simple on condition subsequent. C is incorrect because of the Rule Against Perpetuities, as discussed in D.

49. D is the correct answer. Fixtures the tenant installs during the lease, and that can be removed without damage to the realty, can be removed by the tenant at the end of the lease. Fixtures the tenant installs during the lease and that cannot be removed without damage to the realty become part of the realty. Here, the tenant installed bookcases that were permanently affixed and could not be removed without damage to the realty. They, thus, became part of the realty. Therefore, because the tenant removed the fixtures (the bookcases), causing damage to the realty, the landlord will be successful in his lawsuit against the tenant.

A and B are incorrect because, whether or not the bookcases are considered trade fixtures and removable at the end of the lease (answer A), or non-trade fixtures and removable per the modern trend (answer B), the removing tenant must remove them without doing damage to the realty – a requirement contradicted by the facts here. C is incorrect for the reasons discussed in D.

50. D is the correct answer. Under the common law doctrine of ameliorative waste, a tenant cannot make any alteration to the premises – even those that improve the property, such as the improved steps and banister here. Therefore, the tenant will not be successful in his lawsuit against the landlord to recover the cost of the steps and banister. A and B are incorrect because, although modernly a long-term or life tenant

A PROPERTY

may be permitted to set off the value of the improvements against any money owed the landlord, at common law he could not. However, the facts state that this is a common law jurisdiction. C is incorrect because permissive waste (failure to make repairs) does not apply to this situation, since the tenant made an improvement.

51. D is the correct answer. Under the common law doctrine of ameliorative waste, a tenant cannot make any alteration to the premises – even those that improve the property. Here, the tenant added a sink, which was an alteration to the premises because sinks are permanent fixtures. Even the sink improved the property, under the doctrine of ameliorative waste, the landlord will prevail in his lawsuit regarding the sink because the common law is followed in this jurisdiction. A and B are incorrect because, although modernly a long-term or life tenant may be permitted to set off the value of the improvements against any money owed the landlord, at common law he could not. Furthermore, the tenant has not brought the lawsuit here. The suit was brought by the landlord. C is incorrect because permissive waste (failure to make repairs), does not apply to this situation.

52. D is the correct answer. The Rule Against Perpetuities forbids future interests that will not vest within a life in being plus twenty-one years. A life in being is any person who is in existence at the time the conveyance takes effect. Here, the interest in the charity violated the Rule Against Perpetuities because there is no life in being such that at that person's death, we will know whether the property has ceased being used for residential purposes. Therefore, the executory interest in the charity fails. It was replaced by a possibility of reverter in the woman. When the woman devised all of her real property to her niece, upon the death of the woman, the niece as devisee of all the woman's real property, held a possibility of reverter in the property. Therefore, the niece had to be included with the woman's son and the man in order to properly sell the property. The suit by the woman's son and the man against the investor for specific performance will, thus, be denied. A, B, and C are incorrect for the reasons discussed in D.

53. D is the correct answer. The interest in the soup kitchen follows a defeasible fee in the neighbor and was, therefore, an executory interest, rather than a remainder. However, the interest in the charity runs afoul of the Rule Against Perpetuities. The Rule Against Perpetuities forbids future interests that will not vest within a life in being plus twenty-one years. A life in being is any person who is in existence at the time the conveyance takes effect. Here, the interest in the soup kitchen violates the Rule Against Perpetuities because there is no life in being such that at that person's death, we must know whether the property has been used as a campground. Therefore, the interest in the charity fails.

A and B are incorrect because the interest in the soup kitchen is an executory interest, rather than a remainder, as discussed in D. C is incorrect because the interest violates the Rule Against Perpetuities for the reasons discussed in D.

54. A is the correct answer. The neighbor has a written document from the owner of the land (the man), entitling the neighbor to enter the property and remove wheat from it. This describes a profit a prendre, which is a protectable property interest under the Due Process Clause of the federal Constitution. B and D are incorrect since this interest is not a license, since a license is a limited land use that does not involve extracting materials (such as wheat in this case) from the land, unlike a profit a prendre. C is incorrect for the reasons discussed in A.

55. A is the correct answer. As between the original parties to a covenant, there is no requirement that the covenant (burden or benefit) run with the land. The arrangement need only be in writing. Here, the original parties to the covenant (that the woman would not construct anything other than a single-family dwelling on the land) are the man and the woman, and the lawsuit is between them. The man and the woman are in privity of contract regarding the covenant. Because the woman breached the contract by constructing a multi-family dwelling, which decreased the value of the man's adjacent property, the man will be successful in his lawsuit against her for the decreased value of his adjacent property. B, C and D are incorrect for the reasons discussed in A.

56. C is the correct answer. In order to run with the land, the covenant must have an intent to run with the land to subsequent successors and assigns; the covenant must touch and concern the land; the subsequent purchasers must have notice of the covenant; and horizontal and vertical privity. If these elements are met, the covenant will run with the land to bind successive owners of the property, regardless of their use of the facilities. A subsequent purchaser may enforce a covenant that runs with the land if that covenant benefits the purchaser.

Here, the covenant to not construct anything other than a single-family dwelling burdens the owner of the property that has the restriction (here, the sister). The covenant benefits the owner of the adjacent property containing the schoolhouse (originally the man and now the teacher), because the value of the property containing the schoolhouse is higher with the single-family dwelling on the sister's property than with a multiple-family dwelling on the sister's property.

The teacher presumably meets all the elements for the covenant to run to her, since she purchased directly from the man. Since this covenant is sought to be enforced by the teacher, who as discussed is the recipient of the benefit of the covenant, only the benefit side of the promise must run with the land. In this case, the benefit does run with the land because it is the value of that particular land (namely, the property containing the schoolhouse) that will be increased if the sister's covenant is followed. Thus, the teacher may enforce this covenant against the sister, a party to the original covenant.

B and D are incorrect for the reasons discussed in C. A is incorrect because the requirements for the benefit of a covenant to run are met on these facts, as discussed in C.

57. A is the correct answer. As between the original parties to a covenant, there is no requirement that the covenant (burden or benefit) run with the land. The arrangement need only be in writing, as this one is. Similarly, there is no requirement of horizontal privity either; it is irrelevant to this problem that the neighbor and the man do not have an interest in the same land at the same time (horizontal privity).

B and C are incorrect for the reasons discussed in A. D is incorrect because the difference in remedies is relevant to whether the agreement can be enforced as a covenant (damages) or servitude (injunction). This promise could be enforced as either. Furthermore, the neighbor has not yet broken the promise; he only plans to do so. Thus, there are no damages that the man can recover.

58. C is the correct answer. The woman, a grantee from an original party to the covenant (the man), is seeking to enforce the covenant against the daughter. The daughter was not one of the original parties to the covenant but, rather, received her lot from someone who was an original party to the covenant (the brother). The woman must show intent, notice, touch and concern, and both horizontal and vertical privity in order to bring a suit for damages to enforce a covenant. The woman and the daughter are not in horizontal privity because only the woman is an original party to the covenant, as discussed above. Therefore, there is no horizontal privity between the woman and the daughter. As a result, the woman will lose her suit for damages, and the daughter will win.

A is incorrect because, even though the daughter violated the restriction, the woman will not prevail in a suit for damages against the daughter for the reasons discussed in C.

B is incorrect because, even though the burden and benefit of the covenant touch and concern land, the element of horizontal privity has not been met, as discussed in C.

D is incorrect because the validity of a covenant is not affected solely by economic efficiency or the zoning of adjacent properties.

59. B is the correct answer. At common law, a landowner is entitled to lateral and subjacent support of his property in its natural condition. Furthermore, the man may be strictly liable for damage to the house and garage, if the woman could show that the weight of the house and garage did not contribute to the subsistence damage. Here, the house had been standing since 1990 with no problem, until the damage occurred thirteen years later. Thus, it is very unlikely that the weight of the house contributed to the damage. However, the garage was built in 2002, just one year before the damage occurred, so the woman will not be able to demonstrate that the weight of the garage did not contribute to the damage. A, C, and D are incorrect for the reasons discussed in B.

60. C is the correct answer. The Rule Against Perpetuities forbids future interests that will not vest within a life in being plus twenty-one years. A life in being is any person who is in existence at the time the conveyance takes effect. Here, the sister and the daughter are in existence at the time the conveyance takes effect. They are, therefore, measuring lives. The condition "if my sister should ever have a son" can only occur during the life of the sister. It will, thus, occur within a life in being (even without the twenty-one years). The sister's son's interest is an executory interest.

A is incorrect because the sister's hypothetical sons do not yet exist. Thus, their interest is not vested. B is incorrect because the Rule Against Perpetuities applies to all executory interests. Here, however, the Rule is not violated, since using the sister as the measuring life, one must know at her death plus 21 years whether or not she has a son, as discussed in C. D is, therefore, incorrect.

61. D is the correct answer. At common law, a piece of property that was granted to more than one person could be held by those people in one of three ways. If it was held by people who were validly married, it was known as a tenancy by the entirety. In a tenancy by the entirety, both spouses owned the entire property as a whole, and the property could not be severed, unless there was a divorce, an agreement by both the man and the woman, or death of either. In a joint tenancy, the parties hold the property both by the whole and by the part. The tenancy could be severed unilaterally during the lifetime of either party. In a tenancy in common, each tenant only held by the part, and they could sever the tenancy by inter vivos deed or by will.

Here, the conveyance to the woman and the man stated, "to woman and a man, jointly and forever." This did not expressly create a joint tenancy because a joint tenancy is created only by a conveyance that states, "as joint tenants with rights of survivorship," which was not the case here. Thus, the conveyance created a tenancy in common.

A

PROPERTY

Since tenants in common may fully transfer their property interest during their lifetime or by will, when the man died, his 1/2 interest passed to the brother by will. As a result, upon the man's death, the woman and the brother shared the property as tenants in common.

A and B are incorrect for the reasons discussed in D. C is incorrect because the interest shared by the woman and the brother is not a joint tenancy, as discussed in D.

62. B is the correct answer. In a tenancy in common, each of the co-tenants has an exclusive right to possess the whole of the property. However, each co-tenant owes a proportionate share of the taxes and other expenses in the property. Here, the brother lived on the property exclusively and paid all of the property taxes. Therefore, he is entitled to reimbursement of 1/2 of the property taxes from the sister. However, because the brother has an exclusive right to possess the whole of the property (as discussed above), the sister is not entitled to the fair market rental value of the brother's use of the property. A, C, and D are incorrect for the reasons discussed in B.

63. D is the correct answer. The class gift to the grandchildren is void under the Rule Against Perpetuities. In 1980 (the time of the conveyance), the boyfriend had no grandchildren. Thus, at the time of the conveyance, no person existed as a "measuring life" such that, at that person(s)' death, plus 21 years, one would know who all the grandchildren are. Since it is possible for the boyfriend to have children born after the date of the instrument, the class of his children cannot be used as measuring lives. Therefore, by the "all or nothing" rule, since it is possible for one member of the class (grandchildren) to vest (be born) after the perpetuities period, the gift to the class must completely fail, and the interest is void.

A and B are incorrect for the reasons discussed in D.

C is incorrect because, although in a per stirpes distribution the children of a deceased parent do step up to take their parent's share, that principle is irrelevant to this problem.

64. C is the correct answer. The will originally gave the nephew a life estate, his children a vested remainder subject to open (one child is alive in 2012), and a contingent remainder in the nephew's heirs. The Rule in Shelly's case changes the remainder in the nephew's heirs to a vested remainder in the nephew. This interest cannot merge with the nephew's life estate because, upon the nephew's death, the nephew's children will get a life estate. Upon the death of the children, their life estate will terminate and the estate will then go to the nephew. (Since the nephew will be dead at this point, the nephew's heirs will take the property, but as representatives of the nephew.) The

interest in the nephew is vested because the nephew is alive and is guaranteed to take his interest in the property in the future. A, B, and D are incorrect for the reasons discussed in C.

65. B is the correct answer. To gain title to a piece of property through adverse possession, a person must hold the property hostilely, openly, actually and continuously for the statutory period and file an action to quiet title after the statutory period has run. Here, the facts state that the jurisdiction follows the common law; under common law, the statutory period is 20 years.

Here, the woman entered the property illegally, which demonstrates hostility. She planted a vegetable garden, paid all taxes and assessments on the property, and received mail and telephone service at that address, which demonstrates openness (i.e., that she lived "out in the open" on the property). She has also lived on the property since 1980 continuously, according to the facts. However, the statute of limitations for adverse possession does not begin in 1980 when the woman enters the property because the young man (the owner) was only 18 at the time. Rather, the statute of limitations begins in 1983 when the young man's disability of infancy is terminated because, according to the facts, the age of majority in this jurisdiction is 21. Therefore, if the woman files an action to quiet title in 2003, she will gain title to the property through adverse possession.

A is incorrect because the year 2000 is not twenty years since the young man (the owner) turned 21; it is merely twenty years since the woman initially entered the property, which, as discussed in B, is too soon to bring an action to quiet title.

C is incorrect because it is possible to file an action to quiet title within one year, and woman's right to file an action to quiet title arose in 2003, as discussed in B. D is incorrect because the young man, not the parents, was the owner of the property. Therefore, an action to quiet title must be filed against the young man, not the parents. Furthermore, an action to quiet title filed in 2000 would be three years too early, as discussed in B.

66. C is the correct answer. The Rule in Dumpor's case states that once the landlord gives consent to one assignment, any covenant in a lease requiring consent is terminated. Here, because the landlord had already consented to the assignment to the woman, the landlord did not need to consent to the woman's assignment to the man. A is incorrect because, although lease covenants may be construed against the landlord, that principle is merely a generalized policy statement and would not necessarily determine the outcome of a case, like answer C. B is a correct statement of principle, but is inapplicable to these facts because these facts are about a subsequent assignment, not a sublease. D refers to the Rule in Spencer's case,

A PROPERTY

which states that a covenant relating to a thing not yet in existence must expressly bind successors. That rule is also inapplicable to the facts.

67. A is the correct answer. The facts state that the parking garage was not yet in existence when a promise was made concerning the maintenance of the spaces. That promise did not expressly mention assigns and, therefore, does not bind successors. Here, the woman was a successor who would, therefore, not be bound by the covenant to maintain the parking spaces according to the city code. Thus, the landlord will lose for this reason. B is incorrect because there is horizontal privity in that the landlord and the man were landlord and tenant respectively. C and D are incorrect because the benefit and burden do touch and concern land in that the parking spaces would be maintained, causing a benefit to the landlord's reversion and a detriment through the expenditure of time/labor/money by the tenant.

68. C is the correct answer. The original tenant and the landlord were in privity of estate while the tenant lived on the property and remained in privity of contract, even after the tenant had assigned his interest because, under contract law, an assignor remains liable in the absence of a novation (a contract with a new party that supersedes the original contract). Thus, the landlord could collect rent from the tenant.

    While the mother was on the property, she was in privity of estate with the landlord. Thus, the landlord could collect rent from her, as well.

    A and B are incorrect because the girlfriend was never in privity of contract with the landlord, and after she moved out of the apartment, she was no longer in privity of estate with the landlord, either.

    D is incorrect for the reasons discussed in C.

    When the original tenant assigned his interest in the apartment to his girlfriend, Tina possessed the office space for nine months, thus, constituting an obligation of $200 per month under privity of estate for that time. Since she never signed a lease agreement with Laurette, she is not bound by privity of contract for any amount of money. Thus, C is incorrect. Since Tomasso never signed a lease nor moved into the building, he is bound by neither privity of contract nor privity of estate, respectively. Therefore, A and B are incorrect.

69. B is the correct answer. To gain title to a piece of property through adverse possession, a person must hold the property hostilely, openly, actually and continuously for the statutory period and file an action to quiet title after the statutory period has run. Normally, the "continuous" requirement is not met by intermittent use. However, when the nature and character of the property are

such that intermittent use is considered normal use, then intermittent use will fulfill the "continuous" requirement. Here, the facts that the property is a ski cabin, which would normally only be used during the ski season (i.e., the winter). The woman did use the cabin consistently every winter during the twenty-year period. Thus, she has met the "continuous" requirement for adverse possession.

Her use of the ski cabin was open because she held several parties there, paid all taxes and assessments on the property, and received mail and telephone service at that address. Lastly, her use of the ski cabin was hostile because did not have the man's permission to be there.

Hence, because she has met all the elements of adverse possession, she will be declared the owner of the property.

A is incorrect because intermittent use does not prevent the "continuous" requirement from being met in this case, for the reasons discussed in B. C is incorrect because this is the reason why the woman will be declared the owner of the ski cabin, for the reasons discussed in B. D is incorrect because, while factually true, a person may obtain title to property, if they meet all the requirements of adverse possession, including being there without permission (i.e., the "hostility" requirement).

70. B is the correct answer. In a general warranty deed, the grantor makes six covenants of title. These covenants are seisin, right to convey, covenant against encumbrances, quiet enjoyment, warranty, and further assurances. If there is a breach of the covenants of seisin, right to convey, and against encumbrances, this breach occurs immediately. Here, there was a breach of the covenant of seisin. The covenant of seisin states that the original grantor (here, the woman) is the rightful owner of the property. Here, however, the woman was not the rightful owner of 100% of the property, since she held a 1/4 interest as a tenant in common with one other person (who held a 3/4 interest in the rest of the property). The measure of damages for a breach of the covenant of seisin is the purchase price (plus interest). Since the woman was only an owner of 1/4 of the interest promised in the deed, the damages here would be 1/4 the purchase price ($40,000/4= $10,000). A, C and D are, therefore, all incorrect figures.

71. B is the correct answer. The measure of damages for breach of a title insurance contract is normally the diminution in fair market value of the property caused by the defect. Since the value of the property as promised was $30,000 and the value of the property with an easement is $20,000, the damages equal $30,000 – $20,000, i.e., = $10,000. A, C and D, therefore, are all incorrect figures.

A

PROPERTY

72. B is the correct answer. In a general warranty deed, the grantor makes six covenants of title. These covenants are seisin, right to convey, against encumbrances, covenant quiet enjoyment, warranty, and further assurances. If there is a breach of the covenants of seisin, right to convey, and against encumbrances, this breach occurs immediately. If there is a breach of the covenants of quiet enjoyment, warranty, and further assurances, this breach occurs in the future, after the property has been conveyed to the new owner. Here, although there was a breach of the covenant against encumbrances because the property was encumbered by an easement, the easement was not being used at the time of the transfer of the property, and the woman did not disclose the easement to the man.

    As discussed above, the covenant against encumbrances is breached when made, and the covenant of quiet enjoyment occurs in the future, after the property has been conveyed. Here, when the easement holder returned and began using the easement, this was an interference with the man's use and enjoyment of his property, and it occurred after the man purchased the property. Thus, a breach of the covenant of quiet enjoyment is the man's best theory of recovery.

    A is incorrect because, as discussed in B, the covenant against encumbrances is breached immediately, and the man was not aware of the encumbrance until a later point in time.

    C and D are incorrect because there is nothing in the facts to indicate that the woman was not the rightful owner of the property.

73. B is the correct answer. A quitclaim deed contains no title covenants and offers no warranties regarding the property title. When a piece of property is conveyed by quitclaim deed, the grantor merely conveys the interest that he has in that property, if any, at the time of the conveyance. Here, because the property was conveyed by quitclaim deed, there was no warranty to be breached. Thus, the sister will recover $0. Answers A, C, and D are incorrect for the reasons discussed in B.

74. C is the correct answer. To gain title to a piece of property through adverse possession, a person must hold the property hostilely, openly, actually and continuously for the statutory period and file an action to quiet title after the statutory period has run. Here, the facts state that this jurisdiction follows the common law. Under the common law, the statutory period is twenty years. Although the man went into possession of the property without permission, and he continuously lived there in excess of the twenty years, his possession was not open and notorious because the shack was totally covered by woods. Therefore, the man failed to meet all the elements of adverse possession, and his sister would not be successful in her action to quiet title.

A is incorrect for the reasons discussed in C. B and D are incorrect because there are no such common law rules.

75. A is the correct answer. To gain title to a piece of property through adverse possession, a person must hold the property hostilely, openly, actually and continuously for the statutory period and file an action to quiet title after the statutory period has run. Here, the facts state that this jurisdiction follows the common law. Under the common law, the statutory period for adverse possession is twenty years.

In 1949, when the woman began possession of the property, the estate in existence was a fee simple in the original owner. The subsequent conveyance and division of the estate was irrelevant to the statutory period for adverse possession. The twenty-year period was completed in 1969. Assuming that she files an action to quiet title in 1969, she will, therefore, become the owner of the property.

B, C, and D are incorrect for the same reasons that A is correct.

76. C is the correct answer. Prior appropriation gives rights in water to the first taker, regardless of his or her ownership or use on riparian land. It is the only water rights theory available to the man. A and B are incorrect because the man's land is not located adjacent or beneath the river; it is, therefore, not riparian land. A and B are riparian theories, which only permit water to be taken for use on riparian land and are, thus, not available for the man's use. D is incorrect for the same reason that C is correct.

77. C is the correct answer. The Statute of Frauds requires that contracts for the sale of land, and also agency contracts, be in writing. Therefore, although the land sales contract and the contract between the man and his agent were in writing, the contract between the woman and her agent was not in writing. Thus, A and B are incorrect. D is incorrect, since there is no requirement that the parties to a contract personally sign the agreement. An agent's signature is binding on the principal.

78. C is the correct answer. An easement may be created by express grant, implication, prescription, or strict necessity. Here, the teenager was given written permission to walk across the property. This was an express grant of an easement and the teenager could continue to use this easement, whether or not the property was sold to someone else. Thus, the sale of the property to the woman did not terminate the teenager's easement.

A is incorrect for the reasons discussed in C. B and D are irrelevant factors under this fact pattern.

79. D is the correct answer. Under dower rights, a wife received a dower interest in 1/3 in all land in which her husband

was seised at his death. A, B, and C are, therefore, incorrect because they do not correctly state the law.

80. D is the correct answer. A land sales contract must be in writing that contains the essential terms, including the price term, in order to satisfy the Statute of Frauds. If a price term is not recited in the writing, the contract will not be enforceable. Here, the facts state that the contract did not contain the price term. Thus, the contract is not enforceable under the Statute of Frauds and the woman will not be successful in her lawsuit for specific performance. A, B, and C are incorrect because, as discussed in D, the price term must be in the written contract in order for it to be enforceable; all other considerations (fair market value, etc.) are irrelevant.

81. C is the correct answer. A fee tail is created by a grant to the grantee "and the heirs of his (or her) body." After the death of the holder of a fee tail, the property in question must transfer to that person's lineal descendants or, if none, it must revert to the original grantor. Here, the conveyance created a fee tail in the daughter because of the language "to my daughter and the heirs of her body" in the conveyance. Since the facts do not indicate anything about the daughter having any lineal descendants, the man (the original grantor) retained a reversion. A and B are incorrect for the reasons discussed in C. D is incorrect because a remainder is an interest that is held by a third party, rather than the original grantor (here, the man).

82. A is the correct answer. A life estate is created by a grant to the grantee "for life." After the death of the holder of a life estate, the property must transfer to the remainderman (if one is named) or revert to the original grantor (a reversion).

A fee tail is created by a grant to the grantee "and the heirs of his (or her) body." After the death of the holder of a fee tail, the property in question must transfer to that person's lineal descendants or, if none, it must revert to the original grantor.

Here, the conveyance to the wife created a fee tail because of the language "to my wife and the heirs of her body" in the conveyance. Since the wife had a fee tail, after her death the property must transfer to her lineal descendants or, if none, it must revert to the grantor (here, the man). Therefore, the uncle's interest must end at the wife's death. Moreover, since the wife gave the uncle a life estate, that life estate must also end at his death, assuming that he survives the wife.

B, C, and D are incorrect for the reasons discussed in A.

83. D is the correct answer. A fee tail is created by a grant to the grantee "and the heirs of his (or her) body." After the death of the holder of a fee tail,

the property in question must transfer to that person's lineal descendants or, if none, it must revert to the original grantor.

Here, the husband had a fee tail, which descended to his lineal heirs because of the language of the woman's conveyance, "to my husband and the heirs of his body." Since the son of the husband and the woman was one of the husband's lineal heirs, he, too, had a fee tail. A, B and C are incorrect for the reasons discussed in D.

84. C is the correct answer. A fee tail is created by a grant to the grantee "and the heirs of his (or her) body." After the death of the holder of a fee tail, the property in question must transfer to that person's lineal descendants or, if none, it must revert to the original grantor.

    Here, the husband's 2005 conveyance created a fee tail in the wife because of the language of the conveyance "to my wife and the heirs of her body." After the wife died, her fee tail passed to her child (her lineal descendant). The husband still retained a reversion, which will go into possession, if ever, after the wife's lineal heirs all die. A, B, and D are incorrect for the reasons discussed in C.

85. A is the correct answer. The natural-flow riparian rights theory gives a downstream owner the right not to have the flow of water diminished in either quality or quantity from its natural state. This is true, even if the downstream owner had sufficient water for her needs. The reasonable-use theory only permits injunction if the downstream owner has insufficient water for her needs. Here, the facts indicate that the woman was a downstream owner, and when the man increased his use of the water, he diminished the flow of water to the woman's property. A is the only option that presents the natural-flow theory alone. It is, therefore, the only correct answer. B, C, and D are incorrect for the reasons discussed in A.

86. C is the correct answer. A cumulative zoning ordinance is one in which higher, but not lower, uses are permitted. Here, since single-family residential is a higher use than multi-family residential, both those uses are permitted in a multi-family zone. A, B, and D are incorrect since they do not state that combination.

87. B is the correct answer. An easement is a legal right to enter and use the real property of another without actually possessing it. Here, the man gave the telephone company a written grant of the right to enter his land and install and maintain telephone equipment. This written instrument gave the telephone company the right to use the man's land, but not to possess it. The written instrument, therefore, created an easement in the telephone company. Thus, the man will lose the lawsuit to have the telephone wires removed because

the telephone company had a legal right to put and keep them there, due to the easement.

A is incorrect because a license is granted orally. Here, there was a written instrument. It created an easement, rather than a license. If a license had been granted, the man could have forced the telephone company to remove its equipment by withdrawing his permission.

C is incorrect because the telephone company did not acquire title to the man's property nor an easement by prescription because the telephone company had written permission to install and maintain telephone poles across the man's land. An easement by prescription is only created when there is no permission to enter and use the land in question.

D is incorrect because an easement by necessity is only created when one is landlocked and needs to cross neighboring land in order to reach the nearest public road. There is no easement by necessity for phone service.

88. A is the correct answer. A non-exclusive easement is one in which the owner of the servient estate (here, the electric company) retains the right to make the same use of the owner's land that was granted by the easement. Therefore, the owner of a non-exclusive easement (but not the owner of an exclusive one) cannot apportion/transfer it to another, since to do so would be in derogation of the rights of the owner of the property (here, woman) to sell another easement to the internet service provider. Here, the electric company permitted the internet service provider to lay cables on the electric poles. This would be an apportionment of the non-exclusive easement, which is not allowed because only the woman had the power to grant a new easement to the internet service provider. Thus, this will be the woman's best argument.

B, C, and D are incorrect for the reasons discussed in A.

89. D is the correct answer. A license is created orally, rather than by written agreement. Here, the man made his grant to the city orally. This oral agreement created a license, rather than an easement. The license was made irrevocable through the expenditure of money and labor by the city in installing and maintaining the sewer lines.

A is incorrect because there was no easement here, for the reasons discussed in D. B is incorrect because the license was irrevocable, for the reasons discussed In D. C is incorrect because the city was given permission by the man. An easement by prescription is only created when no permission is given.

90. A is the correct answer. Although the conveyance is somewhat ambiguous, it does not state the limitation for school purposes in such a way as to cut down

the estate granted (the length of time that the school board is given title to the property). Therefore, given the courts' policy preference for the estate that will least result in forfeitures, the most likely result of the conveyance is that the man granted the school board a fee simple absolute with a covenant that the property would be used for school purposes. In that event, in 2011, the school may be liable in damages for breach of the covenant, but its estate continues.

B and C are incorrect for the reasons discussed in A. D is incorrect because economic inefficiency cannot change the estate granted.

91. C is the correct answer. A fee simple determinable is created by a grant or conveyance containing the language "so long as," "until," or "while." A fee simple determinable is followed by a possibility of reverter in the grantor (or an executory interest in a third party). The possibility of reverter takes effect automatically when the event in question occurs.

Here, conveying the property "to my church, so long as the property is used as a church" will create a fee simple determinable in the church and a possibility of reverter in the woman (the grantor). Thus, if the conveyance to the church uses the wording set forth in C, the woman will automatically get the property back if the property ceases to be used as a church, which is precisely what the woman wants to occur.

A and D are incorrect because conveyances containing the wording of either answer choice would create a fee simple on condition subsequent (which is created when the conveyance contains the language "but if," "upon," "provided," or "however"). A fee simple on condition subsequent is followed by a right of reentry in the grantor, if the condition in question occurs. However, the right of reentry does not take effect automatically; the grantor must affirmatively exercise this right. Thus, if the conveyance to the church is a fee simple on condition subsequent, and the church ceases to use the property as a church, the woman will not get the property back automatically; she will need to re-enter the property to assert her right. Since the woman wants to get the property back automatically if the property ceases to be used as a church, A and D are incorrect.

B is incorrect because the language "if and only if" does not create any particular type of estate under the common law.

92. D is the correct answer. The lease states that it is to run for 24 months. Therefore, it has a definite ending date, December 31, 2011, and consequently, must be a tenancy for years. The provision of annual rent or monthly rental installments cannot contradict the fixed term in the lease. A and B are incorrect because periodic tenancies continue for period-to-period because they do not have a definite ending point. C is

incorrect because a tenancy at will is an agreement between a landlord and tenant for an unspecified period of time. Here, there was a lease with a specified period. Therefore, the woman did not have a tenancy at will.

93. A is the correct answer. Under modern law, the landlord has a duty to deliver actual possession of the leasehold to the tenant at the beginning of the lease. Actual possession means exclusive possession. Here, although the landlord delivered the keys to the new tenant, he failed to ensure that the new tenant had exclusive possession because the apartment was still occupied by the former tenant. B is incorrect because, while it is a true factual statement, the landlord would still have to eject the former tenant, and while that process was occurring, the new tenant would not have exclusive possession, as required under modern law. (See discussion in B above.) C and D are incorrect because they state the common law rule of delivery of the legal right to possession only.

94. A is the correct answer. An easement by implication arises from the original subdivision of land for continuous and obvious use of the adjacent parcel, such as to enable a person on a "landlocked" parcel to reach the nearest public road. The difference between an easement by implication and an easement by necessity is that an easement by necessity requires strict necessity, while an easement by implication requires only reasonable necessity. Here, the man was landlocked and he cleared a dirt road from his house to the only public road. The man's actions met the definition of both an easement by implication and of an easement by necessity. B, C, and D are incorrect because there have only been eleven years of use by the man and only one year of adverse use against the woman (from 2010 to 2011). He, therefore, did not have an easement by prescription because an easement by prescription requires twenty years of adverse use.

95. B is the correct answer. An easement by implication arises from the original subdivision of land for continuous and obvious use of the adjacent parcel, such as to enable a person on a "landlocked" parcel to reach the nearest public road. The difference between an easement by implication and an easement by necessity is that an easement by necessity requires strict necessity, while an easement by implication requires only reasonable necessity. Here, once the new public road was built in 2005, the woman no longer had any strict necessity to cross over the man's property. Furthermore, an easement will terminate whenever the necessity does. That limitation does not apply to the easement by implication. Here, the strict necessity ended when the new road was built in 2005. However, the woman would still have an easement by implication because the previous easement by implication was still effective. A is incorrect because there was no prescriptive use because the man gave the woman permission to cross his property

and never revoked that permission. C is incorrect because there was no longer an easement by necessity here, for the reasons discussed in B. D is incorrect because an express easement requires a writing. Here, the facts indicate that man granted the woman permission orally.

96. A is the correct answer. In order to be valid, the covenant must have an intent to run with the land to subsequent successors and assigns; the covenant must touch and concern the land; the subsequent purchasers must have notice of the covenant; and horizontal and vertical privity. If these elements are met, the covenant will run with the land to bind successive owners of the property, regardless of their use of the facilities. Here, the uncle is suing the original promisor, the man. Thus, only the benefit side of this covenant needs to run with the land. All those elements are met: intent (the parties intended the promise to run "forever"); notice (the promise was recorded, which constitutes constructive notice); touch and concern (the promise will raise the value of the uncle's land by limiting the uses to be made on the man's land, which is adjacent to the uncle's land); and vertical privity (the uncle was the grantee of the woman, who was herself one of the original contracting parties). B and D are incorrect for the reasons discussed in A. C is incorrect because only the benefit needs to run: as discussed in A, horizontal privity is, therefore, not required.

97. C is the correct answer. In order to be valid, the covenant must have an intent to run with the land to subsequent successors and assigns; the covenant must touch and concern the land; the subsequent purchasers must have notice of the covenant; and horizontal and vertical privity. If these elements are met, the covenant will run with the land to bind successive owners of the property, regardless of their use of the facilities. Here, the following elements are met: intent (the parties intended the promise to run "for our lives and for the lives of any of our heirs and assigns"); notice (the promise was recorded, which constitutes constructive notice); touch and concern (the promise prevents the land from being used as anything but a farm); and vertical privity (the father was the grantee of the woman, who was herself one of the original contracting parties).

Both the benefit and the burden of the covenant need to run because the promise was allegedly breached by a subsequent party (the father was a subsequent grantee, after the 2005 promise was made), and the person bringing the suit is one of the original parties (the man).

As stated above, the benefit does run with the land. However, the burden cannot, since the man and the father did not have an interest in the same land at the same time that the promise was made (horizontal privity) since the father was not one of the original parties. Therefore, because the element of horizontal privity has not been met, the covenant does not run with the land here.

A is incorrect because the covenant does not run with the land, as discussed in C. B is incorrect because there is vertical privity, as discussed in C. D is incorrect because the covenant does touch and concern the land, as discussed in C.

98. D is the correct answer. This is a suit for specific enforcement, in equity. Therefore, the question is whether the promise can be enforced as an equitable servitude. In order to be valid, an equitable servitude must have an intent to run with the land to subsequent successors and assigns; the servitude must touch and concern the land; and the subsequent purchasers must have notice of the servitude.

Notice can be constructive (if the promise is recorded), actual (if subsequent parties are told about the promise), or inquiry (found through a reasonable inspection of the property). If these elements are met, the servitude will run with the land to bind successive owners of the property, regardless of their use of the facilities. Here, this servitude will run because the above elements are met: intent ("the two parcels of land would remain forever undeveloped"), touch and concern (the servitude is a direct restriction on the use of the land, in that it prevents the land from being developed).

The element of notice has been met, as well: while the promise was not recorded, and neither the sister nor the brother had actual notice of the restriction in the promise, a reasonable inspection of the land would reveal that it was not developed property. Thus, D is the correct answer because notice was sufficient, and the sister will be able to specifically enforce the promise.

A is incorrect because horizontal privity (the parties owning the properties in question at the time the promise is made) is not required for the servitude to run. B is incorrect because the servitude does touch and concern the land, as discussed in D. C is incorrect because privity is not required to enforce an equitable servitude.

99. B is the correct answer. In order to be valid, an equitable servitude must have an intent to run with the land to subsequent successors and assigns; the servitude must touch and concern the land; and the subsequent purchasers must have notice of the servitude.

Notice can be constructive (if the promise is recorded), actual (if subsequent parties are told about the promise), or inquiry (found through a reasonable inspection of the property). If these elements are met, the servitude will run with the land to bind successive owners of the property, regardless of their use of the facilities.

Here, there was nothing in the promise indicating an intent for it to run to subsequent heirs and assigns, and the promise was a personal promise that did not touch and concern the land.

A is incorrect because privity is not a requirement of an equitable servitude. C is incorrect because a servitude does not need to be in writing to be enforceable. D is incorrect because, when a person purchases land subject to a servitude, he voluntarily subjects himself to the terms of the servitude. Therefore, there is no involuntary servitude.

100. C is the correct answer. A tenant who wrongfully holds over on her lease is a tenant at sufferance until such time as the landlord chooses to treat her as a trespasser and evict her or treat her as a tenant for a new term.

A is incorrect because, until the tenant pays a new month's rent and the landlord accepts that rent, she cannot be a periodic tenant.

B is incorrect because, unless there is an express agreement between the landlord and the tenant to fix the ending date of the new term of tenant's holdover tenancy, she cannot be a tenant for years.

D is incorrect because the tenant legally entered possession of the property initially. She is, therefore, not a trespasser;

101. D is the correct answer. On default of a deed of trust the lender/beneficiary has the right to sell the property at either a judicial or private sale. A mortgage permits only a judicial sale. Therefore, D is correct, and A, B, and C are incorrect.

102. B is the correct answer because the parties entered into a contractual arrangement leading to transfer of title. The agreement states that payments will be made in installments with title passing to the woman when the full price, plus interest, is paid. That arrangement is characteristic of an installment sale.

A is incorrect because, in a deed of trust, the legal title would be vested in a third party (trustee) by the debtor (the woman) for the benefit of the lender (the man). No such arrangement exists here. C is incorrect because in a mortgage, the title to the property transfers immediately to the mortgagor. D is incorrect because neither a present transfer of leasehold nor a future interest in a fee simple appears contemplated.

103. A is the correct answer. The general rule is that when property burdened with a mortgage is sold, the property is transferred "subject to" the mortgage. Therefore, the man is still personally liable to the woman for the debt as the original mortgagor. The transfer does not release him from liability. B and C are incorrect because the brother is not personally liable on the mortgage,

unless he "assumes" the mortgage, a fact not present here. D is incorrect for the reasons discussed in A.

104. D is the correct answer. The woman is the lender/mortgagee in this transaction. When she transferred her interest in the mortgage to her cousin, he stepped into her shoes. The phrases "subject to" or "assuming" a mortgage have to do with the debtor's/mortgagor's interest, not the lender's interest. Therefore, A, B, and C are incorrect.

105. C is the correct answer. When a person takes property and assumes a mortgage, he or she becomes personally liable on the debt. The original debtor is not released from personal liability, unless there has been a novation. Here, the sister was the original debtor, and the boyfriend assumed the mortgage after the transfer to him. Thus, both the sister and the boyfriend are liable on the debt. A, B, and D are incorrect for the reasons discussed in C.

106. B is the correct answer. When a person takes property and assumes a mortgage, he or she becomes personally liable on the debt. The original debtor is released from personal liability when there has been a novation (release from liability). Here, the man released the woman from the debt. There was, thus, a novation, and the woman is no longer liable. A, C, and D are incorrect for the reasons discussed in B.

107. A is the correct answer. This question tests differences between property and contract law. Under contract law, as the facts state, the brother did not assume the mortgage (and is, therefore, not personally liable on the debt). However, under property law, he still took the house burdened with the mortgage. Consequently, if the original mortgagor (the man) defaults, the house can be sold out from under the brother. B is incorrect because the brother's consent is irrelevant. C is incorrect because the man was not obligated to pay the woman when he sold the house to his brother. D is incorrect because the fact that the brother paid more than the amount of the outstanding debt to the original mortgagors is irrelevant to this question because the brother took the house burdened with the mortgage, as discussed in A.

108. C is the correct answer. When there is more than one mortgage on a property and the mortgagor defaults, the mortgagee on whom the mortgagor has defaulted may foreclose and sell the property at a judicial sale. If the amount realized at the sale exceeds the amount owed on the mortgages, the proceeds are distributed according to the priority of the mortgages, with senior interests paid before junior ones. Any excess is given to the mortgagor. Thus, $80,000 to the man, $35,000 to the sister, and $5,000 to the woman. A, B, and D are incorrect for the reasons discussed in C.

109. D is the correct answer. When there is more than one mortgage on a property and the mortgagor defaults, any mortgagee on whom the mortgagor has defaulted may foreclose and sell the property at a judicial sale. If the amount realized at the sale exceeds the amount owed on the mortgages, the proceeds are distributed according to the priority of the mortgages with senior interests paid before junior ones. Any excess is given to the mortgagor. If there is a shortfall, the senior claims are paid in full before the junior, who may have a right to go against the mortgagor personally.

Here, the woman owed the man $80,000 and she owed her sister $40,000, for a total of $120,000 owed. Only $90,000 was realized at the sale. Consequently, there was no excess, so the woman will get nothing. The man (the senior mortgagee) will get all $80,000 he is owed, and the sister (the junior mortgagee) will get the remaining $10,000.

A, B, and C are incorrect for the reasons discussed in D.

110. C is the correct answer. When there is more than one mortgage on a property and the mortgagor defaults, the mortgagee on whom the mortgagor has defaulted may foreclose and sell the property at a judicial sale. If the amount realized at the sale exceeds the amount owed on the mortgages, the proceeds are distributed according to the priority of the mortgages with senior interests paid before junior ones. Any excess is given to the mortgagor.

If a junior mortgagee is not given notice at a foreclosure sale, the junior mortgage is not extinguished. The property is taken by the new buyer (at the foreclosure sale), subject to the mortgage. Here, the sister promptly recorded her mortgage. Thus, the bank was on notice of the sister's mortgage. The bank did not give the sister notice of the sale. Consequently, the sister's mortgage (which is a junior mortgage) was not extinguished.

A and B are incorrect for the reasons discussed in C. D is incorrect because, when there is a shortfall, the senior claims (here, the bank) are paid in full before the junior (here, the sister) who may have a right to go against the mortgagor (here, the woman) personally, as discussed in C.

111. A is the correct answer. After a foreclosure sale by a senior mortgagee, if there is no excess realized, any properly noticed junior interests are extinguished. The property can then be sold free and clear. However, the junior mortgagee has a personal right to recover against the mortgagor. Here, the senior mortgagee (the man) gave notice of the sale to the junior mortgagee (the sister), and the man received all $90,000 that he was owed. Since there was no excess, the sister's

mortgage was extinguished. B, C, and D are incorrect for the reasons discussed in A.

112. B is the correct answer. A foreclosure sale by a junior interest cannot affect the rights of a senior interest. The property can be sold, but it is taken by the buyer, subject to the senior interest. Here, first mortgage was from the man, making him the senior interest. The second mortgage was from the cousin, making her the junior interest. The cousin foreclosed and sold the home at a judicial sale. Therefore, the investor (buyer) took the property subject to the senior interest (i.e., the man's interest). A and D are incorrect for the reasons discussed in B. C is incorrect because the buyer is under no obligation to pay that debt of the original mortgagor.

113. C is the correct answer. A foreclosure sale by a junior interest cannot affect the rights of a senior interest. The property can be sold, but it is taken by the buyer, subject to the senior interest. Here, first mortgage was from the man, making him the senior interest. The second mortgage was from the sister, making her the junior interest. The proceeds from the judicial sale are paid to the junior claimant (the sister), who foreclosed, with the balance given to the mortgagor (the woman). The man's interests are still secured by the mortgage on the property and the personal debt of the mortgagor (the woman). A, B, and D are incorrect for the reasons discussed in C.

114. A is the correct answer. If a mortgage is a recordable interest in land and if it is not duly recorded, it is void as against a subsequent bona fide purchaser (a person who gives value without notice). Notice can be either actual, constructive, or inquiry. Here, the facts state that the cousin did not have actual notice of the man's mortgage. In addition, the man failed to record his mortgage. Thus, the cousin did not have constructive notice of the man's mortgage, either. Finally, the man did not move into the home, so the cousin did not have inquiry notice (i.e., he could not have discovered the man's mortgage through reasonable inspection). B, C, and D are incorrect because they assume that the man's mortgage survives as against the cousin. For the reasons discussed in A, it does not.

115. B is the correct answer. If a mortgage is not a recordable interest in land then priority is not determined by the recording act, but rather, by the common law rule of first in time, first in right. Here, the facts indicate that mortgages are not recordable interests in this jurisdiction. Therefore, the woman's mortgage could not be recorded. Applying the first in time, first in right rule, the brother takes the land, subject to the woman's interest because the woman's mortgage preceded the brother's ownership. A is incorrect for the reasons discussed in B. C and D are incorrect because the covenants of seisin or warranty concern defects in title, and a mortgage is an encumbrance/lien.

116. B is the correct answer. A general warranty deed contains six covenants of title: the covenant of seisin, the covenant of right to convey, the covenant against encumbrances, the covenant of quiet enjoyment, the covenant of further assurances, and the covenant of warranty.

The first three covenants can only be breached immediately upon sale of the property. The second three covenants can be breached in the future, after the sale of the property.

Here, the mother discovered the man's mortgage shortly after escrow closed. The mortgage is an encumbrance on the property. Therefore, the mother can sue the woman for breach of the covenant against encumbrances.

A is incorrect because the mother would be suing immediately, rather than waiting until a future date to sue. As discussed above, the covenant of quiet enjoyment is breached in the future. Thus, because the mother is suing immediately, this covenant could not have been breached yet. Also, there is nothing in the facts to indicate that the man is using the property, which would be a breach of the covenant of quiet enjoyment.

C and D are incorrect because the covenants of seisin or warranty concern defects in title and a mortgage is, in most states, considered to be a lien, not affecting title to property.

117. C is the correct answer. Since the father assumed the mortgage, he agreed to be personally bound by the debt. However, the man is not released from liability by the father's assumption of the mortgage, unless there is a novation, which did not occur under these facts.

A and D are incorrect because recording, or lack of it, is only used to determine priority among claimants to the same property. As between the transacting parties, it is not relevant. Here, the father is a transacting party because he assumed the mortgage. B is incorrect for the reasons discussed in C.

118. D is the correct answer. The man never recorded his mortgage from the woman. When the man transferred his interest to the father, the father simply recorded that interest. If the cousin did a proper search of the records, the mortgage from the woman to the man would not be found because it is outside the chain of title. Therefore, since the father stepped into the shoes of the man, his interest would effectively not be recorded, and between the father and cousin, the cousin's interest would have priority. Thus, the cousin will receive all that is owed to her ($70,000), and the father will receive the remainder ($10,000).

A is incorrect because, although the father is the senior interest, he lost his seniority because of the man's non-recordation. B is the right conclusion, for the wrong reason. C is incorrect because the father needed to be within the chain of title to claim recording act priority

119. B is the correct answer. This is an after-acquired title problem/estoppel by deed issue. The deed from the man to the woman, although recorded, is a wild deed outside the chain of title because at the time of that deed, the property was owned by the man's uncle, not the man. This issue was rectified in 2000 when the uncle sold the property to the man, making the man the actual owner of the building (after-acquired title/estoppel by deed). At this time, the woman gained title in the building because the man, who had originally attempted to sell the building to her in 1990, was now finally empowered to do so as the rightful owner of the building.

In 2010, the man gave a mortgage on the building to the mortgagee. When the mortgagee traced title, he would not find the original 1990 deed from the man to the woman, even though it was recorded because the man was not the rightful owner of the building at that time.

Consequently, the mortgagee gave value without notice, making the mortgagee a bona fide purchaser. The mortgagee should, therefore, be the person with first priority in the building. Thus, title is in the woman, subject to the mortgagee's mortgage.

A is incorrect for the reasons discussed in B. C and D are incorrect because the man no longer has any interest in the building, since he has sold it to the woman, as discussed in B.

120. D is the correct answer. Although the cousin is the junior mortgagee, she was the only one to record. Recording then determines priority, not the common law first in time, first in right.

Under a race statute, the first to record will have priority. Here, the cousin was he first to record, so she will collect all $65,000 under a race statute.

Under a race-notice statute, the first to record without notice will have priority. Here, the cousin was the first to record, as discussed. The facts also indicate that she had no notice, so under a race-notice statute, the cousin will collect all $65,000, as well.

Under a notice statute, the last person to take without notice will collect. Here, the facts indicate that the cousin was the last person to take the property without notice, so she will collect all $65,000 under a notice statute, also. A, B, and C are incorrect because they do not state all three types of recording statutes.

121. B is the correct answer. The majority rule is that the grant of a mortgage by one joint tenant does not sever the joint tenancy; it merely places a lien on it to the extent of the joint tenant's share.

Therefore, when the brother died, his undivided 1/2 passed to the sister by right of survivorship, subject to the bank's mortgage. A is incorrect since the brother's interest could not pass to the beneficiary by will because, when a joint tenant dies, his interest automatically passes to the other joint tenant, regardless of the terms of any will or other instrument. C and D are incorrect statements of law, for the reasons discussed in B.

122. D is the correct answer. In a title theory state, the conveyance of a mortgage affects title and severs the joint tenancy. Here, the facts state that this is a title theory state. Therefore, when the mother sold her share, the joint tenancy was severed; when the daughter mortgaged her share, the joint tenancy was also severed; and when the son died, he had a tenancy in common share, which could be passed on to a beneficiary. Therefore, in 2011, title was held in the daughter for 1/3 subject to the bank's mortgage, in the woman for 1/3, and in the beneficiary for 1/3 – all as tenants in common. A, B, and C are incorrect for the reasons discussed in D. In addition, C is incorrect because the total shares cannot exceed 100% (in this case, 3/3/).

123. A is the correct answer. The facts do not state which type of concurrent estate the wife and husband have. Modern law presumes that a tenancy in common was created when the type of concurrent ownership was not specified. Therefore, the wife could mortgage her interest and, on her death, it went to her heirs subject to the mortgage. B and C are incorrect for the reasons discussed in A. D is incorrect because the facts do not indicate that the husband and wife held the home as tenants by the entirety.

124. A is the correct answer. If a junior interest is not given notice at a foreclosure sale, that interest is not extinguished. The property is taken by the buyer subject to the deed of trust. Here, the cousin held the junior interest, and the man did not give her notice of the foreclosure sale. Therefore, her interest was not extinguished. B and D are incorrect for the reasons discussed in A. C is incorrect because, even though no notice was given to the junior mortgagee (the cousin) on sale, the proceeds are still distributed according to the priority of the deeds of trust with senior interests paid before junior ones. If there is a shortfall, the senior claims are paid in full before the junior who may have a right to go against the trustor personally.

125. C is the correct answer. If a junior interest is not given notice at a foreclosure sale, that interest is not extinguished. The property is taken by the buyer, subject to the mortgage. Here, the brother (the junior interest) was not given notice of foreclosure, even though his interest was recorded, which put the man (the senior interest) on constructive notice of the brother's

interest. Therefore, the investor took the home subject to the brother's mortgage. When the woman defaulted on the loan to the brother, the brother could foreclose on the home.

A is incorrect because the investor did not have actual notice of the brother's interest, but did have constructive notice under the recording act because the brother recorded, as discussed in C.

B is incorrect because, although the investor did not have actual notice of the brother's mortgage, he had constructive notice via the recording act, as discussed in C.

D is incorrect because the investor was not a bona fide purchaser, since a bona fide purchaser gives value without notice. Here, although the investor gave value, he was on constructive notice of the brother's recorded mortgage, as discussed in C.

END OF ANSWERS